ARTHURIAN   III

THE LEGEND OF THE GRAIL

ARTHURIAN STUDIES

ISSN 0261-9814

General Editor: Norris Lacy

Previously published volumes in the series
are listed at the back of the book.

FLEET

To buy any of our books and to find out
more about Fleet, our authors and titles, as well
as events and book clubs, visit our website

www.littlebrown.co.uk

and follow us on Twitter

**@FleetReads
@LittleBrownUK**

To order any Fleet titles p & p free in the UK,
please contact our mail order supplier on:

+ 44 (0)1832 737525

Customers not based in the UK should contact
the same number for appropriate postage
and packing costs.

THE LEGEND OF THE GRAIL

Compiled and translated by
Nigel Bryant

D. S. BREWER

First published 2004
D. S. Brewer, Cambridge
Reprinted in paperback 2006

ISBN 1 84384 006 5 Hardback
ISBN 1 84384 083 9 Paperback

D. S. Brewer is an imprint of Boydell & Brewer Ltd
PO Box 9, Woodbridge, Suffolk IP12 3DF, UK
and of Boydell & Brewer Inc.
668 Mt Hope Avenue, Rochester, NY 14620, USA,
website: www.boydellandbrewer.com

A catalogue record for this book is available
from the British Library

Library of Congress catalog card number 2003024685

Printed in Great Britain by
CPI Cox and Wyman, Reading

Contents

Introduction

THE QUEST FOR THE HOLY GRAIL is the single most important element in the story of King Arthur. Even to the many who have only the haziest knowledge – or no knowledge at all – of things Arthurian, the Grail itself is an emblem, a metaphor for an ultimately challenging but supremely desirable goal: it has, indeed, become something of a journalistic cliché. Yet very few people, even those interested in the wonderful stories of the Round Table, have ever read at first hand the medieval masterpieces which, over a period of some forty years in the late twelfth and early thirteenth centuries, constructed what might be called the legend of the Grail. Most people's mental images of the Grail quest are more likely to be dependent on Burne-Jones tapestries and Tennysonian idylls, themselves dependent principally on the comparatively late borrowings 'oute of certeyn bookes of Frensshe' by Thomas Malory.

Complexities

There is a good reason for this. The original Grail romances did not develop a consistent, coherent narrative: there never appeared a clear and definitive 'legend of the Grail'. The romances were created by a series of writers working with different preoccupations, different purposes and different interpretations of their predecessors' stories – and in some cases almost certainly at the same time as each other, with no knowledge of one another's work. The manuscripts that have come down to us, therefore, were in many cases compiled by redactors – scribe/editors – struggling valiantly to make sense of the contradictory, half-adapted, subtly altered and rearranged inter-borrowings of the storytellers who had created a vast series of extraordinary adventures that constituted the Grail quests of many different knights.

Some of these romances contain huge digressions as well as contradictions: the *First Continuation* of the unfinished *Perceval* by Chrétien de Troyes, for example, contains a story about a young knight named Carados, unrelated to the Grail quest, which runs (albeit very entertainingly) for several thousand lines, and *Gerbert de Montreuil*'s *Continuation* devotes the best part of 2,000 lines to a substantial story about Tristran, Iseult and King Marc.

The massive and unwieldy nature of this material has led to a body of magnificent literature, a major component of the European imagination, being unknown to the point of being effectively lost. This priceless material deserves to be presented in an accessible form. But to provide, for example, condensed versions of each major Grail text individually would, if anything, merely accentuate the contradictions and increase the modern reader's sense of bewilderment.

This volume is designed instead to interweave the principal motifs and narrative strands of all the original Grail romances in order to construct a single, consistent and completely accessible version of the Grail story. Avoiding all contradiction and repetition, it aims to accentuate instead what the medieval romances have in common. In spite of what has been said above, it is surprising how much common ground there is between the different writers, as they looked over their shoulders to the work of their predecessors and were remarkably aware of the gradual development of their potent and absorbing theme.

The development of the legend

So how did this development take place? A defeatist, but not entirely untrue, answer is that we shall never know. The order – let alone the precise dating – of the composition of the Grail romances will forever be a matter of conjecture and scholarly dispute. There is not even agreement about fairly long-standing assumptions that the mighty theme of the Grail was (a) initiated by the poet Chrétien de Troyes with his unfinished *Perceval* and (b) was based upon an amorphous body of much older Celtic tales of a maimed king and magic feeding vessels and cauldrons of regeneration.

What follows is, therefore, merely one of a number of possible accounts of the development of what might be called the legend of the Grail.

In the mid-1180s the great poet Chrétien de Troyes, borrowing and reworking various narrative elements from existing Celtic tales, wrote just over 9,000 lines of a romance in verse called *Perceval – the Story of the Grail*. The dating of this poem is fairly reliable: it was certainly written no later than 1191, when Count Philip of Flanders, to whom it is dedicated, died at Acre during the Third Crusade. It tells of a young knight who sees a procession of mysterious objects including a shining, bejewelled vessel referred to as a grail. Chrétien died with the poem unfinished. Its tantalising theme was, however, far too good to leave, and during the 1190s were composed at least two of the anonymous *Continuations* – the so-called First Continuation and Second Continuation – which are added to *Perceval* in most of the surviving manuscripts. Simultaneously (though some scholars would claim that he was writing at the same time as, or even before, Chrétien de Troyes was working on *Perceval*), one Robert de Boron looked back rather than forward in time and created a prehistory of the Grail in his *Joseph of Arimathea*. In this crucial work, a kind of apocryphal gospel, Robert identified the Grail as a vessel used by Christ at the Last Supper and by Joseph of Arimathea at the Crucifixion.

This clear, unambiguous identification of the Grail as a holy relic of supreme importance was made at a time when, to the East, the forces of Christendom were losing holy places and relics to the Saracens in no uncertain manner – in 1187 the True Cross itself was lost to Saladin at the catastrophic battle of Hattin. Small wonder, then, that around 1200, with the situation in the Holy Land so critical, the anonymous writer of the next great treatment of the Grail theme, *The High Book of the Grail*, developed the story to stress a crucial connection between striving to recover the Grail and crusading – with ruthless violence if necessary – against the infidel.

By now Perceval and Gawain were well established as protagonists in the Grail quest, but a different anonymous writer with a different didactic purpose felt the need to create a new, unsullied Grail hero in the form of Galahad, who brings a decisive conclusion to the story in *The Quest of the Holy Grail*, probably composed around 1220–25. But it was by no means the only conclusion, or the first or the last. The writer of *The High Book of the Grail* had already decided to kill off the Fisher King, the maimed guardian of the Grail, without his having been healed; and two further Continuations of Chrétien's *Perceval* – despite the fact that they almost certainly post-date *The Quest of the Holy Grail*, being composed probably as late as 1230 – provide conclusions to the Grail story that have nothing to do with Galahad, who does not even appear. These are the so-called Third Continuation attributed to one Manessier, and Gerbert de Montreuil's Continuation. To continue the complication, Gerbert's work exists in two surviving manuscripts as a long interpolation between the Second and Third Continuations, and probably gave an independent ending to the story which was edited out to make possible the inclusion of the Third which would otherwise have been redundant.

A modern redaction

Given all this complexity, what might a scribe in, say, 1240, with *all* the available Grail texts before him and commissioned to compile a new and complete 'story of the Grail,' have produced? Who knows? But the likelihood is that he would have selected episodes, as all scribes did, to create a narrative as consistent as possible unto itself. He would surely have put Robert de Boron's 'prehistory' of the Grail, whether or not it was composed first, at the start. He would have edited out one ending at the expense of another, but tried to make sure that every narrative strand was satisfactorily brought to a conclusion.

That is what this volume sets out to do. It is no more and no less than a modern redaction, a compilation of existing material of a kind that medieval scribes were constructing in the late twelfth and early thirteenth centuries. The only difference is that it invents nothing: apart from an occasional linking phrase to clarify connections between various characters and incidents, there is no scribal interpolation of any kind.*

It is compiled by interweaving all the key narrative strands in the eight great French romances which, between the mid-1180s and some time around 1230, created and developed the legend of the Grail: Robert de Boron's *Joseph of Arimathea*, Chrétien de Troyes' *Perceval – the Story of the Grail*, the anonymous First Continuation and Second Continuation, the Third Continuation attributed to Manessier and Gerbert de Montreuil's Continuation, and the anonymous *High Book of the Grail* (also known as *Perlesvaus*) and *Quest of the Holy Grail*.

The first and the last two of these were written in prose, the other five in verse. But whether verse or prose, it is vital to recognise that they were scripts. They were intended to be read aloud. The notion of sitting alone, reading a manuscript in silent isolation, was alien to the medieval mind; it would have been as strange and anti-social to our forebears as solitary drinking might be to us. The dramatic qualities of this medieval writing, and the power of its unfamiliar rhythms, become startlingly evident when read aloud. It is not by chance that the first three words of *Perlesvaus*, which open this modern redaction of the legend of the Grail, are:

Hear the story.

---

* With a rare exception: it has been necessary to take a very occasional liberty to overcome significant inconsistencies in the original. Readers with a detailed knowledge of the texts may notice, for example, that on page 61, when Perceval breaks the sword given to him by the Fisher King, an invented phrase states that the sword vanishes, to account for its otherwise inexplicable reappearance when Perceval next visits the Grail Castle.

Joseph of Arimathea

HEAR THE STORY OF THAT HOLY VESSEL which is called the Grail, in which the precious blood of the Saviour was gathered on the day when He was crucified to redeem mankind from Hell. Such was His purpose in coming to this world, being born of the Virgin Mary at Bethlehem.

At the time when Our Lord was upon the Earth, most of the land of Judaea was answerable to Rome, and the governor's name was Pilate. This Pilate had in his service a soldier named Joseph of Arimathea, who followed Christ to many places and loved him deeply in his heart, but dared not show it openly, for Our Lord had many enemies set against Him. And not only enemies: He had a disciple, too, who was not as a follower should be. He was ill-disposed towards his fellow disciples, and began to distance himself from them, serving them harshly and unkindly; they were very wary of him. But Our Lord, being God, knew all. This disciple's name was Judas, and his hatred towards Our Lord was conceived on account of an ointment; I shall tell you now of his treachery.

At this time it was the custom that a chamberlain received a tenth of all moneys that came into his lord's purse, and when Mary Magdalene poured an ointment upon Our Lord's feet Judas was enraged, counting in his heart that the ointment was worth three hundred pence. He did not want to lose his due; he reckoned his tenth was worth thirty pence, and was determined to secure that amount. At the earliest opportunity he sought to recover those thirty pence from God's enemies.

Three nights before the Passover, Christ's enemies were at the house of a man named Caiaphas, discussing how they could capture Him. Joseph of Arimathea was present as they talked, and their wicked words grieved him terribly. In the middle of their discussion Judas appeared, and when they saw him they fell silent, for they distrusted him, believing him to be a good disciple of Jesus.

Judas spoke out and asked them: 'Why are you assembled here?'

And they replied: 'Where is that master of yours?'

And he told them where Jesus was and why he had come to them, and when the Jews heard Judas's words of treachery they were overjoyed and said: 'Tell us how we can take him prisoner!'

And he replied: 'I'll sell him to you if you wish.'

'Yes indeed,' they said, 'most gladly!'

And he said he would give them Jesus for thirty pence. One of them had the money to hand, and paid it. And so Judas recovered his tenth of the three hundred pennies' worth of ointment.

Then they discussed how they would capture Jesus: they fixed the day and an early hour; Judas would inform them where Jesus would be, and they would be armed and ready to seize Him. But Judas warned them to be sure they did not seize James, for he looked very much like Jesus – understandably, for James was His cousin. And they asked him: 'How then will we recognise Jesus?'

And he replied: 'Take the man that I shall kiss.'

And so it was resolved.

Joseph of Arimathea was present throughout all this, and it weighed heavily upon his heart, but he dared do nothing. They went their several ways and waited till the Thursday.

On the Thursday evening Our Lord was at the house of Simon the Leper. I cannot and should not tell you everything He said to His disciples, but this much I can say for sure: He told them that eating and drinking with Him was one who would betray Him. The disciples were dismayed and swore they were not guilty. But Christ assured them it was true, and Judas asked Him: 'Are you saying it's me?'

And Jesus answered: '*You* say so.'

It was then that the men whom Judas had informed burst into the house, and the disciples were terrified. And once the house was full, and Judas was sure they had the upper hand, he stepped forward and kissed Jesus. Seeing this, the Jews seized Him from all sides, and Judas cried to them: 'Hold him fast!,' for he knew how great was Christ's strength. And they led Him away, leaving the disciples filled with grief.

And the vessel in which He had made the sacrament was there at Simon's house, and one of the Jews took it and kept it until the next day.

Jesus was taken before Pilate, and they charged Him with everything they could – though it wasn't much: they could find no justification for putting Him to death. But the weakness of the law was such, and Pilate felt so powerless before all the Jews, that he had to accept it. Then he spoke as governor, saying: 'Who will take responsibility if the emperor asks about this? I can see no reason for this man to suffer death.'

And they all cried out together: 'May his blood be showered upon us and all our children!'

And while they seized Jesus and led Him away, Pilate called for water and washed his hands, and said that, just as his hands were clean, so was he clean of responsibility for that man's death.

It was then that the Jew who had taken the vessel from Simon's house came to Pilate and gave it to him. Pilate took it and kept it safe.

When the news came that they had put Jesus to death, Joseph of Arimathea was overcome with grief and anguish, and he came to Pilate and said: 'Sir, my knights and I have served you for a long while, and you've given me nothing for my service.'

'Ask,' said Pilate, 'and I'll give you whatever you wish in payment.'

And Joseph thanked him and said: 'I would like the body of the prophet whom the Jews have wrongfully put to death.'

Pilate was astonished that he should ask for such a poor reward, and said: 'I thought you'd ask for a greater gift! If that's the payment you desire, you shall have it.'

'Many thanks, sir,' said Joseph. 'Give orders that it should be mine.'

'Go and take it,' Pilate said.

But Joseph replied: 'Sir, the Jews are strong in numbers, and won't want to give it to me.'

But Pilate was sure they would; so Joseph made his way to the Cross. When he saw Jesus hanging there he was filled with pity and wept bitter tears, for he had loved Him deeply. He came to the Jews who were guarding Him and said: 'Pilate has given me permission to remove the prophet's body from this shameful place.'

But all the Jews together said: 'You're not having it, for his disciples say he's going to revive. But however often he comes back to life, we'll kill him!'

'Let me take him, sirs,' said Joseph, 'for Pilate has granted him to me.'

But the Jews cried: 'We'd sooner kill you!'

Joseph left them and returned to Pilate and told him of the Jews' response. Pilate was amazed; but he saw before him a man named Nichodemus, and he commanded him to go with Joseph and take Christ's body from the Cross himself. And then he remembered the vessel that the Jew had given him, and he called Joseph and said: 'Joseph, you loved that prophet dearly.'

'Yes indeed, sir,' he replied.

And Pilate said: 'I have a vessel of his, given to me by one of the Jews who were present at his capture, and I've no wish to keep anything that belonged to him.'

And he gave the vessel to Joseph, who received it with the greatest joy.

Joseph and Nichodemus set off together, and Nichodemus went to a smith to borrow pincers and a hammer; then they came to the Cross where Christ still hung, and Nichodemus said to the people there: 'You've dealt wickedly with this man. But now he's clearly dead, and Pilate has granted the body to Joseph and has commanded me to deliver it to him.'

They all replied that he was sure to come back to life, and refused to let the body go; but Nichodemus said that nothing they could do would stop him taking it. So they all marched off to Pilate, while Joseph and Nichodemus climbed up and took Jesus Christ from the Cross.

Joseph held Him in his arms and laid Him on the ground, cradling Him tenderly and washing Him most gently. But when he had washed Him, he saw His wounds still bleeding and was dismayed to see the blood spilling into the ground; and then he remembered his vessel, and thought the falling drops of blood would be better gathered there. So he placed it beneath Christ's wounds; and blood from the wounds in His hands and His feet dripped into the vessel. Then Joseph set it to one side, and took Jesus' body and wrapped it in a sheet that he had bought for his own use.

Meanwhile the crowd who had gone to Pilate gained his agreement that, wherever Joseph might put the body, it should be closely watched in case it came back to life, and they arranged for a large armed guard.

While all this was happening, Our Lord descended into Hell, broke in and set free Adam and Eve and as many others as He pleased. And He returned to life, unknown and unseen by those who were standing guard, and He went forth and appeared to Mary Magdalene and to other disciples where He chose.

When the Jews heard He had come back to life they all assembled to hold council, and said to each other: 'This man will do us great harm if he's truly alive again!'

And those who had been guarding the body declared that they knew for sure it was not where Joseph had put it. 'It's his fault we've lost him!' they cried. 'And if harm befalls us it'll be because of him and Nichodemus!'

They discussed what they could do if the emperor demanded the body; and they agreed to say they had handed it over on the orders of Nichodemus.

'But if anyone says "You had the body guarded at the tomb: ask the guards what happened", what answer could we give?'

And one replied: 'There's a way around that. Let's seize Joseph and Nichodemus tonight in secret, and put them to a grim death. Then afterwards, if anyone asks us for Jesus' body, we'll say we gave it to them!'

They all agreed to this, and praised the man for his cleverness. So it was agreed they would seize them by night.

But friends of Nichodemus were present, and they informed him of the plan and he fled; and when the Jews arrived at his house they found no sign of him. So they moved on to the house of Joseph, and seized him naked in his bed; they made him dress and then led him to the house of one of the richest men in the land, where there was a tower with a dismal dungeon. Having Joseph there alone, they beat him and asked him what he had done with Jesus.

'Those who were guarding him will know,' he replied, 'for I did nothing secret or underhand.'

'You've stolen him from us, we know it!' they replied. 'We're going to throw you in this dungeon, and you'll die there unless you tell us where the body of Jesus is!'

And Joseph, knowing nothing of its whereabouts, said: 'I'm willing to die, if that's the will of the Lord – the Lord on whose account I'm your captive.'

Then the Jews seized him and beat him dreadfully, and flung him down into the dungeon vault. They sealed it with a stone, so that if anyone came in search of him, they would never find him.

And so it was that Joseph was abducted and imprisoned. When Pilate learned he was missing he was distressed and heavy-hearted, for he had been the best of friends to him. And Joseph was missing for a long time.

But the one in whose cause he had suffered did not forget him. Being Lord and God He watched over him, and came to the dungeon where he lay, and brought him his vessel. A shining light appeared to Joseph, and he was filled with joy and with the grace of the Holy Spirit, and he marvelled and said: 'Almighty God, where can such a brilliant light come from unless from You?'

And Jesus answered: 'Joseph, Joseph, do not be afraid, for my Father's power will guard you.'

'Who are you?' Joseph asked Him. 'You're so fair – I don't know you – I cannot look upon you.'

And Jesus said: 'Hear me, Joseph. I am Jesus Christ, the Son of God. I came to Earth to suffer death at the command of my Father, who made Adam and from Adam made Eve, but the Enemy deceived Eve and made her sin, and she caused Adam to do likewise. They were cast into misery; and they conceived and had children and a great line of descendants, and when they died the Devil was determined they should all be his. But it was my Father's will that I should come to Earth and be born of woman. It was through a woman, Eve, that the Enemy took possession of men; and as a woman had caused man's soul to be imprisoned, it was only right that it should be recovered and redeemed through a woman: that is why I was born of the Virgin.

'And you saw the torment I suffered on the Cross. Just as the tree in Eden bore the apple that tempted Eve, so the Son of God died on a tree to save His Father's creation. I came on Earth to work this salvation, and suffered worldly pain. Blood flowed from my body in five places.'

'Oh Lord,' said Joseph, 'have pity and mercy on me: it's for your sake I'm imprisoned here. I've always loved you dearly, but never dared to speak to you, for I feared you wouldn't trust me because of the people I conversed with, keeping company as I did with the ones who meant you harm.'

'Joseph,' Our Lord replied, 'it's good to have a friend amongst enemies – as you can see now for yourself! I knew you were a good friend to me, so I left you with them, knowing you would feel grief at my torment and would come to my aid when none of my disciples could. I knew you would help me out of love for my Father, who gave you the courage to do the service for which I was given to you.'

'Oh, dear Lord,' said Joseph, 'don't say that you're mine!'

'But I am,' Our Lord replied. 'I belong to all the good, and all the good are mine. And do you know what reward you'll have because I was given to you? Lasting joy will be yours at the end of this mortal life. None of my disciples knows of the love between us: you have loved me in secret as I have loved you.

But know this: our love will be revealed to all – and will be a curse to the wicked – for you shall have the sign of my death in your keeping; see: it is here.'

And Our Lord took hold of the precious vessel with the holy blood that Joseph had gathered from His body when he washed Him; and as soon as Joseph saw it he went down on his knees and cried for mercy, saying: 'Lord, am I worthy to keep such a holy thing as this vessel?'

And Our Lord replied: 'You, Joseph, must be its keeper, you and whoever else you may command. But there are to be no more than three keepers, and those three shall guard it in the name of the Father, the Son and the Holy Spirit, which three powers are one and the same being in God.'

And He held out the vessel and Joseph, still kneeling, took it; and Our Lord said: 'Joseph, you are holding the blood which contains these three powers. Do you understand your reward? Your reward is that the sacrament shall never be made without remembrance of your good work by those who recognise it.'

'Lord,' replied Joseph, 'please tell me what I did, for I don't know.'

And Jesus said: 'You took me from the Cross. And know this: when I sat at the table of the Last Supper on the night I was betrayed, I said that many tables will be established in my service, where the sacrament shall be made in my name, which will be a reminder of the Cross; and the vessel of the sacrament will be a reminder of the stone tomb in which you laid me, and the paten which will be placed on top will be a reminder of the lid with which you covered me, and the cloth called the corporal will be a reminder of the winding-sheet in which you wrapped me. And so your work, Joseph, will be remembered until the world's end. And all who see the vessel and remain in its presence will have lasting joy and fulfilment for their souls.'

And so saying, Christ gave the vessel to Joseph. And when he had taken it, Our Lord spoke sacred words that He had prepared for him, and said: 'Whenever you have need, seek the help of the three powers that are one being, and of that blessed lady Mary who gave birth to God the Son, and ask for whatever counsel your heart desires, and you will hear the voice of the Holy Spirit. And be assured, you will not remain imprisoned in this dark dungeon; and your deliverance will astound your wicked captors.'

With that, Christ left him, and for the time being Joseph remained in prison. Of his imprisonment nothing is said by the apostles or the writers of the Gospels, for they knew nothing about Joseph except that, because of his affection for Christ, he had asked to be granted His body. Some of the apostles did hear of Joseph's disappearance, but they did not speak of it, for they committed nothing to the Scriptures except what they had seen or heard themselves.

Joseph stayed imprisoned for a long time.

* * *

Meanwhile there was a pilgrim who had been in Judaea and seen Our Lord performing miracles upon the blind and the lame, and had seen Him crucified, too, under the authority of Pilate. This worthy man journeyed through many lands until at last he came to Rome, at the time when Vespasian, the son of the emperor Titus, was sick with leprosy: he was shut away in a stone chamber with only a tiny window through which they passed his food. The worthy pilgrim came to Rome and took lodging with a rich man in the city. In conversation that evening, the rich man told his guest how pitiful it was that the emperor's son was sick and shut away, and said that if he knew of any possible remedy he should say so. And the pilgrim replied:

'No, I don't; but I can tell you that in the land of Judaea there was a prophet through whom God worked many miracles. I saw Him heal the lame who couldn't walk and the blind who couldn't see. He healed anyone He wished to heal, and the rich and powerful of Judaea came to hate him because they could do nothing to match His words and deeds. They put Him to death by crucifying Him. And I swear to you,' said the pilgrim, 'had He still been alive and brought before the emperor's son, if He'd wished to cure him He'd have surely done so.'

And his host said: 'Did you ever hear why He was crucified?'

'No,' said the pilgrim, 'except that they hated Him.'

'Where did this happen, under whose jurisdiction?'

'Pilate's,' said the pilgrim, 'the emperor's governor in that city.'

'Truly now, would you come with me and tell this to the emperor?'

'I'd tell it to anyone,' he replied.

And when they came before the emperor and his counsellors and the pilgrim repeated his story, they were utterly amazed, for they had always thought Pilate a good and wise man who would never have permitted such an outrage. And one of them said: 'I love Pilate dearly, and can't believe he'd have allowed the killing of such a great healer, if he could have prevented it.'

But the pilgrim assured them it was true. 'And I'd wager my life that Pilate would not deny it. I also believe that if anyone found anything that had belonged to the prophet, and brought it to the emperor's son, if he had faith and touched it, he would be healed.'

They were all astounded at his words, and one of them said: 'If my lord the emperor sends me to learn the truth, what would you have us do with you?'

'Keep me fed until your return, and if you say my story isn't true, I shall accept death by beheading.'

They all agreed he had said enough, and they had him taken and placed in a chamber under guard. When the emperor's son Vespasian heard the news he begged his father to send messengers as soon as he could. The emperor did so, sending the wisest men of his court to confirm the pilgrim's story and, if the prophet was dead, to bring back something He had touched to heal his son.

The emperor's messengers crossed the sea to the land of Judaea, and ordered Pilate to meet them at Arimathea. When he arrived there was no rejoicing, for they feared they might be taking him back to Rome to execute him. They gave him the emperor's letters, which told him everything the pilgrim had said. He read them, turned back to the messengers, looked kindly upon them, and said:

'Sirs, everything these letters state is true: it was exactly as they say.'

They were amazed at his admission, and said: 'You're acknowledging great folly! If you can't excuse yourself, you'll surely die!'

Pilate called the messengers into a chamber, and made sure the doors were firmly shut so that they could not be overheard by the Jews. Then he began to tell them everything he knew or had heard about Christ's life: how the rich had come to hate Him; how He had healed whoever He wished; how the Jews had accused Him and bought His betrayal by a disciple who did not love Him. And he told them of the foul treatment they had dealt Him, and how they had brought Christ before him and demanded that he condemn Him to death.

'I saw no reason to sentence the man, but they were so many, and so aggressive and rich and powerful! I told them that if the emperor asked me about it, it would be on their heads, and they replied that they wished Christ's blood might be showered on them and their children! Then they seized Him and led Him away and did with Him as you've heard. I wanted it known that I was blameless, and called for water and washed my hands and said: "May I be as clean of this man's death as my hands are clean in this water." When the prophet was dead, one of my knights asked to be given His body, which I gladly granted, and he took it from its place of shame and laid it in a stone tomb. I don't know what became of it after that. But I believe they've killed Joseph, my knight. That's my story: now judge whether I did wrong.'

Having heard all this, the messengers thought Pilate less guilty than before, and said: 'We don't know if what you say is true, but if it is, you may well absolve yourself of blame.'

'The Jews know the truth of it,' said Pilate. 'I'll have them confirm my story.'

'Call them,' the messengers replied. 'Command all who were involved in the prophet's crucifixion to gather in this city a month from today.'

Pilate sent messengers throughout the land to summon all who had been present at Christ's death, and to let them know that the emperor's envoys wished to speak to them. While waiting for the month to pass, Pilate had people search the country for anything touched by Jesus Christ, but they could find nothing.

At the end of the month the Jews assembled at Arimathea. Pilate said to the emperor's messengers: 'Let me speak to them first: you'll hear my words and their replies, and when you've heard what both sides say, act accordingly.'

When they were all assembled, Pilate said: 'Sirs, here are the emperor's envoys, who wish to know who it was that you put to death, the one held to be King of the Jews. For the emperor has heard He was a great healer, and has commanded that He be taken to him, if He can be found. But I've told his envoys He's dead, and that you yourselves, the powerful men of this land, put Him to death because He said He was your king – and you did so without the emperor's leave.'

'Because you were so poor a governor,' the Jews replied, 'that you dared not punish Him! Instead you seemed upset when we said we'd put Him to death.'

And one of the messengers addressed them, saying: 'Sirs, this man who claimed to be a greater lord than the emperor, did Pilate then not pass sentence upon Him?'

'No indeed!' they replied. 'We had to take responsibility upon ourselves and our children, or Pilate would never have agreed!'

'And who was this prophet of whom so much has been spoken?'

They replied that He performed the greatest miracles and wonders in the world; He was an enchanter. Then the messengers asked all those present to tell them if they knew of anything that had ever been touched by the prophet, but they replied that they knew of nothing, for everything he owned had been thrown away and anyone might have taken it. With that the assembly broke up, and Pilate was cleared of the envoys' suspicion.

Then, a while later, while they were still distressed at their failure to find anything that had touched the body of Our Lord, a man came to them saying that he knew a woman who had an image of Christ that she revered, but did not know how she had come by it. Pilate sent for her and she came. And when Pilate saw her he rose to greet her, and embraced her and asked her name, and the good woman, baffled by Pilate's joyful welcome, told him her name was Veronica. He drew her aside, and said: 'Veronica, I hear you have the image of a man in your keeping; I beg you to show it to me.'

'I know nothing about this!' the woman said, greatly alarmed, and denied it vigorously. Then the emperor's messengers approached and greeted her with joy, and told her why they had come to the land and about the illness of the emperor's son Vespasian. 'We believe that if he were given the image, he'd be healed.' If she would sell it to them, they would pay whatever she asked.

Hearing the plight of the emperor's son, she realised she must reveal the truth, and said: 'Sirs, I could never sell the thing you seek, however much you paid me. But if you swear by all you believe in that you'll not keep what I give you, I'll come with you to Rome.'

They were overjoyed at this and said: 'We'll take you to Rome most gladly, and as you've requested, so we swear.' They made their vow all together, and then said: 'You'll be made a rich woman. Now show us the thing we seek.'

So Veronica went back to her house and fetched the image of the face and returned to where they were waiting.

'Sit down,' she said when she arrived, and they did so, and she took out the image. When they saw it they were overcome with joy and all rose to their feet. 'Why have you stood up?' she asked, and they replied: 'When we saw the face we couldn't help it. Ah, lady, tell us where you found it and how it came to be yours.'

'I will,' she said. 'I'd made a length of linen cloth and was carrying it to market to sell it, when I met the people who were driving the prophet through the streets, His hands bound, leading Him to His death. And He asked me to wipe away the sweat that was running down His face. So I took one end of the cloth and wiped His face; then I went on my way while they drove Him on, flogging Him and abusing Him. And when I got home and looked at the cloth, I found it bore this image of His face. That's exactly how it happened. And if,' she said, 'you think it would be of use to the emperor's son, I'll go with you and take it to him.'

'Many thanks,' they replied. 'We believe it would be of use to him indeed!' This image was the only thing they found which had touched Our Lord.

* * *

The emperor was overjoyed when they arrived back in Rome, and they confirmed that every word the pilgrim had told them was true. The emperor asked if the prophet was such a great man as was said, and they replied: 'Yes, and a good deal more!'

'And have you brought back anything that touched Him?'

'Yes!' they said, and they told him how they had found Veronica and her image of the prophet's face.

'This is a great wonder,' said the emperor. 'I've never heard of the like.'

And he went to Veronica and gave her a joyful welcome, and said he would make her a rich woman for what she had brought him. And Veronica showed him the face on the cloth; and when he saw it, the emperor, filled with wonder, made three deep bows and said: 'This is the most beautiful face I've ever seen.'

Then he took it in both hands and carried it into the chamber where his son was shut away. He was sleeping; so the emperor placed the cloth at the window, and called to his son and showed him the face. As soon as Vespasian set eyes upon it he was healed, in better health than he had ever been in his life. And he said: 'Dear Lord God, whose face is this that has healed me of all sickness? Father!' he cried to the emperor. 'Have this wall knocked down at once!'

It was done with all possible speed, and Vespasian left the chamber in perfect health and spirits, to the great joy of the emperor and everyone. He asked where the image of the face had been found, and whose it was, which had healed him as no man on Earth could do. And when the emperor told him the pilgrim's story of Christ and all His miracles, Vespasian asked the messengers: 'Sirs, did they truly put to death such a worthy man as He?'

'They did,' they said; and when he heard this he was deeply angry and said they had done a shameful deed, and that he would never be content until they had paid for it. And he said to his father: 'Sir, you are not our king or emperor: the true lord is the man who by His very image has healed me as neither you nor anyone else could do. He is the lord of men and women and of all things, and I beg you now, let me go and take revenge upon His killers.'

'Dear son,' the emperor replied, 'do exactly as you wish.'

And Vespasian crossed the sea and ordered Pilate to come to him; and when Pilate saw he had come with a great company he was filled with fear and said: 'Dear sir, I am at your command. Let me know your will.'

'I have come to avenge the death of Jesus Christ,' Vespasian replied, 'the prophet who healed me.'

Pilate was terrified, imagining Vespasian had been told he was responsible; and he said: 'Sir, would you like to see the men who were present at His death and know who was guilty and who was not?'

'Indeed I would,' said Vespasian.

'Then have me taken and imprisoned,' said Pilate, 'and say it's because I wouldn't sentence Him. Pretend to despise me.'

Vespasian did as Pilate said, and summoned those involved from every corner of the land. When they had all assembled, Vespasian asked them about the prophet who was a higher lord than his father, and said: 'You committed treason, allowing Him to make Himself your king.'

And they all replied: 'It was Pilate, your governor, who stood up for Him! He said that even if the prophet claimed to be our king, it wasn't enough to merit death. But we said it was, and that we wouldn't allow Him to be lord above our masters, but Pilate said the man was lord above all kings!'

'That's why I've thrown him in prison,' Vespasian said. 'I'd heard about his actions, and how he loved the prophet more than us. Now I wish to know,' he said, 'which of you inflicted most pain on the prophet, who was most offended at His claim to be king, and which of you were most involved in the plot against Him. Tell me everything, exactly as it happened.'

Imagining it was for their benefit and Pilate's downfall, they were delighted, and told him exactly what they had done: they pointed out the one who had paid Judas the thirty pence and the ones who had captured Christ. Each one of them bragged of the foul things they had said and done. Then they told him how they had led Him before Pilate.

'But he wouldn't pass judgment, so we killed Him without leave. We had to take his death upon ourselves and our children. We pray you now, declare us relieved of this responsibility.'

Without another word Vespasian had them all seized and kept under guard; and then he sent for Pilate and said: 'You're not as guilty of wrongdoing as I thought. But I mean to destroy all who were involved in the killing of the Lord who has cured me.'

And he called for a great number of horses, and with four horses to each man he began to have the guilty torn to pieces. They were astounded to see him mete out such justice and asked him why, and he said it was because they had killed Jesus Christ, and now they were all to suffer the same death unless they delivered Christ's body to him.

'We gave it to Joseph!' they cried. 'And we don't know what he's done with it. But if Pilate gives us Joseph, we'll give you Jesus!'

'You didn't trust Joseph at all,' said Pilate. 'You had the body watched by your own guards. And now Christ's disciples say they've seen Him since, and that He is resurrected.'

'All these people must die,' said Vespasian, 'unless they return the body to me.'

He began to have more of them put to death, commanding them to deliver up either Jesus or Joseph. When they saw they were all destined to die, one of them said: 'Would my children and I be spared if I told you where to find Joseph?'

Vespasian said they would; and the man led him to the tower where Joseph had been locked away, and said: 'I saw him imprisoned here, sealed up under this great stone slab.'

'How long ago was this?' Vespasian asked.

'On the third day after the prophet was crucified.'

'Did you kill him before you threw him in prison?'

'No,' the man replied, 'but we gave him a good beating for his crazy words!'

'Do you think he's dead now?'

'How could he possibly be alive,' said the man, 'after so long in here?'

And Vespasian replied: 'He might well have been saved by the one who healed me of my sickness. He healed me, even though I had never done anything for Him – I had never even seen Him! But Joseph was imprisoned for His sake; Joseph asked to be granted His body, and cleaned it, and buried it: I can't believe He would let Joseph die so wretchedly.'

Then the stone slab was lifted, and Vespasian bent down and called to Joseph; but there was no reply. The others said: 'This is incredible. Do you really think this man could have survived so long?'

'I'll not believe he's dead,' Vespasian replied, 'until I've seen him.'

And he took a rope and called to Joseph again. And when no reply came he clambered down into the vault. When he reached the bottom he looked all around, and in one corner of the dungeon he saw a brilliant light. He commanded that the rope be pulled back up, leaving him alone there in the dungeon. Then he moved towards the light.

'Welcome, Vespasian.'

He stood motionless, astonished, and said: 'Who are you who call my name, but wouldn't reply when I called?'

And the answer came: 'I am Joseph of Arimathea.'

Vespasian was elated, and cried: 'Blessed be the Lord who has saved you, for none but He could have done so!'

They embraced each other with the greatest joy, and Vespasian asked Joseph: 'Who told you my name?'

And Joseph said: 'The one who is omniscient.'

Then Vespasian asked if he knew the man who had healed him, and he replied: 'Of what sickness did he cure you?'

And Vespasian told him of his illness in every detail. Joseph was amazed by the story, and said: 'I know Him very well. Do you want to know His name and who He is? If you do, I'll let you know what He bade me tell you.'

'Yes indeed,' said Vespasian, 'I'd be very glad to hear it.'

'Believe then,' said Joseph, 'that it is the Holy Spirit that created all things: Heaven and Earth, night and day and the four elements. The Holy Spirit created the angels, too; but the evil angels became full of pride and envy, and God cast them out of Heaven and for three days and three nights they fell like the heaviest rain that ever was, bringing to Earth all evil, deceit and wickedness. The angels who remain in Heaven strive to guide men, to keep them from sin – in the face of those who rebelled against Christ and whose reward was to lose all spiritual joy. It was in contempt of them that Our Lord created man from the very basest mud, and gave him intelligence and light; and Our Lord declared that with this new creation He would fill the place vacated by the fallen angels. When the Devil realised that so base a being had risen to the glory from which he had fallen, he was enraged, and pondered deeply on how he could deceive him. By tricking Eve he succeeded, and when she and Adam had been led astray, Our Lord, who will not countenance sin, cast them out of Paradise. And they conceived and gave birth to mankind; and the Devil wanted all mankind to be his. But to save mankind, the Father, the Lord of all things, sent His son to Earth to save His people, being born of the Virgin Mary at Bethlehem. He it was who walked the Earth for thirty-three years. He it was who performed the great miracles and wondrous deeds beyond compare. He it was that the Jews put to death on the Cross. He is one being with the Father and the Holy Spirit, and His power is manifest in the fact that He healed you and brought you here and saved me. And know this in all certainty: He is risen again, and has returned to His Father in the same flesh in which He walked the Earth.'

'Joseph,' Vespasian replied, 'you have shown me clearly that He is Lord of all things, and that God is the Father and the Son and the Holy Spirit. Just as you have said, so I believe, and will do so all the days of my life.'

And so it was that Joseph converted Vespasian to a firm belief in the true faith. Then Vespasian called to the people in the chamber above, and said he had found Joseph and wanted the dungeon broken open. They were amazed, and said the man could not possibly be alive. But he commanded them to do as he said quickly; and as soon as it was done, Vespasian came out first and Joseph after. And when they saw him they were filled with wonder, and declared it was a mighty power indeed that had saved him.

And so Vespasian freed Joseph from prison, and led him to where the Jews were gathered. When they saw him they were astounded; and Vespasian said to them: 'Will you deliver Jesus to me, if I give you Joseph?'

'We gave Him to Joseph!' they replied. 'Let him tell you what he's done with Him!'

'You know very well what I did,' said Joseph, 'and you set your own guards to watch the place where I laid His body. But know this now: He is risen again, as Lord and God.'

They were horrified by his words; and Vespasian asked him: 'Do you wish to save any of these people?'

And Joseph answered: 'Unless they believe in the Trinity of Father, Son and Holy Spirit, and that the Son of God was born of the Virgin Mary, they will perish in body and in soul.'

Now, Joseph had a sister named Enigeus whose husband's name was Bron, and Bron loved Joseph dearly; and when Bron and his wife heard that Joseph had been found they were overjoyed and came to meet him and said: 'Sir, we have come for your blessing.'

'Not for mine,' said Joseph, 'but for the blessing of the one who was born of the Virgin and who kept me alive in prison, and in whom you should believe for evermore.'

And he asked if they could find more people who would be willing to believe in the Trinity and in God; and they went and spoke with others, who came before Joseph and declared they would believe in his words, and he said: 'Don't tell me lies or you'll suffer for it, for Vespasian says you'll pay a more terrible price if you do.'

'We could never lie to you,' they said.

'If you wish to follow my belief,' said Joseph, 'you'll not stay in your homes and estates, but will come with me into exile and give up everything for the sake of God and me.'

Vespasian pardoned these; but upon those who would not believe, he exacted such terrible justice as he pleased. And thus it was that he avenged the death of Christ.

* * *

Joseph now took his people into exile. He taught them many of the good words of Our Lord, and set them to work upon the land. For some while they prospered; but as time passed all their work and labour began to be fruitless. Their plight grew worse and worse, until they could bear it no more. They came to Bron, who was very dear to Joseph, and said to him:

'The good and plentiful harvests that we used to enjoy are failing us; no people ever suffered such hunger – we're close to eating our children! We beg you in God's name to talk to Joseph, and find out whether it's because of some sin of ours or his.'

And Bron came to Joseph and told him of his people's plea.

'I shall pray to the one who was born of the Virgin,' said Joseph, 'to tell me why this famine has befallen them.' He was afraid that he had failed to fulfil one of Our Lord's commands. 'If I can find the answer, I'll tell you.'

And Joseph came and knelt before his vessel, the vessel Christ had brought him in his prison, and said: 'Lord, I saw you truly both alive and dead, and saw you again – in the tower where I was imprisoned – after you had suffered the agonies of death, and you bade that, whenever I needed you, I should come and pray before this precious vessel which held your holy blood; so truly, Lord, I beg you now to guide me in answering my people's plea, so that I may act according to your will.'

And when Joseph had made this prayer, the voice of the Holy Spirit descended and said: 'Joseph, do not be afraid: you are not the one who is guilty of this sin.'

'Ah, Lord,' said Joseph, 'help me remove from my company the sinners who have brought this famine upon us!'

And the voice replied: 'Joseph, you will give your people a great sign, testing the power of my flesh and blood against those who have sinned. Remember, Joseph, that I was sold and betrayed on Earth – and knew that it would be so: as I sat at the table of the Last Supper, I said that eating and drinking with me was one who would betray me. Make another table in its name; and when you have made it, summon your brother-in-law Bron – he is a good man and more good will spring from him – and bid him go and fish on the water and bring you the first he catches. While he is fishing, lay the table and take your vessel and place it where you will be sitting, and cover it with the edge of the tablecloth. When you have done so, call your people and tell them they are about to see the cause of their distress. Then take Bron and seat him at your right hand; and you will see him move one seat away, leaving an empty place between you. Know this: that seat will signify the place abandoned by Judas when he betrayed me, and it cannot be filled until the son of Bron's son fills it. Once Bron is seated, call your people and bid those who have true faith in the Trinity of Father, Son and Holy Spirit, and are willing to obey the commandments, to come forward and take their seats.'

With that the voice departed; and Joseph did as Our Lord had commanded, and a great number of his people sat down at the table; but there were many more who did not. The table was full except for the place that could not be filled. And when those who had sat down to eat sensed the sweetness and the fulfilment of their hearts, they very soon forgot the others. One who was seated at the table, whose name was Petrus, looked at those who were standing and said: 'Do you feel what we feel?'

'We feel nothing,' they replied.

And Petrus said: 'Then you are guilty of the sin which has brought the famine upon us.'

Hearing Petrus's words, they were overcome with shame and left the house. And when the service was over, all rose from the table and went off with the others, but Joseph commanded them to return each morning. And so it was that, by the will of God, Joseph came to discover who had sinned, and this was the first place in which the vessel was put to the test.

So things remained for a long time, until those who were excluded asked those who attended about the grace they were given, saying: 'What is it you receive and feel each day?'

'Our hearts could not conceive,' they replied, 'the great joy and delight we feel while we are sitting at that table, and we remain in a state of grace until we return the next day.'

'Where can such grace come from, which so fills man's heart?'

And Petrus replied: 'It comes from the one who saved Joseph in prison.'

'And tell us of the vessel we've seen, of which we know nothing.'

'By that vessel,' he replied, 'we are separated, for it will allow no sinner in its presence. And those who wish to name it rightly will call it the Grail, for it gives such joy and delight to those who can stay in its presence that they feel as elated as a fish escaping from a man's hands into the wide water.'

And hearing this, they said: 'This vessel should indeed be called the Grail*.'

Both those who went and those who stayed named it so, and when Joseph heard the name it pleased him greatly. And to the service of the Grail they all came each morning at the third hour**.

Now, among those who were excluded was a man named Moyse, and he stayed behind when the others left. And every time he saw one of those who had been granted grace he would beg for mercy most earnestly, with an apparently good heart and good intentions, saying: 'In the name of God, sir, ask Joseph to have pity on me and let me share in the grace that you enjoy!' He made this entreaty many times, desperate to join them, until one day, when all the company of the Grail were gathered together, they said they felt sorry for Moyse and would plead to Joseph on his behalf. They all came to him and fell at his feet and implored his mercy. Joseph was taken aback and asked them what they wanted.

'Most of the people leave,' they replied, 'when we come before the Grail. But there's one, sir, named Moyse, who stays behind, and he seems to be full of penitence, and begs you to grant him the grace we share in the company of your vessel.'

When Joseph heard this he replied: 'Grace is not mine to bestow. Our Lord has granted it as He pleases, and those He chooses shall have it. And this man Moyse may not be all he seems. He may well be tricking us – but if so, he'll be his own victim.'

'We'll never trust him again,' they replied, 'if he's been deceiving us by his behaviour. But please invite him to join us.'

And Joseph said: 'I'll pray for Our Lord's guidance in this.'

Then Joseph went alone and prayed, prostrate, before his vessel, that Christ might reveal whether Moyse was truly as he seemed. And thereupon the voice of the Holy Spirit spoke to him, saying: 'Now the time has come when you will see what I told you about the seat left empty between you and Bron.

---

*   An untranslatable play on words runs through this passage, linking the name 'graal' to the verb 'agreer' (to delight).

** The third canonical hour: nine o'clock in the morning.

Moyse claims to seek the grace of the Holy Spirit. Let him come forward then, and sit in its presence, and you will see what becomes of him.'

So Joseph returned to those who had pleaded for Moyse and told them: 'Say to Moyse that if he is as he claims and deserves to be granted grace, no man can deprive him of it. But if he is other than good, he should not come, for he could betray no-one so badly as himself.'

They went and told Moyse what Joseph had said, and he was delighted and said: 'My only fear was that he'd think me unworthy!'

'You have his leave to come,' they replied, 'if you share our faith.'

So they welcomed him into their company, and took him to the service, and when Joseph saw him he said: 'Moyse, Moyse, stay away from anything of which you're not worthy. No-one can deceive you so thoroughly as yourself.'

'As I am truly a good man,' he replied, 'may God permit me to remain in your company.'

'Then step forward,' said Joseph, 'if you're as you say. Be seated, and we'll clearly see your goodness.'

Then Joseph sat down, along with his brother-in-law Bron and all the others, each in his rightful place. And when they were all seated, Moyse, still standing, felt suddenly afraid. He went around the table, but could see nowhere to sit – except in the seat left empty between Joseph and Bron. So he sat there. And the moment he did so he was swallowed up. It was as if he had never been.

When they all rose from the table at the end of the service Petrus spoke to Joseph, saying: 'We've never been so bewildered! By all the powers you believe in, tell us what's become of that man!'

'I've no idea at all,' Joseph replied, 'but if it please the one who has revealed so much to us, we'll find out.'

And Joseph returned and knelt before his vessel, and said: 'Dear Lord God, your powers are wonderful and your ways are wise. Free me from doubt and tell me truly what has become of Moyse.'

Then the voice of the Holy Spirit came to Joseph once more and said: 'Now is revealed the significance of my words when you established this table. I told you that the place left empty beside you would be a reminder of Judas – who lost his seat on the night he betrayed me – and that it would remain empty until one of Bron's lineage came to fill it. The third man of Bron's line will fill that place at the table – or another established in its name. As for the one who was swallowed up, I will tell you what became of him. When he stayed behind after his fellows left, he did so only to deceive you, for he did not believe that those of your company could have such great grace as they did. And be assured that he has fallen into abysmal depths and will never be heard of again. Tell this to your disciples, and consider what you have gained in serving me.'

* * *

A long while now passed, in which Joseph and his followers lived in this state of grace. And the time came when Joseph's sister Enigeus and his brother-in-law Bron decided to ask Joseph for advice about their children's future.

'Sir,' said Bron, 'your sister and I have twelve fair sons, but we wish to take no decision about their future life except with God's advice and yours.'

Joseph promised to pray for guidance, and he came in private before the Grail and remembered his nephews. And when he had finished his prayer, an angel appeared to him and said:

'Joseph, Jesus Christ has sent me to you in answer to your prayer. His will is this: those of your nephews who wish to take wives should do so, but the one who does not shall have the others as his disciples. And when they are married, command Bron the father and Enigeus the mother to bring the unmarried son to you. Then come with him before your vessel and you will hear the word of Jesus Christ, who will speak to you and your nephew together.'

The angel departed, and when Joseph told his sister and Bron how his prayer had been answered, Bron searched far and wide to find wives for his sons according to the command of Holy Church.

Eleven of the sons were glad to marry, but the twelfth, whose name was Alain li Gros, said he would take none of the women, even if he were to be flayed alive. His father was amazed by this and said: 'Dear son, why won't you marry like your brothers?'

'Sir,' he replied, 'I've no desire to do so yet; I'll take none of those wives.'

And so Bron saw eleven of his children married, and the twelfth he took to Joseph and said: 'Sir, here is your nephew who will not take a wife either at my bidding or his mother's.'

And Joseph said to Bron: 'Will you and my sister give him into my keeping?'

And they replied: 'Yes, sir, most willingly.'

Joseph was overjoyed at this, and he took Alain in his arms and embraced him, and said to the father and mother: 'Go now, and leave him with me.'

So Bron and his wife departed, and the child stayed with Joseph, who said to him: 'My good, dear nephew, you should feel joy indeed, for Our Lord has chosen you to serve Him and exalt His name. Stay with me now, and you shall hear the mighty words of Jesus Christ Our Saviour.'

Then Joseph prayed to Our Lord to reveal the truth about his nephew's future life. And when his prayer was done, he heard the voice saying:

'Joseph, your nephew is chaste and honest and good, and will believe your words in all matters. Tell him of the love I have shown you, and of why I came to Earth; and show him your vessel and tell him to read what is written about me inside, for it will confirm his faith. And let him know this: that from him will be born a male child to whom my vessel is to come. Then entrust to him the guardianship of his brothers, and let him go to the West, to the most distant parts he can find, and wherever he goes let him do all he can to exalt my name.'

With that the voice departed, and Joseph took Alain back to his father and said: 'Bron, this son shall be guardian on Earth of his brothers and sisters. They must trust in him and take his advice in all things; if they believe in him, it will be to their advantage. Give him your blessing in their sight and they will trust him and love him the more; he will be a fine leader for as long as they are willing to believe in him.'

Then Bron summoned his sons and their wives and said: 'I want you to be obedient to one of our number. All I can give that is of worth or grace I bestow upon my son Alain, with my prayer that he keep you all in God's name. And I command you to obey him and take his advice in all your troubles, and he will give you guidance. Be sure to undertake nothing against his will.'

With that the children left their father's house, knowing they had a protector. And Alain led them into strange lands; and wherever he went, to all the worthy men and women he met he recounted the story of the death of Jesus Christ. Alain was blessed with so much of God's grace that no man could have more.

Then Our Lord, who had arranged how everything was to be, sent his messenger to Joseph once more, with the words:

'Joseph, your vessel will have an end as well as a beginning. Our Lord knows that Bron is a worthy servant, and He wishes him to be guardian of the vessel after you. Tell him how to behave as its keeper, and tell him everything you have learned in your life of Christ's deeds, so that you confirm him in his faith. And tell him the words Christ taught you when He brought the Grail to you in prison: they are the holy words of the sacrament of the Grail. When you have told Bron all this, commend the vessel into his keeping; and all who hear of him will call him the rich Fisher King because of the fish he caught on the day the table of the Grail was first established. And know this: just as the world is and always will be moving towards night, so must Bron and his people move towards the setting sun – into the West. As soon as the Fisher King has the vessel bestowed upon him, he must journey westward, wherever his heart leads him. And where he comes to rest, there he must await the coming of Alain's son, and when the time is right, pass on to him the vessel and the grace that he will have received from you. Between you then you will have completed a sign of the Trinity, which is in three parts. As for the third of you – the son of Alain li Gros – what befalls him will be determined by Jesus Christ, who is Lord of all.'

Joseph did as Christ's messenger commanded, and remained in the company of the Fisher King for three days and three nights, bequeathing to him the vessel and entrusting to him all Christ's secret words. Then Bron said to Joseph: 'Sir, a great desire to leave has come upon me; is it your will that I should go?'

'It is indeed,' Joseph replied, 'since it is the will of Our Lord. You are well aware of what you will be taking with you, and who will be watching over you; no-one knows as well as you and I. Go when you will.'

And so it was that the rich Fisher King departed and, like his son Alain, made his way into the West.

The Welsh Boy

NOW BEGINS THE HOLY TALE ABOUT A GOOD KNIGHT who was born of Joseph's line. A good knight he was indeed, for he was chaste and pure in body, bold of heart and strong, and in him there was no wickedness. But his face did not suggest such courage, and he had no way with words; indeed, through just a few words which he failed to say, such great misfortunes befell Britain that all the isles and all the lands fell into great sorrow; but he then restored them to happiness by the valour of his fine chivalry. And a good knight he should have been, being descended from Joseph of Arimathea. Joseph was his grandmother's brother, and had asked no reward for his service to Pilate but permission to take Christ's body from the Cross. Pilate had supposed that he would drag it shamefully through the city of Jerusalem and leave it in some foul place outside; but the good soldier had no such intention: rather did he honour the body as highly as he could, laying it to rest in the holy tomb; and he kept the lance with which Christ's side had been pierced and the holy vessel in which he gathered the blood that flowed from Our Saviour's wounds.

Descended from this line was the Good Knight: Joseph was his grandmother's brother, and the Fisher King was his grandfather; his mother's name was Yglais, by whom he had an uncle, the King of Castle Mortal, in whom there was as much evil as there was good in her; by his father, Alain li Gros, he had eleven uncles, but those eleven – Gosgallian, Brun Brandalis, Bertolet the Bald, Brandalus of Wales, Elinant of Escavalon, Calobrutus, Meralis, Fortimet of the Crimson Heath, Meliarman of Albanie, Galerian of the White Tower and Aliban of the Waste City – all died in battle in the service of the Holy Prophet who renewed the Law by His crucifixion, as they strove to check His enemies as much as they could. From such a line was the Good Knight descended, of whose name and ways you soon will hear.

It was in the time when trees burst into leaf, and fields and woods and meadows are green, and the birds in their own Latin sing so sweetly in the morning, and every soul is aflame with joy, that the son of the Widowed Lady of the wild and lonely forest rose, and with all eagerness he saddled up his hunting-horse and took three javelins, and set out from his mother's house.

As he passed into the forest his heart leaped for joy at the sweetness of the season, and taking the bridle from his hunting-horse he let him go free to graze amongst the fresh green grass.

The boy was very skilled with his javelins, and all around he went throwing them, back and forth, high and low, until he heard, coming through the woods, five knights – all fully armed from head to foot. And their arms made a terrible din as they came, as oak- and elm-branch crashed against them; their lances clashed upon their shields, the mail-rings of their hauberks ground; the wood beat, the iron rang, upon their mail-coats and their shields. The boy could hear but could not see them as they came towards him at a walk. He was filled with awe, and said:

'By my soul, my mother's words were true when she told me that devils are the foulest things in the world! She taught me that to counter them a man should always cross himself; but never mind that! I'm going to strike the fiercest with one of my javelins; for then none of the others will dare come near me!'

So he said before he saw the knights; but when he saw them openly, no longer hidden by the trees, and saw their mail-coats shimmering, their helmets, burnished, dazzling, saw the white and the red shining brightly in the sun, and the gold and blue and silver, he thought it glorious indeed, and cried:

'Oh, thank you, God! These are angels I see here! My mother was telling no fable when she said that angels were the fairest things there are – except God, whose beauty surpasses all other. But there, I think, I see God Himself! For I can see one who's ten times fairer than all the rest! My mother told me we should worship God above all things, and so I shall!'

And he threw himself to the ground and said such creed and prayers as his mother had taught him. And the foremost of the knights saw this and said:

'Stay back! A boy who's seen us has collapsed in fear. If we all advance at once he'll die of fright, I think, and won't be able to answer my question.'

So they drew rein, while the foremost knight rode on and greeted the boy and reassured him, saying: 'You needn't be afraid, lad.'

'I'm not, but tell me,' the boy replied, 'are you God?'

'No, in faith!'

'Who are you, then?'

'I'm a knight.'

'I've never met a knight before,' the boy said, 'or ever heard of them; but you're more beautiful than God! Oh, I wish I were the same – made like you, and shining so!'

Then the knight asked him: 'Have you seen five knights and three young ladies pass this way today?'

But the boy had questions of his own to ask: he reached for the knight's lance and, taking hold, said: 'What's this thing you're holding?'

'I see I'm to have fine guidance here!' the knight said. 'I'd thought to learn some news from you, dear friend, but you want some from me! And I'll tell you: this is my lance.'

'Do you throw it,' asked the boy, 'as I do my javelins?'

'Why no! What a simpleton you are! You strike with it directly.'

'Then one of my javelins is better! With these I can kill as many birds or beasts as I like, and with fully the range of a crossbow.'

'That's not really my concern! Come, boy, answer my question about the knights. Tell me, do you know where they are, and did you see the young ladies?'

The boy grabbed the bottom of his shield and said: 'What's this? What's it for?'

'Boy,' said the knight, 'is this some trick? I thought you'd tell me news rather than learn from me! But so you shall, come what may, for I've taken a liking to you: this thing I'm carrying is called a shield.'

'A shield?'

'And truly,' he said, 'it's such a faithful friend to me that if anything's thrown or aimed at me it sets itself against the blows.'

Just then the knights who had stayed behind came briskly up to their lord and said: 'What's this Welshman saying, sir?'

'He doesn't quite know his manners,' their lord replied. 'He won't give me a straight reply to anything I ask him. Instead he asks the name and use of everything he sees!'

'Oh, I promise you, sir, the Welsh are all more stupid than the beasts in pasture; and so is this one – just like a beast! Only a fool would dally with him.'

'I don't care,' the lord said. 'Before I carry on I'll tell him whatever he wants to know.' Then he asked him again: 'If you don't mind, boy, tell me of the five knights and the girls; have you seen them today?'

The boy clutched him by his mail-coat and tugged at it, saying: 'What's this thing you're wearing here?'

'Don't you know, boy?' said the knight.

'No, I don't.'

'This is my hauberk, and it's as heavy as iron – because that's what it's made of, as you can see.'

'I don't know anything about that,' he said, 'but it's very beautiful. What do you do with it? What's it for?'

'That's easily answered, boy. If you threw a javelin or shot an arrow at me, you couldn't do me any harm.'

'Oh, sir knight! God keep the hinds and stags from getting hauberks, or I'd never kill one! I'd have to give up hunting them!'

The knight said to him yet again: 'Now, boy, can you tell me news of the knights and the girls?'

But he, in his simplicity, said to him: 'Were you born like that?'

'No, lad, that's impossible! How could a man be born like this?'

'Who was it, then, made you so?'

'Very well, I'll tell you.'

'Go on, then.'

'Five years ago I was given these arms by King Arthur, who dubbed me knight. But come, lad, tell me now: what became of them – the knights who passed this way with the three girls? Were they riding fast or slowly?'

And the boy replied: 'Up there, sir, where the woods encircle the mountain, are the passes of Valbone.'

'What of it?' said the knight.

'That's where my mother's harrowers are, who plough and sow her lands. And if those people passed that way and they saw them, they'll tell you.'

They said they would go with him if he would guide them there, and so the boy took his hunting-horse and rode to where the harrowers were working in the barley-fields. But when they caught sight of their lady's son accompanied by armed knights they all trembled with fear; for they knew all too well that if the knights had told him of their life and ways, then he would want to be a knight; and his mother then would lose her mind, for she had been trying to keep him from ever seeing knights or learning anything of their business. The boy said to the men who drove the oxen:

'Have you seen five knights and three girls ride this way?'

'They went through the pass this very day,' the ox-drivers said.

And so the boy said to the knight who had talked to him so long: 'Sir, the knights and girls did go this way; but tell me more now of the king who makes men knights: where does he live?'

'At present, boy, the king is staying at Cardoeil. He was there not five days ago, for I was there and saw him; and if he's not there now, there'll be someone who'll give you news of him for sure, and tell you where he's gone.'

With that the knight rode off at a gallop, anxious to catch up with the others. Nor did the boy delay in riding home, where his mother was waiting, her heart black with grief because he had been away so long. But the moment she saw him she was filled with joy; she could not hide her happiness, she loved her son so much, and ran to meet him, crying: 'Dear son! Dear son! You've been away so long! Where have you been? I could have died!'

'I'll tell you, and without a word of a lie; I've seen something that made my heart rejoice. Mother, didn't you always say that God and the angels were so beautiful that there was nothing in the world so fair?'

'I said so, truly, and still do.'

'Say so no more, mother! Haven't I seen the fairest things alive, that pass through the lonely forest? They're more beautiful, I think, than God and all His angels!'

His mother took him in her arms and said: 'God protect you, dear son! I do believe you've seen the angels who cause people such grief, killing whoever they come across.'

'No, truly, mother, no, I didn't! They told me they were called knights.'

On hearing him utter this word his mother fainted; and when she came to, she cried, now filled with grief and anger: 'Oh, no! Oh, no! My sweet, dear son, I'd planned to guard you so well from knights that you'd never hear of them or

ever see one! You should indeed have been a knight, if God had guarded your
father and others close to you. There was no knight of such high worth, or as
feared and respected, as your father, in all the islands of the sea. You may be
proud indeed of your descent, both on his side and on mine: for I too was born
of a line of knights, and the finest in the land. In all the ocean's isles there was
no finer lineage than mine in my time; but now the greatest of my line have
fallen: it's often the case that misfortunes befall the worthy men who strive to
live in honour. Your father, though you don't know this, was wounded in the
leg and crippled. Then his great land and his great treasures all were lost, and
he fell into utter poverty. And after the death of King Uther Pendragon, the
father of good King Arthur, the lands were laid waste and all who could do so
took refuge elsewhere. Your father had this manor-house out here in the wild
forest; he couldn't flee, but with all possible speed he had himself borne here
in a litter, for he didn't know where else to go. And you, who were very small
– not yet weaned – had two dear brothers, and when they grew older, at your
father's advice they went to two royal courts, to receive arms and horses. The
elder went to the king of Escavalon, and served him a long while, and the
younger served King Ban of Gomorret. On one and the same day both boys
were dubbed and knighted; and on one and the same day they both set out to
return home, wanting to delight me and their father; but we never saw them
again, for they were both killed in combat and left for the crows and rooks to
peck out their eyes. Your father died of grief for his sons, and I've suffered a
bitter life since his death. You were all my consolation then, and all that I
possessed, for nothing else remained to me. God had left me nothing more to
give me joy and comfort.'

The boy had heard very little of what his mother had been saying. 'Give me
something to eat,' he said. 'I don't know what you're talking about. I'd be very
glad to go to the king who makes men knights; and I *shall* go, whatever grief it
brings.'

His mother kept him there as long as she could, and dressed him in a great
canvas shirt, and breeches made in the Welsh fashion, where shoes and leggings
are made together in one piece; and she gave him a hooded tunic of deer-hide,
stitched tight all round; that was how his mother clothed him. She held him
back for three days, but that was all; after that all her ploys were vain. Then she
was overcome with grief. Weeping, she kissed and embraced him, and said:

'I can't bear to see you leave! You'll go to the king's court and tell him to give
you arms. And he won't refuse: he'll give you them, I know he will. But when
it comes to trial of arms, what will happen then? How will you fare at something
you've never done before – and never seen another do? Badly, I fear! Dear son,
I want to give you some advice which you'd do very well to heed. Soon you'll
be a knight. Well, if you encounter, near or far, any lady or girl in need of help,
be ready to aid her if she asks, for when a man fails to honour ladies, his own
honour is dead. But if you should desire the love of any, take care. A maid who
kisses gives much; so if she consents to kiss you, I forbid you to take more: leave

with the kiss! But if she has a ring on her finger or a purse at her waist, and out of love she should give it to you, then I'd be happy that you should take her ring; yes, I give you leave to take the ring or purse. And one thing more: on the road, or in lodging, share no-one's company for long without asking him his name; for know this: the name reveals the man. Dear son, seek the company of worthy men, for they never give bad advice. Above all I beg you to go to minster or to church, to pray to Our Lord to give you honour in this world and grant that you so lead your life that you may come to a good end.'

'Mother,' he said, 'what's a church?'

'It's where one pays service to God, who made Heaven and Earth and set us men and women here.'

'And what's a minster?'

'The same: a beautiful and holy house where sacred relics and treasures are kept; and there we sacrifice the body of Jesus Christ, the holy prophet. He was betrayed and wrongly judged, and He suffered death's anguish for all men and women; for their souls went to Hell when they left their bodies, but He set them free. He was bound to a stake and scourged, and then crucified, and made to wear a crown of thorns. To hear masses and matins, and to worship this lord, I would have you go to church.'

With that he would delay no more and took his leave. His mother wept. He was dressed in the style and manner of the Welsh, with shoes of coarse hide on his feet, and he carried a switch in his right hand to goad his hunting-horse along. He always bore three javelins: he wanted to take them with him now, but his mother took two of them because he would have looked too Welsh. She would have taken all three of them if she could. And as he left, she kissed him, weeping, for she loved him dearly, and prayed to God to keep him safe.

'Dear son!' she cried. 'God guide you! May he give you more joy than I have now, wherever you may go.'

When the boy had gone a stone's throw he looked back and saw his mother in a heap at the bridge's foot; she lay there in a faint, as though she had fallen dead. But the boy lashed his hunting-horse hard on the rump and departed; and his mount was sure of foot and bore him swiftly through the forest, great and dark. He rode on from early morning till the day drew to a close. He slept in the forest that night, until the bright new day appeared.

* * *

In the morning when the birds began to sing the boy rose and mounted, and rode on until he caught sight of a pavilion pitched in a beautiful meadow beside a stream from a spring. The pavilion was a wonder, it was so fair: one side was vermilion, the other embroidered with a thread of gold, and on the top was a golden eagle. Upon this eagle the sun fell, bright and blazing, and the whole meadow shimmered with the pavilion's light. All around it were leafy bowers, and lodges made in the Welsh manner, of interwoven branches. The boy rode towards the pavilion, and as he approached he said:

'God, I see your house! It would be shameful not to go and worship you. My mother was telling the truth when she said that a church was the fairest thing there is, and she told me that whenever I came across a church I should go and worship the Creator. I'll go and pray to Him to give me food: I'm starving!'

Then he came up to the pavilion and found it open; and inside he saw a bed covered with a rich silken cloth; and in the bed, all alone, lay a young girl, sleeping. Her companions were out in the wood: her maids had gone to pick fresh flowers with which to strew the pavilion. As the boy entered, his horse neighed so loudly that the maiden heard it and awoke with a start. And the boy, in his simplicity, said:

'I give you greeting, girl, as my mother taught me to do. She told me I should greet girls whenever I met them!'

The girl trembled with fear, thinking the boy was mad – and she charged herself with madness for letting him find her alone.

'Go away, boy!' she cried. 'Be off, or my love will see you!'

'No, by my life! I'm going to kiss you!' said the boy. 'I don't care who it upsets, for my mother told me to!'

'I'll never kiss you, truly I won't!' cried the girl. 'Be off! If my love finds you here you're dead!'

But the boy had strong arms and embraced her – but gauchely, for that was the only way he knew. Then he laid her down full-length beneath him, and she struggled with all her might to get away; but she fought in vain, for whether she liked it or not the boy kissed her seven times – until he saw a ring on her finger crowned with a brilliant emerald.

'My mother also told me,' he said, 'to take the ring from your finger, but to do no more with you. So now for the ring! Let me have it!'

'You'll never have my ring,' the maiden cried, 'unless you tear it from my hand by force!'

The boy took her by the hand, forced her fist open, snatched the ring from her finger and set it on his own; then he said: 'I wish you well, girl! I'm off now, and with good reward! It's much better kissing you than any of the maids at my mother's house: your lips don't taste sour!'

The girl began to weep and begged him: 'Don't take my ring, boy! I'll be sorely treated for it, and it'll cost you your life, I promise you!'

He took in not a word of this, but he knew he hadn't breakfasted; he was dying of hunger, horribly. He found a cask full of wine and beside it a silver goblet; and then he saw a fresh, white cloth on a bundle of rushes. He picked it up, and underneath he found three venison pies, new-baked – a dish of which he was not unfond! To quell the hunger that beset him he broke off a hunk of pie and ate with a vengeance, and started pouring wine into the silver cup; it wasn't bad; he drank great and frequent draughts, and said:

'I can't eat all these pies myself, girl. Give me a hand, they're very good! We can have one each and there'll still be a whole one left!'

But the girl just wept and couldn't say a word. She wrung her hands and shed piteous tears, while the boy ate and drank till he had had his fill. Then he covered up what was left and took his leave at once, commending her to God – little though his good wishes pleased her.

'God save you, friend!' he cried. 'I'm off now, by your leave.'

The girl wept on and said she would never commend him to God, for he had betrayed her, and because of him she would suffer shame and distress such as no girl had ever known. And so he left her there, in tears.

It was not long before her lover returned from the wood; and when he saw the hoofprints left by the boy, who had now set off on his way, he was most aggrieved. He found his love weeping, and said: 'Girl, from the signs I see, I think a knight has been here!'

'No, sir, no, I promise you! It was a Welsh boy, a tiresome, base and foolish thing, who drank as much of your wine as he pleased, and ate some of your pies!'

'Is that why you're weeping? If he'd eaten and drunk it all it would have been as I'd have wished.'

'That's not all, sir,' she said. 'There's also my ring: he seized it from me and carried it off. I'd rather have died than have had him take that!'

Her love was downcast then, and anguished in his heart. 'What? This is outrageous! Since he's taken it, let him keep it; but I think he did more! If he did, don't hide it.'

'Sir,' she said, 'he kissed me.'

'Kissed you?'

'Yes, truly, but it was against my will.'

'No!' he cried, struck through with jealousy. 'It was as you wished, and pleased you well! He found no great resistance! You think I don't know you? I'm not blind to your falseness! You've taken a wicked course – and a course to suffering: your horse shall be neither groomed nor fed until I've taken my revenge! If he loses a shoe he'll not be re-shod; and if he dies you'll have to walk! And the clothes you wear will not be changed; you'll follow me on foot and naked until I have his head; I'll settle for no less.'

With that he sat down and began to eat.

* * *

Meanwhile the boy rode on, until he saw a charcoal-burner coming along his path, driving an ass before him.

'Worthy sir,' said the boy, 'tell me the quickest way to Cardoeil. They say King Arthur makes men knights there.'

'Boy,' he said, 'this way lies a castle overlooking the sea. That's where you'll find King Arthur, both joyful and grieving.'

'Oh? Why's that, sir? Tell me, please.'

'He fought with all his army against King Rion, the King of the Isles, and Rion was defeated, which brought King Arthur joy. But now his companions have left him, deciding they'd rather stay at their own castles, and he has no news of them: that's what's caused him grief.'

The boy cared little for the charcoal-burner's news, but set off along the road he had shown him, until he caught sight of a castle standing by the sea, finely positioned and strong and handsome. And then he saw, riding out through the gate, an armed knight carrying a cup of gold; he held his lance and his reins and his shield by his left hand, and the cup of gold in his right. His arms were quite magnificent, and from head to foot they were entirely red. The boy saw these arms, so handsome and all brand new, and they appealed to him greatly, and he said:

'In faith, I'll ask the king to grant me those; how I'd love it if he gave them to me! A curse on the man who'd seek any others!'

With that he hurried on towards the castle, so eager to reach the court; but as he drew near, the knight stopped him and asked: 'Where are you scurrying off to, boy?'

'To the king's court,' he said, 'to ask him for those arms!'

'And well you might, lad!' the knight laughed. 'Off you trot, then, and hurry back. And tell this to that worthless king: if he doesn't wish to hold his land as my vassal, he should yield it to me or send a champion to fight me for it, for I say it's mine. To prove my point, I've just taken this cup from under his nose, with the very wine he was drinking!'

The knight should have sought another messenger, for the boy hadn't heard a word. He rode straight on to the court, where the king and his knights were seated at dinner. The hall was paved with flagstones, and was as long as it was wide – and it was on ground level, so the boy rode his horse straight in. King Arthur was sitting at the head of the table, lost in troubled thought; but while he was sombre and silent, all his knights were laughing and joking. The boy came forward, not knowing whom to greet, for he did not know the king at all. Then Yvonet came towards him, holding a knife in his hand.

'Vassal,' the boy said, 'show me which of these men is the king.'

Yvonet, who was courteous indeed, replied: 'There he is, friend.'

And the boy went up to him at once and gave him such greeting as he knew. But the king was still lost in thought and did not say a word. The boy addressed him a second time; the king thought on and said nothing.

'By my life,' said the boy, 'this king never made anyone a knight! How could he when you can't get a word out of him?'

So he prepared to go back and turned his hunting-horse about; but he pulled his mount so near the king, like the rude soul that he was, that he sent the king's hat flying from his head to the table. The king turned his bowed head to the boy and awoke from his thoughts and said: 'Dear brother, welcome. Please don't take it ill that I didn't return your greeting. I couldn't reply for grief and anger, for my greatest enemy, the one who hates and torments me most, has now contested my land; he's mad enough to claim that he'll have it all, uncon-ditionally, whether I like it or not! His name is the Red Knight of the Forest of Quinqueroi. I wouldn't have cared about his words, but he took my cup from in front of me, and snatched it up so recklessly that he poured the whole cupful of wine over the queen! It was a base, ugly, shameful deed; the queen has run back to her chamber, suicidal with anger.'

The boy didn't care a jot about the king's story, or about his grief or shame – and just as little about the king's wife.

'Make me a knight, lord king,' he said, 'for I want to go.'

The eyes of the simple, untaught youth were bright and laughing. No-one who saw him thought him wise, but all who saw him thought him handsome and fair.

'Friend,' said the king, 'dismount and give your horse to a boy, who'll care for it and do your bidding. You'll shortly be a knight, to my honour and your profit.'

But the boy replied: 'The ones I met in the glade never dismounted. Why do you want *me* to? By my life, I won't get down! Just hurry up, then I can go. And I shan't be a knight without being a *red* knight! Grant me the arms of the one who took your golden cup – I met him outside the gate.'

Kay the seneschal was angered by these words and said: 'How right you are, friend! Off you go and take his arms: they're yours! How wise of you to come and ask!'

The king heard this and was enraged, and said to Kay: 'It's very wrong of you to mock the boy, and no mark of a worthy man. Though the boy be simple, his upbringing may be to blame, at the hands of a bad master; he may yet prove a worthy vassal.'

So said the king to Kay. Then the boy, just as he was leaving, noticed a fair and lovely girl and greeted her; and she returned his greeting, and then laughed, and as she laughed she said: 'If you live long, boy, I feel in my heart that in all the world there will not be, nor will there ever have been known, a finer knight than you.'

The girl had not laughed for more than six years; but she said these words so loud and clear that everyone could hear her. And the words enraged Kay. He leaped forward and slapped her so hard across her tender cheek that he laid her full-length on the floor. And turning back after hitting the girl he found the court fool standing by a chimney, and he kicked him into the blazing fire in rage, because the fool had always said: 'That girl will not laugh until she sees the one who is to be the greatest of all knights.'

The fool wailed, the girl wept, and the boy delayed no longer: without a word from anyone he set off after the Red Knight. And Yvonet, who was a keen bringer of news to court, ran off, all alone, through a garden beside the hall and down through a postern gate, and came straight to the path where the Red Knight sat, waiting for adventure and a test of chivalry. The boy was racing towards him to take his arms, and the knight, while he was waiting, had placed the golden cup on a rock of grey stone. When the boy had ridden within earshot he cried:

'Lay down your arms! Carry them no more, for King Arthur commands you!'

And the knight called back: 'Boy, is anyone coming to defend the king's right?'

'What? By the Devil, sir knight, are you mocking me, that you haven't laid aside my arms? Take them off now, I command you!'

'Boy,' he said, 'I asked you if anyone was coming from the king to fight with me.'

'Sir knight, take off those arms or I'll take them off you! They're not yours any more! I'm warning you, I'll hit you if you make me say it again!'

The knight was angered then: he raised his lance with both hands and gave the boy such a blow across the shoulders with the shaft that he rocked forward on to the neck of his horse. The boy was enraged by the pain from the blow; he aimed for the knight's eye and let fly his javelin so fast that the knight neither saw nor heard it; it struck him through the eye and into the brain, and out through the nape of his neck the blood and brain gushed. The knight's heart burst with the pain, and he toppled over and crashed to the ground, stone dead. The boy dismounted and laid the knight's lance to one side and took his shield from his neck; but he didn't know how to tackle the helmet on the knight's head: he couldn't think how to remove it. And he wanted to ungird the knight's sword but he didn't know how, nor how to draw it from its scabbard; he just took the sword and heaved and pulled. Yvonet began to laugh when he saw the boy's bewilderment.

'What are you doing, friend?' he said.

'I don't know. From what your king said I thought he'd granted these arms to me, but it seems I'll have to butcher the knight first: they're stuck to the body so tight that inside and out are one piece, it seems.'

'Don't worry,' said Yvonet. 'I can separate them if you wish.'

'Go on, then,' said the boy, 'and give them to me, quickly.'

So Yvonet set to work, and stripped the knight right down to his toes; he left neither hauberk nor shoe, nor the helm on his head nor any other armour. But the boy would not lay aside his own clothes; in spite of Yvonet's pleas he would not take the sumptuous tunic of quilted silk that the knight had worn beneath his hauberk. Nor could Yvonet take from the boy the old ankle-boots he wore; the boy said:

'You must be joking! Swap the clothes my mother made me for this knight's useless stuff? My lovely thick canvas shirt for his, all soft and thin? My tunic never leaks: his wouldn't keep out a drop! Hang the man who'd change good clothes for bad!'

Teaching a fool isn't easy. All pleas were vain: he would take nothing but the arms. Yvonet laced them on for him, and tied the spurs to his ankle-boots, and clad him in the hauberk – a finer one was never seen; and over the mail hood he set the helmet, which fitted him very well; and he taught him to gird on the sword so that it hung loose and free; then he set the boy's foot in the stirrup and mounted him on the knight's charger. He had never seen stirrups before, and knew nothing of spurs – he had never used anything but sticks and switches. Yvonet brought him the shield and the lance and gave them to him. And before Yvonet turned back, the boy said:

'Friend, have my hunting-horse – take him with you. He's very good, but I don't need him now. And take the king his cup with my greetings. Oh, and tell this to the girl that Kay struck on the cheek: that if I can, I mean to deal with Kay so that she may consider herself avenged.'

And Yvonet replied that he would return the cup to the king and deliver his message faithfully. And with that they parted and went their ways.

Yvonet came into the hall where the barons were, and carried the cup to the king, saying: 'Sire, be joyful now, for your knight returns your cup to you.'

'Which knight do you mean?'

'The one who's just left here,' said Yvonet.

'You mean the Welsh boy,' said the king, 'who asked me for the red arms of the knight who's done me every possible shame?'

'Yes indeed, sire!'

'And how did he get my cup? Did the knight love and esteem him so much that he returned it of his own free will?'

'No indeed. The boy made him pay dearly for it: he killed him.'

'What? How was that, friend?'

'I saw the knight strike him with his lance most painfully, and the boy replied with a javelin clean through the eye, so that blood and brain spilled out behind, and laid him dead on the ground.'

Then the king said to the seneschal: 'Ah, Kay! You've done me ill service today! With your offensive tongue, which has uttered so many insults, you've robbed me of the boy who has been of such worth to me.'

'And, sire,' said Yvonet to the king, 'he gave me a message for the queen's maid whom Kay struck out of spite and hatred: he says he'll take revenge on him if he gets the chance.'

The fool, who was sitting beside the fire, heard this and leaped to his feet; he came happily up to the king, hopping and jumping for joy, and said: 'God save me, sire, adventures are now about to befall us, and many of them will be hard and cruel! And I promise you, Kay can be quite certain that his foot and his hand and his base and foolish tongue will bring shame upon his life, for before a fortnight has passed the knight will have avenged the kick he gave me, and the slap he gave the girl will be well repaid, for his right arm will be broken between the elbow and the armpit: he'll carry it in a sling for half a year, indeed he will; he can escape it no more than death!'

These words upset Kay so much that he nearly burst with fury; he would have killed the fool in front of everyone, but he refrained from attacking him for fear of incurring the king's displeasure. And the king cried:

'Ah, Kay! You've earned my rage today! If someone had guided the boy in the art of arms, so that he could handle a shield and lance, he would have made a good knight without question; but he knows so little that he couldn't even draw a sword if he needed to! Now he's sitting in the saddle, fully armed, and he's sure to meet some hardy knight who won't hesitate to wound him to win his horse; he'll kill or maim him in an instant, for he won't know how to defend himself. He's so naive and untaught, he won't last long.'

Thus the king lamented and grieved for the boy, and his face was downcast. But lamenting would do no good, and he said no more.

* * *

Meanwhile the boy went riding through the forest without a stop, until he came to a flat land beside a river, great and roaring and wider than a crossbow's range. He rode across a meadow towards it, but he did not venture into the water: he saw that it was dark and rushing, and a good deal deeper than the Loire. And so he rode along the bank; and on the far side of the river there rose a jagged crop of rock, the water thundering at its foot, and on a side of the rock sloping down towards the sea there stood a rich, strong castle. Where the river opened into a bay the boy turned to his left, and there he saw the castle's towers being born: for in his eyes they were being born there, issuing from the rock. In the middle of the castle loomed a great, strong tower, and a mighty barbican faced the bay and made its stand against the sea, which pounded at its foot. At the four corners of the castle wall, which was made of great, square, solid stones, were four handsome turrets. The castle was finely situated, and well arranged inside. Before the round gatehouse was a bridge built of stone and sand and lime, stretching across the water; it was strong and high, with battlements all the way along, and before it was a drawbridge, built to serve its special purpose: by day it was a bridge, by night a gate.

The boy rode on towards it. Dressed in a rich and deep-hued robe, a nobleman was strolling on the bridge. Up rode the boy. He was very mindful of what his mother had told him, for he gave the nobleman his greeting, and said: 'Sir, my mother taught me that.'

'God bless you, brother,' the nobleman replied, seeing he was a simpleton. 'Where have you come from?'

'From the court of King Arthur!'

'Oh yes? What were you doing there?'

'The king made me a knight!'

'A knight! God save me, I thought he'd forgotten about such matters; I thought he had other things on his mind than making men knights. But tell me, brother, who gave you those arms?'

'The king!' he said.

'He gave them to you? How was that?'

And the boy told him the whole story. Then the nobleman questioned him further, and seeing him mounted on the magnificent charger, asked him about his horsemanship.

'I run him up and down nicely, just like I did with the hunting-horse I took from my mother's house.'

'Tell me more, friend. How do you manage with your arms?'

'I know all about getting them on and off, just the way the fellow did when he disarmed the knight I killed and put them on me. They're so light to wear, they're no trouble at all.'

'By my life, that's good,' the noble said, 'I'm glad of that. Now tell me, what was it brought you here?'

'Sir, my mother told me to seek the company of worthy men wherever I found them, and to trust in what they said, for there was much to gain by heeding them.'

And the nobleman replied: 'God bless your mother, for she gave you good advice. Have you anything else to tell me?'

'Yes.'

'What's that?'

'Just one thing: give me lodging tonight.'

'Gladly,' said the nobleman, 'provided you grant me a favour – one from which you'll greatly benefit.'

'What's that?' he said.

'Trust in your mother's advice – and also mine.'

'In faith,' said the boy, 'I promise you that.'

'Dismount then.'

And the boy stepped down. One of the two boys who were there took his horse, while the other disarmed him; that left him in his ridiculous outfit – the ankle-boots and the ill-made, ill-cut coat of deer-hide that his mother had given him. The nobleman was then fitted with the sharp steel spurs that the boy had brought, and he mounted the boy's horse, hung the shield from his neck by its strap and took up the lance, and said:

'Now, friend, learn the art of arms: note how a lance should be held, and a horse spurred on and reined in.'

Then he unfurled the pennon and showed the boy how a shield should be carried. He made it hang a little forward until it touched the horse's neck, and he set the lance in its rest and spurred the horse on. It was worth a hundred marks, that horse: none ever charged with more will, more speed or more power. The nobleman was highly skilled with shield and horse and lance, for he had learned the art from his youth, and everything he did filled the boy with delight and he watched with rapt attention. When he had finished his splendid mock-combat before the boy, the nobleman came back to him with his lance raised and asked him:

'Well, friend, could you handle the lance and shield like that, and spur and guide the horse?'

And straight away the boy replied that he did not wish to live a day longer without knowing how to do those things.

'Dear friend,' said the nobleman, 'what a man can't do he can learn to do, if he's willing to apply himself. All crafts can be learned with will and work and practice. And you shouldn't be ashamed or blamed if you can't do what you've never done and have never seen others do.'

Then the nobleman told him to mount, and the boy began to carry the lance and shield as perfectly as if he had spent his life in tournaments and wars, and ridden through every land in search of battle and adventure; for it came to him quite naturally, and with nature instructing him and his whole heart determined, he was bound to have no difficulty. He gave such a fine account of himself that the nobleman was greatly pleased, and said to himself that if the boy had spent his whole life engaged in arms this would still have seemed a fine display.

When the boy had done his turn he came back to the nobleman with his lance raised, just as he had seen him do, and said: 'Did I do it well, sir? Do you think my effort will pay off, if I keep on trying? I've never seen anything I desired so much. I'd love to know as much about it all as you.'

'My friend,' said the nobleman, 'if that's your heart, you will; you need have no fear of that.'

Three times the nobleman mounted, three times he taught the boy as much as he could, until he had taught him a good deal; and three times he bade the boy do likewise. The final time he said to him:

'If you met a knight and he struck you, what would you do?'

'I'd hit him back.'

'And if your lance broke?'

'Then there'd be nothing else for it: I'd lay into him with my fists.'

'No you wouldn't, friend.'

'What should I do, then?'

'Join combat with the sword.'

Then the nobleman plunged the lance bolt upright in the ground before him, eager to teach the boy to defend himself with the sword if he were attacked, and to go on the offensive if the chance arose; and grasping the sword he said to the boy: 'This is how to defend yourself if anyone attacks you.'

'God save me,' said the boy, 'no-one knows as much about that as I; I learned all about it at my mother's house, practising with cushions and shields, often till I was quite worn out.'

'Then let's go to my house at once,' said the nobleman, 'I can give you no better advice! Tonight we'll enjoy the finest lodging – no-one shall stand in our way!'

They both set off then side by side, and the boy said to his host: 'Sir, my mother taught me that I should never share a man's company for long without knowing his name. So I'd like to know yours.'

'Dear friend,' the nobleman replied, 'my name is Gorneman de Gorhaut.'

And with that they walked into the castle, holding each other by the hand.

As they began to climb the steps a young lad came up eagerly, carrying a short mantle; he ran and dressed the boy in it, in case he caught some harmful cold after getting so hot. The nobleman's house was rich and handsome, and he had fine retainers; and the table was already laid, with dishes good and appealing and well prepared. The knights washed and sat down to dine. The nobleman seated the boy next to him, and had him eat with him from the same platter. They ate and drank their fill. And when they had risen from the table the nobleman, who was most courteous, begged the boy to stay for a month. He would gladly keep him a full year if he wished, and in that time would teach him things, if he cared to learn, which would be of great use in time of need. And the boy replied:

'Sir, I don't know if I'm near the house where my mother lives, but I pray to God to lead me to her so that I may see her again, for I saw her faint and fall at the foot of the bridge outside the gate, and I don't know whether she's alive or dead. She fainted with grief because I left her, I know it. So I can't stay, not until I know how she is.'

The nobleman could see it was no use pleading with him. They said no more, and retired to their rest without another word, for the beds were already made.

The nobleman rose early next morning and went to the boy's bed where he found him still lying, and had a shirt and breeches of fine linen brought to him as a present, and hose dyed with Brazil-wood, and a tunic of violet silk woven and made in India; he sent him all these things to wear, and said to him: 'If you'll take my advice, friend, you'll wear *these* clothes.'

And the boy replied: 'How can you say that? Aren't the clothes my mother made me twice as good as these?'

'By the eyes in my head, boy, these are far better!'

'Far worse, you mean!'

'You said, friend, when I brought you here, that you'd do everything I told you.'

'And so I will,' said the boy. 'I won't break my promise to you in any way.'

And so he delayed no longer in donning the clothes, and abandoned the ones his mother had made. Then the nobleman knelt down and fastened the boy's right spur; for it was the custom that whoever made a man a knight should put on his spur. And the nobleman took the sword and girded it on the boy and kissed him, and said that with the sword he had given him the highest order that God had created: the order of chivalry, which should always be clean of all wickedness. Then he said:

'Good brother, listen to me now: if you ever have to fight a knight, I pray you, if you gain the upper hand and he begs for mercy, make sure you grant it and don't kill him. Another thing: don't be too keen on talking. Anyone who talks too much is bound to say things that make him look a fool. In the words of the wise: "He sins who speaks too much". That's why I warn you, friend, not to have too loose a tongue. I beg this, too: if you find a man or a woman, or an orphan or a lady, in any kind of distress, lend them your aid if you can. And one more lesson I have for you – and don't scorn it, for it's not a lesson to be scorned: go willingly to church to pray to the One who made all things, that He may have mercy on your soul, and in this life here on Earth He may guard you as His Christian.'

The boy said to the nobleman: 'May you be blessed by all the popes, sir, for my mother said the same!'

'Never say, dear brother,' said the nobleman, 'that your mother taught you such and such: say it was I. I don't blame you for having said so hitherto, but henceforth please refrain, for if you keep saying it people will think you're mad.'

'What shall I say, then, sir?'

'You can say that the vassal who fastened your spur taught and instructed you so.'

And the boy gave him his word that for as long as he lived he would not mention anyone but him, for he felt that his advice was good. Then the nobleman raised his hand and made the sign of the Cross over him, and said:

'Since you've no desire to stay and are determined to go, go with God and may He guide you.'

The Fisher King

THE NEW KNIGHT TOOK HIS LEAVE OF HIS HOST, most anxious now to return to his mother and to find her alive and well. He made his way into the lonely forest, for he was more at home there than in the open country, knowing the ways of the woods. He rode on until he caught sight of a castle: it was strong and impressive, but outside its walls there was nothing but sea and river and wasteland. He hurried on until he neared the gate; but before he could reach it he had to cross a bridge so weak that he feared it would hardly take his weight. He managed to get across without mishap, but when he reached the gate he found it locked fast. He wasn't one to hammer gently, and his cries were none too soft. He pounded away until a thin, pale girl rushed to the windows of the hall and cried:

'Who's that calling?'

He looked up towards the girl and said: 'Dear friend, I'm a knight who prays that you let me in and give me lodging tonight.'

'Sir,' she said, 'you shall have lodging, though you'll give me little thanks for it. But we'll lodge you as well as we can.'

The girl drew back from the window then; and he, waiting at the gate, thought they were making him stand around too long and began to shout again. Then four retainers came, each clutching an axe and bearing a sword at his waist, and unlocked the gate and said to him: 'Come this way.'

If the retainers had been in a happy state they would have been handsome men indeed; but they had suffered so much hardship from lack of food and sleep that they were a pitiful sight. And just as he had found the land outside all bare and deserted, so he found precious little within. Everywhere he went the streets were empty and the houses in ruins, with not a man or woman anywhere. There were two churches in the town which had both been abbeys: one of nuns, lost and fearful, the other of monks, confused, bewildered. He found these churches well adorned neither with ornament nor tapestry; instead he saw their walls crumbling and broken, their towers open to the sky; and the doors of all the houses hung open at night as they did by day. No millstone ground, no oven baked in any part of the town, and there was not a pennyworth of anything to be had: no bread, no pastry, no wine, no cider, no ale.

The four retainers led him to a palace roofed with slate, and there they helped him dismount and disarm. Then a boy came down a staircase from the hall carrying a grey mantle, and draped it on the knight's shoulders. Another took his horse to the stable, where there was only the tiniest amount of hay or oats. The others ushered him up the steps to the hall, which was handsome indeed, and two noblemen and a girl came to meet him. The noblemen were grey with age but not altogether white; they would have been in their prime of blood and strength had it not been for their troubles and their woe. As for the girl who came with them, she was more gracious, comely and elegant than a hawk or bird of paradise. Her mantle and tunic were of a rich black cloth starred with gold, and there was no sign of wear on the ermine lining. The neck of her gown had a border of black and white sable, of perfect length and breadth. Her hair was so fair and shining that anyone who saw it would have thought it strands of purest gold. Her forehead was high and white and smooth, as if it had been carved by a man's hand from stone or wood or ivory. Her eyebrows were fine and perfectly spaced, and her eyes were bright and clear and well set; her nose was straight and smooth; and in her face the red and white made a finer blend than red and silver in heraldry. God had made in her a prodigy for stealing men's hearts; He had never made her like before and has never done so since. When the young knight saw her he greeted her, and she greeted him, as did the noblemen with her. She took him by the hand most courteously and said:

'Good sir, your lodging tonight will certainly not be such as befits a worthy man. If I told you now the full extent of our plight, you might think I was saying it in a base attempt to make you go. But come now, please, and take lodging, such as it is, and may God give you better tomorrow!'

And she led him by the hand to a chamber with a painted ceiling, long and wide and beautiful, where they sat together on a bed spread with a quilt of samite. Knights came in and sat in groups of four and five and six, and looked at the one who was sitting beside their lady – not saying a word. He was refraining from talking because he remembered the advice the nobleman had given him, and all the knights began whispering to each other about his silence.

'God,' they all said, 'is this knight dumb? It would be a great shame, for never was such a handsome knight born of woman. He looks so well beside our lady, and our lady beside him – if only they weren't both stricken dumb! He is so handsome, and she so beautiful, that it looks as if God made them for each other.'

The girl waited for him to broach some subject or other, until she realised he was not going to say a word unless she spoke to him first. So she said, most courteously: 'Where have you come from today, sir?'

'Young lady,' he replied, 'I stayed last night at the castle of a nobleman where I had fine lodging. It had five strong and splendid towers, one big and four small; I could describe it all to you, but I don't know what it was called – though I do know the worthy man's name was Gorneman de Gorhaut.'

'Oh, dear friend!' cried the girl. 'May God the King reward you well for calling him a worthy man, for you never said a truer word. I'm his niece, you know, but I haven't seen him for a very long time. But certainly, since you left your home you won't have met a worthier man. He'll have given you delightful lodging, being the courteous soul he is – and powerful, too, and well served and rich. But here there are only five small loaves which another uncle of mine – a prior, a most holy and religious man – sent me for supper tonight, and a small cask of sour wine. There's no other food here.'

She gave orders then for the tables to be set; her bidding was done and everyone sat down to supper. It did not last long, but the food was taken eagerly. When they had finished they parted: those who had kept watch the previous night stayed there to sleep, and those whose turn it was to be on guard made themselves ready. Fifty retainers and knights kept watch that night, while the others did everything they could to make their guest comfortable. The one who took charge of making his bed laid out white sheets and a costly coverlet, and a fine pillow for his head. That night he had all the comfort and pleasure one can imagine in a bed – except for the enjoyment of a girl, if that had been his wish, or a lady, if that had been allowed. But he knew as little about love as he did about anything else, and fell asleep quite soon, untroubled by any cares.

But his hostess, in her chamber, could get no rest. While he slept at ease she was burdened with thought, for she had no defence in a battle that threatened her. She tossed and turned this way and that, until finally she threw a mantle of silk over her shirt, deciding in her boldness and courage to take the risk; and it was no easy decision: she had decided to go to her guest and tell him of her worries. So she rose from her bed and left her chamber, in such fear that she trembled in every limb and broke into a sweat. She came to the bed where he lay sleeping, and began to grieve and sigh, and went down on her knees and wept so much that her tears spilt all over his face until he awoke, startled to find his cheeks all wet and to see her kneeling beside his bed, hugging him tightly round the neck. He was courteous enough to take her in his arms and draw her towards him, saying:

'What do you want, dear girl? Why have you come here?'

'Oh, gentle knight, have pity! In God's name, don't think ill of me! Although I'm almost naked I had no thought of folly or sin. There's no-one living in the world so beset by grief and misery as I! Nothing I have brings me any comfort, and I haven't had a day free of misfortune. But I shall see no night after tonight, nor any day after tomorrow, for I'm going to kill myself with my own hand! Of three hundred and ten knights who used to man this castle only fifty now remain; for 260 have been killed or captured by an evil knight named Engygeron, the seneschal of Clamadeus of the Isles. I grieve as much for those held captive as for those who've been killed, for I know they'll die – they'll never escape. Engygeron has besieged us here for a whole winter and summer, never moving; and his strength increases constantly, while ours has diminished and our provisions have been exhausted. We're now in such a plight that tomorrow, unless God intervenes, this castle will be surrendered, for it can no longer be defended, and I shall be surrendered with it as a miserable prisoner. But truly, I'll kill myself before he takes me alive. He'll have me dead; then I shan't care if he carries me off. Clamadeus, who thinks to have me, never will in any way, except bereft of life and soul. In a jewel-case of mine I keep a knife of the finest steel which I shall bury in my heart. That's what I had to tell you; I'll go now and leave you in peace.'

The knight could soon earn great praise if he had the courage, for whatever she may have given him to understand, the only reason she had come and wept on his face was to inspire him to take up the battle to defend her land. He said to her:

'Dear friend, take comfort now and stop your weeping; come here beside me and wipe the tears from your eyes. If God pleases, He'll send you better fortune tomorrow than you say. Lie here beside me on this bed – it's wide enough for both of us.'

And she said: 'I will, sir, if that's your wish.'

And he kissed her and held her close, and drew her gently and softly under the coverlet. She let him kiss her, and it didn't displease her. She found great comfort that night, as they slept lip to lip, in each other's arms, until day broke. At dawn the girl returned to her chamber; and without the help of a maid or waiting-woman she dressed and made herself ready, waking no-one.

As soon as they saw the day break those who had been keeping watch that night woke the sleepers, rousing them from their beds. At the same time the girl returned to her knight, and said to him most graciously:

'Sir, may God give you a good day today; I don't think you'll be staying here: what would you gain by doing so? You'll leave, I know; but I don't object to that – I'd be discourteous if I did, for we've done you no honour or service here. I pray that God may have better lodging in store for you.'

'Dear lady,' he replied, 'I shan't be looking for other lodging today. I'll be bringing peace to all your land instead. I'll not have your enemy stay to harass you longer. But if I kill and vanquish him, I ask, as my reward, that your love may be mine. I'll take no other payment.'

'Sir,' she replied, 'you've asked of me a small, poor thing; but if it were denied you, you'd take it as pride, so I won't refuse it. But don't say that the condition of having my love is that you go and die for me, for that would be a grievous shame. Be sure of this: your body and your age are not such that you could endure combat against so hard and strong and great a knight as the one who waits outside.'

'You'll see if that's so today,' he said, 'for I'm going to fight with him. Nothing you can say will stop me.'

She fashioned her speech cleverly, pretending to plead against his plan when it was exactly what she wanted, inspiring him to do what she staunchly deplored. He called for his arms; they were brought to him, and he was armed

and mounted on a horse made ready for him in the middle of the square.
Everyone there looked dismayed and said:

'Sir, may God lend you aid today, and heap misfortune upon Engygeron the
seneschal who has destroyed all this land.'

They led him in a convoy to the gate, and having seen him outside the castle
they all cried with one voice:

'Good sir, may the True Cross on which God allowed His son to suffer guard
you today from mortal danger, and lead you back safely to where you may
rest in happiness and pleasure.'

Such was the prayer of every man and woman.

Then the men of the besieging army saw him coming, and pointed him out
to Engygeron. He was sitting outside his tent, expecting either that the castle
would be surrendered to him before nightfall, or that someone would come to
fight with him in single combat. His men were in high spirits, thinking they
had conquered the castle and the whole country. Engygeron, mounted on a
sturdy charger, rode calmly up to the knight at a walk and said:

'Who sent you here, boy? Tell me your business: have you come in search
of peace or battle?'

'What are you doing in this land?' replied the boy. 'You'll tell me first why
you've been killing their knights and ravaging the country.'

And Engygeron answered, like the haughty and arrogant man he was:
'I want that castle cleared forthwith and the keep surrendered. It's been held
against me too long. And my lord will have the girl.'

'Damn that decree and the one who uttered it!' cried the boy. 'You'll
renounce every claim you've made!'

'By Saint Peter!' cried Engygeron. 'What nonsense are you talking? It's often
the way that one who's not to blame pays the penalty!'

The boy was incensed at this and set his lance in its rest; and they charged
at each other as fast as their horses could carry them. With their anger and
rage, and the strength in their arms, they made their lances shiver and fly into
pieces. But Engygeron was the only one to fall, with a terrible wound in his
arm and side. The boy dismounted, not knowing how to attack him on horseback; down he jumped, sword in hand, and strode up to Engygeron and assailed
him fiercely. The battle lasted a long while, with awesome blows exchanged,
until Engygeron collapsed and cried for mercy. The boy said he would have
no mercy whatever; but then he remembered the nobleman, who had taught
him never to kill a knight deliberately once he had vanquished him and had
mastery. And Engygeron cried:

'Oh, gentle friend, don't be so cruel as to refuse me mercy! I grant victory
to you; you're a true and a splendid knight indeed, but no-one would have
believed from seeing you that you'd have killed me in battle by your own arms
alone. But if I testify in the presence of my men that you've defeated me in
combat, my word will be taken and your honour will be enhanced beyond any
other knight's. And if you have a lord who's done you some kindness or service,

send me to him, and I'll tell him on your behalf how you vanquished me in battle, and yield myself as his prisoner to do with me as he pleases.'

'Curse anyone who would sue for more!' said the boy. 'I'll tell you where to go, then: to that castle; and you'll tell the fair girl who's my love that never, as long as you live, will you ever trouble her again, and you'll put yourself entirely at her mercy.'

'Then kill me,' Engygeron replied, 'for she would have me killed! She desires nothing so much, for I was involved in her father's death; and I've incurred her greatest wrath by killing and capturing all her knights this year. Anyone who sent me to her would be committing me to a terrible imprisonment; it's the worst he could possibly do! Have you no other friend or sweetheart?'

So the boy told him to go to a castle belonging to a worthy man: there is not a mason in the world who could have described the castle better. He told him with high praise of the river and the bridge, and the turrets and the tower and the mighty walls around it, until Engygeron realised all too well that the boy wanted to send him as a prisoner to the place where he was hated most.

'You're sending me to no haven there! God help me,' he said, 'you mean to put me in the direst plight of all! I killed one of his brothers in this war. Kill me yourself, friend, rather than make me go to him: if you force me there it'll be my death.'

So the boy replied: 'Then go as a prisoner to King Arthur; give the king my greetings, and ask him to show you the girl whom Kay the seneschal struck because she laughed when she saw me. You're to yield yourself her prisoner and tell her that I hope to God I live long enough to avenge her.'

And Engygeron replied that he would do that service as finely as he could. The victorious knight turned back towards the castle, while Engygeron set off to his imprisonment, giving orders that his standard should be taken down. The besieging army departed, till neither a fair nor a dark-haired head remained.

The people of the castle poured forth to meet the knight on his return, and joyfully helped him dismount and disarm, but they all said: 'Since you've not brought Engygeron back, why didn't you cut off his head?'

'In faith, sirs, how could I properly do either? He's killed your kinsmen, and I couldn't have protected him: you'd have killed him in spite of me. And it wouldn't have been very good of me to refuse him mercy when I had the better of him. He's to present himself as a prisoner to King Arthur.'

Just then the girl appeared and greeted him with the greatest joy, and led him to her chamber to rest and take his ease. She did not resist his embraces and kisses; instead of eating and drinking they sported and kissed and exchanged sweet words.

Meanwhile Clamadeus, in his delusion, was expecting to have the castle without contest that day, until he met a boy along his way, lamenting bitterly, who told him the news about Engygeron the seneschal.

'In God's name, sir, things are going badly!' cried the boy, who was grieving so much that he was tearing at his hair with both hands; and Clamadeus said: 'What's wrong?'

'Truly, sir, your seneschal's been defeated in combat, and is to yield himself prisoner to King Arthur: he's on his way to him now.'

'Who did this, boy? Speak up! How could it happen? Where could they have found a knight who could beat such a mighty, valiant man into submission?'

'I don't know who the knight was, sir,' the boy replied. 'But I know this much, for I saw it myself: he came out of Beaurepaire, and was armed with red arms.'

'Tell me, boy, what shall I do now?' he cried, nearly going out of his mind.

'Go back the way you came, sir. You'll gain nothing by carrying on.'

Just as he said this there appeared a white-haired knight, Clamadeus's counsellor, who said: 'Those are base words, boy! You should give wiser and better advice than that: he'd be mad to listen to you! Sir, do you want to know how to get the knight and the castle? It'll be done with ease! Within the walls of Beaurepaire there's nothing to drink or eat and the knights are weak, while we are strong and healthy, neither hungry nor thirsty, and could endure a long battle if they dared to come out and engage us. We'll send twenty knights to fight outside the gate. This knight of theirs, sporting with his fair love Blancheflor, will want to prove his chivalry; and he'll be captured or killed, for the others, who'll be weak, will give him little help. The twenty will do nothing except draw them into the trap and keep them occupied while we creep up through this valley and close in on them from behind!'

'Truly,' said Clamadeus, 'I approve of that! We have four hundred armed knights here, and a thousand footmen fully equipped, all chosen fighting men. Our enemies are as good as dead!'

So Clamadeus sent twenty of his knights to the castle gate, with pennons and banners unfurled in the wind. And when the men of the castle saw them they rashly flung open the gates at the boy's request, and with everyone watching he rode out to do combat with the knights. Bold and strong and confident, he met them all together; and no-one who felt his onslaught guessed he was an apprentice in the art of arms! He showed great skill that day: he gutted many with his lance, here pierced their chests and there their bellies, here broke an arm and there a collar, this one he killed and that one wounded, this one unhorsed and that one seized, and gave the captives and the horses to those who had need of them.

But then they caught sight of the great battalion that had come up through the valley: four hundred armed knights and a thousand footsoldiers. The men of the castle drew up close to the open gate, while the besiegers beheld their wounded and dead companions and came charging towards the gate in impetuous disarray. The defenders were ranged in serried ranks and received them boldly; but they were few in number and weak, while their attackers were boosted by the men-at-arms who followed them; and finally they could resist no longer and fell back into the castle. Above the gate there were archers shooting into the great crowd who were burning and raging to break into the castle, until finally, violently, a band forced their way in. The men above dropped a gate on to those below, killing and crushing all it caught as it fell. Clamadeus could not have seen a more grievous sight: the falling gate had killed huge numbers of his men and locked him out; there was nothing for it but to go and rest: to continue such a furious assault would be a waste of effort now.

But his counsellor said: 'Sir, good or ill befalls us all according to God's will. The long and the short of it is: you've lost. But every saint has his feast-day! The tempest has fallen on you, your men are wounded and the men of the castle have won; but they'll lose yet, be sure of that! Tear out both my eyes if they survive in there for three more days! The castle and the keep will be yours; they'll put themselves entirely at your mercy. If you can stay here just today and tomorrow – that's all – the castle will fall into your hands. Even the girl who's refused you for so long will beg you in God's name to take her!'

So the besieging army pitched a great camp of tents and fine pavilions.

Meanwhile the men of the castle disarmed the knights they had captured; but they did not lock them up in dungeons or irons, on condition that they promised as loyal knights to stay in captivity honourably and to do their captors no harm.

And then, that very day, a mighty wind drove a vessel across the sea with a huge cargo of wheat and other supplies, and by God's will it arrived safe and sound below the castle. When they caught sight of it the men of the castle sent down to enquire who they were and what they wanted. And they replied: 'We're merchants carrying provisions to sell: bread and wine and salted bacon, and we've plenty of cattle and pigs to slaughter if need be.'

The men of the castle cried: 'God be praised for giving the wind the power that brought you drifting here! You are welcome indeed! Start unloading! You can sell the lot, as dear as you dare! Come quickly now and take your payment! We'll give you bars of gold and silver for your wheat. And for the wine and meat you'll have riches enough to fill a cart – more, if need be!'

The buyers and sellers did a fine job as they set about unloading the ship and sending all the goods ahead to fortify the people in the castle. When they saw them coming with the provisions you can imagine how they rejoiced! And with all possible speed they gave orders for dinner to be prepared.

Clamadeus, loitering outside, could now stay as long as he liked, for in the castle they had cattle and pigs and salted meat in abundance, and enough wheat to last till the next harvest. The castle cooks were not idle, and boys lit the kitchen fires to cook the dinner. Now the new knight could sport with his love at his ease; she embraced him, and he kissed her, and they delighted in each other's company. The hall was far from silent now: it rang with a mighty, joyful din. The cooks laboured with all their might until finally they told them to sit down to dine – and how they needed that dinner!

News of the castle's provisioning now reached Clamadeus and his men; they were filled with anguish, and all said they should leave, for there was no way now of starving out the castle: they had besieged the town for nothing. Clamadeus was furious, and without anyone's advice he sent a message to the castle, telling the red knight that until noon the next day he could come and meet him alone in the plain to do battle with him if he dared. When the girl heard this she was filled with grief and anger; but he sent word back that, come what may, Clamadeus would have battle since that was what he wanted. At that the girl's distress grew deeper still, but no amount of tears from her would ever have made him stay. All the women and all the men implored him not to go and fight the one whom no knight had ever withstood in battle; but the boy said:

'Save your breath, my friends: no man in the world could hold me back.'

Thus he stopped their tongues, and they went to their beds and rested until the sun rose next morning. They were still most distressed for their lord, but no matter how much they implored him they could not change his mind. And his love, too, begged him not to go to battle but to stay there in peace, for they had nothing to fear any longer from Clamadeus and his men. But all this entreaty was in vain – which was remarkable indeed, for her coaxing words to him were as sweet as could be, and with each word she kissed him so softly and gently that she slid love's key into the lock of his heart. Yet still she found no way of dissuading him from going to battle; instead he called for his arms, and they were brought with all speed. But there was the greatest sorrow as the boy was armed; all the men and women were heavy-hearted. He commended them all to the king of kings and mounted the swarthy horse which had been brought to him; and then in a moment he was gone.

When Clamadeus saw his opponent coming he was in such a wild mood that he imagined he would empty the knight's saddle in no time. The plain was beautiful and smooth, and there was no-one there but the two of them, for Clamadeus had dismissed his men and sent them all away. Each had his lance fixed in its rest before the saddle-bow, and they charged at each other without a challenge or wasting words. Both had the sharpest heads on their ash-wood lances, stout and fine to handle; and they charged full tilt, and the knights were strong and filled with mortal hatred; and they struck each other so hard that their wooden shields split and their lances smashed and they brought each other down; but they both leaped up and came straight at each other, fighting with swords for a long while. It was an even battle, but in the end Clamadeus, against his will, had to cry for mercy. But he swore most earnestly, as his seneschal had done, that on no condition would he submit to imprisonment in Beaurepaire; nor, for all the Roman Empire, would he go to the nobleman who owned the fine castle. But he willingly promised to yield himself prisoner to King Arthur, and to give the boy's message to the girl whom Kay had struck so basely: that he longed to avenge her, if God gave him strength. Then the boy made Clamadeus swear that before dawn the next day he would set free, safe and sound, all he held captive in his dungeons; and that, as long as he lived, if ever there were an army besieging Beaurepaire he would drive them off if he could; and that the girl would never again be troubled either by him or by his men. And so Clamadeus returned to his land, and when he arrived he commanded that all his captives be released from prison, and said they could go their ways now, completely free. As soon as he had given the word his bidding was done: out came the prisoners, freed from the dungeons, and they set off immediately with all their belongings, for nothing was kept from them.

Clamadeus set out on a different path, travelling all alone. It was the custom at this time that a knight had to yield himself prisoner dressed just as he was when he was vanquished, without removing or donning anything. Thus attired, Clamadeus set off after Engygeron, who was heading for Disnadaron where King Arthur was to hold court.

Meanwhile there was great jubilation in the castle of Beaurepaire, where those who had spent so long in foul captivity had now returned. The hall and the knights' lodgings rang with rejoicing, and in the chapels and churches all the bells pealed with joy. Every monk and nun gave thanks to God, while through the streets and squares all the men and women danced their rounds. How the castle celebrated, now that no-one was besieging them or waging war!

And meanwhile Engygeron rode on; and Clamadeus followed him, staying three nights in a row at the house where Engygeron had lodged before. Lodging by lodging, he followed him to Disnadaron in Wales, where King Arthur was holding a packed court in his halls. They saw Clamadeus coming, armed as custom required, and he was recognised by Engygeron, who had already given the boy's message to the court on his arrival the night before, and had been retained for the king's household and council. He now saw his lord covered in crimson blood, and said at once:

'My lords, my lords, just look at this! Believe me, the boy with the red arms has sent this knight here! He's vanquished him, I'm sure of it, for he's covered in blood! I know the man well, for he's my lord and I'm his vassal. Clamadeus of the Isles is his name, and I thought there was no finer knight in the Empire of Rome, but misfortune befalls even the worthiest.'

So said Engygeron; and then Clamadeus arrived, and they ran to meet each other in the middle of the hall. It was Pentecost, and the queen was sitting beside King Arthur at the head of the table, surrounded by a good many kings and queens and dukes and counts and countesses. Kay the seneschal strode through the hall, a staff of office in his hand and a hat of rich cloth upon his fair-haired head. His tunic was coloured with a fine, deep dye, and girdled with a belt of which the buckle and all the links were gold. There was not a more handsome knight in all the world; but his beauty and his prowess were tainted by his wicked, mocking tongue. Everyone stepped out of his path as he strode through the middle of the hall; they all feared his base jests and his evil tongue. Any wise man fears open spitefulness, whether it be in jest or not. In view of them all, Kay marched up to where the king was sitting and said:

'If you wished, sir, you could dine at once.'

'Kay,' said the king, 'leave me in peace. Never, by the eyes in my head, will I eat on so great a feast-day when I hold so full a court, until some news arrives.'

It was while they were talking thus that Clamadeus entered to yield himself a prisoner, armed as custom demanded; and he said: 'God bless the finest king alive, the noblest and most generous: such is the testimony of all who have heard of his great deeds. Now hear me, sire,' he said, 'for I have a message to give. Much as it grieves me, I acknowledge that I'm sent here by a knight who's defeated me. I have to yield myself prisoner to you on his behalf, whether I like it or not. If anyone asked me if I knew the knight's name, I would have to say no. But I can tell you that he bears red arms, and he said you gave them to him.'

'God guide you, friend,' said the king. 'Tell me truly: is he in good health and spirits?'

'You may be sure he is, sire,' said Clamadeus. 'He's the most valiant knight I've ever known. And he told me to speak to the girl who laughed at him, which made Kay shamefully strike her: he says he'll avenge her, if God grants him the power.'

The court fool, when he heard these words, jumped for joy and cried: 'God bless me, lord king, that blow will indeed be avenged, without a word of a lie; for Kay will have his arm broken and his shoulder dislocated – there's nothing he can do to stop it!'

Kay heard this and thought it the most insulting folly; you may be sure it was not cowardice that stopped him beating the fool about the head, but the presence of the king and the risk of shame. The king shook his head and said to Kay:

'It grieves me deeply that he's not here with me. It was you and your foolish tongue that made him go, and it saddens me.'

Then Gifflet rose at the king's command, along with Sir Yvain, who improved all who shared his company; and the king told them to take Clamadeus and escort him to the chambers where the queen's maids were playing. They did so, and pointed out the girl, and he told her the news that she so wished to hear, grieving as she still was for the shame that rested on her cheek: she had recovered from the blow, but had not forgotten or forgiven the shame. And so it was that Clamadeus delivered his message; and the king retained him in his court and household for life.

Meanwhile the one who had fought him for Beaurepaire and for the beautiful girl Blancheflor, his love, was now taking his ease beside her. The land could now have been his, entirely and undisputed, had his heart not been elsewhere; but he was thinking more of someone else: his heart was fixed on his mother whom he had seen faint and fall, and he longed more than anything to go and see her. He did not dare to ask leave of his love, for she refused and forbade it and commanded all her people to beg him to stay. But all their pleas were vain, except that he made them a promise: if he found his mother alive he would bring her back with him, and from that day forward would be lord of the land; and if she were dead, he would return likewise.

And so he set out, promising to return, leaving his beautiful love filled with anguish and sorrow, as was everyone else. There was such a procession as he rode from the town that it was like Ascension Day, for all the monks were there, dressed in their rich silk copes, and all the nuns in their veils; and they all said:

'Sir, you've rescued us from exile and restored us to our homes: it's no wonder that we grieve when you mean to leave us so soon.'

And he said to them: 'There's no need to cry any more. With God's guidance I'll return, and what's the use of weeping? Don't you think it's right that I should go and see my mother, whom I left on her own in the wild forest? I shan't fail to come back, not for all the world; and if she's alive, I'll have her take the veil as a nun in your church; and if she's dead, I'll have a service sung for her soul each year.'

At that the monks and nuns and everyone turned back. And the boy set out, his lance in its rest, fully armed, just as he had come.

* * *

All day long he rode on, meeting no earthly being who could guide him on his way. He prayed constantly to God the sovereign father that he might find his mother full of life and health. He was still praying when he caught sight of a river flowing down a hill. He saw that the water was swift and deep and he did not dare to ride in; and he said:

'Oh! If only I could cross this river I think I'd find my mother on the other side, if she's still alive.'

He rode along the bank until he came to a high, jutting rock, and the river washed all round it so that he could go no further. But suddenly he noticed a boat with two men on board, sailing downstream. He stopped and waited, thinking that they would sail on down to him. But they stopped and stayed dead still in midstream, anchored fast. The one at the front was fishing with a line, baiting his hook with a little fish slightly bigger than a minnow. The boy, not knowing what to do or where to find a crossing, greeted them and asked them:

'Tell me, sirs, is there a bridge across this river?'

And the one who was fishing replied: 'No indeed, brother; nor is there any boat, I think, bigger than the one we're in, which wouldn't carry five men. You can't cross on horseback for twenty leagues upstream or down, for there's no ferry or bridge or ford.'

'Then tell me, I pray you, where I could find lodging.'

And the man replied: 'You've need of that and more besides, I think. *I* will give you lodging tonight. Ride up through the cleft in that rock, and when you come to the top you'll see a house in a valley ahead of you. That's where I live, between the river and the woods.'

So the boy climbed up the rock; but when he reached the top he peered all around and saw nothing but earth and sky, and said: 'God bring disgrace upon the one who sent me here! What a dance he led me, telling me I'd find a house when I reached the top! Fisherman, that was an unworthy deed!'

But just then, in a valley nearby, the top of a tower caught his eye. You wouldn't find one more handsome from here to Beirut. It was square and built of grey stone, and flanked by two smaller towers. A hall stood before the tower, and lodges before the hall. The boy rode down towards it, saying that the one who had sent him there had guided him well, and he praised the fisherman, no longer calling him treacherous or dishonest. He headed towards the gate; and before it he found a drawbridge, and it was lowered. Over the bridge he rode and in, and four boys came to meet him; two of them disarmed him, while the third led away his horse to be fed and stabled; the fourth dressed the boy in a fresh and brand-new mantle of scarlet cloth. Then they led him to the lodges; and he could have searched as far as Limoges without finding any so fine.

The boy stayed there until two servants came to escort him to their lord. He returned with them to the hall, which was square, being as long as it was wide. And in the middle of the hall he saw, sitting in a bed, a most handsome nobleman with greying hair; on his head he wore a hat of sable, dark as mulberry, covered in a deep rich cloth on top, and his whole gown was the same. He was leaning on his elbow, and before him was a huge fire of seasoned logs, blazing brightly, surrounded by four columns supporting a tall, wide chimney of heavy bronze. Four hundred men could easily have sat around that fire and each would have had an excellent place. The two servants who were escorting the boy, one at each shoulder, came before their lord, who greeted him at once, and said:

'Forgive me if I don't rise to meet you, for I'm unable.'

'Think no more about it, sir,' the boy replied. 'It doesn't bother me at all.'

But the worthy man made an effort and strained to be as upright as he could; then he said: 'Come here, my friend. Don't be afraid of me: sit down here beside me, you're quite safe.'

The boy did so, and the nobleman asked him: 'Where have you come from today, dear friend?'

'Sir,' he said, 'I rode this morning from Beaurepaire – that was its name.'

'Before God, you've travelled a very long way. You must have left before the watch blew the dawn signal.'

'No indeed,' said the boy. 'The first hour* had already been sounded, I promise you.'

While they were talking thus, a boy came through the door; he was carrying a sword hung round his neck, and presented it to the nobleman. He drew it half out of its scabbard, and saw clearly where it was made, for it was written on the blade. And he also learned from the writing that it was of such fine steel that there was only one way it could ever be broken, which no-one knew except the one who had forged and tempered it. The boy who had brought it to him said:

---

* The first canonical hour: six o'clock in the morning.

'Sir, that beautiful fair-haired girl, your niece, has sent you this gift; you never saw a finer sword as long and as broad as this. You may give it to whoever you like, but my lady wishes it to be put to good use where it's bestowed. The one who forged the sword has only ever made three, and he's not long to live, so this is the last he'll ever make.'

And straight away the lord girded his guest with the sword by its belt, which itself was worth a fortune. The sword's pommel was made of the finest gold of Arabia or Greece, and the scabbard was of golden thread from Venice.

'Good brother,' he said, 'this sword was intended and destined for you, and I very much want you to have it; come, draw it now.'

The boy thanked him, and fastened it so that it was not restricting, and then drew it, naked, from the scabbard; and after gazing at it for a while, he slid it back into the sheath. And truly, it sat splendidly at his side, and even better in his hand, and it seemed indeed that in time of need he would wield it like a man of valour. Behind him he saw some boys standing around the brightly burning fire; he noticed the one who was looking after his arms, and entrusted the sword to him. Then he sat down again beside the lord, who treated him with the greatest honour. And no house lit by candles could ever provide a brighter light than shone there in that hall.

While they were talking of one thing and another, a boy came from a chamber clutching a white lance by the middle of the shaft, and he passed between the fire and the two who were sitting on the bed. Everyone in the hall saw the white lance with its white head; and a drop of blood issued from the lance-head's tip, and right down to the boy's hand this red drop ran. The lord's guest gazed at this marvel, but restrained himself from asking how it came to be, because he remembered the advice of the nobleman who had made him a knight, who had taught him to beware of talking too much; he feared it would be considered base of him if he asked – so he did not. Then two other boys appeared, and in their hands they held candlesticks of the finest gold, inlaid with black enamel, and in each burned ten candles at the very least. A girl who came in with the boys, fair and comely and beautifully attired, was holding a vessel between her hands. And when she entered holding this vessel, so brilliant a light appeared that the candles lost their brightness like the stars or the moon when the sun rises. The vessel was made of fine, pure gold; and in it were set jewels of many kinds, the richest and most precious stones in the earth or the sea. Another girl followed, holding a silver trencher. The procession passed before the bed and disappeared into another chamber. The boy saw them pass, but did not dare to ask who was served from the vessel, for he had taken the words of the wise nobleman to heart. I fear he may suffer for doing so, for I've heard it said that in time of need a man can talk too little as well as too much. I don't know whether it will bring him good or ill, but he asked nothing.

The lord commanded boys to bring them water and to lay the cloths. They did as they were bidden, and the lord and the new knight washed their hands in warm water. Two boys brought in a wide table of ivory, and held it in front of their lord until two others came bringing trestles of ebony. Then the cloth was laid, and no cardinal or pope ever dined at one so white. The first dish was a haunch of venison, seasoned with hot pepper. There was no shortage of clear, delicious wine to drink, from golden cups. Before them a boy carved the peppered venison, drawing the haunch to him with the silver trencher, and presented pieces to them on a slice of perfectly baked bread. And meanwhile the vessel passed before them again, but the boy did not ask who was served from it: he refrained because of the nobleman's well-meaning warning not to talk too much – he had taken it to heart and had it constantly in mind. But he held his tongue more than he should have done, for as each dish was served he saw the vessel pass before him, right before his eyes, and he did not know who was served from it and he longed to know. He said to himself that before he left he would certainly ask one of the boys of the court, but would wait until the morning when he took his leave of the lord and the rest of the household. And so he put it off till a later time, and concentrated on eating and drinking.

They did not stint with the wines and food, which were delicious indeed: the worthy man and the boy were served that night with all the dishes befitting a king or a count or an emperor. And after they had dined they stayed together and talked, while the boys prepared the beds and provided fruit to eat – and there were fruits of the dearest kind: dates and figs and pomegranates. Then there were many different drinks to taste: sweet, aromatic wine, made with neither honey nor pepper, and old mulberry wine and clear syrup. The boy, who had never tasted the like, was filled with wonder. Then the nobleman said:

'Good friend, it's time to take to our beds for the night. I'll go now, if you don't mind, and sleep in my chamber, and whenever you wish you can go to sleep in here. I've no strength in my body: I shall have to be carried.'

Then four strong and hearty servants came from the chamber, and taking hold of the four corners of the blanket that was spread across the bed beneath him, they carried their lord where he directed. Other boys stayed with his guest and served him and fulfilled his every need: when he wished they took off his shoes and clothes and put him to bed in sheets of fine white linen.

He slept until the morning when day had broken and the household had risen; but he could see no-one as he looked about him, and he had to get up alone whether he liked it or not. He did the best he could, and put on his shoes without waiting for help; then he went to don his arms again, finding that they had been brought and left at the head of a table. When he had fully armed he headed for the doors of the chambers which he had seen open the night before; but he found them shut tight. He called and beat and barged a good deal, but no-one opened up for him or uttered a single word. After calling in vain for quite a while he turned back to the door of the hall. This was open, and he went down the steps to find his horse saddled and his lance and shield leaning against a wall. He mounted and went looking everywhere, but could not see a living soul. So he came straight to the gate and found the drawbridge lowered: he thought the boys must all have gone into the woods to check their traps and snares. He had no wish to stay longer, and decided to go after them to see if anyone would tell him why the lance bled – if perhaps there were something wrong – and where the beautiful vessel was being taken. And so he rode out through the gate; but before he had got across the bridge, he felt his horse's hooves rise high into the air. The horse made a great leap; and if he had not jumped so well both horse and rider would have been in a sorry plight. The boy looked back to see what had happened, and saw that the bridge had been raised. He called out, but no-one replied.

'Hey!' he cried. 'Whoever raised the bridge, talk to me! Where are you? I can't see you. Come out and let me look at you: there's something I want to ask.'

But he was wasting his time calling out like this, for nobody would answer him.

* * *

He headed towards the forest, and came upon a path where he found fresh hoofprints.

'I think,' he said, 'the ones I'm looking for went this way.'

So he went galloping through the wood as far as the tracks led him, until he chanced to see a girl beneath an oak tree weeping and lamenting, filled with sorrow and misery.

'Alas!' she cried. 'How unfortunate I am! Cursed be the hour I was born! Oh, would to God my love had lived and I had died! With him gone I care nothing for my life. Come, Death, and take my soul! Let it be the chambermaid and companion of his, if he'll accept it.'

Such was the girl's lament for a knight she was cradling in her lap: he had been beheaded. As soon as he saw her the boy rode towards her and said: 'Young lady, who killed this knight?'

'Good sir,' she replied, 'another knight killed him, this very morning. But there's something that amazes me: you could ride forty leagues the way you've come and you wouldn't find any decent lodging, yet your horse is well fed and his coat smooth. If he'd been washed and groomed and given a manger of oats and hay he wouldn't have had a fuller belly or a sleeker coat. And you seem yourself to have had a comfortable and restful night.'

'Truly,' he said, 'I had every possible comfort. But if you shouted loudly from here it would be heard quite clearly where I lodged last night! You can't have explored this country much, for without a doubt I had the finest lodging I've ever known.'

'Oh, sir! Then you lodged at the house of the rich Fisher King!'

'I don't know if he's a fisher or a king, but he's very wise and courteous. I came across two men in a boat late yesterday, sailing gently along. One of them was rowing, the other was fishing with a hook, and he told me the way to his house last night, and gave me lodging there.'

And the girl said: 'Good sir, he *is* a king, I can assure you. But he was crippled years ago by a wound in the thighs, so that he's helpless now; he can't even mount a horse. But when he wants to engage in some sport he has himself carried to a boat and goes fishing with a hook, and is known as the Fisher King. He finds his enjoyment that way because he couldn't manage any other sport: he can't hunt in the woods or along the riverbanks and marshes. But he has men to hunt the wildfowl, and archers who go shooting with their bows in the forests. That's why he likes to live in this house just here; for in all the world he could find no retreat so suited to his needs, and he's had a house built befitting a rich king.'

'It's true what you say, young lady, and I wondered at it when I came into his presence last night. I stood a little way from him, and he told me to come and sit beside him, and not to take it for haughtiness if he didn't rise to greet me, for he didn't have the strength or power; so I went and sat at his side.'

'Truly, he did you a great honour when he seated you beside him. And tell me now: as you sat there, did you see the lance which bleeds from its tip, though it has neither flesh nor veins?'

'Did I see it? Yes, in faith!'

'And did you ask why it bled?'

'So help me God, I didn't say a word.'

'Then I tell you,' she said, 'you've done great wrong. And did you see the Grail?'

'The Grail?'

'The beautiful, bejewelled vessel.'

'I saw it clearly.'

'Who was holding it?'

'A girl.'

'Where did she come from?'

'From a chamber.'

'And where did she go?'

'Into another chamber.'

'Did anyone go ahead of the Grail?'

'Yes.'

'Who?'

'Two boys, that's all.'

'What were they holding?'

'Candlesticks full of candles.'

'And who came after the Grail?'

'Another girl.'

'What was she holding?'

'A small silver trencher.'

'Did you ask where they were going?'

'Not a word crossed my lips.'

'God help me, so much the worse. What's your name, friend?'

And the boy, who did not know his name, guessed and said it was Perceval the Welshman, not knowing if it were true or not. But it was true, though he did not know it. And when the girl heard this she stood up before him and said, distressed:

'Your name is changed, friend.'

'To what?'

'Perceval the wretched! Oh, luckless Perceval! How unfortunate you are to have failed to ask all this! You would have healed the good king who is crippled, and he would have regained the use of his limbs and the rule of his land – and you would have profited greatly! But know this now: many ills will befall both you and others. And know this, too: this has come upon you because of the sin against your mother, for she has died of grief on your account. I know you better than you know me; you don't know who I am, but I was brought up with you for a long time at your mother's house: I'm your cousin and you are mine. And I grieve no less for your misfortune in not learning what was done with the Grail or where it's taken, than I do for your mother who has died – and for this knight whom I adored.'

'Oh, cousin!' cried Perceval. 'If what you've told me is true, tell me how you know.'

'I know it to be true,' said the girl, 'for I saw her laid in the earth.'

'God have mercy on her soul,' said Perceval. 'It's a cruel tale you've told me. And now that she's been buried, what would be the use of going on? I was on my way to see her; I'll have to take a different course. If you wanted to come with me I'd be very glad, for the one who lies here dead will be of no service to you now. The dead with the dead, the living with the living; let's go together. It seems foolish to stay here on your own watching over this body: let's follow the one who killed him. And I swear this: we'll fight to the bitter end if I can track him down.'

But his cousin, unable to suppress the grief in her heart, replied: 'I won't leave him at any price until I've buried him. If you'll take my advice you'll follow the road down here, for the wicked knight who killed my sweetheart went this way. Not that I want you to pursue him – though I wish him as much ill as if it were *me* he'd killed. But listen: where did you get that sword that hangs at your side? It's never spilled a man's blood and has never had occasion to be drawn. I know very well where it was made, and I know very well who forged it. Beware! Don't ever put your trust in it! It'll betray you, I promise you, when you find yourself in a great battle, for it'll fly into pieces.'

'Dear cousin, it was sent to my host last night by a niece of his, and he gave it to me, and I consider it a fine present. But you alarm me if what you've said is true. Tell me: if it came to be broken, do you know if it could be repaired?'

'It could, but there'd be great hardship for whoever took the road to the lake below Cothoatre. There you could have the sword tempered anew and made whole once more, if adventure* led you there. You must go to a smith named Triboet, and to him alone, for he made it and will remake it; it will never be repaired by any other man who tries.'

'Truly,' said Perceval, 'it would grieve me deeply if it broke.'

And with that he set off, and his cousin stayed behind, not wanting to leave the body of the one whose death weighed so heavily on her heart.

* * *

On Perceval rode, following the horse's tracks, until he came upon a palfrey, thin and weary, plodding along before him. The palfrey was so skinny and wretched that he thought he must have fallen into bad hands. He seemed to have been well worked and ill fed – like a borrowed horse: overtaxed all day and neglected at night. He shivered as if frozen stiff, his neck was mangy and his ears drooped. He would soon be fodder for mastiffs and mongrels, for his hide was all that covered his bones. On his head was a bridle and on his back was a saddle, and in the saddle was a girl – and one more wretched was never seen. She would have been comely enough if she had been well cared for, but she was in such a sorry state that there was not a hand's breadth of her gown untorn: her breasts showed through the rips. It was held together here and there with knots and coarse stitches; and her flesh looked as if it had been slashed with a lancet, it was so beaten and burned by heat and gale and frost. She was bareheaded, without veil or wimple, so her face was clearly visible, with many an ugly stain left in the paths of her endless tears, which flowed down to her breast and over her robe and right down to her knees. Well might she have had a heavy heart, being in such distress.

As soon as Perceval saw her he rode swiftly to meet her. She clasped her clothes around her to cover up her skin, but she was bound to open other gaps: whenever she covered one spot she closed one hole and opened a hundred. Thus Perceval found her, pale and wan and wretched, and as he approached he heard her complaining bitterly of her suffering and misery.

'God,' she cried, 'let me live no longer! I've lived in misery too long and suffered too much misfortune, and through no fault of my own. Dear God, you know very well that I've done nothing to deserve it, so send me, I beg you, someone who'll free me from this torment; or deliver me from the one who makes me suffer this shame, for I can find no mercy in him. I don't know why

---

* In medieval French the word 'aventure' meant a great deal more than its modern equivalent. It could mean 'chance' or 'phenomenon' or perhaps 'fortune', and was frequently, and importantly, a sign of God's intervention in the world – or of His favour. A knight would not even encounter an 'aventure' (let alone succeed in whatever test it might present) if he were unworthy of doing so, or unable to recognise it as a sign of God's presence and guidance.

he wants my company when he keeps me like this, unless he relishes my shame and misery.'

'God save you, fair lady,' said Perceval, who was now beside her.

The girl bowed, and answered softly: 'May you, sir, have all that your heart desires – but I shouldn't be wishing you that.'

And Perceval, blushing with shame, replied: 'In God's name, lady, why not? Truly, I don't think I've ever seen you before or done you any wrong.'

'Yes, you have!' she cried. 'For I mustn't be greeted by anyone! That's the torment I have to bear, wretch that I am. I sweat with anguish whenever anyone addresses me or even looks at me.'

'I wasn't aware of my misdeed,' said Perceval. 'I certainly didn't come here to do you shame or wrong: my path just led me here. And once I'd seen you in such a plight, so poor and naked, I couldn't rest until I'd learned the truth: what adventure has brought you such sorrow and hardship?'

'Oh, sir!' she cried. 'Have pity on me! Ride on! Fly from here and leave me in peace!'

'I want to know,' he said, 'what fear or threat should make me fly, when nobody's pursuing me?'

'Sir,' she replied, 'fly as fast as you can, in case the Proud Knight of the Heath should see us talking! If he found you here he'd kill you on the spot. No-one who stops me can leave with his head – he killed one just a short while ago!'

And just as they were talking thus, the Proud Knight rode out of the wood and came like a thunderbolt across the sand and dust, crying at the top of his voice: 'Woe betide you! Your end has come for stopping that girl for a single pace!' And as he approached he drew rein and said: 'But I won't kill you until I've told you why I'm making her live in shame; so listen now, and you'll hear the tale. Just recently I'd gone into the wood and left this girl in my pavilion; and I loved no-one but her. But a Welsh boy chanced to come there. I don't know who he was, but he went so far as to kiss her – by force, so she told me. And if she lied, then what was to stop him doing more? And even if it was against her will, wouldn't he then have done all he wanted? Yes! No-one would believe he kissed her and did no more, for one thing always leads to the other. If a man kisses a woman and does no more when they're alone together, then I think it's *his* decision; for a woman who yields her lips gives the rest most easily to whoever makes the effort! And though she may defend herself, we all know that a woman wants to win in all things but one: that struggle in which she grabs the man by the throat and scratches and bites and wrestles, but wants to be beaten! She struggles, but she longs for it; too cowardly to grant it, she wants it to be taken by force, but then shows neither willingness nor thanks! That's why I think he lay with her. And he took from her a ring of mine and carried it off, much to my annoyance; and before that he drank and ate his fill of strong wine and good pies that were being kept for me. So now my love has a charming reward as you see! I vowed that her palfrey would have no oats to eat and would not be groomed or shod again, and that she would have no coat or mantle but the ones that she was wearing then, until I found the one who'd violated her, and killed him and beheaded him.'

When Perceval had heard him out he answered exactly thus: 'Know this, friend, without a doubt: she's done her penance, for it was I who kissed her – and it was against her will, and grieved her deeply. And I took the ring from her finger, but that was all – I did nothing more; though I ate, I admit, one of the pies and half of the other, and drank as much wine as I pleased. But I did nothing stupid.'

'By my life!' cried the Proud Knight. 'What an incredible confession! You've deserved death, that's for sure!'

'My death's not as near as you think,' said Perceval.

Without another word they sent their horses charging at each other, and clashed with such fury that their lances flew into splinters. Both saddles were emptied as they brought each other down, but they leaped to their feet at once and unsheathed their swords and dealt each other mighty blows. Perceval struck him first with the sword he had been given, because he wanted to test it. And he dealt him so great a blow upon his steel helmet that he broke the Fisher King's good sword in two. The Proud Knight was not cowed; he repaid him well upon his decorated helmet, smashing off the flowers and gems that adorned it. Perceval was bitterly sad at heart that his sword had failed him; but he gathered up the pieces and put them back in the sheath; and in that very instant they vanished, sword and sheath together; Perceval was astounded, but he cast off his bewilderment and drew the sword that had belonged to the Red Knight. Then they came at each other on equal terms and began a bitter battle: you never saw one greater. The combat raged, hard and mighty, until the Proud Knight of the Heath admitted defeat and cried for mercy. And Perceval said:

'By my life, knight, I'll not have mercy on you until you have mercy on your love; for she hasn't deserved the punishment you've made her suffer, I can swear to that.'

And the knight, who loved her more than his own eyes, replied: 'Good sir, I'll make amends to her as you wish: I'll do whatever you command. My heart is sad and dark indeed for the suffering I've made her bear.'

'Then go,' said Perceval, 'to the nearest house you have in these parts, and let her bathe at leisure until she's healed and well. Then get ready and take her, properly dressed and attired, to King Arthur, and greet him on my behalf and yield yourself to his mercy. If he asks who sent you, tell him it was the one he made a red knight by the advice of Sir Kay the seneschal. And you must tell the court of the penance and suffering you've made your girl endure; tell it aloud to all those present, so that all the men and women hear it, and the queen and her maids, too – there are many lovely ones in her company. I hold one in special esteem, whom Kay, because she'd laughed at me, dealt such a blow that he knocked her out. Find her, I command you, and give her this message from me: that I will never, on any account, enter any court King Arthur may hold until I've avenged her.'

And the knight replied that he would go there most willingly and say everything he had commanded, and without delay – except that he would first let his sweetheart rest, and clothe her as she needed. He would gladly have taken Perceval to rest as well, and to heal and dress his wounds, but Perceval said:

'Go now, and good luck to you; just take care of her – I'm going to look for other lodging.'

The talking ended there, and neither party dallied longer: they both set out without more ado. And that evening the knight had his love bathed and richly clothed, and he cared for her so lovingly that she was restored to her former beauty. Then they both set out and went straight to Carlion, where King Arthur was holding court – and a most intimate affair it was, with only three thousand knights of high repute! In the sight of them all he yielded himself a prisoner to King Arthur, saying:

'Lord king, I am your prisoner and will do whatever you wish: I was commanded to do so by the boy who asked you for red arms, and got them.'

As soon as the king heard this he knew exactly who he meant. 'Disarm, good sir,' he said. 'May the one who's sent you here have joy and good fortune. For his sake you'll be cherished and honoured in my house.'

'My lord, there's something else I wish to tell you before I disarm. And I'd like the queen and her maids to come and hear my news, for it'll be told only in the presence of the one who was struck on the cheek for no other crime than uttering a single laugh.'

Then the knight paused, and the king sent for the queen; she came, and all her maids with her, hand in hand. When the queen was seated beside her lord King Arthur, the Proud Knight of the Heath said to her:

'My lady, a knight I hold in great respect, who vanquished me with his skill in combat, sends you greetings. He also sends you my beloved – the girl you see here.'

'My thanks to him, friend,' said the queen.

Then he told her of all the baseness and shame he had inflicted upon her for so long, and the suffering she had endured, and the reason for it all: he told her everything, concealing nothing. When he had finished they showed him the girl whom Kay the seneschal had struck, and he said to her:

'The one who sent me here asked me to greet you on his behalf, and to tell you that he'll never enter any court King Arthur holds until he's avenged you for the blow you received on his account.'

When the court fool heard this he leaped to his feet and cried: 'Kay! Kay! God bless me, you'll pay for it, you really will, and soon!'

When the fool had finished, the king in turn said: 'Ah, Kay! How courteous you were to mock the boy! You've robbed me of him with your mockery; I don't think I'll ever see him again.'

Then the king seated his captive knight before him, and declared him free from imprisonment and bade that he be disarmed. And Sir Gawain, who was seated at the king's right hand, asked:

'In God's name, sire, who can that young man be who could defeat such a fine knight as this in single combat? In all the isles of the sea I've never heard of any knight who could equal the Proud Knight in arms and chivalry.'

'Dear nephew,' said the king, 'I don't know who he is. I saw him only once, and didn't have time to ask anything. He told me to make him a knight that instant, and I saw how fair and handsome he was, and said: "Gladly, brother, but dismount while they bring you golden arms". But he said he'd never dismount until he had red arms – those of the knight who'd stolen my golden cup! And Kay, insulting as ever, said to him: "Friend, the king grants you the arms – they're all yours – go and take them!" And the boy, not realising it was a joke, went after the knight and killed him with a javelin. I don't know how the quarrel began, except that the Red Knight of the Forest of Quinqueroi hit him with his lance most haughtily, and the boy struck him clean through the eye with his javelin and killed him, and took his arms. Since then his service to me has been so good that, by Saint David of Wales, I shan't lie in a chamber or hall for two nights in a row until I know if he's alive! I'm setting out to search for him – this instant!'

And once the king had made the vow, everyone knew there was nothing for it but to go. Sheets and blankets and pillows were packed, coffers filled, packhorses loaded and carts and wagons piled high, for they were not sparing with the number of tents and pavilions they took. If he had taken all day, a bright, well-lettered clerk could not have kept account of the baggage train, for the king rode from Carlion as if he were going on campaign, with all his barons following. Not even a girl remained behind: the queen took them all as a display of power and authority.

That night they camped in a meadow beside a forest, and in the morning they found that it had snowed heavily, and the country round about was freezing cold.

Perceval had risen early as usual, eager to find adventure and deeds of chivalry; and he came straight towards the frozen, snowy meadow where the king's army was encamped. But before he reached their pavilions, a flock of wild geese, dazzled by the snow, came flying overhead. He saw them and heard them as they fled, screeching, from a falcon that swooped after them like a flash, until it found one of them alone, cut off from the flock, and swept down and struck the bird so hard that it sent it plummeting to the ground; but it was very early in the morning, and the falcon flew off, not wanting to attack it. Perceval spurred on to where he had seen it fall. The goose was wounded in the neck, and it bled three drops of blood which spilled on to the whiteness of the snow: it looked like a natural colouring. The goose was not hurt badly enough to keep it grounded, and by the time Perceval arrived it had already flown away. When Perceval saw the crushed snow where the goose had lain, and the blood spilled around it, he leaned on his lance to gaze at the vision; for the blood and snow together resembled for him the fresh hues in the face of his beloved Blancheflor, and he became quite lost in the thought that in her face the red was blended with the white like those three drops of blood in the whiteness of the snow. As Perceval mused upon the drops, enraptured, all the early morning passed him by.

At length some squires emerged from the tents and, seeing him in his contemplation, thought he was asleep. Before the king, still slumbering in his pavilion, was awake, the squires met Saigremor outside the royal tent, who because of his impetuosity was called the Rash.

'Come on!' he cried. 'Don't hide it from me: why have you come here in such a hurry?'

'Sir,' they said, 'we've seen a knight outside the camp, asleep upon his charger.'

'Is he armed?'

'Yes, in faith.'

'I'll go and speak to him,' said Saigremor, 'and bring him back to the court.' And he ran straight to the king's tent and woke him. 'Sire,' he said, 'out on the heath there's a knight sleeping.'

And the king commanded him to go and bring the knight back without fail. Saigremor called for his arms and his horse; his bidding was done at once, and he left the camp, fully armed, and rode on until he reached the knight.

'Sir,' he said, 'you must come to the king!'

The knight did not move, and seemed not to have heard him. He addressed him again, but he made no reply, and Saigremor was annoyed and said: 'By Saint Peter, you'll come whether you like it or not! I'm sorry I ever deigned to ask – I wasted my breath!'

Then he unfurled the pennon that was rolled around his lance, and the horse beneath him leaped forward; he called out to the knight once more, warning that he would strike him unless he defended himself. Perceval glanced up and saw him coming full tilt. He snapped out of his dreaming and spurred forward to meet him. Saigremor smashed his lance as they met, but Perceval's neither broke nor bent: he struck him with such force that he brought him crashing down in the middle of the field. His horse did not linger but fled away, head high, towards the camp; those who were rising saw the horse from their tents and were most distressed.

But Kay, who could never resist a cruel joke, said to the king: 'Look, sire, here's Saigremor! He's got the knight by the reins and is bringing him back against his will!'

'Kay,' said the king, 'it's bad of you to mock worthy men. Go yourself, and let's see you do better.'

'Truly,' said Kay, 'I'll be only too glad to go, and I'll bring him back by force, whether he likes it or not, and make him give his name.'

He had himself armed with great attention, and then mounted and set off towards the knight, who was so intent upon gazing at the three drops that he was oblivious to everything else. Kay shouted to him from far away: 'Vassal! Vassal! Come to the king! You'll come right now, or pay most dearly!'

Perceval, hearing this threat, turned his horse's head about; and thrusting in his spurs of steel he came galloping at Kay – who was not riding slowly himself. Both were anxious to do well, and they clashed full-bloodedly. Kay struck with all his force, so hard that his lance smashed and crumbled like a pie-crust. Nor did Perceval hold himself back: he hit Kay smack upon the boss, and brought him crashing down upon a rock so that he dislocated his shoulder and broke his right arm between the elbow and the armpit like a dry twig – just as the fool had foretold: the fool's prediction had come true. Kay fainted with the pain, while his horse fled towards the camp at a gallop.

The Britons saw the horse return without the seneschal, and boys and knights and ladies set out and found him still unconscious, and felt sure that he was dead. They began to mourn for him bitterly. Meanwhile Perceval was leaning on his lance again over the three drops.

The king was most upset about his wounded seneschal, but he sent for a learned doctor and two girls who were pupils of his, and they put his shoulder back in place and bandaged his arm and joined the broken bone. Then they carried him to the king's tent and did all they could to comfort him.

Then Sir Gawain said to the king: 'Truly, sire, it isn't right – as you've always said yourself – that a knight should disturb another from his thoughts as Saigremor and Kay have done. The knight was thinking, perhaps, of some loss he's suffered, or maybe his love has been stolen from him and it's weighing on his mind. Let me go and see how he looks, and if I find that he's left his musing I'll ask him to come back here to you.'

Kay was enraged at this and said: 'Oh yes, Sir Gawain, you'll lead the knight back by the reins whether he likes it or not, of course you will – provided victory's handed to you on a plate! You've conquered many a knight like that! When the knight's worn out and has fought long enough, then the worthy Gawain asks leave to try his hand – and of course he goes and conquers him! Oh Gawain, you're no fool! There are plenty of tricks to learn from you! And you're good at spinning fair and courteous phrases, aren't you? You could do this job in a silk tunic! You won't need to draw a sword or break a lance. If you can just get your tongue round "Sir, God save you and give you joy and health", he'll do your will! You'll cosset and coax him like a cat, while everyone's saying "Now Sir Gawain's engaged in a mighty combat!"'

'Oh, Sir Kay,' said Gawain, 'there was no need to speak so unkindly. Why do you vent your rage on me? By my faith, I'll bring back the knight if I can. And I shan't have my arm injured for it or my shoulder dislocated – that's not my idea of a reward.'

'Go now, nephew,' said the king. 'You've spoken most courteously. Bring him back if you can – but take all your arms with you: you're not to go unarmed.'

Gawain, renowned and esteemed for all knightly virtues, armed at once and mounted a strong, keen horse, and rode straight up to the knight who was leaning on his lance, still not tired of the musing that so enraptured him. But the sun had dried up two of the drops of blood that had lain upon the snow, and was fast drying the third, so he was not as absorbed in thought as he had been.

Sir Gawain cantered gently up to him, suggesting no hostility, and said: 'Sir, I'd have greeted you if I'd known your heart as well as my own. I'm a messenger of the king, who summons and requests you to come and speak to him.'

'There have already been two,' said Perceval, 'who tried to take my life and lead me off as a captive. I was musing so deeply upon a delightful thought that whoever tried to draw me from it was asking for trouble; for just in this spot there were three drops of fresh blood gleaming in the whiteness, and as I gazed at them I thought I saw the fresh colour of my fair love's face, and I didn't want to leave.'

'Truly,' said Sir Gawain, 'there was nothing base about that thought: it was most courteous and sweet; and the one who turned your heart from it was cruel and harsh. But tell me: what do you want to do now? I'd gladly take you to the king, if you don't object.'

'Tell me first, dear friend,' said Perceval, 'if Kay the seneschal's there.'

'Indeed he is. And I tell you, he was the one who jousted with you here just now – and the joust cost him dearly, for you've broken his right arm and dislocated his shoulder.'

'Then I think I've avenged the girl he struck!'

When Sir Gawain heard this he was startled and said: 'God save me, sir, it's you the king's been looking for! What's your name, sir?'

'Perceval, sir; and yours?'

'I was baptised with the name of Gawain.'

'Gawain?'

'Yes, good sir.'

Perceval was overjoyed and said: 'I've heard tell of you, sir, in many places, and longed to meet you: I hope it may please you as well.'

'Truly,' said Sir Gawain, 'it pleases me no less than you, but more, I think!'

And Perceval replied: 'Then I'll gladly go where you wish, and consider myself honoured to be your companion.'

With that they embraced each other, and began to unlace their helmets and the necks of their hauberks, opening their mail-hoods; then they made their way back, rejoicing in each other's company. Some boys watching from a hillock saw them returning, and came running down to the king.

'Sire! Sire!' they cried. 'Sir Gawain's bringing back the knight, and they seem pleased to see each other!'

All who heard the news rushed from their pavilions and went out to meet them.

And Kay said to the king: 'Now Sir Gawain, your nephew, has won esteem and honour! My word, it's been a hard and perilous battle! He's coming back as hearty as he left: he hasn't had a blow from anyone, and no-one's felt a blow from him. He hasn't uttered a word of challenge! How right that he should be esteemed and praised, and that people should say he's done what we all failed to do, for all our might and effort!'

So, rightly or wrongly, Kay spoke his mind, as he always did.

Sir Gawain did not want to take his companion to court in his armour, so he had him disarmed in his tent, and a chamberlain took a robe from a coffer and presented it to Perceval. Once he was finely and handsomely dressed, in a tunic and mantle which suited him splendidly, they both came hand in hand to the king, who was sitting outside his pavilion.

'Sire,' said Sir Gawain to the king, 'I bring you the one you've been longing to meet, the one you've been out searching for; I present him to you – here he is.'

'Many thanks, dear nephew!' said the king. And overcome with joy, he leaped to his feet to greet him, saying: 'Welcome, sir! Now tell me, please, by what name I should call you.'

'Lord king,' he replied, 'my name is Perceval the Welshman.'

'Oh, Perceval, dear friend, now that you've come to my court I'd have you never leave it! I've been worried about you, for when first we met I didn't know what a great future God had in store for you. Yet it was clearly predicted by the girl and the fool whom Kay the seneschal struck; and you've verified their prediction in every way! No-one now can be in doubt that we've heard the truth about your chivalry.'

As he said this the queen arrived, having heard the news about the knight's arrival. As soon as Perceval saw her and was told that it was she, and saw the girl behind her who had laughed when he had looked at her, he stepped straight up to meet them and said:

'May God give joy and honour to the fairest and finest of all ladies living, as all who have seen her testify.'

And the queen replied: 'It's a great joy that you've been found, for you've proved yourself to be a knight of high prowess.'

Then Perceval greeted the girl who had laughed at him, and embraced her, saying: 'Dear girl, if ever you need me, I shan't fail to come to your aid.'

And she thanked him. The king, the queen and the barons gave the most joyful welcome to Perceval the Welshman, and led him back to Carlion, returning there that day. They celebrated all that night and all the day that followed.

And then, on the third day, they saw a girl coming on a tawny mule, clutching a whip in her right hand. And there was no creature so utterly ugly even in Hell. There is no iron as black as her neck and hands, but that was little compared to the rest of her ugliness: her hair hung in two tresses, black and twisted; her eyes were just two holes, tiny as a rat's; her nose was like a cat's or monkey's, her lips like an ass's or a cow's, and her teeth were the colour of egg-yolk. She had a beard like a billy-goat, a hump in the middle of her chest, a curving spine and legs that bent like willow-wands. None such was ever seen at a royal court.

She greeted the king and all his knights together – except for Perceval. Seated on the tawny mule she said:

'Ah, Perceval! Fortune has fair tresses in front but is bald behind! A curse on anyone who wishes you well, for you didn't take Fortune by the hand when you met her! You entered the house of the Fisher King and saw the lance that bleeds, but it was so much trouble to you to open your mouth and speak that you never asked why that drop of blood sprang from the tip of the white head; nor did you ask what worthy man was served from the vessel that you saw, the Grail. How wretched is the man who sees the perfect opportunity and still waits for a better one! And you, you are wretched indeed: you saw that it was the time and place to speak and yet stayed silent; you had ample opportunity! It was an evil hour when you held your tongue, for if you had asked, the rich king who is so distressed would now have been healed of his wound and would have held his land in peace, which now he will never do. And do you know what will happen because that king will not now rule his land or be healed? Ladies will lose their husbands, lands will be laid waste, girls will be left in distress and orphaned, and many knights will die; all these evils will happen because of you!'

Then turning to the king she said: 'Don't be displeased if I leave now, for my lodging tonight will be far from here. I don't know if you've heard of the Proud Castle, but that's where I have to go tonight. In that castle there are 566 knights of worth; and I tell you, each of them has his sweetheart with him, a noble, fair and courtly lady. I'm telling you this because no-one who goes there can fail to find a joust or battle. Anyone eager for chivalrous deeds is sure to find them if he seeks them there. But if he wants to gain the whole world's esteem, I know where he could win it best, if he dared. On the peak of Montesclaire a girl lies besieged; whoever could raise the siege and free the girl would win the greatest honour and all possible praise; and the one to whom God granted such good fortune could safely gird on the Sword of the Strange Belt.'

With that the girl fell silent, having said all she wished, and set off without another word. And Sir Gawain leaped up and said he would go to Montesclaire and do all in his power to rescue the girl. And Gifflet the son of Do said that he would go, with God's aid, to the Proud Castle. All the knights pledged themselves to a host of great adventures: 'I,' said Kahendin, 'shall climb Mount Dolorous.'

But Perceval spoke quite differently: he said that as long as he lived he would not lodge in the same place for two nights together, nor hear word of any perilous passage but he would go and attempt it, nor hear of a knight greater than any other but he would go and do combat with him, until he knew who was served from the Grail and had found the bleeding lance and learned the certain truth about why it bled; he would never give up, whatever happened.

And so up to fifty of them rose, vowing to each other that they would go and seek out any wonder or adventure they might hear of, no matter in how terrible a land.

* * *

April and May passed by five times. Five years went by. And in that time Perceval lost his memory to such a degree that he no longer remembered God. In five years he failed to set foot in a church or worship God or His Cross. That's not to say that he stopped seeking deeds of chivalry: he went in search of strange, hard and terrible adventures, and encountered so many that he tested himself well. In five years he sent sixty worthy knights as prisoners to King Arthur's court. But for five years he lived without a thought for God.

It was at the end of these five years that he was riding across a wilderness, fully armed as always, when he met three knights and ten ladies, all in hair-shirts, bare-footed and with their heads hidden in their hoods. For the salvation of their souls they were doing penance on foot for the sins they had committed, and were astonished to see Perceval coming in armour, holding a lance and a shield. And one of the three knights stopped him and said:

'Dear friend, don't you believe in Jesus Christ, who laid down the New Law and gave it to the Christians? Truly, it's very wrong to carry arms on the day when Jesus died.'

And he who had no sense of day or hour or time, in such turmoil was his heart, replied: 'What day is it, then?'

'Don't you know, sir? It's Good Friday, the day when a man should worship the Cross and weep for his sins, for on this day the one who was sold for thirty pieces of silver was nailed to the Cross. He saw the sins with which the whole world was stained and bound, and became a man to save us from them. It's certain truth that He was both God and man, for the Virgin bore a son conceived by the Holy Spirit, so that the Deity was housed in the flesh of man. And those who will not believe that will never see Him face to face. And it was on this day that the son born of the Virgin Lady was nailed to the Cross and freed all His friends from Hell. It was a most holy death, which saved the living and brought the dead to life. All who believe in Him should be spending today in penitence. No man who believes in God should be carrying arms today, either in the field or on the road.'

'Where have you just come from now?' Perceval asked.

'From a worthy hermit who lives in this forest. He's such a holy man that he lives solely by the glory of God.'

'And why were you there? What did you ask? What were you looking for?'

'We asked him for guidance from our sins,' said one of the ladies. 'And we did the greatest thing any Christian can do who wants to come to God – we made confession.'

What Perceval had heard made him weep, and he longed to go and talk to the worthy man.

'I would very much like to go there,' he said, 'if you'd tell me the way.'

'Go straight along the way we've come, through the thick, dense wood, and look out for the branches that we knotted together as we came. We left such signs so that no-one going to the holy hermit should lose his way.'

With that they commended each other to God and no more questions were asked. Perceval set off along the path, sighing from the depths of his heart, for he felt he had wronged God and regretted it deeply. He rode on, weeping, right through the wood.

When he came to the hermitage he dismounted and disarmed and tethered his horse to an elm tree. Then he entered the hermit's cell. In a little chapel he found the hermit and a priest and a clerk beginning the highest and sweetest service that can be held in a holy church. Perceval went down on his knees as soon as he entered the chapel, and the good man, seeing him so humble and weeping, with tears streaming from his eyes to his chin, beckoned him to draw near. And Perceval bowed down before him and clung to the hermit's foot, and then, with hands clasped, begged him to give him guidance, for he had great need of it. The good man told him to make confession, for he would never have remission if he did not confess and repent.

'Sir,' said Perceval, 'fully five years ago I lost my bearings, and stopped loving God and believing in Him; and since then I've done nothing but ill.'

'Oh, good friend,' said the worthy man, 'tell me why you did this, and pray to God to have mercy on His sinner's soul.'

'Sir, I was once at the house of the Fisher King, and I saw the lance with the head that most certainly bleeds, but I asked nothing about the drop of blood I saw hanging from the tip of that white head. And truly, I've done nothing since then to make amends. Nor do I know who was served from the vessel I saw, the Grail, and I've suffered such grief ever since that I would gladly be dead; for I've forgotten God because of it, and not once since then have I asked Him for mercy – and I don't think I've done anything to earn it.'

'Oh, my dear friend,' said the worthy man, 'tell me your name.'

And he said: 'Perceval, sir.'

At that the hermit gave a sigh, for he recognised the name, and said: 'Friend, a sin of which you perhaps know nothing has done you great harm: it's the grief you caused your mother when you left her. She fell to the ground in a faint at the foot of the bridge outside the gate, and she died of that grief. I know this well, for she, your mother, was my sister. It was because of the sin you committed there that you came to ask nothing about the lance and the vessel, and many misfortunes have befallen you because of that. And I tell you this: you wouldn't have survived this long if she hadn't commended you to God. It was sin that stopped your tongue when you saw the lance-head with its ceaseless flow of blood, so that you didn't ask the reason; and folly seized you when you failed to learn who was served from that vessel, the Grail. The one who is served from it, I believe, is the father of the rich Fisher King. And don't imagine he's given pike or lamprey or salmon; he's served with a single host* which is brought to him in the Grail. It comforts and sustains his life – the Grail is such a holy thing. And he, who is so spiritual that he needs no more in his life than the host that comes in the Grail, has lived there for twelve years without ever leaving the chamber which you saw the Grail enter. Now I want to direct you and give you penance for your sin.'

'I want that with all my heart, good uncle,' said Perceval. 'And since my mother was your sister, you ought to call me nephew and I should love you the more.'

'That's true, dear nephew, but listen now: if pity has taken hold of your soul, repent in all truthfulness, and go in the name of penitence to church each morning before anywhere else, and you'll benefit greatly: don't fail to do so on any account. If you're in a place where there's a minster, church or chapel, go there when you hear the bell ring, or sooner if you're awake. And if mass is begun there'll be even more profit in being there: stay there until the priest has said and sung it all. If you do this with a will, you may come to redeem yourself and win honour and a place in Paradise. Love God, believe in God, worship God; honour godly men and women; and if a girl or a widow or an orphan requests your help, grant it, and it'll be the better for you. I'd have you do this if you'd recover all your former virtues. Now tell me if you'll do so.'

'Yes, sir, most gladly.'

'Then stay here with me for a while, and in penitence eat such food as I eat.'

Perceval agreed to all of this, and the hermit whispered a prayer in his ear, repeating it to him until he had learnt it. Many of the names of Our Lord appeared in this prayer, including the greatest ones, which the tongue of man should never utter except in fear of death. And when he had taught him the prayer he forbade him ever to utter those names except in times of grave peril.

'I shan't, sir,' said Perceval.

And so he stayed there and heard the service, which delighted him. And after the service he worshipped the Cross and wept for his sins. That night he ate as the holy hermit pleased: beets, chervil, lettuce and cress and millet, and bread made of barley and oats, and water from a clear spring. And his horse had straw and a full trough of barley.

Thus Perceval came to recognise that God received death and was crucified on the Friday. And at Easter, most worthily, Perceval received communion.

The story leaves Perceval with his uncle for now, and before saying any more about him, it first recounts the adventures of Sir Gawain.

---

* Communion bread or wafer. The references to fish are less strange than they appear, for the word 'graal' is almost certainly derived from the Latin 'gradalis', a broad, shallow dish or platter.

Sir Gawain's Quest Begins

KING ARTHUR HAD HAD LETTERS SEALED and sent to every land summoning lords and knights to attend a court at Pennevoiseuse by the Welsh sea at the feast of Saint John. The knights of the Round Table, who were scattered throughout the lands and forests, heard the news and were filled with joy, and returned to the court with all speed. Sir Gawain and Lancelot did not come on the day decreed, but the other knights of the court made their arrival, every one.

Saint John's Day came. The weather was fine and clear and the hall was high and wide and filled with a great throng of knights. Cloths were laid on the tables, of which there were many in the hall, and when the king and queen had washed and were seated at the head of one table, all the knights sat down – and there were at least five hundred present. Kay the seneschal and Sir Yvain, son of King Urien, were serving at the table that day along with twenty-five knights, and Lucan the butler served the king with his cup of gold. The sun streamed in through the windows all around the hall, and the floor was strewn with rushes and flowers and wild mint, filling the air with a heady fragrance.

The first course had been served and everyone was waiting for the second when three maidens suddenly entered the hall. The first was riding a mule, whiter than snow, with a head-piece of gold and an ivory saddle inlaid with precious stones, and a saddle-cloth of red samite traced with gold. The maiden had a most comely body, and she was clad in a rich silken gown, with a fine head-dress flowing all around her head, laden with jewels that blazed like fires. And it was well that her head was covered thus, for she was quite bald. Her right arm was hung in a sling embroidered with gold, and rested on the richest cushion ever seen, set about with little golden bells. And in her hands she held the head of a king, sealed with silver and crowned with gold.

The second maiden, more beautiful still, was mounted on a horse such as a squire might ride, and from her neck a shield hung: pure white it was, with a red cross, and in it was fixed a piece of the True Cross on which Christ was crucified.

The third maiden came in on foot. She was about the height of a boy and wore a short skirt, and carried a whip in her hand with which she drove the two mounts. She was the most beautiful of all.

The first maiden rode up to the king and queen where they were seated at the table, and said: 'Sire, may the Saviour of the world grant honour and joy to you and the queen and all those present; and don't take offence if I remain mounted, for I cannot dismount in the company of knights, nor must I, until the Grail is won.'

'Damsel,' said the king, 'nothing would please me more than that.'

'I know that, sire; and I've a request to make.'

'Speak your will.'

'Sire,' she said, 'the shield this maiden bears belonged to Joseph of Arimathea, the good soldier who took Our Lord from the Cross, and I now present it to you, on these conditions: that you keep the shield for a knight who'll come to collect it, and that you hang it on that pillar in the middle of the hall and keep it there; for none but he must take it down or hang it from his neck. With this shield he will win the Grail, and he'll leave another shield here, a red shield emblazoned with a white stag.'

'Damsel,' said the king, 'the shield we will gladly keep, and I thank you deeply for bringing it here.'

'Sire,' she said, 'I've more to say. I bring you greetings from the greatest, most loyal and upright king on earth – the Fisher King, who is to be pitied indeed, for he has fallen into a grievous weakness.'

'That is a great shame, damsel,' said the king, 'and may God grant him what his heart desires.'

'But sire, do you know why this weakness has beset him? It's because of a knight he lodged at his castle, to whom the Grail appeared. Because the knight failed to ask who was served from it, all lands were engulfed by war; whenever a knight met another in a forest or glade they would do battle without any real cause. And I have my own grievance, sire, against the knight, and I'll show you why.'

And so saying she took off her rich head-dress and showed the king, the queen and all the assembly her bald, quite hairless head.

'Sire,' she said, 'I had a beautiful head of hair, all braided into golden tresses, until the knight came to the house of the Fisher King; because he failed to ask the question I'm now bald, and my hair will not return until a knight goes and asks the question properly, or goes and wins the Grail. But sire, you've not yet seen the full harm this has wrought. Outside this hall is a cart pulled by three white stags. I tell you, the harness is of silk and gold, and all the timber is ebony. It's draped in black samite, with a gold cross on top as long as the cart itself. And on the cart beneath the drape are the heads of 150 knights, some sealed in gold, some in silver and others in lead. And the rich Fisher King wants you to know that this calamity is all the fault of the knight who failed to ask who was served from the Grail. Sire, the maiden with the shield is holding in her hand the head of a queen, sealed in lead and crowned with copper, and by her were betrayed the king whose head I am carrying and the knights whose heads are in the cart outside. Send someone, my lord, to witness the richness and finery of the cart.'

So the king sent Kay the seneschal, who looked all over, inside and out, and returned to the king and said: 'Sire, I've never seen such a handsome cart. And the three white stags that pull it are the sleekest you ever beheld. But if you'll take my advice, you'll take the one at the front; he's the best of the lot, and would make fine venison!'

'Kay!' cried the king. 'You've spoken basely! I wouldn't do such a thing for all the kingdom of Logres!'

'Sire,' said the maiden, 'Sir Kay may speak his mind, but I know you'll take no heed of what he says. Command that the shield be hung on that pillar. We'll leave you now, for we've stayed long enough.'

At the king's command Sir Yvain took the shield from the maiden's neck and hung it on the pillar in the middle of the hall. Then the maidens took their leave of the king and turned away, and the king commended them to God.

When the banquet in the hall was over, the king and the queen and all the knights went to the windows to see the three maidens and the cart with the three stags. The bald maiden was riding in front, and did not don her head-dress again until she had entered the forest and the knights watching from the windows could no longer see her: only then did she cover her head once more. When the maidens were lost to view the king and the knights came down from the windows, and most said that she was the first bald maiden they had ever seen.

* * *

Now the story leaves King Arthur and tells of the three maidens and the cart pulled by the three stags. They made their way into the forest and rode hard until, with the castle seven leagues behind them, they saw a knight coming along their path. He was riding a big horse, but it was all skin and bone; his hauberk was turned to rust, his shield was holed in more than seven places, and its colour was so faded as to be indiscernible; and he had a great lance in his hand. As he came up to the first maiden he greeted her most nobly, saying:

'Damsel, may God guide you and your company!'

'Sir,' she said, 'may God give you joy and good fortune.'

'Where have you ridden from today?' he asked.

'From a great court, sir, held by King Arthur at Pennevoiseuse. Are you going there?'

'No,' he said, 'but I've been there many times.'

'Where are you headed, then?' she asked.

'To the land of the Fisher King, if it please God.'

'Tell me your name, sir, and tarry awhile with me.'

The knight drew rein and the maidens and the cart halted.

'Damsel,' he said. 'It's only right that you should know my name. I'm the nephew of King Arthur, and my name is Gawain.'

'By my life!' she cried. 'Sir Gawain? But in truth, my heart told me so. And

God be praised, so fine a knight as you should indeed go and see the rich Fisher King. And now I entreat you, by the valour that is in you and for the sake of all that's noble, to return with me and guide me past a castle which stands in this forest, for it's a perilous place.'

'As you wish,' said Sir Gawain.

So he turned back and rode with the maiden through the forest, which was high indeed and thick with leaves and little frequented by people. The maiden recounted the story of the heads they were carrying in the cart, just as she had done at King Arthur's court, and also of the shield that they had left there. But Sir Gawain was more concerned about the maiden who was following behind them on foot.

'Lady,' he said, 'why does the maiden walking behind us not ride on the cart?'

'That she will not, sir. Henceforth she must travel only on foot. But if you're as fine a knight as they say, her penance will soon be done.'

'How so?' asked Sir Gawain.

'I'll tell you,' she said. 'If God should lead you to the castle of the Fisher King and the Holy Grail appears to you, and you ask who is served from it, her penance will be done, and I who am bald shall have tresses once more. But if you fail to do so, we shall have to suffer our afflictions until such time as the Good Knight wins the Grail. For because of the knight who went there first and failed to ask the question, all lands have fallen into misery and war, and the good Fisher King is languishing.'

'Damsel,' said Sir Gawain, 'may God give me the courage and the will to do what will find favour in His eyes and win the world's praise.'

Sir Gawain and the maidens journeyed on and passed through the high forest, green with leaves and filled with birdsong, and entered the most terrible and forbidding forest that ever a man beheld. It seemed it had never been blessed with green: all the branches were bare of leaves and shrivelled, the trees were black as though burnt by fire, and the ground was charred, devoid of grass and full of great crevices.

'Damsel,' said Sir Gawain, 'this forest is grim indeed. Does it go on like this for a long way?'

'A good ten leagues, sir, but you'll not have to suffer them all.'

From time to time Sir Gawain looked back at the maiden walking behind, and worried about how he could help her. They rode on until they came to a great valley. Sir Gawain looked down a wide defile, and there before him was a black castle enclosed by a great ring of wall, forbidding and ghastly; and the nearer he came to the castle the more hideous it seemed. He could see great halls looming, of foul aspect; and a river tumbled from the peak of a lowering black mountain and surged through the castle with such a terrible roar that it sounded like bolts of thunder. Sir Gawain saw the gateway, as ugly as the mouth of Hell, and from within came a great wailing and weeping, with many people crying:

'God! What has become of the Good Knight? When will he come?'

'Damsel,' said Sir Gawain, 'what castle is this, so ugly and foul? There seems to be great suffering here, and people are crying for a good knight to come.'

'It's the castle of the Black Hermit. And no matter what the ones within may do to me, I beg you not to intervene, for you might very well die: you'd have no strength or power against them.'

They rode to within two bowshots of the castle; then through the gates they saw knights on black horses pouring forth, armed all in black. There were 152 of them, and they were hideous to behold. They galloped up to the maidens and the cart, and each took one of the 152 heads, spiking them on the ends of their lances; then they rode back into the castle rejoicing. Sir Gawain had seen what the knights had done, and felt deeply ashamed for not intervening.

'Sir Gawain,' said the maiden, 'now you can see that your strength would be worth little here!'

'Damsel,' he said, 'this is a wicked castle if they rob people so.'

'But there'll be no amends for this outrage, sir, nor will the evil-doers be overcome, nor will those who wail and weep be released from their imprisonment, until the coming of the Good Knight for whom you heard them crying.'

'Damsel,' said Sir Gawain, 'that knight should be happy indeed if he has the valour and strength to overcome such a wicked people.'

'That knight, sir, is the finest in the world and is still quite young. And my heart grieves that I've no news of him, for I'd rather see him than any man alive.'

'So would I, damsel,' said Sir Gawain. 'But may I turn back now, by your leave?'

'No, sir, not until we're past the castle. Then I'll show you the path you should take.'

With that they all moved off together. Just as they were about to leave the castle walls behind, a knight suddenly rode out from a hidden postern, mounted on a great horse and fully armed, lance in hand, and from his neck hung a red shield emblazoned with a golden eagle.

'Sir knight!' he cried to Gawain. 'Stop there, I pray you.'

'What do you want, good sir?' Gawain said.

'You must joust with me,' he cried, 'and try to win this shield; it's a splendid shield, and you should be at great pains to win it, for it belonged to the greatest knight there ever was of his religion, the strongest and the wisest.'

'And who was that?' asked Sir Gawain.

'Judas Machabeus, the creator of falconry.'

'Truly,' said Gawain, 'he was a good knight.'

'So you should be glad indeed,' said the knight, 'if you won this shield, for your own is the most pitiful and battered I've ever seen; I can hardly tell what colour it is!'

'Then you can plainly see,' said the Maiden of the Cart, 'that the knight and his shield have not been idle; and his horse is not as well rested as yours, sir.'

'Damsel,' said the knight, 'there's no need for all this talking. He must fight with me to the death. I challenge him!'

And Sir Gawain said: 'I heard you.'

He drew back and prepared to charge. The knight did likewise, and they came at each other as fast as their horses could bear them, lances levelled. The knight struck Sir Gawain on his shield where he had little protection and rammed it a full yard through, breaking his lance in the thrust; and Sir Gawain struck him full in the chest with his lance and sent him tumbling over his horse's rear and crashing to the ground, impaled on the lance with a full hand's breadth of steel in his breast. Gawain withdrew the lance, and when the knight found himself unpinned he climbed to his feet and came back to his horse. He was about to step into the stirrups when the Maiden of the Cart cried:

'Sir Gawain, take the knight now, for if he remounts you'll have great trouble beating him!'

When the knight heard Sir Gawain named he drew back. 'What?' he said. 'Is this the good Gawain, the nephew of King Arthur?'

'Yes indeed,' said the maiden.

'I admit defeat, sir, and it grieves me that I didn't know who you were before I began fighting you.' He took the shield from his neck and handed it to Gawain. 'Sir,' he said, 'take the shield that belonged to the good Machabeus, for I know of none on whom it could be better bestowed than you. With this shield were beaten all the knights who are held prisoner in this castle.' Sir Gawain took the shield, which was most handsome and rich, and then the knight said: 'Now give me yours, sir, for you'll surely not carry two?'

'You're right,' said Sir Gawain, and he lifted the shield-strap from his neck. But just as he was about to hand over the shield, the maiden on foot cried out:

'No! Sir Gawain, what are you doing? If he takes your shield back to the castle, all those within will think you've been beaten and will come out after you! They'll force you back inside and throw you into the terrible dungeon! For no man carries back a shield except from a vanquished knight.'

'Sir knight,' said Gawain, 'you seek to do me ill, if this maiden's words are true.'

'Have mercy on me, sir, I pray you,' said the knight. 'Once more I admit defeat. But I'd be very glad to take your shield back to the castle, for never will the shield of so fine a knight be seen there. And I'm delighted you've come, even though you've wounded me, for you've delivered me from the greatest hardship that ever a knight endured.'

'What hardship's that?' said Sir Gawain.

'I'll tell you, sir: many knights have passed this castle, both valiant and cowardly, and I've had to joust and do combat with them all, offering them the shield as a prize just as I did with you. I found most of them courageous and bold in defending themselves, and they wounded me in many places, but never did a knight strike me down or give me such a blow as you. And since you've carried off the shield and beaten me, never again will any knight who passes this castle need to fear me or any of the knights within.'

'By my life,' said Sir Gawain, 'I prize my victory even more now!'

'Sir,' said the knight, 'I'll go now by your leave. I won't be able to hide my shame at the castle; I'll have to show it openly.'

'May God give you courage,' said Sir Gawain.

Then the Maiden of the Cart told Gawain to give her the shield which the knight had asked to carry off.

'Gladly, damsel,' he said, and the maiden on foot took the shield and placed it in the cart, while the vanquished knight remounted and rode back to the castle. When he was inside, so great a commotion and shouting arose that all the forest and valley resounded.

'Sir Gawain,' said the Maiden of the Cart, 'the knight is disgraced: he's being thrown into that dread prison. But hurry! Now we can go!'

And with that they all set off together and left the castle a league behind.

'Damsel,' said Sir Gawain, 'when it shall please you I'll take my leave.'

'May God keep you, sir, and I thank you deeply for escorting us.'

'Damsel,' he said, 'I shall always be at your service.'

'Many thanks, sir,' she said. 'There's your path, by that tall cross at the edge of the forest. There you'll find the most beautiful wood in the world, once you've passed through this one that's so grim.'

Sir Gawain turned away, and suddenly the maiden on foot cried out: 'Sir! Sir! You're not as alert as I thought!'

Sir Gawain, startled, turned his horse back. 'Why do you say that, damsel?'

'Because,' she said, 'you didn't ask my lady of the Cart why she carries her arm in that golden sling. Will you be as alert at the court of the Fisher King?'

'Oh sweet friend,' said the Maiden of the Cart, 'don't hold Gawain alone guilty, but King Arthur before him, and all the knights of his court, for none had the presence of mind to ask. Sir Gawain, go your way. It's no use asking the question now, for I won't tell you, and you'll never have the answer except from the most cowardly knight in the world, who's in my service and trying to find me – though without success.'

'Damsel,' said Sir Gawain, 'I shall press you no further.'

And with that the maiden took her leave, while Gawain rode off along the path she had shown him.

* * *

The story now leaves the three maidens and the cart and tells how Sir Gawain passed through the dismal forest and entered a beautiful, vast and lofty wood, full of wild creatures. He rode on at a good pace; but he was greatly disturbed by what the maiden had said, and feared he would be widely reproached.

He rode all day until evening fell and the sun was sinking. Then looking ahead he saw the cell of a hermit and its chapel deep in the forest. Before the chapel leaped a spring, clear and swift, shaded by a wide-spreading tree. A maiden was seated beneath the tree, holding a mule by the reins, and from her saddle-bow hung the head of a knight. Sir Gawain rode up and dismounted.

'God keep you, damsel,' he said.

'And you, sir, all the days of your life.'

Then she rose to meet him, and he said: 'Damsel, what are you waiting for here?'

'For the hermit, sir, who's gone out into the woods. I want to ask him news of a knight.'

'Do you think he'll have the news you seek?'

'Yes, sir; so I've been told.'

Just then the hermit appeared and greeted the maiden and Sir Gawain. He opened the door of his cell and led their mounts inside, where he unbridled them and gave them hay and barley. He was just about to take off their saddles when Sir Gawain stepped forward and said: 'Leave that, sir; it's not a task for you.'

'I'm quite capable of it,' replied the hermit, 'for I was in King Uther's household as a squire and a knight for forty years; and now I've been a hermit here for more than thirty.'

Sir Gawain gazed at him in wonder. 'Sir,' he said, 'you don't look even forty years old!'

'I know,' said the hermit.

Sir Gawain saw to the unsaddling, taking more care of the maiden's mule than of his own horse, and then the hermit took Gawain and the maiden by the hand and led them to the chapel, which was a most beautiful place.

'Sir,' said the hermit to Sir Gawain, 'you mustn't lay aside your arms, for this forest is full of adventures, and no worthy man should be unarmed here.'

So he went and fetched his lance and shield and placed them inside the chapel. Then the hermit brought them such food as he had and water from the spring; and when they had eaten, the maiden said to the hermit:

'I've come here, sir, to ask you news of a knight I'm seeking.'

'And who is that?'

'A chaste knight of the most holy lineage. He has a head of gold, the gaze of a lion, a heart full of valour and a mind quite free of baseness.'

'Damsel,' said the hermit, 'I can tell you nothing, for I don't know for certain where he is. But he's slept in this chapel twice in less than a year.'

'Is that all you can tell me?'

'Yes, damsel.'

'And you, good sir?' she said to Gawain.

'Damsel,' he said, 'if he's the youth I think you mean, I'd be as glad to see him as you, but I've met no-one who had news of him.'

'And the Maiden of the Cart, sir, have you seen her?'

'Yes, indeed,' he said, 'and just a short while ago.'

'Did she still have her arm in a sling?'

'Yes,' said Sir Gawain.

'She'll carry it so for a long time,' said the maiden.

Then the hermit said: 'What's your name, sir?'

'Gawain, the nephew of King Arthur.'

'Then I love you the more,' said the hermit. 'God save King Arthur, for his father made me a knight. But now I'm a priest, and ever since I came to this hermitage I've served the Fisher King, by Our Lord's command. And all who serve him are well aware of his grace, for his holy house is so sweet that a year's stay seems no more than a month. And because of his holiness and the sweetness of his house, where I've many times held service in the chapel where the Grail appears, I, and all who serve him, retain the appearance of youth.'

'Sir,' said Sir Gawain, 'can you show me the way to his house?'

'No-one,' said the hermit, 'can show you the way; the will of God must lead you there. Do you wish to go?'

'There's nothing I desire more.'

'Then may God grant,' said the hermit, 'that you ask the question that the other knight to whom the Grail appeared failed to ask, for because of him many misfortunes have since befallen a great many people.'

With that they ceased their talking, and the hermit led Sir Gawain to his cell to rest, while the maiden stayed in the chapel.

As soon as dawn broke next day, Sir Gawain, who had slept all night fully armed, arose to find his horse and the maiden's mule saddled and bridled. He went to the chapel and saw the hermit dressed for mass and the maiden kneeling before the altar of Our Lady, praying to God and His mother for guidance and weeping most tenderly, the tears running down her cheeks.

When she had prayed for some time she rose, and Sir Gawain said to her: 'May God bless your day.'

And she returned his greeting.

'Damsel,' he said, 'you don't seem very happy.'

'I've no reason to be, sir, for I'm near to being disinherited since I can't find the Good Knight. Now I must go to the castle of the Black Hermit and take the head that hangs on my saddle-bow, for otherwise I'll not be able to pass through the forest without being taken captive or dishonoured, but this will buy me safe passage. Then I'll seek out the Maiden of the Cart and travel through the forest in safety.'

At that the hermit began mass. Sir Gawain and the maiden heard it, and when it had been sung Gawain took his leave of the hermit, and the maiden likewise. He rode off in one direction and the maiden in another, and they commended each other to God.

Sir Gawain passed into the high forest and rode swiftly on, praying to God to show him the path that would lead him to the land of the Fisher King. On he rode until midday when, deep in the forest, he saw a youth beneath a tree, sitting beside his hunting-horse.

Sir Gawain greeted him, and the youth called back: 'God guide you, sir.'

'Where are you headed, friend?' said Sir Gawain.

'I'm looking for the lord of this forest.'

'Why, to whom does the forest belong?'

'To the finest knight in the world, sir. Perhaps you've news of him: he should be bearing a red shield with a white stag. I say he's a good knight, but in faith I shouldn't praise him, for he killed my father in these woods with a javelin. He was just a boy when he killed him, and while I'm just a boy I'll avenge my father if I find the knight, for when he killed my father he robbed me of the greatest knight in the kingdom of Logres. And he robbed me well, killing him with a javelin without so much as a proper challenge! I'll never rest until I've avenged him.'

'Dear friend,' said Sir Gawain, 'since he's such a good knight, take care you don't bring misfortune upon yourself; I pray you may meet him on peaceful terms.'

'That can never be,' said the youth, 'for if I once catch sight of him I'll attack him as a mortal enemy.'

'Whatever you say, good friend,' said Sir Gawain. 'But can you tell me if there's a house in this forest where I could find lodging tonight?'

'I know of no house on your path within twenty leagues of here. So you mustn't delay, for it's long past noon.'

And so Sir Gawain bade the youth farewell and rode swiftly away. He knew none of the paths or tracks: he galloped on as chance took him, rejoicing at the beauty of the forest and the great herds of wild beasts that wandered across his path. He rode on until he came at twilight to the forest's edge. The dusk was soft and tranquil and the sun was about to set. He had ridden fully twenty leagues since leaving the boy, yet he feared he was going to find no lodging. Gawain now found himself in the most beautiful meadowland in the world, and after riding on a little way he looked ahead, and there before him appeared a castle, standing close to the forest upon a mountain. It was bounded by a great wall lined with battlements; rich, windowed halls peered out above them, and in the middle of the castle loomed an ancient tower. All around were great rivers, wide meadowlands and deep forest. Sir Gawain spurred on towards the castle, and just as he came in sight of the gate he saw a youth ride out towards him, mounted on a packhorse. As the boy approached he greeted Sir Gawain courteously, saying: 'God keep you, sir.'

'And bring you good fortune,' replied Gawain. 'Good friend, what castle is this?'

'The castle of the Widowed Lady, sir.'

'And what's it called?'

'Kamaalot, sir. It belonged to Alain li Gros, a most fair and noble knight, but he died a long time ago, and so, more lately, did his widow. And now the castle's at war, for the Lord of the Fens and another knight are trying to take it by force, and indeed, they've already seized seven of her castles. Only the widow's daughter and five elderly knights are left to defend this castle, and they long for the return of the widow's son. Sir,' said the boy, 'the gate is shut and the drawbridge raised, for the castle is on the alert. But if you'll tell me your name, I'll ride ahead and have the bridge lowered and the gate unbarred, and tell them you'll lodge there tonight.'

'Many thanks,' said Sir Gawain. 'Truly, my name shall be known before I leave the castle.'

So the youth rode off at a gallop while Sir Gawain sauntered along behind, for he had had a long day's ride. Between the forest and the castle he came across a chapel, its roof supported by four marble columns, and inside was a beautiful tomb, which was wide open to view since the chapel had no walls. Sir Gawain stopped to take a look. Meanwhile the boy rode into the castle and had the drawbridge lowered and the gate opened. Then he dismounted and ran to the hall where the Widowed Lady's daughter was sitting. She said to the boy:

'Why have you turned back from delivering my message?'

'Lady, I've just met the finest knight I've ever seen! He wishes to lodge here tonight; he's fully armed and riding alone.'

'Well, what's his name?' she asked.

'He told me that we'd know his name before he left the castle.'

At that she began to weep for joy, and raising her hands to heaven she cried: 'Dear Lord God, never will I have known such joy if this is my brother: I would not then lose my honour or my castle, which they're wrongfully trying to take from me because I've no lord or defender.'

Then the Widow's daughter rose and walked out across the drawbridge, and there she saw Sir Gawain still gazing at the tomb in the chapel.

'Ah!' she said. 'The tomb will tell us if it's really he!'

She hurried on to the chapel, and when Sir Gawain saw her coming he dismounted.

'Good day, young lady,' he said.

She made no reply and came straight up to the tomb; but when she saw that it was not open she collapsed in a swoon, much to Sir Gawain's dismay. As she recovered from her faint she began to cry out in grief; but at last she said: 'Sir, I bid you welcome. But I thought you were my brother and was overjoyed, and now I see you're not I can't help but grieve. For the tomb is to open as soon as he returns, and until then no-one will know what lies within.'

She rose to her feet and took Sir Gawain by the hand and said: 'What's your name, good sir?'

'Gawain, damsel, the nephew of King Arthur.'

'I bid you welcome, sir, out of love for my brother and you.'

Then she bade the boy take Sir Gawain's horse into the castle, while she led him up to the hall, where his arms were laid aside and water was brought for him to wash his face and hands, for he had been bruised and chafed by his hauberk. Then she robed him in a rich gown of silk and gold, lined with ermine, and seated him beside her.

'Sir,' she said, 'have you any news of my brother? I haven't seen him for a long time and I've great need of him. His name is Perceval.'

'Perceval? I'm sorry, damsel, I can tell you nothing at all. But there's no knight in the world I'd rather see.'

'He was a fair youth indeed, sir, when he left here. And I've since heard he's the fairest knight alive, and the boldest. His bravery now would serve me well, for he left me embroiled in war when he departed. That was a good seven years ago, but I've never seen him since. He killed the Red Knight of the Forest of Quinqueroi, and now that knight's brother and the Lord of the Fens are waging war upon me and trying to seize my castle, so I pray that God will help me, for most of my uncles are dead. King Pelles is not, but he's given up his lands for God and retired to a hermitage. And another of my uncles, the King of Castle Mortal, would give me no support or aid, for he has as much evil in his heart as King Pelles has goodness, which is a great deal; he has designs on the lands of my grandfather the Fisher King, and on the Holy Grail and the lance with the head that bleeds each day; but if it please God they'll never be his.'

Sir Gawain was astonished to hear of the Welsh boy's family, and wondered how much his sister knew. 'Damsel,' he said gently, 'at the house of the Fisher King there was once a knight to whom the Grail appeared three times, but he failed to ask what was done with it or who was served from it.'

'True, sir,' said Perceval's sister. 'Yet they say he was the finest knight in the world. I would curse him indeed, but out of love for my brother I love all knights. Yet because of that knight's folly, my grandfather the Fisher King is now languishing. Sir,' she said, 'all good knights should go and see the house of the rich Fisher King. Will you go?'

'Oh yes, damsel, and as soon as may be. I had no other goal in mind.'

'Then sir,' she said, 'tell my brother and my grandfather the Fisher King of my plight, if you see them. But make sure, Sir Gawain, that you're more alert than the other knight.'

Sir Gawain could not bear to tell her what he knew of her brother Perceval, and said no more than: 'Damsel, I shall do as God guides me.'

While they were talking thus the five elderly knights who guarded the castle came riding back from the forest bearing stags and hinds and boars. They dismounted, and greeted Sir Gawain with joy when they knew that it was he.

When the food was ready they all sat down to dine and were served most graciously. Just then in came the boy who had opened the gate for Sir Gawain. He knelt before the Widow's daughter and said he had delivered her message.

'And what news?' she said.

'My lady, there's to be a great tournament in the vales which once belonged to you: the pavilions are already set. Both your enemies are there, with a great host of other knights, and they've declared that the one who wins the prize at the tournament will become guardian of this castle and hold it against all comers for a year.'

The Widow's daughter began to weep, and said to Sir Gawain: 'Now you know, sir: this castle is no longer mine; those knights have laid claim to it.'

'Truly, my lady, they're wicked and sinful men.'

When the tables had been cleared away the Widow's daughter came to Sir Gawain and fell at his feet, weeping. He raised her up at once, saying: 'Come, damsel; no tears, I pray you.'

'Sir,' she said, 'for God's sake, have pity on me.'

'I have, damsel, by my life.'

'Then our plight will reveal whether you're truly a good knight.'

With that she retired to her chamber, while a bed was set up for Sir Gawain in the hall; and there he lay down to sleep, and the five elderly knights likewise. But thoughts filled Gawain's mind that night, and when he rose next morning he went to hear mass in the castle chapel and then, after eating three pieces of bread soaked in wine, he armed himself at once and asked the five knights if they would go with him to the tourney.

'Oh yes, sir,' they said, 'if you're going!'

'In faith,' cried Sir Gawain, 'I wouldn't miss it for the world!'

So the knights donned their armour, and their horses were brought along with Sir Gawain's. Then he went to take his leave of the Widow's daughter, who was filled with joy when the knights told her that Sir Gawain was going to the tournament.

Gawain and the knights mounted and rode from the castle, galloping on with all speed. When they reached the edge of the forest Sir Gawain looked before him and saw the most beautiful valley he had ever beheld, so great that he could not see a quarter of it; in between patches of deep green forest lay wide stretches of rich meadowland, abounding with game.

'Sir,' said the knights, 'behold the Vales of Kamaalot, which have been taken from our lady the Widow's daughter, along with seven splendid castles in Wales.'

'It's a crime and a sin,' said Sir Gawain.

They rode on until at last they spied the pennants and shields where the tournament was to take place; and already they could see most of the knights mounted and fully armed, spurring their horses down the meadow, and the lodges and pavilions pitched all around in the shade of the woods. Sir Gawain and his companions drew rein beneath a tree and watched as knights gathered on all sides for the tourney, and they pointed out the Lord of the Fens and the brother of the Red Knight, whose name was Cahot the Red. As soon as the tourney was assembled, Sir Gawain and the knights rode down and joined in: Gawain charged a Welsh knight and sent him and his horse crashing to the ground in a heap. Behind him galloped his five companions, each felling an enemy, elated at being with so fine a knight. Cahot the Red saw Sir Gawain, and not realising who he was, came charging at him full tilt. Gawain met him with the head of his lance and struck him so fiercely that he shattered his collar-bone and sent his lance flying from his hand. All over the field Gawain rode seeking out opponents, and every knight he met he unhorsed or wounded: the five knights rejoiced at the feats they saw him perform. But suddenly they pointed out the Lord of the Fens, who was advancing with a great body of knights. Sir Gawain turned his horse and galloped straight towards him; they struck each other at such close quarters that their lances bent and flew into splinters, and they and their horses collided so hard that the Lord of the Fens lost his stirrups, his rear saddle-bow was shattered, and he came crashing down behind his horse so that the spike on his helmet plunged a full hand's breadth into the ground. Gawain took his horse, a fine mount indeed, and in full view of all the Lord's followers gave it to one of the five knights, who bade a squire take it back to the castle of Kamaalot. Meanwhile Sir Gawain rode on, seeking opponents all over the field and performing impossible feats of arms. And the five knights themselves, inspired by his example, summoned all their courage and did greater feats of arms that day than they had ever done before, each taking knights captive and winning their horses.

But the Lord of the Fens was now remounted on a fine charger, full of shame at being toppled by Sir Gawain. So he picked out Gawain and came galloping at him, thinking to avenge his disgrace. They clashed; Sir Gawain had but a broken shaft of lance, but he struck him with it full in the chest to balk him, and the Lord of the Fens in turn broke his lance as he struck his foe. Sir Gawain drew his sword and cast away his broken lance, and the Lord of the Fens did likewise, shouting to his men not to intervene, for he had never failed to vanquish any knight he met. They rained great blows on each other's helm, until sparks flew and the swords were notched. But Sir Gawain's blows were the greater, so fierce and terrible that blood poured from his foe's mouth and nose until his hauberk was drenched. The Lord of the Fens could take no more, and he yielded himself prisoner and liegeman to Sir Gawain, who was exultant, as were his five companions. The Lord of the Fens then rode to his tent and dismounted; Gawain took the Lord's horse and said to one of the five knights: 'Keep it for me.'

Meanwhile all the knights of the tournament had retired to their pavilions, all agreeing that the knight with the red shield emblazoned with the eagle of gold had won the day. They asked the Lord of the Fens if he agreed and he did so.

'Then sir,' they said to Sir Gawain, 'the castle of Kamaalot is in your keeping for a year.'

'Many thanks, my lords!' said Sir Gawain, and calling to the five knights he said: 'Sirs, it's my wish that you keep the castle on my behalf, and that you do so with the consent of these knights here.'

'We grant your wish most gladly, sir.'

'And you, sir,' said Sir Gawain to the Lord of the Fens, 'I give as my prisoner to the Widow's daughter who gave me lodging last night.'

'That is not yours to do,' he replied. 'A tournament is not warfare, and I'll not be taken captive back to the castle: I'm quite able to pay my ransom. But tell me your name, sir.'

'My name is Gawain,' he said.

'Oh, Sir Gawain, I've heard tell of you many times, but never seen you until today. Since the castle of Kamaalot is now in your keeping, I swear that for a year and a day the castle and the Widow's lands will have nothing to fear from me – or from anyone else, if I can help it: that I swear before all these knights. And if you want gold or silver of me I'll give it willingly.'

'I thank you, sir. Your pledge gives me joy enough.'

Sir Gawain took his leave and turned away, riding back towards the castle of Kamaalot. To the daughter of the Widowed Lady he bade a squire take the horse of the Lord of the Fens, and she was overjoyed by the gift. The five knights likewise sent all their spoils before them, and there was great rejoicing when they arrived at the castle and he announced that the castle was now in the keeping of the five knights and himself. It is no wonder that Sir Gawain was highly honoured and given fine lodging that night.

When morning came, Sir Gawain took his leave and left the castle; but first he heard mass, for such was his custom. The Widow's daughter, Perceval's sister, commended him to God, and truly, he left the castle a happier place than he had found it.

* * *

Sir Gawain rode on, as God and adventure took him, searching for the land of the Fisher King. Fully armed, his shield hung from his neck and lance in hand, he passed into a great forest, praying to Our Lord to guide him on the high quest he had undertaken, so that he might win through with honour. He rode on until he came as evening fell to a house deep in the forest, built on an island in the middle of a river. It was surrounded by tangled woods so that he could scarcely make out the hall; but it was handsome indeed, and Sir Gawain, thinking it must be the house of a great nobleman, headed that way to seek lodging.

Just as he neared the drawbridge, he noticed a dwarf sitting on one of the pillars of the bridge. He jumped up and cried: 'Welcome, Sir Gawain!'

'I wish you good fortune, friend,' said Gawain. 'So you know my name?'

'Indeed I do, sir!' said the dwarf. 'I saw you at the tournament. You couldn't have come here at a better time, for my lord's away but my lady's stayed behind, and she's the most beautiful, wise and noble lady in all the kingdom of Logres, though she's only twenty!'

'My friend,' said Sir Gawain, 'what's the name of the lord of this castle?'

'He's called Marin the Jealous, sir, of the Castle of Gomorret. I'll go and tell my lady that the good Sir Gawain has come, and to make merry!'

Sir Gawain was astonished by the dwarf's welcome, for in most dwarfs he had found great villainy.

The dwarf ran to his lady's bedchamber. 'Quickly, madam,' he said. 'Prepare! The good Sir Gawain has come to lodge with you!'

'Truly,' she said, 'that brings me both joy and sorrow: joy that such a fine knight should lie here, and sorrow, too, because he's the knight my lord fears most in all the world, for he's told me many times that Gawain never won the trust of a lady or a maiden but he had his way.'

'That's not true, my lady,' said the dwarf, 'whatever they may say.'

At that moment Sir Gawain rode into the courtyard and dismounted, and the lady came down to meet him.

'I wish you joy and good fortune, sir.'

'My lady,' he replied, 'may your life be graced with honour.'

The lady took him by the hand and led him to the hall where she seated him on a cloth of golden silk, while a boy went to stable his horse. The dwarf called two other boys to disarm Sir Gawain, and was most anxious to help, calling for water to be brought to wash his face and hands.

'Sir,' he said, 'your hands and nose are still swollen from the blows you received at the tournament.'

Sir Gawain made no reply. The dwarf ran to the bedchamber and brought back a gown of rich scarlet cloth lined with ermine in which he dressed Sir Gawain. And now the food was all ready and the tables were set, and Gawain and the lady could sit down to dine. From time to time he would sit and gaze at the lady because of her great beauty, and if he had given way to his heart and his eyes he would soon have lost his resolve; but because of the high quest he had undertaken he had so bound and restrained his heart that he would not permit any thoughts to turn to baseness. And so his eyes began to turn away from the lady and her shining beauty.

After they had dined a bed was set up for Sir Gawain and he made ready to lie down to sleep. He and the lady wished each other a good night, and when she had gone to her bedchamber, the dwarf said to Sir Gawain: 'I'll lie down here at the foot of your bed, sir, and make sure you're comfortable until you're asleep.'

'Many thanks,' he said. 'And may God grant that I soon earn such kind treatment.'

So the dwarf lay down on a couch before Sir Gawain. And as soon as he saw that he was asleep he got up as quietly as he could and ran down to where a boat was moored on the river that flowed behind the hall. He clambered in and rowed downstream until he came to a fishing-lodge, a fine-looking hall on a little islet, where Marin the Jealous had gone to find sport. The dwarf jumped from the boat and ran inside, where he lit a fistful of candles and came to where Marin was lying on a couch.

'How now?' he cried. 'Are you asleep?'

Marin awoke with a frightened start; he asked the dwarf what was wrong.

'You don't sleep like Sir Gawain,' came the reply.

'What do you know about that?'

'A lot,' said the dwarf. 'I've just left him asleep in your hall – arm in arm with your wife, I do believe!'

'What?' he cried. 'But I forbade her ever to give Sir Gawain lodging!'

'Well truly,' said the dwarf, 'she gave him a more joyful welcome than I ever saw her give anyone! But come quickly, for I fear he'll carry her off!'

'By my life,' cried Marin, 'I'll not return while he's there, but she'll pay for it when he's gone!'

'Then you'll be too late!' said the dwarf.

Meanwhile Sir Gawain was lying in the hall, suspecting nothing; and seeing the dawn break bright and clear, he arose. But just then the lady came to the door of her chamber, and when she saw the dwarf was not in the hall she realised at once his treachery.

'In God's name, sir,' she cried to Gawain, 'have pity on me – the dwarf has betrayed me! If you leave now and don't try to save me from the punishment my lord will make me suffer on your account, then shame upon you! For you know there's nothing you've done to me or I to you for which my lord or anyone else should reproach me!'

'That's true indeed, my lady,' said Sir Gawain, and he armed and rode out of the castle and hid among the trees close by. At that very moment the jealous knight appeared with the dwarf and ran into the hall. The lady came to meet him.

'I bid you welcome, sir,' she said.

'And I wish you,' he cried, 'shame and ill fortune! You're the most faithless woman alive! Last night you lodged in my castle and my bed the man I most despise!'

'Sir, I lodged him in your castle, but your bed I never dishonoured, nor shall I ever!'

'You're lying, false woman!' he cried; and hurriedly arming himself he called for his horse, while his wife, crying for mercy and weeping bitterly, was stripped to her shirt. He mounted, took his shield and lance, and bade his dwarf seize the lady by her hair and drag her after him into the forest. He halted beside the pool of a spring and forced her in where the water was coldest. Then he dismounted and gathered switches among the trees, and began to beat her and flog her across the back and breasts until the stream was running with blood. She cried with all her strength for mercy, and when Sir Gawain heard her he came out of the bushes and galloped towards them.

'Sir!' cried the dwarf. 'Here comes Sir Gawain!'

'In faith,' said the knight, 'now I know there's been evil done – it was a conspiracy!'

'For God's sake, sir,' cried Sir Gawain as he rode up, 'why would you kill the most noble and faithful lady I ever saw in the world? Never has a lady done me such honour, and you should be most grateful to her. In her conduct, her speech and her person I found only virtues, and all the virtues that can be found in a good and faithful lady, and it's a grievous sin to ill-treat her so! I pray you in the name of honour and love to forgive her your anger and fetch her from the water. I swear I did her no harm or dishonour, nor did I wish to.'

The knight was filled with anger when he saw that Sir Gawain would not be gone; a bitter jealousy inflamed his heart, and he conceived an insane and wicked plan.

'Sir Gawain,' he said, 'I'll let her out if you'll joust with me. And if you can vanquish me, she'll be absolved of all guilt and wrong; but if I vanquish you she'll be most surely accused. So shall it be decided.'

'I ask for nothing more,' said Sir Gawain.

And so the knight bade his dwarf take the lady from the pool and seat her in the glade where they were to joust. The knight drew back ready to charge and Sir Gawain came at him as fast as his horse could go. But when he saw him coming Marin the Jealous swerved away from the attack; and lowering his lance he rode up to his wife who was weeping in her innocence, and thrust his lance clean through her and struck her dead. Then he turned and galloped off towards his castle. Sir Gawain saw the lady lying dead and the dwarf running off after his master; he raced after him and trampled him under the hooves of his horse, bursting open the heart in the dwarf's chest, and then rode on towards the castle in the hope of finding a way in. But the drawbridge was raised and the gate bolted, and he could hear Marin shouting to him from within:

'Sir Gawain, this shame and misfortune has befallen me because of you; but, as I live, you'll pay for it yet!'

Sir Gawain had no desire to argue with him, and seeing there was no way in, he turned away and rode back to where the lady lay dead. Across the neck of his horse he laid her body, covered in blood, and wept for her most tenderly. Then he carried her to a chapel outside the castle, and took the body down and laid it inside the chapel, his heart filled with grief and anger. Then he closed the door to keep out the wild beasts, and trusted that someone would come and shroud her and give her burial when he had gone.

And so Sir Gawain departed, grieving so much that he was scarcely in command of himself. Never had any misfortune weighed so heavily on his heart; and with his head hung low, burdened with thought, he rode on through the forest.

Suddenly he saw a knight coming towards him in a most curious manner: he was riding backwards, with the reins of his horse tied round his chest, his shield back to front, his lance upside down, and his hauberk and greaves hanging round his neck. Sir Gawain gazed at him in wonder.

The knight could hear Gawain coming but could not see him, and so he cried aloud: 'Good, gentle knight there, for God's sake don't hurt me, for I'm the Coward Knight!'

'In faith,' said Sir Gawain to himself, 'you don't look like a man that anyone would try to hurt.' And had it not been for the grief that burdened him he would have laughed at his strange appearance. 'You need have no fear of me,' he said, and he rode up to the Coward Knight and looked him in the face. The Coward Knight looked back.

'Sir,' said the knight, 'well met!'

'Well met, indeed,' replied Sir Gawain. 'In whose service are you, sir knight?'

'The Maiden of the Cart's, sir.'

'By my life, I love you the more for that.'

'Then you won't hurt me?' said the knight.

'No,' said Sir Gawain, 'have no fear.'

Just then the knight noticed Sir Gawain's shield and recognised it at once. 'Sir,' he said, 'I know who you are! I'll dismount and ride properly now, and put my armour on the right way round, for you're Sir Gawain, I know, for you alone were to win that shield.'

The knight dismounted to put his armour on properly, asking Sir Gawain to wait until he had armed himself; and Gawain did so, and gave the knight some help. At that moment a knight came galloping through the forest like thunder, and he bore a shield quartered in black and white.

'Sir Gawain,' he cried, 'stop there! I challenge you on behalf of Marin the Jealous, who has murdered his wife because of you!'

'Sir knight,' said Gawain, 'my heart is full of grief for her death, for she'd done nothing to deserve it.'

'I don't care!' cried the Motley Knight. 'I want you dead. If I vanquish you then you're in the wrong, and if you vanquish me then the guilt and shame will lie with my lord – though if you grant me mercy he'll hold his castle as your vassal.'

'God knows in truth,' Gawain replied, 'that I'm guilty of no wrongdoing.'

'Sir Gawain,' said the Coward Knight, 'I hope you're not relying on me; please don't imagine I'll be any help.'

'I've accomplished many things without you,' said Gawain, 'and I'll do so now, with God's aid.'

With that they charged at each other full tilt; their lances shattered on their shields, and as Sir Gawain galloped past he collided with the knight and sent him and his horse crashing to the ground in a heap. Then he drew his sword and returned to the attack, but the knight shouted:

'No! Sir Gawain, do you mean to kill me? I admit defeat; I've no wish to die through another man's folly; have mercy, I pray you!'

Sir Gawain decided to do him no harm, for he wanted him to do as his master had said. So the knight rose to his feet and held out his hands to Gawain, and did him homage on his lord's behalf for the castle and all his lands, and thus he became his vassal. Without another word the knight departed.

'Oh, sir!' said the Coward Knight. 'I'm glad I'm not as brave as you! If he'd challenged me like that I'd have run straight off or fallen at his feet and begged for mercy.'

'You don't seem to like battle,' said Sir Gawain.

'Which is only right,' said the knight, 'for nothing but ill comes of war. I've never been injured or wounded, except once when I was hit by a branch in the woods. But look at *your* face – cut and scarred all over! I commend you to God; I'm going to look for the Maiden of the Cart.'

'Stay,' said Sir Gawain. 'Tell me first why the Maiden of the Cart carries her arm in a sling.'

'Willingly, sir,' he said. 'With that hand she presented the Holy Grail to the knight who came to the castle of the Fisher King but failed to ask what was done with the Grail. And because she held in that hand the precious vessel into which the hallowed blood drips from the point of the lance, she won't hold anything else in it until she returns to the holy house of the Grail. And now, sir,' said the Coward Knight, 'I'll take my leave, if it please you; but here, take my lance, for I shan't be needing it.'

Sir Gawain accepted it gratefully, for his own was broken, and then took his leave of the knight, commending him to God.

Gawain rode swiftly on through the forest, until he was tired and weary. Then, just as the sun was about to set, he saw a knight galloping through the trees towards him, and speared he was, and filling the forest with his cries:

'Sir knight! What's your name, sir knight?'

'Good sir, my name is Gawain.'

'Oh, Sir Gawain!' he cried. 'See my wounds, received in your service!'

'In my service?' said Gawain. 'What do you mean?'

'I went to bury the lady, sir, whom you bore to the chapel, but Marin came and attacked me, and wounded me as you see; I'd just dug a grave with my sword when he seized the body from me and abandoned it to the wild beasts. Now I'm going to find the hermit who lives in this forest so that I can make confession, for I know I've not long to live: the wound lies close to my heart. But I shall die the more at ease for having shown you the grief I've come to on your account.'

'By my life,' said Sir Gawain, 'it pains me deeply.'

The knight departed and Sir Gawain rode on until, deep in the forest, he came upon a handsome, splendid castle. Out of the castle an aged knight had ridden to hunt, with a hawk perched on his wrist. He greeted Sir Gawain, who returned the greeting and asked the name of the fine castle he could see. It was the castle, said the knight, of the Proud Maiden, who never deigned to ask any knight his name. 'And we who are in her service dare not ask on her behalf. But you'll be well lodged here, for in other ways she's a most gracious lady, and the most beautiful in all the land. She's never had a husband, nor ever deigned to love a knight unless she heard he was the finest knight in the world. But come, I'll accompany you on your way.'

'Many thanks,' said Sir Gawain.

They rode into the castle together, and dismounted at the steps of the great hall. The knight took Sir Gawain by the hand and led him upstairs to be stripped of his arms, and brought him a coat of rich scarlet cloth all lined with fur, which he fastened for him. Then he brought the lady of the castle to greet Sir Gawain, who rose as she came and said: 'My lady, may good fortune ever follow you!'

'I bid you welcome, sir knight,' she said, and taking him by the hand she led him to the castle chambers. 'Would you like to see my chapel, sir?' she said.

'As you wish, damsel,' said Sir Gawain, and she led him there.

Gawain looked about him and thought he had never entered a chapel so beautiful or so richly adorned. Before him were four tombs, the finest he had ever seen; and on the right-hand side were three recesses in the wall, set all about with gold and precious stones, at the back of which could be seen crosses and amulets and the bright gleam of candles, and they smelt sweeter than balsam.

'Sir,' said the maiden, 'do you see those tombs?'

'Yes, damsel.'

'Three of them have been made for the three finest knights in the world, and the fourth is for me. One of the knights is named Gawain, and another is Lancelot of the Lake, and each of them I love deeply; but the third, whose name is Perceval, I love more than either. In those three recesses relics have been placed out of love for them. But look; I'll show you what I'd do to them if they were here – and if I can't do it to all three, I'll do it at least to one or two.'

She reached towards the recesses and pulled on a golden bolt fixed in the wall, whereupon a steel blade, sharper than a razor, flashed down and closed the three holes.

'This is how I'll cut off their heads when they go to worship the relics in the recesses. Then I'll take their bodies and lay them in these tombs with much honour, richly shrouded. For I can have no joy of them while they're alive, but joy I shall have of them dead; and when I die, I'll be laid to rest in the fourth coffin in the company of the three good knights.'

Sir Gawain heard all this and was amazed, and wished the night were already over.

That night the maiden did Sir Gawain much honour. She had a great company of knights to serve her and to help her defend the castle, and they honoured Gawain highly, though they did not know that it was he, and no-one asked his name for that was not the custom of the castle. But the maiden knew that the three knights she sought often rode through the forest, and she had given orders to four of her knights to keep watch on the forest's paths and bring her any of the three if they should pass by.

Next morning Sir Gawain went to hear mass, and then armed and took his leave of the maiden and her knights and galloped out of the castle with no pressing wish to return. Into the deep forest he went, and had ridden a full league when he came upon two knights sitting in a defile. As soon as they saw him coming they leaped on to their horses, fully armed, and with shields hung from their necks and lances in hand they came to meet him.

'Halt there, sir knight,' they cried, 'and tell us your name!'

'Sirs,' he said, 'I've never kept my name from anyone who asked it. My name is Gawain, the nephew of King Arthur.'

'Oh, you are welcome, sir!' they said. 'We wished for nothing more! Come with us now to the lady on the hill: she's very eager to see you, and will give you a joyful reception at the Proud Castle where she lives!'

'I've no time to go there, sirs,' said Sir Gawain. 'I'm headed elsewhere.'

'You have to come with us, sir! We've been ordered to take you there by force if you won't come with a good grace.'

'I say I will not come,' said Sir Gawain.

At that they seized his bridle, but Gawain, filled with indignation, drew his sword and struck one of the knights with such fury that he cut off his arm. The other dropped the bridle and turned swiftly away, and he and his wounded companion galloped back to the castle where they found the Proud Maiden at the gate and showed her what had befallen them.

'Who did that to you?' she said.

'Sir Gawain, my lady!'

She called for a horn to be sounded at once, and all the knights of the castle took up arms, but just as they were about to set off in pursuit of Gawain, two other knights who had been on watch in the forest appeared, both speared through the body. Sir Gawain had inflicted these terrible wounds, they said, and the knights all agreed that it would be folly to pursue him.

'And it's my lady's fault that she's lost him!' said one. 'We all know it was he who lodged here last night. Was he carrying a red shield with a golden eagle?'

'Indeed he was,' said one of the wounded.

'Then it was he!' said the maiden. 'And I admit I lost him through my pride. Never again shall I lodge a knight in my castle without asking him his name. But now it's too late: I've lost that one forever, unless God leads him back to me, and through him I'll lose the other two.'

And so the pursuit of Sir Gawain was abandoned, and he rode on, praying to God for guidance and direction in his quest, that he might find news of the castle of the rich Fisher King.

* * *

Sir Gawain travelled on until evening was approaching, when he saw to the right of his path a narrow track which seemed to be frequented by people. So, seeing the sun about to sink, he turned that way and found, deep in the heart of the forest, a great chapel with a splendid house beside it. Before the chapel was an orchard enclosed by a row of palings, though they were less than the height of a man, and a hermit of noble appearance was leaning on them and peering into the orchard; and from time to time he laughed and clapped his hands with joy. He saw Sir Gawain approaching and came to meet him, saying: 'I bid you welcome, sir.'

'God give you the joy of Heaven,' Gawain replied.

The hermit bade a boy take Gawain's horse to be stabled, and then he took him by the hand to lean beside him at the orchard fence.

'Now, sir, you'll see why I was so delighted.'

Sir Gawain followed his gaze and saw two maidens and a boy, and a child who was riding on a lion.

'Sir,' said the hermit, 'have you ever seen a child so fair?'

'No indeed,' said Sir Gawain.

They went and sat down in the orchard, for it was a fine and tranquil evening, and as Gawain took off his armour a maiden brought him a coat of rich cloth lined with ermine. Sir Gawain sat and watched with delight as the child rode the lion, and the hermit said:

'Sir, no-one but that child dares look after or master that lion, yet the boy is only young. He's of noble descent, sir, but is the son of the most cruel and wicked knight alive: his father is Marin the Jealous, who murdered his wife because of an incident with Sir Gawain. And since his mother died the boy hasn't wanted to live with his father, for he knows he murdered her wrongfully. I'm his uncle, and he's being looked after by those maidens and two young boys. But there's no-one in the world he desires to see so much as Sir Gawain, for he wants to be his liegeman when his father dies. If you have news of Sir Gawain, sir, do tell us.'

'In faith,' said Gawain, 'I've very reliable news of him. There are his shield and lance, and you'll be lodging him in your house tonight!'

'Good sir, are you Gawain?'

'That's my name; and I saw the lady murdered in the forest, and it grieved me very much.'

'Ho there! Nephew!' cried the hermit. 'Here is Sir Gawain, whom you've so longed to see! Come and greet him!'

The boy jumped down from the lion's back and goading it with a whip he led it to its den and shut the gate so that it could not escape. Then he came up to Sir Gawain, who met him with an embrace.

'Welcome, sir!' said the boy.

'And may God ever enhance your honour,' said Sir Gawain. He kissed him and greeted him most affectionately. Then the boy knelt before him and held out his joined hands.

'Sir,' said the hermit, 'is that not a moving sight? He is offering you his homage. He should indeed be your liegeman, and have your help and guidance, for his mother met her death because of you.'

Sir Gawain took the boy's hands between his own, saying: 'Truly, I greatly value your love and homage, and will come to your aid whenever you need it. But tell me your name.'

'Meliot of Logres, sir.'

Sir Gawain was lodged well there that night; and in the morning after mass, the hermit asked him where he was headed, and he said towards the land of the Fisher King, if it pleased God.

'Sir Gawain,' said the hermit, 'may God grant that you do better than the knight who went there before you, for because of him great misfortunes have befallen all lands, and the good Fisher King is languishing.'

'Sir,' said Sir Gawain, 'may God grant that I do His will.'

And with that he took his leave and rode off, the hermit commending him to God.

Sir Gawain rode so hard each day that he left the forest and the hermitage far behind, and found himself in the fairest land in the world, with the most beautiful meadowland ever seen, stretching a full two leagues. Beyond that he could see another forest, and as he rode on he met a boy who had just emerged from it, looking most downcast and dejected.

'Good friend,' said Sir Gawain, 'where have you come from?'

'From the forest, sir.'

'You don't seem very happy.'

'Nor should I be,' said the boy. 'Anyone who loses his good master has no reason to be joyful.'

'And who's your master?'

'The finest knight in the world.'

'And he's dead?'

'No, sir, please God; if he were it would be a grave misfortune to the world. But he's been in distress for some time.'

'What's his name?'

'Where he is now, he's called Par-lui-fet.'

'And where's that? May I not be told?'

'Not by me, sir,' said the boy. 'I'll tell you he's in yonder forest, but I'll say no more of his whereabouts – I must do nothing against my master's will.'

Suddenly the boy bowed down to the ground, with tears streaming from his eyes. Gawain asked him what was wrong.

'Sir,' he said, 'I shall never be happy until I can enter a hermitage to save my soul, for I've committed the greatest sin anyone can commit: I've killed my mother – and a queen she was – because she said I wouldn't be king when my father died; she was going to make me a monk or a priest and have my younger brother inherit the kingdom. When my father knew I'd killed her, he went off into that forest and built a hermitage and abandoned his kingdom, but because of the crime I've committed I don't want to take his place: I've decided to go into exile like him.'

'What's your name?' asked Sir Gawain.

'Joseus, sir. King Pelles is my father, and the Widowed Lady of Kamaalot was my aunt, so the good knight Par-lui-fet is my cousin.'

At that the boy took his leave and Sir Gawain commended him to God. He felt very sorry for him.

Gawain plunged into the forest and rode swiftly on until he came upon the rill of a spring running through the woods, and nearby was a path which seemed much used. He left the main track and followed the line of the stream for a good league until he spied a fine house and a chapel surrounded by a hedge. And seated beneath a tree outside the entrance he could see one of the most handsome men he had ever beheld of such an age: dressed like a hermit he was, with white hair and a white beard, and he was resting his cheek in his hand. Before him stood a youth holding a fine, sleek horse and a shield that shone in the sun, and the hermit was gazing at the hauberk and iron greaves that he had bade the boy bring. When he saw Sir Gawain coming, he rose to his feet and came to meet him.

'Dear sir,' he said, 'please ride on quietly and make no noise, for we don't want any more trouble than we have already. I beg you not to take offence: I'd gladly have you lodge here if we didn't have such troubles. For a knight is lying sick within who is held to be the finest in the world, and I wouldn't like him to know there'd been a knight here, or he'd get up, ill as he is, and no-one could keep him from donning his arms, mounting his charger and going off to joust with you, and it might well make him worse. That's why we're keeping him inside the house: I don't want him to see you or any other knight, for it would be a grave misfortune to the world if he died.'

'What's his name?' asked Sir Gawain.

'Sir,' replied the hermit, 'he has made his own name, and so I call him Par-lui-fet – "Self-made" – out of affection and love.'

'May I see him?' said Sir Gawain.

'No, sir,' said the hermit. 'No stranger may until he's restored to health and happiness.'

'Then will you give him a message from me?'

'I'll say nothing to him unless he speaks to me first.'

Sir Gawain was most upset that he could not speak to the knight. 'What is his lineage?' he asked the hermit.

'He's descended,' he replied, 'from the good soldier Joseph of Arimathea.'

Just then a maiden appeared at the chapel door and called softly to the hermit, who rose and took his leave of Sir Gawain, and shut the door of the chapel behind him, while the youth took the horse and the armour inside the house and closed the door. Sir Gawain was left outside, quite bewildered, not knowing for certain whether the ailing knight was the son of the Widowed Lady, for there can be many good knights in one family.

He rode away, most disturbed, and passed into the forest; and he wandered far until he found himself in a beautiful, rich and fertile land, in the middle of which stood a magnificent castle. He turned that way and rode towards it, and soon he could see the great wall that surrounded it and the mighty castle gate. And lying in the middle of the gateway he saw a lion, chained to the wall, and on either side of the gate stood two awesome figures of copper, which by an ingenious device could fling forth crossbow-bolts with the utmost strength and fury. Seeing the lion at the gateway and these dread figures, Sir Gawain did not dare go any nearer. He looked along the top of the walls and saw priests dressed in albs, and old white-haired knights clothed like monks or clerics, and on each of the battlements was a cross. A chapel stood on the wall, and on the chapel's roof were three crosses, each one topped with an eagle of gold. The priests and the knights on the wall knelt towards the chapel, and from time to time they would look up at the sky, rejoicing, as if they could see God and His mother on high. Sir Gawain sat watching from a distance, not daring to approach the castle because of the figures that could loose bolts with such fury that no armour could withstand them. But he could see no path to right or left: he would have to turn back or go on to the castle. He did not know what to do. But just then he looked ahead and saw a priest coming out of the gate.

'Good sir,' he cried to Sir Gawain, 'what's your business here?'

'I pray you, tell me what castle this is.'

'This is the entrance to the land of the rich Fisher King, and inside the service of the Holy Grail is begun.'

'Then permit me to ride on,' said Sir Gawain, 'for I've been heading for the land of the Fisher King!'

'I tell you truly,' said the priest, 'you cannot enter the castle or go any nearer the Grail, unless you bring the sword with which Saint John was beheaded.'

'Oh,' said Sir Gawain, 'then I'm in a sorry plight.'

'But you may trust me that it's so,' said the priest, 'and I tell you, it's now in the possession of the most wicked and heathen king alive. But if you bring the sword, you'll be gladly admitted to the castle and celebrated wherever the Fisher King holds sway.'

'Then I must turn back,' said Gawain, 'and that grieves me deeply.'

'You shouldn't grieve, for if you win the sword and bring it here, then all will know you worthy to look upon the Holy Grail. But remember the knight who failed to ask what was done with it.'

At that Sir Gawain rode off, so downcast and troubled that he forgot to ask in what land he would find the sword, or the name of the king who then possessed it; but he would know of the sword when it pleased God.

He rode on until, one beautiful clear day, he found himself outside a city, and looking ahead he could see a townsman in the middle of a field mounted on a great charger which looked fine and handsome indeed. The man caught sight of Gawain and came towards him, and they greeted each other most nobly.

'Sir,' said the townsman, 'I'm sorry you've such a thin and scraggy horse. Such a worthy knight as you seem to be should be better mounted.'

'Alas, sir,' said Gawain, 'there's nothing I can do about that – I'll have another when it shall please God.'

'Where are you headed, good sir?'

'I'm on the quest for the sword with which Saint John was beheaded.'

'Oh sir,' said the townsman, 'you're riding into great danger! It's in the possession of King Gurgaran – a wicked and cruel man, and an infidel. Many knights have passed this way in search of the sword, and they never returned. But if you promise to come back here and let me see the sword if you win it, I'll give you this horse.'

'Will you?' said Sir Gawain. 'Then you're a most courteous man, sir, for you don't even know me.'

'You seem so noble that I've no doubt you'd keep a promise.'

'And I do promise,' said Sir Gawain, 'that if God lets me win the sword, I'll bring it for you to see on my return.'

And so the townsman dismounted and exchanged horses with Gawain, who bade farewell and departed. On he rode into a great forest beyond the city, and he journeyed on until the sun began to set, but could find neither house nor castle. But then, in the depths of the forest, he came across a wide clearing through which a stream flowed from a spring, and looking towards the head of the clearing, right at the edge of the woods, he could see a great tent with ropes of silk and pegs of ivory to fix them in the ground, and golden pommels on the tent-poles with an eagle of gold on top of each. The tent's walls were white and the roof was red, of a rich silken cloth like samite. Sir Gawain rode up and dismounted at the door. He took off his horse's bridle and set it free to graze, and propping his shield and lance outside the tent he took a look inside. He could see a rich golden couch, with a silken sheet on top as fine as white linen, and a coverlet of ermine and green samite with drops of gold. And at the head lay two pillows, so sweetly perfumed that the tent was filled with a balmy fragrance. All around the couch rich silken cloths were spread on the ground, and on either side of the couch's head was an ivory chair with cushions of gold cloth, and above the couch's foot hung a golden candlestick holding a great candle. A table had been set in the middle of the tent: of ivory it was, and edged with gold and precious stones; and a cloth had been laid upon it with a silver trencher and ivory-handled knives and golden plate.

Sir Gawain sat down upon the couch fully armed, wondering for whom the tent could have been so richly furnished, and puzzled at seeing no-one around. But just as Gawain was about to take off his armour, a dwarf appeared at the door and greeted him, and kneeling down he began to disarm him. But Sir Gawain remembered the dwarf who had caused the death of Marin's wife, and said:

'Please leave me, friend, for I don't wish to lay aside my armour yet.'

'Indeed you shall, sir,' said the dwarf, 'for you've nothing to fear until tomorrow, and tonight you'll be lodged more richly and with more honour than ever before!'

And so Sir Gawain, with the dwarf's assistance, began to remove his armour, and placed it beside the couch along with his sword and shield and lance. Then the dwarf brought two silver basins and a white towel and bathed Sir Gawain's face and hands. He then unlocked a handsome chest from which he took a rich gown of gold cloth and silk, all lined with ermine, and with this he robed Sir Gawain.

'Sir,' said the dwarf, 'don't worry about your horse, for you'll have him again in the morning when you rise. To put you more at ease I'll bring him close by, and then I'll be back.'

Sir Gawain agreed. Then two boys came in bearing wine and food for the table, and they seated Sir Gawain to dine. They lit two great candles in golden candlesticks and then left at once. But before Sir Gawain had finished eating, into the tent came two maidens who greeted him most nobly, and he returned their greeting as graciously as could be.

'Sir,' they said, 'may God give you the power and strength tomorrow to destroy the evil custom of this tent.'

'Is there an evil custom?' said Gawain.

'Yes, sir, and it grieves us much, but you seem to be a knight fine enough to put an end to it.'

At that he rose from the table, and a boy was called to remove the cloth. The two maidens took Gawain by the hands and led him outside, where they sat down together in the middle of the clearing.

'Sir,' said the elder maiden, 'what's your name?'

'Gawain, damsel.'

'Then we love you the more!' she said. 'Now we know for certain that the evil custom of the tent will be cast out – on condition that you choose tonight which of the two of us will please you most!'

'Thank you, damsel,' he said.

With that he rose, and as he was tired he made his way back to the couch, where the maidens attended him as he lay down. Then they sat before him, lit the candle, and rested on the couch, offering him their service. Sir Gawain made no reply except to thank them, for his only thought was to sleep and rest.

'In faith,' said one, 'if this were Gawain, the nephew of King Arthur, he'd speak to us differently! And we'd find in him more entertainment than in this man: this Gawain's an impostor! The honour we've paid him was ill-spent!'

'But what does it matter?' said the other. 'Tomorrow he'll repay us well enough!'

Just then the dwarf appeared.

'Watch over this knight, friend,' said the maidens, 'and see he doesn't leave. He rambles from lodging to lodging like a beggar and calls himself Sir Gawain, but he can't be, for if this were he, and we wished to go sleepless for three nights, then he would do so for four!'

'Damsels,' said the dwarf, 'he can't escape except on foot, for his horse is in my keeping.'

Sir Gawain had heard every word of this but said nothing in reply, and they departed, bidding him an ill night since he was so base, half-hearted and cowardly. And they ordered the dwarf not to leave on any account, but to guard him closely.

Sir Gawain did not sleep much that night, and as soon as he saw day break he rose and found that his arms were all ready and his horse had been brought to the tent, fully harnessed. He armed as fast as he could, and the dwarf helped him, saying:

'Sir, you haven't served the maidens very well; they're complaining a lot about you!'

'I'm sorry,' said Sir Gawain, 'if I've deserved it.'

'It would be a great shame if one as handsome as you were as bad a knight as they say.'

'They may say what they like,' said Sir Gawain, 'for that's their right. I don't know who to thank for the fine lodging I had last night, but if I meet the lord or lady of the tent I'll thank them deeply.'

Just then two knights came riding past the tent, fully armed, and saw Sir Gawain, who was mounted with his shield at his neck and lance in hand, expecting to take his leave without any more ado. They rode up to him, crying:

'Sir, you must pay for your lodging! We put ourselves out for you last night, and left you the tent and all quite freely, yet now you'd just ride off!'

'What would you have me do?' said Sir Gawain.

'You must earn the food you ate and the honour you were paid.'

At that moment the two maidens appeared, and beautiful they were indeed, and said: 'Now, sir knight, we'll see if you're Gawain, the nephew of King Arthur!'

'Truly,' said the elder, 'I don't think he'll be able to break the evil custom and free us of these knights, but if he could I'd forgive him my harsh words.'

Sir Gawain heard these insults just as he had done that night, and felt deeply ashamed. But he saw he could not depart without combat. One of the knights had drawn back and dismounted, but the other was on horseback, fully armed, his shield at his neck and lance in hand, and he came charging full tilt at Sir Gawain, and Gawain charged him, and struck the knight such a furious blow that he pierced his shield, pinned his arm to his side and thrust his lance into his body before crashing into him so hard that he brought both the knight and his horse tumbling to the ground in a heap.

'By my life,' said the elder maiden, 'the false Sir Gawain is doing better than he did last night!'

He pulled out the lance, drew his sword and charged to the attack; but the knight cried for mercy and admitted defeat. Sir Gawain tried to decide what to do, and he looked to the maidens.

'Sir knight,' said the elder, 'you've nothing to fear from the other knight while this one's alive, but the evil custom will not be broken as long as he lives, for he's the lord of the tent, and because of his wickedness I've seen no knight here for a long time.'

'Just listen,' the knight said to Sir Gawain, 'to her disloyalty! There's no-one in the world she seemed to love as much as me, and now she condemns me to death!'

'And I say again,' she cried, 'that the evil custom will never be broken unless he kills you!'

Thereupon Sir Gawain lifted the skirts of the knight's hauberk and ran him through with his sword. The other knight, seeing his companion slain, was filled with rage and grief and hatred, and he and Gawain came charging and struck one another with such fury that they smashed through their shields, rent their hauberks and tore into their flesh with the heads of their lances; and both men and horses collided with such force that their stirrups stretched, their saddle-girths snapped, their lances shivered and the knights crashed to the ground so hard that blood gushed from their mouths and noses. And in his fall Sir Gawain's enemy broke his arm and collar-bone, and the dwarf cried:

'Girls, your Gawain's fighting well!'

'He will indeed be our Gawain henceforth,' they said, 'if he's willing!'

Sir Gawain drew away from the knight and returned to his horse, and had it not been for the maidens he would gladly have let the knight live, for he had appealed for mercy and Gawain felt pity for him. But the maidens were shouting:

'If you don't kill him, the evil custom won't be broken!'

'Sir,' said the younger, 'if you want to kill him, you must strike him with your sword in the sole of his foot; it's the only way he'll die!'

'Damsel,' cried the knight, 'your love for me has turned to hatred! A knight should never trust in a maiden's love. But may God grant that others are not like you!'

Sir Gawain was astonished by the maiden's words and drew back, feeling very sorry for the knight. He went behind the tent and took the saddle from the dead knight's mount and placed it on his own, and then drew his horse away. But the wounded knight had remounted with the dwarf's help, and was fleeing towards the forest as fast as he could ride. The maidens were crying:

'Sir Gawain, your pity for him will bring you to your death! That knight has no mercy: he's gone to find help, and if he escapes, we shall die and so will you!'

Hearing this, Sir Gawain leaped into his saddle, and seizing a lance propped against the tent he went galloping after the knight, and struck him so hard that he knocked him to the ground, crying: 'You'll go no further!'

'That grieves me,' said the knight, 'for I would soon have had revenge on you and the maidens!'

At that Sir Gawain thrust his sword a full hand's breadth into the sole of the knight's foot, and the knight stretched out dead. Then he rode back to be greeted with joy by the maidens, who told him how that was the only way the knight could have been killed, for he was of the line of Achilles, whose descendants could die in no other way. Sir Gawain dismounted, and the maidens tended to the wound in his side. Then they said: 'Sir, we offer you our service once more, for now we know for certain that you're the good knight Gawain. Take as your lady which of us you wish!'

'I thank you, damsels,' said Sir Gawain. 'I shan't refuse your love. I commend you to God.'

'What?' they cried. 'Do you mean to leave us? You'd do better to stay with us in our pavilion and take your ease!'

'It's no use,' said Sir Gawain. 'I've no time to spare.'

'Let him go,' said the younger maiden. 'He's the most foolish knight in the world!'

'By my life,' said the elder, 'it grieves me to see him depart.'

But Sir Gawain left them at once and mounted his horse, and away he rode into the forest.

On he journeyed until he reached the edge of the woods and saw before him a rich and pleasant land bounded by a huge wall which stretched a great way. As he drew nearer he found there was only one gate; and when he passed through he saw the fairest and most abundant land that ever a man beheld, filled with the most beautiful orchards. It was no more than three leagues wide, but in the middle stood a great tower upon a rock, and at the top of the tower a crane had built its nest, and cried out whenever a stranger entered the land. Sir Gawain rode forward, but the crane gave such a clamouring call that the King of the Watch, the lord of the land, sent two knights galloping after Sir Gawain, shouting:

'Halt there, sir knight! You must come and answer to the king of this land. No stranger passes through without seeing him.'

'My lords,' said Sir Gawain, 'I wasn't aware of the custom. I'll willingly come.'

And so they rode back to the king's hall and dismounted. Sir Gawain left his shield and lance outside and then climbed the stairs to the hall. The king gave him a joyful welcome and asked him where he was heading.

'To a land, sire, where I've never been before.'

'Ah,' said the king. 'Since you're passing through my country, you'll be going to the land of King Gurgaran on the quest of the sword with which Saint John was beheaded.'

'Exactly so, sire. And may God grant that I win it.'

'You'll not win it so soon,' said the king, 'for you'll not leave my land until a year has passed.'

'No, sire, I beg you!' cried Sir Gawain.

'It must be so,' said the king, and with that he had Gawain disarmed and called for a gown to be brought for him. He did him much honour, but Sir Gawain was uneasy, and said:

'Sire, why do you want to keep me here so long?'

'Because I know you'd win the sword and would not return by way of my country.'

'I promise you, sire,' said Sir Gawain, 'that if it please God that I win it, I shall return through this land.'

'Then I'll let you go as you wish, for there's nothing I desire to see as much as that sword.'

And so Gawain slept there that night and departed next day with a glad and joyful heart, and journeyed on towards the land of King Gurgaran. He passed into the grimmest forest in the world, but just on the hour of noon he came across a fountain set about with marble; it was shaded by the forest as if by a bower, and rich pillars of marble stood all around inlaid with bands of gold and precious stones, and from the central pillar hung a vessel of gold on a silver chain. And in the middle of the fountain stood a statue so finely sculpted that it seemed to be alive; and the moment Sir Gawain appeared before the fountain the statue plunged into the water and vanished. Gawain dismounted, but just as he went to take hold of the golden vessel a voice cried out: 'You are not the Good Knight who is served from the vessel and cured by it.'

Sir Gawain drew back and saw a priest approaching the spring: a young man he was, dressed in white robes, with his arm in a sling, and he was holding a square golden vessel. He walked up to the vessel which hung from the marble pillar and looked inside; then he rinsed the vessel he was holding and poured what he found in the other into his own. Then three maidens of fabulous beauty appeared, all draped in white robes over body and head; one of them carried bread in a vessel of gold, another brought wine in a vessel of ivory, and the third bore meat in a vessel of silver. They came to the golden vessel which hung from the pillar and in it they placed their offerings. And after sitting awhile at the foot of the pillar they began to walk back; but as they went, it seemed to Sir Gawain that there was but one of them, and he marvelled at this miracle. He went after the priest who bore the other vessel, and said:

'Good sir, speak to me.'

'What do you want?' said the priest.

'Where are you taking that golden vessel and whatever it holds?'

'To the hermits,' he replied, 'who live in this forest, and to the Good Knight who lies sick at the house of his uncle, the Hermit King.'

'Is that far from here?'

'It would be for you,' said the priest. 'But I'll get there sooner than you could.'

'In faith,' said Gawain, 'I wish I were there now, so that I could see him and talk to him!'

'That I can well believe, but the time is not yet ripe.'

So Sir Gawain took his leave and departed, and on he rode until he came across a hermitage. Out of it came a hermit, old and white, a most good-living man, and he said to Sir Gawain:

'Where are you heading, sir?'

'To the land of King Gurgaran. Is this the right road?'

'It is,' said the hermit, 'but many knights have passed this way and never returned.'

'Is it far?'

'His land is near enough, sir, but it's a long way to the castle where the sword lies.'

Sir Gawain spent the night at the hermitage, and the next morning after hearing mass he set out, and rode on until he came to the land of King Gurgaran, where he heard the people everywhere wailing with grief. Then he met a knight riding swiftly towards a castle, and Gawain asked him: 'Sir, why are the people of this land lamenting so? Everywhere I go I hear them weeping and beating their palms with grief.'

'I'll tell you, sir,' said the knight. 'King Gurgaran has but one son, and he's been abducted by a giant who's done the king much harm and laid waste a great part of his country. And now King Gurgaran has proclaimed throughout his land that to anyone who rescues his son and kills the giant he'll give the finest sword in the world, which is in his possession, and as much of his treasure as he wishes to take. But he can find no knight bold enough to go, and he curses his own religion even more than Christianity, and has said that if any Christian knight enters his land he'll receive him.'

Sir Gawain was elated at this news, and taking his leave of the knight, he rode on until he came to the castle of King Gurgaran. The king rejoiced when word reached him that a Christian knight had arrived at his castle, and he summoned him to come before him, and asked him his name and country.

'My name is Gawain,' he said, 'and I'm from the land of King Arthur.'

'A land of good knights,' said the king. 'But in my land I can find no knight brave enough to bring order to my affairs. If you would help me, I would reward you well. A giant has carried off my son whom I dearly love, and if you'll risk your life to save my son, I'll give you the finest sword ever forged, the sword with which Saint John was beheaded. It bleeds each day at noon, because that was the hour when they severed that good man's head.'

The king called for the sword to be brought, and he showed Gawain the scabbard first, all inlaid with precious stones; and the belt was made of silk with golden studs; and the hilt was of gold likewise; and the pommel was a holy, sacred stone which Evalus, a noble emperor of Rome, had mounted there. Then the king drew the sword from its sheath, and out it came, bleeding, for it was then noon, and he commanded that it be held before Gawain until that hour had passed. Thereupon the sword became as bright and green as emerald. Sir Gawain gazed at it in wonder, coveting it more than ever, and he saw that it was as big as any other sword, but that when it was sheathed neither the scabbard nor the sword looked longer than two spans.

'Sir knight,' said the king, 'I will give you this sword – and I will do something else which will bring you great joy.'

'And I, sire,' said Sir Gawain, 'will do as you've asked, if it please Our Lord and His sweet mother.'

With that the king pointed out the path the giant had taken and the place where he lived, and Sir Gawain set out along that road, commending himself to God. The men of the castle prayed for him in the manner of their religion, that he might return in joy and safety, for he was riding into grave danger.

On he rode until he came to a great high mountain, and bounded by its peaks was a land that the giant had completely laid waste, a land some three leagues across. And there within was the giant, so huge and cruel and terrible that he feared no-one in the world. Nor had any knight sought him out for a long time, for none dared linger there. The entrance to his mountain home was so narrow that a horse could not pass through; so Sir Gawain had to dismount and leave his horse and shield and lance behind, and with great difficulty he clambered up the mountain, the path being a cleft between sharp rocks. Then he came to the open plain, and looking ahead he could see the giant's stronghold upon a crag; and there in the plain beneath a tree the giant and the king's son were playing chess. Sir Gawain was armed and his sword was girded on. He advanced towards them. The giant, seeing him coming, leaped to his feet and seized a great axe that lay beside him, and strode towards Gawain ready to strike, aiming to deal him a two-handed blow full on the head. But Sir Gawain dodged aside and attacked the giant with his sword, and gave him such a blow that he cut off the arm that clutched the axe. The giant reeled back when he felt himself wounded and seized the king's son by the throat with his other hand, and crushed and strangled him to death. Then he turned back to Sir Gawain and took hold of him, squeezing him hard around the waist and hauling him three feet off the ground. He intended to carry him back to his stronghold on the crag, but on the way he stumbled and fell, along with Sir Gawain; the giant ended up beneath him, and before he could get to his feet Sir Gawain thrust his sword right through the giant's heart and hacked off his head. Then he came back to where the king's son lay, and when he found that he was dead it grieved him deeply. He lifted the boy on to his shoulders, and with the giant's head in his hand he returned to where he had left his horse and shield and lance. Then he mounted and rode back, carrying the king's son and the giant's head before him.

The king and all the men of the castle came down to meet him full of joy, but when they saw the dead boy their jubilation turned to grief. Sir Gawain dismounted and presented to the king his son and the giant's head.

'Truly, sire,' he said, 'I'd have been happy indeed if I could have presented him to you alive.'

'I know,' said the king, 'but I'm grateful to you for doing as much as you've done, and you shall have your reward.'

But he and all the men of the castle began to lament for his son most bitterly; and the king commanded that a great fire be kindled in the heart of the city, and that his son be placed in a brass vessel full of water to be cooked and boiled over the fire, while the giant's head was hung above the gate. And when his son's flesh was cooked, he had it cut into the smallest pieces possible, and summoned all the people of his land and gave each a piece until all the flesh was gone.

Then he called for the sword to be brought and presented it to Sir Gawain, who thanked him deeply.

'I'll do still more for you,' said the king, and summoning all the men of his land to his castle hall, he said: 'Sir, I wish to be baptised.'

And Sir Gawain said: 'God be praised!'

The king then summoned a hermit from the forest and was baptised with the name Archier, and he declared that all those who refused to believe in God were to be beheaded by Gawain. So it was that the king who was lord of Albanie was baptised by the miracle of God and the chivalry of Sir Gawain, who departed from the castle with a heart full of joy.

He now retraced his path, and rode on until he came to the land of the King of the Watch where he decided to go and fulfil his promise. He dismounted before the hall. The king was overjoyed to see him coming, and Sir Gawain said to him: 'I've come to do as I promised; here is the sword.'

The king took it in his hand and gazed at it in delight, and filled with joy, he went and placed it among his own treasures.

'Sire!' said Sir Gawain. 'Do you mean to betray me?'

'I've more right to it than you,' said the king. 'I'm descended from the king who beheaded Saint John!'

'Sire,' said the king's men, 'Sir Gawain is a true and worthy knight and kept his promise; you should return to him what he's won: it would be a grave disgrace to do him wrong!'

The king sighed, and said: 'Very well – on one condition: that he will grant to the first maiden who has a request of him whatever she asks, no matter what it may be.'

Sir Gawain agreed to this quite willingly, but by doing so he was soon to suffer much humiliation.

The king returned the sword to him, and after sleeping there that night, Gawain left in the morning as soon as he could, and rode on until he came to the city where the townsman had exchanged horses with him. He remembered his promise to this man, too; so he halted for a long while, leaning on the butt of his lance until the townsman appeared. They rejoiced to see each other, and Sir Gawain showed him the sword. The townsman took it, plunged his spurs into his horse and galloped off towards the city. Gawain was astounded, and raced after him, shouting to him that he was acting wickedly. He pursued him into the city, but ran into a great procession of priests and clerks bearing crosses and censers. Sir Gawain dismounted because of the procession, and saw the townsman enter the church and the procession after him.

'Sirs,' said Gawain to the priests, 'return to me what that man in your church has stolen!'

'We're well aware,' replied the priests, 'that it's the sword with which Saint John was beheaded, and that man has brought it to us to add to our relics. He says it was given to him in his honour.'

'Indeed it was not! I showed it to him because I'd promised to do so, and he carried it off like a rogue!'

He told them all that had happened, and the priests ordered that it be returned to him. He took his leave with joy in his heart, remounted and took up his arms, and rode out of the city.

On he journeyed, and made his way back to the castle at the entrance to the land of the Fisher King. And he saw now that the ghastly copper statues were no longer shooting, and the lion was not at the gate. Then he caught sight of the priests and men of the castle coming towards him in a great procession, and he dismounted, and a squire took his arms and his horse. Gawain held the sword aloft before the procession; it was noon; and when he drew the sword from its scabbard, he saw that it was bleeding. Down they bowed before it, worshipping it and singing '*Te Deum laudamus*'. He slid the sword back into its scabbard and guarded it closely; and he never let it be known in any of the places where he lodged what sword it was. And so the priests and the knights greeted him with great joy, and earnestly begged him to promise that if God led him to the castle of the Fisher King and the Grail appeared before him, he would not be as negligent as the other knight had been. And Gawain replied that he would follow God's guidance.

'Sir,' said the head priest, 'you must have great need of rest now, for you seem very tired.'

'If I do,' he replied, 'it's because I've seen many bewildering things that I don't understand.'

'This, sir,' said the priest, 'is the Castle of Enquiry, where you'll be told the significance of anything you ask.'

'In faith,' said Sir Gawain, 'I'm greatly puzzled about three maidens who came to the court of King Arthur, bearing two heads – the head of a king and the head of a queen; and in a cart they were carrying the heads of 150 knights, some sealed with gold, some with silver and others with lead.'

'Indeed,' said the priest, 'but the maiden said that by the queen the king was betrayed and killed, along with the knights whose heads were in the cart. She was telling the truth; for by Eve was Adam betrayed, and all the people who have lived since then and every age to come will suffer for it. Because Adam was the first man, he is called king, for he was our earthly father, and his wife is queen. And the heads of the knights sealed in gold signify the New Law of Christ, the heads sealed in silver the Old Law of the Jews, and the heads sealed in lead the false law of the Saracens. Of these three kinds of men is the world composed.'

'Sir,' said Sir Gawain, 'I wonder much about the castle of the Black Hermit, where all the heads were taken; the maiden told me that the Good Knight would set free all those within when he came, and the people imprisoned there are calling for him.'

'You surely know,' said the priest, 'that because of the apple that Eve gave Adam to eat, the good went to Hell as well as the wicked, and to free His people from Hell God came as a man and through His goodness and power He set His friends free. And thus the castle of the Black Hermit signifies Hell, from which the Good Knight will set the imprisoned free; and the Black Hermit is Lucifer, who is lord of Hell just as he wished to be of Paradise.'

'In God's name,' said Sir Gawain, 'I wonder also about the maiden who's completely bald, and says she'll never have hair again until the Good Knight conquers the Grail.'

'She must indeed be bald, sir,' replied the priest. 'She's been bald ever since the Fisher King gave lodging to the knight who failed to ask the question. The bald maiden signifies Fortune, who was bald before the Crucifixion of Our Lord, and never had hair until the hour when the Saviour redeemed His people with His blood and His death. The cart which the maiden brought with her signifies Fortune's wheel, for just as the cart is borne by its wheels so is the world governed by the wheel of Fortune. This can be clearly seen from the two maidens who followed her, for the most beautiful went on foot and the other on a lowly packhorse and they were poorly attired, while the third was much better dressed. The shield with the red cross which was left at King Arthur's court signifies the holy shield of the Cross for which none but God ever dared pay the price.'

Sir Gawain was delighted to hear these explanations. And he thought of the shield hanging in King Arthur's hall which no-one dared take up, as he had heard in many places; everyone was waiting daily for the Good Knight who was to come for it.

'Many thanks,' said Sir Gawain to the priest, 'for explaining the things that have puzzled me so. But I was most grieved for a lady whose husband killed her because of me, though neither she nor I was guilty of any wrong.'

'Sir,' said the priest, 'her death was of great significance, for the Old Law was irreparably overthrown by the thrust of a lance; to overthrow the Old Law God suffered Himself to be stabbed in the side with a spear, and by that blow and His crucifixion the Old Law was cast down. That lady signifies the Old Law. Have you anything else to ask me?'

'Sir,' said Sir Gawain, 'I met a knight in the forest who was riding backwards and carrying his arms upside down and back to front; he said he was the Coward Knight – and he had his hauberk tied round his neck! But as soon as he saw me he carried his arms properly and rode along like any other knight.'

'Religion,' said the priest, 'was turned the wrong way before the death of Our Lord, but once He was crucified it was set right.'

'One more thing,' said Sir Gawain. 'Another knight came to joust with me with arms quartered in black and white, seeking satisfaction for that lady's death on behalf of her husband Marin. And he told me that if I vanquished him, then he and his lord would be my vassals. I did vanquish him and he paid me homage.'

'Which was only right,' said the priest, 'for when the Old Law was overthrown all those who upheld it were brought into subjection, and always will be. Have you anything more to ask?'

'I wonder much,' said Sir Gawain, 'about a child who was riding a lion at a hermitage, when none but he dared go near it. He was only young, and the lion was a most ferocious beast. He was the son of the lady who was murdered because of me.'

'You've spoken well,' replied the priest, 'in reminding me of that. The child signifies the Saviour of the world, who was born into the Old Law and was circumcised, and the lion he was riding signifies the world and the people in it, and the animals and birds, for only He with His divine power could govern them and bring them justice.'

'Oh, sir!' cried Sir Gawain. 'Your words fill me with joy! But I came upon a fountain in the forest, sir, the most beautiful ever seen, and a statue was there which vanished as soon as it saw me. Then a priest came bearing a golden vessel, and he went up to another which hung from the pillar and took what was inside and placed it in his own. Then three maidens came and filled the vessel with whatever they were carrying, and thereupon it seemed to me that there was but one maiden.'

'Of that,' said the priest, 'I'll tell you no more than you've heard, for no-one should reveal the secrets of the Saviour.'

'Sir,' said Sir Gawain, 'I'd like to ask about a king I saw who took his dead son and had him boiled and cooked, and then gave him to all the people of his land to eat.'

'Sir,' replied the priest, 'he had brought his heart to the Saviour and wanted to make a sacrifice to Our Lord with his son's blood and flesh, and so he gave him to be eaten by all his people, wishing them to share his belief. And he's so entirely cleared his land of all wrongful religion that none now remains.'

'Blessed be the hour I came here!' said Sir Gawain, and the priest replied: 'Amen.'

Sir Gawain slept there that night and was given good lodging. The next morning after hearing mass he departed, and after taking his leave and riding out of the castle he found himself in the fairest land in the world, with the most beautiful meadows and rivers that ever a man beheld. He rode on until, just as evening was setting in, he came to a hermit's cell, a hut so low that a horse could not enter, and the chapel was no bigger. The good man had not set foot outside his house for at least forty years. He leaned out of his window when he saw Sir Gawain, and cried: 'Welcome, sir!'

Gawain wished him God's blessing, and said: 'Sir, would you give me lodging here?'

'None but God finds lodging here, sir,' said the hermit. 'No earthly man has come in here with me for forty years. But just ahead is a castle where good knights are given lodging.'

'To whom does the castle belong?' asked Sir Gawain.

'To the Fisher King. It's surrounded by great rivers, rich in fish, or would be if only he weren't languishing. But he gives lodging only to good knights.'

'May God grant that I be one,' said Sir Gawain.

Knowing now that he was near the castle, he dismounted and made confession to the hermit, telling him of all his sins for which he was deeply and truly repentant.

'Now, sir,' said the hermit, 'don't forget to ask what the other knight forgot; and don't be afraid of anything you see at the entrance to the castle. Ride on without fear, and worship the holy chapel that you'll find at the castle, where the flame of the Holy Spirit descends each day because of the Holy Grail which they serve there along with the sacred lance with the head that bleeds.'

'Sir,' said Sir Gawain, 'may God guide me to do His will.'

He took his leave and departed, and rode on until a valley opened before him, flourishing with good crops; and there stood the castle. And Sir Gawain saw the holy chapel appear; he dismounted and went down on his knees, bowing to it and worshipping it with a gentle heart. Then he remounted and rode on until he came across a magnificent tomb with a beautiful lid; there appeared to be a little cemetery there, for it was fenced all around, and yet there seemed to be no other tombs. And just as he was passing the cemetery, a voice cried out to him:

'Do not touch the tomb, for you are not the knight who shall learn who lies within.'

Hearing the voice Sir Gawain rode on past; but as he approached the castle entrance he saw that there were three long and terrible bridges to cross, with three great rivers rushing beneath. It seemed to him that the first bridge was about the length of a bowshot but less than a foot wide. It looked narrow indeed, and the river beneath was wide and deep and swift. He did not know what to do, for it seemed to him that no-one could cross it either on foot or on horseback.

Just then an aged knight appeared from the castle and came to the head of the bridge, which was called the Bridge of the Needle, and cried at the top of his voice: 'Sir knight, come across now! It'll soon be dark and the people of the castle are waiting for you!'

'But sir!' shouted Sir Gawain. 'Tell me how I can cross!'

'In faith,' the knight called back, 'I know of no other way but here at this gate, so if you want to come to the castle, take courage and cross now.'

Sir Gawain felt ashamed for having tarried so long, and thought again of how the hermit had told him to fear nothing he saw at the entrance to the castle; and he had made confession in all truthfulness and repented of his sins, and feared death the less for having done so. So he blessed himself with the sign of the Cross and, thinking he was about to die, commended himself to God; then he spurred forward. And as soon as he began to ride ahead he found that the bridge was as wide as he could wish. Many knights who wanted to enter the castle had been tested by this crossing. Sir Gawain was astonished to find the bridge so wide when it had looked so narrow; and it was a drawbridge, and by an ingenious device it rose by itself when he had crossed so that no-one then could enter the castle, for the river below flowed swiftly indeed.

The knight had now withdrawn beyond the second bridge, and once again the thought of crossing filled Sir Gawain with fear, for it seemed just as long as the first. And he looked at the river beneath, which was no less swift and no less deep, and it seemed to him that the bridge was made of ice, weak and fragile and rising high above the water. But because of the other he ceased to fear this bridge, and he rode on, commending himself to God; whereupon he found that the bridge was the strongest and finest he had ever seen, with statues all along the way; and when he had crossed it rose up just as the other had done. But when Gawain looked ahead he could not see the knight, and so he came up to the third bridge. Because of what he had now seen he felt no fear, and the third bridge was not like the others: all across it were marble columns, each one topped with a golden pommel. Then he looked at the gate ahead of him, and there he saw depicted Our Lord on the Cross, with His mother on one side and Saint John on the other; all in gold they were, inlaid with precious stones that blazed like fires. And on the right he saw a beautiful angel, his finger pointing to the chapel of the Holy Grail. There was a precious stone in the middle of his chest, and letters written above his head saying that the lord of the castle was as pure and clean of all sins as the jewel. Suddenly Gawain saw at the gateway a huge and terrible lion, standing there on all fours, but as soon as it saw Sir Gawain it lay down on the ground, and he passed by quite freely.

Into the castle he rode and dismounted, and leaving his lance and shield propped against the wall he climbed the marble steps and entered a magnificent hall, set all around with images in gold. And in the middle he found a rich, high couch, at the foot of which was a handsome chessboard, finely wrought, and a golden cushion studded with jewels and beautifully embroidered; but the chessmen were not set up. Sir Gawain was gazing at the beauty and splendour of the hall when two knights appeared from a chamber.

'Welcome, sir!' they said.

'May God bring you joy and good fortune,' replied Sir Gawain.

They bade him be seated on the couch, and then had two boys remove his armour; and when that was done water was brought in two basins to wash his face and hands. Then two maidens came, and dressed him in a fine gown of golden cloth.

'Sir,' they said, 'be thankful for what is done for you here, for this is the lodging of good and true knights.'

'That I will,' said Sir Gawain. 'Many thanks.'

He was suddenly aware that, although the night was very dark, in the hall, without candles, it was as bright as if the sun had been shining, and he wondered where the light could be coming from.

Dressed in the fine gown, Sir Gawain was handsome indeed to behold: he had all the appearance of a worthy knight. Then the knights said: 'Sir, will you come now to see the lord of the castle?'

'I'd be glad to see him, sirs,' replied Sir Gawain, 'and I wish to present to him a most sacred sword.'

And so they led him to the chamber where the Fisher King lay. It was strewn with grass and flowers, and the king was lying in a bed hung on cords, with posts of ivory and a mattress of brocaded silk, and his coverlet was of sable with the finest of sheets; and on his head he wore a sable hat covered with red samite and emblazoned with a cross of gold. His head rested on a pillow perfumed with a balmy fragrance, and a jewel was set at each corner, shining with a brilliant light. And there in the room stood a pillar of copper, and on it sat an angel, holding a golden cross bearing a piece of the real Cross where God was crucified, as big as the Cross of gold itself, and this the worthy king worshipped; and in four golden candlesticks stood four tall candles which burned throughout the hours when light was needed.

Sir Gawain came up to the Fisher King and greeted him, and the king welcomed him with great joy.

'Sire,' said Sir Gawain, 'I present to you the sword with which Saint John the Baptist was beheaded.'

'Many thanks, sir,' said the king. 'Neither you nor anyone else could have entered this castle without the sword; and had you not been a knight of great worth, you would never have won it.'

He took the sword and held it to his lips and cheek, kissing it very gently and rejoicing at its touch. Then a most beautiful maiden came and sat at his head, and he gave the sword into her keeping. Two others sat at his feet, gazing at him with gentle eyes.

'What's your name?' said the king.

'Sire,' he replied, 'my name is Gawain.'

'Gawain, the light that is now about us comes to us from God out of love for you. Each time a knight comes to lodge at our castle, the light appears in this way. I'd give you a much finer welcome than I do if I could only help myself, but I've been languishing ever since the knight of whom you've heard came to lodge here. Because of just one thing he neglected to say this weakness has beset me, and I beg you in God's name to be mindful of it, for you should be glad indeed if you could restore me to health. But look: here's my grand-daughter, whose land, her inheritance, has been seized from her, and it can be restored to her only by her brother – she's searching for him desperately. We've heard he's the finest knight in the world, but we can get no proper news of him.'

'Sire,' said the maiden to her grandfather the king, 'thank Sir Gawain for the honourable deed he did for me: when he came to our house he brought peace to all our land, and won the guardianship of our castle for a year's term. He left five knights to serve as my guard, but now that year is out and the great war has reopened, and if God doesn't help us and I can't find my brother, our land will surely be lost.'

'Damsel,' said Sir Gawain, 'I'd do everything in my power to help you if I had the opportunity. And there's no knight in the world I'd more gladly see than your brother; but I can give you no certain news of him, except that I came across a hermitage where there was a hermit king, and there I was told to make no noise because the finest knight in the world was lying there in distress. His name, the hermit told me, was Par-lui-fet. I saw his horse being cared for by a boy outside the chapel, and his arms and shield had been laid in the sun.'

'Sir,' said the maiden, 'my brother's name is not Par-lui-fet but Perceval: that was his name in baptism. And those who have seen him say he's the most handsome of knights.'

'Well truly,' said the king, 'I never saw a more handsome knight than the one who came to this castle, and I know he must indeed have been a good knight, for otherwise he could not have gained entrance. But I was poorly rewarded for his lodging, for I'm now of no help to myself or others. In God's name, Sir Gawain, be mindful of me tonight, for I've great faith in your worth.'

'Truly, sire,' said Sir Gawain, 'if it please God, I shall do nothing here for which I may be reproached.'

With that Sir Gawain was led into the hall, and there he found twelve aged, white-haired knights; yet they did not look as old as they were, for each was one hundred or more, though they did not look more than forty. They seated Sir Gawain to dine at a splendid table of ivory, and then sat down all around him.

'Sir,' said the foremost knight, 'remember what the king asked of you tonight.'

And Sir Gawain replied: 'May God keep me mindful.'

At that moment in was brought a loin of stag and other venison in great plenty, and rich golden plates adorned the table, with great lidded goblets of gold, and magnificent golden candlesticks bearing great candles. But the light of these was dimmed by the other light in the room. And suddenly two maidens appeared from a chapel: in her hands one was carrying the Holy Grail, and the other held the lance with the bleeding head. Side by side they came into the hall where the knights and Sir Gawain were eating. So sweet and holy a fragrance came forth that their feasting was forgotten. Sir Gawain gazed at the Grail and thought he saw therein a chalice, which at that time was a rare sight indeed; and he saw the point of the lance from which the red blood flowed, and he thought he could see two angels bearing golden candlesticks with candles burning. The maidens passed before Sir Gawain and into another chamber. Sir Gawain was deep in thought, so deep in joyful thought that he could think only of God. The knights stared at him, all downcast and grieving in their hearts. But just then the two maidens returned and passed once more before Sir Gawain. And he thought he saw three angels where before he had seen but two, and there in the centre of the Grail he thought he could see the shape of a child. The foremost knight cried out to Sir Gawain, but he, looking before him, saw three drops of blood drip on to the table, and was so captivated by the sight that he did not say a word. And so the maidens passed on by, leaving the knights looking at one another in dismay. Sir Gawain could not take his eyes off the three drops of blood, but when he tried to kiss them they moved away from him, and it grieved him deeply that he could not touch them with his hand or anything within his reach. Thereupon the two maidens passed once more before the table, and to Sir Gawain it seemed that there were three; and looking up it appeared to him that the Grail was high in the air. And above it he saw, he thought, a crowned king nailed to a cross with a spear thrust in his side. Sir Gawain was filled with sorrow at the sight and could think of nothing but the pain the king was suffering. Again the foremost knight cried out to him to speak, saying that if he delayed longer the chance would be lost forever. But Sir Gawain remained gazing upwards in silence, hearing nothing the knight had said. The maidens disappeared into the chapel with the Grail and the lance, the knights cleared the tables, left the feast and moved off into another chamber, and Sir Gawain was left there alone.

He looked around him and saw all the doors shut tight, and then, looking towards the foot of the couch, he could see two candlesticks burning before the chessboard with all its pieces in place; one set was of ivory and the other of gold. Sir Gawain began to move the ivory men, whereupon the gold pieces countered his moves and checkmated him twice. In the third round Gawain hoped to gain revenge, but seeing that he was heading for defeat once more he broke up the game. A maiden then came from a chamber and bade a boy remove the chessboard and the pieces and take them away.

Sir Gawain, exhausted from wandering for so many days in search of the castle where he now found himself, fell asleep on the couch and remained there until day had dawned, when he heard the loud blast of a horn. At that he donned his armour and went to take his leave of the Fisher King; but the doors were bolted fast against him: there was no entrance for Gawain. He could hear a most beautiful service being sung in a chapel, and it grieved him deeply that he could not hear mass. Just then a maiden came into the hall and said:

'Sir, you can now hear the service and the great rejoicing for the sword you delivered to the good king. It would have gladdened your heart to be in the chapel now, but your silence has lost you the right of entry. For this chapel is so holy – because of the sacred relics which lie within – that no-one can enter from noon on Saturday until the Monday after the mass.'

In his bewilderment Sir Gawain could make no reply, and the maiden said: 'Sir, may God keep you safe, whatever you may have done; for it seems to me that your only failing was to neglect to say those words which would have restored joy to the castle.'

With that the maiden departed, and once again Sir Gawain heard the horn sound, and a voice cried aloud: 'Let anyone who does not belong here be gone. The bridges are lowered, the gate is open and the lion is in its den. And after this the bridges must be raised again, because the King of Castle Mortal is besieging this castle, for which he will surely die.'

At that Sir Gawain left the hall, and at the foot of the steps he found his horse and arms ready for him. He mounted and rode out of the castle, to find the bridges high and wide, and galloped on beside a great river which flowed through a valley and into a forest. Rain and storm and thunder arose in the wood, so great that it seemed as if all the trees would be uprooted. So furious a tempest was it that Sir Gawain had to lay his shield over his horse's neck to save it from drowning in the torrential rain. In this dreadful plight he rode on beside the river as it coursed through the forest until he saw, in a meadow on the further bank, a knight and a maiden riding gracefully along; beautiful saddles they had, and the knight was carrying a bird on his wrist, with two hunting-dogs following behind, and the maiden wore a hat embroidered with gold. There in the meadow the sun was shining down beautifully, and the air was clear and pure. Sir Gawain marvelled that the rain should be driving down so hard along his path when in the meadow where the knight was riding the sun was beaming through with weather fair and tranquil; and he watched them ride contentedly along. He could not call out to them because they were too far away, but looking along a nearer part of the riverbank he caught sight of the knight's squire, and he cried:

'Dear friend, how is it that the rain's pouring down on me but over there it's not raining at all?'

'Sir,' said the boy in reply, 'you've deserved it, and it's the custom in this forest.'

'Will the storm last long?'

'It'll stop at the first bridge you come to,' said the boy.

Then Sir Gawain left him, and the storm grew even stronger until he finally came to a bridge. He rode across and found himself in the meadow, where he could sling his shield around his neck again. Just then he saw before him a castle where he could hear a multitude of people rejoicing, and he rode on until he arrived at the castle and saw great crowds of knights and ladies and maidens. Sir Gawain dismounted; but nowhere in the castle could he find anyone who would speak to him: all were intent on their rejoicing. Sir Gawain presented himself here and there, but everyone ignored him. He could plainly see that he would gain nothing by staying, so he mounted once more and left. He met a knight at the gate and said: 'What castle is this, sir?'

'Can't you see?' replied the knight. 'It's a Castle of Joy.'

'In faith,' said Sir Gawain, 'they're not very polite here: no-one's spoken to me yet!'

'They can't be accused of discourtesy for that,' said the knight, 'for you've deserved it. They take you to be as negligent in deed as you are in speech. They saw you'd come through the Perilous Forest, and that's the road taken by all who've failed: it's obvious from your arms and your horse.'

With that the knight took his leave, and Sir Gawain rode on for a great part of the day, sunk in grief and bewilderment.

Perceval's Recovery

MEANWHILE THE SON OF THE WIDOWED LADY was still staying at the hermitage of his uncle King Pelles, and because of his distress from the suffering he had endured since his failure at the house of the Fisher King, he had made confession to his uncle and told him of his lineage and that his name was Perceval. But the good hermit, the good king, had named him Par-lui-fet, because he was a self-made knight. But one day, when the hermit had gone out to work in the forest, the Good Knight Perceval felt stronger and happier than usual, and hearing the birds singing in the forest his heart began to burn with chivalry, and he recalled the adventures he had found in the forest and the maidens and knights he had met; never had he felt such an eagerness for feats of arms as then: he had lingered there so long. And so, feeling a vigour in his heart, a surging in his limbs and a resolve in his spirit, he armed at once, saddled his horse and mounted, praying to God to lead him to an adventure where he might meet a worthy knight. Then he left his uncle's hermitage and rode off into the forest, deep and shadowed.

On he rode until he came to a glade wide and long and beautiful, and there he saw a tree green with leaves and spreading wide with many branches. There in its shade he dismounted, thinking to himself that two knights could joust handsomely on that ground, for it was a most fair and pleasant place. Just as he was thinking this, he heard a horse in the forest neigh three times very loudly, and he rejoiced at the sound.

'Oh God!' he cried, 'grant in Your gentleness that there may be a knight coming with whom I can test my strength and valour, for I don't know now what my strength may be, except that I feel a health in my heart and a rejoicing in my limbs. But if a knight has no courage in him, then another knight cannot properly test his chivalry. So I pray to the Saviour that if it be a knight coming this way, he may be strong and valiant in defending himself, for I long to attack him!'

At that moment he looked towards the edge of the clearing and saw the knight emerge from the forest and pass into the glade. He was fully armed, and bore a white shield round his neck emblazoned with a cross of gold, and his lance was lowered. He was mounted on a great charger and advancing at a walk. As soon as Perceval saw him he set himself firmly in his stirrups, gripped his lance and with a burst of joy plunged in his spurs. He came at the knight in an impetuous charge, crying:

'I challenge you to joust, sir, and may you be a good knight, for more can be learned from good knights than from bad!'

And he struck the knight such a furious blow that he made him lose one of his stirrups, and smashed through his shield right on the boss. He went galloping past, leaving the knight bewildered at his demand, saying: 'Good sir, what wrong have I done you?'

Perceval fell silent, and his heart was filled with rage at having failed to unhorse the knight; but he would not be so easily overcome, for he was one of the finest knights in the world at defending himself in combat. He charged at Perceval as fast as his horse could bear him and Perceval charged too, and they struck each other on their shields with such force that the heads of their lances smashed through and rent their hauberks; Perceval struck the knight full in the chest and thrust a good two finger-lengths of lance into his flesh, and the knight made no mistake but thrust his lance right through Perceval's arm. The shafts flew into pieces, and as the knights passed they crashed into each other so hard that the mail of their hauberks stamped rings on their foreheads and faces, and blood burst from their mouths and noses and drenched their mail-coats. They drew their swords in a rage and the knight with the white shield shouted to Perceval:

'I'd like to know who you are and why you hate me so, for you've given me a grievous wound, and you're a fearsome opponent and a knight of great strength.'

But Perceval did not say a word; he flew at the knight, sword drawn, and the knight came at him, and they gave each other such terrible blows on their helms that they saw stars before their eyes, and the forest rang with the sound of their swords. The battle was fierce and terrible, for they were both great knights, and though the blood that poured from their wounds weakened them somewhat, their ardour and the rage they bore each other had so enflamed them that they were hardly aware of their wounds, and rained blows on each other mercilessly.

The Hermit King Pelles returned from working in the forest and was deeply distressed when he could not find his nephew at the hermitage. He mounted a white mule he kept there, whose forehead was marked with a red cross. This mule had belonged to Joseph of Arimathea when he was a soldier of Pilate, and he had bequeathed it to Pelles. The good Hermit King rode from the hermitage on this mule, praying to God to let him find his nephew. Through the forest he rode until he neared the clearing where the Good Knight was fighting. There he heard the ringing of the swords, and he raced towards the knights and set himself between them to stop the blows.

'Oh, sir!' he cried to the knight with the white shield. 'You're very wrong to fight this knight: he's been lying sick in the forest for a long while, and you've wounded him sorely!'

'And he has wounded me, sir!' cried the knight. 'I would never have attacked him if he hadn't sought combat first! And he won't tell me who he is, or what cause he has to hate me!'

'And who are you, good sir?' said the hermit.

'The son of King Ban of Benuic,' the knight replied. 'My name is Lancelot of the Lake.'

'Oh, dear nephew!' cried the hermit to Perceval. 'This knight is your cousin! You should greet him with joy!'

He made them take off their helmets and open the hoods of their hauberks, and bade them kiss one another. Then he led them back to the hermitage where they dismounted together, and he called a boy to their service to help them gently from their armour. There was a maiden present who was a cousin of King Pelles and had been caring for Perceval in his illness. She gently bathed their wounds and washed away the blood, and she saw that Lancelot's wounds were graver than Perceval's.

'What do you think, damsel?' said the hermit.

'Sir,' she said, 'this knight will have to stay with us until his wound has healed, for it's in a dangerous place.'

'Is he in danger of death?'

'No,' she said, 'not from this wound, so long as it's well tended.'

'God be praised,' he said. 'And how does my nephew seem?'

'His wound will soon heal. No harm will come of it.'

The maiden, who was skilful indeed, nursed the knights' wounds and cared for them as well as she could, with the help of the Hermit King. But if Perceval had been carrying his shield, which he had left there at the hermitage, of red emblazoned with a white stag, then Lancelot would have recognised him and they could have avoided the combat, for he had heard tell of that shield at King Arthur's court.

When Perceval was restored to health and fully cured he left his uncle's hermitage, leaving Lancelot behind because his wound was not yet healed, but promising to return as soon as he could.

Fully armed, he rode on through a forest until, just as evening fell, he came to the edge of the woods and saw a castle before him, fine indeed and well situated. He turned towards it to find lodging, for the sun was setting, and rode inside and dismounted.

The lord came down to meet him, a great red-faced knight with an evil look and scars across his face in many places; he was the only knight there, alone with his retinue. As soon as he saw Perceval dismount he ran and bolted the gate, but Perceval came up to him all the same and greeted him.

'Before you leave here,' cried the knight, 'you'll have your just reward! You're my mortal enemy and rash indeed to come here, for you killed my brother, the Red Knight of the Forest of Quinqueroi, and I am Cahot the Red and

I'm waging war on your sister! I took this castle from her, and I'll take your life before you leave here!'

'I came to this castle,' said Perceval, 'to lodge with you, and it would be shameful of you to do me harm. Now give me lodging as a knight should give another, and in the morning when it's time to leave, let each do the best he can.'

'By my life,' cried Cahot the Red, 'my mortal enemy will never lodge here except as a corpse!'

And he ran up to his hall, armed himself as fast as he could, and clutching his naked sword he returned to where Perceval stood, his heart heavy at learning that the knight was waging war on his sister and had seized that castle from her. Perceval cast aside his lance and came at Cahot on foot, sword drawn, and gave him such a mighty blow on the hood of his hauberk that he smashed through the mail rings and cut away a chunk of flesh to send him staggering. Cahot the Red was filled with anguish when he felt himself wounded, and he came at Perceval and dealt him such a terrible blow on the helm that he sent sparks flying and made his neck bow and his eyes reel. He rained blows on Perceval's shield and split it down to the boss. Perceval felt the fearsome blows and saw that his enemy was a tough and powerful knight; he returned to the attack, aiming to strike him full on the head, but Cahot dodged aside and Perceval's blow caught him on the right arm and hacked it off at the shoulder, sending the arm with the sword flying to the ground. Cahot attacked him in a rage, trying to seize him with his left arm, but although he was desperate for revenge, his strength was grievously sapped. And Perceval, his heart filled with hatred for the knight, assailed him a final time and struck him full on the head with such a blow that his brains were sent scattering. His retinue and servants were watching from the windows of the hall, and seeing this mortal blow to their lord they began to shout to Perceval:

'Sir, you've killed the boldest knight in the kingdom of Logres, and the most feared by all his enemies. But we can do nothing about that; we know this castle belongs to your sister and is rightfully yours, and we'll not challenge you. You may do as you wish with the castle, but let us take our lord Cahot's body and lay it in a proper place, for the sake of his chivalry and because it's our duty.'

'Your request is granted,' said Perceval.

And so they bore his body to a chapel where they took off his armour and laid him to rest. Then they led Perceval into the hall, where they helped him to disarm and said: 'Sir, we present to you the keys of the castle.'

'I order you to guard it for me henceforth,' said Perceval. 'What's it called?'

'The Key of Wales, sir, for this is the entrance to that land.'

Perceval slept that night at his sister's castle which he had recaptured, and the next day when he departed, Cahot's retinue promised to guard the castle faithfully in his name.

He rode on until he came to a meadow where he saw pavilions pitched, and all he could hear was the sound of bitter grieving. But he would not turn back, and he rode up and dismounted amidst the pavilions, and laid aside his shield and lance. He could see a group of maidens wringing their hands and tearing their hair, and wondered what could be the matter. One of the maidens came forward; she was from the castle where he had killed the knight, and she said: 'May it be to your shame and ill-fortune that you've come here!'

Perceval looked at her and marvelled at her words; and she cried: 'My lady! My lady! Come and see the man who killed the finest knight in all your family! And you, Clamadoz, he killed your father and your uncle! Now we'll see what you'll do with him!'

Another maiden now stepped forward; she was the Maiden of the Cart, and she recognised Perceval by his red shield with the white stag.

'Sir,' she said, 'I bid you welcome. They may mourn, but I rejoice at your coming.'

She led him inside a pavilion and seated him on a fine couch, and bidding her two maidens disarm him, she dressed him in a rich gown. Then she led him before the Queen of the Pavilions, who was still lost in grief, and said: 'My lady, behold the Good Knight for whose coming these pavilions were set up, and for whom you were rejoicing until today.'

'Ah!' she cried. 'Is this then the son of the Widowed Lady?'

'Indeed it is,' said the maiden.

'Oh,' she said, 'he's killed the finest knight in all my family, who always defended me against my enemies.'

'My lady,' replied the maiden, 'this man could be your protector and defender now, for he's the finest knight in the world, and the fairest.'

The queen took him by the hand and bade him be seated beside her. 'Sir,' she said, 'whatever may have happened, my heart bids me rejoice at your coming.'

'Thank you, my lady,' he said. 'Cahot tried to kill me in his castle, and I defended myself as well as I could.'

The queen looked him straight in the face, and her heart lit up with such love that she almost threw herself upon him. 'Sir,' she said, 'if you'll grant me your love, I'll forgive you for killing Cahot the Red.'

'My lady, I'd gladly earn your love, and I give you mine.'

'How can I be sure of that?' she said.

'I'll tell you, my lady: I'd do everything in my power to help you against any knight in the world who tried to harm you.'

'Such a love,' she said, 'should be commonly borne by a knight to a lady. You might well do as much for another.'

'That may be, but a man offers his service more gladly in some places than in others.'

But the queen wanted Perceval to swear himself to her more than that, and the more she looked at him the more he pleased her and the more she burned and longed for his love. But Perceval could not think of loving her; he beheld her with great pleasure, for she was beautiful indeed, but he said nothing to make her think that he loved her with a complete love. But she could not restrain her heart, or divert her gaze, or lose her desire. The maidens were astonished to see that she had forgotten her grief so soon.

But Clamadoz was coming. He had been told that this was the knight who as a boy had killed his father and had now killed his uncle, Cahot the Red. He burst into the tent to see Perceval seated beside the queen, who was gazing at him most tenderly.

'My lady!' he cried. 'You do great shame to all your line in seating our mortal enemy beside you! No-one should ever trust in your love or support!'

'Clamadoz,' said the queen, 'this knight has been received by me, and I must do him no harm, but give him lodging and care for him, for he's done nothing to earn accusations of murder or treachery.'

'My lady!' said Clamadoz. 'He killed my father, unchallenged, with the treacherous throw of a javelin, and I'll never rest until I've gained revenge; I accuse him here in your court of murder and treachery, and I beseech you to decide in my favour – not as a relative but as a stranger, for I see that kinship is meaningless here!'

Perceval looked at the knight, who was stalwart, of good height and fair of face, and said: 'Dear sir, I must free myself entirely of the charge of treachery, for never was my heart or my mind set against your father or any other man, and may God keep me from such baseness, as from other sins. I shall earnestly defend myself against your accusation.'

Clamadoz was about to throw down his gage, but the queen said: 'By my life, there'll be no challenge now! Tomorrow we'll see light and sense, and each shall make amends to the other!'

Clamadoz was filled with rage, but the Queen of the Pavilions honoured Perceval as highly as she could: this grieved Clamadoz deeply, and he swore that no man should ever have faith in a woman; but he was wrong to reproach her so, for she honoured Perceval because of the great love she bore him; she knew that he was the finest knight in the world, and the fairest. She could find in him no secret intimacy, however, either in deed or in word, and that grieved her much.

That night the knights and maidens lay down to sleep until the morning, when they went to hear mass in a chapel which stood amidst the pavilions. Just as mass had been sung, a very young knight rode up in full armour with a white shield slung around his neck. He dismounted amidst the tents and came, fully armed, before the queen.

'My lady,' he said, 'I have a grievance against a knight here who killed my lion, and if you don't grant me satisfaction for this, I'll despise you as much as I do him, and do you as much harm as I can. So I pray and entreat you, out of love for Sir Gawain whose vassal I am, to help me obtain amends.'

'What is the knight's name?' asked the queen.

'Clamadoz of the Shadows, lady, and I think I see him there.'

'And what's your name?' she asked.

'Meliot of Logres.'

Then Clamadoz came before the queen, saying: 'My lady, I beg you once more to grant me satisfaction of the knight who killed my father and my uncle.'

'I need to be gone at once, lady,' said Meliot of Logres. 'I don't know who this knight is pleading against, but I accuse him of villainy for killing my lion.' And taking a strip of his hauberk he said: 'I hereby offer my gage.'

'Clamadoz,' said the queen, 'did you hear what this knight said?'

'I heard him well. It's true I killed his lion, but it attacked me first and gave me the wounds for which I've been treated here; and you surely know that the one who came here last night has done me a greater wrong than I've done this knight! I pray you let me take vengeance first.'

'But you've heard,' she said, 'that the knight who's come here, ready armed, wishes to leave at once. So defend yourself first against his accusation. We'll consider the other after.'

'Many thanks, my lady,' said Meliot. 'Sir Gawain will be most grateful to you, for this knight killed the lion who protected me from my enemies, nor was the entrance to your land ever exposed while my lion guarded it. And he contemptuously hung the lion's head on my own gate.'

'My lady,' said Clamadoz, 'I'll do whatever he wishes, but I beg you then to grant me satisfaction of the other knight.'

'That I will,' she replied, 'for no-one shall have cause to reproach me.'

So Clamadoz armed and mounted his great charger; he looked a bold and valiant knight indeed. He made his way to the middle of the pavilions where it was good and level, and there he found Meliot of Logres fully armed upon his horse; a fine and skilful knight he was, despite his youth. The ladies and maidens gathered on every side.

'Sir,' said the queen to Perceval, 'I pray you, be referee for these two knights.'

'As you wish, my lady.'

At that moment Meliot came charging at Clamadoz and Clamadoz at him, and they struck each other so hard on their shields that they pierced them and tore through their hauberks with the heads of their lances; blood came streaming from the wounds. But the lances were unbroken, and the knights drew back to prepare for a second charge, and came back at one another at a terrible pace; and they struck each other with such fury full in the chest that their hauberks could not save them from being speared deep into the flesh; and they collided so hard that horses and knights came crashing down together in a heap. The queen and the maidens were deeply distressed, for they could see the two knights were sorely wounded. But they had climbed to their feet and were clutching their bare, drawn swords, for their lances were broken. With all the strength they could summon they assailed each other in a fury, and the queen cried to Perceval:

'Go, sir, and part those knights before one kills the other, for they're grievously wounded!'

And so Perceval went to separate them, and: 'Stop now, sir,' he said to Meliot of Logres, 'you've done enough.' And Clamadoz, knowing the wound in his chest was very deep, drew back likewise.

The queen now approached and said to her nephew: 'Clamadoz, you're sorely wounded. It grieves me, but there's nothing I can do; I've never seen a knight whose will for fighting didn't at some time serve him ill. A man can never attain all his rights.'

She had him carried on his shield into a tent, where he was stripped of his arms and his wounds were tended to: there was nothing to fear from one of them, but the other was dangerous indeed.

'I beg and entreat you once more,' he said to the queen, 'as my lady and my aunt, not to let the knight who killed my father leave here, unless he gives assurances that he'll return when I'm cured.'

'I'll do so,' she said, 'since that's your wish.'

And she came to Perceval and said: 'Sir, you must stay with us till my nephew's healed; you're well aware of the charge he's made against you, and I wouldn't have you go while under accusation.'

'My lady,' he said, 'I've no desire to make a speedy departure or go without your leave, and I'll always be ready to defend myself against reproach. But I can't stay here so long; I swear to you that I'll return within forty days or however long it takes his wounds to mend.'

'Sir,' said the Maiden of the Cart, 'I'll stay here as your hostage.'

'Oh, but beg him,' the queen cried to her, 'to stay here with you!'

'I can't, my lady,' said Perceval, 'for I left Lancelot sorely wounded at my uncle's hermitage.'

'Sir,' said the queen, 'I wish that staying here could please you as much as it would please me.'

'It should displease no-one to be with you,' he said, 'but every man must keep his word, and I promised Lancelot that I'd return as soon as I could – and no-one should lie to so fine a knight.'

'Then do you promise me,' she said, 'that you'll return by the time Clamadoz is healed to defend yourself against his charge of treachery?'

'And if he should die, my lady, would I be absolved of having to return?'

'Of course, sir, unless you'd return out of love for me, for your return would give me great joy.'

'My lady, there'll never be a day,' Perceval replied, 'when my service will not be freely given you, if I'm in a position to be of help.'

With that he took his leave and departed, fully armed, and the Maiden of the Cart commended him to God.

Perceval galloped swiftly away, and rode hard each day until he reached his uncle's hermitage. He expected to find Lancelot there, but his uncle told him that he had left, fully healed of his wound. Perceval was sorry not to find Lancelot, but he rejoiced to hear his uncle say that he had departed in good health and spirits.

Lancelot's Quest

WHEN LANCELOT LEFT THE HERMITAGE he rode on until he passed out of the forest and found before him a waste land, a land stretching far and wide where there dwelt neither beasts nor birds, for the earth was so poor and dry that there was no pasture to be found. Lancelot gazed far before him, and a city appeared to view; he rode on towards it at a swift pace, and found that the city was so huge that it stretched to every horizon. But he could see its walls crumbling round about, and the gates leaning with age. He rode inside to find the city deserted, its great palaces derelict and waste, its markets and exchanges empty, its vast graveyards full of tombs, its churches crumbling. Through the great streets he rode until he found a huge palace which seemed to be less ruined than the others. He drew rein before it, to hear knights and ladies lamenting bitterly and saying to a knight:

'Oh God! What a shame and sorrow it is that you must go and die, and your death cannot be delayed!'

Lancelot heard all this but could see no-one. But just then the knight came down from the hall: he was young and handsome, and was dressed in a red coat girdled with a rich belt of silk and gold; a beautiful brooch was pinned at his neck clustered with precious stones; his head was crowned with a golden hat; and in his hands he clutched a huge axe. As he approached he said to Lancelot: 'Dismount, sir.'

'Gladly,' said Lancelot, and he climbed down and tethered his horse to a silver ring set in the mounting-block. 'What do you want, sir?' he said to the knight.

'Sir,' came the reply, 'you must cut off my head with this axe, for I'm condemned to death with this weapon; if not, I'll cut off yours.'

'By my life!' cried Lancelot. 'What are you saying?'

'What you hear, sir,' said the knight. 'This you must do since you've come to the city.'

'Sir,' said Lancelot, 'only a fool would fail to see how to get the better in this game! But it would be to my shame to kill you without cause.'

'Truly,' said the knight, 'you cannot leave otherwise.'

'Dear sir,' said Lancelot, 'you look so fine and noble: how can you go so calmly to your death? You surely know I'd sooner kill you than have you kill me, since that's the choice.'

'I'm well aware of that,' said the knight, 'but you must swear to me before I die that you'll return to the city in a year's time and offer your head freely, without contest, just as I offer mine.'

'Upon my soul!' cried Lancelot. 'Nothing you could say would dissuade me from deferring death rather than dying here and now. But I'm amazed you're so well prepared to die.'

'Sir,' the knight replied, 'a man about to go before the Saviour of the world must cleanse himself of all the sins he's ever committed, and I'm now truly repented of mine, and I want to die so.'

And with that he handed him the axe. Lancelot took it and saw how keen and sharp it was.

'Sir,' said the knight, 'stretch out your hand towards that church you can see.'

'Very well,' said Lancelot.

'Will you now swear to me on the relics in that church,' said the knight, 'that you'll return here a year from this day, at the hour at which you kill me, and offer your head freely, without defence, as I shall in a moment offer mine?'

'I swear it,' said Lancelot.

And with that the knight knelt down and stretched out his neck as straight as he could. Lancelot clutched the axe in both hands and said: 'For God's sake, sir knight, have mercy on yourself.'

'Willingly, sir. Let me cut off your head. Only thus can I find mercy.'

'That mercy I will not grant you,' said Lancelot, and he raised the axe and struck off the knight's head with such a terrible blow that he sent it flying seven feet from the body. The headless knight crashed to the ground, and as Lancelot threw down the axe he thought he would do ill to linger there, and he returned to his horse, took up his arms and mounted. When he looked back he could see neither the body of the knight nor his head, and he could not think what had become of them; but he heard a great, mournful crying of knights and ladies far off in the city: they were bewailing the Good Knight, and saying that he would be avenged, God willing, at the agreed time or sooner. Lancelot rode out of the city, hearing every word the knights and ladies said.

On he rode through a forest until he came upon a castle which lay across his path at the edge of a glade. At the entrance to the castle he saw an aged knight and two maidens sitting on a bridge. He rode that way and the knight and the maidens rose to meet him. Lancelot dismounted, and the old vassal said: 'Welcome, sir!'

And the maidens greeted him joyfully and led him into the castle.

'Sir,' said the vassal, 'we sorely needed you to come!'

Lancelot was led up to the hall and disarmed, and the maidens served him with the greatest kindness.

'These two girls,' the vassal said, 'are my daughters, and are in a sorry plight.

Certain men are trying to seize this castle from them, because they've no aid or support except from me, and I can provide no strong defence, for I'm old and frail. For a long while I've found no-one bold enough to defend me from our attackers, but you seem to be of such great valour that you'd surely go to my defence tomorrow, for our truce ends tonight.'

'What?' cried Lancelot. 'I came to this castle only to find lodging, and you'd engage me so soon in battle?'

'Thus, sir,' said the vassal, 'we'll test whether there's as much valour in your heart as there seems from your appearance; and in defending the fief of these maidens, my daughters, you'll win God's love and the world's honour.'

At that the maidens fell weeping at his feet, begging him to have mercy on them for God's sake, that they might not be robbed of their inheritance. And Lancelot, filled with pity, asked them to rise at once, saying: 'Damsels, I'll do all in my power to help you, but may the time be near.'

'Sir,' they replied, 'the day is fixed for tomorrow, and if by then we've not found a knight to be our champion, this castle will be lost to us for sure. This hateful attack is being levelled at us because we once gave lodging to Sir Gawain.'

Lancelot lay that night at the castle and was treated with all honour. The next day after hearing mass he armed, and as soon as he had done so, he heard three loud blasts of a horn ring out beyond the castle gate.

'Sir!' cried the vassal to Lancelot. 'The knight has arrived! He thinks there's no-one here to defend us.'

'But there is, by my life!' said Lancelot.

The knight sounded his horn once more, and Lancelot went down to find his horse saddled and he mounted at once. The maidens were at his stirrups, begging him in God's name to defend their honour, for if he failed, they would face a wretched flight to other lands. Once more the knight sounded his horn, and Lancelot would tarry no longer; out he rode, his lance in his hand and his shield slung at his neck. He could see the knight at the far end of the meadow, fully armed, waiting beneath a tree. Lancelot spurred towards him, and seeing him coming the knight cried:

'What do you want, sir knight? Have you come to do me harm?'

'Yes indeed!' cried Lancelot. 'For you mean to do mischief here, and I challenge you on behalf of the vassal and his daughters!'

And he struck the knight full on the shield, smashing through the boss with such a furious thrust that he pinned his arm to his side and felled both him and his horse. Then he leaped down and came running to the attack, sword drawn.

'Oh, sir!' cried the knight. 'Stand back! Don't kill me! Tell me your name.'

'What use is my name to you?'

'I'd gladly know it, sir,' he said, 'for you seem a fine knight indeed, as I've learned only too well in our first meeting!'

'My name, sir knight, is Lancelot of the Lake. And yours?'

'Marin, sir, of the Castle of Gomorret, and I'm the father of Meliot of Logres. And I beg you by all you hold most dear in the world not to kill me.'

'By all that I hold most dear in the world I will,' cried Lancelot, 'unless you abandon your hostility towards this castle!'

'Then truly, I shall,' said the knight. 'I promise they'll never have anything more to fear from me.'

'I'll not trust your word,' said Lancelot, 'unless you come with me to the castle.'

'Sir, you've wounded me gravely; I can't easily mount.'

So Lancelot helped Marin on to his horse, and then led him to the castle and made him present his sword to the vassal and the maidens and surrender his shield and his arms, and swear on holy relics that he would never again wage war upon them. With that he left the castle, while Marin made his way back to Gomorret, leaving the vassal and his two daughters to live in happiness.

Lancelot now journeyed through strange forests in search of adventure, and rode on until he found himself in open country outside a huge city which seemed to be of great importance. As he rode across the fields he saw a great company ride out amid a mighty noise of bagpipes and flutes and viols. They were coming down the road towards Lancelot, and when the foremost neared him they halted and redoubled their joy, crying: 'Welcome, sir!'

'My lords,' said Lancelot, 'who are you preparing to meet with such celebration?'

'Our masters will tell you that,' they said. 'They're following behind.'

And up came the provosts and the lords of the city to meet Lancelot. 'Sir,' they said, 'this whole city is overcome with jubilation for your sake, and all these instruments are sounding their joy at your coming!'

'Why should they sound for me?' said Lancelot.

'We'll tell you,' they said. 'This city has begun to burn in one quarter ever since the death of our king, and the fire will never be quenched until we find a king to be lord of our city and its fief for a year's term. At the end of that year he must cast himself into the fire, and then it will be extinguished. Until then it cannot be quenched, nor will it die. So we've come to meet you to bestow our kingdom upon you, for we've heard that you're a great knight!'

'My lords,' said Lancelot, 'I've no need of such a kingdom, and may God save me from the honour!'

'Sir,' they said, 'you can't be saved from it now that you've come to our land; and it would be a great pity if such a beautiful city were to fall to ruins to avoid the death of one man. And its fief is great indeed – it would be a high honour for you. And at the year's end you'll be crowned in the fire to save the city and its people and win high praise indeed!'

Lancelot was filled with awe by their words, but they crowded round him on every side and bore him into the city. Ladies and maidens stood at great stone windows to cry their joy, saying to one another:

'Behold, they bring the new king! In a year's time the fire will be quenched!'

'But God!' cried some. 'What a shame it is that such a handsome knight should die so.'

'Silence!' said others. 'It's a great joy that so fine a city as ours should be saved by his death, for all the kingdom will pray for his soul evermore.'

Rejoicing, they led him into the palace and said they would crown him. Lancelot found the palace strewn with reeds and hung with rich silken drapes, and all the lords of the city were standing ready to pay him homage; but he staunchly refused, saying he would never be their king or their lord in this way.

It was just then that a dwarf entered the city with one of the most beautiful maidens in the kingdom, and he asked what had caused such rejoicing and commotion. He was told how they wanted to make a knight their king and how he would not agree, and he was told about the fire, too; whereupon the dwarf and the maiden dismounted before the palace and climbed the steps, and the dwarf cried out to all the lords and the most powerful men of the city:

'My lords, since this knight has no wish to be king, I'll accept your crown most willingly, and govern this city at your pleasure and do all that you require.'

'In faith,' they said, 'since the knight has refused this honour and you wish to accept it, we grant it to you gladly. Now he may resume his journey, for we declare him free.'

With that they set the crown on the dwarf's head, and Lancelot, filled with joy, took his leave and commended them to God. But as he rode through the city in all his armour, the ladies and maidens whispered of how he was not willing to be king and die so soon.

He was glad indeed to leave the city behind, and he passed once more into a great forest and rode on until the sun went down; and then, looking ahead, he caught sight of a hermitage: it had been set up very recently, for the dwelling and the chapel were newly built. He turned that way to find lodging, and as he dismounted, the hermit, a young man without a beard or a moustache, came out of the chapel.

'Welcome, sir!' he said to Lancelot.

'I wish you good fortune,' he replied. 'But I've never seen one so young as you in a hermitage.'

'Sir, my only regret is that I didn't come here a long time ago.'

With that, he stabled Lancelot's horse and led him into the hermitage, where he took off his armour and made him as comfortable as he could.

'Sir,' said the hermit, 'can you give me news of a knight who lay for a long time at the house of a hermit king?'

'Oh, it's only a short while since I saw him.'

'Where was that, sir?' he said.

'At that very house, for the Hermit King cared for me and tended the wounds the knight gave me!'

'Then the knight is now cured?'

'Yes, sir,' said Lancelot, 'which is a great joy indeed. But why do you ask?'

'It's only right that I should,' he said, 'for my father King Pelles is his uncle, and his mother is my father's sister.'

'Oh, sir, then the Hermit King is your father?'

'Indeed he is.'

'Then I love you the more,' said Lancelot, 'for I never met a man who did me such honour as he. What's your name?'

'Joseus; and yours?'

'Sir,' he said, 'my name is Lancelot of the Lake.'

'Then we're closely related, you and I!'

'Truly,' said Lancelot, 'that gladdens my heart!'

Then he looked around the hermit's dwelling and saw a shield and a lance, a sword, a hauberk and javelins.

'Sir,' he said, 'why do you keep those weapons?'

'This forest is a lonely place,' he replied, 'far from any people, and there's no-one here but me and my boy. When robbers and villains come to attack us, we defend ourselves.'

'I didn't think,' said Lancelot, 'that anyone would kill or hurt a hermit.'

'And may God keep me,' said the hermit, 'from ever killing or wounding a man.'

'Then how do you defend yourself?'

'When robbers come we arm ourselves; if I can get hold of one with my hands he'll not escape, and my boy is tough and brave and will kill him at once or render him harmless.'

'By my life,' said Lancelot, 'I can see that if you weren't a hermit you'd do likewise!'

'True enough,' said the hermit's boy, 'for I think there's none as strong and bold as he in all the kingdom of Logres!'

That night the hermit lodged Lancelot as well as he could. But just as they had fallen asleep, four robber knights came riding up from the forest, for they knew that a knight was lodged there, and coveted his horse and arms. The hermit, who was in the chapel, spotted them first, and he woke his boy and told him to fetch his arms as quietly as he could. Then he armed at once and told the boy to do likewise.

'Shall I wake the knight, sir?' asked the boy.

'No, not until we have good reason.'

Then snatching up a piece of rope he opened the chapel door, and they ran outside to find the robbers in the stable, about to steal Lancelot's horse. The hermit shouted out at them, and the boy ran forward and brought one down with his lance; the hermit seized him and bound him to a tree so tightly that he could not move, while the other three set about defending themselves and tried to rescue their companion. Lancelot heard the commotion and jumped up in alarm and armed himself as fast as he could; but by the time he arrived the hermit had caught the other three and tied them up with the fourth.

'Ah, sir,' said the hermit to Lancelot, 'I'm sorry you were woken up.'

'It was very wrong of you,' he said, 'not to call on me before!'

'Oh,' said the hermit, 'we often have attacks like this.'

The four robbers begged Lancelot for mercy, imploring him to ask the hermit to take pity on them; but Lancelot said: 'May God never aid a man who has pity on thieves.'

And as soon as it was day, Lancelot and the boy led them out into the forest, their hands tied behind their backs, and hanged them in a wild place far from the hermitage.

Then Lancelot took his leave of the young hermit Joseus, saying that it was a great loss to the world that he was not a knight.

'But it's a great joy, too, sir,' said the boy, 'for many men may find a model in him.'

Lancelot mounted and Joseus commended him to God, and begged him to greet his father and cousin for him when he saw them, and Sir Gawain, too, who had met him in the forest as he came in tears to the hermitage.

Lancelot took to the road again. He journeyed on through great forests, finding many castles and hermitages, until he came at last upon a beautiful meadowland where flowers bloomed everywhere; and through it flowed a great river, clear and wide. Looking ahead, Lancelot caught sight of a big boat; on board were three aged, white-haired knights, and a maiden who seemed to be resting in her lap the head of a knight who lay upon a mattress covered with brocaded silk and blanketed with ermine. Another maiden was sitting at his feet. There was a knight in the boat fishing; the shank of his hook seemed to be of gold, and he was catching a great number of big fish, which he placed in a little craft behind the boat. Lancelot rode down to the bank as fast as he could and hailed the knights and maidens, who returned his greeting most courteously.

'My lords,' said Lancelot, 'is there a house or a castle near here?'

'Indeed there is, sir,' they said, 'on the other side of that mountain; a fine and handsome castle, and this river flows all round it.'

'To whom does it belong, my lords?'

'To the Fisher King,' they said. 'He gives lodging to good knights who come to this land. But lodging has been taken there by knights whom he has good cause to reproach.'

The knights sailed on down the river while Lancelot made his way to the foot of the mountain, where he found a hermitage beside a spring; and he thought to himself that, since he was about to go to so great and noble a house as that in which the Grail appeared, he would make confession to the holy man. So he dismounted and did so, owning to all his sins; and he said that he repented of all of them but one. The hermit asked him which sin that was.

'Sir,' said Lancelot, 'it seems to me the sweetest and most beautiful sin I ever committed.'

'Dear sir,' said the hermit, 'sins are sweet to commit, but the reward is bitter indeed; and no sin is beautiful or noble, though some are more base than others.'

'My tongue will tell,' said Lancelot, 'of the sin that my heart cannot repent. My lady, who is a queen, I dearly love more than anything in the world, and one of the finest kings alive has her for his wife. My desire for her seems to me so fine and noble that I cannot abandon it, and it is now so rooted in my heart that it can never leave me. And whatever is of most worth in me comes from that desire.'

'Oh, mortal sinner!' cried the hermit. 'What are you saying? Nothing of worth can come from such lust, and it will be most dearly bought! You are traitor to your earthly lord and a crucifier of the Saviour. Of the seven deadly sins you are burdened with one of the greatest. The joy it gives is pure deception, and you'll pay most dearly for it if you do not soon repent.'

'Never again, sir,' said Lancelot, 'will I confess it to any man on earth.'

'So much the worse!' cried the hermit. 'You should have confessed it long ago, and ceased your sinning forthwith, for as long as you hold to such ways you are an enemy of the Saviour.'

'Oh, sir!' cried Lancelot. 'There is so much beauty and worth and wisdom and courtesy in her that no man on whom she bestowed her love should abandon it!'

'The more beauty there is in her and the more worth,' said the hermit, 'the more she is to blame, and you likewise, for there is far less shame in a man of little worth than in one who ought to be worth much. And she is a blessed and sacred queen, sworn from the beginning to God, but now she has given herself to the Devil because of your love, just as you have done. My good, dear sir, abandon this folly of yours, repent of this sin, and each day I shall pray for you to the Saviour, that as truly as He gave forgiveness for His death to the man who pierced Him in the side with his lance, so may He forgive you for this sin you have clung to, so long as you confess yourself and are truly repentant. And I will take the penance upon myself.'

'I thank you, sir,' said Lancelot, 'but I've no desire to abandon my love, nor do I wish to say anything to you that my heart would deny. I will gladly do as great a penance as is laid down for this sin, for I wish to serve my lady the queen as long as she will have me as her love. And God is so gentle and full of kindness, as all holy men testify, that He will have mercy on us, for I've never been untrue to her, nor she to me.'

'Oh, my dear friend!' said the hermit. 'Nothing I say to you will be of any avail, but may God give both her and you the will to do the Saviour's bidding and save your souls. But now I must tell you this: because of the mortal sin that lies in your heart, if you lodge at the house of the rich Fisher King you will never see the Grail.'

'May God and His sweet mother guide me,' said Lancelot, 'by His will and pleasure.'

'May He indeed,' said the hermit. 'I, too, would have it so.'

Then Lancelot took his leave and mounted and left the hermitage. Night was near: he saw that it was time to find lodging, and there before him he could see the castle of the Fisher King. He saw its bridges great and wide, for they did not seem to him as they had seemed to Sir Gawain. He gazed at the fine gateway where God was pictured, nailed to the Cross; and he saw two lions guarding the entrance, and thought that Sir Gawain must have passed between the lions, and so would he. He rode on towards the gate, and the lions on their chains pricked up their ears and watched him; but Lancelot passed through with no fear; and neither did him any harm.

He dismounted before the great hall and climbed the steps. Two aged knights came to greet him, and received him with the greatest joy, seating him on a couch in the middle of the hall and bidding two servants take off his armour. Two maidens brought Lancelot a rich gown and elegantly dressed him, while he gazed at the splendour of the hall, adorned with holy images and hung on every side with silken drapes. Then the two knights led him into the richest of chambers; and there lay the Fisher King, on a bed so rich and so finely decked that never was one more splendid seen; and there was a maiden at his head and one at his feet. Lancelot greeted him most highly and the king replied in comely words befitting such a noble man; and the room was filled with such a brilliant light that it seemed as if the sun were streaming in on every side, yet it was far into the night, and Lancelot could see no candle burning anywhere.

'Sir,' said the Fisher King, 'can you give me news of my grandson, the son of Alain li Gros of the Vales of Kamaalot, who is called Perceval?'

'I saw him, sire,' said Lancelot, 'just a short while ago at the house of his uncle, the Hermit King.'

'I've heard he's a fine knight indeed.'

'The finest in the world, sire,' said Lancelot. 'I myself have tasted his merit and valour, for he wounded me sorely before we recognised each other.'

'And what is your name?' said the king.

'Sire, my name is Lancelot of the Lake, the son of King Ban of Benuic.'

'Ah,' said the king, 'then you are of our line. You should be a fine knight indeed, and so you are, as I've heard tell. Lancelot,' he said, 'behold the chapel of the Holy Grail. It appeared to two knights who came here: I don't know the name of the first, but I never saw one so calm or so composed, nor one who looked a finer knight. But because of him I've fallen into languor. The other knight was Sir Gawain.'

'Sire,' said Lancelot, 'the first was your grandson, Perceval.'

'Oh!' cried the Fisher King. 'Take care that you speak true!'

'I do, sire,' said Lancelot. 'I ought to know him.'

'Oh, God!' cried the king. 'Then why did I not realise? Because of him I'm languishing, but if I'd known that it was he, I would now have been sound in limbs and body! I pray you, when you see him, tell him to come and see me before I die, and to go and aid his sister, for her men are being slain and her land is being taken, and he alone can win it back. His sister has gone in search of him through every realm.'

'Sire,' said Lancelot, 'I'll gladly tell him so if I find him anywhere; but it'll be a great stroke of luck if I do, for he goes under many disguises and conceals his name in many parts.'

The Fisher King honoured Lancelot most highly. The knights led him into the hall and seated him to dine at an ivory table. When they had washed, the table was laid with the richest vessels of gold and silver, and they were served with fine dishes of venison and boar. But the Grail did not appear at the feast. It did not appear, because Lancelot was not one of the three finest knights in the world, because of his sin with the queen; he would not repent of his love for her, for he thought more of her than of anything else and could not restrain his heart. When they had eaten they rose from the tables, and two maidens attended upon Lancelot as he went to his bed; he lay that night on the finest of couches, and they would not leave his side until he had fallen asleep.

He rose next morning as soon as he saw day break and went to hear mass. Then he took his leave of the Fisher King and the knights and maidens, and rode out of the castle between the two lions, praying to God that he might soon see the queen, for that was his greatest desire. He rode on until he had left the castle far behind, and passed into the forest, dearly hoping to meet Perceval, but he was not to hear news of him for quite some time.

The Castle of Marvels

MEANWHILE SIR GAWAIN HAD BEEN JOURNEYING ON, and one morning, between nine o'clock and noon, he came riding up a hill and saw a massive oak tree, thick with leaves, giving plenty of shade. He could see a shield hung on the oak, and beside it a good, straight lance. He hurried on towards the tree until he noticed a small, dark palfrey beside it; he was astonished by this, for it did not seem right to him: arms and a palfrey – usually a lady's mount – did not go together. Had it been a charger he would have supposed that some knight, roaming the country in search of honour and glory, had climbed the hill. But then he looked beneath the oak and saw a girl sitting there, who would have seemed most beautiful to him if only she had been happy; but her fingers were thrust into her tresses and tearing out her hair: she was going wild with grief. She was grieving for a knight, and was kissing him over and over on the eyes and lips and forehead. Sir Gawain came closer and saw that the knight was wounded, with his face cut all over and a terrible sword-wound in his head, and down both his sides blood flowed in great streams. The knight had fainted many times from his pain and now was lying motionless, and when Sir Gawain arrived he could not tell whether he was alive or dead.

'How does he seem, dear girl?' he said.

And she replied: 'You can see his wounds are dangerous: he'd die of the very smallest.'

'Good friend,' said Gawain, 'try to wake him, please; I want to ask him about the affairs of this land.'

'I'd sooner be flayed alive!' said the girl. 'I've never loved a man so much, and never will as long as I live. Now that he's sleeping and at rest I'd be a wretched fool to disturb him.'

'Then truly, I'll wake him if I can!' said Sir Gawain, and turning his lance around he nudged him on the ankle with the butt. It did not disturb the knight to be woken, for Sir Gawain shook his spur so gently that he did not hurt him. Instead the knight thanked him, saying:

'A thousand thanks, sir, for waking me so gently that I've suffered no harm. But for your own sake I beg you, go no further: you'll be a fool if you do. Take my advice and stop here.'

'Stop? Why should I?'

'No knight who's ever gone this way, by road or field, has ever come back, for this is the border of Galvoie, and no knight can cross it and return. I'm the only one who's ever done so, and look at the state I'm in: I won't last the day. I met a knight, bold and strong and fearsome: I've never tested myself against his equal. So turn back.'

'In faith,' said Sir Gawain, 'it would be foul cowardice in me if I turned back having taken this path. I'm going on until I find out why no-one can return.'

'I see,' said the wounded knight, 'you're eager to increase your honour. But I ask this of you: if God should grant you the honour which no knight has ever had – and I don't think any ever will – please return this way and see if I'm alive or dead. And if I'm dead, then in the name of charity and the Holy Trinity I beg you take care of this girl, and see that she suffers no shame or harm. Please do so, for God never made one more noble or kind-hearted.'

Sir Gawain granted his wish, promising that, if he were not prevented by capture or some other misfortune, he would return to him and give the girl such assistance as he could. With that he left them and rode on without stopping, over plains and through forests, until he caught sight of a mighty castle, one side of which was a sea-port with a fleet resting at anchor. This noble castle was worth little less than Pavia. On its other side lay a vineyard, and beneath it flowed the great river which girded its walls, enclosing the castle and town on every side. Sir Gawain rode into the castle over the bridge, and when he had climbed to the strongest part of the city he found, beneath an elm tree in a courtyard, a sweet girl, whiter than snow, gazing at her face and lips in a mirror. She had made a crown around her head with a thin circlet of golden thread. Sir Gawain dug in his spurs and cantered up towards the girl, but she shouted to him:

'Easy, sir, easy! Go gently now! You're riding like a madman. There's no need to hurry and wear out your horse: it's foolish to rush for nothing.'

'God bless you, girl,' said Sir Gawain. 'What made you so quick to tell me to go easy?'

'Oh, I had good reason, knight, truly I did; for I know exactly what you're thinking.'

'What's that?' he said.

'You want to carry me off across the neck of your horse.'

'True enough, girl!'

'I knew it,' she said, 'but curse the thinker of such a thought! I'm not one of those simpletons that knights sport with and carry off on their horses when they go in search of chivalry. And yet you *could* take me with you, if you dared do what I ask.'

'What's your wish?' asked Gawain, remembering his vow to the King of the Watch that he would grant whatever was asked by the first maiden who had a request of him.

'Go and fetch my palfrey from that garden,' she replied. 'If you do I'll go with you – and mishap and hardship and grief and shame will befall you in my company.'

'Is anything needed but courage, friend?' said Gawain.

'I don't think so, vassal,' she replied.

'Where shall I leave my horse if I go? He won't be able to cross that plank.'

'No, he won't. Give him to me and cross on foot. I'll keep your horse for you. But come back quickly, for I couldn't keep hold of him if he refused to be calm, or if he were taken from me by force before you came back.'

'That's true,' he said. 'But I shan't hold you to blame if he escapes or is snatched from you.'

So he gave her the horse and set off, but decided to take all his arms with him, for if there were someone in the garden who refused him the palfrey and forbade him to take it, there would be trouble and combat before he brought it back. And just as he crossed the plank he saw a great crowd of people gathered together; they stared at him in dismay and cried:

'May a hundred demons burn you, girl, for being so wicked! You've sent so many worthy men to lose their heads. What a grievous shame! You want to fetch the palfrey, knight, but you don't know what'll befall you if you touch it! Oh, knight! Turn back!'

So said all the men and women, but it was not going to change his mind; Sir Gawain headed straight for the palfrey, and was just reaching for the bridle when a great knight, sitting beneath a lush, green olive tree, said: 'Don't lay a finger on it. I advise you to be gone, for if you take that palfrey you'll find a fearsome challenge.'

'That won't stop me, sir,' said Sir Gawain, 'for the girl by the elm tree with the mirror sent me for it, and if I don't take it back I'd be damned on Earth as a cowardly good-for-nothing.'

'Then you'll suffer for it, brother,' said the knight, 'for by God the sovereign father, no knight has ever dared take the palfrey and escaped the grim fate of being beheaded.'

Sir Gawain would not linger a moment more. He drove the palfrey, whose head was black on one side and white on the other, across the plank before him. It had no trouble in crossing, for it had often done so and was well schooled in it now. Sir Gawain took it by its silken rein and came straight to the elm tree where the girl was gazing at herself in her mirror; she had cast her mantle and wimple to the ground so that she could see her face and body freely. Sir Gawain presented the saddled palfrey to her and said: 'Come now, girl, and I'll help you to mount.'

'May God never let it be said,' she replied, 'that you held me in your arms. If your bare hand touched any part of me I'd think myself disgraced. I'd rather have the flesh flayed from my bones! And God grant that I see what I expect: disaster befalling you before the day is out! Go where you like: I'll follow your every step until you've suffered some grave disgrace and mishap. I'm sure I'll make you come to grief – you can't escape it any more than death!'

Sir Gawain heard every word the haughty girl said, but made no reply. He just gave her the palfrey and she returned his horse. Then he bent down, meaning to pick up her mantle from the ground and drape it round her; but the girl, who was never slow in saying shameful words to a knight, said: 'Vassal, what business have you with my mantle? Your hands aren't fit to touch anything I wear.'

So the girl mounted, and donned and fastened her clothes herself, and said: 'Now, knight, go where you please, and I'll follow you everywhere, until I see you disgraced because of me – and that'll be today, if it please God!'

Sir Gawain, feeling humbled and embarrassed, was silent, unable to find a word in reply. He mounted, and they set off; and with his head bowed he turned back along the path towards the oak where he had left the girl and the knight who was in sore need of a doctor. Sir Gawain knew more than any man about healing wounds, and he saw a herb in a hedgerow which was very good for taking the pain from a wound, and he went and picked it; then he carried on until he found the girl beneath the oak tree, lamenting; and as soon as she saw him she said: 'Dear sir, I think this knight is dead now: he hears nothing any more.'

Sir Gawain dismounted, and found that the knight had a firm pulse, and his mouth and cheek were not very cold.

'No, girl,' he said, 'this knight's alive; and I've brought a herb which will relieve the pain of his wounds as soon as it touches him; no finer herb can be set upon a wound, and if it were bound to the bark of an infected tree, the roots would recover and the tree would return to leaf and flower. We'll need a wimple of fine cloth to make a bandage.'

'Take the one I'm wearing,' she said without hesitation. And she took the wimple from her head, and it was very fine and white; and Sir Gawain cut it up as necessary and bound the herb on all the knight's wounds. Then Gawain stayed motionless until the knight gave a sigh and spoke, saying:

'May God reward the one who's restored my speech, for I was greatly afraid of dying without confession. Demons came here in procession, seeking my soul. I know a chaplain near here, and if only I had something to ride I'd go and confess my sins and take communion – then I'd no longer fear death. So do me this service, I pray you: give me the packhorse of that squire who's trotting this way.'

Sir Gawain turned and saw a squire coming, of most unpleasant appearance: his hair was red and stood stiffly on end like the spines of an angry porcupine, and his eyebrows were the same; and he had a great slit of a mouth, and a wide beard, forked and curled, and a short neck and a swollen chest.

Sir Gawain said to the knight: 'God help me, sir, I don't know who this squire is, but I'd rather give you seven chargers than his packhorse, whoever he may be.'

'I tell you,' said the knight, 'he's intent on one thing only: to do you harm if he can.'

Sir Gawain went to meet the squire and asked him where he was going. And he, being far from amiable, replied: 'What business is it of yours, vassal? Whatever my path may be, I wish ill-fortune on your body!'

In an instant Sir Gawain gave him his just deserts, striking him with his open palm; and, his arm being armoured and his will to strike keen, he toppled him and emptied his saddle; and when the squire tried to rise he staggered and fell down flat again.

'You hit me, vassal!'

'Indeed I did,' said Gawain, 'and I'm sorry, but you spoke most offensively.'

'Well, you'll pay for it! You'll lose the hand and the arm that dealt that blow, for it'll never be forgiven you!'

While this was happening, the wounded knight's heart, which had been so weak, returned to him, and he said to Sir Gawain: 'Leave that squire: you'll never have an honourable word from him. But bring me his packhorse: I need to make confession – I shan't stop until I've received the last sacrament.'

Sir Gawain took the packhorse at once and gave it to the knight; his sight had now returned and cleared, and he saw Sir Gawain and recognised him for the first time. Gawain took the girl and, like the kind and courteous knight he was, set her upon the dark palfrey; and while he was helping her into the saddle, the knight took Gawain's horse and mounted, and began to send him charging hither and thither in all directions. Sir Gawain saw him galloping about the hill and laughed in amazement; but as he laughed he said:

'By my faith, sir knight, you're foolish to make my horse leap about like that! Dismount and give him to me, for you could easily reopen your wounds.'

But he replied: 'Hold your tongue, Gawain! You'd better take the packhorse, for you've lost your charger! I like the way he goes, and I'm taking him with me for my own!'

'What! I come here to help you and you'd do me wrong? Don't you dare take my horse: it would be treachery.'

'Gawain, I'd like to tear your heart from your belly with both hands!'

'This reminds me of a proverb,' Gawain replied. '"Do some men a good deed and your neck will bleed"! I'd like to know why you'd have my heart, and why you're taking my horse; for never in my life have I done you any harm. I've never seen you before, as far as I know.'

'Yes, you have, Gawain. And you did me a great disgrace. Don't you remember the man you humiliated by making him eat with the dogs for a month, with his hands tied behind his back? I tell you, that was a foolish deed! But now you're paying for it!'

And Gawain, recalling an incident from many years before, remembered the knight's name and said: 'Are you then Greoreas, who abducted the girl and had your way with her? Yet you knew full well that in King Arthur's land girls are protected; the king has given them a safeguard, and watches over them and ensures their safe conduct. The punishment I dealt you was for the sake of justice, which is imposed throughout the king's land.'

'And now *you* must suffer the justice that *I'*ll exact: I'm taking your charger Gringalet, for that's the best revenge I can have for now; and you'll have to make do with the squire's packhorse – you've not much choice, I'd say!'

With that Greoreas left him and raced off after his sweetheart, who was riding swiftly away. And the haughty girl laughed at Sir Gawain and said: 'Oh, vassal, vassal, what are you going to do? It may well be said of you now: "There's one born every day"! By God, it's great fun following you! If only the packhorse were a mare! Then your disgrace would be greater still!'

Then Sir Gawain, having no choice, mounted the stupid, trotting packhorse. It was an ugly beast, with a bent spine, a thin neck, a fat head and long, limp ears, and all the imperfections of age: its lips sagged, its eyes were cloudy and dim, its hooves covered in sores, and its flanks were hard and slashed by spurs. The reins and bridle were made of old rope, and the saddle, which had seen better days, had no blanket. And the stirrups were so short and weak that he did not dare stand up in them.

'Oh,' cried the girl, plaguing him, 'what a noble escort you look for a girl! Give your horse a bit of a spur and test him – but watch out: he's like lightning! I'll follow you, yes, and I'll never leave you till total disgrace has befallen you – as it surely will.'

'Dear friend,' he replied, 'it isn't right for a girl to speak so impolitely when she's past the age of ten; she should be well-mannered and courteous, if she has the wit to learn.'

'What! You want to teach me lessons, do you, Sir Hapless? I don't need instruction from you! Ride on and hold your tongue, for you're equipped now as I wanted you to be.'

And so they rode on till evening, and neither of them said a word. Sir Gawain went ahead and she rode behind. He didn't know what to do with his pack-horse: it went at a walk whether he liked it or not, for if he dug in his spurs he had a dreadful ride: it shook up his insides so much that he couldn't bear to have it go above walking-pace.

On the packhorse carried him through wild and lonely forests, until he came to a flat land beside a deep river, so wide that no mangonel or catapult could have thrown a stone across. On the further bank, overlooking the river, very well appointed and immensely strong, stood a castle on a cliff, with a great palace set upon a sheer rock, built entirely of grey marble. There were a good five hundred open windows in the palace, and all were filled with girls and ladies, gazing out before them at the meadows and flowery gardens. Many of the girls were dressed in samite, and most wore silken gowns of different colours, all brocaded with gold. From outside they could be seen from the waist up, with their shining heads and comely bodies.

The most evil woman in the world, who was now riding ahead of Sir Gawain, came straight down to the river. There she stopped and dismounted from her little mottled palfrey; and on the bank she found a boat, fastened and padlocked to a stone. But there was an oar on board, and on the stone lay the key to the lock. The evil-hearted girl climbed into the boat and drew her palfrey in after her, as she had done many times before.

'Vassal,' she called to Gawain, 'dismount now and climb in here with your packhorse – it's as skinny as a chicken! – and take up the anchor. I tell you, you'll be in a sorry plight unless you cross this river quickly – or can swim fast!'

'What, girl? Why?'

'You haven't seen what I can see: if you had you'd flee with all speed!'

Sir Gawain looked round and saw a knight riding towards him across the meadow, fully armed. 'Who's that?' he asked. 'He's mounted on my horse, which that traitor stole this morning after I healed him of his wounds!'

'I wouldn't tell you if I thought it was good news!' said the girl. 'But since I'm sure it's not I shan't hide it from you: he's Greoreas's nephew! He's sent him after you, and I'll tell you why: Greoreas has commanded him to track you to your death and to take him back your head! That's why I advise you to climb aboard and flee, unless you want to die right here!'

'I certainly won't flee because of him, girl. I'll wait for him.'

'Well I shan't stop you!' said the girl. 'Oh, what a fine charge you'll make in front of all those beautiful girls at the windows! They'll love it, with you mounted on that mighty packhorse!'

'Whatever it may cost me, girl, I'm not going to shirk this. I want to win back my horse.'

And he turned his packhorse to face the knight who was spurring across the sandy riverbank. Sir Gawain prepared to meet him, and braced himself so firmly in the stirrups that he snapped the left one clean off; and the packhorse wouldn't move: for all his spurring he couldn't make it stir.

'Oh!' he cried. 'A packhorse is no mount for a knight when he wants to do battle!'

And the knight gave Gawain such a blow with his lance that it bent like a bow and snapped clean across, leaving the head in his shield. And Sir Gawain struck him above the boss, and with such force that it smashed through both shield and mail-coat and brought him crashing down in the fine sand. Sir Gawain reached out and seized his horse and leaped into the saddle. This adventure was so sweet to him that he had never felt happier in his life. He rode back to the girl who had climbed into the boat – but there was no sign either of the boat or of her. He had no idea what had become of them.

While he sat there thinking about the girl he saw a skiff coming from the castle, guided by a pilot. And when the pilot reached the bank he said: 'Sir, I bring you greetings from the girls at the windows yonder; and they send you word not to withhold my rightful possession.'

'God bless you and all that fair company,' Gawain replied. 'What is it you want from me?'

'I saw you topple a knight here whose horse I should rightfully have. Unless you mean to do me wrong you ought to hand the horse to me.'

And Gawain said: 'It would be a great hardship for me, my friend, to give up what you say is yours, for I'd have to continue on foot.'

'Shame upon you! Those girls will think you most disloyal now, refusing to return what is rightfully mine. Whenever a knight's been unhorsed on this bank I've always claimed his mount. And if I didn't get the horse I was given the knight.'

'I'll not refuse you the knight, my friend: you're welcome to him!'

'That's no gift!' said the pilot. 'I'd never be able to take him if he decided to defend himself! If you've got it in you, go and capture him and bring him to me; then you can keep what's rightfully mine.'

'Friend, if I dismount and go on foot, can I trust you to keep my horse in good faith?'

'Certainly,' he said. 'I'll keep him and return him faithfully, I swear it.'

So Gawain climbed from Gringalet and entrusted him to the pilot, and set out, sword drawn; but the knight had no need of further trouble, for he was badly wounded in the side and had lost a good deal of blood.

'It's no use pretending, sir,' he said, in great difficulty. 'I've such a grievous wound that I can do without receiving worse; I've lost a gallon of blood – I submit to your mercy.'

'Get up, then,' said Sir Gawain.

And the knight struggled up, and Gawain led him back to the pilot, who thanked him deeply. Then Gawain asked him to tell him about the girl he had led there, and where she had gone.

'Forget about her, sir,' the pilot replied. 'She's not a girl: she's worse than Satan! On this bank she's caused many a knight to be beheaded. Come now and accept such lodging as I can offer, for it's no good staying here on the riverbank: it's a wild place, and full of strange marvels.'

Sir Gawain did as the pilot advised. His horse was taken aboard, and he climbed in after, and they set out and sailed to the other bank. The pilot's house was close to the water, and was such that a count could have disembarked there: he had every comfort in that house. The pilot led his guest and his prisoner inside, and gave them the finest welcome that he could. Sir Gawain was served with everything befitting a worthy man: he dined on plover and pheasant and partridge and venison, and the wines were strong and clear, white and red, new and old. Sir Gawain's host and lodging that night were much to his liking: he deeply appreciated the pilot's hospitality.

Next morning he rose as soon as he saw day break, as was his custom, and the pilot rose likewise to look after his guest. They went together and leaned at the windows of a turret, and Sir Gawain gazed out over the countryside, which was beautiful indeed, and saw the forests and the plains and the castle on the cliff.

'Kind host,' he said, 'who is the lord of this land and the castle?'

But the pilot replied: 'I don't know, sir.'

'Truly? You astonish me: you're a retainer of the castle and it brings you a handsome living, yet you don't know who its lord is?'

'I promise you,' he said, 'I don't know and have never known.'

'Then tell me, who defends the castle?'

'It's very well guarded, sir: there are five hundred bows and crossbows always at the ready. If the castle were ever threatened they'd shoot ceaselessly and never tire, so ingeniously are they arranged. And I tell you this: there's a queen at the castle, a noble, rich and wise lady of the highest lineage. She came to live in this land with a great treasure of gold and silver, and built the mighty castle you see before you; and she brought with her a lady whom she dearly loves: she's her daughter, and a queen likewise. She, too, has a daughter, who does nothing to debase or shame her line, for I don't think there's a girl of fairer looks or manners beneath heaven. And the hall, let me tell you, is protected by magic and enchantment. In that great hall a clerk versed in astronomy has created unheard-of marvels; for no knight can enter there and live if there's any vice in him. No coward or traitor or perjurer can survive: all die there in an instant. But there are many squires from many lands serving at the castle as a training for arms – well over five hundred. And there are old ladies without husbands or lords: they've been wrongfully deprived of their lands and inheritance since their husbands died. And with the two queens are orphaned girls who are kept with great honour. All these people go about their lives at the castle, nursing a wild and impossible hope: they're waiting for a knight to come and support them, who'll restore the ladies to their lands, give husbands to the girls, and make the squires knights. But all the sea will turn to ice before they find a knight who can stay in that hall, for he'd have to be handsome and wise, worthy and bold, noble and loyal, and clean of all baseness and wickedness. If such a knight came he could be lord of the castle, and cast out the enchantments of the hall.'

This news enthralled Sir Gawain. 'Let's go down,' he said. 'Have my arms and my horse brought to me at once. I'm not dallying here – I want to go!'

'Where, sir? Oh, stay – God keep you – today and tomorrow and longer still!'

'Bless your house, good host, but that shall not be. I'm going to see the girls and the marvels of the hall!'

'No, sir! Please God, you'll not do such a foolish thing. Take my advice and stay.'

'Do you take me for a faint-hearted coward? God forsake my soul if I ever take such advice.'

'In faith, sir, I'll hold my tongue, for I can see I'll be wasting my breath. Go, since you want to go so earnestly – though it grieves me. But I'll guide you there – and I tell you, no escort could be more valuable to you than I.'

Then Gawain called for his horse and his arms again, and he armed and mounted and set off, the pilot leading him faithfully to where he did not wish him to go.

They rode on until, at the foot of the steps before the hall, they found a one-legged man sitting all alone on a bundle of straw. He had a false leg made of silver, inlaid here and there with gold and precious stones. His hands were not idle: he was holding a knife and was busy sharpening a stick of ash-wood. He did not address the two riding past him, and they said nothing to him. The pilot drew Sir Gawain to him and said: 'Sir, what do you make of that one-legged man?'

'His false leg's not made of poplar, that's certain,' said Sir Gawain. 'It looks beautiful.'

'Truly,' said the pilot, 'he's rich indeed, with great and handsome revenues. You'd hear news now that would distress you much if I weren't escorting you.'

They climbed up to the hall. One of the doors was of ivory, magnificently carved; the other was of ebony, and likewise sculpted on its face; and both of them shone with gold and jewels. The paving in the hall was of many colours: green and red, indigo and deep blue, finely worked and polished. And in the middle of the hall there stood a bed, and not one part of it was wooden: every bit of it was gold, except the cords on which the mattress sat, which were made of silver, and wherever they interlaced there hung a bell; and across it was spread a huge coverlet of samite; and on each of the bed-posts was mounted a garnet, which yielded more light than four brightly burning candles. The bed stood on grotesque carved dogs with grimacing cheeks, and the dogs were mounted on four casters, so smooth and swift that the bed could be sent from one end of the hall to the other at the push of a single finger. No bed like it was ever made for any king or any count. And there it stood in the middle of the hall. And all around the hall's marble walls were windows, four hundred closed and a hundred open, with glass so clear that anyone watching could see all who entered the hall as soon as they came through the door.

'Dear host,' said Gawain, 'I can't see anything here to make a man afraid! I'm going to sit on this bed and rest for a while: I've never seen one so luxurious.'

'Oh, good sir! If you go near that bed you'll die the most dreadful death that any knight has ever known! Turn back, sir – leave this castle – leave this land!'

'For all the world I shan't give up sitting on this bed and seeing the girls I saw from across the river!'

'There's no chance of your seeing them! Though, God save me, they can see you clearly at this very moment – through those windows: their chambers are on the other side.'

'Well if I can't see the girls I'll at least sit on the bed. Such a bed can have been made for one thing only: to have a worthy man or noble lady lie upon it. And – by my soul – I'm going to sit on it, whatever may befall me!'

The pilot saw there was no stopping him, and said nothing more; but he had no desire to stay and see him sit on the bed, and he took his leave, saying: 'Sir, your death upsets me deeply. No knight has ever sat upon that bed and left it alive, for it is the Bed of Marvels! May God have mercy on your soul!'

With that he left the hall. Sir Gawain, armed as he was, with his shield hung at his neck, sat down upon the bed. And the moment he did so, the bed-cords made a deafening din as all the bells began to ring until the whole hall resounded; then all the windows opened, and the marvels and enchantments were now uncovered and revealed, for down through the windows flew arrows and crossbow-bolts: more than seven hundred smashed into Sir Gawain's shield, and he didn't know what had hit him – the enchantment was such that no man could see where the bolts and arrows came from or the archers who had loosed them. Gawain would not have been there then for a thousand marks! The windows closed in an instant, without anybody's touch. Sir Gawain began to pull out the bolts embedded in his shield, and they had wounded him in several places and he was losing blood. But before he had drawn out all of them he was presented with another test: the bed suddenly began to career about the hall on its casters, smashing from wall to wall; and while Sir Gawain was busy clinging on, a door was kicked open, and a ravenous lion, ferociously strong and wondrously huge, leaped from a vault and in through the door and hurled itself at Gawain in a furious attack. Its claws ripped into his shield as though through wax; but Gawain wrestled free and drew his naked sword and dealt the beast such a blow that he cut off its head and its forefeet together. That very instant the bed stopped its mad careering and all was still. And Sir Gawain was jubilant, for the lion's feet were left hanging on his shield by the claws.

Having killed the beast he sat down on the bed again, and his host came running back into the hall, his face beaming, and said: 'You've nothing more to fear, sir, I promise you! Take off all your armour now, for you've cast out the enchantments of the hall for evermore, and you'll be served and honoured here by young and old – may God be praised!'

Then a stream of squires appeared, dressed in the finest tunics, and they all went down on their knees and said: 'Good sir, we offer you our services: we've longed for your coming!'

Then they began to disarm him, while others went to stable his horse. And while he was being disarmed a most beautiful girl entered, with a circlet of gold upon her head, and her hair was as bright as the gold or brighter. Her face was white, and illumined by Nature with a pure red hue. She was lithe and fair, with a comely figure and a tall, fine bearing; and behind her came other girls, all of considerable beauty. Sir Gawain gazed in wonder, and rose to meet them, saying: 'Welcome, young ladies!'

The first of them bowed to him and said: 'Good sir, my lady the queen sends you greetings, and commands all her people to acknowledge you as their right-ful lord. I shall be the first to offer you my service in all faithfulness, and these girls here all hold you as their lord and have long desired your coming. They're overjoyed to see you, the finest of all worthy men.'

And with that they all knelt before him, vowing to serve and honour him. Then the girl said: 'My lady sends you this gown to don before she sees you, for she thinks you'll have suffered great toil and hardship. So put it on and see if it fits you: wise men guard against the cold after being hot, for it endangers and benumbs the blood.'

And Sir Gawain replied, like the most courteous knight in the world: 'May that Lord in whom no good thing is lacking guard my lady the queen – and guard you, too, for speaking so kindly and being so courteous and fair. Give her my deepest thanks.'

'I shall, sir,' said the girl, 'most willingly. In the meantime put on this gown and enjoy the view from the windows; or if you like, climb the tower and look at the forests and meadows and rivers until I return.'

With that the girls turned away; and Sir Gawain donned the gown, which was rich indeed, all lined with ermine, and set off with his host to survey the land. They climbed a spiral staircase at the side of the vaulted hall, until they reached the top of the tower and saw the country all around, fairer than any man could describe. Sir Gawain gazed at the river and the meadowlands and the forests, teeming with game, and turned to his host and said: 'By God, I'd love to live here and go hunting in those forests!'

'Sir,' said the pilot, 'you'd better say no more of that. For it was decreed that whoever came to be lord and protector here would never be able to leave this house. So it's no good talking of hunting, for this is where you stay: you'll never leave here again.'

'Silence, host!' he cried. 'You'll drive me out of my mind! I tell you, if I couldn't go out when I wanted I could no more live here for seven days than for seven score years!'

And with that he came down from the tower and back into the hall. Lost in anger and vexation, he sat down on the bed again, crestfallen, until the girl who had been there earlier returned. When Sir Gawain saw her he rose to meet her, angry as he was, and greeted her. She saw that his countenance had changed, and realised that something had disturbed him. But she did not dare refer to it; instead she said:

'Sir, whenever you wish my lady will come and see you. And dinner is ready now, and you may eat.'

Sir Gawain replied: 'I've no wish for food. A curse upon my body if I eat or make merry before I hear news I badly need.'

The girl returned at once in consternation, and the queen summoned her and asked her for news, saying: 'Dear granddaughter, how did you find the good lord whom God has sent us?'

'Oh, my lady, honoured queen, I'm dying of grief for the good, kind-hearted lord; for the only words he'll utter are of anger and rage. When I first saw him I found him so polite and fair of speech that one could never tire of listening to his words or gazing at his joyful face. Now suddenly he's changed and would gladly be dead, I think.'

'Don't worry, granddaughter. He'll soon calm down when he sees me. However great his rage may be, I'll cast it out and set joy in its place.'

So saying, the queen came to the hall, accompanied by the other queen, her daughter, who was only too pleased to go; and with them they took a good 250 girls and at least as many squires. As soon as Sir Gawain saw her coming, holding her daughter by the hand, his heart told him that she was the queen, guessing with ease by her white tresses which hung down to her hips, and by the white mottled silk she wore, finely embroidered with golden flowers. He was not slow to go and meet her, and he greeted her, and she him. And she said:

'I am lady of this palace, sir, second to you. I yield the lordship to you, for you've well deserved it. But are you of King Arthur's household?'

'Yes indeed, lady.'

'And are you one of the Round Table, who are the most esteemed in all the world?'

'Lady,' he said, 'I wouldn't dare to say I'm one of the most esteemed; I don't consider myself one of the finest, nor do I think I'm one of the worst.'

'That is a most courteous reply, good sir. But tell me now of King Lot: how many sons did he have by his wife?'

'Four, my lady.'

'Tell me their names.'

'Gawain was the eldest, lady, and the next was Engrevain, the proud one with strong hands; the other two are named Gaheriet and Guerrehet.'

And the queen said: 'Those were indeed their names. I would to God they were all together here with us! But tell me now, do you know King Urien?'

'Yes, lady.'

'Has he a son at court?'

'Yes, lady, he has two, of great renown: one of them is named Sir Yvain, the courteous and polite. I'm happier all day if I see him in the morning, for I find him so wise and generous. The other is also called Yvain, but he's not his full brother: that's why he's called the Bastard. He outfights any knight who does battle with him. They're both at court, and are most worthy, wise and courteous knights.'

'And King Arthur, good sir,' she said, 'how is he faring now?'

'Better than ever: in finer health and spirits, and stronger.'

'In faith, sir, that's as it should be, for King Arthur is a child: why, he's surely no more than a hundred years old – no, he can't be. But I'd like you to tell me just one thing more, if you will: how is the queen, how is she faring?'

'Truly, lady, she's so courteous and beautiful and wise that God never made so fair a lady. There has never been a lady of such renown since God made the first woman from Adam's rib. And she's justly renowned: all goodness stems and passes down from her. No man does any good or honourable deed who hasn't learned it from my lady. No man, however unhappy, leaves her with his grief intact.'

'Nor will you, sir, leave *me* so.'

'I believe you, lady,' he said, 'for before I saw you I didn't care what happened to me, such was my despair and grief. But now I'm as happy as I could ever be.'

'In the name of God who gave me life,' said the queen with the white tresses, 'your happiness will double yet, and your joy will increase constantly and never fail. And since you're now at ease and happy, dinner is ready, and you may eat whenever you wish and wherever you like.'

'Lady, has any knight dined here in this hall before?'

'No, sir, none that ever left again or stayed alive so much as half an hour.'

'Then I shall dine here, my lady, by your leave.'

'I grant you that, sir, willingly. You shall be the first knight who has ever dined here.'

With that the queen departed, leaving 250 of her most beautiful girls with him. They dined there with him in the hall, and served him and ensured his comfort, providing for his every wish. And squires served him joyfully at dinner; two knelt before him, one of them cutting meat for him and the other pouring wine. Sir Gawain seated his host at his side. And the dinner was not short: it was deep black night and many great torches were burning before the meal was over. There was lively conversation all the while, and afterwards much dancing before they took to their beds, as they rejoiced with all their hearts for their lord whom they dearly loved.

And when he decided to retire he lay down on the Bed of Marvels. Beneath his head one of the girls placed a pillow, which made him sleep most peacefully.

* * *

When the time came to wake next morning, a gown of ermine and samite had been prepared for him, and the pilot came and roused him, and arranged his dressing and washed his hands. And Clarissant was there, too, the fair, honourable, wise and courteous granddaughter of the queen. And when she went into her grandmother's chambers, the queen asked her: 'Has your lord risen yet?'

'Yes, lady,' she said, 'some while ago.'

'Where is he, dear granddaughter?'

'He went to the tower, my lady; I don't know if he's come down yet.'

'Granddaughter, I shall go to him; and if it please God, he shall have only joy and happiness today.'

With that the queen rose, anxious to go and see Gawain, and she and her daughter found him high up at the windows of a tower, watching a girl and a fully armed knight riding across a meadow. The two queens came, side by side, to where Sir Gawain was standing with his host.

'Sir,' said the queens together, 'a happy rising. May that glorious Father who made His daughter His mother grant you a good day.'

'May the one who sent His son to Earth grant you joy, lady. But come to this window if you will, and tell me who that girl can be who's riding this way: there's a knight with her, carrying a quartered shield.'

The lady, looking down at them, said: 'It's the one who accompanied you here last night – may an evil fire consume her! But don't concern yourself with her – she's an arrogant and wicked woman. And forget about the knight she's brought with her. He doesn't fight for amusement's sake: I've seen him kill many knights at this landing-place.'

'Lady,' said Sir Gawain, 'I wish to go and speak to the girl, by your leave.'

'No, sir! Leave her to her own affairs – she's a terrible girl! Please God, you'll never leave this hall for such a pointless cause. And you must never leave here at all, unless you wish to do us wrong.'

'Oh, come now! That distresses me! I'd think myself ill-rewarded if I could never leave. God keep me from being a prisoner here!'

'Lady,' said the pilot, 'let him do as he wishes. Don't hold him back against his will or he might die of grief.'

'Then I'll let him go,' said the queen, 'on condition that, if God guards him from death, he'll return here tonight.'

'Have no fear, lady,' said Gawain. 'I'll return if I can. But I beg a favour of you: please don't ask my name until seven days have passed.'

'If that's your wish, sir, I'll refrain from asking,' said the queen, 'though if you hadn't forbidden it, your name would have been the first thing I'd have asked you.'

And so they came down from the tower, and squires came running to arm him. Then they fetched his horse and he mounted, fully armed, and rode down to the landing-place accompanied by the pilot, and they both climbed into the boat. Oarsmen rowed them from the bank and across to the other side, and Sir Gawain stepped forth.

The other knight said to the pitiless girl: 'Tell me, my dear, this knight coming towards us – do you know him?'

'No,' the girl replied, 'but I know he's the one who brought me here last night.'

'God save me,' he said, 'he's the very man I've been looking for! I was afraid he'd escaped me, for no knight crosses the border of Galvoie to boast that he's passed through this land!'

Thereupon the knight, without a challenge, set his shield on his arm, thrust in his spurs and charged. And Sir Gawain headed for him and struck him such a blow that he wounded him gravely in the arm and side; but it was not a mortal wound, for his mail-coat held together so well that the lance-head could not fully break through; but a finger's length of the tip pierced his body and bore him to the ground. He climbed to his feet and saw, to his dismay, the blood flowing down his hauberk. He attacked Sir Gawain with his sword, but he was soon so tired that he could hold out no longer and had to cry for mercy. Sir Gawain received his assurances, and then handed him to the waiting pilot.

Meanwhile the evil girl had climbed from her palfrey. Gawain came up to her and greeted her, and said: 'Remount, dear friend, for I'm not going to leave you here. You're coming with me across the river.'

'Oh, knight!' she cried. 'How high and mighty you are now! You'd have had a battle on your hands if he hadn't been tired by old wounds of his. He'd have put an end to your lies and silenced your prattling tongue. Have you ever been checkmated in the corner of the board? That's how silent you'd have been! Do you really think you're of greater worth than he? The best man doesn't always win! But listen: if you left this landing-place and came with me beneath that tree, and did something that he did for me when I desired, then I'd admit you were his equal, and wouldn't despise you any more.'

'If it's only that far, girl,' he said, 'I've no reason to refuse your wish.'

And she whispered: 'God grant you never return from there.'

And with that they set off, she in front and he behind. And the girls and ladies in the hall tore their hair and rent their gowns in dismay, crying: 'Oh, alas! Alas! Why do we not die, when we see our lord going to his death? That evil girl goes at his right hand, leading him to the place from where no knight returns! Alas! We're accursed just when we thought our luck was blessed!'

The girl and Sir Gawain arrived at the tree.

'Tell me now,' he said, 'have I done my duty, or do you want me to do something more? I'll do it if I can, rather than lose your favour.'

And she replied: 'Do you see that ford, where the banks are so high? My love used to cross there, and I don't know any lower spot.'

'Dear girl, that's impossible; the bank's too high at every point.'

'You're afraid!' cried the girl. 'I didn't think you'd have the heart to try, for this is the Perilous Ford, which no-one dares cross on any account, unless he's exceptional.'

Sir Gawain instantly rode his horse to the bank. He saw the deep water below and the sheer bank beyond; but the river was narrow enough, and Sir Gawain felt Gringalet had cleared many greater ditches; and he had often heard that whoever could cross the deep water of the Perilous Ford would be renowned as the finest knight in the world. So he drew his horse away from the river and came galloping back to leap across; but he failed, for he didn't take the jump well, and came down in the middle of the ford. But Gringalet swam on until he got all four hooves on land, and gathering himself for a mighty leap he launched himself on to the great, high bank. Once there, he stood stock still, unable to go another step, and Sir Gawain dismounted of necessity, for he saw that Gringalet was exhausted. He decided to take off his saddle, and turned it upside down to dry. Then he removed the saddle-cloth and wiped the water from Gringalet's back and flanks and legs.

After a good rest he put the saddle on again and mounted once more, and rode on at a walk until he caught sight of a knight out hunting with a sparrowhawk; and in the field before him were two small retrievers. The knight was more handsome than any tongue could tell. Sir Gawain rode up and greeted him and said:

'Good sir, may God who made you fairer than any living man give you joy and good fortune.'

And the knight was quick to reply: 'You are the fair one, sir, and good and worthy. But tell me, how did you come to leave the evil girl alone over there? What happened to her companion?'

'Sir,' replied Sir Gawain, 'a knight with a quartered shield was with her when I met her, but I defeated him in combat.'

'And what became of him then?'

'The pilot took him away, for he said he should be his prisoner.'

'True enough. That girl was once my love, but she would never deign to call me her sweetheart. And I promise you, I never kissed her except by force, and never had my way with her for I loved her against her will. I had robbed her of a love of hers whose company she used to share; I killed him and led her off and strove in every way to serve her. But my service was fruitless, for she sought the chance to leave me as soon as she could, and took for her love the knight you've just vanquished. And he's no joke, that knight! Today you've done something that no knight has ever dared do; and your valour has made you the finest and most praised knight in the world. It took the greatest courage to leap into the Perilous Ford, and I tell you truly, no knight has ever come through it before.'

'Then the girl lied to me, sir,' said Sir Gawain. 'She said her sweetheart crossed it every day out of love for her.'

'She told you that? She must be possessed by a host of demons! That devil – God confound her! – meant to drown you in the deep and roaring water. But promise me something now: that you'll tell me truthfully all I wish to know, and in return I'll promise to tell you the truth about anything you ask me.'

They exchanged these promises, and Sir Gawain was the first to start questioning, saying: 'Tell me about the city I can see over there: who does it belong to, and what's it called?'

'I can certainly tell you that, friend, for it belongs to me entirely: I owe no part of it to any man born – I'm vassal to God alone. It's called Orqueneseles.'

'And what's your name?'

'Guiromelant.'

'I've often heard that you're most worthy and valiant, and lord of a very great land. And what's the name of the girl of whom no-one has a good word to say?'

'I can assure you, sir, she's greatly to be feared, for she's full of scorn and evil. That's why she's called the Haughty Maiden of Nogres – her birthplace.'

'And who is her love who's gone to be the pilot's prisoner?'

'He's an extraordinary knight, and he's known as the Proud Knight of the Narrow Pass; he guards the border of Galvoie.'

'And what's the name of the handsome castle where I ate and drank last night?'

At that Guiromelant turned his back in sorrow and began to move away. But Sir Gawain reminded him: 'Sir, sir, remember our promise and tell me.'

Guiromelant stopped and turned his head, and said: 'Be gone; I declare you free of your promise, and you absolve me of mine. I'd planned to ask you news from there, but it seems you know as much about that castle as you do about the moon.'

'I stayed there last night,' said Gawain, 'and lay upon the Bed of Marvels. There's none like it in the world; no man has ever seen its equal.'

'By God,' he replied, 'it's great fun listening to your fantasies: like being entertained by a storyteller! I see it now – you're a minstrel! Why, I thought you were a knight and had done some feat of prowess yonder! Come now, tell me truly: what did you see at the castle?'

And Sir Gawain told him: 'Sir, the moment I sat upon the bed there was a great commotion in the hall. Without a word of a lie, the bed-cords groaned and the bells upon them rang, and closed windows opened by themselves and crossbow-bolts and smooth arrows smashed into my shield. And in it were stuck the claws of a huge, bristling lion that had been chained in a vault: it leaped at me and struck at my shield and plunged in its claws so hard that it couldn't pull them free. If you doubt my words, look: the claws are still hanging here! I cut off its head, thanks be to God, and its feet, too. What do you think of these marks of proof?'

With that, Guiromelant jumped from his horse and went down on his knees and clasped his hands together, and begged Gawain to forgive his foolish words.

'I forgive you,' he said. 'Remount now.'

And Guiromelant did so, filled with shame for his foolishness, and said: 'God save me, sir, I didn't think any knight would ever have the honour that's befallen you. But tell me, did you see the white-haired queen? Did you ask her who she was and where she was from?'

'I never thought to ask her that,' he replied, 'but I saw her and spoke to her.'

'Then I'll tell you,' said Guiromelant. 'She's King Arthur's mother.'

'By God and His power, King Arthur's not had a mother for sixty years or more!'

'But it's true, sir: she's his mother. When his father Uther Pendragon was buried Queen Ygerne came to this country, bringing all her treasure, and built that castle on the rock with its rich and beautiful hall. You doubtless saw the other lady, too, the other queen.'

'Indeed I did,' said Sir Gawain.

'She was the wife of King Lot and the mother of the one whom I wish every misfortune.'

'Who's that, sir?'

'Sir Gawain.'

'Indeed? I know Gawain well, and I've heard he's not had a mother for at least twenty years.'

'But she's his mother, you may be sure. And when she came here she was with child; the child was the noble and beautiful girl who is my love and, sad to say, the sister of Gawain – may God bring him the deepest shame! I swear he wouldn't escape with his head if he was within my reach as you are now: I'd behead him on the spot! And his sister herself couldn't stop me tearing his heart from his chest with my bare hands – I hate him so much!'

'Upon my soul,' said Sir Gawain, 'if I loved a girl, then for her sake I'd love and serve all her family.'

'You're right, but when I remember how Gawain's father killed mine, I can't feel any goodwill towards him; and Gawain himself killed one of my closest cousins, a valiant and worthy knight, and I've never had the chance to take revenge. But do this favour for me now: return to the castle and take this ring to my love and present it to her as a gift from me; and tell her I believe her love for me is such that she'd rather her brother Gawain died a foul death than that I should hurt my smallest toe! Send my love my greetings and give her this ring from me, her sweetheart.' Sir Gawain set the ring on his little finger, and Guiromelant said: 'In return I'll tell you the name of that castle, as you asked: it's called the Rock of Canguin. Do you wish to ask me anything else?'

'No, sir, only that I may leave.'

Then Guiromelant said: 'Before you go, sir, tell me your name if you don't mind.'

And Sir Gawain said: 'Before God, my name shall never be kept from you. I am the one you hate so much. I am Gawain.'

'You are Gawain?'

'Yes, truly, the nephew of King Arthur.'

'Then you're very brave or very foolish to tell me your name when you know I hate you mortally! If only I had my helmet and shield! If I were armed as you are I'd cut your head off instantly – nothing would stop me! But if you dare to wait for me I'll fetch my arms and return to do battle with you, and bring three or four men to watch our combat. Or if you wish, we'll wait for seven days, and on the seventh we'll return here fully armed; and you will summon the king and the queen and all their people, and I shall assemble all the knights from my kingdom. Then our battle won't be fought in secret: all who come will witness it. For a battle between such worthy men as we are deemed to be shouldn't be fought without witnesses; it's only right that ladies and knights should be present, for when one of us is vanquished and everybody knows of it, the victor will have a thousand times more honour than if he alone knew.'

'Sir,' said Sir Gawain, 'I'd gladly do without all this. If I've done you any wrong I'll willingly make amends acceptable both to your friends and mine, so that all is just and fair.'

But Guiromelant said: 'I can't think what justice there can be if you won't do battle with me! I've suggested two courses of action; now choose which one you like: either wait for me here, if you dare, while I go and fetch my arms, or summon all the people of your land to come here in seven days. At Pentecost

King Arthur will be holding court at Orquenie, I'm told, which is only two days' ride from here.'

And Sir Gawain replied: 'Then God save me, I swear by this hand that I'll send him word before I sleep a wink.'

'Gawain,' he said, 'I'm going to take you to the finest bridge in the world. This river's very deep and swift, and no man alive could cross it or jump to the other bank.'

But Sir Gawain replied: 'I'm not going to seek any bridge, for the treacherous girl will think it cowardice. No, I'll keep my promise to her and go straight across.'

Without another word he thrust in his spurs and his horse leaped nimbly across the water; and when the girl who had so misled him saw him coming, she tethered her horse to the tree and came towards him on foot. And her heart and will had now changed, for she greeted him in all humility, and said that she had come to plead for mercy, admitting her guilt, for she knew she had made him suffer greatly.

'Good sir,' she said, 'listen now, and I'll tell you why I've been so haughty towards all the knights who've come to share my company. That knight – God damn him! – who was talking to you on the other bank, he ill-bestowed his love on me: I hated him – he'd caused me great pain by killing the knight I adored. Then he thought to woo me; but his efforts were vain, for at the first opportunity I escaped from him and joined company with the one from whom you took me today. Losing him doesn't bother me at all, but ever since death took my first love from me I've been mad and spoken haughtily and acted wickedly; I didn't care who I crossed – I tormented them deliberately, because I wanted to find one whose temper was such that I could drive him and anger him into cutting me to pieces, for I've yearned for death for a long time. Mete out justice now, sir; such justice that no girl who ever hears of me will dare speak shamefully to a knight again!'

'Dear girl,' said Sir Gawain, 'why should I punish you? God forbid that you suffer any harm from me. Mount now, without delay, and we'll go back to the castle. The boatman's at the landing-place, waiting to ferry us across.'

'I'll do exactly as you wish, sir,' said the girl.

Then she climbed into the saddle of her little palfrey with its long mane; and they rode down to the pilot, who ferried them across the river without the slightest trouble.

The ladies and girls, who had been lamenting bitterly for him, saw them coming. All the squires at the hall, too, had been out of their minds with grief. But now their rejoicing was the greatest ever seen. The queen was awaiting him outside the hall, and had commanded all the girls to take each other by the hand and to dance and celebrate. And so they began their rejoicing to greet Sir Gawain, singing and dancing all around, and he came and dismounted in their midst. The ladies and girls and both the queens embraced him joyfully, and the girl he had brought was greeted with joy, as well: everyone served her willingly – but for his sake, not for hers. They went then to the hall and all sat down. Sir

Gawain took his sister and seated her beside him on the Bed of Marvels, and whispered to her softly:

'I bring you a golden ring from across the river, mounted with a brilliant green emerald. A knight sends it to you as a love-token.'

'I believe it, sir,' she said. 'But if I love him at all it's from a distance, for he's never seen me, nor I him, except from across the river.'

'Oh! He's boasting that you'd rather your brother Sir Gawain were dead than that he had hurt his toe!'

'What! How could he say such a foolish thing? My brother doesn't even know I'm born, and has never seen me. Guiromelant's quite wrong: by my soul, I wouldn't have my brother harmed, any more than myself.'

While they were talking together, the aged queen said to the other queen, her daughter, who was seated beside her: 'What do you make of the lord sitting next to my granddaughter? He's been whispering to her for a long while; and I'm delighted, as we both should be: it's a mark of great nobility that he's drawn to the fairest and wisest in the hall! I wish to God he'd married her, and that she was as pleasing to him as Lavinia to Aeneas!'

'Oh, lady,' said the other queen, 'may God so incline his heart that they may be like brother and sister; that he may love her so dearly, and she him, that they may be as one flesh.'

The lady meant by her prayer that Gawain should love her and take her for his wife; she had not recognised her son.

Sir Gawain spoke with his beautiful sister for a long time; then he called to the boy who seemed the brightest and most able of all the squires in the hall, and went down to a chamber, taking only the boy with him. There Sir Gawain said to him: 'I'm going to tell you a secret, and I advise you to keep it: you'll profit greatly if you do. I'm going to send you to a place where you'll be received with joy.'

'Sir, my tongue will be torn from my throat before a single word you want hidden escapes my lips.'

'Then, brother,' said Sir Gawain, 'you're to go to my lord King Arthur – for I'm his nephew, Gawain. The way is neither long nor hard, for the king has established court for Pentecost at the city of Orquenie. When you come before the king you'll find him in low spirits; but when you give him my greetings he and all the court will be filled with joy. You're to tell the king that, since he's my lord and I'm his vassal, he mustn't fail to appear before me in the meadow below this castle on the fifth day of the feast of Pentecost. And he's to bring all the company that has gathered at his court, nobility and common folk alike, for I'm committed to battle with a knight, Guiromelant, who hates me mortally. You're to tell the queen, too, that she must come for my sake, and bring all the girls and ladies who are at court that day. But one thing worries me: have you a good hunting-horse to take you there swiftly?'

The boy replied that there was a fine one, sturdy, fast and strong, that he could take for his use.

'Excellent!' said Sir Gawain.

The boy took him quickly down to the stables and led out some strong, well-rested hunting-horses, one of which was ready to ride and travel, for he had had it newly shod, and it lacked neither saddle nor bridle.

'Go now, boy,' said Sir Gawain, 'and may the lord of all kings be your guide.'

So he sent the boy on his way, and led him down to the river where he told the pilot to ferry him across, and the boy was soon on the right road for the city of Orquenie.

Sir Gawain now returned to the hall, where he spent the night in great joy and pleasure, for everyone loved and served him. The queen had baths of hot water prepared in five hundred vats, and bade all the squires go in to wash and bathe. New robes were ready when they left the baths: the cloth was woven with golden thread and the lining was of ermine. The squires stayed in the chapel until after matins, standing all the while, never kneeling. And in the morning Sir Gawain, with his own hands, fastened the right spur on each of them and girded their swords and dubbed them. He was now accompanied by fully five hundred new knights.

Meanwhile the boy had reached the city of Orquenie, where the king was holding a court befitting such a high feast-day. Those who watched him gallop through the streets, the crippled and the sick, said: 'He's come on urgent business! He must have brought some message to the court from afar. Whatever his news may be, he'll find the king deaf and dumb – he's so full of grief and anguish, having lost the one who defended us all and brought us so much good.'

Throughout the city the poor people were lamenting thus for Sir Gawain whom they dearly loved.

The boy found the king seated in his hall, with a hundred counts and a hundred kings and a hundred dukes seated around him. The king was deep in mournful thought, seeing the great host of nobility but no sign of his nephew; and such was his distress that, at the very moment the boy arrived, he fainted and fell. The first to reach him and help him to his feet was certainly not idle, for everyone rushed to his aid. The lady Lores was sitting in a gallery, and saw the alarm that had stricken the hall. She hurried down from the gallery and ran to the queen who, seeing her troubled face, asked her what was wrong.

'Oh, noble queen! I've just seen a messenger arrive, and the king has never been so dismayed by a message! All his men are grieving equally: he must have brought some news that's upset all the court. The king has fainted!'

The queen turned pale; and her ladies and girls lamented loudly, tearing at their dresses and their hair: no man ever saw such bitter grieving.

But in the hall the king had recovered from his faint, and the boy came up to him and said: 'God bless you, sire, and all your good company. I bring you such greetings as befit a king from your nephew, Gawain.'

And hearing this, King Arthur leaped to his feet; the news was such a joy to him that he took the boy in his arms and swept him from his hunting-horse.

'Friend,' he said, 'may God guard and aid my dear nephew Gawain! I love him no less than myself. Tell me, how is he? Is he in good health and spirits?'

'I left him well and happy, sire, in a castle he's conquered: there's none more splendid in all the world. And he summons you, as his uncle and his lord, to aid him. He's accepted a challenge to single combat, and he begs you to come without fail and guard him against treachery. He wants to rebut Guiromelant's boast that he'll dishonour him. I tell you truly, neither you nor Gawain has a more mortal enemy.'

Never was a grieving court so soon restored to joy. Everyone's heart, without exception, exulted at the news, knowing that the one held to be the most courteous of the age, unsurpassed by count or king, the most great-hearted, most valiant and the finest at arms, was alive. Harps sang and hurdy-gurdies churned and the whole hall rang with music. No man could describe the sweet melodies they made.

Lady Ysave of Carahet heard the rejoicing in the hall, and from the gallery where she was sitting she ran straight to the queen and said: 'My lady, I think we're about to hear *good* news! The king has greeted the messenger with joy; it's a most reassuring sign!'

The queen left in such a hurry that she didn't think to don a mantle. She ran to the hall and hurried in, with all the ladies and maids rushing after her and entering the hall in disarray. The king leaned towards the boy and said: 'Go to the queen quickly, friend, and tell her the news that's delighted me.'

The boy went to her without more ado and said: 'May God who dwells above and sets the good at His right hand protect you and your dear company, lady: so Sir Gawain wishes.'

The fair-faced queen replied: 'God save you and give him joy and happiness! Is he safe and in good health?'

'Yes, lady, and full of joy. And as your dear friend he bids you go to his aid by the faith you owe him, with all the girls and maids and ladies who have come to this court.'

'My lords,' said Kay the seneschal, 'we should all thank God that Sir Gawain is alive; we were more dejected at his absence than joyful at the presence of the rest! It's true what they say: no-one knows what a worthy man is worth until he's gone! There were a good thirty thousand of us grieving and downcast, but God has brought light and day to us, now that the one who's full of courtliness is alive and well.'

With that he ordered that two trumpets be sounded, and water was brought in basins of fine gold and bright silver, and everyone in the hall sat down to dine. Never has such a splendid feast lasted a shorter time or been received with such joy: their love for Gawain drove them to finish their feast with speed. And then you'd have seen so many mules and chargers and palfreys saddled! Everyone was terrified of not being packed in time. King Arthur mounted and rode from the city with fully thirty thousand knights and fifteen thousand ladies and girls and maids: no man has ever seen such an army raised as rode that day from Orquenie. The baggage-train was of an astounding length: the line stretched out across the plains, and those at the rear had to camp a league from the place where the foremost lodged, in a meadow beside a river.

They set out again early the next day; and the boy led them through forests and fair open land, with plenty of feasting all the way, straight to the castle where Sir Gawain now was lord. The king reached there on the seventh day, and the boy came to him and said: 'There is the castle, sire, that your good nephew has won.'

The king dismounted, and ordered all to pitch their tents and pavilions. And the Welshmen among them, most skilled in the craft, built a great number of lodges in the Welsh manner, of interwoven branches; and they made shelters for their horses, too, by taking boughs from the forest and stripping off their leaves. Yvain, King Urien's son, and Gifflet, the son of Do, arrived escorting the queen. And in their company, which was well endowed with ladies, came three thousand knights, and none of them lacked a fine warhorse; and behind them came the huge convoy of wagons – none so great was ever seen. The queen dismounted at her tent, already pitched for her.

Meanwhile, from the upper chambers of the castle hall, Queen Ygerne saw the great host stretching all along the meadow. She was terrified at the sight, and her heart was faint and trembling. She took her daughter by the hand and said:

'Norcadet, we've lived a long while, and now our time has come, for we're besieged! I've never seen so many men amassed, so many shining helmets and shimmering shields. Look at all the swords and lances! And are they ladies or fairies down there on the riverbank?'

'God help me, I don't know, dear lady. But I've never seen girls or ladies in such a throng, and leading an army and going off to war!'

Just then Sir Gawain and his sister Clarissant came from a chamber, and as soon as she saw him Ygerne rushed to him and said: 'Dear friend, look at the mighty army besieging us, all along the meadows! And look – on that side there are only girls and ladies! Sir, you asked a favour of me: that I shouldn't ask your name for seven days, or enquire about your lineage. I refrained completely, but now the seventh day has passed, and I'd like to know your name.'

'I shall indeed tell you, lady, for I've never hidden my name from anyone. It is Gawain.'

She embraced him on the instant, and smothered his lips and face with kisses. And her daughter was beside herself, her heart leaping and soaring for joy, such joy as had kept her wide awake on the day she gave him birth, and she kissed his face and breast.

'My good, dear friend,' said Queen Ygerne, 'by the faith I owe almighty God, I am the mother of King Arthur, and this is my daughter: she is your mother.'

But when Gawain's sister Clarissant, standing there beside him, heard this, she rushed to her chamber and began to grieve desperately – because her brother knew all about her love for Guiromelant, the very one who had challenged him to battle.

'Gawain, dear grandson,' said Queen Ygerne, 'you can see our plight: they're besieging us without a doubt. For the love of God, what are we to do?'

'My lady, there's no danger. That's King Arthur, your son!'

'Is that true?'

'Yes, lady. Have no fear.'

'I can't wait to see him! I've never been so happy in my life!'

And Gawain said: 'By your leave, my lady, I'd like to cross the river and speak to him.'

She could not stop kissing him. He had many a willing kiss from his grandmother and his mother alike; then he left the ladies and mounted a swift horse, and took ten worthy and able knights with him across the river.

Kay was the very first to see him, as he came from the tent of King Do. He galloped with all his might to King Arthur's pavilion and joyfully announced: 'Here comes your nephew, sire!'

Without a word the king mounted a palfrey, in too much haste to wait for another horse, and rode to meet his nephew with all the speed his mount could summon. And as soon as he reached him he kissed him twenty times before he had said a word.

'Great joy awaits you, sire,' Gawain said at last, 'for your mother is longing to see you and speak to you.'

The king smiled at the knights and then said: 'My dear nephew, by the faith I owe my father's soul, I haven't had a mother for fifty years!'

'With respect, sire, yes, you have – I can say so in all truthfulness. When Uther Pendragon died, Ygerne fled with a great treasure, seeking the loneliest land there was, until she found this place. And with the great wealth she'd brought she had this castle built and made it her home. I know of none finer. And when my father King Lot lost his life, my mother – your sister – came to this castle and lived with her mother and yours, relinquishing all our land. She was left with child, and bore a daughter who's there in the castle – a beautiful, comely and most worthy girl.'

The king and all those present were overjoyed at this astounding news. And the queen kissed Gawain sweetly, as did a hundred other ladies and girls of worth. And as for King Arthur's mother, up in the castle hall, listen now to what she did that night.

With her in the castle she had five hundred newly dubbed knights, all of high lineage, of excellent families, and wise. She gave orders that all their arms – which were wonderful, smothered with precious stones – should be placed at all the windows of the chambers and the hall and on the battlements, so that the jewels, truly, shed as brilliant a light on King Arthur's host as if it had been noon. They were astounded by the light, and thought a spell had been cast on them; and the king was stricken silent, thinking he had been bewitched, and greatly fearing that Gawain had been tricked by sorcery. But Gawain managed to convince the king that he should go with four companions, secretly summoned, and take Queen Guinevere and just three of her maids; and they slipped down to the river, passed across, and hurried on to the castle. And Queen Ygerne, her head crowned with flowers, received her son King Arthur with indescribable joy, and welcomed the gracious Queen Guinevere, too, with the greatest happiness.

The mood was different in the king's camp. No sooner had the king gone than Kay the seneschal arrived with three others for private consultation with his lord, and when they found the king missing from his tent they were horrified. As for the girls and the ladies and maids, they went to look for the queen in her pavilion and were filled with dismay. The whole host was in turmoil – they had never been so distraught: all the men were grieving for their lord and all the women for their lost lady. Such was their despair that, if day had been approaching rather than night, they would certainly have fled in consternation and disarray. They all armed rapidly, donning their mail-coats. The army kept guard earnestly that night, for fear of being taken by surprise.

As soon as day broke King Arthur heard mass, and then rode back to his army with the five hundred newly dubbed knights of the castle; and he brought with him fifty beautiful ladies and girls. The whole host were amazed when they saw their lord King Arthur coming. If he had arrived a moment later they would all have been striking camp and setting fire to the lodges, but they were so overjoyed at seeing him return that all such plans were forgotten. He dismounted at his pavilion, and the queen at hers with many gracious ladies. Then Sir Gawain told the king exactly why he had summoned him: how he had agreed to do battle, and that it was due to be fought that day. Then he made confession to one bishop Solomon, who addressed many good words to him, giving him kind instruction. Sir Gawain humbly confessed all his sins; and when the holy man heard them, and saw that he repented from the heart, he gave him absolution in the name of God and Holy Mary. Then he blessed him with the sign of the Cross, and told him to have complete faith in God; now that he was truly confessed he had nothing to fear, for God would always protect him when he called on Him with a good heart.

With that their talking ceased. And thereupon there was no fine charger anywhere in the king's host that was not brought and presented to Gawain. And he could boast likewise that there was no fine sword, helmet or lance in the entire army that was not offered to him. He would not change his arms for anyone's, but he did take one of the horses: he was called Guilodien, and there was no finer, bolder horse in all this earthly world; his dappled coat was so sleek and fine that they did not add a saddle-cloth. They clad Sir Gawain in his armour splendidly, with a smooth padded doublet of cotton beneath, and equipped him with all the arms he would need both for attack and for defence: everything was perfect – he needed nothing more or less. Gifflet and Yvain, who loved him dearly, armed him with great skill.

As soon as he was ready Sir Gawain looked towards the Perilous Ford and saw a great company of knights emerge from behind a hill: they numbered a good three thousand. First he caught sight of the heads of their lances, and then he saw their pennons and banners; then their shining helms and dazzling shields, and then the heads of the worthy knights and the heads of their swift horses. They advanced at a walk in serried ranks across the plain, until they reached a tree close to King Arthur's army, and there they halted. And behind them Gawain saw another company advancing, in fine and impressive order, and there were as many knights in this company as in the first. And then a third company appeared, the most splendid ever seen, and without a lie there were four thousand of them, each equipped with a handsome shield and a good, straight lance. The plain was broad and long and level. And the one at their head did not let a single knight break rank or any horse move ahead of another: they advanced in tight formation. Then the three companies joined together into one, and King Arthur's men estimated their numbers at ten thousand. And after them came another company: at least three thousand ladies and girls of worth, with bright and shining faces. Before them came musicians playing tunes on the hurdy-gurdy, and harpers playing sweet airs on their harps. They came joyfully to the tree where they saw their knights gathered, and dismounted alongside them, in the middle of the plain.

King Arthur in turn commanded fifteen thousand of his men to arm and assemble in battalions; whatever happened, he did not like to think that his army might be caught off guard. They did the king's bidding without delay. Meanwhile the queen sat down beneath a clump of trees in the middle of the plain, accompanied by a good three thousand of the most worthy and beautiful ladies and girls living at that time. The plain was filled with ladies and knights, magnificent arms and horses. No man has ever seen, or will ever see, so many all together.

Sir Gawain called to Gifflet and Sir Yvain. 'Go,' he said, 'out into the plain. In that great company by the tree I think you'll find the one who's challenged me to battle. You needn't ask for a description: you'll know him as soon as you set eyes on him, for there's no nobler or more handsome knight in the world – nor one more fierce. Tell him that I'm ready to fulfil my promise.'

They mounted at once and galloped straight to Guiromelant's army. And every knight in all the isles of the sea who bore any hatred for King Arthur had come to face him in that host. Sir Gawain's messengers soon found Guiromelant: he was standing on a sumptuous cloth from Africa, resting his arms on the shoulders of two knights, while boys and squires knelt before him, lacing on his iron leggings. He wore a long gown, half deep purple cloth and half rich padded stuff, as is necessary with armour; and his forehead was protected with quilt to stop the chain-mail being driven into the flesh. No-one has ever seen a more handsome creature of human shape; no man could possess more beauty. There was a chamberlain before him who had dressed him in his hauberk, and two squires were taking the greatest care that nothing needed altering or adding or removing. They had soon arranged everything perfectly, wanting nothing to be amiss and hamper him in battle.

As soon as his knights saw Gifflet and Sir Yvain coming, they made the crowd give way. The messengers dismounted, and Guiromelant addressed them, saying: 'Welcome, worthy knights.'

Yvain replied most courteously: 'You've forestalled us, sir: we should have greeted you first. Sir Gawain has sent us to tell you that he's ready to fulfil his pledge without delay.'

And he replied: 'As God's my witness, so am I! But tell me your names if you will.'

'Gladly,' said Gifflet. 'His name is Sir Yvain, and he's the son of King Urien. And my name is Gifflet, the son of Do.'

Guiromelant replied immediately: 'Sir Gawain is courteous indeed, it seems: he's sent me the two knights I most desired to see in all the world. But you're to tell him from me that I'm his most deadly enemy. Listen! I swear to you, Sir Yvain, that if I can overcome him in battle, the whole world together couldn't save him: I'll have his head before I leave him.'

'That will never happen, sir, if it please God,' said Sir Yvain, 'for he's such a wise and worthy man, and so are you, that the battle you've undertaken will be judiciously abandoned, and peace made to the honour of both parties.'

'So help me God who made the world,' replied Guiromelant, 'I consider you so worthy and wise that I shall send no messengers to Gawain but you. But you're to tell him this: I'm ready to fulfil our agreement. Go now: I've nothing more to say.'

And so they mounted and set off, and returned to the king's pavilion where Sir Gawain was waiting for them, fully armed. Sir Yvain told him: 'Your adversary sends you this message pure and simple: he's ready to fulfil his promise at once.'

'Then what is there to do but mount?' said Sir Gawain.

Yvain held his stirrup and Sir Gawain mounted Guilodien, fully armed. And as soon as he was in the saddle he took his shield by the strap and slung it round his neck. There were at least ten squires before him, each holding a lance, waiting to see which one he would choose. He examined them carefully, and chose one with a stout, square shaft of ash and a bright, sharp head of steel. Upon it he fixed a rich pennon, subtly embroidered with gold; the lovely lady Guilorete had sent it to him as a love token, and it was sure to boost his courage when the time came.

Out he rode from the king's army, and Guiromelant from the other side as swiftly, lance in hand and shield shining in the sun. He looked every inch a knight, and his horse was clad in yellow samite at the rear and red at the head.

The plain was beautiful and level, and incredibly full of knights and ladies. More than a thousand girls made their way through the ranks to sit and get a better view of the combat.

They wasted no time in talking; as soon as they entered the field and saw each other, without any oaths or discussion of terms, the two knights fixed their shields on their arms like the skilled warriors they were and set them firmly between their chests and the necks of their swift horses; then they lowered their pennons and thrust in their spurs. Both horses surged forward, faster than a bolt loosed from a crossbow; and there were no ruts or rocks to upset their charge – to all who watched it seemed they would surely fly! Their riders were not sparing with their spurs; and when they were about to meet, to give greater power to their blows they supported their lances on their shields and struck with such force that they pierced their hauberks, tearing clean through the chain-mail and the tunics next to their skin. Their horses were charging with such fury that the knights, as they passed, couldn't help but collide so heavily, bodies and shields together, that they grazed all the skin from their faces and knees, and all four, knights and mounts, came crashing to the ground in a heap. But they were great and splendid knights and leaped nimbly to their feet, and drew their naked swords and raised their shields high. They came at each other in a fury, and dealt such fearsome blows with their swords that they struck sparks from their helmets and smashed leather and wood from their shields. They hated each other mortally. Blow after mighty blow they struck, and won and yielded ground in turn. But they recovered so fast from every blow that the watching host were amazed they could endure so long. Neither had any intention of leaving the other as long as he had breath left in him. These fine and valiant knights were locked together till noon.

And then, truly, as soon as that hour arrived, Sir Gawain recovered his courage and strength and vigour. He shook off his weariness and the effects of the heat, and once past noon he felt stronger and fresher than he had at the start. With his strength revived, he came swiftly with his naked sword in hand and attacked Guiromelant in a fury. He struck him on the helm and stove it in right on the forehead; he would have cut right through to his head if his sword had not slipped; but it came down on his shield with such might that it sliced a great wedge off the side. Gawain prepared to strike again, and Guiromelant did likewise; and such was their fury that with the hewing of their sharpened blades all that remained of their shields were the straps and nails. Blood flowed down to their heels from their flushed, stained bodies; for with no shields left to protect them they rained mighty blows on each other's mail-coats and wounded each other terribly: they cut and hewed the tender flesh beneath their shirts with the great and awesome blows they dealt. But it was Guiromelant who tired and weakened. For every blow he gave Gawain, Gawain returned three. The king's host, who had earlier been downcast, could rejoice again, seeing the good knight Gawain harrying the other and driving him back, and they began to whisper that he would soon have vanquished him. And those who loved Guiromelant, and had earlier been rejoicing, were now dismayed; all his people were lost in grief.

But whoever had the better or worse of the combat, Clarissant's sorrow was the same. If either of them were disgraced or killed, she would surely die. She came before the king her uncle and fell at his feet and begged him to have mercy.

'For the love of God, sire,' she cried, 'end this battle between my brother and Guiromelant! Give him to me as a husband, for he's bestowed his love on me, and I've granted mine to him; I'll never take another on any account!'

The king replied with sympathy, but said: 'I can't, dear niece, I tell you truly, and my heart is so much the sadder. It's a custom of chivalry that once a knight has entered the field of battle, and has his helmet laced on and his right spur fastened, he must not be drawn from the combat unless he requests it. But go to your brother now, quickly, and beg him to stop the battle, and to give Guiromelant to you as a husband since you love him. He's a noble man of high renown, and such a fine and handsome knight that there's no king or count who could surpass him; it would be a great shame if anything but good befell him.'

Then Clarissant set out eagerly; and it was a most courageous deed she did, as she ran before that great assembly to the combat in the middle of the plain, and begged Sir Gawain for mercy, to stop the battle for the love of God, and to give her Guiromelant for her husband: he would be doing her a great honour if he did, for she would then have a fine man for her love. And Sir Gawain instantly replied:

'God help me, sister, I'd rejoice in my heart if he could be persuaded, but I'll not grant your request until he's withdrawn his accusation of treachery.'

The king delayed no longer but went straight after his niece. The debate lasted a long while, with Clarissant weeping constantly. Sir Gawain promised that, if Guiromelant retracted his accusation, he would certainly grant him his sister's hand. 'But if he won't withdraw the charge, let him don his mail-coat again tomorrow and return to battle armed as he is now.'

They agreed to this, and nothing more was said. Then Sir Gawain departed, riding slowly off towards his lodging in the castle, while King Arthur had Guiromelant disarmed at once, and mounted him on a palfrey and led him away with the fair Clarissant.

And then, at the crack of dawn next morning, the king told his niece to dress; and when she was ready she was led to the church, looking fair and elegant and beautifully attired; and the worthy knight Guiromelant received her from an archbishop's hand. There were many bishops and priors and abbots at the wedding, and much laughter and merriment. The musicians made a glorious sound and the whole court rejoiced: it was a great service indeed.

But before they had left the church Gawain returned to the king's camp, fully armed. Sir Kay ran to him, and asked him why he was armed at such a happy hour. And Sir Gawain answered: 'I'm going to do battle. Is the king up yet?'

'Oh, sir! You've put yourself out for nothing! Peace has been made! He's married your sister!'

'Married? You don't mean it?'

'I tell you, sir,' said Kay, 'they're still in church, listening to the holy service.'

'How could my uncle deal me such an insult? Giving my sister to the man who was charging me with treachery! Marrying her without my consent! You can go and tell the king that I shall never be his vassal or return to him, until he comes and seeks me in a distant land with three thousand knights of worth!'

With that Gawain turned and rode swiftly away. And Sir Kay went straight to the church and was not slow to speak; he said: 'I have to tell you, sire, you've lost your nephew. He's sworn never to return to court, because you've given his sister to his enemy before he'd withdrawn his charge. He'll no longer hold you as his friend or his uncle or his lord.'

When the king heard this he was stricken with the deepest anguish he had ever felt in his life; he nearly went out of his mind with grief. The king and his noble company were all downcast; the joy they had been feeling fled away and they were lost in sorrow. Guinevere was woebegone, and Ygerne fainted; and Clarissant held herself to blame, grieving bitterly that Gawain had left the king's court because of her impulsive act.

The king gave orders for his palfrey to be saddled at once, and told the squires to fill the chests and load the ponies. They cleared the lodgings straight away, taking mantles and cloaks and robes, goblets and blankets, and filling coffers and cases with golden cups and drinking-bowls. No-one was left behind, knight or girl or lady. Guiromelant and his wife and the three queens mounted, and princes, barons, dukes and counts set out with King Arthur. But there was no laughter or joy in the king's host; they could not have been more sorrowful. Nothing could comfort them now that they had lost Gawain. No-one has ever seen so many nobles all together in search of a single knight: they were reckoned to number sixty thousand. And the king rode on, deep in troubled thought; and the queen went, too, as distracted as he.

* * *

Meanwhile Gawain had been riding steadily through a forest, until he suddenly found himself by a river, deep and wide and swift. He looked at the high, rocky bank and saw no ford or bridge where he could cross. He carried on down the river's edge, looking for a plank or a boat or a crossing. On he rode along the bank, fully armed and deeply troubled.

Then his thoughts began to turn, and he remembered the lance he had been seeking; but he did not know where chance had now led him: all he knew was that it was a day in Lent. He told himself he had been a fool, and felt he had delayed too long; he was desperate now to fulfil his vow, but there was no-one to approach to ask the way. He decided to ride on until he met a knight or girl who could give him the information he needed. And so he turned away from the bank and began to clamber up a rock. He goaded his horse with his spurs and finally reached the top.

He gazed far along the riverbank, and suddenly saw something to raise his spirits, for just at the edge of a forest he caught a glimpse of a lofty tower. Gawain set off towards it at once, happier now and greatly cheered. He rode on until he reached the castle, where he found the drawbridge lowered. He passed through the gate – it was wide open – and dismounted. More than a hundred boys appeared, all eager to serve him, and gave his horse to the master of the stables who provided him with oats and hay. They led Sir Gawain to be disarmed in an antechamber, paved with marble and strewn with fresh grass. They brought him a brand-new gown lined with grey and white fur, and then, without the slightest delay, the boys led him from the chamber to the hall.

There they found a most handsome, white-haired nobleman sitting on a bed; he was certainly not a penitent or an ill-bred man, or a servant or a layabout: his gown alone was worth a hundred marks, and his hat was not made of straw but of rich sable covered with silk, and on top of the hat was a beautiful circle of gold, studded with jaspers and sardonyx and other precious stones. He was lying on the bed, leaning on his elbow; and it seemed indeed that he could have lived in great happiness, for he would have been a lord of great riches, if his body had not been maimed, rendering him helpless.

He greeted Gawain as soon as he approached, and Sir Gawain, filled with joy as he realised where he was, returned his greeting. And the good man entirely forgot his troubles and received Gawain at his side. Together they talked of many things, for they were comfortable and at ease, and everyone in the house was happy, lord and knight alike.

When the cooks had prepared and arranged the dinner, the servants brought two basins of hot water to wash their hands, and a towel for their drying. And as soon as they had dried their hands, two servants brought trestles of cypress-wood on which they placed the table, spread with a tablecloth of the purest whiteness. The whole hall was equally white, for there were many candles burning there, radiating a brilliant light.

Thereupon they sat down to dine; but they had not been seated long before they saw a boy come from a chamber. In his hand he was holding a white lance with a rounded shaft. He came across the crowded hall and passed before Sir Gawain. And the lance-head bled, and did not stop bleeding until he had passed through the hall. And after him Gawain saw a beautiful girl come from the same chamber, and he couldn't take his eyes off her, so delightful did he find her. In her hands she was carrying a small silver trencher, and she passed before all the people there, following the lance. And next Sir Gawain saw two boys holding candlesticks laden with candles. Gawain was burning to ask who these people were and from what land. And while he was thus absorbed he saw, coming through the hall behind the boys, another girl, slim and straight, of lovely appearance, but grieving desperately. Between her hands she held aloft the Holy Grail for all to see. Gawain saw it quite clearly, and longed to know why she was weeping so bitterly. As everyone watched she went swiftly past and straight into another chamber. And when she had disappeared with the Grail, four servants followed carrying a bier covered with a royal silk, and on the bier there was a body. And on the silken covering lay a sword which was broken across the middle. But anyone who did not already know would have found it hard to see the break, for the sword looked quite intact. The four carried the bier onward and passed through the hall.

None of the people gathered there addressed them in any way; nor did the bearers say a word. Gawain was filled with wonder. All four servants with the bier passed into a chamber. But they had only just vanished and been gone but an instant when the boy reappeared carrying the white lance with the head that bled – though it had neither flesh nor veins; and the girl with the silver trencher passed again before everyone; and the two boys reappeared with the candlesticks; and back came the bejewelled Grail, carried by the weeping girl; then the bier, after only the briefest pause. That night they passed through the house three times, so that everyone in the hall saw them with perfect clarity. And Gawain, too, saw them and was lost in wonder.

And then he remembered how he had failed before; and he drew close to the worthy man and, with the utmost eagerness, asked the significance of the Grail and the lance, and why the girl was crying; and why the bier was being carried thus; and why the burnished sword was lying on the top. And the one who was full of nobility replied that he would certainly tell him – if he was worthy to know such things. Then he called four boys and said:

'Go; bring me my good sword.'

They did so; and know this: it was broken. Two of the boys gave it to him, placing the pieces in his hands. He took the sword and passed it to Sir Gawain, who was so eager to find out the truth, and said to him, without further explanation:

'If you can mend this blade and make the pieces join together so that the sword is whole again, you'll be able to know the truth and significance of the bier and the Grail and the lance, and why the girl weeps.'

Without a moment's hesitation Gawain took the pieces and put them together; and they joined perfectly as though they were one again: everyone who saw it thought it was repaired. Then the lord said:

'Take the blade by the point and pull. If you don't pull one piece from the other, you can be sure I'll tell you the secret and the purest truth about the Grail and the lance and the bier.'

And Gawain took the sword and pulled; and he broke one piece from the other at the first tug. The lord said:

'Ah, Gawain, you have not yet achieved enough as a knight to be able to know the truth about these things; for I promise you, the one who'll come to know the truth will be esteemed and praised as the finest knight in the world. But you may well yet come to know the truth, and win by your chivalry glory and influence above all others.'

While he was speaking Sir Gawain listened, and with such intense attention to his every word that he fell asleep upon the table.

Gawain stayed fast asleep until he awoke next day; and he was astounded to find himself in a marsh with his weapons and armour beside him and his horse tethered to a tree. He was dismayed and downcast to find himself there. And he was distressed and furious with himself at having failed to learn the truth about the mysteries: it pained his heart most bitterly – he wouldn't have missed that at any price. His whole body shivered and shook with anguish.

He took up his arms and came to the elm where his horse was tethered, and mounted and set off, deep in troubled thought.

The Broken Sword

MEANWHILE PERCEVAL, HAVING LEFT his uncle's hermitage, had journeyed long through a great forest until one day, about noon, he emerged into a beautiful country, richly farmed on every side, filled with wheat and barley like the lands of the abbeys of Citeaux or Clairvaux. Perceval wondered to what country he had come, for it was at least two years since he had seen a land so abundantly endowed with all good things, so plentiful and populous. Then he caught sight of a splendid castle, of which all the walls and battlements were whiter than new-fallen snow. It had five handsome towers, all identical: one in the middle and four all round. But they were not all the same colour: the one in the centre was red and the others were whiter than snow settled on a bough. The sea beat at the wall's foot, and a river flowed on the other side, full of salmon, pike, perch and sturgeon. There was a great township inside the walls, nobly peopled with knights and serving-men, burgesses and merchants, liberal, courteous and well-bred, trading in furs of white and grey, in silk, samite and the finest cloth, in Byzantine and Norman coin, in horses and vessels of gold and silver, in pepper and wax, in cloves and spices of many kinds, most precious and expensive. Never has there been such plenty in any city. It all came by sea from Alexandria and Slavonia, from Babylon, from Mecca and Calabria, from Jerusalem and Caesarea, from Acre, which stands at the ocean's edge, and from far beyond the Saracen lands: the abundant riches of the castle came from all over the world.

There were two abbeys in the town, magnificently housed, with beautiful churches, handsome towers and splendid belfries, richly roofed with lead. Perceval, ravished by the sight, spurred his horse on until he reached the bridge, which stood upon vaulted arches and was so designed that it could be raised permanently at night; and there were crenellated barbicans at each end; and many other fine fortifications, all newly built, surrounded the whole castle.

Perceval rode through the gate, gazing about him in delight, and there in the streets he saw many knights and servants and townsmen and girls and rich young ladies, most nobly dressed. He did not stop until he reached the great hall; then four boys came running to meet him, and helped him from his horse at once and took his shield and lance, and without delay they led him into the handsome hall.

A young lady came to meet him, and she was of the greatest beauty; and twenty knights accompanied her. They all greeted Perceval and honoured him most highly, for they thought him very handsome and of noble bearing. They seated him on a carpet embroidered with silver flowers, and disarmed him, and brought him a short mantle of silken cloth lined with ermine.

Meanwhile the young lady confided in a girl, whispering to her secretly so that no-one else could hear: 'I've never seen a man in this mortal world who more resembled Perceval, my sweet friend whom I love so much and who suffered such danger on my account, winning back all my land for me, and vanquishing my enemies, Engygeron and Clamadeus.'

'Before God, my lady,' the girl replied, 'I do believe it *is* Perceval!'

And thereupon the young lady took him by the hand and seated him beside her on a rich silken cloth decorated with wheels. Perceval was in no way disconcerted and had no desire to hold his tongue; he was quick to ask her the name of the castle, and her own. The girl was only too pleased at this, for she didn't want him to stay silent.

'Sir,' she said, 'all who live in these parts call the castle Beaurepaire. And my name is Blancheflor. And now,' she said, 'tell me *your* name, good sir.'

Perceval gave a sigh, and blushed; and he looked anew at the girl and became so lost in thought that for a while he couldn't utter a word. But finally he replied, saying:

'Young lady, I shan't make a long sermon out of telling you my name. God preserve me, I'm called Perceval: I was born and raised in Wales.'

When the girl heard this her heart leaped for joy, and she couldn't hide her feelings but began to smother him with kisses. And knights and servants and girls and squires came to see the knight, and Blancheflor said to them:

'This is the good, the worthy, the noble Perceval, who rescued my land when Clamadeus was waging war on me! You're to treat him as your lord.'

Then there was jubilation in the hall, and the news spread through the city and the whole town rang with joy: there were more than thirty thousand souls rejoicing for Perceval. The bells rang in all the churches, and silken cloths adorned with gold were hung from the windows, beautifying the place still more. The celebration lasted all that day, not ceasing until late at night as the moon shone down serenely. The hall was filled with a brilliant light, for so many candles were blazing there that no-one could tell their number.

Now Perceval was a lord indeed; now he had everything he could wish; now his heart had no cause for sorrow; now it was filled with joy and happiness; now he no longer knew any sadness; now he could see his beautiful love, who was fairer than a flower upon a sapling; now he had the one of whom he had dreamed when he found the three drops of blood in the frozen snow.

They called for water, and it was brought at once in silver basins; great cloths were spread upon the tables, with knives and salt-bowls and rich and costly cups. Such abundant riches appeared there that no man's tongue could tell them all and no clerk's pen could ever record them. Perceval sat beside Blancheflor, whose colour was finer than a rose in bud, and he was more than contented, for before his eyes was the one he had thought he would never see again.

After they had eaten at their leisure they had the cloths removed; and the gentle-hearted Blancheflor had Perceval's bed made in the richest of chambers, lined with wooden panelling. And in the hall there was a high, clear, ringing music, wonderful to hear.

The celebration continued till nearly midnight, and then everyone departed, retiring to their houses in the town. The great hall was left quite empty; only the household now remained, and they took Perceval and laid him down in a magnificent and costly bed. And Blancheflor, filled with happiness and joy, lay down to rest in a chamber next to his. Then the candles, which burned brightly in the chambers and lit the whole palace, were taken away. And all who had been serving there that night went to bed and fell asleep, for they were very tired and weary.

But though they might sleep, Perceval stayed wide awake, still overwhelmed at having found his love. Nor had Blancheflor's thoughts drifted: she rose without delay and donned a white gown of ermine and left her chamber. All alone, without a chambermaid, she came to Perceval's bed, drew back the blanket and lay down beside her love.

She whispered to him: 'Don't think it wicked or foolish that I've come here: I've longed for you so much! And I tell you in all truthfulness, I would never take a husband if it meant being untrue to you.'

Perceval took her in his arms, for he greatly desired the pleasure of her embrace, and he found it pleasing indeed. He kissed her a hundred times without stopping.

They spoke of many things, and asked each other all kinds of questions. 'My lady,' he said, 'when was this castle rebuilt? The walls seem brand-new – the towers, too – and there are many ladies and girls and knights and burgesses and serving-men, all rich and well-to-do. It's well peopled with all kinds of folk, and the town and country are beautiful.'

'In faith, sir,' she said, 'this castle was badly damaged after it had been besieged by Engygeron – as you know very well, for it was you who raised the siege and delivered me and my land. But I couldn't be married to you then, for that was not yet your wish. So I remained alone and lost, while you set off for other lands in search of adventures to enhance your glory. And truly, I wished then that I were dead and buried, and that my soul had left my body! My heart was quite distraught, until the people of this land, who had fled because of the war, heard the news and came back to the castle; their return delighted me! Then I sent for craftsmen, a host of masons and carpenters, and had the walls rebuilt and new towers constructed. There: that's the story; now I've told you everything. And in the morning you'll marry me and the land will be yours; and you'll keep it in peace: there'll be no war. There are a thousand knights who'll all accept you as their lord.'

'Truly, my love,' said Perceval, 'I can't do that yet, for I've undertaken a journey that I wouldn't give up for all the wealth of Rome. But as soon as it's done I'll come straight back to you.'

'Sir,' said Blancheflor, 'I don't know what will come of this, but it isn't right for such a worthy man as you to abandon what he's vowed to do – not even for his love's sake. When you left me the other year I remember you told me you'd go and find your mother, and that once you'd seen her you'd return to me without delay. So I waited for you from then till now, and I'll wait again, for I'd rather suffer agony, and have my heart made dark and sad, than go against your will. I'll do just as you wish, since I can't hold you back by force or pleading. And even if I could it would be a great wrong if I did so and angered you, for a lady shouldn't do anything to displease or annoy her love. If she's come to love him with a noble love that's true and sure, then she should bear the pain that wrings her heart.'

Then she embraced him tightly and kissed him sweetly twenty times, and with a heart full of sorrow she said: 'There's nothing for it: you'll leave when you wish. But stay just two days more, and then you can go freshly equipped.'

Perceval agreed to this, but unwillingly, for he was eager to be on his way.

Then day began to break, and Blancheflor rose, grieving bitterly in her heart at what had been said, but she showed no outward sign of it. She returned to her own bed; and in spite of all her troubled thoughts she fell asleep at once, for she was very tired after staying awake all night. And Perceval, too, fell fast asleep.

The weather was beautiful and calm, and the sun shone brightly through the windows, filling the handsome hall with light. And soon the bells rang, summoning people to mass. Perceval awoke when he heard them; and his fair love Blancheflor sent a maid to him with a gown of silk embroidered with gold. Perceval was delighted, and rose and donned the gown; and without more ado he left the chamber and entered the great hall, and found it filled with knights and ladies who greeted him with the high honour that they owed their lord who had rescued them from the terrible plight into which Engygeron had plunged them. Then the fair Blancheflor appeared from her chamber, clothed in white samite adorned with golden flowers and silver stars; her mantle was made of the same cloth and richly lined with ermine; no man of woman born ever beheld such a beautiful girl. Perceval went to meet her; they greeted each other, and then went to the church together to hear mass. And everyone who saw them side by side was filled with wonder, and said that if you searched all the lands and seas you could never find a couple as beautiful as those two.

When mass was over they returned to the hall, where feasting and merry-making began such as no-one could describe; the festivities and gaiety lasted all day long, without interruption. There was not a word of sadness, of poverty or of growing old, only of joy and happiness. Everyone present was blissfully happy.

Perceval stayed thus for three days, for his sweetheart begged him so earnestly. And when the fourth morning came Blancheflor rose, grieving bitterly that he meant to leave; she began to weep, imploring him to postpone his journey just one more day for her sake. But Perceval said he could delay no longer. He called for his arms and armed at once, and then bade that his charger be brought to him; it had been well cared for, and was richly harnessed with a brand-new saddle. And that was that. He kissed his love, whose heart was distraught and full of sorrow: her eyes filled with tears and her heart with sighs, but she stood there in silence.

Perceval addressed her most tenderly, saying: 'In God's name, my love, don't be so upset and sad at heart, for by Saint Gilles of Provence, I'll return to you as soon as I can!'

Blancheflor said not a word in reply, for her heart was so gripped by grief and sorrow that she couldn't have spoken at any price. The hall was packed with ladies and knights and townsfolk: they numbered more than four thousand. The highest among them spent a long while in consultation with him, begging him not to refuse to marry Blancheflor, who was beautiful and wise and rich. Perceval said he couldn't do so yet, but asked them not to be displeased, for he would return from the task he had undertaken just as soon as he could. Then he wouldn't leave the lady and the land for the rest of his life.

That was the end of their debate, and Perceval mounted his charger. A red quartered shield with a lion rampant of silver, newly made and decorated, was presented to him, and he hung it at his neck. Then, clutching a lance of apple-wood with a great, sharp head of steel, Perceval took his leave, commending them all to God. And he rode from the castle and was on his way.

Blancheflor was left desolate and mournful, and everyone with her grieved bitterly for Perceval; knights, townsmen and servants, ladies, girls and children all wept and lamented. To the one who had suffered martyrdom and accepted the agony of the Cross to free His people from Hell, to the almighty King of all, they commended him a hundred thousand times.

* * *

The good and loyal knight Perceval rode for fifteen days and met with no adventure worth relating, until he passed into a vast and beautiful forest. And high up in a tall tree, so high that he couldn't have been touched even with a lance, a child was sitting on a branch. In his hand he was holding an apple, and from here to Rome you wouldn't find so beautiful a being. He didn't look so much as five years old, too young to be without his mother. Perceval looked long at him, and turned his horse towards the tree. He halted beneath it and greeted him, and the child was quick to return his greeting. Perceval asked him to climb down, but he said he would not.

'You have no authority over me,' said the child. 'Although you're a knight I owe you homage for nothing I possess, and if I do I renounce all rights to it and yield it to you. Many words have reached my ears and truly had no effect on me: yours affect me not at all.'

'So it seems,' said Perceval. 'But tell me, am I on the right road for the house of the Fisher King?'

'You may well be, gentle friend; but I don't think I'm yet so learned as to be able to answer all your questions.'

'In faith,' said Perceval, 'none of the things I want to ask requires great thought before you reply. I want to know your name, and where you're from, and why you're sitting on that branch, and if you can tell me anything about the Fisher King. That's all.'

The child replied that he would tell him nothing about any of those things – neither truth nor falsehood. But he should know this much: 'You could go tomorrow to the pillar on Mount Dolorous, where you'll hear news, I believe, that will delight you.'

Then he stood up on the branch and climbed swiftly to a higher one; he hardly lingered there at all, but climbed from branch to branch right to the top of the tree, which was wondrously high. Perceval watched in astonishment. And unseen by Perceval the little child vanished from the tree, leaving him down below, peering all around. Unable to see any sign of him, Perceval set off on his way again, just as the day was fading. He slept that night at the house of a hermit, who received him most happily and gave him all he could provide.

Morning came, and before the sun had fully risen Perceval armed once more and took to the road. He drove his horse hard until almost noon; then he caught sight of Mount Dolorous far off in the distance: it was the most beautiful mountain in all the world, and so colossally high that Perceval was filled with wonder.

He reached the mountain's foot and paused awhile and then dismounted, for he saw that his horse was sweating and tired from the swift ride, and he took off the bridle and saddle and left him to graze and rest. Then he looked up and saw a girl approaching from the top of the mountain; she was riding a greyish palfrey which bore her swiftly along. He greeted her, and she replied most graciously and said:

'In God's name, sir, have mercy on yourself and me.'

'How do you mean, dear girl?'

'Don't go to the top of this mountain: it would be the utmost folly! No-one goes there and returns alive! My love went there this morning, the most esteemed of all men living in the world, and I don't know what's become of him. I've searched high and low but can see no sign of him at all, and my heart is dark and sad. A lady I met told me he'd lost his mind and rushed away like a man turned wild. Now I'm all alone and lost in this distant land. I don't know what to do or say; my heart is filled with grief and despair! But if you'll remount and avoid this mountain, I'll gladly come with you and serve you at your will.'

Perceval wouldn't lie to her: he swore that he would not depart, which grieved her deeply, for she was terrified of the great forest, so vast and lonely. But she crossed the plain and rode on until she disappeared into the wood. Then Perceval took his bridle and remounted, and rode on alone to the top of Mount Dolorous.

And there he found the pillar. He gazed at its magnificent workmanship: it was made of copper, and polished from head to foot; and it was as high as a crossbow-bolt could fly. It was surrounded by fifteen crosses, all at least sixty feet in height and made of solid stone to last forever. No human soul has seen so fine a piece of work: Perceval was astounded. Five of the fifteen crosses were red, five were whiter than snow on a branch, and the rest were a beautiful shade of blue; and all the colours were natural. Perceval gazed long at them, and then at the pillar, golden and tall and beautiful, and saw a ring attached to it. Around it was written in letters of fine silver – and in Latin, not a word of any other language – that no knight should dare to tether his horse to the pillar unless he was the equal of the finest knight in the world. Perceval dismounted and took the reins and tied them to the ring. He left his horse standing quietly, and propped his shield and his sharp, steel-headed lance against the pillar. Then he stood quite still, and took off his helmet as he waited to see if anything would happen. And suddenly a girl appeared, riding a white mule. To describe her beauty would take the longest day of summer. She rode steadily up and dismounted on the green grass before Perceval. She greeted him graciously in the name of God who never lies, and bowed to him with a true and humble heart. Perceval returned her greeting, gazing at her in wonder. The girl said nothing more, but walked straight up to the fine charger tethered to the ring and stroked his head and neck with her mantle, giving him the kindest and gentlest of welcomes.

'Sir,' she said, 'I know beyond all doubt that the whole world should worship and honour and bow to you and your horse, more than to any saint at any altar, for there is no knight to be found in all this world to equal you, who have brought your horse to Mount Dolorous and tethered him to the pillar's ring. You can now boast that you have greater honour than any knight of woman born has ever had in all his life!'

'Say what you like, friend,' said Perceval, 'but there are a good many finer than I. It would be quite wrong of me to consider myself the best.'

'You speak most nobly, sir,' she said. 'But enough: you must come down now to my pavilion. You'll be treated with all possible honour, before God you will!'

They mounted and set off, and rode straight down to her beautiful, rich pavilion, pitched on a heath below the mountain in the shadow of a fir. There they dismounted, and were received with joy by knights and a host of beautiful girls and ladies; and a bevy of servants came and disarmed Perceval from head to toe most courteously. Then the lady with the shining face led him into the pavilion and gave him a splendid gown of green samite bedecked with fur. The squires now hurried to set up the tables, and they all sat down to dine. By the time they had eaten and the tables had been cleared, the sun was fading and night fast approaching. In that grassy spot, so pleasant and broad and long and fair, Perceval and the young lady sat down together on the green grass while the squires made the beds in the pavilion. Perceval was questioning her, asking her kindly to tell him her name and where she was from, and why she had pitched her pavilion there beside the mountain, so wild and forbidding.

'My name,' she said, 'is the Lady of the High Peak of Mount Dolorous. I've a castle just beyond the mountain, but ten days ago a boy brought me word that he'd been at the court of King Arthur, where a good fifty of his finest knights made a vow that they would come to the pillar on Mount Dolorous; that's why I had my pavilion pitched here: I wanted to see the cream of all knighthood. But enough of them: if you'd like to hear the true story of the pillar, I'll gladly tell you.'

'Indeed I would,' said Perceval.

'Then listen, sir. When King Arthur was born, he was the most beautiful creature that Nature had ever made, applying all her powers to his creation. The king his father was told that three ladies had been present at his birth. The mistress of the three said that Arthur would have esteem and valour and wisdom and prowess greater than any man of woman born. When Uther Pendragon heard this he rejoiced in his heart. One day he was in his castle in the forest of Gloucester, sitting at a window overlooking a lake. He was gazing at the water and the meadow and the beautiful forest when a girl appeared before him, most splendidly dressed.

'"Sir", she said to him, "the other day I went out riding, and as evening fell I found a girl sitting in a beautiful meadow beside a stream from a spring; I sat down beside her to rest awhile, and we began talking of one thing and another, until finally she told me that you had a son who would be held in greater esteem and awe than his father who was a king and an emperor. I've been searching for you to tell you this, so that you may cherish the child, who'll be of great service to many men".

'The king had a magician called Merlin, and while the girl was talking he'd been standing nearby, listening but not saying a word. The king saw him and called to him, saying: "Wise sir, do you know anything about this?"

'"Sire", said Merlin, "I know indeed that he'll be of very great might, and of higher nobility than any Christian man before him. In his household he'll have many kings and princes and barons, and a hundred more in his company as good as he at enduring the fiercest battle. I trust this will not displease you, sire".

'Uther Pendragon began to laugh with joy at what he'd heard, for he trusted Merlin more than anyone in his land, great and wide and filled with worthy men though it was. Then the king summoned Merlin to tell him one thing more: how he could identify the finest knight in his land at enduring battle and combat, and the most endowed with all knightly qualities. Merlin said he would tell him, but he needed a fortnight's respite; and he left the court and began searching the forests and mountains and heaths and plains, until he found this great peak. Then he set to work and made the crosses and the pillar – by the art of necromancy. My mother was then still young, and she became his mistress; and he built for her the beautiful house which is now my castle. When the time came for him to return to Uther Pendragon, he found him at Carlion in Wales. There in his hall, in the presence of a thousand knights or more, he told the king he'd found a pillar to which no-one could tether his horse except the finest knight in all his land. The king was delighted; and he led several fine knights of high esteem to the pillar, but ill befell them there. Merlin left the court and came to live with my mother – and became my father. You shouldn't doubt my words, for I've told you the story as true as the Paternoster. But enough: night's upon us; let's go and sleep and rest.'

Squires and serving men appeared bringing wine, and they drank; and without much further talking the young lady went to her bed in a beautiful chamber made for her in the pavilion. And in a rich and luxurious bed, most handsomely prepared, the worthy Perceval lay down. He slept all night without stirring, until God, the lord of all things, made the blazing sun appear to light up the world. Then the brave and mighty knight rose and dressed, and clad himself in all his armour. With his helmet laced, his shield slung round his neck, his sword at his waist and his lance in hand – sullied only with dark, congealed blood – he mounted his fine charger; and the young lady mounted likewise and they set out from the tent.

They rode on through the valley until they found a broad path through the great, leafy forest.

'Sir,' she said then, 'tell me, if you will, to which land you're going.'

'I'm going to the court of the Fisher King,' he replied, 'if I can find the way.'

'Take the path you see ahead. Have no doubt – it'll lead you straight there. If you ride swiftly and keep to the path you'll be there tomorrow morning.'

With that she took her leave. And Perceval commended her to God and rode swiftly away.

He rode on along the wide, beaten track until noon. Then a great swirl of cloud began to churn the air, and thunder and lightning and rain swept down with such violence that Perceval could barely see for the mighty storm. All the beasts of the forest shook with fear of the tempest, and even the hugest trees were torn down on every side. Until three o'clock neither the storm nor the wind abated. But Perceval battled on, not stopping despite the terrible weather, and rode on until night fell. And when the moon appeared, the night became so calm and soft and tranquil that never since the day he was born had he seen a night so clear. And the stars gleaming in the firmament shone so sharply that each one could be clearly seen. Perceval rode on through the beautiful moonlight. All his heart and mind were set on recalling what he had seen before when the good king had given him lodging and the bleeding lance had appeared. And he longed above all to know about the Grail – the rich and precious Grail, so beautiful and glorious and encrusted with gems. Pondering deeply on these things he rode along, and swore that if he ever found that house again, he would ask the king the truth about them all.

He was still thinking about this when he looked ahead and saw, a long way off, a huge and leafy oak, right in the middle of his path. And on the tree were more than a thousand candles – of miraculous size, it seemed to him; twenty or thirty on every branch. Perceval didn't linger but rode straight on towards the tree, which seemed to be ablaze with candles; but with each approaching step, the dazzling light faded away to nothing. By the time he arrived he found not a single candle, large or small. But he caught sight of a chapel beyond the tree, and through the open door he could see a candle inside, burning. He dismounted, leaving his horse standing quietly by the wall. Then he entered the chapel and looked up and down, and saw not a mortal man or woman or any living thing; but on the altar there lay a slain knight. Over him was spread a cloth of samite, richly dyed, embroidered with many golden flowers, and before him burned a single candle, no more, no less. Perceval listened hard for approaching footsteps, but none came. He suffered this frustration for a long while, neither happy at having to linger there nor wanting to leave, until midnight drew near. Then he stepped out of the chapel to unbridle his horse. But he'd not gone two paces from the door when the light which had lit the chapel was suddenly snuffed out. Perceval was well aware of it, but refused to be alarmed, and didn't shake or tremble. He mounted without delay and soon left the chapel and the tree far behind.

Pondering deeply in his heart upon the wonders he had seen, he rode on until he came to a beautiful oak tree, tall and wide. The grass beneath it was long and thick, and he dismounted at once and unbridled his horse, and left him there to graze till daybreak.

Then he mounted again and journeyed on all morning. He found himself crossing a dismal waste of barren ground. Suddenly he heard a great horn sound three long blasts far off in the distance; he turned that way immediately and headed on with all speed, eager to find its source, until he saw a pack of dogs in pursuit of a huge boar, and four hunters following behind on fine hunting-horses. Perceval rode to meet them and greeted them most courteously, and one of them drew rein and asked him where he was going. Perceval replied that he was searching for the house of the rich Fisher King.

'By God the Creator,' said the huntsman, 'we're all in his service; and if you cross the peak you can see ahead; you'll find the hall and the tower beside the river, not a league and a half away!'

At that Perceval left him and rode on, overjoyed at the news. Then he saw a girl coming straight towards him, mounted on a dappled palfrey. She was richly dressed in indigo samite embroidered with silver flowers, and had a fine, pure beauty. She rode down at an easy pace, and as soon as Perceval met her he greeted her nobly in the name of God who never lies.

'May He bring you joy and honour,' the girl replied. 'Now tell me, please, where you lodged last night.'

'In the forest,' he said; and he told her about the tree and the brilliant light, and how he had been in the chapel with the body of the dead knight, and how, when he stepped outside to unbridle his horse, the candle had been snuffed out.

'Truly,' said the girl, 'this is of great significance. You are to learn the truth about the lance and the Holy Grail.'

Perceval was elated; and he told her how he had seen the child in the tree, so very young that he did not believe he could yet have left his mother. 'Dear girl,' he said, 'I wish you could tell me why he wouldn't speak to me, and why he disappeared.'

'I couldn't, sir, before God,' said the wise girl, 'but everything you've told me is a sign of the holy secret of which you'll soon hear news.'

With that she promptly rode away, and for all his calling after her she would not say another word. So he set off towards the court of the Fisher King, following the path that the huntsmen had shown him, over the mountain-top.

He rode on until he caught sight of the castle standing near the river; then he spurred his horse on eagerly. As soon as Perceval entered the castle servants came from all sides and greeted him with the utmost joy. They disarmed him and dressed him in a long mantle; then they passed through the great hall and led him into a chamber. Never had its like been seen: it was not painted as other chambers are, for looking up he saw the ceiling illuminated with gold and tiny silver stars; but there was no other decoration: on the walls round about there was no blue or vermilion, or green or red or any other colour – they were lined instead with panels of gold and silver. And there were images worked into the gold, inlaid with a thousand precious stones which filled the chamber with light. Anyone entering that room could not fail to wonder who could have created such a place, and Perceval was spellbound.

He found the king sitting inside, and greeted him nobly in the name of the king of Paradise; and the good king replied like the kindly man he was, and seated him at his side. Perceval was dying to see the Grail for which he had been striving so long, and the lance, too, with the bleeding head. His heart was set upon it, but he did not see it yet. The good king gently asked him to tell him where he had slept the night before; Perceval replied that it was in the forest, and told him straight away about the chapel he had found, and how he had gone inside and seen the knight lying upon the rich cloth; and how, the moment he went out, the candle had been extinguished.

'And sire,' he said, 'I found a child in a great, leafy tree, sitting high up on a branch, who vanished after saying just a word or two. And he told me no secrets about anything except Mount Dolorous: he told me that there I would encounter something very pleasing to me – and that was true, indeed: what I saw and heard delighted me, for there are many wonders in that place.'

The king heard this and sighed, and asked him if he had seen anything else that had puzzled him. And Perceval replied: 'No, sire; but if it's no trouble to you, I'd gladly ask about the child in the tree. What was the significance of his climbing from branch to branch, right to the very top? And I'd like to know about the slain knight in the chapel, and the tree of candles: all these things have mystified me.'

The king was silent, and Perceval fell to thinking. All the knights then washed, and the king invited Perceval to eat with him from his own bowl. They had not been seated long when a girl, fairer than an April flower upon a sapling's branch, appeared from a beautiful chamber. She was holding the Holy Grail in her hands. She passed before the table, and was followed a moment later by another girl dressed in white, embroidered silk. She was carrying the lance which dripped blood from its tip. And a boy followed after her, carrying a naked sword broken clean in half across the middle. He laid it on the table, on the corner by the king. Perceval was in turmoil, not knowing what to ask first – about the Grail or the lance, or the broken sword. The king kept summoning him to eat well, asking him repeatedly. And back came the girl, holding in her hands the Grail, so glorious and holy; and behind her came the one with the lance. Perceval leaned towards the king, and said to him:

'Truly, sire, I'd dearly love to hear the truth about the Grail which has passed before us twice, and also about the lance that bleeds; who does it serve and what is done with it? And tell me about that broken sword, and if it will ever be repaired?'

The king replied: 'Dear friend, you've asked me a very great deal, but I'll tell you the truth about it all. I'll tell you first about the child, for that is the beginning. I tell you, with all certainty, that he was a divine being, and felt such hatred for you, because of the dreadful sins with which you were stained, that he wouldn't say a word to you. And know this: he gave you an important lesson when he climbed from branch to branch to the top of the great tree, and I'll tell you why. When God first made the Earth and all the creatures in it, the birds and fishes and wild beasts, they were made with their faces always earthward, searching for their food. But God didn't wish to make man thus; instead He raised man's face to see the vast height of the firmament and the riches with which the Lord God lit the whole world He had made. And so that he should remember the one who had made him so beautiful and so noble, like Himself, God made man in no-one's likeness but His own. And now they repay Him by straying from His commandments and devoting themselves to sin. The child who vanished from the tree and mounted heavenwards was showing you symbolically that you should think of the Creator high in Heaven, and without delay, so that He may be sure to receive your soul and place it in His Paradise; for, my good dear friend, you've been enmeshed in folly for a long while. He's a fool indeed who forgets God for the sake of earthly gain, for then he loses the praise and riches that God promises to His faithful. But of the tree of candles, which so astonished you, and of the chapel and the body of the dead knight, and of the lance and of the Grail, you'll hear me say neither good nor ill until you've eaten.'

With that he fell silent: for the moment he would say no more. Perceval was so on edge that he could neither eat nor drink, and the good king very gently summoned him again to dine. Perceval was very troubled, and said to the king:

'Before dinner's finished I'd be very glad to hear at least about the broken sword.'

And the king replied: 'Since you're so eager I'll tell you. If some worthy man – a man full of chivalry and free of wickedness, who loved and honoured God and Holy Church – if such a man laid his hand upon the sword and set the pieces together, I think that in a moment it would be whole again. Look: here it is. Take it, I pray you, and join the two pieces. If you can do so, I'll tell you about the knight at the chapel, and then about the rich Grail and the lance, and anything else you wish. Have no fear: you'll hear about the adventures which have been so strange and taxing, and when you hear them you'll be amazed. But first, I beg you, place your hand upon the sword, for by you, I believe, it will be repaired.'

So Perceval took the pieces and put them together; and the steel blade joined so finely that the day it was made it had not seemed better burnished or more handsome. But just by the join there remained a very small notch; and the king said:

'Listen, dear sir. You've striven hard at the art of arms, I know you have. From this test I know for sure that, of all men now living in the world, there is none of greater worth than you in combat or in battle; but you've not yet done enough to have God bestow on you the praise, esteem and courtesy, the wisdom and the chivalry, to enable us to say that of all knights you were the most endowed with all high qualities.'

Perceval was so lost in astonishment that he did not know what to say; and he sighed so deeply that all those seated at dinner marvelled. But the king looked at Perceval and flung his arms around his neck with the utmost joy, and said:

'My good, dear friend, be lord of my house! I willingly bestow upon you everything I have, and henceforth will hold you dearer than any man alive.'

Perceval was greatly comforted by the Fisher King's words, but he felt a sinner indeed since he could not know the truth about the Grail. But he eagerly asked the king to tell him where it was being taken and who was served from it, and why the lance bled. The king replied immediately, saying:

'After dinner you shall hear things that will delight you, but I shall not speak about the Grail, nor will you know the secret of the lance – not until the notch in this sword has been repaired by your hands. But I'll tell you this: I know of no man in the world who can learn these things but you; but make sure you don't lose that prize through sin. And if you do fall into sin and anger God, then confess and repent and do thorough penance. And know this, too, and never doubt it: if you can return here, it may well be that you'll repair the notch, and then you could ask about the Grail and the lance; and then you would know the profound truth, the secrets and the divine mystery.'

Perceval sighed, and wondered what sin or offence prevented him from learning the secrets of the Grail; but the king would reveal no more, except that he made him realise that it was a dire sin he had committed towards his mother when she had fallen dead at the foot of the bridge on the day he left her. And he said that until he had atoned for that sin, and others, the secrets of the Grail would not be told or revealed to him. Then four servants opened the door of a chamber and carried the king away to his bed; others removed the table and made a bed for Perceval beside the fire, most rich and splendid: it was set upon a silver frame, and the sheets were fine indeed. And there Perceval lay down and slept very deeply.

But at midnight bells rang out so loud and clear that Perceval, who had been asleep awhile, started up, wide awake. He peered ahead, and saw a light so bright that, in the fields on the fairest summer's day, none brighter is ever seen. Then he heard a song so sweet that it seemed to him quite glorious, and it grieved him deeply that it was so short-lived, that beautiful, precious song of God and His sweet mother. Perceval laid his head down again, but heard a voice that cried out to him, saying:

'Perceval, I have been sent to you. Go tomorrow, my good, dear friend, and seek the house where you were born, and go to the aid of your sister who is at the mercy of strangers. I commend you to God.'

With that the voice departed, leaving Perceval pondering on the thought that he was to suffer still more toil before he saw the Grail again. He was longing to be off once more, for he had no wish to stop until he could learn all the mysteries of the Grail. But he laid his head down again, and after a while he fell asleep, and slept and rested till daybreak.

When it was light he awoke, but was astonished to see neither hall nor house; instead he found himself in a beautiful meadow beneath a flowering bush, and his horse beside him, saddled and bridled. And hanging from the saddle-bow was a magnificent sword, with a pommel of gold and a scabbard of golden thread from Venice, just like the one he had received on his first visit to the Fisher King. He was quite bewildered; but at last he stirred himself and armed and mounted.

'Truly,' he said to himself, 'I don't think any earthly man has experienced such wonders! By the Saviour, I was lodged last night, I remember clearly, at the house of the rich Fisher King; and I saw the Grail and the ever-bleeding lance, and the broken sword which I joined together – except for the notch which has still to be repaired. And now I find myself here all alone! By your grace, my dear lord God, show me the way to my mother's house.'

Thus praying, Perceval rode through the meadow until he saw a crenellated ring of wall, and was filled with wonder, for one half of the wall was red and the other white. Perceval swore that before he went on he would learn who was within; and he rode around it until he found a gate. He thought he would be able to enter, but the gate was shut fast. So he cried out, calling for it to be unlocked, but no-one said a word; yet he could hear loud sounds of rejoicing inside, with pipes and organs, harps and hurdy-gurdies playing; and the melodies were so beautiful and sweet that Perceval forgot every trouble he had known since the moment he was born. Then he called out again, saying:

'Open the gate! Let me come in and see your rejoicing!'

But he heard not a word in reply.

'In faith,' he said, 'I see they scorn my call.'

And he drew his new sword at once, and hammered on the gate with the pommel; but at the third blow he dealt, such terrible thunder and lightning fell that it seemed like the end of the world; and the sword of fine steel broke in half across the middle. Perceval was distressed indeed to see his good, new sword broken, just as the other had broken so easily before. Then suddenly a man with hair as white as snow came to the gate. He opened the wicket just a crack and saw Perceval clad in iron, and said:

'What do you want, vassal, shouting and hammering at our gate? The devil who drove you to it has brought you much misfortune! Your sword now needs to be repaired, I see, for it's broken across the middle; and you've thus lengthened by seven whole years your toil to see the lance that bleeds; nor, I promise you, will you learn the secrets of the Grail until all your sins are washed away by confession, with true repentance and deeds of penance, which will free you of all evil.'

'Oh, good sir!' cried Perceval. 'Open your wicket-gate wide, for I can see so great a light shining inside that it seems a glorious place to be – I can see everyone laughing with joy!'

'Vassal,' the white-haired man replied, 'you'll see no more till you return here. But if you can return, it may well be that you'll witness all our joy, and know the certain truth about the Grail, and why the lance bleeds – those things for which you've toiled so hard.'

'Oh, sir!' cried Perceval. 'Tell me if my sword will ever be repaired!'

'Yes,' the worthy man replied. 'The one who made it knows the hazard which caused it to be broken. Take it to him, and it'll be repaired; but no-one else will ever do so.' Then he said: 'Wait here: I'll be back with something that will help you, for I feel very sorry for you.'

He went at once, and was soon back at the gate, carrying a small, round, neatly written letter. It looked as if it could be swiftly read, but anyone who tried would find it a tiring task, for if he read all year he would not have finished it. He handed it to Perceval.

'Vassal,' he said, 'you may be sure of this: you'll never be tricked or defeated by an enemy, nor will any man, however lost or wild his mind, fail to recover his senses if he lays this letter on his head. Vassal, you're seeking something so holy that it will never be attained by any man unless he is clean of all sins, and you are deeply stained with them. You have seen quite openly the earthly Paradise; we, hereafter, shall have the celestial Paradise of ultimate glory. All men should desire to win the perfect joy which lasts forever. Go, you shall know no more for now; but remember the letter I gave you, friend.'

With that he turned away. And Perceval, having listened to the worthy man's words, held the round letter in his hand and said: 'Wherever I may go from here, I'll hang this from my neck; I'll do it now.'

He did so, and then gathered up the pieces of his good sword and slid them into the scabbard. Then he turned his horse about and set off, riding swiftly across the meadow. But, chancing to glance back, he could see no sign of the ring of wall; he had not yet ridden a bow-shot's length, yet all he could see was open ground.

* * *

He drove his horse on swiftly until, towards evening, he left the meadow-land behind. He now beheld rich pasture and ploughed fields and vineyards and rivers and townships of many kinds, populous and supplied with great riches. Perceval was astonished, and said:

'This is a marvel. Last evening when I came this way I found the land waste and deserted, and now it's teeming with all kinds of wealth.'

And he looked ahead and saw a fortified tower, two hundred feet high, surrounded by a wall with many splendid turrets; and below it was a town more noble and beautiful than any as far as Constantinople. Then Perceval turned his gaze and saw, just outside the town, a great house in the middle of a lake: in no romance or any lay will you hear of one so delightful. He saw a peasant sowing corn in a field, and rode straight to him and asked him who was the lord of the castle. And the peasant replied:

'Go there, sir: they're all waiting for you, and will receive you with jubilation!'

So he rode on at once, without delay, wondering what he meant. And everyone at the castle was filled with joy when they saw him, and rushed to meet him with crosses, in procession, saying:

'Sir, you've restored to us everything we'd lost: thanks to you we've recovered our riches and our meadowlands, our goods and all our pasture-lands, and all temporal wealth!'

Perceval, baffled by their words, was led with much rejoicing to take lodging in the castle. And when they had disarmed him, a beautiful girl brought him a fur-lined robe, a surcoat and a mantle to wear, with a splendid purse on a belt which was fastened with a golden buckle inlaid with rich jewels; and when Perceval was thus arrayed there was not a more handsome man in all King Arthur's kingdom, nor any so bold and strong. Then a lady appeared from a chamber, and Nature never made a fairer, wiser or more courteous creature. She had the comeliest body and a charming face; she was tall and young and elegant, upright in bearing and shapely, with fine shoulders, a slender waist, and hips as wide as one would wish. Her hair shone bright as gold – it seemed indeed to be threads of gold, it was so fair; and her forehead was whiter than snow; she had sparkling eyes, wide and laughing, and warm, red lips. The colour of her cheeks was a thousand times brighter than a rose on a May morning: white blended with red so perfectly that it was a marvel. She was dressed in two layers of samite, one green and one red, and on her head she wore a chaplet emblazoned with two lion cubs. Her name was Escolasse. As soon as Perceval caught sight of her he stepped forward to greet her – but she did not give him time to do so: she greeted him first.

'Sir,' she said, 'you've restored us to wealth and honour and freed us from great misery through your unmatchable valour and goodness. Welcome to this house! And welcome you shall be, if I can make you so.'

'Lady,' he replied, 'I'm glad I've been of service. But upon my soul, I don't know what I've done for you!'

'Sir,' she said, 'you've been to the house of the Fisher King and asked about the Grail, which has brought us great benefit, for in this kingdom every river and spring was dry and the land was waste and barren; now they're full of health once more. And when you asked why the lance bled, you repaired the whole country, so that now it's rich and plentiful, well stocked with all the good things of which we were in dire need before. You've brought help to us all! But when you were there the first time and saw the Grail and the bleeding lance, you would have learned the truth and all its meaning if you'd asked at once, and the rich king would have been healed of the wound which brings him grief and anguish; but I think that, if you devote unceasing energy and thought, you may yet earn the right to learn the perfect truth.'

With that the young lady took Perceval's hand and led him to a window to entertain him with conversation until nightfall when supper would be ready. Perceval leaned there and looked down at the beautiful lake below the castle and noticed again the house that stood in the middle; and he saw the flame of a great furnace, bluer than azure, rising from a chimney. He asked the girl how a fire came to fling forth such a flame; and she replied:

'I'll tell you, sir. In that house on the lake lives an aged smith. A king gave him the house in return for three swords: he has a forge there where he made all three. One of them consumed his efforts for a whole year, and it was sharp and solid, magnificently made; and he said that it would never be broken except by one hazard which he alone knew: by that hazard the splendid sword would be broken, and it would never be repaired except by him. And that strange, deep blue flame has never since gone out; yet no fire is kept there, and he's never since wished to forge again: were he given a coffer full of gold he still would not return to forging, for he knows he won't live long after he's repaired that other sword. I'm telling you the truth, and I tell you this: at the foot of his bridge are two serpents in chains, and no man of woman born could pass through his gate and return with life and limb, though the doors are always open. Now hear, dear friend, why the serpents have been placed there: it's so that, if someone came to this land to repair the sword, the evil serpents would kill him as soon as he tried to enter the forge. Unless he flew like a bird, I promise you, he'd be torn to pieces!'

When Perceval heard this he was overjoyed, for it seemed he had found the place where the pieces of his sword would be joined once more. Then he questioned the girl again, saying: 'Lady, tell me the name of this castle; it's a delightful place.'

'It's called Cothoatre; and the house below is called the Lake. Let's go and have supper now, for it's time.'

So they went and washed, for all was ready, and dined at the high table. That night Perceval was served most handsomely, and after supper they went to their beds. Perceval's was spread with two sheets from Constantinople, and at each corner there hung a little golden bell, so perfectly tuned that when they rang together they made a delightful melody. Any man, however ill, who lay upon that bed would be released from all pain. Perceval lay down, and found it rich and beautiful indeed; and the girl whispered sweetly in his ear that if he wanted pleasure she would lie there with him in the bed, for he had deserved it. She looked so lovely to Perceval that he did not know whether to refuse or accept – and he trembled in every limb as he remembered the quest he had undertaken for the Grail.

'In faith,' he said, 'I think she means to deceive me, or else she always asks knights for love, and I'm not the first! But a man should always fear sin, both in word and deed, if he wants to conquer Paradise.'

Perceval shivered at the thought, and said to the girl: 'Fair lady, I've no need of that just now. But truly, I refuse you only because it would be a great sin if I ruined your virginity or mine.'

The girl was filled with shame, and said: 'As God's my witness, sir, I said what I said to fulfil your wishes. Now that I see your desire is to shun the sport I offered you, it is my desire as well.'

At that she left without another word, and went to her chamber to sleep. Perceval, thinking about the Grail and nothing else, fell asleep, and slumbered on until daybreak when the watch sounded the dawn.

Then he arose at once, impatient to be off. The girl came and begged him earnestly to stay, for she would honour him most highly if he would accept her service. But no plea or promise could persuade Perceval to delay. She led him to a handsome chapel to hear mass, where they were told about Our Lady, the jewel of them all. After mass she had food brought to him: a roast salted capon; and when he had eaten Perceval quickly armed, girding on his broken sword, and then mounted at once with his shield and his lance. To see him safely on his way the girl mounted, too, and all her people with her. Perceval noticed an axe hanging on a hook, and he went and took it; then he rode down through

the castle with Escolasse at his side. As he passed through the streets all the
people came thronging, and bowed low to him on every side and loudly cried:

'Sir, you've restored our joy and prosperity: how can we help feeling grief
when you leave so soon?'

Perceval, with the axe in his hand, left the castle and rode towards the house
in the middle of the lake. Outside the gate, at the head of the bridge, were
chained two serpents, huge and fierce and hideous. No man ever beheld such
a perilous passage. But he advanced towards them swiftly and dismounted.
And the girl cried:

'Sir, what do you mean to do?'

'To repair my sword, lady, by overcoming these serpents and entering
this house!'

'Oh, gentle knight! Do you want to die?'

'It's no use trying to stop me. I want to know if there's a man here who
can repair my sword, for I was told that if it were broken it would be mended
here.'

Hearing this, all the people present begged him to have mercy, warning him
to stay away from there. But Perceval would not delay a single moment. He
advanced towards the bridge, holding his shield before his face and praying
earnestly. He clutched the axe in both hands and stepped on to the bridge to
meet the demon beasts. When the serpents saw him coming they turned wild,
rearing up in rage and lashing and clawing at the sandstone slabs of the bridge.
Then they surged towards him, blazing in their eagerness; Perceval waited until
they had reached the full extent of their chains, and then charged at them in
a fury, brandishing the great axe, and struck one such a blow that he sent both
its feet flying. It recoiled in horror, but the other flung itself at Perceval and
plunged both feet into his shield; no weapon, however sharp, could have
smashed through with such ease. When Perceval, alert as ever, saw that its
claws had broken through, he thrust the beast back with the shield and threw
the strap off over his head. It was a fine ploy, for hampered by the shield it
could not use its legs, and Perceval, seeing the serpent's plight, swung his
axe and sliced clean through its neck to send the black and hideous head flying into the water. But the first serpent lashed its tail at Perceval, and sent
him crashing to the ground two yards behind; then it coiled itself into a ball
and grasped so firmly with its hind legs' claws that it fixed them in a marble
stone; then out it snaked in a lashing attack; but Perceval leaped up with his
axe and with an awesome blow he hacked through the serpent's throat and
chest and down into its bowels, and from its loathsome body a red smoke
belched. Perceval took the shield that the serpent had seized and pulled it from
its claws; he hung it at his neck by the strap, and stood staring at the marks of
the serpent's blow.

When Escolasse and her people saw that Perceval had killed the two hideous
serpents, the anguish they had felt turned to joy. And they brought him his
horse and he mounted and set off, and rode through the gate of the house on

the lake and found its master. Perceval greeted him with great respect – as was proper, for he saw that he was very old.

'God save you, sir,' said Perceval.

But hearing this, the old man, white with age, was distraught and said: 'Curse your coming! I know what it is you want! Did you enter here on wings?'

'No,' said Perceval. 'I defeated the two crested serpents. I battled with them and killed them both, thanks be to God; show me now, without delay, where I can find the smith who used to forge here.'

'What do you want with him?'

'God save me,' said Perceval, 'he must repair my sword.'

When the lord of the house heard this he trembled and turned pale; and he saw the sword at Perceval's side which he himself had made, and knew very well where it had been broken.

'Vassal,' he said, 'you have greatly sinned in breaking your sword, which I made many years ago. You broke it at the gate of Paradise, I see; and I tell you, unless I repair it, it will remain forever broken.'

With that he unlocked a wicket-gate and said: 'Dismount, vassal, and give me your sword. I'll join the pieces together; and there will never be any risk of it breaking again, whatever blow may be struck with it.'

Perceval handed him the sword at once. And the aged lord took a great pair of bellows and blew on the ever-burning fire. He took the pieces and set to work, and reforged the sword so perfectly that there was no sign that it had ever been broken. He burnished it with exceeding care, and repaired the inscription; then he returned it to its scabbard and said:

'I'll tell you now, vassal: you should be counted the finest knight in the world. You've been through many perilous tests, I know, and many winters and summers, too, for the sake of the Grail – but you've more to go through yet, I think. And I can tell you this as well: I've not much longer to live.'

So saying, he handed him the sword. Perceval girded it on and courteously took his leave; then he mounted and set off on his way, passing back through the gate and over the bridge. The young lady Escolasse and her people came to meet him, giving him a joyful welcome, and they detained him as long as they could; but try as they might they could not keep him: he set out once more, and they accompanied him and guided him to a great road.

There Perceval bade them farewell, and Escolasse made her way back to her castle. With his shield at his side, Perceval rode on without further delay; but he had not gone far from the castle when he heard bells ringing in all the churches, for Triboet, who had repaired his fine, sharp, sturdy sword, was dead.

* * *

Perceval rode hard all day, following a path through a great forest, until he saw a cross and a small church, old and ruined. He dismounted there, tethered his horse to a stake, laid down his lance and shield and composed himself; then he entered the chapel. He appealed over and over to the mother of God, for her image was upon the altar, praying that she might keep him from harm and misfortune, and grant that he might find the lance that bled unceasingly, and the Grail. Then he returned to his horse and removed his bridle, and wiped his head and flanks with his silken surcoat; and he tossed him some grass in place of hay, scything it with his sword. Then he lay down beneath a thorn-bush, still fully armed, and soon he was fast asleep.

Suddenly a demon appeared in the semblance of a girl, the most beautiful seen in any land, and she was mounted on a black mule. She kept saying: 'When will I find my love? I've been seeking him so long!'

Perceval awoke and raised his head, surprised to hear the voice. The evil creature dismounted and said: 'Perceval, dear friend, you've caused me a great deal of trouble: I've been seeking you for more than a year! I tell you truly, if you wish to know all the secrets of the Grail and the bleeding lance, you'll learn them swiftly through me, and be free of the toil you've suffered so long – if you'll do my will completely and lie with me, for I adore and desire you so much that I'm dying for your love! I tell you, dear friend, I'm the Fisher King's daughter, and for love of you I'll reveal all the truth about the Grail to you tomorrow, for it's in my possession; and have no doubt: you'll also know the truth about the sword that you repaired except for the notch; just do as I wish, and quickly!'

The demon was desperate to make Perceval sin, to destroy his chastity and prevent him knowing about the Grail. For the Devil goes wild when he sees a man committed to doing good. The demon kept pressing him in his effort to deceive him, but Perceval said:

'I can see you've a lot to learn, young lady: you're misguided, and pursuing foolish goals, unworthy of a girl as beautiful as you. Remember your honour, and remember God, and the Holy Cross where He was crucified.'

And Perceval made the sign of the Cross; and the moment the demon saw that sign he flew off through the forest, creating such a tumult, such a tempest, that for a league and a half on every side all the birds and beasts shook with fear.

Perceval, seeing this astounding sight, drew his sword and marked a circle on the ground around his horse and himself; then he lay down in the middle, fearing nothing now, and slept securely till dawn.

When he saw day break he rose, not wishing to linger, and saddled and bridled his horse. Then he crossed himself and mounted.

He rode on all that day and all that week. He suffered a good deal of toil and hardship, but pressed on until he came to the passes of Valbone, to the tall, wild forest surrounded by mountains. He recognised the pass very well, for it was near that spot, while out on his hunting-horse with his javelins as a boy, that he had met the five knights and asked the first if he was God or an angel. Yes, he recognised the area well, for near there, as he realised, stood the house where his mother had lived. He wanted to go there right away, and he rode on and was filled with joy when he caught sight of his boyhood home. He rode up at once; but the bridge was raised, for his beautiful sister was seated at dinner – and grieving bitterly, weeping over and over: she hated her life; when she thought and pondered on her lot she found nothing at all to please her. Perceval arrived at the gate and called out at the top of his voice.

'God help me!' said the girl. 'Who can that be, crying so loudly?'

She came down to the courtyard with her household running after her. And when she saw Perceval she recognised him instantly, for all that he was older now and armour-clad, and tears of joy streamed down her radiant face as she cried: 'Dear brother, welcome!'

She could not wait to lower the bridge, and she released the chain and brought it down and Perceval rode across. His sister kissed him more than a hundred times before he had dismounted; and all the servants offered a hand to take his horse, and stabled him splendidly with plenty of fodder, for their labouring had provided enough barley, oats and feed to last a hundred horses for months.

When Perceval was disarmed, his sister gave him clothes to wear which were worth at least a thousand silver marks. Perceval washed his hands in two basins of pure gold, and then sat down to dinner. His sister had plenty of venison to offer; nor was the wine scarce – it was plentiful and clear, as if it had been drawn from a pool in a great vase; the boys and servants had so much that the cups were always full. After Perceval had eaten all he wished, he sat down at the fireside with his sister and began to talk of the matter that weighed so heavily upon his heart: his mother's death.

'It was fully ten years ago,' his sister said. 'When she saw you leave to become a knight she collapsed and fainted, and passed away there and then.'

'I know,' said Perceval, 'and it grieves me deeply. And what became of her body?'

'An uncle of ours, a hermit who lives nearby in this wood, carried her to his hermitage for burial.'

His sister had a delightful bed made for Perceval in the hall, for he wanted to lie down and rest, being very tired and weary. And down he lay, and all around him lay the servants, who loved him dearly; and his sister went to her chamber and slept most happily that night.

Perceval, fearing that he might stay too long out of love for his sister, arose when day had dawned. His sister, who was already awake and dressed, asked him why he had risen so early, and where he was planning to go. And Perceval said:

'By the faith I owe you, I want us both to mount now and ride to my uncle's hermitage; for this may be the only time I go there: I don't know if I'll ever return to these parts.'

With that he bade that her mule and his horse be harnessed. Then he armed swiftly, and when he had done so his horse was brought to him promptly, as commanded. The servants asked him if his sister was going with him, and he said: 'Yes, but we'll be back this evening, if it please God.'

And, weeping, each of the servants said: 'God grant that it be so.'

Perceval and his sister rode through the forest together until they came to the hermit's chapel. Perceval called at the wicket-gate – the hermitage was all enclosed for fear of wild beasts – and the hermit, who had been deep in prayer, rose and opened it. He recognised his niece at once and welcomed her with embraces. He asked her what had brought her there, and why she was accompanied by an armed knight.

'Sir,' she said, 'I've joyous news, for the Lord God has brought me help by sending me the brother I thought I'd lost! Here he is – it's Perceval, dear uncle!'

'The boy who brought your mother such distress,' said the hermit, and he sighed from the heart. Then he seated Perceval at his side and said to him: 'My good, dear friend, your mother lies nearby; I had her brought here and buried before my altar.'

So saying, he rose and led Perceval into the chapel, which was very beautiful, and showed him the tomb: it was covered with a silken cloth and yielded a fragrance of indescribable sweetness. Perceval began to weep as he remembered his mother, and he prayed to God in His gentleness to have mercy on her soul; and he said:

'Oh, dear mother, the sins I've committed towards you have so burdened me that I shall never expiate them or gain God's love, unless He will look on me with pity.'

And he told the hermit of all the toil and hardship he had suffered in the quest for the Grail.

'Dear friend,' said the hermit, 'abandon all evil vices: he is a miscreant and a hypocrite who thinks to gain God's love and glory through proud and boastful ways. No! It takes suffering, fasting, prayer and true repentance. Such are the arms with which a knight should arm himself if he wishes to love God and be worthy and valiant. Think of this: a knight's sword has two cutting edges – do you know why? It should be understood, I tell you truly, that one edge is for the defence of Holy Church, while the other should uphold all temporal, earthly justice, protecting the rights of Christian people. But know this: Holy Church's edge is notched and blunted; only the earthly edge is sharp – oh, sharp indeed! Yes, every knight cuts and hews the poor and holds them to ransom, though they've done him no wrong. Yes, that side of the sword is very sharp! And a knight who carries such a sword is deceiving God; and if he fails to mend his ways, the gate of Paradise will be closed to him. God keep you,' said the hermit, 'from such a sword, which might damn your soul.'

At the end of his sermon the hermit said a beautiful, glorious, most holy prayer, imploring God to keep him from affliction. Then Perceval politely took his leave at once, and the hermit, with great affection, blessed them with the sign of the Cross.

* * *

After seeing her safely home Perceval bade his sister farewell. She was distressed to see him go, swearing she would die of grief at being abandoned once more, and the whole household wept with her inconsolably; but he promised to return as soon as he could, and bade her behave nobly and to stop grieving, for he could not postpone the work he had undertaken. He thrust in his spurs and was gone.

For a long while he wandered through a vast forest. But when he emerged on the other side he looked ahead and in the middle of a plain he saw a castle, of which all the walls and battlements were of smooth-hewn stone. But before the bridge was a barrier of fresh-cut oak, its bark still on. Perceval spurred forward, for night was fast approaching, and saw, riding ahead of him, five knights. They were fully armed and equipped, but their arms were battered, their gold shields pierced, their helmets split and dented, their horses exhausted, and their swords notched and bent. Four of them were wringing their hands and lamenting bitterly, for they were gravely wounded, with blood spilling from their bodies: they had been in a grim battle indeed. And they were grieving desperately for the fifth, for he was wounded through the body by four spears and in the head by two swords, which had bitten through his helmet and down to the bone. They were certainly not galloping, but riding at a walk. Perceval was shocked to see them in such a state, and before he left he wanted to know what had befallen them. And he was amazed, too, to see the land laid waste and desolate: all around the castle there was not a cottage or a house to be seen.

Perceval hailed the knights with friendly words, and one of them, most kindly and soft in speech, said: 'May God through His power keep you from harm and send you the fullest joy, as He most certainly can.'

'Noble and kindly knight,' said Perceval, 'before I go, please tell me what's been happening.'

'Never, sir,' he replied, 'has such misfortune befallen anyone. But come and lodge with us tonight and I'll tell you everything; for you won't find lodging anywhere else within a long day's ride of here.'

And Perceval said: 'Many thanks.'

So they rode on towards the castle and the gate was opened for them. The people of the castle saw the loss they had suffered with the wounds to their lord, and cried: 'Alas! Oh, he's suffered strife and torment for so long!'

Such was their lament; and the four sons carried their father into the hall, and removed his armour and bandaged his wounds, and treated him with an ointment – and themselves likewise, for they needed it: their bodies were covered in wounds.

They laid their father in a bed beside the fire; then he tried to speak, calling his four sons to him and saying: 'Make our guest comfortable and honour him. If I could I'd welcome him with joy, for he looks very like the boy I once made a knight.'

When Perceval heard these words, he realised that this was the worthy man

who had bestowed upon him the order of knighthood, established in the world
by God to uphold justice and to protect Holy Church. He looked again and
recognised him now, but nonetheless asked him his name. And the worthy man
replied at once:

'Dear guest, my name is Gorneman de Gorhaut.'

Perceval felt both joy and sorrow: joy at hearing his name, but sorrow at his
wounds. 'Sir,' he said, 'it's a great calamity to me that you're wounded; and
all my happiness will be turned to grief until I've taken revenge upon the one
who wounded you: he'll find a fearsome adversary if I can track him down!
Avenging you is my solemn duty, for I'm the boy you equipped with arms
and dubbed a knight. So tell me the whole story from beginning to end: explain
why you've been done such grievous harm.'

With a great struggle Gorneman heaved himself on to one elbow and
said: 'Let me tell you the dreadful story. It's been going on for a long while; nor
will it cease as long as this castle stands – and until I'm destroyed. Every single
morning I find forty mighty knights, well armed, on horses big and strong
and swift, with lances chisel-sharp. Every single day my four sons and I have
to do battle with them: they've killed all my people. Every morning they
come and attack me at the gate, and they're terrible and furious; and I have to
go out against them, with no support except my sons here. But that's not the
whole story. Listen: each and every day we have to fight them until we've
destroyed them and left them dead in the field; then when evening comes
we return home, but the following morning, by some miraculous power, we
find them all quite safe and sound, and the battle begins all over again! So
we spend our lives in torment, and have done so for a long time now, and will
do so still, that's certain. We're in despair! We fought them today as ever,
but our efforts will have been in vain, for they'll be back tomorrow to join battle
yet again! But I'm so gravely wounded that I shan't be there – my sons will have
to go, just the four of them, to withstand their attacks.'

'My good, dear sir,' said Perceval, 'I swear to you by this hand that I'll go
with your sons tomorrow to defend both them and you, for it's only right that
I repay the great service and kindness I found in you before. I knew nothing
of the world except what my mother had told me – and I still know little enough!
When I saw the Grail and the lance which bleeds incessantly, I was dreadfully cautious and asked nothing about them, which has caused me a great
deal of pain and anguish. If I'd asked then, I'd have known the whole truth;
but I hadn't the sense! But since then I've searched and scoured and found it
once more, and asked to be told the truth; and the king would have told me,
but first I had to mend a splendid sword which was broken across the middle,
and when I came to join the pieces a notch remained in the blade. And the
king said I could ask as much as I liked, but I'd learn nothing until I'd repaired
and mended the notch in the sword; and he also said I'd done something that
made me unworthy of knowing the secrets either by word or sign. It worries
me, for I can't think of any sin, great or small, that I haven't now confessed and

atoned for – except one: I gave a promise of marriage to a beautiful and lovely girl; she was your niece, I know, for she told me so: it was Blancheflor of Beaurepaire. It's only right that I recognise that sin. I brought an end to a war in which she was embroiled, and she loved me with a true heart and wanted me to take her and make her my wife. And I promised to be her love and to marry her and to do no wrong with any other. Now I remember: that's the sin, I think, with which I'm most tainted.'

Gorneman reached towards Perceval, and said, like the worthy man he was: 'Dear friend, seek God's pardon and set your mind on marrying Blancheflor as soon as you leave here. God is so full of mercy that He grants the requests of anyone who prays to Him with a true heart. And go willingly to hear mass: whoever hears that precious service can see with his own eyes the body of Jesus Christ when the priest consecrates the host and holds it in his hands – the very same, no more, no less, as was born of the Virgin and crucified. If you believe this firmly, and fulfil the promise you made to Blancheflor when you undertook to marry her, you'll repair the notch and learn all the secrets of the lance and the Grail.'

Perceval took in every word; and he bowed his head and prayed to God to grant by His power that he might deliver his host from the ones who meant to destroy both him and his land. Then they washed and took to their beds.

Perceval lay down to sleep but felt no joy or comfort, being so worried about his host. He would be distraught indeed if he could not free him from his suffering and torment.

When day broke the four brothers, despite their wounds, were quick to rise; and so was Perceval, still deeply troubled though he was. When he saw the four knights armed to meet the attack of the forty, who had already come and were awaiting them outside the gate, Perceval called for his arms. They were brought immediately, and presented to him on a carpet of rich silk; and two boys knelt before him to arm and equip him. Now all five were fully armed – and there was nothing to mock in their appearance! Like noble souls they heard the mass of God and His sweet mother; then each of the sons took his leave of his father, who was still gravely wounded.

'My sons,' he said, 'may it please God to lead you back, for I ask nothing more than to see you again, safe and sound!'

With that Perceval mounted outside the chapel door, and gently called to the four knights, saying that bread and wine should be brought for them and that each should eat a sop. A boy brought them clear, bright wine in a large cup, while another cut bread and dropped it into the vessel, which was not of aspen or fir but of the finest silver. Each knight ate and drank of the wine just once, that was all; then the gate was opened and they all rode out, their helmets laced. The enemy knights came charging at them like wild things, and Perceval, his lance levelled, rode to meet them at full speed, with all the brothers following him as fast as their horses could go. And Perceval thrust his lance of apple-wood and struck the first knight such a blow that he smashed through his shield, tore through his mail-coat and rammed the head clean through his body – and may his soul be sent to the hundred devils of Hell! Then he struck another so mightily that all his armour was of little use, as he drove both head and shaft through his chest, parting body and soul before he hit the ground. But the match was very far from even: there were still thirty-eight against five in the contest, and all thirty-eight were more than eager. Perceval killed eight with his lance before it shattered; and then they harried him hard indeed, hammering at him with their swords of steel like smiths upon an anvil. Perceval, now with drawn sword, was frothing with rage and fury, and beheaded one of his fiercest attackers; he was giving them awesome treatment! And the four brothers were proving their worth, throwing themselves into the thickest press. Perceval struck one knight such a blow that he smashed off his helmet along with an ear, and his sword turned red as it plunged into the brain; he sliced another to the nape of the neck; in all he severed seven heads. But he was sorely hurt as they struck and smote at him; they broke and battered rings from his mail-coat and smashed and split his helmet. But the four brothers were not half-hearted: they were all dealing mighty blows. They had been badly wounded before, but this time a good deal more: all their helmets were split, their shields smashed, their hauberks pierced and their bodies wounded from head to foot. One of them was caught by a sword-blow to the scalp, and the other three pulled him from the fray before returning to the combat. So now there were only four of them; but they battled on and struck at the enemy until only twenty of the forty remained, and they withdrew and paused awhile to rearrange their arms. But Perceval charged after them, shield held firm before his breast; and the three brothers were at the ready, and galloped after Perceval, determined to do well. Battle was joined again, and as the afternoon passed and evening approached still Perceval spurred his horse on, determined to kill the enemy, and the three brothers were right behind him; but the fourth was helpless, and watched the combat motionless. Perceval charged in to hew his enemies with his steel sword; but they, who had little fear of death and little love for Perceval, rained a storm of blows upon him, wounding him most fearfully. And the three brothers gained nothing: such were their wounds that the enemy knights cast them to the ground with their entrails spilling out; and then they turned on Perceval in a terrible assault, though now there were only four of them. They were sure they would bring him down, but he returned to attack them in a fury, and beheaded one and clove another to the chin. With that the remaining two cried out:

'Oh, Perceval! It's useless! Tomorrow the attack will begin again: your exhaustion's all for nothing! Tomorrow, before you wake, we'll all be back at the castle together to recommence battle: of that you can be sure!'

'May you all be damned!' cried Perceval. 'But come what may, before I leave here the battle will end for you as it has for your companions!'

'We don't fear you in the slightest – nor do we fear death.'

At that Perceval spurred his horse and clutched his sword, and beheaded one and hacked an arm from the other and sent him toppling from his horse: all were now dead and slain. Perceval went to his companions and did enough to enable them to mount, bandaging their wounds which were giving them grave pain, for they kept splitting open and bleeding. Then they began to say:

'Good sir, we can go home now and give you and your horse rest and comfort for the night; and in the morning you can be on your way. I don't think any of us will see beyond noon tomorrow. And even if we recovered we'd face a terrible plight once more. Those last two knights told you the position: the battle will begin again tomorrow. We won't have the strength to return, and they'll destroy us and burn our castle to ashes.'

'God save you from that!' said Perceval. 'But tell me, do you know how they come back to life?'

'No indeed! And we fear the danger too much to stay: anyone who stayed to find out would die without question!'

But Perceval said: 'However terrible the danger, I'm not leaving here until I know their secret.'

'Oh, sir, do you want to die?'

'I shan't leave for anything,' he replied. 'Go now.'

They saw that their words and warnings were vain, and they rode away, silent and grieving for Perceval.

Perceval dismounted and sat down on a rock, while the wounded brothers spurred on towards the castle, not drawing rein at all. They crossed the bridge and passed through the gate, each carrying a grievous wound for which they expected no cure by any medicine or potion. They dismounted, and when they had disarmed they told their father of Perceval's great deeds of prowess, and of the jousts and charges he had made during the battle.

'And we promise you, we would all have been killed on the spot, but Perceval drove them to defeat. But now he's stayed behind to find out how they return to life! It's a terrible loss, that a man so full of noble qualities should stay to receive certain death! But no words of ours could persuade him to return with us. As for ourselves, we're finished: in the morning our end will come, for we've no strength left. And our hearts should break with utter grief for the death of the bravest man who ever rode a horse.'

'Oh, Perceval!' cried Gorneman. 'What a loss it will be if you die! If you stay out there, no-one can save you!'

And tears began to stream from his eyes and down his cheeks. All night, unceasingly, they cried their lament for Perceval.

Meanwhile Perceval was holding his horse by the bridle and sitting on a marble stone beside a tree, overlooking the dead. He had no wish to sleep, but his body began to shiver because of the cold, and he paced about, back and forth, and so stayed awake until midnight had passed. He surely cannot have enjoyed it much, but he was about to witness a marvel.

As he peered ahead towards the foot of a hill he saw a light appear, accompanied by such a tremendous groan that the ground shook and trembled.

Perceval was filled with awe, and he raised his hand and made the sign of the Cross in the name of the heavenly Father: the sign the Devil fears most. Then he saw an open door, the source of the shining light. And through the door came a tall old woman. She was carrying two small casks of handsome ivory, bound by hoops of pure, bright, brilliant gold, embedded with many precious stones: all King Arthur's wealth could not have matched the value of those casks. And never was there such a hideous creature as the old woman who carried them. Her eyes were fouler than any beast's: one, red and tiny, was buried in her head; the other seemed stuck out on a stalk, and it was huge and dark as dregs. Her tresses hung like two skinned rats, her neck was thin, her face all hairy, and she was gnarled and hunch-backed. Never was iron or steel blacker than her face and hands; and her skin and flesh looked so dry and wizened that she'd have burned like tinder if you'd set fire to her. Her mouth was a yawning maw, splitting open from ear to ear.

'God,' said Perceval, 'what foul demon sired such a loathsome creature? Is it by charm or magic that she's so hideously formed? She seems to have hung in the smoke of Hell-pit – she's blacker than any iron.'

But Perceval's courage was unimpaired. He wanted to know more about the old woman and the casks; so he sat there in silence while she, thinking to go about her business in secret, limped up the path and in among the dead, and put down the casks that were hung about her neck. The ugly, twisted hag now picked up the head of one of the corpses lying in the field, beheaded by Perceval that night, and placed it on the body. Perceval watched with rapt attention as she took the stopper from one of the casks and poured into her palm a drop of liquid clearer than any rose water. She dabbed her finger in the drop, and rubbed it on the dead knight's lips. And thereupon all his veins and joints were full of life, and his wounds were healed, every one, as though he had never been hurt at all; and he was up on his feet again before you could count to three. The potion had the power to restore the dead to life, for with it Christ was anointed and embalmed when He was laid in the sepulchre. The old hag replaced the heads of four more and brought them back to life. She rubbed the potion on another's lips, and up he leaped. Perceval was dismayed, and said to himself that he would soon be in a sorry plight if he dallied any longer. So he leaped into the saddle, took up his shield and drew his sword, thrust in his spurs and rode towards the hag crying: 'The potion you've used to restore them to life will do you little good!'

The old woman was astonished, and cried: 'What foul devil has brought you riding here? You're Perceval! I know you well, and I've always known you're the only man on Earth I need to fear! You don't yet know who is served from the Grail or what is done with it, or why the lance bleeds, and never, as long as I live, will you learn one jot about them, I swear it!'

'May you be damned!' cried Perceval. 'And for eternity! I've endured so much toil in the quest. Now answer me this: why has Gorneman been attacked and assailed so many times?'

'A fine question!' she replied. 'It was commanded by the King of the Waste City, who cannot and will not believe in God. By the power of demons and devils he made me set these strange and terrible men here. He wanted to destroy Gorneman utterly because he made you a knight, and because if you follow Gorneman's guidance you'll do such a deed as will undo the Devil's work: for by you God's friends, whom the Devil has been striving to destroy, will be restored to joy and well-being. So with the potion in the casks I'm returning to life all who lie here, and I'll keep doing so until Gorneman is finished! That's why the sodomite tyrant sent me here – he wanted to stop you learning anything about the Grail!'

'Oh God!' cried Perceval. 'I've sought it for so many Aprils and Mays and achieved precious little – I've not been able to learn a thing!'

'Nor will you, truly,' said the hag, 'as long as I live!'

'Glorious God,' thought Perceval, 'what an evil old woman this is. I don't know if she's telling the truth or if it's just boasting and trickery.'

While he was thinking this, the hag bent down to one of the dead and anointed him, and up he leaped. Then Perceval spurred towards them, clutching his whetted sword, and with a single blow he struck off the old woman's head and sent her body crashing to the ground. Thereupon the six who had been restored to life came charging at Perceval in mortal fury, and they and he began to rain blows upon each other's helmets. Perceval beheaded three, but the other three came to the attack, cursing him for having killed their lady. Perceval did not spare his blows, and cut one of them clean in two; but the other two fought back so well that they killed his horse beneath him and brought him to the ground, and struck at him ferociously; but Perceval leaped to his feet and attacked them in a fury, slicing through the head of one before slaughtering the last. Then he sat down and rested for a long while beside his horse, who lay dead before him on the battle-ground. His sword, which shone as clear as ice, was smeared and stained with blood. He picked up the splendid, precious casks, and said:

'Oh dear and glorious Father God, how beautiful these vessels are! But I don't care a jot for the gold and jewels, though they're worth King Arthur's land and treasure; I'm going to see if I can do as she did with the potion, and restore them to life and health.'

With that he picked up one of the rich casks, poured a drop of the balm into the palm of his hand, and gently moistened his finger in the drop. Then he said: 'I'll try it on this one, who did best of all in the battle yesterday, and wounded me the most.'

And he came up to the knight and dabbed the potion on his lips. Up he jumped at once, feeling no ill. He saw Perceval before him and stepped towards him. He was still holding his drawn sword, and he struck Perceval so mightily that he cut through his helmet and the hood of his hauberk, and from his forehead the red blood ran.

'God blind the man,' cried Perceval, 'who would ever heal you again! Well might the proverb apply to me: "who seeks folly finds it"! You don't care about my forgiveness – you've repaid me wretchedly!'

At that the knight returned to the attack, and harried Perceval so fiercely that he inflicted heavy wounds. But Perceval recovered vigour and will and drove himself so hard that he robbed the knight of strength and breath. The knight fell back in retreat, so full of despair that he had neither the heart nor the power to beg for mercy. Now you can clearly see that a sinner who despairs, and thinks he has committed so many sins that he cannot have forgiveness, is a fool; for God is full of pity and mercy to any man who wants to make peace with Him and begs His forgiveness with a true heart. The knight did not dare to cry for mercy, and the one who was so highly praised for his courage and prowess bore down on him and dealt him such a blow that he severed his head, and his body crashed to the ground. Then Perceval sat down and took the casks once more; he carefully poured a little of the balm and this time dabbed it on his own lips; and at once he felt as lithe as any fish, bursting with health and vigour, and said: 'I wouldn't give up this potion for all the world! It has healed and cleansed me of my wounds.'

And he carefully stopped the casks – and not with hemp or oakum, but with two rich, cut rubies; and emeralds and chalcedony, sapphires, diamonds and topaz were thickly inlaid in the golden hoops and collar-bands.

Meanwhile Gorneman saw dawn break and was fearful and dismayed. He arose and had a palfrey saddled, and told his sons there was no time to lose.

'Come on, get up, get up! Stir yourselves and mount and let's be off!'

'Truly, sir, we can't, for we're sorely wounded. We'll soon be condemned to torment: we can't escape it, for we'll be assailed by the wild devils who're sure to have killed our dear friend Perceval. It'll be our last battle, and there'll be no deliverance, for we've little strength or power left.'

Gorneman was white with grief when he saw his sons so broken. At the thought of Perceval he shook in every limb with rage and sorrow; he would gladly have died.

But suddenly, at the foot of the bridge, there was Perceval, calling out. His voice was heard by a girl as she sat, weeping with despair; and she said: 'Oh, Holy Mary! Who was that calling?' She came to the battlements and cried: 'Who's there, in God's name?'

'It's me, young lady, Perceval. I've put an end to the great torment your people have been suffering. Open the gate for me.'

At this the girl ran straight to the hall and told them the news that Perceval was at the gate. Gorneman was so filled with joy that he forgot about his wounds. He came running to the gate and opened it with all speed, and was astounded to see Perceval carrying the casks. In jubilation he led him to the hall, where he said: 'What's happened to your horse? Why have you returned on foot?'

'He was killed,' replied Perceval, 'but I promise you, thanks be to God, I've gained more than I've lost.'

And Perceval recounted the whole story from beginning to end. He told how the old woman had come and what had happened then: how she had revived the dead, and how he had taken the casks from her and killed the knights who had returned to life. He told everything, and especially about the balm. Then he said: 'Please, dear sir, send for your sons,' for he longed for their cure most earnestly.

The gentle and pious Gorneman had his sons carried down to the hall on two large couches, side by side. The knights were overjoyed when they saw their guest, but they were so terribly wounded that they were fainting with pain. Perceval took his balm, and pouring a little into his hand, he set about healing the wounded knights, placing a little in the mouth of each. And as soon as the potion touched their lips, they were all fitter than a river fish swimming in the Oise or Seine! Every wound was healed and they felt neither pain nor sadness. Now the rejoicing began! If God had descended from Heaven and appeared in person He would not have been embraced more fervently than Perceval was by Gorneman and his sons! They sat together then and addressed him fondly, saying:

'Sir, stay with us awhile and take your ease.'

But Perceval replied: 'No, it's no use; I'm not going to stay. I want to go to my sweetheart Blancheflor, your kinswoman. And I'll be most grateful if your father will take me to her, for I want to marry her. I shall live more chastely then; and the man who lives a holy life and keeps himself pure and preserves his chastity will find it to his advantage: for he's loved and cherished in this life and his soul will be secure in the next. So I'll leave tomorrow morning.'

'I'll go with you,' said Gorneman, 'and honour you in every way I can. Meanwhile there's no-one here who'll fail to serve you with whatever you desire.'

Perceval thanked him deeply. Then the table was set and they sat down to dine; and when they had eaten and drunk and the cloths had been cleared there was great rejoicing and singing in honour of Perceval, and all day long they laughed and talked of joyful things. And when evening came they sat down to supper: they had five or six dishes of meat and as many of fish. And when it was time to sleep and rest, the boys did not dally but made the beds most handsomely. In a panelled room, painted gold, they made a gorgeous bed with a grey coverlet and a rich silken quilt. Perceval was soon asleep, for he was very weary.

Everyone in the castle slept securely, feeling no fear or terror now: their fear and dread had gone. And truly, the ivory casks that Perceval had won shed such a brilliant light in the hall that it was as bright as noon; Perceval awoke suddenly and was astonished by the light, but he sensed there was no danger, for since the light was coming from the casks he knew that it must be holy. So he fell asleep again, and slept until day broke and the watch sounded the dawn. Then Perceval awoke, but he was still tired and weary, for it was a long time since he had had pleasant lodging; and he lay in bed all the first part of the morning until the bell was rung for mass to be sung in a chapel. Then he summoned the servants, who came running to him and dressed him. And Gorneman and his sons dressed, too, and they all went to hear mass together, which filled their hearts with joy – for truly, the man who loves God and hears mass knows great joy indeed.

As soon as mass was over, Perceval, eager to go and fulfil his promise, said to Gorneman: 'Sir, please keep your word and come with me to Beaurepaire, to Blancheflor who seems to me the flower of all womanhood.'

'I shall be only too happy,' said Gorneman. 'But we'll have a little breakfast before we leave.'

And Gorneman ordered plovers and pheasants and pies to be brought at once, and they washed their hands and ate. Then they set off hurriedly and mounted, and Gorneman wisely took both the casks, for it would not do to forget them. Then off they rode, and a great crowd gathered to see them go.

They journeyed on without delay until they caught sight of Beaurepaire. It was quite the richest and most handsome place that anyone has ever seen, and excellently fortified. A river bearing a fleet of boats flowed along one side, and on another were great, thick forests full of game; and then there were meadows and open ground, and farmland, fishing lakes and pasture, gardens and fine arable, and vineyards and orchards, rich and wide. And on another side it was bounded by the sea, crashing at the foot of its walls. Perceval recognised it at once, but Gorneman was bewildered, for he had not been there since Clamadeus had laid waste the land. Perceval sent two boys on horseback to tell Blancheflor he was coming, and that he would keep his promise forthwith to take her for his wife. They set off swiftly, and rode through the thronging streets until they found the girl sitting at the door of the hall: she was dressed in samite, glittering with gold, and surrounded by a great crowd of her people. The two boys dismounted and stepped towards the girl – and then stopped, so stunned by her beauty that they could not say a word. The girl bowed her head towards the ground, and carried on thinking of Perceval like the lovesick girl she was.

'Oh God!' she said. 'My love has been away so long! If he'd set his heart on me as I have mine on him, he wouldn't delay in returning. But I'll continue to wait, for his wish is my wish, too. The hope I have in him comforts me in my pain.'

The two messengers now regained the power of speech, and they stepped forward and swept back their hoods. They stood side by side and then knelt and said: 'Lady, your friend the worthy Perceval sends you greetings.'

The lady was amazed. And when she heard them say that he was coming with her uncle Gorneman, she was so lost in joy that if her fingernails had been pulled out she would have been none the wiser! She was about to run off through the streets to meet him when her maids caught hold of her.

'Oh, lady!' they said. 'All your dignity is lost when you're so carried away!'

But the girl replied: 'I can't help it, leave me be! If you were in love you wouldn't reproach me for this. But yes,' she said, 'I'll take your advice.'

Then she had her finest clothes prepared; and her people were not idle, but adorned the streets with silk and samite. So much richness was draped at the windows that it seemed like an earthly paradise, and they spread carpets on the ground, not caring that they might be harmed. Knights and clerics and burgesses all dressed themselves in gowns of gold-embroidered cloth; and the sons of these burgesses equipped themselves splendidly and set about a festive joust; and elsewhere bears and lions, boars and leopards went fighting through the streets. And a cavalcade of more than ten thousand rode from the town to meet Perceval. Those who were jousting had draped their horses with silken cloths of many kinds, and there was a great scaffold for spectators on every side. And the drummers were not dressed in cheap stuff but in samite embroidered with golden thread, and were mounted on palfreys with brand-new harnesses, rich and handsome. The jousting was magnificent, and created such a din that the whole town shook and rumbled. Blancheflor was mounted on a mule harnessed more richly than any mule has ever been, and everyone gazed at her in wonder: she was dressed in a deep red silken gown lined with new ermine. Escorted by a host of knights and ladies she rode through the gate, and as she came to the open country Gorneman called to Perceval, saying:

'Sir, my niece certainly can't be ill-disposed towards you, when she welcomes you so magnificently!'

Perceval turned his horse towards her, and as soon as she caught sight of him she felt embarrassed and turned pale. Perceval was worried when he saw her so subdued, and spurred his horse towards her and greeted her; and she, sighing, returned his greeting, and gazed at him adoringly. And Perceval took her by the hands and then embraced her, for he loved her deeply; and he called her his very sweet love, and she called him her dear sweetheart; and then he began to embrace her at the waist, for Love was spurring him. Thereupon the crowds on horseback rode up and all greeted Perceval, crying:

'Welcome to the one who delivered us from destruction and misery! You've brought us all wealth and comfort and honour!'

They crossed the bridges to the town and rode in through the gates. I don't believe any emperor or king was ever received with such splendour as was Perceval. The cooks prepared supper when the time came, and when it was ready the horn was sounded, and the knights and ladies and lords washed their hands and went to dine. The dishes were not scanty: there were waggon-loads of wine and meat! Everyone had all he wished, and that night there was no doorman or guard: anyone could enter and carry off as much wine and meat, and candles, too, as he liked. The town and the castle shone with the lights from the feasting: the light was so brilliant, indeed, that it seemed as if all the houses were on fire.

When they had eaten their fill and the tables had been cleared, Perceval stood up at once and spoke, addressing the knights who held land as Blancheflor's vassals.

'Sirs,' he said, 'I've come to ask to take your lady as my wife in good faith, as I should: it seems to me that more good should befall me if we're joined in the sacrament of marriage than if I put my body, and she her beauty, to foolish use.'

When the barons heard this they replied: 'Noble sir, if you do so, you'll have brought us joy forever! If she is your lady and you are her lord, we shall never know sorrow or pain again.'

'I'll do so tomorrow,' said Perceval. 'I swear it by this hand.'

The girl heard this and sighed with joy, for she would not have exchanged Perceval for all the empire of Greece or Rome.

Soon they had the beds prepared. In a rich room hung with tapestries and wonderfully painted with gold, they made six soft and beautiful beds with fine and costly sheets. Perceval went to sleep in one, and in the others lay Gorneman and each of his four sons. And over his bed was spread a rich coverlet more speckled than a goshawk's feather shed at the fifth moulting. The fairy Blanchemal had made it, and no-one who slept beneath it would suffer sickness of mind or body.

Meanwhile Blancheflor lay down in her beautiful chamber surrounded by her maids. Much to her delight they all fell into a happy sleep, but she did not: for Love was calling and goading her, not letting her rest at all; and she began to think such sweet thoughts about Perceval that she decided to go and talk with him, and nothing was going to stop her.

'But no, I daren't go.' – 'Why not?' – 'Because he'd love me less for doing so, and think me loose and forward.' – 'If I don't go he'll think I'm leaving him out of excessive pride, and that I'm feeling very sure of myself now that he's promised to marry me!' – 'However he may reproach me, I'm going.'

She sat up in bed and donned a mantle, and slipped away from her maids, passed into the hall and headed on. She no longer cared who saw her; Love had emboldened her so much that she thought whatever she did was for the best. She came to Perceval's bed, naked beneath her mantle, and leaned on the edge. Perceval, who had heard her coming, took her in his arms and held her tightly beneath the sheets and kissed her sweetly. They took great pleasure in each other; and they could feel at ease with their kissing and embracing, for it went no further. They preferred to wait until they could be together without sinning.

And that was how they spent the night; and then, when they saw the dawn, she crept back to her bed and lay happily until the day was bright and fair.

Then the tournament, the jousting and commotion began again. Every lady and high townsman's wife dressed in a brand-new gown; and the chief seneschal bade them all start celebrating in earnest. Perceval, hearing the festive sounds, rose at once and donned a beautifully tailored gown that had been prepared for him, of deep red silken cloth. He was an astonishingly handsome knight: with blond and curly hair, and shining eyes and a bright face, and a straight nose and a forked chin; and he had a small scar on his forehead that suited him so well that it was a delight to see; his body was slim, and his arms were long and stout and strong, powerful in nerve and bone.

'God,' they all said, 'what a handsome, tall and gracious knight!'

Blancheflor had risen, too, the worse for having been awake so long: she had slept very little, having been with her love and awake all night. Her maids dressed her in garments resplendent with gold and jewels. Her gown was of blood-red silken cloth all covered in stars, and fringed with such bright and dazzling gems that they seemed to be aflame.

The people assembled before the hall with a great noise and rejoicing, then moved on to the church, where bishops, prelates, abbots and monks all eagerly awaited a glimpse of Perceval, who was now riding through the street with Blancheflor behind him and a great crowd of people following close after. Perceval dismounted at the door of the church and came to the girl with outstretched arms and lifted her down; and Gorneman hastened to accompany his niece at her right hand. The archbishop conducted the service, taking them both by the hand and joining them in lawful marriage. And so it was that Perceval took Blancheflor as his wife, and the people were filled with joy. Back they came to the palace, where jongleurs played lays and songs and the merry-making knew no bounds. And storytellers told splendid tales to ladies and to counts – and were well rewarded, for all the squires and knights went out of their way to take off clothes to give to them: tunics, surcoats and fur-lined gowns; there were some minstrels who were given five brace of gifts, or six or seven or nine or ten: they arrived as paupers and left rich men! But such practice is a thing of the past, for we've seen a good many celebrations for a knight – at his marriage or his dubbing – where lords have promised minstrels their gowns on a certain day, but when they came for them they left empty-handed, for the lords had used them as payment to their boys, their tailors, their waggoners or their barbers! Damn lords who make such a promise! The world's becoming very stingy now, because no-one's respected if he isn't rich. A curse on worldly wealth! But let's return to Perceval.

The rejoicing at Beaurepaire went on until day waned and night returned, when the knights and ladies, dukes and counts, archbishops and princes all sat down to supper. It was excellent, quite sumptuous, and ablaze with so many magnificent candles that they lit up the whole town.

And later, in Blancheflor's chamber, shining and afire with gold, they had a glorious bed prepared. The archbishops of Rodas and Dinas Clamadas and Saint Andrews in Scotland each took a cross and went to bless the bed. And those who made the responses were no common clergymen, but the bishops of Cardoeil and Cardigan and Cardiff and Saint Aaron in Wales: the dioceses of all these men were under Blancheflor's suzerainty at that time. And in all Britain no queen or king, with the sole exception of King Arthur, had so beautiful a land as Blancheflor had then; and she had made Perceval her lord and thus the lord of all that land. And when the bed had been blessed on every side, and the sign of the Cross had been made over it – both with crosses and with fire – Perceval and the lady lay down together while the people departed and went their separate ways. They lay together arm in arm, skin against skin, beneath the sheets.

Then Blancheflor shook and trembled, and so did he, like a leaf, for they felt unsure: they were both afraid that through bodily pleasure they might lose what the elect have in the great joy of Heaven, and they wanted to save themselves from the perils and torment of Hell. Perceval sighed and lamented as he held Blancheflor in his embrace. She, brought up to be mindful of all good and honour, spoke like a lady afire with love for God, saying:

'Perceval, my sweetheart, let's beware of the Devil having power over us. Chastity is a holy thing; but just as the rose surpasses other flowers in beauty, so virginity surpasses chastity, truly. And the person who possesses both will have a double crown before God in Paradise.'

Perceval agreed entirely, and said: 'My love, let's not cast our lives away, for I too believe that, though chastity is priceless, virginity surpasses all, just as topaz is worth more than crystal, and fine gold more than base metal; and whoever possesses both together will surely win the joy and delight of Paradise.'

With that they rose from their bed and went down on their knees with clasped hands, and turned at once towards the east. They both had their hearts turned to God, inspired by goodness and loyalty and faith, which commanded them not to sully virginity but to be full of charity and humility and to remember God; for then they would win everything. Then they lay down, but did not touch each other in such a way as to have carnal love; they fell asleep without delay.

They had been asleep for a long while when, just as day began to break, Perceval awoke drowsily and stretched a little. Then he listened, and heard a voice and saw a brilliant light. The voice said:

'Perceval, dear brother, you have married a wife who is full of goodness. Now know this, in truth: I have come from God to declare to you that if you now shrink from seeking the bleeding lance and the Grail, for which you have toiled so hard, you will lose your valour and your strength and all the rewards which are to fall to you and your line. I can tell you no more: I commend you to God.'

With that the voice departed, leaving Perceval deep in thought for a long while. He waited until it was time to rise, when boys came and clothed him; and the ladies dressed Blancheflor most graciously. And truly, she lay down a maiden and arose a maiden.

Perceval and all the lords went to the church to hear mass; and after mass he summoned all the knights and lords to him and received the fealty and homage of those who were to be his vassals, who accepted him as their lord with goodwill.

'Sirs,' he said, 'I command you always to do for Gorneman as you'd do for me, and I ask him to be my bailiff and to guard my wife and my land, for I have to go in search of the Grail, which I've been seeking for a long time. I don't wish to dally longer: bring me my arms and my horse!'

When Blancheflor heard Perceval's words she almost died of grief: he was leaving her so soon, and she had thought he would be staying with her in peace now as a worthy man does with his wife. But the lady loved him so deeply that she did not dare to contradict whatever he wished to do or say; she had loved him with such a pure heart from the moment she first saw him and realised his courage, that her love never failed however far he might be from her, nor did his absence ever make her less enamoured.

The Conquest of the Castles

SO PERCEVAL SET OUT ONCE MORE, and soon found himself upon a path which was little trodden. He followed it through the forest until, at the edge of a glade, he saw a magnificent wooden cross. He could see two hermits at the Cross; one was making a great commotion, and was clutching a fistful of twigs with which he kept beating the Cross, as furiously as if he meant to knock it down; and he went on beating it as long as his breath lasted. But the other hermit was on his knees with clasped hands, worshipping the Cross a hundred times over without stopping. Perceval stared at the hermits for a good while, baffled at seeing one beating it so earnestly and the other so intent on its worship. Then he rode swiftly down towards them, and demanded to know of the hermit if it was folly or wisdom that drove him to beat the Cross. He was just about to tell him when Perceval's attention was suddenly seized by something else: for out of the forest ran a beast as white as new-fallen snow, bigger than a hare but smaller than a fox: out into the glade she raced in alarm, for she bore a litter of twelve in her belly who were yelping like a pack of hounds, and she fled across the glade in terror, horrified by their baying. Perceval leaned on the butt of his lance, gazing at the beast in wonder; and he felt great pity for her, for she looked gentle and very beautiful, with eyes like two emeralds. She turned to Perceval for protection, and was just about to leap on to the neck of his horse when the litter burst from her belly: out they came, alive, as dogs. She scrambled across the ground and huddled as close to the Cross as she could; but her brood surrounded her and attacked her and tore her to pieces with their teeth; but they could not eat her flesh or pull her away from the Cross. And thereupon they turned raving mad and went racing off into the woods like wild things. Perceval beheld this amazing sight and was filled with wonder: he had never seen anything like it. And the hermits came to where the beast lay in pieces, and each took a share and placed it in golden vessels. They collected the blood as well as the flesh, and kissed the spot where she had lain, and then made their way back into the forest. Perceval dismounted, and kneeling before the Cross he kissed it and worshipped it, and likewise the ground where the beast had been killed, just as he had seen the hermits do; and thereupon a fragrance rose from that spot and from the Cross, so sweet that none could ever equal it. Then Perceval set off on his way again, amazed by the adventure.

Night was setting in, and he hurried on in search of a house where he could stay and find lodging and have something to eat, for he was certainly in need of it. Night fell and it turned pitch dark. Then suddenly Perceval saw a brilliant light and headed towards it, thinking it a promising sign. As he drew near he found an open gateway covered with broom, and the courtyard beyond was enclosed by a fence; and there inside the house he found thirteen hermits. They were of very pale complexion, and had no great abundance of food for their supper: they had cut a loaf of bread into thirteen pieces, and each of them was breaking his piece before him. A servant stood before the foremost hermit, holding a burning candle; and he began to serve him, while another cut his bread, which looked coarse, not made of wheat. They were all taken aback when they saw Perceval sitting armed upon his horse. But he greeted them, and asked them for lodging out of charity.

'I've been searching for lodging for a good while, but without success.'

'You'll have very little to eat,' said a servant, 'and so will your horse.'

And the one who was lord and master of the hermits gestured to Perceval to dismount. Then the servants took his horse and led him to the stable and gave him a little fresh hay. And when Perceval was disarmed they bade him sit by the fire, where he was served with what little they had; but he ate even less, for he had nothing to his liking – he did not relish the bread.

And just as he was about to finish, a girl entered, carrying an astonishingly handsome shield: all white it was, with a red cross; and in the Cross was such a relic as should certainly not go unmentioned: for in it was embedded a piece of the holy wood on which the flesh of Jesus Christ, the Son of God, suffered torment. And an inscription on the shield revealed that no-one could find the Grail or the lance with the head that bled ceaselessly, except the first to be able to remove the shield from the neck of the beautiful girl; but it was at his peril that any man touched it unless he was the boldest man in the world, both in word and deed, and confessed of all his sins: any other would be destroyed and killed by a thousand stones, and nothing could protect him. The girl had carried it through many lands, searching for the knight who was to bear it, for it had never been collected from the pillar where the Maidens of the Cart had left it in King Arthur's hall. Perceval hurried to help her dismount, and in so doing his first thought was to take the shield from her neck: it was very light, but so strong that it feared no blow from any lance. And when the girl saw he had taken it, she threw herself to the ground, knowing at once that he was the worthiest knight in the world – for confession, which washes away sin, had greatly increased his worth. The girl, without any bidding, went and sat with Perceval, and had two casks full of wine and two rabbit pies unloaded from her horse. The hermit made a sign that they should sit and eat upon a cloak by themselves. The pies and wine were placed before Perceval; but he said to a boy:

'Dear friend, take these pies and casks and give them to the monks to share.'

'Sir,' he replied, 'they don't eat meat and they don't drink wine. And I promise you, they don't talk while they're eating. But eat now with good cheer, and you too, dear lady.'

The servants had made a couch of fresh grass and hay, and when the hermits' meal was done the master of the hermits lay down upon it fully dressed, for he had no quilt. And each of the hermits lay propped against the couch to rest. Then the servants went to attend to Perceval, and made him a bed which offered little comfort, and another for the girl.

When night had passed and they saw day break, the hermits did not delay but went straight to a chapel where their master donned his vestments and sang the holy mass. And Perceval listened most attentively, with all his heart, as did the girl who had brought the shield. And when the hermit had sung the mass, Perceval thanked him for his lodging and asked the servants for his equipment, and armed. The girl held before him the shield with the mighty powers and the precious relic. Perceval had never borne a shield as fine as that: now he feared neither weapon nor fire, for they could never harm him. Perceval did not delay but mounted and hung it at his neck; then he took his leave of the hermits and departed at once. And the girl rode off another way, commending him to God.

But when Perceval had ridden a stone's throw he suddenly thought: 'By Saint Peter, I'm a fool! I didn't ask where the shield I've won came from, or who sent it to me.'

And he looked along the path the girl had taken, wanting to ask her about the shield, but she was nowhere to be seen; he spurred back along the path, but could not find her. He thought it a true marvel that she was not to be found; he hunted for her for a long while, but could find neither scent nor track. He decided she had been whisked away by a fairy or a phantom, and he began to cross himself at this wonder: he could see for three and a half leagues in all directions, but there was no sign of her.

Deeply troubled, he descended a valley and passed into a wasteland. And then he was shocked as he recognised the country: he was near King Arthur's city of Cardoeil – yet all around he found the people in great fear and dismay. He wondered much why this should be, and asked the lowly people why they were so alarmed and the land so afflicted.

'Is King Arthur not still alive?' he said.

'Oh yes, sir,' they replied, 'he's there in yonder castle. But he's never been so distressed and fearful as he is now, for a knight is waging war on him against whom no man can endure.'

Perceval rode on until he came before the great hall, and dismounted at the foot of the steps. Lancelot and Sir Gawain came down to meet him and greeted him with the greatest joy, as did the king and queen and all the court. They had him disarmed and dressed in a splendid gown, and those who had not seen him before gazed upon him gladly, the more so when they saw that he bore the shield that had so long hung on the pillar. And so the court, which had been so troubled, was cheered a little by Perceval's coming.

But that very day, as the king was seated at dinner, four knights burst into the hall fully armed, each bearing a dead knight before him with arms and feet cut off; and although the bodies were still in full armour, the mail-coats were black, as if they had been struck by lightning. They laid the knights down in the middle of the hall and said to the king:

'Sire, you were shown once before the disgrace that's being done to you, yet still it goes unchecked. The Knight of the Dragon is destroying your land and killing your men and is now advancing as close as he can; and he says he'll never find a knight at your court brave enough to meet him in combat.'

The king was filled with shame at this news, and Lancelot and Sir Gawain likewise, who grieved in their hearts that the king had not let them go. The four knights now departed, leaving the bodies in the middle of the hall, and the king bade that they be taken away and buried with the others. Throughout the hall a great murmur arose, with everyone saying they had never heard of a man who killed knights so cruelly or in such numbers; and they said that Sir Gawain and Lancelot should not be reproached for not going, for there was no knight in the world who could vanquish such a man unless God worked a miracle, for he could throw fire and flame from his shield whenever he wished.

While the murmuring continued among the knights in the hall, a maiden entered, and behind her was the body of a dead knight in a litter. She came before the king and said: 'Sire, I beg you to do me justice in your court. Sitting beside you I see the son of the Widowed Lady. He shouldn't refuse what I'm about to ask of him, for the dead knight whom I've so long borne in this litter is the son of his uncle Elinant of Escavalon.'

'Damsel,' said Perceval, 'take care that you speak true. I know that Elinant of Escavalon was my uncle on my father's side, but I knew nothing of his son.'

'Sir,' she said, 'he deserved to be known for his great worth, and it was because of his courage that he was killed. His name was Alain of Escavalon, and the Queen of the Circle of Gold loved him with all her heart, for he was the fairest knight she had ever seen of his age. And because of the great love she bore him, she had him embalmed after he had been killed by the Knight of the Dragon, who's so ruthless that he's destroying all the lands and isles. He's challenged the Queen of the Circle of Gold and has already killed many of her knights, and now she's locked herself in her castle, not daring to leave, and she wishes all knights to know that whoever takes revenge upon this man will have the Circle of Gold; she would never part with it before, and it would be the greatest honour ever bestowed on any knight. Sir,' she said to Perceval, 'it's only right that you should strive to avenge your uncle's son and win the Circle of Gold, because if you kill that terrible knight you'll have saved King Arthur's land, which he's threatening to destroy, for he hates Arthur more than any king on Earth.'

'Damsel,' said Perceval, 'where is this Knight of the Dragon?'

'In the Isle of the Elephants, which was once the richest and most beautiful land in the world. But now he's destroyed it and no-one dares live there. The isle is below the castle of the Queen of the Circle of Gold, so she sees him every day as he bears knights unharmed from the forest and then kills them and dismembers them, and it grieves her deeply.'

Perceval was filled with wonder; and he thought that since the task of seeking vengeance was laid on him, he would be greatly reproached if he failed to do so. He took his leave of the king and the queen and left the court. Sir Gawain and Lancelot went with him, saying they would guide him there if they could, and Perceval cherished their company. But the king and the queen were greatly afraid for Perceval, and everyone agreed that no knight had ever ridden into such grave peril, and that it would be a great loss to the world if he died. The king sent word to all the holy men and hermits of the forest of Cardoeil bidding them pray for Perceval, that God might protect him from this demon knight.

Lancelot and Sir Gawain rode with him through a strange country, and found the forests deserted and the lands on every side destroyed and waste. The maiden followed him with the dead knight, and they journeyed on until they came upon a castle in the middle of open meadows, surrounded by rushing rivers and rings of wall, and within loomed great, windowed halls. And as they approached the castle they saw that it was turning, and faster than any wind; and above the battlements were archers of copper loosing arrows with such power that no armour in the world could withstand their shots. With them were men sounding horns, horns so loud that it seemed as though the earth were quaking. And down below at the gateway were lions and bears in chains roaring with such fury that all the forest and the valley rang. The knights drew rein and gazed at this wonder.

'My lords,' said the maiden, 'there you see the Forbidden Castle. Sir Gawain, and you, Lancelot, draw back. Go no nearer the archers, or your death is assured. And you, sir,' she said to Perceval, 'if you wish to enter the castle, give me your lance and shield; I'll take them ahead as a guarantee, and you can come behind me. Conduct yourself as a good knight should and you'll pass into the castle. But your companions may as well turn back, for it's not yet time for them to enter: the only one who may proceed is the knight who is to conquer the demon knight and the Circle of Gold and the Grail and the false law of the castle.'

It grieved Perceval to hear her say that Sir Gawain and Lancelot could not go with him even though they were the finest knights in the world. He sadly took his leave of them, and reluctantly they departed. They stopped awhile to watch the good knight ride on; and they saw the maiden display Perceval's shield – the white shield with the red cross, containing a piece of the True Cross – to the men of the castle; and she cried out that it was now borne by the knight who was waiting behind her. Perceval sat shieldless in his saddle, clutching his drawn sword; and he planted himself so firmly in the stirrups that he made them stretch and his horse's back bent beneath him. Then he looked back at Lancelot and Sir Gawain.

'My lords,' he cried, 'to the Saviour of the world I commend you!'

And in reply they prayed that the one who suffered on the Cross might be protector of his body and his life. Then Perceval thrust in his spurs and his horse charged forward with all the speed it could summon towards the Turning Castle, and Perceval struck the gate so violently with his sword that he drove it a good three finger-lengths into a marble pillar. The lions and bears in chains who guarded the gate fled to their stalls; the castle suddenly stopped turning; the archers stopped shooting; and there were three bridges before the castle which rose up as soon as he had crossed them. Lancelot and Sir Gawain beheld this wonder and wanted to ride on to the castle when they saw it stop turning, but a knight cried to them from the battlements:

'Sirs, if you come nearer the archers will shoot, the castle will turn and the bridges will be lowered again, which would bring you grave distress.'

They drew back at once, and there in the castle they could hear the greatest rejoicing that ever a man had heard; many were saying that the knight who had come would save both their lives and their souls, if it pleased God to let him conquer the knight who bore the Devil's spirit. And so Lancelot and Sir Gawain turned back, full of sorrow that they could not enter the castle, for they could see no other way in but there.

Virgil, that mechanical necromancer, had built the castle by his magic art, and it was prophesied that the castle would not stop turning until the coming of a knight with a head of gold, the gaze of a lion, the navel of a virgin girl, and a heart free of all wickedness and full of faith and belief in God; and it was prophesied, too, that all the people of that castle would worship the Old Law until the coming of the Good Knight; and the moment he appeared they all ran to be baptised, and firmly believed in the Trinity and adopted the New Law. And so there was great rejoicing in the castle because they had been redeemed from death, when they had feared that they would never be saved and would die in sin because of their false law.

Perceval was overjoyed to see the people of the castle turn to the holy faith of the Saviour; and the maiden said to him: 'Sir, you've done well indeed; but now you must finish your work, for these people will never leave the castle as long as the Knight of the Dragon is alive. And you mustn't delay, for the longer you tarry, the more lands he'll destroy and the more people he'll kill.'

Perceval took his leave of the people of the castle, who cheered him in their joy. They were greatly afraid for him in his coming battle, but said that if Perceval overcame the knight, never would so fine an adventure have befallen any man.

The maiden went in front, for she knew the place where the evil knight lived, and they rode on until they came to the Isle of the Elephants. The knight had dismounted beneath an olive tree, having just killed four knights from the castle of the Queen of the Circle of Gold. She was there at the windows of her palace and had seen her knights being killed, and was grieving deeply, crying:

'Oh God! Will I never find anyone who can take revenge upon this fiend who's destroying my land and killing my men?'

Then, looking up, she saw Perceval and the maiden coming, and the queen cried to him: 'Sir, unless you've greater strength and power than other knights, don't come near this demon! But if you feel in your heart you can vanquish him, I'll give you the Circle of Gold which is here in this castle, and believe in the Law which is newly founded; for I can see by your shield you're a Christian. And if you can overcome him, I shall know then that your Law is of greater worth than ours, and that God was born of a woman.'

Perceval was inspired by her words. He crossed and blessed himself and commended himself to God and His sweet mother; and he blazed with rage and courage like a lion. He saw the Knight of the Dragon mounted now, and he gazed in wonder at his size: never had he seen such a colossal man. And he saw the shield at his neck, huge and black and hideous; and at its centre he saw the dragon's head, belching fire and flame with terrible force, so foul and ghastly that its stench filled the fields. The maiden retreated to the castle, leaving the knight in the litter in the middle of the field; and she said to Perceval:

'Sir, your uncle's son was killed in this plain. Now avenge him as best you can; I leave him to you, for I've done enough to free myself of all reproach.'

And with that she departed.

The Knight of the Dragon saw Perceval advancing all alone, and was filled with contempt for him. He did not deign to take up his lance but came straight at him with his sword drawn: huge it was, and red as blazing coal. Perceval saw him coming and charged towards him, lance lowered, as fast as his horse could go; he aimed to strike him full in the chest with his lance, but the knight thrust out his shield against it, and the flame that burst from the dragon's head burned the lance right down to his fist. The knight went to deal him a blow on the head with his sword, but Perceval covered himself with his shield, and the sword of the demon knight could do it no harm, for Joseph of Arimathea had sealed some of Our Saviour's blood and clothing in the boss. When the knight saw he had damaged neither Perceval nor his shield he was filled with shame, for never before had he struck a knight without giving him a mortal blow. He turned the dragon's head towards Perceval's shield, aiming to destroy it with fire, but the flame that burst from the dragon's head was blown back as though by a wind and could not reach Perceval. The knight was enraged and rushed past him and came up to the litter of the dead knight, and turning his shield with its dragon's head towards it, he set it on fire and burned the knight's body to ashes.

'From burying this man,' he cried to Perceval, 'you are absolved!'

'That grieves me,' he replied, 'but I'll have revenge if it please God.'

The maiden who had been carrying the dead knight was at the palace windows beside the queen, and she cried to Perceval: 'Sir, now the disgrace will be greater and the wrong done will be deeper if you fail to take revenge!'

Perceval was grieved indeed by what had been done to his cousin; but he beheld the knight who bore the strength of the Devil and did not know how he could gain revenge. But he charged at him with his sword drawn and dealt him such a blow on his shield that he smashed it right down to the dragon's head, and the fire leaped on to the sword and it became red and blazing like the blade of his enemy. And the maiden cried to him:

'By my life, sir, now your sword is as strong as his! Now we'll see what you can do! I've been told in truth that the knight can be killed in only one place and by only one blow, but alas, I can't tell you how.'

Perceval gazed at his sword, wrapped in the demon's flame, and was amazed. Then he struck the knight so fiercely that he made his head bow down to his saddle; the knight drew himself up again, enraged that he could not harm him, and struck Perceval such a terrible blow that he broke through the hauberk on his shoulder and cut into the flesh and burned it down to the bone; but as he withdrew the blade Perceval struck him with such force that he cut off his hand while it still clutched the sword. The knight let out an anguished roar, and the queen and the people of the palace heard it and were filled with joy. But the knight was not yet beaten: he came rushing at Perceval and flung more fire at his shield; but it was to no avail: he could do it no harm. Perceval saw the dragon's head, ghastly, foul and terrible, and met it with his sword and thrust it into the roof of its mouth as straight as he could. The dragon's head uttered such a deafening cry that all the plain and forest rang, and it turned upon its lord in a rage and consumed him in flame and burned him to ashes, and then vanished with the speed of a thunderbolt.

The queen was overwhelmed with joy, and came down to meet Perceval with all her knights. They saw that he was sorely wounded in the shoulder, and the maiden said that he would never be healed unless he treated the wound with some of the ash of the dead knight. They led him into the castle, and took off his armour and bathed his wound to help it heal, and put ash from the dead knight on it as a cure. Then the queen called for all the knights of her land, and said:

'My lords, behold the knight who has saved my land and defended your lives and mine! It was prophesied that the Knight with the Head of Gold would come, and that by him we would be saved; and now behold, he has come! The truth of the prophecy cannot be denied, and I would have you be at his command.'

And they replied that they would, most willingly. She led Perceval to where the Circle of Gold was kept, and with her own hand she placed it upon his head. Then she presented to him the sword with which he had destroyed the demon and the knight who bore it on his shield.

'Sir,' she said, 'let all those who will not be baptised and believe in the New Law be killed with your sword; I present it to you.'

She herself was the first to be baptised, and all the others followed after.

Perceval stayed at the castle until he was cured. Word spread through every land that the Knight of the Circle of Gold had come and had killed the Knight of the Dragon, and there was great rejoicing everywhere. The news reached the court of King Arthur, and everyone there was most intrigued when it was said that the Knight of the Circle of Gold had defeated him, for they had no way of knowing who the knight was.

* * *

After leaving Perceval to conquer the Turning Castle, Lancelot and Gawain had passed through many strange lands as they made their way back towards Arthur's court. It was a beautiful, clear day when they found themselves entering a vast forest, and from time to time the sun would stream down upon their shields; but suddenly Lancelot remembered the knight he had killed in the Waste City: he realised that the day of his return was near. As they arrived at a cross where paths forked and branched out through the forest, Lancelot said:

'I must leave you now, Gawain, and keep my promise in an adventure of mortal danger, and I don't know if I'll ever see you again; for I killed a knight, which grieved me deeply, and I had to swear before I killed him that I would return to offer my head as he had offered his. Now the day is near when I must return there, for I've no wish to earn reproach by failing to keep my word. But if God lets me escape alive, I'll follow you with all speed to King Arthur's court.'

Sir Gawain embraced him as he took his leave, and prayed to the Saviour of the world to protect his body and his life so that they might meet again soon. Lancelot would gladly have sent his greetings to the queen if he had dared, for she was dearer to him than anything in the world, but he did not want Sir Gawain to have any suspicion of his love lest he should bear him ill will. But that love was so deeply rooted in his heart, no matter what danger it might bring him, that he could not abandon it; rather did he pray to God each day to deliver him from this perilous adventure so that he might see the queen again.

On he rode until he arrived about noon at the Waste City, which he found as deserted as the first time. On every side stood derelict churches, and magnificent palaces that had crumbled to ruins, and great, deserted halls. And Lancelot had scarcely entered the city when he heard a great wailing and lamentation of ladies and maidens, though he could not tell where it was coming from. They were all saying together:

'Oh God! We've been betrayed by the one who killed the knight, for he doesn't return! The day has now arrived when he should come to keep his promise. We should never believe the words of knights. The others before him have failed us, and now he'll do the same for fear of death: he beheaded the fairest and finest knight in this kingdom, and he should now be beheaded likewise, but he's trying to avoid his fate.'

So said the maidens; Lancelot heard them all too well, but wondered where they could be, for he could see no-one anywhere. He rode up to the palace where he had killed the knight and dismounted, tethering his horse to a ring fixed in a marble stone. He had hardly done so when down from the palace came a knight, tall and fair and strong and assured; dressed he was in a splendid tunic of silk, and in his hand he held the axe with which Lancelot had beheaded the other. And as he came he sharpened it with a whetstone so that it might cut all the better. Lancelot saw him coming and said:

'Good sir, what are you going to do with that axe?'

'Truly,' said the knight, 'you'll find out just as my brother did!'

'What?' cried Lancelot. 'Are you going to kill me, then?'

'You'll know,' replied the knight, 'before you leave. Didn't you agree to put your head at stake, just as my brother did? Otherwise you couldn't have left here. But come forward now and kneel down and stretch out your neck, and I'll cut off your head. And if you won't do so of your own free will, you'll find yourself forced to it – even if there were twenty of you you would. But I know you've returned for no other reason than to keep your promise, and you'll not now refuse.'

Lancelot realised that he was about to die, but he wanted to be true to his vow. He lay down on the ground with his arms outstretched, and prayed to God for mercy. Then he remembered the queen.

'Oh, my lady!' he cried. 'I shall never see you again! If I could have seen you just once before I died it would have given me so much comfort, and my soul could have left me more contentedly. That I shall never see you again distresses me more than death. A man must die when his time comes, but I swear to you that my love will never fail you, and that my soul will love you in the other world as much as my body loved you here.'

Then tears flowed from his eyes, and never in all the time he had been a knight had he wept for any sorrow that had befallen him, save on this occasion. He picked three blades of grass and with them he took communion. Then he crossed and blessed himself, and knelt and stretched out his neck. The knight raised the axe. Lancelot heard the blow coming and ducked and the axe sped past. The knight said:

'Sir knight, that was not how my brother behaved: he kept his head and neck still. So must you.'

And Lancelot, filled with shame, sighed deeply and prepared himself for death. The knight raised the axe for the second blow. At that very moment two maidens appeared at the windows of the palace, and they recognised Lancelot at once. And just as the knight was about to strike, one of them cried:

'If you would earn my eternal love, throw down the axe and declare the knight free! If you don't, my love is denied you forever!'

In an instant the knight threw down the axe and fell at Lancelot's feet, begging him as the truest knight in the world to have mercy on him.

'It's you who need to have mercy on me!' said Lancelot.

'Sir,' he replied, 'I'll not kill you; rather will I aid you against all the knights in the world, even though you killed my brother.'

The maidens now came down from the palace to meet Lancelot. 'Sir,' they said, 'it's only right that we should love you more than any knight in the world. At least twenty knights came here just as you did, and each one killed a brother of ours, or an uncle or a cousin, by cutting off their heads, just as you beheaded the knight; and every one of them swore to return on the day declared. All of them broke their promise, for none had the courage to return; and if you had failed as they did we would have lost this city forever, and the castles which belong to it.'

The knight and the maidens led Lancelot into the palace, and in the forest outside the city the greatest rejoicing in the world could be heard.

'Ah, sir!' said the maidens. 'Now you can hear the townspeople and those who used to dwell in the city rejoicing for your coming, for now they can return!'

Lancelot leaned at the windows of the hall and watched the city fill with the fairest people in the world, and the great halls were brimming, and clerks and priests were coming in great processions, worshipping and praising God and pouring blessings on the knight who had enabled them to return to their churches and their homes. Lancelot was treated, you may be sure, with the utmost honour.

* * *

When Perceval was finally healed of his wounds from his battle with the Dragon Knight, he left the castle of the Queen of the Circle of Gold. All the land was now at his command, and the queen said that she would keep the Circle of Gold for him until he wished to collect it. He left it with her willingly, not wanting to carry it with him, because he had no idea which way he would go.

He followed a path through a vast forest, ever hopeful that he would come once more to the castle of the Fisher King.

But as he emerged from the forest it was another castle he found before him: the Castle of the Copper Tower, where there dwelt many people who worshipped a tower of copper and believed in no other god. This copper tower stood in the middle of the castle, and at all hours of the day it let out such terrible roars that it could be heard for many leagues around; and there was an evil spirit within who gave the people answers to whatever they wished to know. At the gateway stood two men made by sorcery, holding great iron hammers which they drove and dashed together with such fury that nothing in all the world could pass between them without being utterly destroyed. But everywhere else the castle was walled and barred, making entry impossible.

Perceval gazed at the castle's defences and its perilous entrance and was filled with awe. But he summoned up his courage and crossed a bridge and rode towards the guardians of the gate, whereupon a voice cried out above the gateway, saying that he should go on with no fear for the copper men, for they had no power to harm so good a knight as he. He took great comfort in the voice's words; and as he approached the hideous copper figures they stopped their hammering, and he rode straight into the castle where there dwelt so many heathens. There in the middle of the castle he saw the Copper Tower, huge and terrible, and all around it the people had gathered to worship it together, and it was uttering such terrifying roars that nothing else could be heard. The people of the castle stared at Perceval in amazement, wondering how he could have entered; but no-one addressed him, for they believed so firmly in their evil faith that if any man had wished to kill them while they were at worship they would have let him do so and believed themselves safe. They were not used to fighting, for the entrance to the castle had always been impregnable, and the demon in which they believed provided them with such plenty that they wanted for nothing. When Perceval saw they would not address him he drew aside and summoned them to gather round. Most of them came but some would not; and the voice cried that he should make them go through the gate where the copper figures stood, for then he would surely see who would believe in God and who would not. Perceval drew his sword and rounded them up and drove them before him, and those who would not go could be sure of death. He herded them through the gateway where the terrible statues were striking their hammers of iron, and of 1,500 only thirteen remained who did not have their brains beaten out by the hammers; but those thirteen came to believe firmly in Our Lord. The evil spirit that dwelt in the Copper Tower burst out like a thunderbolt, and the tower came crumbling down in ruins – nothing of it remained. Then the thirteen survivors sent for a hermit from the forest and had themselves baptised; and the bodies of the dead heathens were cast into a stream called the river of Hell which flows into the sea, and at whose estuary the waters are so terrible and perilous that hardly any ship passes that way without foundering.

The thirteen stayed at their castle – which was called thereafter the Trial Castle – until the New Law was firmly established, and led good lives indeed; and no-one could go inside to join them without being killed or cut to pieces unless he believed staunchly in God. When the people of the surrounding land had come to a firm belief, the thirteen men of the castle went out and set up hermitages throughout the forests to gain forgiveness for having once upheld the false law, and to win the love of the Saviour of the world.

Perceval had now become a soldier of Our Lord, and God was showing him plainly that he loved his chivalry. And He had further work for him, and did not let him rest. Perceval left the Trial Castle without delay and rode on.

The day was drawing to a close when he passed into a wild, dark forest, ugly and forbidding, where there were no leaves or greenery to be seen or birdsong to be heard; and the ground was scorched and hideous, cracking open into huge crevices. He had not gone far before he met the Maiden of the Cart, who greeted him with the greatest joy.

'The first time we met, sir,' she said, 'when Clamadoz challenged you to battle before the Queen of the Pavilions, I was bald! Now you can see I have hair once more!'

'Yes indeed,' said Perceval, 'and it seems to me a most beautiful head of hair.'

'Sir,' she said, 'I used to carry my arm hung from my neck in a sling of golden silk, because I thought the service I did you at the house of your uncle the Fisher King had been ill-bestowed; but now I see clearly that it was not. So now I carry both arms alike; may you be blessed for having proved your worth by the goodness of your heart and by your origin from your noble line, whom you resemble in all their good ways. And you may prove your worth again,' she said, 'for, sir, I daren't approach that castle.' And Perceval followed her gaze, and saw a huge and hideous fortress at the foot of a lowering mountain. 'It's the castle of the Black Hermit, and archers defend it who shoot with such force that none can endure their shots; and they won't cease, it's said, until you go there. But I know why they will then stop: they'll want to trap you inside the castle to kill and destroy you; but no-one there has the power to harm you save the Black Hermit himself, though he'll do battle with you willingly.'

Without another word Perceval turned towards the castle of the Black Hermit, the Maiden of the Cart following behind. The archers of the castle drew their bows and let fly with terrible power, but Perceval rode swiftly on. They did not recognise him with his white shield with the red cross, and thought he must be some other knight, and many bolts they sent smashing into his shield. Up he came to the drawbridge: it was raised, and beneath it a river ran, foul and terrible. But as soon as he reached it the bridge was lowered. At once the archers stopped shooting, for they knew then that it was Perceval; and the gate was opened to receive him, for the men within felt sure they had the power to kill him. But as soon as they saw him they lost their resolve and were all downcast and powerless, and said they would leave this affair to their lord, who was powerful indeed and had ample strength to kill a man. Perceval, fully armed, entered a great hall and found it filled with a people ugly to behold. The one they called the Black Hermit was standing in the middle of the hall, fully armed.

'Lord,' said his men, 'you'd better defend yourself, for you'll have no counsel or aid from us! We're your men to guard and protect you, and we've done so many times. Now defend us in this hour of need!'

The Black Hermit was mounted on a huge black horse and was magnificently armed. As soon as Perceval saw him he charged at him with such fury that he filled the hall with thunder. The Black Hermit charged, too, and they struck each other with such force that the Black Hermit smashed his lance, and Perceval struck him such a furious blow over his shield that he sent him crashing from his horse, and as he fell he shattered two ribs in his belly; and when the men looking on saw him fall they threw open the cover of a great pit in the middle of the hall, from which belched the foulest stench ever smelt; and they took their lord and flung him into this chasm of filth. Then they turned to Perceval and surrendered the castle to him, and put themselves entirely at his mercy.

Thereupon the Maiden of the Cart appeared, and to her they returned the heads sealed in gold and the heads of the king and the queen. All the people of the Black Hermit's castle were now obedient to Perceval's will and swore to him that no passing knights would ever again be assailed and tormented as they had been thitherto: now they would be received with gladness as they were elsewhere. So it was that Perceval left the castle with joy in his heart, having converted it to a devout and total faith in the New Law.

As he took his leave of the Maiden of the Cart she said to him: 'I pray, sir, that God will guide you now to the house of your uncle, the Hermit King Pelles. He will explain the meaning of your adventures, and will have news that will distress and astound you.'

Perceval was troubled by this but shared her prayer; and that very day he came indeed, by God's will, to his uncle's hermitage. King Pelles greeted his nephew with the utmost joy, and Perceval told him of the great adventures that had befallen him since his departure.

'Uncle,' he said, 'I wonder much about a little white animal I came across in a forest; she had a litter of twelve in her belly which barked and yelped inside her. In the end they burst out and killed her beside a cross, but they never tasted her flesh. Two hermits collected her flesh and blood in golden vessels, while the dogs that had been born from her ran off into the woods, demented.'

'Nephew,' said the king, 'it's a sure sign that God holds you dear when such things appear to you. That sweet and gentle beast in which the twelve dogs were barking signifies Our Lord, and the twelve dogs signify the Jews of the Old Law, whom God created and made in His image. After He had created them He wanted to see how much they loved Him, so He cast them into the wilderness for forty years – but their garments never wore out, and He sent them manna from Heaven. There they dwelt without harm or misfortune, as happy as they could have wished. Then one day they held their council, and the greatest amongst them said that if God became displeased and took back the manna they would have nothing to eat, and it couldn't last forever. They replied that they would hide away a great part of it, so that as soon as God became angry with them they would have plenty to sustain them. But God, who hears and sees all, took back the manna of Heaven; and when they came to their underground caves, expecting to find what they had stowed away, it had all been turned by the will of God into lizards and snakes and vermin; and then they saw they'd done wrong and all dispersed through unknown lands. Dear nephew, the twelve dogs who tore their mother apart but couldn't eat her flesh, and who fled away and turned wild, are the Jews whom God nourished and who were born into the Law which He had established, but would not believe in Him or love Him; instead they crucified Him and broke His body as basely as they could. The hermits who gathered the beast's flesh and blood in their golden vessels signify the deity of the Father, who will not suffer the flesh of the Son to be diminished.'

'Dear uncle,' said Perceval, 'it's only right that they should suffer such an ill reward, for they crucified the one who made them. But tell me about the two hermits: one had been kissing the Cross and worshipping it with the greatest joy, while the other had been beating it, weeping with the bitterest grief in the world. I'd have been angry with him if he hadn't been a holy man.'

'The one who struck the Cross,' said the hermit, 'believes in God just as much as the one who worshipped it. One worshipped it because on it was placed the holy flesh of the Saviour of the world, who would not turn away from death; that hermit was rejoicing because by His death the Saviour redeemed those who loved Him from the anguish of Hell, and they would otherwise have suffered there always. The other was beating the Cross and weeping for the pain that God had suffered there, an indescribable pain, so great that the rocks split*. That's why he beat it and reproached it, because the Saviour had been crucified there, just as I would hate a lance or a sword with which you'd been killed. Whenever he thinks of the pain that God endured he comes to the Cross as you saw. Both of those hermits dwell in the forest; the one who kissed and worshipped the Cross is named Jonas, and the one who beat it is called Alexis.'

Perceval listened eagerly to his uncle's words, and then told him how he had fought with the demon knight who bore the dragon's head on his shield which threw fire and flame, and how it consumed its master in the end.

'Nephew,' said the hermit, 'I rejoice to hear this news of yours, for I'd heard that the Knight of the Circle of Gold had killed him.'

'That may well be so, sir,' said Perceval, 'but truly, I never saw so terrible an enemy.'

'Dear nephew, none but a good knight could have vanquished him. And just as the demon on the shield burned its lord to death, so does one demon torment another in the other world.'

'Uncle,' said Perceval, 'I came by way of a turning castle, where there were copper archers shooting, and bears and lions in chains at the gateway. But as soon as I rode up and struck the gate with my sword, the castle stopped turning.'

'Nephew, the Devil had nowhere more completely in his power than that castle, for it was the entrance to his fastness; and never would its people have been converted had it not been for you.'

'I was very sad that Sir Gawain and Lancelot couldn't enter with me; I'd have dearly loved their company, and they'd have been of great assistance.'

'If they'd been as chaste as you,' his uncle replied, 'they would have entered, for they're the finest knights in the world but for their lust. Nephew, since you became a knight you have greatly advanced the Law of the Saviour, for you've

* Matthew 27:51.

destroyed the falsest religion in the world: the people at the Copper Tower worshipped the Devil. If they had survived and you had failed they would never have been destroyed until the world's end.

'But listen, nephew: now you must accomplish another task: you must recapture the castle of the Fisher King. Yes, all the people of the land which belonged to your grandfather the Fisher King have abandoned the New Law; but most have done so only because of the strength and power of the king who has seized the land – the King of Castle Mortal, who is my brother and your uncle. Oh, it's a grievous shame that one of such holy descent should prove a traitor! Now you must settle this affair: it can be accomplished by no man on earth but you, for the castle and the land of the Fisher King are your inheritance. But nephew,' he said, 'the castle is now greatly strengthened: there are nine bridges newly built, with three knights, huge and strong, defending each; and your uncle is within, guarding the castle. Since he took it the Fisher King and his entire household – knights and priests, boys and maidens – have disappeared, and no-one knows what has become of them. And the chapel in which the Holy Grail used to appear is completely empty. The hermits of the forest yearn for your coming, for no longer do they ever see a knight pass by who believes in God. If you can accomplish this task and reconquer the castle, you are sure to win favour in God's eyes.'

'I'll go, uncle,' said Perceval, 'indeed I will; the castle shouldn't be in the hands of this intruder.'

'Good nephew, I have here a mule, very white and very old, and you're to take her with you: she'll follow you most willingly; and you shall carry a banner, for the strength of God is much greater than your own: twenty-seven knights guard the nine bridges, all picked and tested men of great courage, and no-one should believe that any knight could overcome so many unless Our Lord worked a miracle. And I beg you, be ever-mindful of God and His sweet mother; and when you're hard-pressed, mount the mule and take up the banner, and the strength of your enemies will diminish, for nothing confounds the enemy so swiftly as the power of God. It's well known that you're the finest knight in the world, but you mustn't trust in your strength and chivalry alone against so many, for you wouldn't be able to withstand them.'

Perceval was attentive to all his uncle said, and had the utmost faith in his wisdom.

'Dear nephew,' said the hermit, 'there are two lions at the gateway – one red and the other white. Trust in the white, for he is on God's side; and look to him whenever your strength flags, and he will look at you likewise, and you'll know his mind at once; do what you see in him, for he will think nothing but good, and you will not otherwise succeed in conquering the nine bridges. May God grant that you do conquer them, so that you may save your life and advance the Law of Our Lord, which your uncle is doing all in his power to suppress.'

And with few more words Perceval left the hermitage, carrying the banner as his uncle had advised, with the mule following behind him.

On he rode towards the land which had belonged to the Fisher King, until he met a hermit coming out of his cell. He stopped as soon as he saw the Cross on Perceval's shield, and said: 'Sir, you're clearly a Christian, and I've not seen one for a long time. The King of Castle Mortal is driving us all from the forest, for he has rejected God and His sweet mother, and we daren't dwell here against his decree.'

'By my life,' cried Perceval, 'that you will! God will guide you there first and me after. Are there more hermits in this forest?'

'Yes, sir, twelve, and they're waiting for me at a cross up ahead; we're all going to the kingdom of Logres and leaving our cells and chapels here for fear of the wicked king who's seized the land, for he won't allow any who believe in God to remain.'

Perceval followed the holy man to the Cross where the hermits were meeting. There he found his cousin the young hermit Joseus, the son of King Pelles, and he greeted him with the greatest joy. Then he bade the hermits turn back with him, saying that he would protect them with God's help, and he begged them most tenderly to pray that Our Lord might permit him to win back his rightful inheritance.

He neared the castle, with its great defences at the entrance. Some knew for certain that Perceval would conquer it, for it had long before been prophesied that the one who bore that shield, the white shield with the red cross, would win the Grail from one who rejected God. The knights saw Perceval coming with the company of hermits; a fine sight it was, and they were filled with awe. At a distance of two bow-shots from the bridge stood a chapel, and Perceval halted there with his company and tethered his horse and mule outside and entered. The hermits followed him. Inside was a tomb of exceptional beauty; and as soon as Perceval fixed his eyes upon it, its seal broke and it opened, and the stone lid rose so that they could see the body that lay within. A fragrance of the purest sweetness issued forth; and they found letters inside which testified that the body was that of Joseph of Arimathea. As soon as the hermits saw this, they said to Perceval:

'Sir, now we know for the first time that you are the Good Knight, the chaste and most sacred!'

Perceval left the chapel and mounted his horse once more, fully armed. The hermits blessed him and commended him to God. And clutching his lance he rode down towards the three knights who guarded the first bridge; they came rushing towards him and smashed their lances on his shield; then he struck one with such fury that he sent him plunging into the river below, and though the other two struggled long with him, he overcame them and cut them to pieces and flung their bodies into the water. The knights at the second bridge now came forward and battled hard, for they were fine knights indeed. Then Perceval's cousin Joseus told the other hermits that he would gladly have gone to his aid if he had not thought it a sin, but they said to him that he need have no fear of that, for it would be a great deed to destroy the enemies of Our Lord; so Joseus cast off his grey cloak, and wearing only his cassock he seized one of Perceval's attackers, lifted him on to his shoulders and hurled him into the water. Perceval now killed the other two and flung them in the river like the rest; but by the time he had conquered the two bridges he was weary indeed. Then he thought of the lion of which his uncle had spoken, and looking towards the gate he beheld a white lion, standing on its hind legs and peering at him. Perceval gazed at its eyes and knew at once what the lion was thinking: that the knights at the third bridge were so bold and strong that they would never be beaten by a single knight without the aid of God, so he should ride on the mule and carry the banner. Perceval saw the white lion's thoughts and drew back, and Joseus did likewise. But as soon as they left the bridges behind they looked back and saw that the first bridge had been raised. Perceval went to his mule, which bore the mark of a red cross on her forehead, and mounted, and took up the banner and clutched his drawn sword. And when the white lion saw him returning, it broke from its chains and ran between the knights to the bridge that had been raised, and lowered it at once. Up rode Perceval, sword in hand, upon the white mule, and he attacked the knights who guarded the third bridge and dealt one such a blow that he sent him crashing into the water. Now Joseus came forward, aiming to seize the other two, but they cried for mercy, vowing to do Perceval's will and believe in God and abandon their evil lord; and the knights at the fourth bridge did likewise. Perceval took Joseus's advice and let them live, and they gave up their arms and surrendered the bridges. It now occurred to Perceval that, although the power of God was great indeed, a knight of worth should put his own strength to the test for God; even if all the knights in the world were against God and His will, He would vanquish them in an hour, but He wishes men to labour for Him just as He suffered for His people. So Perceval rode back and climbed from the mule and gave the banner to Joseus; then he mounted his horse once more and returned to attack the knights at the fifth bridge. They defended themselves vigorously, for they were brave knights indeed, and fought fiercely against Perceval; but Joseus the hermit came to join him and assailed them in a fury, and Perceval cut them down and slaughtered them, sending them toppling into the river that rushed beneath the bridges.

When the knights at the sixth bridge saw that all before theirs had been conquered, they cried to Perceval for mercy and yielded to him and surrendered their swords. The knights at the seventh bridge did likewise, and when the red lion saw that the seven bridges had been conquered and the knights at the last two bridges had surrendered to Perceval, it leaped forward in a fury to the limit of its chain, and attacked one of the knights and killed him and devoured him; the white lion flew into a rage and rushed at the red, and tore it to pieces in an instant with its teeth and claws. Then it rose up on its hind legs and looked at Perceval; and Perceval gazed back and saw that the lion was thinking that the knights who guarded the last bridges would be harder to conquer than the others, and would never be destroyed save by the will of God and by the lion himself; and that Perceval should not befriend them, whatever they might promise, for they were treacherous; he should go and mount the white mule, for she was a creature of God, and Joseus should carry the banner, and all the hermits, who were worthy men indeed, should advance at their head to dismay the treacherous king; and when the castle was conquered, then his end would be near.

Perceval had great faith in the lion's thoughts, and he climbed from his horse and remounted the mule, while Joseus took up the banner. Then the company of the twelve hermits, most fair and holy, advanced towards the castle; and the knights at the last bridges saw Perceval advancing with them, and Joseus carrying the banner. They had already seen them attack and destroy their comrades; and the power of Our Lord, the dignity of the banner, the virtue which lay in the mule and the holiness of the good hermits as they offered their prayers to Our Lord all beset the knights' resolve so much that they could scarcely keep control of themselves. But the treachery could never leave their hearts: they were grieved at seeing their kinsmen slaughtered, and they thought to themselves that if they could plead for mercy and escape from there, they would never rest until they had murdered Perceval. And so they came forward, and looking most humble they cried for mercy and promised to do his will, but begged him to let them go alive and unharmed. Perceval looked to the lion for guidance, and saw that the lion thought they were treacherous and disloyal, and that if they were dead their lord would be defenceless. Perceval cried that he would never have mercy on them, and advanced upon them with his drawn sword; they were too terrified to defend themselves, and he almost refrained from killing them when he found no attempt at resistance. But the lion had no such qualms, and leaped at them and tore them to pieces and tossed their limbs and bodies into the river. Perceval left the lion to deal with them, and was pleased with the way he did so; never had he seen a beast he loved so dearly.

Meanwhile the King of Castle Mortal was standing on the battlements. He had seen the lion destroy the last of his knights and realised he was now defenceless. So he climbed to the highest part of the walls and lifted the skirt of his hauberk; then, gripping his drawn sword, he plunged the blade right through his body and tumbled over the wall and into the river, swift and deep; Perceval and all the hermits saw him, and were astonished that he should have killed himself in this way.

It is no surprise if out of three or four brothers there is one who is bad; but it is a great sorrow when a single wicked one injures the greater good of the others. Just as Cain murdered his brother Abel, it is a grievous pity when relatives who should be united betray each other. This wicked king had been treacherous, despite being a brother of the good King Pelles and of the Widowed Lady of Kamaalot, the mother of Perceval. All this family had been in the service of Our Lord, from beginning to end, except for this wicked king who had come to such a sorry end.

Perceval now rode into the castle, and the worthy hermits with him; and as soon as they entered they thought they could hear voices singing '*Gloria in Excelsis Deo*,' and the sweetest praise for Our Lord. They found the halls rich and beautiful indeed, magnificently adorned; and the chapel where the relics had been kept they found open. But they were empty; and the hermits prayed to God to send them soon the Holy Grail and the relics that had been there before.

The aged knights and the priests and maidens of the Fisher King's household had all departed when the King of Castle Mortal had seized the castle, having no wish to be in his power. But God had protected them and guided them to safety; and knowing that the Good Knight had reconquered the castle which was rightfully his, He now sent back all who had been in the Fisher King's service. Perceval greeted them with the greatest joy, just as they greeted him; and they seemed indeed to be ones who had come from a place where God and His will reigned.

And that night the Fisher King himself returned to the castle; and there in the hall, bathed in radiant light, he summoned Perceval to sit at his side and eat from his bowl, most generously and freely.

They had not been sitting long before a lovely girl, whiter than a flower on a sapling's branch, appeared from a chamber; in her hands she was holding the Holy Grail. She passed before the table. And a moment later another girl came, fairer than any ever seen, dressed in a white silken cloth; she was carrying the lance that dripped blood from its tip. And a boy followed after, carrying in his hands the sword still imperfectly repaired; gently and carefully he laid it on a corner of the table by the king. Perceval was very much on edge, and began to say to the king:

'Sire, I've been in your house twice before, but however much I asked you about the affairs of this land, you wouldn't tell me anything; and I almost repaired a sword that was broken across the middle – a fine, a wonderful sword indeed. I see it before me now.'

The king said this: 'Before God, my friend, you've suffered a great deal to accomplish what you've done. But don't be upset or aggrieved. Just take hold of this sword, and it will be joined and made whole.'

Perceval leaned forward and grasped the sword without hesitation. Then he cast his eyes upon it, and saw the notch in the blade and was overcome with anguish. He rubbed his hand up and down the sword – no-one intervened or bade him stop – and then brandished it four times so violently that he almost shattered it. And thereupon the notch was repaired: he had joined it completely, perfectly. He took it by the blade and presented it to the Fisher King in full view of everyone. The king beheld it and was filled with indescribable joy.

'All your toil,' he said, 'is well rewarded, when God declares you worthy to know the truth about all these things!'

Perceval was exultant. Now he felt no grief or sorrow; instead his heart overflowed with joy: he almost burst out singing. The king threw his arms around his neck and said: 'My good, dear grandson, be lord of my house. I willingly bestow upon you everything I have, and henceforth will hold you dearer than any man alive.'

At that the boy who had brought the sword stepped forward and wrapped it in a silken cloth and carried it away; and Perceval was greatly comforted by the great joy and honour that God had sent him that day. The king looked at him and said:

'Eat, dear grandson, and may God who was crucified for our sins grant you every honour and forgiveness.'

At complete leisure they had all the food and wine they could have wished for; no prophet or divine ever drank the like. And just as they were about to rise from dinner, there passed once more before the royal table the lance and the Grail, and a beautiful silver trencher, splendid and handsome, carried by a girl most elegantly. When they had passed the tables, they returned to the chamber from which they had come. Perceval, observing this, sighed, and looked at the king and said at once:

'Dear grandfather, tell me freely now what you promised me before dinner.'

'Come close to me,' the king replied, 'and I'll tell you whatever you wish to ask.'

'I long to know,' said Perceval, 'about the lance and the Grail and the trencher that I've seen: tell me first who is served from them, and where they come from.'

'Grandson,' replied the king, 'I'll tell you first about the lance. Without a word of a lie, it is the holy lance with which Longinus struck Christ when He was hung upon the Cross. And the precious, holy blood which flows from its head is the holy, precious blood that ran from God's side when Longinus pierced Him to the heart. The blow that God received on the Cross was well struck indeed; for through death He overcame the Devil and delivered us from the torment of Hell. That death saved us, you understand, from the evils brought upon us by Adam and Eve when they bit into the apple.'

Perceval leaned on his elbow and listened intently to the Fisher King's words; and he wept at the agony that God had suffered: not for all the Roman Empire would he have stopped. And he said to the king: 'Sire, you've told me about the lance. Now I want to know about the Grail and the trencher, if it's right to ask.'

And the king, governed always by gentleness, granted his every wish, and said: 'When God hung on the holy, glorious Cross and His side was pierced and they withdrew the lance-head, blood ran from the wound right down to his foot. Joseph of Arimathea turned black with grief at the sight of Jesus tortured, and he took this holy vessel and caught the blood therein. The Grail, dear grandson, is Joseph's vessel. And the silver trencher carried by the girl was used to cover the holy vessel so that the blood should not be left exposed. Such, truly, is the Grail, which passed through here with the lance. I've told you the truth about all this: not a word I've said has been a lie. And if there's anything more you wish to know, I'll tell you the truth likewise.'

And Perceval, most eager to hear all, said: 'Sire, please tell me how the Holy Grail came to this country: I long to know that more than anything.'

'Listen then,' the king replied. 'When God was hung upon the Cross, Joseph took Him down with the help of Nichodemus, a smith, the finest that there was. For this he was imprisoned, cast into a dark, black dungeon where he suffered terribly; they wanted him to rot and starve to death. He stayed there for forty days with nothing to eat or drink; but the Lord God sent the Holy Grail to him: he saw it two or three times a day as it visited him in the dungeon, and through the Grail's sweet power he never felt any pain or ill. And the emperor's son Vespasian, although he had not been a Christian, freed him from the dungeon. By God's will the Grail remained in Joseph's keeping. But the time came when a messenger of Our Lord commanded Joseph to bequeath the sacred vessel to me, and bade that I should carry it into the West. I did so, and came to settle in this country and built this house; and Joseph, who was my dear brother-in-law, came to join me here before he died: he lived here at this very house; and when he was dying and departed this life the Grail remained – as it always will, if it please God, as long as I am here.'

Perceval listened with gladness to the story of the Grail, and praised Our Lord for the miracle. Then he said: 'Dear grandfather, tell me also about the beautiful girls who carry the Grail and the trencher; I'm sorry if I'm tiring you with my questions, but all the riches in the world wouldn't give me such joy as this.'

'The girl who carries the Grail,' the Fisher King replied, 'is a maiden and a virgin – otherwise, God save me, she would never have held it in her hands. She's my own daughter – and is certainly no disgrace to me! And the girl who carries the trencher is of royal birth, and wise and courteous indeed: she's the daughter of King Gon of Sert. Now you've heard the stories of the Grail and the lance. And it's time to sleep; let's retire to our beds.'

'Oh, good sir!' cried Perceval. 'Please don't object: I want to know how the sword I've twice repaired was broken.'

'Very well,' said the king. 'I'll tell you: listen, and I'll explain. The sword that you've repaired – for which you should be deeply happy – is the one with which the Mortal Blow was struck. Never will such a grievous and evil blow be dealt, and we're still suffering for it – I and all this kingdom. King Gon of Sert, my brother, the peer of any emperor, was besieged in the castle of Quingragrant by Espinogre, a man of great strength accompanied by a mighty host of knights and men-at-arms. My brother Gon rode out to do battle with him, and fought so well that he routed his whole army. But Espinogre had a nephew of great boldness, who had vowed that he would kill my brother that day; and he did so – by trickery and a foul misdeed. When he saw his side being routed he cast aside his arms and, being well practised in wickedness, stripped a dead enemy of his arms and donned them himself and rejoined the battle, clutching the splendid sword of which you've joined the pieces. He headed for my brother, who had no fear of him, being sure that he was one of his own men, and who, with his helmet off and his mail-hood down, was riding back towards his household who had fought brilliantly that day. And Espinogre's nephew, intent upon his evil plan, struck my unsuspecting brother on the head with his sword and clove him in two right down to the saddle. At this grievous blow the good sword broke in half. And the killer rode off with all speed, throwing away the half he held. He returned to his army who greeted him with the utmost honour, while the men of the castle carried back King Gon of Sert, cloven, cold and dead. And with his body, in deepest sorrow, they also took the sword, broken across the middle, which the knight had thrown down in the press. They carried him to the castle laid out on his shield, with no blanket or serge to cover him. When they had washed and dressed him as well as they could they laid him in a bier and brought him here to me, along with the sword. One of my nieces told me how it had wrought the death of her father, and assured me that if I kept the pieces until a knight came here and repaired the sword, then my brother, whom I loved so dearly, would be avenged by him. But I was so stricken with grief that I took the pieces she had given me, and scythed through my thighs and severed every nerve. That's why I've been helpless ever since, and always will be until revenge is taken upon the false-hearted wretch who treacherously killed the finest knight who ever lived.'

Perceval, hearing the Fisher King's story, responded with a sincere and humble heart, saying: 'Truly, grandfather, he did an evil deed. Tell me the knight's name. The task of vengeance falls to me – I want to know his arms and emblems, too. And as a loyal knight I swear to you that if I can track him down I'll bring him back dead or captive – unless he kills me: that will be his only escape.'

'Dear grandson,' said the Fisher King, 'may the one who forgave Longinus give you the strength and power to do it. The killer's name was Partinial the Wild. He's the Lord of the Red Tower and the land thereabouts. He has wonderfully handsome arms – of silver, emblazoned with two maidens painted in blue. My suffering would be ended if revenge were taken on him, but he has no respect for any knight alive.'

'Sire,' replied Perceval, 'we who ride through the land in search of renown are used to suffering all manner of ills, and with Our Lord's support I'm sure I'll succeed.'

'May He guard you from misfortune,' said the king. 'Let's go and sleep now, for it's well past time, and I think you're tired and in need of rest.'

'Truly, sire, I won't sleep until you've told me the truth about the tree I saw bedecked with candles; and about the altar I saw in the chapel where the dead knight lay: please tell me his name! I've got to know! And the candle in the chapel that was suddenly extinguished – tell me truly, who snuffed it out?'

And his grandfather, sincerely eager to fulfil his wishes, said kindly: 'Hear the truth, then, about the tree of candles. It's the tree of enchantment. The lights which look like candles from afar are fairies who lead astray all who've put their faith in God. And the fact that you went to the tree and saw nothing was a sure sign that you were to accomplish the strange adventures of this land. No-one will ever hear of that tree again, for you chased away the fairies forever as you rode up to the tree. Now it's time to go to our beds and rest awhile.'

'Oh, sire,' said Perceval, 'tell me first about the chapel and the body!'

'I promised to tell you whatever you wished,' said the king, 'so it's only right I do so. Believe me, then, when I say that the chapel was built at the command of Brangemor of Cornwall, the mother of King Pinogres who was so cruel and violent. She became a nun at the chapel, but for less than a day, for then she died: her son Pinogres killed her and beheaded her, burdening himself with a terrible sin. She was buried beneath the altar, and not a day has passed since then without a knight being killed there. More than a thousand have been killed by a hand that ambushes them: no-one knows who their killer is, only that they're killed by a hand with black and swarthy skin. It's the same hand that snuffs out the candle.'

'That's an amazing story,' said Perceval. 'Can no-one rid the chapel of this horror?'

'Dear grandson,' replied the king, 'there's a cupboard in the chapel containing a white veil; and a knight willing to do battle with the Black Hand should know that if he were to drench the veil in holy water and sprinkle it over the altar and the body and the chapel, he would bring an end to the evils of the place. But any man who wanted to fight the Black Hand would need to be brave indeed, possessed of all knightly qualities.'

And with that he rose to his feet and said: 'Go to your bed now, grandson, and sleep, for I can see you're tired from staying awake so long; I fear all the talking I've done has exhausted you, though you seem to have listened with delight. The beds are ready: go and sleep now, if you will.'

Then Perceval rose at once and said: 'I'll do as you say, sire, without fail.'

* * *

Perceval slept in a luxurious bed that night, and next morning he rose early and, after hearing mass sweetly sung in the castle chapel, he took his leave of the Fisher King, vowing that he would not rest until he had found the knight Partinial and taken revenge for the terrible blow, the source of so much suffering.

With his sword girded on and his lance in hand, he rode on all morning, but met no-one at all. Then he passed into a forest and wandered on until late in the afternoon, when he came to the forest's edge. As he passed from the woods the sky began to turn pitch black, though the day was not yet done; and the air was whipped into dusty whirlwinds, and rocks and thunderbolts fell from the sky, so huge and thick and fast that it might have been the end of the world. Perceval and his horse alike received some mighty blows. He did not dare keep his eyes open, and covered his head with his shield; and the rocks that fell upon it made such a crashing din that it was terrible to hear. The thunderbolts and lightning flew until the air and sky seemed ablaze on every side. The forest was toppling and crashing all around. Perceval could see neither fortress nor tower, nor any house, and his horse was going wild at the storming din. Then suddenly the weather cleared, and there before him he saw a chapel. He turned his horse towards it and spurred on urgently. He entered; he was soaking wet and weather-beaten, but greatly relieved to be inside: he swore before God that he had never seen such a storm.

Just then he glanced towards the altar and saw a dead knight lying upon it, with a candle burning beside him; and a moment later he saw, coming through a window, a hand, and it was black right up to the elbow: it was dark and hideous indeed, and it snuffed out the candle. And as soon as the candle was out the air turned dark and dreadful, and Perceval could see no more in there than if he had been down a well. But he refused to be dismayed: he knew he had to fight the hand and prepared to do battle. For a moment he stood in utter darkness, seeing nothing; then suddenly in the flash of a lightning bolt he spotted the hand and darted forward and thrust his lance at it, but the hand seized it in a mighty grip and smashed it to splinters in an instant. Perceval stepped back and drew his sword and leaped towards the hand; but just as he was about to strike he saw a head looming in at the window, followed by its body as far as the waist, and it flung a blazing firebrand, fully twelve feet wide, which scorched Perceval's face and brows. Then Perceval invoked God by His several names, for he knew very well that it was the Devil he had seen. He raised his hand and made the sign of the Cross upon his forehead; and at once he heard a mighty din come crashing from the sky and a lightning bolt rent the very walls asunder. Then Perceval looked up and saw a colossal demon, blazing with fire, with arms as black as coal: it was clearly this demon's hand that had come through the window. And in the same moment he saw a veil lying in an open cupboard – the very veil, he was sure, that the Fisher King had described. He darted towards it, but just as he was about to take it a huge black hand barred his way and a terrible voice cried:

'Knight, you were insolent to enter here – and you've made a grave mistake in staying! Tomorrow it'll be *your* body lying on the altar!'

Perceval uttered not a word in reply, but he raised his hand and made the sign of the Cross. A thunderbolt crashed down, and the demon leaped back through the wall and sprang on to the chapel roof in dire fear of the sign of the Cross; and the lightning bolt struck a wooden beam and sent it bursting into flames and the whole chapel caught fire – nothing could prevent it. But Perceval, still undaunted, came straight to the cupboard to take the veil; but again the hand stopped him, and the voice howled:

'Perceval, cease this folly! Don't believe the Fisher King: you'll be crazy if you do! Be off with you or you'll die here! I've struck down many knights who've fought me – there's one left dead here every day! Make sure you're not left with them!'

Perceval made no reply at all, but advanced towards the cupboard to take the veil. The demon moved to stop him, seizing him by the left hand; but Perceval clutched his sword in the right and strove and struggled to strike the black hand; but to no avail – every blow he dealt failed. He was locked in a terrible battle now, the demon striving with all his might to stop him taking the veil and to inflict all possible pain. He seized Perceval by the hand and pulled and wrenched, sure that he would overpower him. But Perceval made the sign of the Cross with his sword to prevent the demon harming him; and instantly the demon fled in terror as thunder and lightning burst from the sky, the most fearsome ever seen, miraculously wrought by God when the sign of the Cross was made. Perceval crumpled, stricken with awe; and he should not be blamed for that, for no man born encountered such a perilous day in all his earthly life. Beside the altar in the chapel he lay unconscious, stunned by the mighty lightning bolt that had crashed down and dumbfounded him. And meanwhile the fire was spreading everywhere – there was not a rafter, beam or batten left unburnt. Just in time he recovered his senses, and came straight to the cupboard and threw it open and drew forth the white veil. And he did not treat it with contempt, but held it with all reverence. Then he took a vase, brim-full of holy water, and plunged the veil deep in it; then he carried the veil outside and processed all round the chapel, sprinkling the walls, as though it were Ascension Day, Christmas, Easter or Pentecost.

When he had sprinkled every side he entered the chapel again, and dipping the veil in holy water once more he sprinkled the chapel inside; and as he did so, the fire was extinguished, and the storm, which had done so much damage that night, abated. But all the country far and wide had been burnt and consumed by scorching fire.

When Perceval saw that the storm was done he returned the veil safely to the cupboard. Then he hurried back to the body that lay upon the altar, and examined it closely to see if he had seen the man before; but it was impossible to tell, for it was so hideously hacked and battered by the demon that it was as black as pitch. He had never seen such a hideous corpse, and would have dearly loved to find a priest to bury it: he would willingly have lent a hand.

Perceval lay in the chapel until morning, for there was no light at all until day began to break; and just as it did so, the candle began to burn – and it did not go out: nor will it ever until the world's end. When Perceval awoke he was startled by the light from the burning candle. He stared long at it, wondering how it could have been lit – until he realised that it was surely an act of God. Then he noticed a bell hanging in a little belfry and, thinking that if it was rung someone would come, he pulled at the bell-rope. It was not long before a frail old man in a grey cloak appeared. He must have been a hundred years old: his beard had grown right down to his waist and his hair was so long that it touched his heels. Perceval greeted him at once, and the old man returned his greeting, saying:

'I wish you good fortune, sir, for you're the finest knight of more than three thousand who've come here and fought to destroy the terrible marvel.'

'Good sir,' said Perceval, 'do you know where I might find a priest who could bury this body? I wouldn't like to leave him before he's interred.'

And the worthy man replied: 'I'm a priest myself, have no doubt; and I've buried three thousand already, all strangled to death by the Black Hand. But now you've brought this adventure to an end: no more evil will befall this place.'

So Perceval helped the aged priest to prepare the burial. They laid the body in a wooden bed and covered it in a rich sheet of green and indigo silk, and the worthy man placed a cross of gold at the body's head between two elegant golden candlesticks. Then he rang the bell, and two brothers, who dwelt nearby as monks, arrived with a chalice of engraved silver. The priest now began the holy service, to which Perceval listened with deep devotion. And when the service was done the priest came to the dead knight and commended his soul to God. Then the brothers took the body and carried it to a cemetery surrounded by a row of trees; there are many cemeteries in the world, but none as beautiful as this; and all the trees were heavily laden, for on them hung the arms, lances and shields of all those defeated and slaughtered by the demon. The priest walked softly ahead of the bier, and the two who bore it halted beneath a tree where no armour hung, and there they laid it down. Next to the tree was a marble tomb, and they sprinkled it with holy water before laying the body inside; and over the tomb they laid a massive slab of heavy marble, richly inlaid with enamel.

On their way back Perceval, eager to learn about the cemetery and the arms that hung upon the trees, began to question the priest. And the old man told him the true story from beginning to end, saying:

'In this great cemetery I've buried all who died fighting the hand. They all lie in marble tombs, and on each tree hang the arms and shield of the one who lies beneath. Queen Brangemore began the graveyard, and by my life, it was an accursed beginning, for never has a day gone by without a knight being killed here by the hand. The first to be buried was Brangemore herself, and the knight we've just buried will be the last, for no man will ever again be that demon's victim.'

'But where did all these handsome tombs come from?'

'Since the queen was killed,' the hermit replied, 'not a day has passed without a tomb, made to measure for the knight who'd died, being found beneath the tree where he was to lie. And by the faith I owe Christ, the name of the dead knight was written on each one.'

Perceval said that before he left he would go and look at all the inscriptions on the marble slabs.

'So help me God,' said the hermit, 'it'll be noon before you've finished!'

And he left him and went to the chapel to disrobe. Perceval spent all day until nightfall reading the inscriptions; and he found a good number that caused him sorrow. Had he recognised anyone from King Arthur's court it would have been the greatest sorrow of all. But finding no knight of Arthur's he returned to the chapel.

'If you will, sir,' said the old priest, 'accept our lodging and our charity tonight, in the name of the Holy Trinity.'

'Gladly,' said Perceval, 'but I must fetch my horse and bring him here.'

'Your horse is already in the house, and his food has been provided: two basins full of barley; and he has good hay, and a litter of straw that's belly-deep!'

Perceval entered the house, and the worthy man gave him a grey woollen garment – one just like the ewe wears, without any dye or colouring. When the brothers had set up the table – crude though it was – and spread the cloth, they laid it as best they could with barley bread and water, and with cabbages they had cut in the garden; that was all they had to eat, and with that they quelled their hunger.

When they had eaten, the old priest drew his stool close to Perceval and asked him about himself: who he was, and from what land, and what he was seeking in those parts. And Perceval began to tell him, saying:

'I'm a knight, sir, of the Round Table; and I'm wandering in search of chivalry and honour.'

'Honour?'

'Yes indeed, sir.'

'How do you do that?'

'When I go seeking adventures – and I often encounter fearsome ones – I do battle with many knights, and kill and defeat and capture many, and thus I strive to enhance my reputation.'

'Dear friend,' said the hermit, 'that's an astonishing thing to say: you think you win honour and esteem by vanquishing a knight? God help me, you rather win the plainest damnation for your soul! And a man who loses his soul loses everything.'

Perceval was dumbfounded by the worthy man's words. 'By Saint Peter, sir,' he said, 'how then can I save my soul?'

'I'll tell you,' the priest replied. 'If you want to save yourself you must abandon the paths you've followed so long and pacify your heart. A man who kills and murders others and devotes himself to doing ill wins only his own downfall, for he will be in Hell everlastingly.'

Perceval was truly shocked by the worthy man's words, and took them deeply to heart.

Next morning he rose early, and went to the chapel without delay, where the worthy man sang the mass. Then Perceval went to him and confessed all his misdeeds; and as penance the priest emphatically charged him to beware of ever committing such a sin as to kill a man except in self-defence; and Perceval swore he would not. Then he took up his arms and departed, commending the worthy man to God.

Galahad

ERCEVAL RODE OUT INTO OPEN COUNTRY BUT MET no-one; then he passed back into the forest and rode on, his head bowed in thought. Suddenly a knight came thundering through the trees, lance lowered, as fast as his horse could go; and he struck Perceval as he passed and sent him crashing to the ground and seized his horse by the reins. Perceval leaped up swiftly and drew his sword, and began to race after the knight to recover his mount, distraught and furious at being felled. He gave chase right along a valley, not slowing for a moment; but the knight was riding away so fast that a thunderbolt wouldn't have caught him. Perceval lost sight of him and sat down beneath an oak, irate, downcast and troubled, and began to say to himself:

'This morning I unburdened myself of all my sins, wanting to mend my wrongful ways, and now I've lost my horse! I'm in a mess without a mount – I look a proper fool! I don't care what the priest said: I'd pursue that knight to the end of the earth to take revenge! But I'd have to find out his name first – I don't know who he is.'

Such was Perceval's lament as he leaned against the forest oak, sad, dejected and frustrated. While he sat there crestfallen, not knowing what to do, he saw a horse coming straight and swiftly towards him; it lacked neither saddle nor stirrups nor harness: it was a handsome horse indeed, and it galloped up to Perceval like lightning, whinnying and pounding its hooves. And it was as black as any berry. Perceval was roused from his troubled thoughts, and leaped up to catch it as soon as he saw it; the horse baulked and reared, but Perceval grabbed the reins and jumped into the saddle. He was jubilant, and delighted with his fine mount, and said he had had a great stroke of luck in finding this splendid, God-sent horse.

And so it was that he rode on until he found himself in the Waste Forest, where he chanced to meet a knight whose arms he didn't recognise; and taking him for an enemy he charged him and struck him so hard in the chest that he shattered his lance. The knight struck him back, and once again Perceval found himself unseated and crashing to the ground. His own lance being likewise shattered, the knight drew his sword and dealt Perceval such a blow that he split open his helmet and the hood of his mail-coat, and had the sword not turned in his hand he would surely have killed him. Perceval didn't know whether it was day or night.

This combat took place outside the hermitage of a recluse, and when she saw the victorious knight riding away she called out to him: 'Go, and may God be your guide! Truly, if this knight had known you as well as I, he wouldn't have been so bold as to attack you!'

The knight heard this and, seemingly alarmed at being recognised, dug in his spurs and galloped away with all the speed his horse could summon. Perceval remounted as fast as he could, but soon realised he would never catch him; and he turned back, utterly woebegone, and returned to the recluse, hoping to learn something about the knight who had escaped him.

When he arrived at the chapel he beat at the recluse's little window: she was wide awake and opened it at once, and leaned out and asked him who he was. He said he was a knight of King Arthur's court and his name was Perceval the Welshman. When she heard his name she was filled with joy, for she loved him dearly, and rightly so, for he was her nephew. She called to her household and bade them open the door to the knight outside and give him food if he needed and as much as they could, for he was the man she loved most in all the world. They did her bidding, and unbarred the door and admitted Perceval and disarmed him and served him food. He asked if he was allowed to talk to the recluse that evening, and they said:

'No, sir, not until tomorrow after mass.'

He accepted this, and lay down in a bed they prepared for him, and slept all night long, for he was quite exhausted.

When day broke next morning Perceval rose and heard mass, and once he was armed he came to the recluse and said: 'In God's name, lady, tell me about the knight who passed this way yesterday: you said you recognised him – I'm longing to know who he was.'

She asked Perceval why he was so keen to know, and he said: 'I'll never be at ease until I've found him and challenged him to combat. He's done me such dishonour that unless I can pay him back I'll be ashamed!'

'Ah, Perceval!' she said, 'what are you saying? You want to fight with him? Are you so eager to die like your brothers, whose high-handedness brought them to their deaths? Truly, if you die so, it'll be a grievous pity and a disgrace upon your line. And do you realise what you'll lose by fighting this knight? I'll tell you. The great Quest of the Holy Grail is under way, and you are one of its company, are you not? If it please God, it will soon be brought to its conclusion. And a much greater honour awaits you than you imagine, if only you refrain from doing battle with that knight. For we in this land and in many other places know that in the end there will be three supreme knights who, above all others, will achieve the glory and honour of the quest: two will be virgins and the third will be chaste. One of the two virgins will be the knight you seek and the other will be you, and the third will be Bors de Gaunes. By these three knights will the quest be accomplished. And since God has this honour in store for you, it would be a pity indeed if you sought your death in the meantime! And you'll be hastening it for sure if you fight with him, for he is without doubt a much finer knight than you or any man known.'

'From what you say about my brothers, lady,' said Perceval, 'it seems you know who I am.'

'Indeed I do, and so I should, for I'm your aunt and you're my nephew. Don't doubt it just because I'm living here in this poor place: I'm the woman known as the Queen of the Waste Land. Once you'd have seen me in a different state, for I was one of the richest ladies in the world, but that wealth never pleased me as does my present poverty.'

Perceval was moved to tears by her words, and he remembered her now and recognised her as his aunt. He sat down before her and asked her news of his family.

'What?' she said. 'Don't you know about your mother? She died the moment you rode off to Arthur's court. That very same day, as soon as she'd made confession, she died of grief that you'd left her.'

'I know,' said Perceval, 'and she's often appeared to me in my sleep and said she's more reason to rebuke me than to praise me, for I treated her so badly. God have mercy on my soul, for it grieves me deeply. But since it's happened I must bear it, and it's the fate that befalls us all. But tell me, in God's name, do you know who he is, the knight I'm seeking?'

'By my life I do,' she replied. 'Let me explain. You know, don't you, that since the coming of Christ there have been three great tables in the world. The first was the table of Christ Himself, where the apostles ate together many times. At that table souls and bodies were sustained by the bread of Heaven, and the brothers who sat there were united in heart and soul. That table was established by the spotless Lamb who was sacrificed for our redemption. After it, another table was made in its likeness and in its memory: the table of the Holy Grail, which in the days of Joseph of Arimathea, when Christianity was first brought to this land, saw such great miracles as should be remembered forever by the godly and the godless alike. And after that came the Round Table, established by Merlin – and with great significance, for in its name should be understood the roundness of the world and the circular motions of the planets and the stars in the firmament. The Round Table represents the world indeed, for to it come knights from every land where chivalry is known. And when God grants them such grace that they become companions of that fellowship, they count themselves more blessed than if they'd gained the whole world, and forsake mothers, fathers, wives and children for its sake. You've seen this in your own case, for ever since you left your mother and were made a companion of the Round Table you've had no desire to return, captivated as you were by the closeness and fraternal love that unites that brotherhood.

'When Merlin established the Round Table, he declared that its companions would come to know the truth about the Holy Grail, entirely hidden in his own time. "Three knights", he said, "will achieve the quest, two of them virgins and the third chaste. One of the three will surpass his father as the lion surpasses the leopard in strength and courage, and will be master and shepherd of all the others, who'll go mad with frustration in their search for the Grail until Our Lord with wondrous suddenness sends him among them". Hearing this, King Arthur's court said: "Well then, Merlin, if he's as great as you say, you should make a special seat where none should sit except he, so much bigger than the rest that everyone will recognise it". "I shall", Merlin said, and he made a seat of surpassing size and magnificence, and kissed it – out of love, he said, for the Good Knight who would sit there; and he told them: "This seat will give rise to many wonders, for any man who sits therein will be killed or maimed until the True Knight comes to take his place; and for this reason it shall be called the Perilous Seat".

'Now I've told you, dear nephew,' said the noble recluse, 'why the Round Table was created, and the Perilous Seat, too, where many knights unworthy to sit therein have perished. Listen now: it was on the day of Pentecost, when all the companions of the Round Table were gathered with their lord King Arthur, but with the Perilous Seat left empty, that an astonishing thing occurred: just after the first course had been served, all the doors and windows closed by themselves – no-one had so much as touched them; and while they all sat amazed an aged man of most noble bearing appeared, dressed in a white robe – but nobody had seen him enter. And he was holding by the hand a knight in red armour, and he said to the king: "King Arthur, I bring you the Desired Knight, born of the high lineage of King David and of Joseph of Arimathea, through whom the enchantments besetting this and other lands will be cast out. Behold him here".

'"If this is the one we've awaited", said the king, "who'll bring to an end the adventures of the Holy Grail, we'll give him a more joyful welcome than any man has ever known!" And with that the old man led the knight straight to the Perilous Seat beside Lancelot, and raising a silken sheet that had been lain across it he uncovered letters, freshly engraved, and read them aloud so that all could hear: "This seat is Galahad's". And turning to the knight he said: "Sit here, sir, for this place is yours". And the knight sat down in the Perilous Seat – unharmed.

'When the people in the hall saw the knight seated in the dread place where so many terrible wonders had occurred, they were astounded; and seeing he was so young a man they couldn't think how he could be granted such grace unless it were by the will of Our Lord. A boy ran with the news to the queen, saying: "My lady, great wonders have occurred in the hall!" And when she asked him what he meant, he replied: "A knight has overcome the trial of the Perilous Seat!" And all the queen's ladies said: "Ah, God! This is a sign that he's the one who'll bring to an end the adventures of Britain and heal the Maimed King!"

'You know, don't you, nephew, that it was on the day of Pentecost that the apostles were all gathered behind closed doors, and the Holy Spirit descended among them as a flame of fire? And it was on the day of Pentecost that Our Lord came to comfort them. In just such a guise came the knight who is to be your comfort, your master and your shepherd. Just as Our Lord came in the likeness of fire, so did the knight come in arms of fiery red. And just as the doors of the apostles' house were closed at the coming of Our Lord, so were the doors of the palace shut when the knight appeared. Now you know why I say you should never fight him: you're brothers together in the company of the Round Table – and you wouldn't survive against him, for he's a much finer knight than you.'

'Lady, dear aunt,' said Perceval, 'you've said enough to make me never want to do combat with him. But in God's name tell me where I may find him, for if I could share his company I'd never want to leave his side.'

'Go from here to the castle called Gort,' she replied, 'for he has a cousin there with whom he'll doubtless have taken lodging tonight. If she's willing to tell you which way he went, follow his path as fast as you can. If she can't say, go straight to the castle of Corbenic, where the Maimed King lies, and even if you don't find him there you're sure to have reliable news.'

Perceval could not wait to leave, and said: 'Lady, so many things are pressing me that I can't bring myself to stay! I beg you, let me go at once.'

She could not persuade him to stay that night, and Perceval set off into the forest, so vast it was a wonder, and evening was already setting in.

And it was then that the black horse, which he had been so pleased to chance upon, suddenly surged forward with awesome speed and noise, destroying everything in its path, uprooting trees and smashing branches, until it came to a cliff fully six hundred feet in height. It galloped right to the very brink, and Perceval, awe-struck, saw a river below, so deep that no stone could plumb its depths, and the horse was about to fling itself in to bring Perceval to his death. Perceval realised he had been deceived, and in fear of the Devil he did as God had instructed him and raised his hand and made the sign of the Cross. The horse abhorred the sign he had made and reared up on its hind legs to hurl Perceval into the river and drown him; but it flung him only flat on the ground behind, and launched itself from the cliff and plummeted, spinning, down into the river. If a tower had been demolished and cast down in a heap it would not have made such a thunderous din as the horse hitting the water. Perceval was deeply shocked, realising it was a demon that had borne him there; and he blessed himself with the sign of the True Cross more than a hundred times.

He clambered down the mighty cliff and finally reached the riverbank; but then he was even more dismayed, for he found the river was perilous indeed, impossible to cross without a boat: he had not seen a grimmer ford since the day he was born. And on the other side loomed a rock so high that the whole world could be surveyed from the top. He didn't know what to do or which way

to turn. Even were he to swim the river there would be no way to climb the
rock, for he could see it was sheer indeed. So he stayed where he was until night
came.

It brought him no pleasure or comfort. Rain fell, thick and fast, in a torrent.
And from a cloud he saw a whirlwind with three heads appear, and they
were huge and hideous, all hurling scorching fire; and each head's mouth had
a demon's tongue and the teeth and face of a leopard. Perceval averted his
eyes and made the sign of the Cross, and the demon swept away, setting all the
forest and mountain ablaze; Perceval was filled with fear and again blessed
himself with God's sign. Then suddenly he saw a boat covered in black samite;
and a girl was leaning at its side, by all appearances deeply vexed at having
been at sea so long. The boat sped swiftly to where Perceval was sitting on the
bank, downcast and perturbed; and as it reached the shore the rain ceased
and the whirlwind disappeared, and the girl stepped gently and elegantly from
the boat.

When Perceval saw her approach he went eagerly to greet her. And the
girl said: 'Perceval, my dear, I've come here from a distant land to find you! But
it seems you don't recognise me!'

'By the faith I owe God,' replied Perceval, 'I don't remember ever meeting
you.'

Then she came and took him by the hand and said: 'You've never seen me
before, Perceval? Look closely.'

And Perceval looked at her body and her face, and was sure it was his
sweetheart Blancheflor; and he said: 'Well met indeed, lady! How did you get
here? I've never been so pleased to see anyone!'

Then he took hold of her at once and embraced her – it wasn't just a courteous
kiss! And she bade her retinue pitch a rich and splendid pavilion for them;
and they spread a sumptuous quilt in the middle of the tent, and beside it a
table laden with the most delectable dishes imaginable. When they had stripped
him of his arms Perceval sat down to dine. But there was no grace said by
any prior, no blessing or genuflexion by any clerk. When they had eaten their
fill, the lady and Perceval spoke together; he said to her:

'Sweetheart, tell me, in the name of love, what are you seeking in such a
strange and distant land?'

'You!' she said. 'I need your help most urgently, for a wicked knight named
Arides of Escavalon is striving with all his might to do me harm: he's destroying
and laying waste my land, and says that you're lost, or have become a monk
or friar, and he wants to take me as his wife. But I wouldn't marry him for all
the money in the world, nor wrong you in any way; for my life is devoted to
being your wife.'

'My love,' said Perceval, 'mountains, rocks and valleys won't save him from
death at my hands if I can find him! I'll never fail you all the days of my life – I
swear it.'

The lady thanked him, feigning deep affection. And when it was time to sleep she said: 'My love, you may go to bed whenever you like, and lie with me if you wish – I dearly desire it!'

Perceval said he would do just as she wished. The young lady lay down on the rich bed, and Perceval lay beside her; and it pleased him greatly, for he had not seen her for a long time. He felt her naked body. She wanted him to lie with her and to do all he pleased: she was far from coy or reticent. Then Perceval looked up and saw his cruciform sword, and seeing the shape of the Cross he crossed himself, and thus thwarted the demon in the bed – for it was the Devil indeed, you may be sure, who in the semblance of Blancheflor wanted to lure him into sin. When Perceval made the sign of the Cross by God's miraculous inspiration, the Devil leaped up instantly and swept away the pavilion and the bed. Perceval was left all alone, shocked and anguished; and he stretched his hands heavenward and cried:

'Dear Lord who became a mortal man, thank you for your protection here! It was the very same Devil who tried to drown me!'

Then he put on his clothes and shoes and hurriedly armed. And he looked towards the water where the boat had been, but could see no sign of it: there was nothing to be seen in any direction. Then the moon began to shine, which comforted and cheered him, and he spotted the boat sailing down the river and back out to sea the way it had come; and a mighty storm blew up, with thunder, rain and lightning, and rocks fell from the clouds in an endless hail around the boat. For as long as he could see the boat the thunder, rain and lightning fell, but as soon as it was lost to view the storm abated. Perceval rejoiced at this, but he was deeply disturbed by what he had seen.

'Lord God,' he said, 'have mercy and deliver me from this place with my body and soul secure, and I promise I'll strive henceforth to earn your love.'

And there on the shore Perceval sighed and grieved until daybreak, imploring the sovereign father God to cast His divine power over him.

While he was thus immersed in prayer he saw a boat coming with a white sail unfurled; it had no rudder or oars to guide it, but it was surrounded by an air of the utmost joy. It was richly adorned with drapes; but there was no-one aboard except one old man. As the boat touched shore this worthy man, who was well aware of Perceval's plight, stepped out and greeted him in the name of the high master, saying:

'Dear friend, the Lord of the Trinity, who guides sinners back to the right path, has sent me here to comfort and console you: I've no desire to cause you pain, for you've suffered much already. I bring you comfort from Him. You need have no fear or doubt, for Jesus Christ the Saviour, who created Heaven and Earth, has sent me here to find you. Come aboard with me, and have no fear about anything you've seen.'

'Wait a moment, please, dear sir, and tell me first about the black horse that bore me here; and about the young lady who made me lie beside her beneath this cliff, naked, skin to skin.'

The white-haired man replied: 'I promise you, the horse that brought you here last night was the Devil, who longed to plunge you into Hell where his fellows are. I tell you, friend, when you vanquished the Black Hand at the chapel, and then confessed your sins to the priest and assumed penance and repentance, the Devil was deeply vexed at having lost you; and he returned to get you, and saw to it that you lost your horse in the valley in the forest, to make you despair. He then made you mount him, didn't he, in the shape of a fine black horse? And he'd have made you pay dearly, for he'd have drowned you here if God hadn't taken pity on you by having you make the sign of the Cross to work your deliverance. And when he failed to drown you, the horse leaped into the water, baffled and defeated, for he had no force or power left over you: he nearly went mad with grief. But he sent another demon here in the shape of a girl, and the demon told you she was your sweetheart Blancheflor whom you left at Beaurepaire. She lied; she was the Devil, who wanted to drag you down to the shadows of Hell.'

'Truly,' said Perceval, 'I know his ruse would have worked on me if I hadn't blessed myself with the sign of the Cross. That saved me from the Devil, and I saw him sailing away in thunder across the sea, back to where he came from. I was left here; and now I'll go with you wherever you like: it's only right I should when you say you're sent from God.'

'Don't dally, friend,' said the worthy man, 'for you'll be under God's protection for as long as I'm your escort. I'll guide you happily, I promise you, to the road you'll want to take.'

With that they boarded the boat, and the wind filled the sail and bore them away so swiftly that they seemed to be flying over the waves. Perceval looked around the deck but could see nothing clearly because the night was very dark. He went and leaned at the ship's side, and prayed to Christ to guide him to a place where his soul would be safe. And after making this prayer, he fell fast asleep until morning.

When he awoke he looked across the deck and saw a knight, sitting, fully armed; and after a moment this knight recognised him as Perceval the Welshman, and ran and embraced him joyfully. Perceval was taken aback, unaware till now that this other knight had been aboard, and he asked him who he was.

'What?' said the knight. 'Don't you recognise me?'

'Not at all,' said Perceval, 'and I didn't know you were here.'

At this the knight smiled, and took off his helmet. Then Perceval recognised him: it was Bors de Gaunes, the knight of whom the recluse had spoken; he had seen him each time he had been to Arthur's court, and it would be hard to describe the joy with which they greeted each other now. Bors began to tell him how he had come to board the ship, and Perceval for his part told Bors the adventures that had befallen him by the river where the Enemy had appeared to him in the shape of a woman and enticed him to the brink of mortal sin.

And so it was that these two companions were united as Our Lord had planned, awaiting the next adventures He chose to send them. And meanwhile they sailed hither and thither across the sea just as the wind took them, and Perceval said that the only thing lacking for the recluse's promise to be fulfilled was the presence of the third knight, Galahad.

They were just coming into shore when Bors caught sight of a knight in red arms riding down to the water's edge accompanied by a maiden, and he hailed him from afar, crying: 'Welcome, Sir Galahad! We've waited for you so long, and now you've come to us, thanks be to God! Come aboard at once, for nothing remains but to pursue the high adventure that God has prepared for us!'

The knight in red asked the maiden if she would dismount.

'Yes, sir,' she replied. 'But leave your horse here, as I shall mine.'

He dismounted at once and unharnessed both his horse and the maiden's palfrey. Then he made the sign of the Cross on his forehead and, commending himself to Our Lord, he boarded the ship and the maiden followed after. Bors greeted them with the utmost joy, and explained to Perceval that this was the son of the great Sir Lancelot. Then a mighty wind struck up and in an instant the ship was skimming across the sea once more, and before they knew it there was no land to be seen, either near or far.

Bors had removed his helmet and Galahad now did likewise, together with his sword; but he would not lay aside his hauberk. Seeing how beautiful the ship was, both within and without, he asked the two companions where such a handsome vessel had come from. Bors said he had no idea, but Perceval recounted as much as he knew, telling him about his adventure by the river, and how the priest had bidden him come aboard. Galahad said it was a strange place for them all to meet, and they laughed; and then Bors said to Galahad: 'If only your father Sir Lancelot were here it would be perfect!'

But Galahad replied that that was impossible, for it was not Our Lord's will.

They spoke together of their adventures until the middle of the afternoon, and Perceval asked Galahad's pardon for their encounter in the forest outside the recluse's cell. Soon they were far from the kingdom of Logres, for the ship had been travelling under full sail all night and all day. Then they passed between two rocks and came upon a wild island hidden away in a secret cove. And as they sailed in they caught sight of another ship moored behind a rock which they could only reach on foot.

'Good sirs,' said the maiden, 'aboard that ship is the adventure for which Our Lord has brought the three of you together. You must disembark and board that other craft.'

They willingly agreed, and jumped ashore and helped the maiden from the boat before mooring it to prevent the tide carrying it away. Then they clambered over the rocks, one after the other, and made their way to the other ship. They found it to be even finer than the first, and were amazed to see neither man nor woman aboard. They went closer to see what they could find, and as they looked at the ship's side they saw letters inscribed in Chaldean, spelling out a grim warning to any who thought to go aboard. This is what it said:

'Hear you, man who would board me: whoever you may be, take care that you be full of faith, for faith is precisely what I am. So be sure, before you step aboard, that you be stainless, for I am faith and true belief, and as soon as you abandon your belief I shall abandon you entirely: you will have neither aid nor support from me; I shall fail you utterly, no matter how small your failing.'

The three knights looked at each other in amazement. Then the maiden said to Perceval: 'Do you know who I am?'

'No indeed,' he replied, 'I don't think I've ever met you before.'

'I'm your sister,' she said, 'and do you know why I've made myself known to you? So that you'll trust my words the more when I tell you – the dearest person in the world to me – that, if your belief in Christ is not total, you shouldn't think of setting foot in this ship, for you would perish instantly. This vessel is such a precious thing that anyone boarding it stained with vice is in the gravest peril.'

Perceval looked more closely and realised that it was indeed his sister; he was overjoyed and said: 'Truly, dear sister, I shall board this ship, and do you know why? So that, if I prove to be an unbeliever, I may die a traitor's death, and if I am full of faith as a knight should be, I may be saved.'

'Then step aboard,' she said, 'with confidence, and may Our Lord be your guard and defence.'

Hearing this, Galahad, who was closest to the ship, raised his hand and crossed himself and stepped aboard. The others followed without delay and, looking up and down the ship, they declared that no vessel on land or sea could compare to it for perfect beauty. Then, right in the middle of the deck, they saw a sumptuous cloth spread like a canopy over a broad and beautiful bed. Galahad stepped forward and lifted it and looked beneath; and at the head of this splendid bed, the most beautiful he had ever seen, lay a magnificent golden crown, and at its foot lay a sword, shining, glorious, with several inches of its blade drawn from the scabbard. It was truly an exceptional sword; for its pommel was a stone containing every colour to be found on earth, and each colour possessed a special virtue; and its hilt was composed of two ribs, each from a very rare beast. The first was from a kind of serpent, found mostly in Caledonia, called the papalust, whose special quality is that if a man holds any of its ribs or bones he is protected from all heat; and the second rib came from a fish living only in the Euphrates river called the ortenax, and if any man holds one of that fish's ribs he has no thought of joy or sorrow: his whole mind is fixed unswervingly on the purpose for which he took it up. Such were the properties of the ribs which formed the hilt, and they were covered in a rich red fabric embroidered all over with letters saying:

I am a wonder to behold and to comprehend. For no man can or ever will take hold of me save one, and he will surpass in chivalry all who ever were before him or will ever follow after.

So said the letters on the hilt; and the knights looked at each other and said: 'Truly, there are wonders on this ship.'

'In God's name,' said Perceval, 'I'm going to see if I can hold this sword.' And he laid his hand upon it, but could not clasp the hilt. 'By my life,' he said, 'I do believe the inscription's true!'

Bors in his turn tried his hand, but to no avail; and they said to Galahad: 'Sir, try to take the sword. Since we two have failed, it's clear that success will fall to you.'

But he refused, saying: 'These are the greatest wonders I've ever seen.'

Then he looked at the blade, partially drawn as it was from the scabbard, and saw other letters inscribed upon it, red as blood, saying:

None should be so bold as to draw me from this sheath, unless he be more able and more daring than any other, for if he draws me otherwise he will be killed or maimed without a doubt.

'By my life,' said Galahad, 'I wanted to draw this sword, but the warning's so dire I'll not touch it.'

Perceval and Bors agreed, and Perceval's sister said: 'Good sirs, the drawing of the sword is forbidden to all men but one. Let me explain: this ship landed in the kingdom of Logres at a time when deadly war was being waged between King Lambar, a good and noble Christian, and King Varlan, who'd been an infidel all his life. The armies of Lambar and Varlan clashed on the shore where the ship had landed, and Varlan was on the point of defeat, his men being slaughtered. In fear of death, the infidel Varlan leaped aboard this ship; but when he found this sword he drew it and strode back ashore; he searched out King Lambar, the man in all Christendom with the most ardent faith and belief in Christ, and raised his sword and dealt him such a mighty blow upon the helm that he clove both him and his horse in two. This was the first blow struck with this sword in the land of Logres, and it loosed such a plague of miseries upon both their kingdoms that the earth would yield nothing to the farmer: no corn or any other crop would grow, no tree bore fruit, and hardly a fish was to be found in any river. The two kingdoms together came to be called the Waste Land, laid waste as it was by this dreadful blow.

'When King Varlan saw the keenness of the sword he decided to return for the scabbard. He came back to the ship and sheathed the sword; and the moment he did so he fell dead beside this bed, proving that any who drew it would be killed or maimed. The king's body remained here until a maiden cast it overboard, for there was no man bold enough to board the ship because of the dire warning written on her side.'

'Truly,' said Galahad, 'that's an amazing story, and I can well believe it, for I don't doubt that this is a more wonderful sword than any other.'

And with that he stepped forward to draw it.

'Ah, Galahad!' Perceval's sister cried. 'Wait a little longer! We've yet to examine its wonders fully!'

He drew back at once, and they began to study the scabbard. It seemed to be made of nothing other than a serpent's skin, yet it was red as a rose petal, and there were letters inscribed upon it, some gold and some blue. But they were most amazed of all when they noticed the belt; for it was surely not befitting such a magnificent sword: it was made of coarse, cheap material, rough hempen tow, and looked so feeble that they were sure it couldn't take the weight of the sword for an hour without breaking. And the letters on the scabbard said:

The man who carries me will perform greater deeds than any other and will be beyond all danger, so long as he is as clean of sin as he ought to be. I must not be taken into any place where there is uncleanness or sin; if I am, the bearer will be the first to repent. But if he keep me cleanly he may go where he will without any fear, for the man at whose side I shall hang by this belt can suffer no bodily harm. But no man should dare to remove this belt: no man present or future has the right; it may be unfastened only by the hand of a woman, who shall replace it with another, made from the thing she values most, and this woman must be a virgin all the days of her life, both in deed and in desire. Should she have lost her virginity, she may be sure she will die the basest death that any woman can.

When they had read the inscription they began to laugh in astonishment, and declared that what they had seen and heard was truly a wonder. Then Galahad said: 'I think we should go and look for the maiden who's to replace this belt; unless we do, we shouldn't take this sword from here.'

They said they had no idea where to find her, but nonetheless would take up the search, since there was no alternative; and when Perceval's sister heard their troubled words she said: 'Don't be alarmed, sirs, for before we leave here the new belt will be set in place – and it will be fittingly beautiful.'

And so saying, she opened a casket she was holding and brought forth a belt magnificently woven of silk and threads of gold and strands of hair – hair so fair and shining that it could hardly be distinguished from the gold; and it was studded with precious stones, and fastened with two golden buckles of incomparable splendour.

'Here, sirs,' she said, 'is the belt it should bear, made with what I cherished most: my hair. And it's no wonder that I cherished it, for on the day of Pentecost when you, sir,' she said to Galahad, 'were made a knight, I had the most beautiful head of hair of any woman in the world. But as soon as I learned that this adventure was in store for me and that I had to fulfil it, I had my hair cut and made into the braids you see here.'

'God bless you for it!' said Bors. 'You've saved us much hardship!'

And with that she stepped up to the sword, removed the belt of hemp, and fastened the other with such skill and ease that it seemed she had done it every day of her life. Then she said to the companions: 'Do you know the name of this sword?'

'No indeed,' they replied.

'Then know,' she said, 'that it is called the Sword of the Strange Belt.'

'Sir,' they said to Galahad, 'we pray you, in the name of Our Lord Jesus Christ and for the greater glory of all knighthood, gird on this Sword of the Strange Belt, as long desired by the kingdom of Logres as the return of Our Lord was desired by the apostles.'

For they were certain that by that sword the perilous adventures which they daily encountered, and the awesome wonders surrounding the Holy Grail, would be brought to an end.

'Let me first be sure,' said Galahad, 'that I've a right to it, for it'll be a certain sign that I haven't if I cannot clasp the hilt.'

They agreed that that was true; and he took hold of the hilt; and his fingers safely and perfectly encompassed it. Seeing this, the companions said: 'Now we know, sir, that it belongs to you. No-one can deny your right to gird it on.'

And Galahad drew it from its scabbard; and it was so beautiful, so burnished, that he saw his face reflected in the blade, and he prized it more highly than anything could be prized in all the world. Then he slid it back into the scabbard, and Perceval's sister unfastened the sword he had been wearing and, with the belt of silk and hair and gold, fastened this other in its place. And when she had hung it at his side she said:

'Truly, sir, now I don't care when I die, for I consider myself the most blessed of all maidens, having made a knight of the worthiest man in this earthly world. For know this: you were not by rights a knight until you were endowed with the sword which was brought to this land for you alone.'

'Damsel,' Galahad replied, 'for the great boon you have done me I am your knight for evermore. And I thank you deeply for all you've told us.'

'Now we can leave this ship,' she said, 'and return to our own.'

And with that they clambered from the ship and on to the rocks, where Perceval said to Galahad: 'There'll never be a day when I fail to thank Our Lord that I was present at the completion of such a high adventure as this: it's the most wonderful I've ever seen. But there's another mortal blow I've heard of, struck by another sword, that I have vowed to avenge. Until I've done so I cannot stay with you. I pray our paths may cross again soon.'

Galahad and Bors embraced him, wishing the same reunion, and returned to their ship and boarded; and Perceval watched the wind fill their sail and the ship glide swiftly from the shore. Then he set off across country, praying to God to guide him to where he might find Partinial the Wild, the Lord of the Red Tower, and do battle with him as he had promised the Fisher King.

* * *

He had gone but a short way from the sea when he caught sight of a castle crowned by five rich and handsome turrets. It stood beside a river surrounded by fields and woods and meadows: it wanted for nothing. Nor did it need fear attack, for the most earnest assault could not have harmed it: it was so well-placed and strong, enclosed by walls and palisades, that it feared no siege-engines or mangonels or storming. The people of the castle lived pleasantly indeed, for their lord kept and guarded them so well that they had no neighbours who could threaten them. Nor was there anyone who did not hate them, for their lord was more wicked, cruel and ruthless than any man alive. Of the castle's five turrets the one at the centre was the tallest of all, and stood proudly and handsomely indeed, quite wondrously so; and it was redder and brighter than the finest gold. The moment that Perceval beheld it he said:

'That will be the Red Tower; it must be, by my life. There, surely, dwells the one who's caused so much pain for the king who guards the Holy Grail.'

And he drove in his spurs and galloped up to the gate. Two green and lustrous pines were planted outside. On one hung a rich and handsome shield, of silver emblazoned with two elegant maidens painted in blue. Perceval stared at it fixedly, and realised that it was the shield of the one who had caused the Fisher King so much pain and anguish. He longed to know why it had been hung there; and just as he was thinking this a boy came through the gate, and Perceval called to him at once and said:

'Don't keep it from me, friend: what's this castle called? Who is its lord?'

'It's called the Red Tower, sir, and the lord's name is Partinial. He's so fearsome in battle that no knight who comes this way and takes down his shield can survive against him. He's killed 104 worthy knights of renown since he received his arms. As soon as anyone lays a finger on that shield his time is up, his life is over!'

'Indeed?' said Perceval to himself. 'He's a cruel and treacherous knight indeed if he'll kill a man for so little cause.'

And he rode forward and took down the shield, and swinging it by the strap he battered it against the pine until he smashed it to pieces. At that, with all the breath he could summon the boy blew a horn he had hanging at his neck. Partinial heard it and was filled with joy. Sure that someone had come and taken his shield he armed immediately, leaped on to his charger, took an oak-wood lance, gave his mount free rein and rode straight out through the gate. He was carrying no shield, for he expected to use the one that had been hung upon the pine. He nearly died of anguish when he saw it smashed upon the ground, and he charged towards Perceval, crying:

'Vassal! Vassal! You've got a shock in store for you today! You never saw such a precious shield, and you'll be sorry you took it, for it'll cost you your honour and your head!'

When Perceval heard these threats he set his lance in its rest and thrust his sharp steel spurs into his horse's flanks, and they charged at each other as fast as their mounts could go and struck one another with all their might. Partinial struck Perceval upon his shield and smashed right through it; and Perceval, determined to joust well, thrust six feet of his lance's shaft straight through Partinial's shoulder. Both knights came crashing to the ground.

Partinial was in grave trouble with the deep wound he had been dealt; but he was undismayed, and leaped to his feet with his sword drawn; and Perceval likewise jumped up again, ready and eager to defend himself. It was the bitterest combat ever seen. They were both masterly and well-tried in battle, and with their slashing swords, drawing blood with every blow, they dealt each other many fearsome cuts and wounds. Partinial clutched his sword with both hands and gave a fine account of himself – anyone who saw him would have surely said that no finer knight had ever lived. But such was Perceval's response that all the people of the castle declared they had never seen his equal.

The battle lasted from six till noon. They exchanged countless cuts and blows with their steel blades, until neither knight had shield, helmet or mail-hood left to protect him. They were both in grave difficulty, each in turn forced to his knees or full-length on the ground. Neither man would shrink at all, but one had to be the victor; and that victor, through the power of the King of glory, was Perceval. With a final mighty blow he brought Partinial to the ground beneath him, and cried that the battle was over and that he must declare himself his prisoner. But the one who did not believe in God said that he would never descend to yielding himself captive to any knight, and that Perceval need not think he would ever plead for mercy.

'In that case,' said Perceval, 'if I don't kill you, may God never forgive me.'

And he threatened him with instant death if he refused to submit to imprisonment. But Partinial replied: 'I'll never yield as long as I live. If you want to kill me, do it here and now.'

'Then kill you I will, by my life,' said Perceval, 'but it grieves me.'

And he struck him such a blow that he severed the head clean from the body. He left the body there in the grassy field; but he took the head and hung it from his saddle-bow, saying that he would take it to the Fisher King who had done him so much honour. He mounted at once, and set off without delay, leaving Partinial's headless body outside the gate.

* * *

He headed towards the house of the Fisher King, calm now and untroubled; but he did not know how he would find it or ever get there. He rode on, day by day, until one morning, emerging from a vast and bewildering forest, he saw Galahad and Bors crossing the path ahead of him. There is no need to ask if they were pleased at the meeting! They greeted each other with jubilation, and they asked how he had fared, and Perceval showed them Partinial's head and told them the story of how he had avenged the Fisher King.

'And have you returned to his castle? Have you found what we're seeking?'

'No indeed,' he replied, 'but I feel in my heart we shall not part again until we've completed this quest.'

'God grant that it be so,' said Galahad.

And so chance had reunited the three companions; and they rode on for a long while until finally, one day, they came to the castle of Corbenic. And when they had been admitted and the Fisher King recognised them, the rejoicing was great beyond imagining, for everyone knew that their arrival would bring an end to the adventures which had so long beset the castle. The news spread high and low until all the people of the castle came running to see them; and Perceval presented Partinial's severed head to the king, holding it on high and declaring, so that all could hear, that it was the head of the one who had caused the Fisher King such distress. The king looked at the head and recognised it at once; and he took Perceval in his arms with the utmost joy and kissed him more than ten times and said:

'You've brought me the greatest comfort by taking revenge upon this man who was my enemy and had plunged me into misery. Now, by God the Creator, all my sorrow and pain are turned to happiness. I shall fix this severed head upon a stake, in honour and remembrance of the one who took revenge upon the treacherous killer of my brother.'

He bade that a stake be fixed at the top of the castle keep and that the head be stuck upon it, and his bidding was done at once. Then they disarmed Perceval, Bors and Galahad, and every man and woman there rejoiced to a degree unprecedented. The king called for the tables to be made ready, and the servants spread the cloths immediately and set the knives and salt-bowls. When all had washed they took their seats, Perceval sitting beside the king. And thereupon the lance and the Grail appeared, carried by two girls most elegantly; and as they passed before the tables they were spread and arrayed with the most delectable dishes.

And then, when the hour of vespers came, the sky turned dark and a strange and mighty wind struck up and wailed throughout the palace, blasting with such a furious heat that many thought they would be burnt and others collapsed in terror. At that moment they heard a voice, crying:

'All who are not to sit at the table of Christ must go at once, for the time has come for the true knights to be fed with the food of Heaven.'

Thereupon they all departed, leaving the three companions with the king to see what Our Lord would reveal to them. A moment later they saw, coming in through the door, nine armed knights, who took off their helmets and came to Galahad and bowed to him and said: 'Sir, we have made great haste to join you here at the table where the high food of Heaven is to be bestowed.'

He replied that they had made good time, for he and his companions had only just arrived. And so they all sat down together in the middle of the hall, and Galahad asked them where they were from. Three said they were from Gaul, and three from Ireland and three from Denmark.

And at that moment they saw – descending from Heaven, so it seemed – a man in a bishop's raiment, with a crozier in his hand and a mitre on his head, borne on a magnificent throne by four angels; and they seated him at the table on which stood the Holy Grail. His forehead was marked with letters which said:

'Behold Josephus, the first Christian bishop, consecrated by Our Lord at the spiritual palace in the city of Sarras.'

When the knights read this they were filled with wonder, for this Josephus had passed away many years before. Then he spoke to them, saying: 'Ah! knights of God, servants of Christ, do not be amazed at seeing me before you with the holy vessel; for the same service that I performed on earth I still perform in heaven.'

And so saying, he drew close to the silver table and went down on hands and knees. After a long pause he suddenly heard the chamber door fly open; he and all the others looked round and saw the angels who had borne him there processing into the room. Two were carrying candles, the third a cloth of red samite, and the fourth a lance which bled so copiously that the drops were falling into a casket he was holding in his other hand. The two placed the candles on the table, the third laid the towel beside the holy vessel, and the fourth held the lance directly above the vessel so that it could gather the blood that trickled down the shaft. As soon as they had done this, Josephus rose and lifted the lance a little higher and covered the vessel with the cloth.

Then he acted as if he were about to consecrate the mass. After composing himself for a moment, he took from the holy vessel a communion host in the form of bread; and as he raised it on high there descended from above a figure in the shape of a child, his face as radiant and glowing as any fire; and he entered into the bread, so that all those present in the hall distinctly saw the bread assume the substance of human flesh. After holding it aloft for a long moment, Josephus placed it back in the holy vessel.

Having performed the function of a priest at the mass, he came up to Galahad and kissed him and bade him in turn kiss his companions. Then he said to them: 'Servants of Christ, who have toiled and suffered so much to behold the wonders of the Holy Grail, be seated now at this table, and you shall be fed with the most sublime and perfect food that ever passed a knight's lips, and by Your Saviour's own hand. You will know that your labours have been worthwhile, for today you'll receive the highest reward ever bestowed upon any knight.'

At that very instant Josephus vanished; they had no idea what had become of him. They sat down at the table in trepidation, their faces wet with tears. And then, as they looked towards the Grail, they saw rising from the vessel a man, quite naked, bleeding from his hands and his feet and his side; and he said to them:

'My knights, my servants, my loyal sons, who have attained the life of the spirit while still in the flesh, and who have sought me so long that I can hide myself from you no longer, it is only right that you should see some of my mysteries and my secrets, for now you have done enough to earn a seat at my table, where no knight has eaten since the days of Joseph of Arimathea. The knights of this castle and many others have been fed with the grace of the holy vessel, but never as intimately as the three of you shall be now. So come and receive the glorious food that you have so long desired and for which you have suffered so much.'

With that He took the holy vessel in His hands and came to Galahad, who went down on his knees; and He gave him his Saviour. And Galahad, his hands clasped in homage, received the host with joy, as did Bors, Perceval and the other nine knights; and to each and all it seemed that the host placed in his mouth was a piece of bread. When they had all received this food sublime, so wonderfully sweet that it seemed their bodies now contained all the sweetness the heart could ever crave, the One who had fed them said to Galahad:

'Son as clean and undefiled as earthly man can be, do you know what this vessel is that I am holding in my hands?'

'No,' he replied, 'unless you tell me.'

'It is the dish,' He said, 'in which Jesus Christ made the sacrament at the Last Supper. This is the dish which has served and gladdened the hearts of all those faithful to me. This is the dish whose sight has been a torture to the wicked. And because it has given such sublime delight to those it has served, it is rightly called the Holy Grail*. Now you have beheld what you have desired and yearned so long to see.

'But you have not yet seen it as openly as you one day will. Do you know where that will be? In the city of Sarras, in the spiritual palace; that is why you must go from here and accompany this holy vessel, which is to leave the kingdom of Logres tonight, so that neither the Grail nor its attendant wonders will ever be seen here again. It is leaving, because the people of this land pay it neither due honour nor due service. They have turned to base and worldly ways, even though they have been nourished with the grace bestowed by this holy vessel. Because they have repaid this honour so dismally I am now divesting them of it. So I want you to go in the morning down to the sea, where you'll find the ship on which you received the Sword of the Strange Belt. But so that you should not go alone, I would have you take Perceval and Bors with you. And I would not have you leave this land without healing the Maimed King: I want you to take some of the blood from this lance and anoint his legs, for thus and thus alone can he be cured.'

'Ah, Lord,' said Galahad, 'why won't you let the other nine knights come with us?'

'Because,' He replied, 'I would have you be the image of my apostles. For just as they ate with me at the Last Supper, so have you eaten with me now at the table of the Holy Grail. And you are twelve just as the apostles numbered twelve, and I the thirteenth, your master and your shepherd. And just as I sent them out across the world to preach the true law, so do I send you forth by separate ways – and all of you will die in this service.'

---

* The same untranslatable play on words – linking 'agreer' ('to delight') with 'graal' – occurs here as appears in Robert de Boron's account of the Grail's provenance, above, p.20.

With that He gave them His blessing – and then vanished: they did not know what had become of Him, except that they saw Him rising Heavenward.

Then Galahad stepped up to the lance that lay upon the table and dipped his hand into the blood; and then he came before the Fisher King and anointed his legs just where they had been pierced. And in that very instant the king rose from his bed and walked, entirely whole and sound in body once more. He was to live a long time thereafter, not in the world but in an order of white monks.

Around midnight, after they had spent a long while praying to Our Lord to guide their souls to safety wherever they might go, a voice appeared in their midst saying:

'My true sons and my friends indeed, leave this place and go where adventure takes you and where you think you may do most good.'

And hearing this they all replied in one voice: 'Father in Heaven, may you be blessed for calling us sons and friends! Now we know our toils have not been in vain!'

With that they left the palace and went down to the courtyard where they found arms and horses waiting; they armed and mounted at once and rode from the castle.

The three rode on until, in less than four days, they reached the sea and found a ship at the shore – the very ship in which they had found the Sword of the Strange Belt – and saw the letters on the hull declaring that no-one should board it unless he was a firm believer in Christ. They stepped aboard, and at once they saw, lying across the bed that had been made in the middle of the deck, the silver table they had last seen at the castle of the Fisher King. And standing upon it, draped in a veil of red samite, was the Holy Grail. The companions beheld this wonder and spoke of their good fortune, that the object they most adored would be accompanying them to their journey's end. Then they crossed themselves and commended themselves to Our Lord, and the wind, which until then had been calm and serene, blasted into the sail with an awesome force and bore the ship from the shore and on to the open sea, where it blew ever stronger and drove them on at a mighty speed.

A long while they sailed so, not knowing where God was taking them. And each time Galahad lay down to sleep or rose from his bed he prayed to God that whenever he asked for release from this life He would grant it. So many nights and so many dawns did he make this prayer that at last the divine voice said to him:

'Have no fear, Galahad, for Our Lord will grant your wish. Whenever you ask for bodily death you shall have it, and will live in the spirit and have everlasting joy.'

Perceval heard this request, which Galahad had so often repeated, and was amazed, and begged him to explain why he so desired death.

'I'll tell you,' he replied. 'The other day, when we beheld some of the mysteries of the Holy Grail, and I saw the hidden secrets revealed to no-one but the ministers of Jesus Christ, and witnessed what the heart cannot conceive nor the tongue describe, my heart was filled with such sweetness and joy that if I had passed away at that moment I know that no man could have died in such total happiness. For before me was such a mighty company of angels and spiritual beings that I was transported from the earthly to the spiritual plane and shared the bliss of the glorious martyrs and the beloved of Our Lord. I hope death will bring me to an equal or an even better place to behold that joy: that is why I made that prayer. And I hope to pass from this world, by Our Lord's will, while gazing on the wonders of the Holy Grail.'

Thus it was that Galahad announced to Perceval his approaching death as the heavenly voice had promised him.

The companions sailed on for a long while, until one day they said to Galahad: 'Sir, you've yet to sleep on this bed that was prepared for you.'

He said he would do so, and lay down and slept for a long time; and the moment he awoke he looked before him and saw the city of Sarras. Then a voice came amongst them and said:

'Leave this ship now, knights of Christ, and take this silver table and carry it into the city; and do not set it down until you reach the spiritual palace where Our Lord consecrated Josephus the first bishop.'

And so, with Perceval and Bors in front and Galahad behind, they carried the table from the ship and on towards the city. But when they came to the gate Galahad was very wearied by the table's weight. In the gateway he saw a man on crutches, waiting for passers-by to give him alms, and as Galahad drew near him he said:

'Good man, come here and help me carry this table to the palace.'

'Oh, sir!' the man replied. 'What are you saying? It's a good ten years since I could walk unaided!'

'Don't worry,' said Galahad. 'Stand up now, and have no fear, for you are healed.'

No sooner had Galahad said this than the man made an effort to stand; and as soon as he did so he found he was as fit and strong as if he had never had an infirmity in his life. He ran to the table and took hold of a corner alongside Galahad; and as they entered the city he told everyone he met of the miracle God had wrought for him.

When they arrived at the palace they saw the throne that Our Lord had prepared for Josephus, the first bishop, long before; and the people of the city came flocking in wonder to see the cripple who was newly healed.

Now when the king of Sarras, whose name was Escorant, saw the three companions, he asked them where they were from and what it was they had brought upon the silver table. They replied in all truthfulness, and told him of the wonder that was the Grail and of the power that God had invested in it. But the king was treacherous and cruel, descended as he was from a cursed line of infidels, and he whispered that he did not believe their words and took them for base tricksters; and as soon as he saw them disarm he had them seized and thrown in prison.

A whole year they lay imprisoned, never let out of the dungeon; but Our Lord did not forget them: from the moment of their imprisonment He sent the Holy Grail to keep them company and to nourish them daily with its grace.

At the end of that year the day came when Galahad appealed to Our Lord, saying: 'Lord, I have dwelt long enough in this world. I pray you, deliver me from it, and soon.'

That very same day, King Escorant was lying ill, on the point of death, and he summoned the companions before him and begged their forgiveness for so mistreating them. They pardoned him most willingly, and he died upon the instant. And once he had been buried the people of the city were lost in dismay, for they did not know whom they could make king. They deliberated for a long while, and as they sat in consultation they heard a voice saying:

'Take the youngest of the three companions: he will be a fine protector, and give you guidance as long as he is with you.'

They followed the voice's command, and made Galahad their lord and crowned him. And his first decree was that an ark of gold and precious stones be made to cover the silver table and to house the holy vessel. And every morning, as soon as he rose, he and his companions came before the Grail to pray and worship.

At the end of the year, on the very anniversary of his coronation, Galahad and his companions rose early; and when they came to the spiritual palace and looked towards the holy vessel they saw a man of noble appearance, in a bishop's vestments, kneeling before the table and making confession, and surrounded by such a host of angels that he might have been Christ Himself. After a long while he rose and began the mass of the glorious Mother of God. And when he came to the sacrament and raised the paten from the holy vessel, he called to Galahad, saying:

'Come forward, servant of Christ, and your eyes will behold what you have so fervently desired to see.'

And Galahad stepped forward and looked into the holy vessel. And the moment he did so he began to tremble violently as his mortal flesh gazed upon the spiritual mysteries. Then he raised his hands to Heaven and said:

'Lord, I worship you and thank you for fulfilling my desire, for now you have revealed to me what the tongue could not describe nor the heart conceive. Here I behold the spring of all courage, the source of all prowess! Here I see the wonder above all wonders! And since, my good sweet Lord, you have granted my wish and allowed me to see what I have always longed to behold, I pray you, let me now, in this state of utmost joy, pass from this earthly life to the life celestial.'

As soon as Galahad's prayer was done, the worthy man in the bishop's garb took the body of Christ from the table and offered it to him. He received it with all humility and deep devotion. And when he had done so, the worthy man said to him: 'I am Josephus, the son of Joseph of Arimathea, sent by Our Lord to be your companion. And do you know why He sent me rather than another? It is because you resemble me in two ways: you have beheld the wonders of the Holy Grail as I have done, and you are a virgin as am I.'

As soon as he had said this, Galahad knelt before the table; and moments later he fell face down upon the flagstoned floor: his soul had already left his body. It was borne away by angels, rejoicing and praising Our Lord. And no sooner had Galahad passed away than a great wonder occurred. The two companions clearly saw a hand descending from Heaven – though they did not see the body it belonged to – and it clasped both the holy vessel and the lance and carried them away to Heaven, and no man since, however bold, has ever dared claim that he has seen the Holy Grail.

When Perceval and Bors saw that Galahad was dead they were filled with the utmost grief. Their love for him was such that, had they been less good and noble men, they might well have given way to despair. The people of that land, too, grieved and mourned most deeply.

His grave was dug right where he died; and as soon as he was buried, Perceval retreated to a hermitage outside the city and assumed the habit of a monk. Bors stayed with him; but he remained in worldly garb, for he planned to return once more to King Arthur's court. Perceval lived at the hermitage for a year and three days before he passed from this world, and Bors had him buried with Galahad in the spiritual palace.

Then Bors, finding himself alone now in this distant land bordering on Babylon, left Sarras fully armed and made his way to the sea and boarded a ship. So fair was his journey that before long he reached the kingdom of Logres, where he rode day by day until he came to Camelot where King Arthur was holding court. They greeted him with unprecedented joy, for they thought they had lost him forever, so long had he been gone from the land.

And after they had feasted, the king summoned the clerks who were recording the adventures of the knights of the court; and when Bors had related the adventures of the Holy Grail as he had witnessed them, they were set down in writing and preserved in the library at Salisbury, from where they have been translated from Latin into the vernacular.

And that is the end of the story. Nothing more is said of the adventures of the Holy Grail.

Sources

Joseph of Arimathea   The opening lines are from the anonymous *The High Book of the Grail (Perlesvaus)*; the main body of this chapter is from the prose version of *Joseph of Arimathea* attributed to Robert de Boron.

The Welsh Boy   The opening paragraphs are again taken from *The High Book of the Grail*; the rest of this chapter is from *Perceval – the Story of the Grail* by Chrétien de Troyes.

The Fisher King   This continues the story from Chrétien de Troyes' *Perceval*.

Sir Gawain's Quest Begins   From the anonymous *High Book of the Grail*.

Perceval's Recovery   From *The High Book of the Grail*.

Lancelot's Quest   From *The High Book of the Grail*.

The Castle of Marvels   From Chrétien de Troyes' *Perceval* and the anonymous First Continuation; the latter begins when Gawain's messenger arrives at Arthur's court (page 155).

The Broken Sword   From the anonymous Second Continuation of Chrétien's *Perceval* and Gerbert de Montreuil's Continuation; Gerbert takes up the story after Perceval's failure to repair the broken sword (page 180).

The Conquest of the Castles   The encounter with the yelping beast, and Perceval's acquisition of the shield with the red cross, are from Gerbert de Montreuil's Continuation; the episodes involving the conquering of the castles are from *The High Book of the Grail*; the repairing of the broken sword is from Gerbert; the Fisher King's revelations, and Perceval's adventure with the Black Hand, are from the Third Continuation by Manessier.

Galahad   This chapter principally comes from the anonymous *Quest of the Holy Grail*; the episodes involving the demon horse and lady and Perceval's battle with Partinial are from the Third Continuation.

A complete translation of *Joseph of Arimathea* is available in Robert de Boron's trilogy *Merlin and the Grail* (D. S. Brewer, 2001, reprinted in 2003); Chrétien de

Troyes' *Perceval* and its four Continuations are translated as *Perceval – the Story of the Grail* (D. S. Brewer, 1982, reprinted in 1986); the full translated text of *The High Book of the Grail* was published by D. S. Brewer in 1978 and reissued in 1996; a complete translation of *The Quest of the Holy Grail* by Pauline Matarasso is available in Penguin Classics.

For an outstandingly lucid and readable discussion of the inspiration, development and significance of the Grail legend, and for a comprehensive bibliography, see Richard Barber's *The Holy Grail – Imagination and Belief* (Allen Lane/Harvard University Press, 2004).

ARTHURIAN STUDIES

'This thrilling tale of escape from a deep south plantation takes in terror, beauty and the history of human tragedy ... it tells one of the most compelling stories I have ever read. Cora's strong, graceful hands touch on the greatest tragedies of our history'

Cynthia Bond, *Guardian*

'It is a bold way of reimagining the slave experience and, in the capable hands of Whitehead, succeeds triumphantly'

Max Davidson, *Mail on Sunday*

'This bravura novel reimagines that same network as a real subterranean railway, upon which a girl named Cora flees the slave-catcher Ridgeway. Throughout, horrific experiences are rendered in lapidary prose, but it's Cora's daring that provides the story's redemptive oomph'   *Mail on Sunday*, Books of the Year

Colson Whitehead is the *Sunday Times* bestselling author of *The Nickel Boys*, *The Underground Railroad*, *The Noble Hustle*, *Zone One*, *Sag Harbor*, *The Intuitionist*, *John Henry Days*, *Apex Hides the Hurt* and one collection of essays, *The Colossus of New York*. A Pulitzer Prize winner and a recipient of MacArthur and Guggenheim fellowships, he lives in New York City.

Praise for *The Underground Railroad*

'It has invaded both my sleeping and waking thoughts ... Each character feels alive with a singular humanity'

Bim Adewunmi, *Guardian*

'An engrossing and harrowing novel' *Sunday Times*

'An audaciously imagined and profoundly moving novel'

Eithne Farry, *Express*

'A charged and important novel that pushed at the boundaries of fiction' Justine Jordan, *Guardian*, Best Books of 2016

'Brutal, tender, thrilling and audacious'

Naomi Alderman, *Guardian*, Books of the Year

'*The Underground Railroad* is a noble descendant of the great narratives of slavery, and among the very finest of its novels'

Wesley Stace, *Times Literary Supplement*

'A fantastical picaresque through the dark side of American history'

Telegraph, Books of the Year

'One of the best, if not the best, book I've read this year ... Whitehead never exploits his subject matter, and in fact it's the sparseness of the novel that makes it such a punch in the gut'

Sarah Shaffi, *Stylist*

'An utterly transporting piece of storytelling'

Alex Heminsley, The Pool

'A stunning, brutal and hugely imaginative book. It's a favourite of both Oprah Winfrey and Barack Obama. It is painful history re-imagined in a powerful and brilliant way'   Emerald Street

'While *The Underground Railroad* is at times brutal and disturbing, it's also hopeful and an addictive, compulsive read. After reading it, a corner of your heart will always belong to Cora. An instant classic'   Sarra Manning, *Red*

'*The Underground Railroad* isn't the modern slave narrative it first appears to be. It is something grander and more piercing, a dazzling antebellum anti-myth ... Whitehead's prose is quick as a runaway's footsteps'   *New York Review of Books*

'This book should be required reading in classrooms across the country alongside *Huckleberry Finn* and *To Kill a Mockingbird*. If this isn't Colson Whitehead's masterpiece, it's definitely the best book of the year and maybe the most important work of the decade'   *Chicago Tribune*

'Bestselling author Colson Whitehead's novel is a searing indictment of slavery with a detailed inventory of man's inhumanity to man – and Cora's flight is a harrowing and shocking trip for the reader'

Daily Mail

The
Underground
Railroad

The
Underground
Railroad

Colson
Whitehead

FLEET
2021

FLEET

First published in the United States in 2016 by Doubleday
First published in Great Britain in 2016 by Fleet
Paperback edition published in 2017 by Fleet
This edition published in 2021 by Fleet

1 3 5 7 9 10 8 6 4 2

A CIP catalogue record for this book
is available from the British Library.

ISBN 978-0-349-72680-9

Printed and bound in Great Britain by
Clays Ltd, Elcograf S.p.A.

Papers used by Fleet are from well-managed forests
and other responsible sources.

Fleet
An imprint of
Little, Brown Book Group
Carmelite House
50 Victoria Embankment
London EC4Y 0DZ

An Hachette UK Company
www.hachette.co.uk

www.littlebrown.co.uk

For
Julie

CONTENTS

Ajarry

‖‖‖‖‖‖‖‖‖‖‖‖‖‖‖‖‖‖‖‖‖‖‖‖‖‖‖‖‖‖
‖‖‖‖‖‖‖‖‖‖‖‖‖‖‖‖‖‖‖‖‖‖‖‖‖‖‖‖‖‖
‖‖‖‖‖‖‖‖‖‖‖‖‖‖‖‖‖‖‖‖‖‖‖‖‖‖‖‖‖‖

THE first time Caesar approached Cora about running north, she said no.

This was her grandmother talking. Cora's grandmother had never seen the ocean before that bright afternoon in the port of Ouidah and the water dazzled after her time in the fort's dungeon. The dungeon stored them until the ships arrived. Dahomeyan raiders kidnapped the men first, then returned to her village the next moon for the women and children, marching them in chains to the sea two by two. As she stared into the black doorway, Ajarry thought she'd be reunited with her father, down there in the dark. The survivors from her village told her that when her father couldn't keep the pace of the long march, the slavers stove in his head and left his body by the trail. Her mother had died years before.

Cora's grandmother was sold a few times on the trek to the fort, passed between slavers for cowrie shells and glass beads. It was hard to say how much they paid for her in Ouidah as she was part of a bulk purchase, eighty-eight human souls for sixty crates of rum and gunpowder, the price arrived upon after the standard haggling in Coast English. Able-bodied men and childbearing women fetched more than juveniles, making an individual accounting difficult.

The *Nanny* was out of Liverpool and had made two previous stops along the Gold Coast. The captain staggered his purchases, rather than find himself with cargo of singular culture and disposition. Who knew what brand of mutiny his captives might cook up if they shared a common tongue. This was the ship's final port of call before they crossed the Atlantic. Two yellow-haired sailors rowed Ajarry out to the ship, humming. White skin like bone.

The noxious air of the hold, the gloom of confinement, and the screams of those shackled to her contrived to drive Ajarry to madness. Because of her tender age, her captors did not immediately force their urges upon her, but eventually some of the more seasoned mates dragged her from the hold six weeks into the passage. She twice tried to kill herself on the voyage to America, once by denying herself food and then again by drowning. The sailors stymied her both times, versed in the schemes and inclinations of chattel. Ajarry didn't even make it to the gunwale when she tried to jump overboard. Her piteous aspect, recognizable from thousands of slaves before her, betrayed her intentions. Chained head to toe, head to toe, in exponential misery.

Although they had tried not to get separated at the auction in Ouidah, the rest of her family was purchased by Portuguese traders from the frigate *Vivilia*, next seen four months later drifting ten miles off Bermuda. Plague had claimed all on board. Authorities lit the ship on fire and watched her crackle and sink.

Cora's grandmother knew nothing about the ship's fate. For the rest of her life she imagined her cousins worked for kind and generous masters up north, engaged in more forgiving trades than her own, weaving or spinning, nothing in the fields. In her stories, Isay and Sidoo and the rest somehow bought their way out of bondage and lived as free men and women in the City of Pennsylvania, a place she had overheard two white men discuss once. These fantasies gave Ajarry comfort when her burdens were such to splinter her into a thousand pieces.

The next time Cora's grandmother was sold was after a month in the pest house on Sullivan's Island, once the physicians certified her and the rest of the *Nanny*'s cargo clear of illness. Another busy day on the Exchange. A big auction always drew a colorful crowd. Traders and procurers from up and down the coast converged on Charleston, checking the merchandise's eyes and joints and spines, wary of venereal distemper and other afflictions. Onlookers chewed fresh oysters and hot corn as the auctioneers shouted into the air. The slaves stood naked on the platform. There was a bidding war over a group of Ashanti studs, those Africans of renowned industry and musculature, and the foreman of a limestone quarry bought a bunch of pickaninnies in an astounding bargain. Cora's grandmother saw a little boy among the gawkers eating rock candy and wondered what he was putting in his mouth.

Just before sunset an agent bought her for two hundred and twenty-six dollars. She would have fetched more but for that season's glut of young girls. His suit was made of the whitest cloth she had ever seen. Rings set with colored stone flashed on his fingers. When he pinched her breasts to see if she was in flower, the metal was cool on her skin. She was branded, not for the first or last time, and fettered to the rest of the day's acquisitions. The coffle began their long march south that night, staggering behind the trader's buggy. The *Nanny* by that time was en route back to Liverpool, full of sugar and tobacco. There were fewer screams belowdecks.

You would have thought Cora's grandmother cursed, so many times was she sold and swapped and resold over the next few years. Her owners came to ruin with startling frequency. Her first master got swindled by a man who sold a device that cleaned cotton twice as fast as Whitney's gin. The diagrams were convincing, but in the end Ajarry was another asset liquidated by order of the magistrate. She went for two hundred and eighteen dollars in a hasty exchange, a drop in price occasioned by the realities of the local market. Another owner expired from dropsy, whereupon his widow held an estate sale to fund a return to her native Europe, where it was clean. Ajarry spent three months as the property of a Welshman who eventually lost her, three other slaves, and two hogs in a game of whist. And so on.

Her price fluctuated. When you are sold that many times, the world is teaching you to pay attention. She learned to quickly adjust to the new plantations, sorting the nigger breakers from the merely cruel, the layabouts from the hardworking, the informers from the secret-keepers. Masters and mistresses in degrees of wickedness, estates of disparate means and ambition.

Sometimes the planters wanted nothing more than to make a humble living, and then there were men and women who wanted to own the world, as if it were a matter of the proper acreage. Two hundred and forty-eight, two hundred and sixty, two hundred and seventy dollars. Wherever she went it was sugar and indigo, except for a stint folding tobacco leaves for one week before she was sold again. The trader called upon the tobacco plantation looking for slaves of breeding age, preferably with all their teeth and of pliable disposition. She was a woman now. Off she went.

She knew that the white man's scientists peered beneath things to understand how they worked. The movement of the stars across the night, the cooperation of humors in the blood. The temperature requirements for a healthy cotton harvest. Ajarry made a science of her own black body and accumulated observations. Each thing had a value and as the value changed, everything else changed also. A broken calabash was worth less than one that held its water, a hook that kept its catfish more prized than one that relinquished its bait. In America the quirk was that people were things. Best to cut your losses on an old man who won't survive a trip across the ocean. A young buck from strong tribal stock got customers into a froth. A slave girl squeezing out pups was like a mint, money that bred money. If you were a thing—a cart or a horse or a slave—your value determined your possibilities. She minded her place.

Finally, Georgia. A representative of the Randall plantation bought her for two hundred and ninety-two dollars, in spite of the new blankness behind her eyes, which made her look simpleminded. She never drew a breath off Randall land for the rest of her life. She was home, on this island in sight of nothing.

Cora's grandmother took a husband three times. She had a predilection for broad shoulders and big hands, as did Old Randall, although the master and his slave had different sorts of labor in mind. The two plantations were well-stocked, ninety head of nigger on the northern half and eighty-five head on the southern half. Ajarry generally had her pick. When she didn't, she was patient.

Her first husband developed a hankering for corn whiskey and started using his big hands to make big fists. Ajarry wasn't sad to see him disappear down the road when they sold him to a sugarcane estate in Florida. She next took up with one of the sweet boys from the southern half. Before he passed from cholera he liked to share stories from the Bible, his former master being more liberal-minded when it came to slaves and religion. She enjoyed the stories and parables and supposed that white men had a point: Talk of salvation could give an African ideas. Poor sons of Ham. Her last husband had his ears bored for stealing honey. The wounds gave up pus until he wasted away.

Ajarry bore five children by those men, each delivered in the same spot on the planks of the cabin, which she pointed to when they misstepped. That's where you came from and where I'll put you back if you don't listen. Teach them to obey her and maybe they'll obey all the masters to come and they will survive. Two died miserably of fever. One boy cut his foot while playing on a rusted plow, which poisoned his blood. Her youngest never woke up after a boss hit him in the head with a wooden block. One after another. At least they were never sold off, an older woman told Ajarry. Which was true—back then Randall rarely sold the little ones. You knew where and how your children would die. The child that lived past the age of ten was Cora's mother, Mabel.

Ajarry died in the cotton, the bolls bobbing around her like whitecaps on the brute ocean. The last of her village, keeled over in the rows from a knot in her brain, blood pouring from her nose and white froth covering her lips. As if it could have been anywhere else. Liberty was reserved for other people, for the citizens of the City of Pennsylvania bustling a thousand miles to the north. Since the night she was kidnapped she had been appraised and reappraised, each day waking upon the pan of a new scale. Know your value and you know your place in the order. To escape the boundary of the plantation was to escape the fundamental principles of your existence: impossible.

It was her grandmother talking that Sunday evening when Caesar approached Cora about the underground railroad, and she said no.

Three weeks later she said yes.

This time it was her mother talking.

Georgia

||||||||||||||||||||||||||||||||||||||

||||||||||||||||||||||||||||||||||||||

||||||||||||||||||||||||||||||||||||||

THIRTY DOLLAR REWARD

Ran away from the subscriber, living in Salisbury, on the 5th instant, a negro girl by the name of LIZZIE. It is supposed that said girl is in the vicinity of Mrs. Steel's plantation. I will give the above reward on the delivery of the girl, or for information on her being lodged in any Gaol in this state. All persons are forewarned of harboring said girl, under penalty of law prescribed.

W. M. DIXON
JULY 18, 1820

JOCKEY'S birthday only came once or twice a year. They tried to make a proper celebration. It was always Sunday, their half day. At three o'clock the bosses signaled the end of work and the northern plantation scurried to prepare, rushing through chores. Mending, scavenging moss, patching the leak in the roof. The feast took precedence, unless you had a pass to go into town to sell crafts or had hired yourself out for day labor. Even if you were inclined to forgo the extra wages—and no one was so inclined—impossible was the slave impudent enough to tell a white man he couldn't work because it was a slave's birthday. Everybody knew niggers didn't have birthdays.

Cora sat by the edge of her plot on her block of sugar maple and worked dirt from under her fingernails. When she could, Cora contributed turnips or greens to the birthday feasts, but nothing was coming in today. Someone shouted down the alley, one of the new boys most likely, not completely broken in by Connelly yet, and the shouts cracked open into a dispute. The voices more crotchety than angry, but loud. It was going to be a memorable birthday if folks were already this riled.

"If you could pick your birthday, what would it be?" Lovey asked.

Cora couldn't see Lovey's face for the sun behind her, but she knew her friend's expression. Lovey was uncomplicated, and there was going to be a celebration that night. Lovey gloried in these rare escapes, whether it was Jockey's birthday, Christmas, or one of the harvest nights when everyone with two hands stayed up picking and the Randalls had the bosses distribute corn whiskey to keep them happy. It was work, but the moon made it okay. The girl was the first to tell the fiddler to get busy and the first to dance. She'd try to pull Cora from the sidelines, ignoring her protestations. As if they'd twirl in circles, arm in arm, with Lovey catching a boy's eyes for a second on every revolution and Cora following suit. But Cora never joined her, tugging her arm away. She watched.

"Told you when I was born," Cora said. She was born in winter. Her mother, Mabel, had complained enough about her hard delivery, the rare frost that morning, the wind howling between the seams in the cabin. How her mother bled for days and Connelly didn't bother to call the doctor until she looked half a ghost. Occasionally Cora's mind tricked her and she'd turn the story into one of her memories, inserting the faces of ghosts, all the slave dead, who looked down at her with love and indulgence. Even people she hated, the ones who kicked her or stole her food once her mother was gone.

"If you could pick," Lovey said.

"Can't pick," Cora said. "It's decided for you."

"You best fix your mood," Lovey said. She sped off.

Cora kneaded her calves, grateful for the time off her feet. Feast or no feast, this was where Cora ended up every Sunday when their half day of work was done: perched on her seat, looking for things to fix. She owned herself for a few hours every week was how she looked at it, to tug weeds, pluck caterpillars, thin out the sour greens, and glare at anyone planning incursions on her territory. Tending to her bed was necessary maintenance but also a message that she had not lost her resolve since the day of the hatchet.

The dirt at her feet had a story, the oldest story Cora knew. When Ajarry planted there, soon after her long march to the plantation, the plot was a rumble of dirt and scrub behind her cabin, at the end of the line of slave quarters. Beyond that lay fields and after that the swamp. Then Randall had a dream one night about a white sea that ranged as far as the eye could see and switched his crop from dependable indigo to Sea Island cotton. He made new contacts in New Orleans, shook hands with speculators backed by the Bank of England. The money came in as never before. Europe was famished for cotton and needed to be fed, bale by bale. One day the bucks cleared the trees and at night when they returned from the fields they got in chopping logs for the new row of cabins.

Looking at them now as folks chased in and out, getting ready, it was hard for Cora to imagine a time when the fourteen cabins hadn't been there. For all the wear, the complaints from deep in the wood at every step, the cabins had the always-quality of the hills to the west, of the creek that bisected the property. The cabins radiated permanence and in turn summoned timeless feelings in those who lived and died in them: envy and spite. If they'd left more space between the old cabins and the new cabins it would have spared a lot of grief over the years.

White men squabbled before judges over claims to this or that tract hundreds of miles away that had been carved up on a map. Slaves fought with equal fervor over their tiny parcels at their feet. The strip between the cabins was a place to tie a goat, build a chicken coop, a spot to grow food to fill your belly on top of the mash doled out by the kitchen every morning. If you got there first. When Randall, and later his sons, got a notion to sell you, the contract wasn't dry before someone had snatched up your plot. Seeing you out there in the evening calm, smiling or humming, might give your neighbor an idea to coerce you from your claim using methods of intimidation, various provocations. Who would hear your appeal? There were no judges here.

"But my mother wouldn't let them touch her field," Mabel told her daughter. Field in jest, as Ajarry's stake was scarcely three square yards. "Said she'd dig a hammer in they heads if they so much as looked at it."

The image of her grandmother assaulting another slave didn't jibe with Cora's recollections of the woman, but once she started tending to the plot she understood the truth of the portrait. Ajarry kept watch over her garden through prosperity's transformations. The Randalls bought out the Spencer spread to the north, once that family decided to try their luck out west.

They bought the next plantation south and switched the crop from rice to cotton, adding two more cabins to each row, but Ajarry's plot remained in the middle of it all, immovable, like a stump that reached down too deep. After Ajarry's death, Mabel assumed care of the yams and okra, whatever struck her fancy. The fuss started when Cora took it over.

WHEN Mabel vanished Cora became a stray. Eleven years old, ten years, thereabouts—there was no one now to tell for sure. In Cora's shock, the world drained to gray impressions. The first color to return was the simmering brown-red of the soil in her family's plot. It reawakened her to people and things, and she decided to hold on to her stake, even though she was young and small and had nobody to look after her anymore. Mabel was too quiet and stubborn to be popular but people had respected Ajarry. Her shadow had provided protection. Most of the original Randall slaves were in the ground now or sold, some variety of gone. Was there anyone left who was loyal to her grandmother? Cora made a canvass of the village: Not a soul. They were all dead.

She fought for the dirt. There were the small pests, the ones too young for real work. Cora shooed off those children trampling her sprouts and yelled at them for digging up her yam slips, using the same tone she used at Jockey's feasts to corral them into footraces and games. She handled them with good nature.

But pretenders stepped from the wings. Ava. Cora's mother and Ava grew up on the plantation at the same time. They were

17

treated to the same Randall hospitality, the travesties so routine and familiar that they were a kind of weather, and the ones so imaginative in their monstrousness that the mind refused to accommodate them. Sometimes such an experience bound one person to another; just as often the shame of one's powerlessness made all witnesses into enemies. Ava and Mabel did not get along.

Ava was wiry and strong, with hands as quick as a cotton-mouth. Speed that was good for picking and for clopping her little ones across the face for idleness and other sins. She cherished her chickens more than those children and coveted Cora's land to expand her coop. "It's a waste," Ava said, ticking her tongue against her teeth. "All that for her." Ava and Cora slept next to each other every night in the loft and even though they were crammed up there with eight other people Cora could distinguish Ava's every frustration as it moved through the wood. The woman's breath was humid with rage, sour. She made a point of knocking Cora whenever she got up to make water.

"You in Hob now," Moses told Cora one afternoon when she came in from helping with the baling. Moses had made a deal with Ava, using some form of currency. Ever since Connelly had promoted the field hand to boss, to one of the overseer's enforcers, Moses had set himself up as a broker of cabin intrigues. Order in the rows, such as it was, needed to be preserved, and there were things a white man could not do. Moses accepted his role with enthusiasm. Cora thought he had a mean face, like a burl sprouting from a squat, sweaty trunk. She wasn't surprised when his character revealed itself—if you waited long enough, it always did. Like the dawn. Cora slunk over to Hob, where they banished the wretched. There was no recourse, were no laws but the ones rewritten every day. Someone had already moved her things over.

No one remembered the unfortunate who had lent his name to the cabin. He lived long enough to embody qualities before being undone by them. Off to Hob with those who had been crippled by the overseers' punishments, off to Hob with those who had been broken by the labor in ways you could see and in ways you could not see, off to Hob with those who had lost their wits. Off to Hob with strays.

The damaged men, the half men, lived in Hob first. Then the women took up residence. White men and brown men had used the women's bodies violently, their babies came out stunted and shrunken, beatings had knocked the sense out of their heads, and they repeated the names of their dead children in the darkness: Eve, Elizabeth, N'thaniel, Tom. Cora curled on the floor of the main room, too afraid to sleep up there with them, those abject creatures. Cursing herself for her small-mindedness even as she was powerless before it. She stared at dark shapes. The fireplace, the beams undergirding the loft, the tools dangling off nails on the walls. The first time she had spent a night outside the cabin she'd been born in. A hundred paces and as many miles.

It was only a matter of time before Ava implemented the next stage of her scheme. And there was Old Abraham to contend with. Old Abraham, who was not old at all but who had comported himself in the manner of an elderly misanthrope since he first learned to sit up. He had no designs but wanted the plot gone on principle. Why should he and everyone else respect this little girl's claim just because her grandmother had kicked the dirt over once? Old Abraham was not one for tradition. He'd been sold too many times for the proposition to have much weight. On numerous occasions as she passed on errands, Cora overheard him lobby for the redistribution of her parcel. "All that for her." All three square yards of it.

THEN Blake arrived. That summer young Terrance Randall assumed duties to prepare for the day he and his brother took over the plantation. He bought a bunch of niggers out of the Carolinas. Six of them, Fanti and Mandingo if the broker was to be believed, their bodies and temperament honed for labor by nature. Blake, Pot, Edward, and the rest made a tribe of themselves on Randall land and were not above helping themselves to that which was not theirs. Terrance Randall made it known they were his new favorites, and Connelly made sure that everyone remembered it. You learned to step aside when the men were in a mood, or on a Saturday night once they'd emptied all the cider.

Blake was a big oak, a double-ration man who quickly proved a testament to Terrance Randall's investment acumen. The price they'd get for the offspring of such a stud alone. Blake wrassled his buddies and any other comers in a frequent spectacle, kicking up the dust, inevitably emerging the conqueror. His voice boomed through the rows as he worked and even those who despised him couldn't help but sing along. The man had a miserable personality but the sounds that came from his body made the labor fly.

After a few weeks of sniffing around and assessing the northern half, Blake decided that Cora's spread would be a nice place to tie up his dog. Sun, breeze, proximity. Blake had coaxed the mutt to his side during a trip to town. The dog stayed, lingering around the smokehouse when Blake worked and barking at every noise in the busy Georgia night. Blake knew some carpentry—it was not, as was often the case, a lie put out by the trader to bump up his price. He built a little house for his mutt and tried to induce compliments. The kind words were genuine, for the doghouse was a handsome piece of work, of nice proportion, with clean angles. There was a door on a hinge and sun and moon cutouts along the back wall.

"Ain't this a nice mansion?" Blake asked Old Abraham. Blake had come to value the man's sometimes bracing candor since his arrival.

"Mighty fine work. That a little bed in there?"

Blake had sewn a pillowcase and stuffed it with moss. He decided that the patch outside his cabin was the most appropriate spot for his dog's home. Cora had been invisible to him but now he sought her eyes when she was close, to warn her that she was invisible no more.

She tried to call in a few debts owed her mother, the ones she knew about. They rebuffed her. Like Beau, the seamstress Mabel had nursed back to health when she was struck with fever. Mabel had given the girl her own supper portion and spooned potlikker and roots into her trembling lips until she opened her eyes again. Beau said she had paid that debt and then some and told Cora to get back to Hob. Cora remembered that Mabel had extended an alibi to Calvin when some planting tools went missing. Connelly, who had an aptitude for the cat-o'-nine-tails, would have stripped the meat off Calvin's back if she hadn't concocted his defense. Would have done the same to Mabel if he'd found she was lying. Cora crept on Calvin after supper: I need help. He waved her away. Mabel had said that she never discovered to what purpose he used those instruments.

Not soon after Blake made his intentions known, Cora woke one morning to the violation. She left Hob to check her garden. It had been a cool dawn. Wisps of white moisture hovered over the ground. There she saw it—the remains of what would have been her first cabbages. Heaped by the steps of Blake's cabin, the tangled vines already drying out. The ground had been turned and tamped to make a nice yard for the mutt's house, which sat in the center of her plot like a grand mansion in the heart of a plantation.

The dog poked his head out of the door as if it knew it had been her land and wanted to signal his indifference.

Blake stepped out of the cabin and crossed his arms. He spat.

People moved in the corners of Cora's vision: shadows of gossips and scolds. Watching her. Her mother was gone. She'd been moved into the wretch house and no one had come to her aid. Now this man three times her size, a bruiser, had taken her stake.

Cora had been mulling strategy. In later years she could have turned to the Hob women, or Lovey, but this was then. Her grandmother had warned that she would knock open the head of anyone who messed with her land. That seemed out of proportion to Cora. In a spell, she walked back to Hob and plucked a hatchet off the wall, the hatchet she stared at when she could not sleep. Left by one of the previous residents who came to one bad end or another, lung sickness or peeled open by a whip or shitting their insides out on the floor.

By now word had spread and bystanders lingered outside the cabins, heads tilted in anticipation. Cora marched past them, bent as if burrowing her body into a gale. No one moved to stop her, so strange was this display. Her first blow brought down the roof of the doghouse, and a squeal from the dog, who had just had his tail half severed. He scrambled to a hidey-hole beneath his owner's cabin. Her second blow wounded the left side of the doghouse gravely and her last put it out of its misery.

She stood there, heaving. Both hands on the hatchet. The hatchet wavered in the air, in a tug-of-war with a ghost, but the girl did not falter.

Blake made fists and stepped toward Cora. His boys behind him, tensing. Then he stopped. What happened between those two figures in that moment—the burly young man and the slender girl in white shift—became a matter of vantage. To those watching by the first line of cabins Blake's face distorted in surprise and worry, that of a man stumbling into a kingdom of hornets. Those standing by the new cabins saw Cora's eyes dart to and fro, as if she took the measure of an advancing host, not just one man. An army she was nonetheless prepared to meet. Regardless of perspective, what was important was the message imparted by one through posture and expression and interpreted by the other: You may get the better of me, but it will cost you.

They stood a few moments until Alice sounded the bell for breakfast. Nobody was going to forgo their mash. When they came in from the fields, Cora cleaned up the mess that had been made of her plot. She rolled over the block of sugar maple, a castoff from someone's construction project, and it became her perch whenever she had a spare moment.

If Cora didn't belong in Hob before Ava's maneuvering, she did now. Its most infamous occupant, and the most long-term. Eventually the work broke the crippled—it always did—and those in a state of unreason were sold off cheap or took a knife to their own throats. Vacancies were brief. Cora remained. Hob was her home.

She used the doghouse for firewood. It kept her and the rest of Hob warm one night, but its legend marked her for the rest of her time on the Randall plantation. Blake and his friends started telling tales. Blake recounted how he woke from a nap behind the stables to find Cora standing over him with her hatchet, blubbering. He was a natural mimic and his gestures sold the story. Once Cora's chest started to sprout, Edward, the most wicked of Blake's gang, bragged of how Cora flapped her dress at him while she made lascivious suggestions and threatened to scalp him when he refused her. Young women whispered how they watched her slink away from the cabins on the full moon, to the woods, where she fornicated with donkeys and goats. Those who found this last story less than credible nonetheless recognized the usefulness of keeping the strange girl outside the circle of respectability.

Not long after it became known that Cora's womanhood had come into flower, Edward, Pot, and two hands from the southern half dragged her behind the smokehouse. If anyone heard or saw, they did not intervene. The Hob women sewed her up. Blake was gone by then. Perhaps having looked into her face that day, he had counseled his companions against revenge: It will cost you. But he was gone. He ran off three years after she busted up the doghouse, hiding in the swamp for weeks. It was his mutt's barking that gave away his location to the patrollers. Cora would have said it served him right, had his punishment not made her shiver to think about.

They had already dragged the big table from the kitchen and covered it with food for Jockey's celebration. At one end a trapper skinned his raccoons and at the other Florence scraped dirt from a mound of sweet potatoes. The fire under the big cauldron cracked and whistled. The soup roiled within the black pot, bits of cabbage chasing around the hog's head that bobbed up and down, the eye roving in the gray foam. Little Chester ran up and tried to grab a handful of cowpeas, but Alice swatted him away with her ladle.

"Nothing today, Cora?" Alice said.

"Too early," Cora said.

Alice made a brief show of disappointment and returned to supper.

That's what a lie looks like, Cora thought, and marked it. It was just as well her garden had refused. On Jockey's last birthday she had donated two heads of cabbage, which were graciously received. Cora made the mistake of turning back as she departed the kitchen and caught Alice tossing the heads into the slop bucket. She staggered into the sunlight. Did the woman think her food tainted? Is that how Alice had got rid of everything Cora had contributed these past five years, treated every turnip knob and bunch of sour greens? Had it started with Cora, or Mabel, or her grandmother? There was no point in confronting the woman. Alice had been beloved of Randall, and now James Randall, who had grown tall on her mincemeat pies. There was an order of misery, misery tucked inside miseries, and you were meant to keep track.

The Randall brothers. Since he was a young boy, James could be placated by a treat from Alice's kitchen, the sugar apple that cut short a fit or tantrum. His younger brother, Terrance, was a different sort. The cook still had a knot next to her ear where Master Terrance expressed his displeasure over one of her broths. He had been ten years old. The signs had been there since he could walk, and he perfected the more distasteful aspects of his personality as he lurched into manhood and assumed his responsibilities. James had a nautilus disposition, burrowing into his private appetites, but Terrance inflicted every fleeting and deep-seated fancy on all in his power. As was his right.

Around Cora, pots clanged and pickaninnies squealed over the delights to come. From the southern half: nothing. The Randall brothers had flipped a coin years ago to determine stewardship of each half of the plantation and in doing so made this day possible. Feasts like this didn't happen in Terrance's domain, for the younger brother was stingy with slave amusements. The Randall sons managed their inheritances according to their temperaments. James contented himself with the security of a fashionable crop, the slow, inevitable accumulations of his estate.

Land and niggers to tend it were a surety beyond what any bank could offer. Terrance took a more active hand, ever scheming for ways to increase the loads sent to New Orleans. He wrung out every possible dollar. When black blood was money, the savvy businessman knew to open the vein.

The boy Chester and his friends grabbed Cora, startling her. But it was only children. Time for the races. Cora always arranged the children at the starting line, aiming their feet, calming the skittish ones, and graduating some to the older kids' race if need be. This year she kicked up Chester one slot. He was a stray, like her, his parents sold off before he could walk. Cora looked after him. Burr-headed and red-eyed. He'd shot up the last six months, the rows triggering something in his lithe body. Connelly said he had the makings of a top picker, a rare compliment from him.

"You run fast," Cora said.

He crossed his arms and cocked his head: You don't need to tell me anything. Chester was half a man, even if he didn't know it. He wouldn't race next year, Cora saw, but loll at the sidelines, joking with his friends, devising mischief.

The young slaves and the old slaves gathered on the sidelines of the horse path. Women who had lost their children drifted over little by little, to mortify themselves with possibilities and never-would-bes. Huddles of men swapped cider jugs and felt their humiliations slip away. Hob women rarely participated in the feasts, but Nag hustled about in her helpful way, rounding up little ones from their distractions.

Lovey stood at the finish as the judge. Everyone but the

children knew that she always proclaimed her darlings the winner, when she could get away with it. Jockey also presided at the finish, in his rickety maple armchair, the one he used to watch the stars most nights. On his birthdays he dragged it up and down the alley, to give proper attention to the amusements held in his name. The runners went to Jockey after they were done with their races, and he dropped a piece of ginger cake onto their palms, no matter what they placed.

Chester panted, hands on his knees. He had flagged at the end. "Almost had it," Cora said.

The boy said, "Almost," and went for his piece of ginger cake.

Cora patted the old man's arm after the last race. You never could tell how much he saw with those milky eyes of his. "How old are you, Jockey?"

"Oh, let me see." He drifted off.

She was sure he had claimed a hundred and one years at his last party. He was only half that, which meant he was the oldest slave anyone on the two Randall plantations had ever met. Once you got that old, you might as well be ninety-eight or a hundred and eight. Nothing left for the world to show you but the latest incarnations of cruelty.

Sixteen or seventeen. That's where Cora put her age. One year since Connelly ordered her to take a husband. Two years since Pot and his friends had seasoned her. They had not repeated their violation, and no worthy man paid her notice after that day, given the cabin she called home and the stories of her lunacy. Six years since her mother left.

Jockey had a good birthday plan, Cora thought. Jockey awoke on a surprise Sunday to announce his celebration and that was that. Sometimes it was in the midst of the spring rains, other times after harvest. He skipped some years or forgot or decided according to some personal accounting of grievance that the plantation was undeserving. No one minded his caprices. It was enough that he was the oldest colored man they had ever met, that he had survived every torment big and small white men had concocted and implemented. His eyes were clouded, his leg lame, his ruined hand permanently curled as if still clenched around a spade, but he was alive.

The white men left him alone now. Old man Randall said nothing about his birthdays, and neither did James when he took over. Connelly, the overseer, made himself scarce every Sunday, when he summoned whatever slave gal he'd made his wife that month. The white men were silent. As if they'd given up or decided that a small freedom was the worst punishment of all, presenting the bounty of true freedom into painful relief.

One day Jockey was bound to choose the correct day of his birth. If he lived long enough. If that was true, then if Cora picked a day for her birthday every now and then she might hit upon hers as well. In fact, today might be her birthday. What did you get for that, for knowing the day you were born into the white man's world? It didn't seem like the thing to remember. More like to forget.

"Cora."

Most of the northern half had moved to the kitchen to get

fed but Caesar dallied. Here he was. She'd never had occasion to speak to the man since he arrived at the plantation. New slaves were quickly warned against the Hob women. It saved time.

"Can I talk with you?" he asked.

James Randall had bought him and three other slaves from a traveling agent after the fever deaths a year and a half ago. Two women to work the laundry, and Caesar and Prince to join the field gangs. She had seen him whittling, worrying blocks of pine with his curved carving knives. He didn't mix with the more bothersome element on the plantation, and she knew that he sometimes went off with Frances, one of the housemaids. Were they still laying together? Lovey would know. She was a girl, but Lovey kept track of man-and-woman business, the impending arrangements.

Cora felt proper. "What can I do for you, Caesar?"

He didn't bother to see if anyone was in earshot. He knew there was no one because he had planned. "I'm going back north," he said. "Soon. Running away. I want you to come."

Cora tried to think of who put him up to this prank. "You going north and I'm going to eat," she said.

Caesar held her arm, gently and insistent. His body was lean and strong, like any field hand his age, but he carried his strength lightly. His face was round, with a flat button nose—she had a quick memory of dimples when he laughed. Why had she kept that in her head?

"I don't want you to tell on me," he said. "Have to trust you on that. But I'm going soon, and I want you. For good luck."

Then she understood him. It was not a trick being played on her. It was a trick he was playing on himself. The boy was simple. The smell of the raccoon meat brought her back to the celebration and she pulled her arm away. "I ain't trying to get killed by Connelly, or patrollers, or snakes."

Cora was still squinting over his idiocy when she got her first bowl of the soup. White man trying to kill you slow every day, and sometimes trying to kill you fast. Why make it easy for him? That was one kind of work you could say no to.

She found Lovey, but did not ask her what the girls whispered about Caesar and Frances. If he was serious about his plan, Frances was a widow.

It was the most any young man had talked to her since she moved to Hob.

They lit the torches for the wrestling matches. Someone had unearthed a stash of corn whiskey and cider, which circulated in due course and fed the spectators' enthusiasm. By now, the husbands who lived on other plantations had come for their Sunday-night visits. Walking miles, time enough to fantasize. Some wives were happier at the prospect of marital relations than others.

Lovey giggled. "I'd wrestle with him," she said, nodding at Major.

Major looked up as if he heard her. He was turning out to be a prime buck. Worked hard and rarely forced the bosses to raise the whip. He was respectful to Lovey because of her age and it wouldn't surprise if Connelly arranged a match one day. The young man and his opponent twisted in the grass. Take it out on each other if you cannot take it out on the ones who deserve it. The children peeked between their elders, making bets they had nothing to back up with. They pulled weeds and worked in trash gangs now, but one day the field work would make them as big as the men grappling and pinning each other to the grass. Get him, get that boy, teach him what he needs to learn.

When the music started and the dancing commenced, they appreciated the extent of their gratitude for Jockey. Once again he picked the right day for a birthday. He had been attuned to a shared tension, a communal apprehension beyond the routine facts of their bondage. It had built up. The last few hours had dispelled much of the ill feeling. They could face the morning toil and the following mornings and the long days with their spirits replenished, however meagerly, by a fond night to look back on and the next birthday feast to look forward to. By making a circle of themselves that separated the human spirits within from the degradation without.

Noble picked up a tambourine and tapped it. He was a fast picker in the rows and a joyful instigator outside of them; he brought both kinds of dexterity to this night. Clap hands, crook elbows, shake hips. There are instruments and human players but sometimes a fiddle or a drum makes instruments of those who play them, and all are put in servitude to the song. So it was when George and Wesley picked up their fiddle and banjo on days of carousing. Jockey sat in his maple chair, tapping his bare feet on the dirt. The slaves moved forward and danced.

Cora did not move. She was wary of how sometimes when the music tugged, you might suddenly be next to a man and you didn't know what he might do. All the bodies in motion, given license. To pull on you, take both of your hands, even if they were doing it with a nice thought. One time on Jockey's birthday, Wesley treated them to a song he knew from his days up north, a new sound none of them had heard before. Cora had dared to step out among the dancers and close her eyes and twirl and when she opened them Edward was there, his eyes alight. Even with Edward and Pot dead—Edward strung up after shorting the scale by loading his sack with stones and Pot in the ground after a rat bite turned him black and purple—she shrank from the idea of loosening her leash on herself. George sawed with his fiddle, the notes swirling up into night like sparks gusted from a fire. No one approached to pull her into the lively madness.

THE music stopped. The circle broke. Sometimes a slave will be lost in a brief eddy of liberation. In the sway of a sudden reverie among the furrows or while untangling the mysteries of an early-morning dream. In the middle of a song on a warm Sunday night. Then it comes, always—the overseer's cry, the call to work, the shadow of the master, the reminder that she is only a human being for a tiny moment across the eternity of her servitude.

The Randall brothers had emerged from the great house and were among them.

The slaves stepped aside, making calculations of what distance

34

represented the right proportion of fear and respect. Godfrey, James's houseboy, held up a lantern. According to Old Abraham, James favored the mother, stout as a barrel and just as firm in countenance, and Terrance took after the father, tall and owl-faced, perpetually on the verge of swooping down on prey. In addition to the land, they inherited their father's tailor, who arrived once a month in his rickety carriage with his samples of linen and cotton. The brothers dressed alike when they were children and continued to do so in manhood. Their white trousers and shirts were as clean as the laundry girls' hands could make them, and the orange glow made the men look like ghosts emerging from the dark.

"Master James," Jockey said. His good hand gripped the arm of his chair as if to rise, but he did not stir. "Master Terrance."

"Don't let us disturb you," Terrance said. "My brother and I were discussing business and heard the music. I told him, Now that is the most god-awful racket I'd ever heard."

The Randalls were drinking wine out of goblets of cut glass and looked as if they had drained a few bottles. Cora searched for Caesar's face in the crowd. She did not find him. He hadn't been present the last time the brothers appeared together on the northern half. You did well to remember the different lessons of those occasions. Something always happened when the Randalls ventured into the quarter. Sooner or later. A new thing coming that you couldn't predict until it was upon you.

James left the daily operations to his man Connelly and rarely visited. He might grant a tour to a visitor, a distinguished neighbor or curious planter from another neck of the woods, but it was rare. James rarely addressed his niggers, who had been taught by the lash to keep working and ignore his presence. When Terrance appeared on his brother's plantation, he usually appraised each slave and made a note of which men were the most able and which women the most appealing. Content to leer at his brother's women, he grazed heartily upon the women of his own half. "I like to taste my plums," Terrance said, prowling the rows of cabins to see what struck his fancy. He violated the bonds of affection, sometimes visiting slaves on their wedding night to show the husband the proper way to discharge his marital duty. He tasted his plums, and broke the skin, and left his mark.

It was accepted that James was of a different orientation. Unlike his father and brother, James did not use his property to gratify himself. Occasionally he had women from the county to dine, and Alice was always sure to make the most sumptuous, seductive supper at her means. Mrs. Randall had passed many years before, and it was Alice's thought that a woman would be a civilizing presence on the plantation. For months at a time, James entertained these pale creatures, their white buggies traversing the mud tracks that led to the great house. The kitchen girls giggled and speculated. And then a new woman would appear.

To hear his valet Prideful tell it, James confined his erotic energies to specialized rooms in a New Orleans establishment. The madam was broad-minded and modern, adept in the trajectories of human desire. Prideful's stories were hard to believe, despite assurances that he received his reports from the staff of the place, with whom he'd grown close over the years. What kind of white man would willingly submit to the whip?

Terrance scratched his cane in the dirt. It had been his father's cane, topped with a silver wolf's head. Many remembered its bite on their flesh. "Then I recollected James telling me about a nigger he had down here," Terrance said, "could recite the Declaration of Independence. I can't bring myself to believe him. I thought perhaps tonight he can show me, since everyone is out and about, from the sound of it."

"We'll settle it," James said. "Where is that boy? Michael."

No one said anything. Godfrey waved the lantern around pathetically. Moses was the boss unfortunate enough to stand closest to the Randall brothers. He cleared his throat. "Michael dead, Master James."

Moses instructed one of the pickaninnies to fetch Connelly, even if it meant interrupting the overseer from his Sunday-evening concubinage. The expression on James's face told Moses to start explaining.

Michael, the slave in question, had indeed possessed the ability to recite long passages. According to Connelly, who heard the story from the nigger trader, Michael's former master was fascinated by the abilities of South American parrots and reasoned that if a bird could be taught limericks, a slave might be taught to remember as well. Merely glancing at the size of the skulls told you that a nigger possessed a bigger brain than a bird.

Michael had been the son of his master's coachman. Had a brand of animal cleverness, the kind you see in pigs sometimes.

The master and his unlikely pupil started with simple rhymes and short passages from popular British versifiers. They went slow over the words the nigger didn't understand and, if truth be told, the master only half understood, as his tutor had been a reprobate who had been chased from every decent position he had ever held and who decided to make his final posting the canvas for his secret revenge. They made miracles, the tobacco farmer and the coachman's son. The Declaration of Independence was their masterpiece. "A history of repeated injuries and usurpations."

Michael's ability never amounted to more than a parlor trick, delighting visitors before the discussion turned as it always did to the diminished faculties of niggers. His owner grew bored and sold the boy south. By the time Michael got to Randall, some torture or punishment had addled his senses. He was a mediocre worker. He complained of noises and black spells that blotted his memory. In exasperation Connelly beat out what little brains he had left. It was a scourging that Michael was not intended to survive, and it achieved its purpose.

"I should have been told," James said, his displeasure plain. Michael's recitation had been a novel diversion the two times he trotted the nigger out for guests.

Terrance liked to tease his brother. "James," he said, "you need to keep better account of your property."

"Don't meddle."

"I knew you let your slaves have revels, but I had no idea they were so extravagant. Are you trying to make me look bad?"

"Don't pretend you care what a nigger thinks of you, Terrance." James's glass was empty. He turned to go.

"One more song, James. These sounds have grown on me."

George and Wesley were forlorn. Noble and his tambourine were nowhere to be seen. James pressed his lips into a slit. He gestured and the men started playing.

Terrance tapped his cane. His face sank as he took in the crowd. "You're not going to dance? I have to insist. You and you."

They didn't wait for their master's signal. The slaves of the northern half converged on the alley, haltingly, trying to insinuate themselves into their previous rhythm and put on a show. Crooked Ava had not lost her power to dissemble since her days of harassing Cora—she hooted and stomped as if it were the height of the Christmas celebrations. Putting on a show for the master was a familiar skill, the small angles and advantages of the mask, and they shook off their fear as they settled into the performance. Oh, how they capered and hollered, shouted and hopped! Certainly this was the most lively song they had ever heard, the musicians the most accomplished players the colored race had to offer. Cora dragged herself into the circle, checking the Randall brothers' reactions on every turn like everyone else. Jockey tumbled his hands in his lap to keep time. Cora found Caesar's face. He stood in the shadow of the kitchen, his expression flat. Then he withdrew.

"You!"

It was Terrance. He held his hand before him as if it were

39

covered in some eternal stain that only he could see. Then Cora caught sight of it—the single drop of wine staining the cuff of his lovely white shirt. Chester had bumped him.

Chester simpered and bowed down before the white man. "Sorry, master! Sorry, master!" The cane crashed across his shoulder and head, again and again. The boy screamed and shrank to the dirt as the blows continued. Terrance's arm rose and fell. James looked tired.

One drop. A feeling settled over Cora. She had not been under its spell in years, since she brought the hatchet down on Blake's doghouse and sent the splinters into the air. She had seen men hung from trees and left for buzzards and crows. Women carved open to the bones with the cat-o'-nine-tails. Bodies alive and dead roasted on pyres. Feet cut off to prevent escape and hands cut off to stop theft. She had seen boys and girls younger than this beaten and had done nothing. This night the feeling settled on her heart again. It grabbed hold of her and before the slave part of her caught up with the human part of her, she was bent over the boy's body as a shield. She held the cane in her hand like a swamp man handling a snake and saw the ornament at its tip. The silver wolf bared its silver teeth. Then the cane was out of her hand. It came down on her head. It crashed down again and this time the silver teeth ripped across her eyes and her blood splattered the dirt.

⊷⊶◼✦◼⊷⊶

The Hob women were seven that year. Mary was the oldest. She was in Hob because she was prone to fits. Foaming at the mouth like a mad dog, writhing in the dirt with wild eyes. She had feuded for years with another picker named Bertha, who finally put a curse on her. Old Abraham complained that Mary's affliction dated back to when she was a pickaninny, but no one listened to him. By any reckoning these fits were nothing like those she had suffered in her youth. She woke from them battered and confused and listless, which led to punishments for lost work, and recuperation from punishments led to more lost work. Once the bosses' mood turned against you, anyone might be swept up in it. Mary moved her things to Hob to avoid the scorn of her cabin mates. She dragged her feet all the way as if someone might intervene.

Mary worked in the milk house with Margaret and Rida. Before their purchase by James Randall these two had been so tangled by sufferings that they could not weave themselves into the fabric of the plantation. Margaret produced awful sounds from her throat at inopportune moments, animal sounds, the most miserable keenings and vulgar oaths. When the master made his rounds, she kept her hand over her mouth, lest she call attention to her affliction. Rida was indifferent to hygiene and no inducement or threat could sway her. She stank.

Lucy and Titania never spoke, the former because she chose not to and the latter because her tongue had been hacked out by a previous owner. They worked in the kitchen under Alice, who preferred assistants who were disinclined to natter all day, to better hear her own voice.

Two other women took their own lives that spring, more than usual but nothing remarkable. No one with a name that would be remembered come winter, so shallow was their mark. That left Nag and Cora. They tended to the cotton in all of its phases.

At the end of the workday Cora staggered and Nag rushed to steady her. She led Cora back to Hob. The boss glared at their slow progress out of the rows but said nothing. Cora's obvious madness had removed her from casual rebuke. They passed Caesar, who loitered by one of the work sheds with a group of young hands, carving a piece of wood with his knife. Cora averted her eyes and made her face into slate for him, as she had ever since his proposal.

It was two weeks after Jockey's birthday and Cora was still on the mend. The blows to her face had left one eye swollen shut and performed a gross injury to her temple. The swelling disappeared but where the silver wolf had kissed was now a rueful scar shaped like an X. It seeped for days. That was her tally for the night of feast. Far worse was the lashing Connelly gave her the next morning under the pitiless boughs of the whipping tree.

Connelly was one of Old Randall's first hires. James preserved the man's appointment under his stewardship. When Cora was young, the overseer's hair was a livid Irish red that curled from his straw hat like the wings of a cardinal. In those days he patrolled with a black umbrella but eventually surrendered and now his white blouses were stark against his tanned flesh. His hair had gone white and his belly overflowed his belt, but apart from that he was the same man who had whipped her grandmother and mother, stalking the village with a lopsided gait that reminded her of an old ox. There was no rushing him if he chose not to be rushed. The only time he exhibited speed was when he reached for his cat-o'-nine-tails. Then he demonstrated the energy and rambunctiousness of a child at a new pastime.

The overseer was not pleased by what had transpired during the Randall brothers' surprise visit. First, Connelly had been interrupted while taking his pleasure with Gloria, his current wench. He flogged the messenger and roused himself from bed. Second, there was the matter of Michael. Connelly hadn't informed James about Michael's loss as his employer never bothered over routine fluctuations in the hands, but Terrance's curiosity had made it a problem.

Then there was the matter of Chester's clumsiness and Cora's incomprehensible action. Connelly peeled them open the following sunrise. He started with Chester, to follow the order in which the transgressions had occurred, and called for their bloody backs to be scrubbed out with pepper water afterward.

It was Chester's first proper licking, and Cora's first in half a year. Connelly repeated the whippings the next two mornings. According to the house slaves, Master James was more upset that his brother had touched his property, and before so many witnesses, than with Chester and Cora. Thus was the brunt of one brother's ire toward another borne by property. Chester never said a word to Cora again.

Nag helped Cora up the steps to Hob. Cora collapsed once they entered the cabin and were out of sight of the rest of the village. "Let me get you some supper," Nag said.

Like Cora, Nag had been relocated to Hob over politics. For years she had been Connelly's preferred, spending most nights in his bed. Nag was haughty for a nigger gal even before the overseer bestowed his slim favors upon her, with her pale gray eyes and roiling hips. She became insufferable. Preening, gloating over the ill treatment that she alone escaped. Her mother had consorted frequently with white men and tutored Nag in licentious practices. She bent in dedication to the task even as he swapped their offspring. The northern and southern halves of the great Randall plantation exchanged slaves all the time, unloading beat niggers, skulky workers, and rascals on each other in a desultory game. Nag's children were tokens. Connelly could not countenance his mulatto bastards when their curls glowed his Irish red in the sunlight.

One morning Connelly made it clear that he no longer required Nag in his bed. It was the day her enemies had waited for. Everyone saw it coming except for her. She returned from the fields to find her possessions had been moved to Hob, announcing her loss in status to the village. Her shame nourished them as no food could. Hob hardened her, as was its way. The cabin tended to set one's personality.

Nag had never been close to Cora's mother but that didn't stop her from befriending the girl when she became a stray. After the night of the feast and in the following bloody days she and Mary ministered to Cora, applying brine and poultices to her ravaged skin and making sure she ate. They cradled her head and sang lullabies to their lost children through her. Lovey visited her friend as well, but the young girl was not immune to Hob's reputation and got skittish in the presence of Nag and Mary and the others. She stayed until her nerves gave out.

Cora lay on the floor and moaned. Two weeks after her beating, she endured dizzy spells and a pounding in her skull. For the most part she was able to keep it at bay and work the row, but sometimes it was all she could do to stay upright until the sun sank. Every hour when the water girl brought the ladle she licked it clean and felt the metal on her teeth. Now she had nothing left.

Mary appeared. "Sick again," she said. She had a wet cloth ready and placed it on Cora's brow. She still maintained a reservoir of maternal feeling after the loss of her five children—three dead before they could walk and the others sold off when they were old enough to carry water and grab weeds around the great house. Mary descended from pure Ashanti stock, as did her two husbands. Pups like that, it didn't take much salesmanship.

Cora moved her mouth in silent thanks. The cabin walls pressed on her. Up in the loft one of the other women—Rida by the stench—rummaged and banged. Nag rubbed out the knots in Cora's hands. "I don't know what's worse," she said. "You sick and out of sight or you up and outside when Master Terrance come tomorrow."

The prospect of his visit depleted Cora. James Randall was bedridden. He'd fallen ill after a trip to New Orleans to negotiate with a delegation of trading agents from Liverpool and to visit his disgraceful haven. He fainted in his buggy on his return and had been out of sight since. Now whispers came from the house staff that Terrance was going to take over while his brother was on the mend. In the morning he would inspect the northern half to bring the operation in harmony with how things were done in the southern half.

No one doubted that it would be a bloody sort of harmony.

Her friends' hands slipped away and the walls relinquished their pressure and she passed out. Cora woke in the pit of the night, her head resting on a rolled-up linsey blanket. Everyone asleep above. She rubbed the scar on her temple. It felt like it was seeping. She knew why she had rushed to protect Chester. But she was stymied when she tried to recall the urgency of that moment, the grain of the feeling that possessed her. It had retreated to that obscure corner in herself from where it came and couldn't be coaxed. To ease her restlessness she crept out to her plot and sat on her maple and smelled the air and listened. Things in the swamp whistled and splashed, hunting in the living darkness. To walk in there at night, heading north to the Free States. Have to take leave of your senses to do that.

But her mother had.

AS if to reflect Ajarry, who did not step off Randall land once she arrived on it, Mabel never left the plantation until the day of her escape. She gave no indication of her intentions, at least to no one who admitted to that knowledge under subsequent interrogations. No mean feat in a village teeming with treacherous natures and informers who would sell out their dearest to escape the bite of the cat-o'-nine-tails.

Cora fell asleep nestled against her mother's stomach and never saw her again. Old Randall raised the alarm and summoned the patrollers. Within an hour the hunting party tromped into the swamp, chasing after Nate Ketchum's dogs. The latest in a long line of specializers, Ketchum had slave-catching in his blood. The hounds had been bred for generations to detect nigger scent across whole counties, chewing and mangling many a wayward hand. When the creatures strained against their leather straps and pawed at the air, their barking made every soul in the quarters want to run to their cabins. But the day's picking lay before the slaves foremost and they stooped to their orders, enduring the dogs' terrible noise and the visions of blood to come.

The bills and fliers circulated for hundreds of miles. Free negroes who supplemented their living catching runaways combed through the woods and wormed information from likely accomplices. Patrollers and posses of low whites harassed and bullied. The quarters of all the nearby plantations were thoroughly searched and no small number of slaves beaten on principle. But the hounds came up empty, as did their masters.

Randall retained the services of a witch to goofer his property so that no one with African blood could escape without being stricken with hideous palsy. The witch woman buried fetishes in secret places, took her payment, and departed in her mule cart. There was a hearty debate in the village over the spirit of the goofer. Did the conjure apply only to those who had an intention to run or to all colored persons who stepped over the line? A week passed before the slaves hunted and scavenged in the swamp again. That's where the food was.

Of Mabel there was no sign. No one had escaped the Randall plantation before. The fugitives were always clawed back, betrayed by friends, they misinterpreted the stars and ran deeper into the labyrinth of bondage. On their return they were abused mightily before being permitted to die and those they left behind were forced to observe the grisly increments of their demise.

The infamous slave catcher Ridgeway paid a call on the plantation one week later. He rode up on his horses with his associates, five men of disreputable mien, led by a fearsome Indian scout who wore a necklace of shriveled ears. Ridgeway was six and a half feet tall, with the square face and thick neck of a hammer. He maintained a serene comportment at all times but generated a threatening atmosphere, like a thunderhead that seems far away but then is suddenly overhead with loud violence.

Ridgeway's audience lasted half an hour. He took notes in a small diary and to hear the house speak of it was a man of intense concentration and flowery manner of speech. He did not return for two years, not long before Old Randall's death, to apologize in person for his failure. The Indian was gone, but there was a young rider with long black hair who wore a similar ring of trophies over his hide vest. Ridgeway was in the vicinity to visit a neighboring planter, offering as proof of capture the heads of two runaways in a leather sack. Crossing the state line was a capital offense in Georgia; sometimes a master preferred an example over the return of his property.

The slave catcher shared rumors of a new branch of the underground railroad said to be operating in the southern part of the state, as impossible as it sounded. Old Randall scoffed. The sympathizers would be rooted out and tarred and feathered, Ridgeway assured his host. Or whatever satisfied local custom. Ridgeway apologized once again and took his leave and soon his gang crashed to the county road toward their next mission. There was no end to their work, the river of slaves that needed to be driven from their hidey-holes and brought to the white man's proper accounting.

Mabel had packed for her adventure. A machete. Flint and tinder. She stole a cabin mate's shoes, which were in better shape. For weeks, her empty garden testified to her miracle. Before she lit out she dug up every turnip and yam from their plot, a cumbersome load and ill-advised for a journey that required a fleet foot. The lumps and burrows in the dirt were a reminder to all who walked by. Then one morning they were smoothed over. Cora got on her knees and planted anew. It was her inheritance.

NOW in the thin moonlight, her head throbbing, Cora appraised her tiny garden. Weeds, weevils, the ragged footprints of critters. She had neglected her land since the feast. Time to return to it.

Terrance's visit the next day was uneventful save for one disturbing moment. Connelly took him through his brother's operation, as it had been some years since Terrance had made a proper tour. His manner was unexpectedly civil from all accounts, absent his standard sardonic remarks. They discussed the numbers from last year's haul and examined the ledgers that contained the weigh-ins from the previous September. Terrance expressed annoyance at the overseer's lamentable handwriting but apart from that the men got along amiably. They did not inspect the slaves or the village.

On horses they circumnavigated the fields, comparing the progress of the harvest on the two halves. Where Terrance and Connelly made their crossings through the cotton, the nearby slaves redoubled their efforts in a furious wave. The hands had been chopping the weeds for weeks, slashing hoes into the furrows. The stalks were up to Cora's shoulders now, bending and tottering, sprouting leaves and squares that were bigger every morning. Next month the bolls would explode into whiteness. She prayed the plants were tall enough to hide her when the white men passed. She saw their backs as they proceeded from her. Then Terrance turned. He nodded, tipped his cane at her, and continued on.

James died two days later. His kidneys, the doctor said.

Longtime residents of the Randall plantation couldn't help but compare the funerals of the father and the son. The elder Randall had been a revered member of planter society. The western riders commanded all the attention now but it was Randall and his brethren who were the true pioneers, carving out a life in this humid Georgia hell all those years ago. His fellow planters cherished him as a visionary for being the first in the region to switch to cotton, leading the profitable charge. Many was the young farmer suffocating in credit who came to Randall for advice—advice freely and generously given—and in his time came to master an enviable spread.

The slaves got time off to attend Old Randall's funeral. They stood in a quiet huddle while all the fine white men and women paid their respects to the beloved father. The house niggers acted as pallbearers, which everyone thought scandalous at first but on further consideration took as an indicator of genuine affection, one they had indeed enjoyed with their own slaves, with the mammy whose titties they suckled in more innocent times and the attendant who slipped a hand under soapy water at bath time. At the end of the service it began to rain. It put an end to the memorial but everyone was relieved because the drought had gone on too long. The cotton was thirsty.

By the time of James's passing, the Randall sons had cut off social ties with their father's peers and protégés. James had many business partners on paper, some of whom he had met in person, but he had few friends. To the point, Terrance's brother had never received his human portion of sentimentality. His funeral was sparsely attended. The slaves worked the rows—with the harvest approaching there was no question. It was all spelled out in his will, Terrance said. James was buried near his parents in a quiet corner of their abundant acreage, next to his father's mastiffs Plato and Demosthenes, who had been beloved by all, man and nigger alike, even if they couldn't keep away from the chickens.

Terrance traveled to New Orleans to straighten his brother's affairs with the cotton trade. Although there was never a good time to run, Terrance's stewardship of both halves provided a good argument. The northern half had always relished their easier climate. James was as ruthless and brutal as any white man but he was the portrait of moderation compared to his younger brother. The stories from the southern half were chilling, in magnitude if not in particulars.

Big Anthony took his opportunity. Big Anthony was not the most clever buck in the village, but no one could say he lacked a sense for opportunity. It was the first escape attempt since Blake. He braved the witch woman's goofer without incident and made it twenty-six miles before he was discovered snoozing in a hayloft. The constables returned him in an iron cage made by one of their cousins. "Take flight like a bird, you deserve a birdcage." The front of the cage had a slot for the name of the inhabitant, but no one had bothered to use it. They took the cage with them when they left.

On the eve of Big Anthony's punishment—whenever white men put off punishment some theater was bound to be involved—Caesar visited Hob. Mary let him in. She was puzzled. Few visitors ever came to call, and men only when it was a boss with bad news. Cora hadn't told anyone of the young man's proposition.

The loft was full of women either sleeping or listening. Cora put her mending to the floor and took him outside.

OLD Randall built the schoolhouse for his sons and the grandchildren he had hoped to have one day. The lonesome hulk was unlikely to fulfill its purpose anytime soon. Since Randall's sons had finished their education it was used only for assignations and all those different lessons. Lovey saw Caesar and Cora walk to it, and Cora shook her head at her friend's amusement.

The rotting schoolhouse smelled rank. Small animals made regular habitation. The chairs and tables had been removed a long time before, making room for dead leaves and spiderwebs. She wondered if he had brought Frances here when they were together, and what they did. Caesar had seen Cora stripped naked for her whippings, the blood pouring over her skin.

Caesar checked the window and said, "I'm sorry that happened to you."

"That's what they do," Cora said.

Two weeks ago she had judged him a fool. This night he carried himself as one beyond his years, like one of those wise old hands who tell you a story whose true message you only understand days or weeks later, when their facts are impossible to avoid.

"Will you come with me now?" Caesar said. "Been thinking it's past time to go."

She could not figure him. On the mornings of her three whippings, Caesar had stood in the front of the pack. It was customary for slaves to witness the abuse of their brethren as moral instruction. At some point during the show everyone had to turn away, if only for a moment, as they considered the slave's pain and the day sooner or later when it would be their turn at the foul end of the lash. That was you up there even when it was not. But Caesar did not flinch. He didn't seek her eyes but looked at something beyond her, something great and difficult to make out.

She said, "You think I'm a lucky charm because Mabel got away. But I ain't. You saw me. You saw what happens when you get a thought in your head."

Caesar was unmoved. "It's going to be bad when he gets back."

"It's bad now," Cora said. "Ever has been." She left him there.

The new stocks Terrance ordered explained the delay in Big Anthony's justice. The woodworkers toiled all through the night to complete the restraints, furnishing them with ambitious if crude engravings. Minotaurs, busty mermaids, and other fantastic creatures frolicked in the wood. The stocks were installed on the front lawn in the lush grass. Two bosses secured Big Anthony and there he dangled the first day.

On the second day a band of visitors arrived in a carriage,

august souls from Atlanta and Savannah. Swell ladies and gentlemen that Terrance had met on his travels, as well as a newspaperman from London come to report on the American scene. They ate at a table set up on the lawn, savoring Alice's turtle soup and mutton and devising compliments for the cook, who would never receive them. Big Anthony was whipped for the duration of their meal, and they ate slow. The newspaperman scribbled on paper between bites. Dessert came and the revelers moved inside to be free of the mosquitoes while Big Anthony's punishment continued.

On the third day, just after lunch, the hands were recalled from the fields, the washwomen and cooks and stable hands interrupted from their tasks, the house staff diverted from its maintenance. They gathered on the front lawn. Randall's visitors sipped spiced rum as Big Anthony was doused with oil and roasted. The witnesses were spared his screams, as his manhood had been cut off on the first day, stuffed in his mouth, and sewn in. The stocks smoked, charred, and burned, the figures in the wood twisting in the flames as if alive.

Terrance addressed the slaves of the northern and southern halves. There is one plantation now, united in purpose and method, he said. He expressed his grief over his brother's death and his consolation in the knowledge that James was in heaven united with their mother and father. He walked among his slaves as he talked, tapping his cane, rubbing the heads of pickaninnies and petting some of the older worthies from the southern half. He checked the teeth of a young buck he had never seen before, wrenching the boy's jaw to get a good look, and nodded in approval. In order to feed the world's insatiable demand for cotton goods, he said, every picker's daily quota will be increased by a percentage determined by their numbers from the previous harvest. The fields will be reorganized to accommodate a more efficient number of rows. He walked. He slapped a man across the face for weeping at the sight of his friend thrashing against the stocks.

When Terrance got to Cora, he slipped his hand into her shift and cupped her breast. He squeezed. She did not move. No one had moved since the beginning of his address, not even to pinch their noses to keep out the smell of Big Anthony's roasting flesh. No more feasts outside of Christmas and Easter, he said. He will arrange and approve all marriages personally to ensure the appropriateness of the match and the promise of the offspring. A new tax on Sunday labor off the plantation. He nodded at Cora and continued his stroll among his Africans as he shared his improvements.

Terrance concluded his address. It was understood that the slaves were to remain there until Connelly dismissed them. The Savannah ladies refreshed their drinks from the pitcher. The newspaperman opened a fresh diary and resumed his note-taking. Master Terrance joined his guests and they departed for a tour of the cotton.

She had not been his and now she was his. Or she had always been his and just now knew it. Cora's attention detached itself. It floated someplace past the burning slave and the great house and the lines that defined the Randall domain. She tried to fill in its details from stories, sifting through the accounts of slaves who had seen it. Each time she caught hold of something—buildings of polished white stone, an ocean so vast there wasn't a tree in sight, the shop of a colored blacksmith who served no master but himself—it wriggled free like a fish and raced away. She would have to see it for herself if she were to keep it.

Who could she tell? Lovey and Nag would keep her confidence, but she feared Terrance's revenge. Better that their ignorance be sincere. No, the only person she could discuss the plan with was its architect.

She approached him the night of Terrance's address and he acted as if she had agreed long before. Caesar was like no colored man she had ever met. He had been born on a small farm in Virginia owned by a petite old widow. Mrs. Garner enjoyed baking, the daily complications of her flower bed, and concerned herself with little else. Caesar and his father took care of the planting and the stables, his mother the domestic affairs. They grew a modest crop of vegetables to sell in town. His family lived in their own two-room cottage at the rear of the property. They painted it white with robin's egg trim, just like a white person's house his mother had seen once.

Mrs. Garner desired nothing more than to spend her final years in comfort. She didn't agree with the popular arguments for slavery but saw it as a necessary evil given the obvious intellectual deficiencies of the African tribe. To free them from bondage all at once would be disastrous—how would they manage their affairs without a careful and patient eye to guide them? Mrs. Garner helped in her own way, teaching her slaves their letters so they could receive the word of God with their own eyes. She was liberal with passes, allowing Caesar and his family to range across the county as they pleased. It rankled her neighbors. In her degrees, she prepared them for the liberation that awaited them, for she had pledged to set them free upon her death.

When Mrs. Garner passed, Caesar and his family mourned and tended to the farm, awaiting official word of their manumission. She left no will. Her only relative was a niece in Boston, who arranged for a local lawyer to liquidate Mrs. Garner's property. It was a terrible day when he arrived with constables and informed Caesar and his parents that they were to be sold. Worse—sold south, with its fearsome legends of cruelty and abomination. Caesar and his family joined the march of coffles, his father going one way, his mother another, and Caesar to his own destiny. Theirs was a pathetic goodbye, cut short by the whip of the trader. So bored was the trader with the display, one he had witnessed countless times before, that he only half-heartedly beat the distraught family. Caesar, in turn, took this weak licking as a sign that he could weather the blows to come. An auction in Savannah led him to the Randall plantation and his gruesome awakening.

"You can read?" Cora asked.

"Yes." A demonstration was impossible of course, but if they made it off the plantation they would depend on this rare gift.

They met at the schoolhouse, by the milk house after the work there was done, wherever they could. Now that she had cast her lot with him and his scheme, she bristled with ideas. Cora suggested they wait for the full moon. Caesar countered that after Big Anthony's escape the overseers and bosses had increased their scrutiny and would be extra vigilant on the full moon, the white beacon that so often agitated the slave with a mind to run. No, he said. He wanted to go as soon as possible. The following night. The waxing moon would have to suffice. Agents of the underground railroad would be waiting.

The underground railroad—Caesar had been very busy. Did they really operate this deep in Georgia? The idea of escape overwhelmed her. Apart from her own preparations, how would they alert the railroad in time? Caesar had no pretext on which to leave the grounds until Sunday. He told her that their escape would cause such a ruckus that there would be no need to alert his man.

Mrs. Garner had sown the seeds of Caesar's flight in many ways, but one instruction in particular brought him to the attention of the underground railroad. It was a Saturday afternoon and they sat on her front porch. On the main road the weekend spectacle strolled before them. Tradesmen with their carts, families walking to the market. Piteous slaves chained neck to neck, shuffling in step. As Caesar rubbed her feet, the widow encouraged him to cultivate a skill, one that would serve him in good stead as a freeman. He became a woodworker, apprenticing at a nearby shop owned by a broad-minded Unitarian. Eventually he sold his handsomely crafted bowls on the square. As Mrs. Garner remarked, he was good with his hands.

At the Randall plantation he continued his enterprise, joining the Sunday caravan into town with the moss sellers, penny seamstresses, and day laborers. He sold little, but the weekly trip was a small, if bitter, reminder of his life in the north. It tortured him at sundown to tear away from the pageant before him, the mesmerizing dance between commerce and desire.

A stooped, gray-haired white man approached him one Sunday and invited him to his shop. Perhaps he could sell Caesar's crafts during the week, he offered, and they might both profit. Caesar had noticed the man before, strolling among the colored vendors and pausing by his crafts with a curious expression. He hadn't paid him any mind but now the request made him suspicious. Being sold down south had drastically altered his attitude toward whites. He took care.

The man sold provisions, dry goods, and farming tools. The shop was devoid of customers. He lowered his voice and asked, "You can read, can't you?"

"Sir?" Saying it like the Georgia boys said it.

"I've seen you in the square, reading signs. A newspaper. You have to guard over yourself. I'm not the only one can spot such a thing."

Mr. Fletcher was a Pennsylvanian. He relocated to Georgia because, he found out belatedly, his wife refused to live anywhere else. She had a notion about the air down here and its ameliorating effects on the circulation. His wife had a point about the air, he conceded, but in every other way the place was a misery. Mr. Fletcher abhorred slavery as an affront before God. He had never been active in abolitionist circles up north but observing the monstrous system firsthand gave him thoughts he did not recognize. Thoughts that could get him run out of town or worse.

He took Caesar into his confidence, risking that the slave might inform on him for a reward. Caesar trusted him in turn. He had met this sort of white man before, earnest and believing what came out of their mouths. The veracity of their words was another matter, but at least they believed them. The southern white man was spat from the loins of the devil and there was no way to forecast his next evil act.

At the conclusion of that first meeting Fletcher took Caesar's three bowls and told him to return next week. The bowls didn't sell, but the duo's true enterprise thrived as their discussions gave it form. The idea was like a hunk of wood, Caesar thought, requiring human craft and ingenuity to reveal the new shape within.

Sundays were best. Sundays his wife visited her cousins. Fletcher had never warmed to that branch of the family, nor they to him, owing to his peculiar temperament. It was commonly held that the underground railroad did not operate this far south, Fletcher told him. Caesar already knew this. In Virginia, you could smuggle yourself into Delaware or up the Chesapeake on a barge, evading patrollers and bounty hunters by your wits and the invisible hand of Providence. Or the underground railroad could help you, with its secret trunk lines and mysterious routes.

Antislavery literature was illegal in this part of the nation. Abolitionists and sympathizers who came down to Georgia and Florida were run off, flogged and abused by mobs, tarred and feathered. Methodists and their inanities had no place in the bosom of King Cotton. The planters did not abide contagion.

A station had opened up nonetheless. If Caesar could make it the thirty miles to Fletcher's house, the shopkeeper pledged to convey him to the underground railroad.

"How many slaves he helped?" Cora asked.

"None," Caesar said. His voice did not waver, to fortify Cora as much as himself. He told her that Fletcher had made contact with one slave previous but the man never made it to the rendezvous. Next week the newspaper reported the man's capture and described the nature of his punishment.

"How we know he ain't tricking us?"

"He is not." Caesar had thought it out already. Just talking to Fletcher in his shop provided enough grounds to string him up. No need for elaborate schemes. Caesar and Cora listened to the insects as the enormity of their plan moved over them.

"He'll help us," Cora said. "He has to."

Caesar took her hands in his and then the gesture discomfited him. He let go. "Tomorrow night," he said.

Her final night in the quarters was sleepless, even though she needed her strength. The other Hob women dozed beside her in the loft. She listened to their breathing: *That is Nag; that is Rida with her one ragged exhalation every other minute.* This time tomorrow she would be loose in the night. Is this what her mother felt when she decided? Cora's image of her was remote. What she remembered most was her sadness. Her mother was a Hob woman before there was a Hob. With the same reluctance to mix, the burden that bent her at all times and set her apart. Cora couldn't put her together in her mind. Who was she? Where was she now? Why had she left her? Without a special kiss to say, *When you remember this moment later you will understand that I was saying goodbye even if you did not know it.*

Cora's last day in the field she furiously hacked into the earth as if digging a tunnel. *Through it and beyond is your salvation.*

She said goodbye without saying goodbye. The previous day she sat with Lovey after supper and they talked in a way they hadn't since Jockey's birthday. Cora tried to slide in gentle words about her friend, a gift that she could hold later. *Of course you did that for her, you are a kind person. Of course Major likes you, he can see what I see in you.*

Cora saved her last meal for the Hob women. It was rare for them to spend their free hours together but she rounded them up from their preoccupations. What would become of them? They were exiles, but Hob provided a type of protection once they settled in. By playing up their strangeness, the way a slave simpered and acted childlike to escape a beating, they evaded the entanglements of the quarter. The walls of Hob made a fortress some nights, rescuing them from the feuds and conspiracies. White men eat you up, but sometimes colored folk eat you up, too.

She left a pile of her things by the door: a comb, a square of polished silver that Ajarry had scrounged years ago, the pile of blue stones that Nag called her "Indian rocks." Her farewell.

She took her hatchet. She took flint and tinder. And like her mother she dug up her yams. The next night someone will have claimed the plot, she thought, turned the dirt over. Put a fence around it for chickens. A doghouse. Or maybe she will keep it a garden. An anchor in the vicious waters of the plantation to prevent her from being carried away. Until she chose to be carried away.

They met by the cotton after the village quieted down. Caesar made a quizzical expression at her bulging sack of yams but didn't speak. They moved through the tall plants, so knotted up inside that they forgot to run until they were halfway through. Their speed made them giddy. The impossibility of it. Their fear called after them even if no one else did. They had six hours until their disappearance was discovered and another one or two before the posses reached where they were now. But fear was already in pursuit, as it had been every day on the plantation, and it matched their pace.

They crossed the meadow whose soil was too thin for planting and entered the swamp. It had been years since Cora had played in the black water with the other pickaninnies, scaring each other with tales of bears and hidden gators and fast-swimming water moccasins. Men hunted otter and beaver in the swamp and the moss sellers scavenged from the trees, tracking far but never too far, yanked back to the plantation by invisible chains. Caesar had accompanied some of the trappers on their fishing and hunting expeditions for months now, learning how to step in the peat and silt, where to stick close to the reeds, and how to find the islands of sure ground. He probed the murk before them with his walking stick. The plan was to shoot west until they hit a string of islands a trapper had shown him, and then bow northeast until the swamp dried up. The precious firm footing made it the fastest route north, despite the diversion.

They had made it only a small ways in when they heard the voice and stopped. Cora looked at Caesar for a cue. He held his hands out and listened. It was not an angry voice. Or a man's voice.

Caesar shook his head when he realized the identity of the culprit. "Lovey—shush!"

Lovey had enough sense to be quiet once she got a bead on them. "I knew you were up to something," she whispered when she caught up. "Sneaking around with him but not talking about it. And then you dig up them yams not even ripe yet!" She had cinched some old fabric to make a bag that she slung over her shoulder.

"You get on back before you ruin us," Caesar said.

"I'm going where you going," Lovey said.

Cora frowned. If they sent Lovey back, the girl might be caught sneaking into her cabin. Lovey was not one to keep her

66

tongue still. No more head start. She didn't want to be responsible for the girl, but couldn't figure it.

"He's not going to take three of us," Caesar said.

"He know I'm coming?" Cora asked.

He shook his head.

"Then two surprises as good as one," she said. She lifted her sack. "We got enough food, anyway."

He had all night to get used to the idea. It would be a long time before they slept. Eventually Lovey stopped crying out at every sudden noise from the night creatures, or when she stepped too deep and the water surged to her waist. Cora was acquainted with this squeamish quality of Lovey's, but she did not recognize the other side of her friend, whatever had overtaken the girl and made her run. But every slave thinks about it. In the morning and in the afternoon and in the night. Dreaming of it. Every dream a dream of escape even when it didn't look like it. When it was a dream of new shoes. The opportunity stepped up and Lovey availed herself, heedless of the whip.

The three of them wended west, tromping through the black water. Cora couldn't have led them. She didn't know how Caesar did it. But he was ever surprising her. Of course he had a map in his head and could read stars as well as letters.

Lovey's sighs and curses when she needed a rest saved Cora from asking. When they demanded to look in her tow sack, it contained nothing practical, only odd tokens she had collected, like a small wooden duck and a blue glass bottle. As for his own practicality, Caesar was a capable navigator when it came to finding islands. Whether or not he kept to his route, Cora couldn't tell. They started tracking northeast and by the time it got light they were out of the swamp. "They know," Lovey said when the orange sun broke in the east. The trio took another rest and cut a yam into slices. The mosquitoes and blackflies persecuted them. In the daylight they were a mess, splashed up to their necks in mud, covered in burrs and tendrils. It did not bother Cora. This was the farthest she had ever been from home. Even if she were dragged away at this moment and put in chains, she would still have these miles.

Caesar tossed his walking stick to the ground and they took off again. The next time they stopped, he told them that he had to go find the county road. He promised to return soon, but he needed to take measure of their progress. Lovey had the sense not to ask what happened if he didn't return. To reassure them, he left his sack and waterskin next to a cypress. Or to help them if he did not.

"I knew it," Lovey said, still wanting to pick at it despite her exhaustion. The girls sat against the trees, grateful for solid, dry dirt.

Cora filled her in on what there was left to tell, going back to Jockey's birthday.

"I knew it," Lovey repeated.

"He thinks I'm good luck, because my mother was the only one."

"You want luck, cut off a rabbit foot," Lovey said.

"What your mother gonna do?" Cora asked.

Lovey and her mother arrived on Randall when she was five years old. Her previous master didn't believe in clothing pickaninnies so it was the first time she had something on her back. Her mother, Jeer, had been born in Africa and loved to tell her daughter and her friends stories of her childhood in a small village by a river and all the animals who lived nearby. Picking broke her body. Her joints were swollen and stiff, making her crooked, and it anguished her to walk. When Jeer could no longer work she looked after babies when their mothers were in the fields. Despite her torments, she was always tender to her girl, even if her big toothless smile fell like an ax the moment Lovey turned away.

"Be proud of me," Lovey answered. She lay down and turned her back.

Caesar appeared sooner than they expected. They were too close to the road, he said, but had made good time. Now their party had to press on, get as far as they could before the riders set out. The horsemen would wipe out their lead in short order.

"When we going to sleep?" Cora asked.

"Let's get away from the road and then we see," Caesar said. From his comportment, he was spent, too.

They set their bags down not long after. When Caesar woke Cora, the sun was getting down. She had not stirred once, even with her body draped awkwardly over the roots of an old oak. Lovey was already awake. They reached the clearing when it was almost dark, a cornfield behind a private farm. The owners were home and busied themselves in their chores, chasing each other in and out of the small cottage. The fugitives withdrew and waited until the family put out their lamps. From here until Fletcher's farm the most direct route was through people's land, but it was too dangerous. They stayed in the forest, looping around.

Ultimately the pigs did them in. They were following the rut of a hog trail when the white men rushed from the trees. There were four of them. Bait laid on the trail, the hog hunters waited for their quarry, which turned nocturnal in the hot weather. The runaways were a different sort of beast but more remunerative.

There was no mistaking the identity of the trio, given the specificity of the bulletins. Two of the hog hunters tackled the smallest of the party, pinning her to the ground. After being so quiet for so long—the slaves to escape the detection of hunters, and the hunters to escape the detection of their prey—all of them cried out and shrieked with their exertions. Caesar grappled with a heavyset man with a long dark beard. The fugitive was younger and stronger, but the man held his ground and seized Caesar by the waist. Caesar fought like he had struck many a white man, an impossible occurrence or else he would have been in the grave long ago. It was the grave the runaways fought against, for that was their destination if these men prevailed and returned them to their master.

Lovey howled as the two men dragged her into the darkness. Cora's assailant was boyish and slender, perhaps the son of one of the other hunters. She was taken unawares but the moment he laid hands on her person, her blood quickened. She was brought back to the night behind the smokehouse when Edward and Pot and the rest brutalized her. She battled. Strength poured into her limbs, she bit and slapped and bashed, fighting now as she had not been able to then. She realized she had dropped her hatchet. She wanted it. Edward was in the dirt and this boy would join him, too, before she was taken.

The boy yanked Cora to the ground. She rolled over and bashed her head against a stump. He scrambled to her, pinning her. Her blood was hot—she reached out and came up with a rock that she slammed into the boy's skull. He reeled and she repeated her assault. His groans ceased.

Time was a figment. Caesar called her name, pulling her up. The bearded man had fled, as much as the darkness allowed her to see. "This way!"

Cora cried after her friend.

There was no sign of her, no way to tell where they had gone. Cora hesitated and he tugged her roughly forward. She followed his instructions.

They stopped running when they realized they had no inkling of where they were headed. Cora saw nothing for the darkness and her tears. Caesar had rescued his waterskin but they had lost the rest of their provisions. They had lost Lovey. He oriented himself with the constellations and the runaways stumbled on, impelled into the night. They didn't speak for hours. From the trunk of their scheme, choices and decisions sprouted like branches and shoots. If they had turned the girl back at the swamp. If they had taken a deeper route around the farms. If Cora had taken the rear and been the one grabbed by the two men. If they had never left at all.

Caesar scouted a promising spot and they climbed trees, sleeping like raccoons.

When she stirred, the sun was up and Caesar paced between two pines, talking to himself. She descended from her roost, numb in her arms and legs from her entanglement in the rough limbs. Caesar's face was serious. By now the word had spread about last night's altercation. The patrollers knew the direction they traveled. "Did you tell her about the railroad?"

"I don't think so."

"I don't think I did. We were foolish not to think on this."

The creek they waded at noon was a landmark. They were close, Caesar said. After a mile, he left her to scout. On his return they adopted a more shallow track in the woods that permitted them to barely see houses through the brush.

"That's it," Caesar said. It was a tidy one-story cottage that looked out on a pasture. The land had been cleared but lay fallow. The red weathervane was Caesar's sign that this was the house, the yellow curtains pulled shut in the back window the signal that Fletcher was home but his wife was not.

"If Lovey told them," Cora said.

They saw no other houses from their vantage, and no people. Cora and Caesar sprinted through the wild grass, exposed for the first time since the swamp. It was unnerving out in the open. She felt like she had been thrown into one of Alice's big black skillets, fires licking below. They waited at the back door for Fletcher to answer their knock. Cora imagined the posses massing in the woods, girding themselves for a dash into the field. Or perhaps they lay wait inside. If Lovey told them. Fletcher finally ushered them into the kitchen.

The kitchen was small but comfortable. Favorite pots showed their dark bottoms from hooks and gaily colored flowers from the pasture leaned out of thin glassware. An old red-eyed hound didn't stir from his corner, indifferent to the visitors. Cora and Caesar drank greedily from the pitcher Fletcher offered them. The host was unhappy to see the extra passenger, but so many things had gone wrong from the very start.

The shopkeeper caught them up. First, Lovey's mother, Jeer, noticed her daughter's absence and left their cabin to make a quiet search. The boys liked Lovey, and Lovey liked the boys. One of the bosses stopped Jeer and got the story out of her.

Cora and Caesar looked at each other. Their six-hour head start had been a fantasy. The patrollers had been deep in the hunt the whole time.

By midmorning, Fletcher said, every spare hand in the county and from all around enlisted in the search. Terrance's reward was unprecedented. Advertisements were posted at every public place. The worst sort of scoundrels took up the

74

chase. Drunkards, incorrigibles, poor whites who didn't even own shoes delighted in this opportunity to scourge the colored population. Patrol bands marauded through the slave villages and ransacked the homes of freemen, stealing and committing assaults.

Providence smiled on the fugitives: The hunters believed they hid in the swamp—with two young females in tow, any other ambitions must have been curtailed. Most slaves made tracks for the black water, as there were no helpful whites this far south, no underground railroad waiting to rescue a wayward nigger. This misstep allowed the trio to get as far northeast as they did.

Until the hog hunters came upon them. Lovey was back on Randall. Posses had called on Fletcher's house twice already to spread the word and sneak a glance at the shadows. But the worst news was that the youngest of the hunters—a boy of twelve—had not awakened from his injuries. Caesar and Cora were as good as murderers in the eyes of the county. The white men wanted blood.

Caesar covered his face and Fletcher placed a reassuring hand on his shoulder. Cora's lack of a response to the information was conspicuous. The men waited. She tore off a piece of bread. Caesar's mortification would have to suffice for the pair.

The story of the escape and their own account of the fight in the woods did much to alleviate Fletcher's dismay. The three of them in his kitchen meant that Lovey didn't know about the railroad, and they hadn't mentioned the shopkeeper's name at any point. They would proceed.

As Caesar and Cora wolfed down the rest of the pumpernickel loaf and slices of ham, the men debated the merits of venturing now or after nightfall. Cora thought better of contributing to the discussion. This was her first time out in the world and there was much she did not know. Her own vote was for lighting out as soon as possible. Every mile between her and the plantation was a victory. She would add to her collection.

The men decided that traveling right under their noses, with the slaves hidden beneath a Hessian blanket in the back of Fletcher's cart, was the most prudent. It removed the difficulty of hiding in the cellar, negotiating Mrs. Fletcher's comings and goings. "If you think so," Cora said. The hound passed gas.

On the silent road Caesar and Cora nestled among Fletcher's crates. The sunlight glowed through the blanket between the shadows of overhanging trees while Fletcher made conversation with his horses. Cora closed her eyes, but a vision of the boy lying in bed, his head bandaged and the big man with the beard standing over him, forestalled her slumber. He was younger than she had reckoned. But he should not have laid his hands on her. The boy should have picked a different pastime than hunting hogs at night. She didn't care if he recovered, she decided. They were going to be killed whether he woke or not.

The noise of the town roused her. She could only imagine what it looked like, the people on their errands, the busy shops, the buggies and carts navigating each other. The voices were close, the mad chatter of a disembodied mob. Caesar squeezed her hand. Their arrangement among the crates prevented her from seeing his face but she knew his expression. Then Fletcher stopped his cart. Cora expected the blanket to be ripped off the next moment and made a portrait of the ensuing mayhem. The roaring sunlight. Fletcher flogged and arrested, more likely lynched for harboring no mere slaves but murderers. Cora and Caesar roundly beaten by the crowd in preparation for their delivery back to Terrance, and whatever their master had devised to surpass Big Anthony's torments. And what he had already meted out to Lovey, if he was not waiting on a reunion of the three runaways. She held her breath.

Fletcher had stopped at the hail of a friend. Cora let out a noise when the man leaned against the cart, rocking it, but he didn't hear. The man greeted Fletcher and gave the shopkeeper an update on the posses and their search—the murderers had been captured! Fletcher thanked God. Another voice joined to rebut this rumor. The slaves were still about, stealing a farmer's chickens in a morning raid, but the hounds had the scent. Fletcher repeated his gratitude toward a God that looked over a white man and his interests. Of the boy there was no news. A pity, Fletcher said.

Directly, the cart was back on the quiet county road. Fletcher said, "You've got them chasing their tails." It wasn't clear if he was talking to the slaves or his horses. Cora dozed again, the rigors of their flight still exacting their toll. Sleeping prevented thoughts of Lovey. When she next opened her eyes, it was dark. Caesar patted her in reassurance. There was a rumbling and a jingling and the sound of a bolt. Fletcher removed the blanket and the fugitives stretched their aching limbs as they took in the barn.

She saw the chains first. Thousands of them dangled off the wall on nails in a morbid inventory of manacles and fetters, of shackles for ankles and wrists and necks in all varieties and combinations. Shackles to prevent a person from absconding, from moving their hands, or to suspend a body in the air for a beating. One row was devoted to children's chains and the tiny manacles and links connecting them. Another row show-cased iron cuffs so thick that no saw could bite them, and cuffs so thin that only the thought of punishment prevented their wearer from splitting them. A line of ornate muzzles commanded their own section, and there was a pile of ball and chains in the corner. The balls were arranged in a pyramid, the chains trailing off in S shapes. Some of the shackles were rusted, some were broken, and others seemed as if they had been forged that very morning. Cora moved to one part of the collection and touched a metal loop with spikes radiating toward its center. She decided it was intended for wear around the neck.

"A fearsome display," a man said. "I picked them up here and there."

They hadn't heard him enter; had he been there all along? He wore gray trousers and a shirt of porous cloth that did not hide his skeletal appearance. Cora had seen starving slaves with more meat on their bones. "Some souvenirs from my travels," the white man said. He had an odd manner of speech, a queer lilt that reminded Cora of the way those on the plantation sounded after they lost their wits.

Fletcher introduced him as Lumbly. He shook their hands weakly.

"You the conductor?" Caesar asked.

"No good with steam," Lumbly said. "More of a station agent." When not concerning himself with railroad matters, he said, he led a quiet life on his farm. This was his land. Cora and Caesar needed to arrive under the blanket or else blindfolded, he explained. Best they remain ignorant of their location. "I was expecting three passengers today," he said. "You'll be able to stretch out."

Before they could figure his words, Fletcher informed them it was time for him to return to his wife: "My part is finished, my friends." He embraced the runaways with desperate affection. Cora couldn't help but shrink away. Two white men in two days had their hands around her. Was this a condition of her freedom?

Caesar silently watched the shopkeeper and his cart depart. Fletcher addressed his horses and then his voice trailed away. Concern troubled the features of Cora's companion. Fletcher had undertaken a great risk for them, even when the situation grew more complicated than he had bargained. The only currency to satisfy the debt was their survival and to help others when circumstances permitted. By her accounting, at least. Caesar owed the man much more for taking him into his shop all those months before. That is what she saw in his face—not concern but responsibility. Lumbly shut the barn door, the chains jingling with the vibration.

Lumbly was not as sentimental. He lit a lantern and gave it to Caesar while he kicked some hay and pulled up a trapdoor in the floor. At their trepidation he said, "I'll go first, if you wish." The stairwell was lined with stones and a sour smell emanated from below. It did not open into a cellar but continued down. Cora appreciated the labor that had gone into its construction. The steps were steep, but the stones aligned in even planes and provided an easy descent. Then they reached the tunnel, and appreciation became too mealy a word to contain what lay before her.

The stairs led onto a small platform. The black mouths of the gigantic tunnel opened at either end. It must have been twenty feet tall, walls lined with dark and light colored stones in an alternating pattern. The sheer industry that had made such a project possible. Cora and Caesar noticed the rails. Two steel rails ran the visible length of the tunnel, pinned into the dirt by wooden crossties. The steel ran south and north presumably, springing from some inconceivable source and shooting toward a miraculous terminus. Someone had been thoughtful enough to arrange a small bench on the platform. Cora felt dizzy and sat down.

Caesar could scarcely speak. "How far does the tunnel extend?"

Lumbly shrugged. "Far enough for you."

"It must have taken years."

"More than you know. Solving the problem of ventilation, that took a bit of time."

"Who built it?"

"Who builds anything in this country?"

Cora saw that Lumbly relished their astonishment. This was not his first performance.

Caesar said, "But how?"

"With their hands, how else? We need to discuss your departure." Lumbly pulled a yellow paper from his pocket and squinted. "You have two choices. We have a train leaving in one hour and another in six hours. Not the most convenient schedule. Would that our passengers could time their arrivals more appropriately, but we operate under certain constraints."

"The next one," Cora said, standing. There was no question.

"The trick of it is, they're not going to the same place," Lumbly said. "One's going one way and the other ... "

"To where?" Cora asked.

"Away from here, that's all I can tell you. You understand the difficulties in communicating all the changes in the routes. Locals, expresses, what station's closed down, where they're extending the heading. The problem is that one destination may be more to your liking than another. Stations are discovered, lines discontinued. You won't know what waits above until you pull in."

The runaways didn't understand. From the station agent's words, one route might be more direct but more dangerous. Was he saying one route was longer? Lumbly would not elaborate. He had told them all he knew, he maintained. In the end, the slave's choice lay before them, as ever: anyplace but where they had escaped. After consulting with his partner Caesar said, "We'll take the next one."

"It's up to you," Lumbly said. He motioned toward the bench.

They waited. At Caesar's request the station agent told of how he came to work for the underground railroad. Cora couldn't pay attention. The tunnel pulled at her. How many hands had it required to make this place? And the tunnels beyond, wherever and how far they led? She thought of the picking, how it raced down the furrows at harvest, the African bodies working as one, as fast as their strength permitted. The vast fields burst with hundreds of thousands of white bolls, strung like stars in the sky on the clearest of clear nights. When the slaves finished, they had stripped the fields of their color. It was a magnificent operation, from seed to bale, but not one of them could be prideful of their labor. It had been stolen from them. Bled from them. The tunnel, the tracks, the desperate souls who found salvation in the coordination of its stations and timetables—this was a marvel to be proud of. She wondered if those who had built this thing had received their proper reward.

"Every state is different," Lumbly was saying. "Each one a state of possibility, with its own customs and way of doing things. Moving through them, you'll see the breadth of the country before you reach your final stop."

At that, the bench rumbled. They hushed, and the rumbling became a sound. Lumbly led them to the edge of the platform.

The thing arrived in its hulking strangeness. Caesar had seen trains in Virginia; Cora had only heard tell of the machines. It wasn't what she envisioned. The locomotive was black, an ungainly contraption led by the triangular snout of the cow-catcher, though there would be few animals where this engine was headed. The bulb of the smokestack was next, a soot-covered stalk. The main body consisted of a large black box topped by the engineer's cabin. Below that, pistons and large cylinders engaged in a relentless dance with the ten wheels, two sets of small ones in front and three behind. The locomotive pulled one single car, a dilapidated boxcar missing numerous planks in its walls.

The colored engineer waved back at them from his cabin, grinning toothlessly. "All aboard," he said.

To curtail Caesar's annoying interrogations, Lumbly quickly unhooked the boxcar door and slid it wide. "Shall we proceed?"

Cora and Caesar climbed into the car and Lumbly abruptly shut them in. He peered between the gaps in the wood. "If you want to see what this nation is all about, I always say, you have to ride the rails. Look outside as you speed through, and you'll find the true face of America." He slapped the wall of the boxcar as a signal. The train lurched forward.

The runaways lost their balance and stumbled to the nest of hay bales that was to serve as seating. The boxcar creaked and shuddered. It was no new model, and on numerous occasions during their trip Cora feared it was on the verge of collapse. The car was empty apart from hay bales, dead mice, and bent nails.

She later discovered a charred patch where someone had started a fire. Caesar was numb from the series of curious events and he curled up on the floor. Following Lumbly's final instructions, Cora looked through the slats. There was only darkness, mile after mile.

When they next stepped into the sunlight, they were in South Carolina. She looked up at the skyscraper and reeled, wondering how far she had traveled.

Ridgeway

ARNOLD Ridgeway's father was a blacksmith. The sunset glow of molten iron bewitched him, the way the color emerged in the stock slow and then fast, overtaking it like an emotion, the sudden pliability and restless writhing of the thing as it waited for purpose. His forge was a window into the primitive energies of the world.

He had a saloon partner named Tom Bird, a half-breed who took a sentimental turn when lubricated by whiskey. On nights when Tom Bird felt separate from his life's design, he shared stories of the Great Spirit. The Great Spirit lived in all things—the earth, the sky, the animals and forests—flowing through and connecting them in a divine thread. Although Ridgeway's father scorned religious talk, Tom Bird's testimony on the Great Spirit reminded him of how he felt about iron. He bent to no god save the glowing iron he tended in his forge. He'd read about the great volcanoes, the lost city of Pompeii destroyed by fire that poured out of mountains from deep below. Liquid fire was the very blood of the earth. It was his mission to upset, mash, and draw out the metal into the useful things that made society operate: nails, horseshoes, plows, knives, guns. Chains. Working the spirit, he called it.

When permitted, young Ridgeway stood in the corner while his father worked Pennsylvania iron. Melting, hammering, dancing around his anvil. Sweat dripping down his face, covered in soot foot to crown, blacker than an African devil. "You got to work that spirit, boy." One day he would find his spirit, his father told him.

It was encouragement. Ridgeway hoisted it as a lonesome burden. There was no model for the type of man he wanted to become. He couldn't turn to the anvil because there was no way to surpass his father's talent. In town he scrutinized the faces of men in the same way that his father searched for impurities in metal. Everywhere men busied themselves in frivolous and worthless occupations. The farmer waited on rain like an imbecile, the shopkeeper arranged row after row of necessary but dull merchandise. Craftsmen and artisans created items that were brittle rumors compared with his father's iron facts. Even the wealthiest men, influencing the far-off London exchanges and local commerce alike, provided no inspiration. He acknowledged their place in the system, erecting their big houses on a foundation of numbers, but he didn't respect them. If you weren't a little dirty at the end of the day, you weren't much of a man.

Every morning, the sounds of his father pounding metal were the footsteps of a destiny that never drew closer.

Ridgeway was fourteen when he took up with the patrollers. He was a hulking fourteen, six and a half feet tall, burly and resolute. His body gave no indication of the confusion within.

He beat his fellows when he spied his weaknesses in them. Ridgeway was young for patrol but the business was changing. King Cotton crowded the countryside with slaves. The revolts in the West Indies and disquieting incidents closer to home worried the local planters. What clear-thinking white man wouldn't be worried, slaver or otherwise. The patrols increased in size, as did their mandate. A boy might find a place.

The head patroller in the county was the fiercest specimen Ridgeway had ever laid eyes on. Chandler was a brawler and bully, the local terror decent people crossed the street to avoid even when the rain made it a stew of mud. He spent more days in jail than the runaways he brought in, snoring in a cell next to the miscreant he had stopped hours earlier. An imperfect model, but close to the shape Ridgeway sought. Inside the rules, enforcing them, but also outside. It helped that his father hated Chandler, still smarting from a row years before. Ridgeway loved his father, but the man's constant talk of spirits reminded him of his own lack of purpose.

Patrol was not difficult work. They stopped any niggers they saw and demanded their passes. They stopped niggers they knew to be free, for their amusement but also to remind the Africans of the forces arrayed against them, whether they were owned by a white man or not. Made the rounds of the slave villages in search of anything amiss, a smile or a book. They flogged the wayward niggers before bringing them to the jail, or directly to their owner if they were in the mood and it was not too close to quitting time.

News of a runaway sent them into cheerful activity. They raided the plantations after their quarry, interrogating a host of quivering darkies. Freemen knew what was coming and hid their valuables and moaned when the white men smashed their furniture and glass. Praying that they confined their damage to objects. There were perquisites, apart from the thrill of shaming a man in front of his family or roughing up an unseasoned buck who squinted at you the wrong way. The old Mutter farm had the comeliest colored wenches—Mr. Mutter had a taste—and the excitement of the hunt put a young patroller in a lusty mood. According to some, the backwoods stills of the old men on the Stone plantation produced the best corn whiskey in the county. A roust allowed Chandler to replenish his jars.

Ridgeway commanded his appetites in those days, withdrawing before his confederates' more egregious displays. The other patrollers were boys and men of bad character; the work attracted a type. In another country they would have been criminals, but this was America. He liked the night work best, when they lay in wait for a buck who sneaked through the woods to visit his wife on a plantation up the road, or a squirrel hunter looking to supplement his daily meal of slop. Other patrollers carried guns and eagerly cut down any rascal dumb enough to flee, but Ridgeway copied Chandler. Nature had equipped him with weapons enough. Ridgeway ran them down as if they were rabbits and then his fists subdued them. Beat them for being out, beat them for running, even though the chase was the only remedy for his restlessness. Charging through the dark, branches lashing his face, stumps sending him ass over elbow before he got up again. In the chase his blood sang and glowed.

When his father finished his workday, the fruit of his labor lay before him: a musket, a rake, a wagon spring. Ridgeway faced the man or woman he had captured. One made tools, the other retrieved them. His father teased him about the spirit. What kind of a calling was running down niggers who barely have the wits of a dog?

Ridgeway was eighteen now, a man. "We're both of us working for Mr. Eli Whitney," he said. It was true; his father had just hired two apprentices and contracted work out to smaller smiths. The cotton gin meant bigger cotton yields and the iron tools to harvest it, iron horseshoes for the horses tugging the wagons with iron rims and parts that took it to market. More slaves and the iron to hold them. The crop birthed communities, requiring nails and braces for houses, the tools to build the houses, roads to connect them, and more iron to keep it all running. Let his father keep his disdain and his spirit, too. The two men were parts of the same system, serving a nation rising to its destiny.

An absconded slave might fetch as little as two dollars if the owner was a skinflint or the nigger was busted, and as much as a hundred dollars, double that if captured out of state. Ridgeway became a proper slave catcher after his first trip to New Jersey, when he went up to retrieve the property of a local planter. Betsy made it all the way from the Virginia tobacco fields to Trenton.

She hid with cousins until a friend of her owner recognized her at the market. Her master offered the local boys twenty dollars for delivery plus all reasonable expenses.

He'd never traveled so far before. The farther north he got, the more famished his notions. How big the country was! Each town more lunatic and complicated than the last. The hurly-burly of Washington, D.C., made him dizzy. He vomited when he turned a corner and saw the construction site of the Capitol, emptying his guts from either a bad oyster or the hugeness of the thing stirring rebellion in his very being. He sought out the cheapest taverns and turned the stories of the men over in his mind as he scratched at lice. Even the shortest ferry ride delivered him to a new island nation, garish and imposing.

At the Trenton jail the deputy treated him like a man of standing. This was not scourging some colored boy in the twilight or breaking up a slave festival for amusement. This was man's work. In a grove outside Richmond, Betsy made a lewd proposition in exchange for freedom, pulling up her dress with slender fingers. She was slim in the hips, with a wide mouth and gray eyes. He made no promises. It was the first time he lay with a woman. She spat at him when he fastened her chains, and once again when they reached her owner's mansion. The master and his sons laughed as he wiped his face, but the twenty dollars went to new boots and a brocade coat like he'd seen some worthies wear in D.C. He wore the boots for many years. His belly outgrew the coat sooner than that.

New York was the start of a wild time. Ridgeway worked

retrieval, heading north when constables sent word they'd captured a runaway from Virginia or North Carolina. New York became a frequent destination, and after exploring new aspects of his character, Ridgeway picked up stakes. The fugitive trade back home was straightforward. Knocking heads. Up north, the gargantuan metropolis, the liberty movement, and the ingenuity of the colored community all converged to portray the true scale of the hunt.

He was a quick study. It was more like remembering than learning. Sympathizers and mercenary captains smuggled fugitives into the city ports. In turn, stevedores and dockhands and clerks furnished him with information and he scooped up the rascals on the threshold of deliverance. Freemen informed on their African brothers and sisters, comparing the descriptions of runaways in the gazettes with the furtive creatures slinking around the colored churches, saloons, and meeting houses. *Barry is a stout well made fellow five feet six or seven, high small eyes and an impudent look. Hasty is far advanced in her pregnancy and is presumed to have been conveyed away by some person, as she could not undergo the fatigue of traveling.* Barry crumpled with a whimper. Hasty and her pup howled all the way to Charlotte.

Soon he owned three fine coats. Ridgeway fell in with a circle of slave catchers, gorillas stuffed into black suits with ridiculous derbies. He had to prove he was not a bumpkin, but just once. Together they shadowed runaways for days, hiding outside places of work until opportunity announced itself, breaking into their negro hovels at night to kidnap them. After years away from the plantation, after taking a wife and starting a family, they had convinced themselves they were free. As if owners forgot about property. Their delusions made them easy prey. He snubbed the blackbirders, the Five Points gangs who hog-tied freemen and dragged them south for auction. That was low behavior, patroller behavior. He was a slave catcher now.

New York City was a factory of antislavery sentiment. The courts had to sign off before Ridgeway was permitted to take his charges south. Abolitionist lawyers erected barricades of paperwork, every week a new stratagem. New York was a Free State, they argued, and any colored person became magically free once they stepped over the border. They exploited under-standable discrepancies between the bulletins and the individual in the courtroom—was there proof that this Benjamin Jones was the Benjamin Jones in question? Most planters couldn't tell one slave from another, even after taking them to bed. No wonder they lost track of their property. It became a game, prying niggers from jail before the lawyers unveiled their latest gambit. High-minded idiocy pitted against the power of coin. For a gratuity, the city recorder tipped him to freshly jailed fugitives and hurriedly signed them over for release. They'd be halfway through New Jersey before the abolitionists had even gotten out of bed.

Ridgeway bypassed the courthouse when needed, but not often. It was a bother to be stopped on the road in a Free State when the lost property turned out to have a silver tongue. Get them off the plantation and they learned to read, it was a disease.

While Ridgeway waited at the docks for smugglers, the magnificent ships from Europe dropped anchor and discharged their passengers. Everything they owned in sacks, half starving. Hapless as niggers, by any measure. But they'd be called to their proper places, as he had been. His whole world growing up in the south was a ripple of this first arrival. This dirty white flood with nowhere to go but out. South. West. The same laws governed garbage and people. The gutters of the city overflowed with offal and refuse—but the mess found its place in time.

Ridgeway watched them stagger down the gangplanks, rheumy and bewildered, overcome by the city. The possibilities lay before these pilgrims like a banquet, and they'd been so hungry their whole lives. They'd never seen the likes of this, but they'd leave their mark on this new land, as surely as those famous souls at Jamestown, making it theirs through unstoppable racial logic. If niggers were supposed to have their freedom, they wouldn't be in chains. If the red man was supposed to keep hold of his land, it'd still be his. If the white man wasn't destined to take this new world, he wouldn't own it now.

Here was the true Great Spirit, the divine thread connecting all human endeavor—if you can keep it, it is yours. Your property, slave or continent. The American imperative.

Ridgeway gathered renown with his facility for ensuring that property remained property. When a runaway took off down an alley, he knew where the man was headed. The direction and aim. His trick: Don't speculate where the slave is headed next. Concentrate instead on the idea that he is running away from you. Not from a cruel master, or the vast agency of bondage, but you specifically. It worked again and again, his own iron fact, in alleys and pine barrens and swamps. He finally left his father behind, and the burden of that man's philosophy. Ridgeway was not working the spirit. He was not the smith, rendering order. Not the hammer. Not the anvil. He was the heat.

His father died and the smith down the road assumed his operation. It was time to return south—back home to Virginia and farther, wherever the work led—and he came with a gang. Too many fugitives to handle by himself. Eli Whitney had run his father into the ground, the old man coughing soot on his deathbed, and kept Ridgeway on the hunt. The plantations were twice as big, twice as numerous, the fugitives more plentiful and nimble, the bounties higher. There was less meddling from the lawmakers and abolitionists down south, the planters saw to that. The underground railroad maintained no lines to speak of. The decoys in negro dress, the secret codes in the back pages of newspapers. They openly bragged of their subversion, hustling a slave out the back door as the slave catchers broke down the front. It was a criminal conspiracy devoted to theft of property, and Ridgeway suffered their brazenness as a personal slur.

One Delaware merchant particularly galled him: August Carter. Robust in the Anglo-Saxon tradition, with cool blue eyes that made the lesser sort pay attention to his mealy arguments. That worst sort, an abolitionist with a printing press.

"A Mass Meeting of the Friends of Freedom Will Be Held at Miller's Hall at 2 p.m. to Testify Against the Iniquitous Slave Power That Controls the Nation." Everyone knew the Carter home was a station—only a hundred yards separated it from the river—even when raids came up empty. Runaways turned activists saluted his generosity in their Boston speeches. The abolitionist wing of the Methodists circulated his pamphlets on Sunday morning and London periodicals published his arguments without rebuttal. A printing press, and friends among the judges, who forced Ridgeway to relinquish his charges on no less than three occasions. Passing Ridgeway outside the jail, he'd tip his hat.

The slave catcher had little choice but to call upon the man after midnight. He daintily sewed their hoods from white sacks of flour but could barely move his fingers after their visit—his fists swelled for two days from beating the man's face in. He permitted his men to dishonor the man's wife in ways he never let them use a nigger gal. For years after whenever Ridgeway saw a bonfire, the smell reminded him of the sweet smoke of Carter's house going up and a figment of a smile settled on his mouth. He later heard the man moved to Worcester and became a cobbler.

The slave mothers said, Mind yourself or Mister Ridgeway will come for you.

The slave masters said, Send for Ridgeway.

When first summoned to the Randall plantation, he was due for a challenge. Slaves eluded him from time to time. He was extraordinary, not supernatural. He failed, and Mabel's disappearance nagged at him longer than it should have, buzzing in the stronghold of his mind.

On returning, now charged to find that woman's daughter, he knew why the previous assignment had vexed him so. Impossible as it seemed, the underground railroad had a spur in Georgia. He would find it. He would destroy it.

South Carolina

30 DOLLARS REWARD

will be given to any person who will deliver to me, or confine in any gaol in the state so that I get her again, a likely yellow NEGRO GIRL 18 years of age who ran away nine months past. She is an artfully lively girl, and will, no doubt, attempt to pass as a free person, has a noticeable scar on her elbow, occasioned by a burn. I have been informed she is lurking in and about Edenton.

BENJ. P. WELLS
MURFREESBORO, JAN. 5, 1812

THE Andersons lived in a lovely clapboard house at the corner of Washington and Main, a few blocks past the hubbub of stores and businesses, where the town settled into private residences for the well-to-do. Beyond the wide front porch, where Mr. and Mrs. Anderson liked to sit in the evenings, the man scooping into his silk tobacco pouch and the woman squinting at her needlework, were the parlor, dining room, and kitchen. Bessie spent most of her time on that first floor, chasing after the children, preparing meals, and tidying up. At the top of the staircase were the bedrooms—Maisie and little Raymond shared theirs—and the second washroom. Raymond took a long nap in the afternoon and Bessie liked to sit in the window seat as he settled into his dreams. She could just make out the top two floors of the Griffin Building, with its white cornices that blazed in the sunlight.

This day she packed a lunch of bread and jam for Maisie, took the boy for a walk, and cleaned the silver and glassware. After Bessie changed the bedding, she and Raymond picked up Maisie from school and they went to the park. A fiddler played the latest melodies by the fountain as the children and their friends diverted themselves with hide-and-seek and hunt the ring. She had to steer Raymond away from a bully, careful not to upset the rascal's mother, whom she could not pick out. It was Friday, which meant that she ended the day with the shopping. The clouds had moved in, anyway. Bessie put the salt beef and milk and the rest of the supper makings on the family's account. She signed with an X.

Mrs. Anderson came home at six o'clock. The family doctor had advised her to spend more time out of the house. Her work raising funds for the new hospital assisted in this regard, in addition to her afternoon lunches with the other ladies of the neighborhood. She was in good spirits, rounding up her children for kisses and hugs and promising a treat after dinner. Maisie hopped and squealed. Mrs. Anderson thanked Bessie for her help and bid her good night.

The walk to the dormitories on the other side of town was not far. There were shortcuts, but Bessie liked to take in the lively activity of Main Street in the evening, mingling with the townsfolk, white and colored. She strolled down the line of establishments, never failing to linger by the big glass windows. The dressmaker with her frilly, colorful creations draped on hooped wire, the overstuffed emporiums and their wonderland of goods, the rival general stores on either side of Main Street. She made a game of picking out the latest additions to the displays. The plenty still astounded her. Most impressive of all was the Griffin Building.

At twelve stories, it was one of the tallest buildings in the nation, certainly it towered over any structure in the south. The pride of the town. The bank dominated the first floor, with its vaulted ceiling and Tennessee marble. Bessie had no business there but was not a stranger to the floors above. The previous week she took the children to see their father on his birthday and got to hear the clopping of her footsteps in the beautiful lobby. The elevator, the only one for hundreds of miles, conveyed them to the eighth floor. Maisie and Raymond were not impressed with the machine, having visited many times, but Bessie never failed to be both delighted and frightened by its magic, bracing herself with the brass rail in case of disaster.

They passed the floors of insurance agents, government offices, and export firms. Vacancies were rare; a Griffin address was a great boon to a business's reputation. Mr. Anderson's floor was a warren of lawyer's offices, with rich carpets, walls of dark brown wood, and doors inlaid with frosted glass. Mr. Anderson himself worked on contracts, primarily in the cotton trade. He was quite surprised to see his family. He received the small cake from the children with good cheer, but made it clear he was anxious to get back to his papers. For a moment Bessie wondered if she was in for a scolding, but none came. Mrs. Anderson had insisted on the trip. Mr. Anderson's secretary held open the door and Bessie hustled the children out to the confectioner.

This evening Bessie passed the shiny brass doors of the bank and continued home. Every day the remarkable edifice served as a monument to her profound change in circumstances. She walked down the sidewalk as a free woman. No one chased her or abused her. Some of Mrs. Anderson's circle, who recognized Bessie as her girl, sometimes even smiled.

Bessie crossed the street to avoid the jumble of saloons and their disreputable clientele. She stopped herself before she searched for Sam's face among the drunkards. Around the corner came the more modest homes of the less prosperous white residents. She picked up her pace. There was a gray house on the corner whose owners were indifferent to their dog's feral displays, and a line of cottages where the wives stared out of the windows with flinty expressions. Many of the white men in this part of town worked as foremen or laborers in the larger factories. They tended not to employ colored help so Bessie had little information about their day to day.

Presently she arrived at the dormitories. The two-story red brick buildings had been completed only a short time before Bessie's arrival. In time the saplings and hedges on the perimeter would provide shade and character; now they spoke of fine intentions. The brick was a pure, unsullied color, without so much as a dot of mud splashed from the rain. Not even a caterpillar crawling in a nook. Inside, the white paint still smelled fresh in the common spaces, dining rooms, and bunk rooms. Bessie wasn't the only girl afraid to touch anything apart from the doorknobs. To even leave a speck or scratch mark.

Bessie greeted the other residents as they crossed each other on the sidewalk. Most were returning from work. Others departed to watch over children so their parents could partake of the pleasant evening. Only half of the colored residents worked on Saturdays, so Friday night was busy.

She reached number 18. She said hello to the girls braiding their hair in the common room and darted upstairs to change before dinner. When Bessie arrived in town, most of the eighty beds in the bunk room had been claimed. A day earlier and she might have been sleeping in a bed beneath one of the windows. It would be some time before someone moved away and she could switch to a better position. Bessie liked the breeze afforded by the windows. If she turned her body the other way she might see stars some nights.

Bessie opened the trunk at the foot of her bed and removed the blue dress she bought her second week in South Carolina. She smoothed it over her legs. The soft cotton on her skin still thrilled her. Bessie bunched her work clothes and put them in the sack under the bed. Lately she did her washing on Saturday afternoons following her school lessons. The chore was her way of making up for sleeping in, an indulgence she allowed herself those mornings.

Supper was roast chicken with carrots and potatoes. Margaret the cook lived over in number 8. The proctors felt it prudent that the people who cleaned and cooked in the dorms did so in buildings other than their own. It was a small but worthy idea. Margaret had a heavy hand with the salt, although her meat and poultry were always exquisitely tender. Bessie mopped up the fat with a crust of bread as she listened to the talk of evening plans. Most of the girls stayed in the night before the social, but some of the younger ones were going out to the colored saloon that had recently opened. Although it wasn't supposed to, the saloon accepted scrip. Another reason to avoid the place, Bessie thought. She brought her dishes to the kitchen and headed back upstairs.

"Bessie?"

"Good evening, Miss Lucy," Bessie said.

It was rare Miss Lucy stayed this late on a Friday. Most proctors disappeared at six o'clock. To hear the girls from the other dormitories tell it, Miss Lucy's diligence put her colleagues to shame. To be sure, Bessie had benefited from her advice many times. She admired the way her clothes were always so crisp and fit just so. Miss Lucy wore her hair in a bun and the thin metal of her eyeglasses lent her a severe aspect, but her quick smile told the story of the woman beneath.

"How are things?" Miss Lucy asked.

"Think I'm gonna spend a quiet night in the quarter, Miss Lucy," Bessie said.

"*Dormitory*, Bessie. Not *quarter*."

"Yes, Miss Lucy."

"*Going to*, not *gonna*."

"I am working on it."

"And making splendid progress!" Miss Lucy patted Bessie's arm. "I want to talk to you Monday morning before you head out for work."

"Anything wrong, Miss Lucy?"

"Nothing at all, Bessie. We'll talk then." She gave a little bow and walked to the office.

Bowing to a colored girl.

BESSIE Carpenter was the name on the papers Sam gave her at the station. Months later, Cora still didn't know how she had survived the trip from Georgia. The darkness of the tunnel quickly turned the boxcar into a grave. The only light came from the engineer's cabin, through the slats in the front of the rickety car. At one point it shook so much that Cora put her arms around Caesar and they stayed like that for a good while, squeezing each other at the more urgent tremors, pressed against the hay. It felt good to grab him, to anticipate the warm pressure of his rising and falling chest.

Then the locomotive decelerated. Caesar jumped up. They could scarcely believe it, although the runaways' excitement was tempered. Each time they completed one leg of their journey, the next unexpected segment commenced. The barn of shackles, the hole in the earth, this broken-down boxcar—the heading of the underground railroad was laid in the direction of the bizarre. Cora told Caesar that on seeing the chains, she feared Fletcher had conspired with Terrance from the very beginning and that they had been conveyed to a chamber of horrors. Their plot, escape, and arrival were the elements of an elaborate living play.

The station was similar to their point of departure. Instead of a bench, there was a table and chairs. Two lanterns hung on the wall, and a small basket sat next to the stairs.

The engineer set them loose from the boxcar. He was a tall man with a horseshoe of white hair around his pate and the stoop that came from years of field work. He mopped sweat and soot from his face and was about to speak when a ferocious coughing wracked his person. After a few pulls from his flask the engineer regained his composure.

He cut off their thanks. "This is my job," he said. "Feed the boiler, make sure she keeps running. Get the passengers where they got to be." He made for his cabin. "You wait here until they come and fetch you." In moments the train had disappeared, leaving a swirling wake of steam and noise.

The basket contained victuals: bread, half a chicken, water, and a bottle of beer. They were so hungry they shook out the crumbs from the basket to divvy. Cora even took a sip of the beer. At the footsteps on the stairs, they steeled themselves for the latest representative of the underground railroad.

Sam was a white man of twenty-five years and exhibited none of the eccentric mannerisms of his co-workers. Sturdy in frame and jolly, he wore tan trousers with braces and a thick red shirt that had suffered roughly at the washboard. His mustache curled at the ends, bobbing with his enthusiasm. The station agent shook their hands and appraised them, unbelieving. "You made it," Sam said. "You're really here."

He had brought more food. They sat at the wobbly table and Sam described the world above. "You're a long way from Georgia," Sam said. "South Carolina has a much more enlightened attitude toward colored advancement than the rest of the south. You'll be safe here until we can arrange the next leg of your trip. It might take time."

"How long?" Caesar asked.

"No telling. There are so many people being moved around, one station at a time. It's hard to get messages through. The railroad is God's work, but maddening to manage." He watched them devour the food with evident pleasure. "Who knows?" he said. "Perhaps you'll decide to stay. As I said, South Carolina is like nothing you've ever seen."

Sam went upstairs and returned with clothes and a small barrel of water. "You need to wash up," he said. "I intend that in the kindest way." He sat on the stairs to give them privacy. Caesar bid Cora to wash up first, and joined Sam. Her nakedness was no novelty, but she appreciated the gesture. Cora started with her face. She was dirty, she smelled, and when she wrung the cloth, dark water spilled out. The new clothes were not stiff negro cloth but a cotton so supple it made her body feel clean, as if she had actually scrubbed with soap. The dress was simple, light blue with plain lines, like nothing she had worn before. Cotton went in one way, came out another.

When Caesar finished washing up, Sam gave them their papers.

"The names are wrong," Caesar said.

"You're runaways," Sam said. "This is who you are now. You need to commit the names and the story to memory."

More than runaways—murderers, maybe. Cora hadn't thought of the boy since they stepped underground. Caesar's eyes narrowed as he made the same calculation. She decided to tell Sam about the fight in the woods.

The station agent made no judgments and looked genuinely aggrieved by Lovey's fate. He told them he was sorry about their friend. "Hadn't heard about that. News like that doesn't travel here like it does some places. The boy may have recovered for all we know, but that does not change your position. All the better that you have new names."

"It says here we're the property of the United States Government," Caesar pointed out.

"That's a technicality," Sam said. White families packed up and flocked to South Carolina for opportunities, from as far as New York according to the gazettes. So did free men and women, in a migration the country had never witnessed before. A portion of the colored were runaways, although there was no telling how many, for obvious reasons. Most of the colored folk in the state had been bought up by the government. Saved from the block in some cases or purchased at estate sales. Agents scouted the big auctions. The majority were acquired from whites who had turned their back on farming. Country life was not for them, even if planting was how they had been raised and their family heritage. This was a new era. The government offered very generous terms and incentives to relocate to the big towns, mortgages and tax relief.

"And the slaves?" Cora asked. She did not understand the money talk, but she knew people being sold as property when she heard it.

"They get food, jobs, and housing. Come and go as they please, marry who they wish, raise children who will never be taken away. Good jobs, too, not slave work. But you'll see soon enough." There was a bill of sale in a file in a box somewhere, from what he understood, but that was it. Nothing that would be held over them. A confidante in the Griffin Building had forged these papers for them.

"Are you ready?" Sam asked.

Caesar and Cora looked at each other. Then he extended his hand like a gentleman. "My lady?"

She could not prevent herself from smiling, and they stepped into the daylight together.

The government had purchased Bessie Carpenter and Christian Markson from a bankruptcy hearing in North Carolina. Sam helped them rehearse as they walked to town. He lived two miles outside, in a cottage his grandfather had built. His parents had operated the copper shop on Main Street, but Sam chose a different path after they died. He sold the business to one of the many transplants who'd come to South Carolina for a fresh start and Sam now worked at one of the saloons, the Drift. His friend owned the place, and the atmosphere suited his personality. Sam liked the spectacle of the human animal up close, as well as his access to the workings of the town, once the drink loosened tongues. He made his own hours, which was an asset in his other enterprise. The station was buried beneath his barn, as with Lumbly.

At the outskirts Sam gave them detailed directions to the

Placement Office. "And if you get lost, just head for that"—he pointed at the skyscraping wonder—"and make a right when you hit Main Street." He would contact them when he had more information.

Caesar and Cora made their way up the dusty road into town, unbelieving. A buggy rounded the turn and the pair nearly dove into the woods. The driver was a colored boy who tipped his cap in a jaunty fashion. Nonchalant, as if it were nothing. To have such bearing at his young age! When he was out of sight they laughed at their ridiculous behavior. Cora straightened her back and held her head level. They would have to learn how to walk like freemen.

In the following months, Cora mastered posture. Her letters and speech required more attention. After her talk with Miss Lucy, she removed her primer from her trunk. While the other girls gossiped and said good night one by one, Cora practiced her letters. The next time she signed for the Andersons' groceries, she would write *Bessie* in careful print. She blew out the candle when her hand cramped.

It was the softest bed she had ever lain in. But then, it was the only bed she had ever lain in.

Miss Handler must have been raised in the bosom of saints. Even though the old man was utterly incompetent with regards to the rudiments of writing and speaking, the teacher was never less than polite and indulgent. The entire class—the schoolhouse was full on Saturday mornings—shifted at their desks while the old man sputtered and choked on the day's lessons. The two girls in front of Cora made cross-eyes at each other and giggled at his botched sounds.

Cora joined the class in exasperation. It was nigh impossible to understand Howard's speech under normal circumstances. He favored a pidgin of his lost African tongue and slave talk. In the old days, her mother had told her, that half language was the voice of the plantation. They had been stolen from villages all over Africa and spoke a multitude of tongues. The words from across the ocean were beaten out of them over time. For simplicity, to erase their identities, to smother uprisings. All the words except for the ones locked away by those who still remembered who they had been before. "They keep 'em hid like precious gold," Mabel said.

These were not her mother's and grandmother's times.

Howard's attempts at "I am" consumed precious lesson time, already too short after the work week. She had come here to learn.

A gust sent the shutters wheezing on their hinges. Miss Handler put down her chalk. "In North Carolina," she said, "what we are doing is a crime. I would be fined a hundred dollars and you would receive thirty-nine lashes. That's from the law. Your master would likely have a more severe punishment." The woman met Cora's eyes. The teacher was only a few years older than her but she made Cora feel like an ignorant pickaninny. "It's hard to start from nothing. A few weeks ago, some of you were where Howard is now. It takes time. And patience."

She dismissed them. Chastened, Cora snatched up her things, wishing to be the first one out the door. Howard wiped his tears with his sleeve.

The schoolhouse lay south of the rows of girls' dormitories. The building was also used for meetings in need of a more serious atmosphere than that of the common rooms, Cora noticed, such as the assemblies on hygiene and feminine matters. It looked out on the green, the colored population's park. Tonight one of the bands from the men's dormitory was playing in the gazebo for the social.

They deserved Miss Handler's scolding. South Carolina maintained a different attitude toward colored progress, as Sam had told Cora on the platform. Cora had savored this fact in a multitude of ways over the months, but the provision for colored education was among the most nourishing. Connelly once put out a slave's eyes for looking at words. He lost Jacob's labor, though if the man had been talented the overseer would have subjected him to a less drastic punishment. In return he gained the eternal fear of any slave with a notion to learn his letters.

Don't need eyes to shuck corn, Connelly told them. Or to starve yourself to death, as Jacob did presently.

She put the plantation behind her. She did not live there anymore.

A page slipped out of her primer and she chased it onto the grass. The book was falling apart, from her use and that of the previous owners. Cora had seen little children, ones younger than Maisie, use the same primer for their lessons. New copies with fresh spines. The ones from the colored schoolhouse were well-thumbed and she had to squeeze her letters above and in between other people's scribblings, but there was no whipping attached just for looking at it.

Her mother would be proud of her. As Lovey's mother was likely proud of her daughter for running away, for a day and a half. Cora replaced the page in her book. She pushed the plantation from her again. She was getting better at it. Her mind was wily though, twisty. Thoughts she did not like wormed in from the sides, from beneath, through the cracks, from places she had battened down.

Of her mother, for example. Her third week in the dormitory, she knocked on the door of Miss Lucy's office. If the government kept records of all the colored arrivals, perhaps among the many names was that of her mother. Mabel's life after her escape was an enigma. It was possible she was one of the freemen who came to South Carolina for the opportunities.

Miss Lucy worked in a room down the hallway from number 18's common room. Cora did not trust her, yet there she stood. Miss Lucy admitted her. The office was cramped, with filing cabinets the proctor had to squeeze through to get to her desk, but she kept it pleasant with samplers on the walls detailing farming scenes. There was no room for a second chair. Visitors stood for their audience, which kept the visits short.

Miss Lucy regarded Cora over her glasses. "What's her name?"

"Mabel Randall."

"Your name is Carpenter," Miss Lucy said.

"That my daddy's name. My mother, she a Randall."

"*That is,*" Miss Lucy said. "*She is.*"

She stooped before one of the cabinets and ran her fingers over the blue-tinted papers, glancing in Cora's direction every so often. Miss Lucy had mentioned that she lived with a group of proctors in a boardinghouse near the square. Cora tried to picture what the woman did when she was not managing the dormitory, how she spent her Sundays. Did she have a young gentleman who took her places? How did an unattached white woman occupy herself in South Carolina? Cora was getting braver but still stuck close to the dormitories when not attending to the Andersons. It seemed prudent, those early days out of the tunnel.

Miss Lucy moved to another cabinet, tugging open a series of drawers, but came up empty. "These records are only of who's here at our dormitories," she said. "But we have locations all over the state." The proctor wrote down her mother's name and promised to check the master records in the Griffin Building. For the second time she reminded Cora of the lessons in reading and writing, which were optional but recommended, in keeping with their mission of colored uplift, especially for those with aptitude. Then Miss Lucy returned to her work.

It had been a whim. Once Mabel ran, Cora thought of her as little as possible. After landing in South Carolina, she realized that she had banished her mother not from sadness but from rage. She hated her. Having tasted freedom's bounty, it was incomprehensible to Cora that Mabel had abandoned her to that hell. A child. Her company would have made the escape more difficult, but Cora hadn't been a baby. If she could pick cotton, she could run. She would have died in that place, after untold brutalities, if Caesar had not come along. In the train, in the deathless tunnel, she had finally asked him why he brought her with him. Caesar said, "Because I knew you could do it."

How she hated her. The nights without number she spent up in the miserable loft, tossing about, kicking the woman next to her, devising ways off the plantation. Sneaking into a cartload of cotton and leaping to the road outside New Orleans. Bribing an overseer with her favors. Taking her hatchet and running through the swamp as her wretched mother had done. All the sleepless nights. In the light of morning she convinced her-self that her scheming had been a dream. Those were not her thoughts, not at all. Because to walk around with that in your mind and do nothing was to die.

She didn't know where her mother had fled. Mabel hadn't spent her freedom saving money to buy her daughter out of bondage, that was certain. Randall would not have allowed it, but nonetheless. Miss Lucy never did find her mother's name in her files. If she had, Cora would have walked up to Mabel and knocked her flat.

"Bessie—you all right with yourself?"

It was Abigail from number 6, who came by for supper occasionally. She was friendly with the girls who worked on Montgomery Street. Cora had been standing in the middle of the grass, staring. She told Abigail everything was fine and returned to the dormitory to do her chores. Yes, Cora needed to keep better guard over her thoughts.

If Cora's own mask was occasionally askew, she proved adept at maintaining the disguise of Bessie Carpenter, late of North Carolina. She had prepared herself for Miss Lucy's question about her mother's surname and for other tracks the conversation might have taken. The interview at the Placement Office that first day had concluded after a few brief questions. The newcomers had toiled either in the house or in the field. In either case, the majority of the openings were domestic work. The families were told to exercise forbearance with inexperienced help.

The doctor's examination gave her a scare, but not on account of the questions. The gleaming steel instruments in the examination room looked like tools Terrance Randall might have ordered from the blacksmith for sinister purposes.

The doctor's offices were on the tenth floor of the Griffin. She survived the shock of her first elevator ride and stepped into a long corridor lined with chairs, all of which were full of colored men and women awaiting examinations. After a nurse in a stark white uniform checked her name off a list, Cora joined the group of women. The nervous talk was understandable; for most, this was their first visit with a doctor. On the Randall plantation, the doctor was only called when the slave remedies, the roots and salves, had failed and a valued hand was near death. In most cases there was nothing for the doctor to do at that point but complain about the muddy roads and receive his payment.

They called her name. The window in the examination room granted her a view of the configuration of the town and the verdant countryside for miles and miles. That men had built such a thing as this, a stepping-stone to heaven. She might have stayed there all day, gazing at the landscape, but the examination cut short her reverie. Dr. Campbell was an efficient sort, a portly gentleman who buzzed around the room with his white coat flapping behind him like a cape. He probed about her general health as his young nurse recorded it all on blue paper. From which tribe did her ancestors originate and what did she know of their constitutions? Had she ever been sick? How was the condition of her heart, her lungs? She realized the headaches she had suffered since Terrance's blows had disappeared since she came to South Carolina.

The intelligence test was brief, consisting of playing with wooden shapes and a series of illustrated quizzes. She undressed for the physical examination. Dr. Campbell looked at her hands. They had softened but were still those of one who had worked the fields. His fingers traced the scars from her whippings. Hazarding a guess as to the number of lashes, he was off by two. He examined her privates with his tools. The exam was painful and made her ashamed, the doctor's cold attitude doing nothing to ease her discomfort. Cora answered his questions about the assault. Dr. Campbell turned to the nurse and she wrote down his speculations over her ability to mother a child.

A collection of imposing metal instruments lay on a nearby tray. He picked up one of the most terrifying, a thin spike attached to a glass cylinder. "We're going to take some blood," he said.

"What for?"

"Blood tells us a lot," the doctor said. "About diseases. How they spread. Blood research is the frontier." The nurse grabbed Cora's arm and Dr. Campbell stabbed the needle in. This explained the howls she had heard in the hall outside. She made her own contribution. Then she was done. In the hall, only the men remained. The chairs were full.

That was her last visit to the tenth floor of the building. Once the new hospital opened, Mrs. Anderson told her one day, the offices of the government doctors were relocating. The floor was already fully leased, Mr. Anderson added. Mrs. Anderson's own doctor ran his practice on Main Street, above the optician. He sounded like a capable man. In the months that Cora had worked for the family, the mother's bad days had markedly reduced in number. The tantrums, the afternoons she spent locked in her room with the drapes shut, her severe manner with the children occurred less frequently. Spending more time outside the house, and the pills, had worked wonders.

When Cora finished her Saturday washing and had supper, it was almost time for the social. She put on her new blue dress. It was the prettiest one at the colored emporium. She shopped there as little as possible on account of the markup. From shopping for Mrs. Anderson, she was horrified that things in their local establishment cost two or three times as much as those in the white stores. As for the dress, it had cost a week's wages and she was forced to use scrip. She had been careful about her spending for the most part. Money was new and unpredictable and liked to go where it pleased. Some of the girls owed months of wages and resorted to scrip for everything now. Cora understood why—after the town deducted for food, housing, and miscellany like upkeep on the dormitories and schoolbooks, there was little left. Best to rely on scrip's credit sparingly. The dress was a one-time affair, Cora assured herself.

The girls in the bunk room were in a state of great excitement over the evening's gathering. Cora was no exception. She finished primping. Perhaps Caesar was already on the green.

He waited on one of the benches affording a view of the gazebo and the musicians. He knew she was not going to dance. From across the green, Caesar seemed older than he had in his

Georgia days. She recognized his evening clothes from the stacks in the colored emporium, but he wore them with more confidence than other men his age who hailed from plantations. The factory work agreed with him. As well as the other elements of their improved circumstances, of course. In the week since they last saw each other, he had cultivated a mustache.

Then she saw the flowers. She complimented him on the bouquet and thanked him. He complimented her on her dress. He had tried to kiss her a month after they emerged from the tunnel. She pretended it didn't happen and since then he had joined this performance. One day they would address it. Maybe at that time she would kiss him, she didn't know.

"I know them," Caesar said. He pointed at the band as they took their places. "I think they might even be better than George and Wesley."

Cora and Caesar grew more casual about referring to Randall in public as the months passed. Much of what they said could apply to any former slave who overheard them. A plantation was a plantation; one might think one's misfortunes distinct, but the true horror lay in their universality. In any event, the music would soon cover their talk of the underground railroad. Cora hoped the musicians wouldn't think them rude for their inattention. It was unlikely. Playing their music as freemen and not chattel was probably still a cherished novelty. To attack the melody without the burden of providing one of the sole comforts of their slave village. To practice their art with liberty and joy.

The proctors arranged the socials to foster healthy relations between colored men and women, and to undo some of the damage to their personalities wrought by slavery. By their reckoning, the music and dancing, the food and punch, all unfolding on the green in the flickering lantern light, were a tonic for the battered soul. For Caesar and Cora it was one of their few opportunities to catch each other up.

Caesar worked in the machine factory outside town and his changing schedule rarely overlapped with hers. He liked the work. Every week the factory assembled a different machine, determined by the volume of orders. The men arranged themselves before the conveyor belt and each was responsible for attaching his assigned component to the shape moving down the line. At the start of the belt there was nothing, a pile of waiting parts, and when the last man was finished, the result lay before them, whole. It was unexpectedly fulfilling, Caesar said, to witness the complete product, in contrast to the disembodied toil on Randall.

The work was monotonous but not taxing; the changing products helped with the tedium. The lengthy rest breaks were well distributed throughout the shift, arranged according to a labor theorist often quoted by the foremen and managers. The other men were fine fellows. Some still bore the marks of plantation behavior, eager to redress perceived slights and acting as if they still lived under the yoke of reduced resources, but these men improved every week, fortified by the possibilities of their new lives.

The former fugitives traded news. Maisie lost a tooth. This

week the factory manufactured locomotive engines—Caesar wondered whether they would one day be used by the underground railroad. The prices at the emporium had gone up again, he observed. This was not news to Cora.

"How is Sam?" Cora asked. It was easier for Caesar to meet with the station agent.

"In his usual temper—cheerful for no reason you can tell. One of the louts at the tavern gave him a black eye. He's proud of it. Says he'd always wanted one."

"And the other?"

He crossed his hands on his thighs. "There's a train in a few days. If we want to take it." He said that last part as if he knew her attitude.

"Perhaps the next one."

"Yes, maybe the next one."

Three trains had passed through since the pair arrived. The first time they talked for hours over whether it was wiser to depart the dark south immediately or see what else South Carolina had to offer. By then they had gained a few pounds, earned wages, and begun to forget the daily sting of the plantation. But there had been real debate, with Cora agitating for the train and Caesar arguing for the local potential. Sam was no help—he was fond of his birthplace and an advocate of South Carolina's evolution on matters of race. He didn't know how the experiment would turn out, and he came from a long line of rabble-rousers distrustful of the government, but Sam was hopeful. They stayed. Maybe the next one.

The next one came and went with a shorter discussion. Cora had just finished a splendid meal in her dormitory. Caesar had bought a new shirt. The thought of starving again on the run was not attractive, nor was the prospect of leaving behind the things they had purchased with their toil. The third train came and went, and now this fourth one would, too.

"Maybe we should stay for good," Cora said.

Caesar was silent. It was a beautiful night. As he promised, the musicians were very talented and played the rags that had made everyone happy at previous socials. The fiddler came from this or that plantation, the banjo man from another state: Every day the musicians in the dormitories shared the melodies from their regions and the body of music grew. The audience contributed dances from their own plantations and copied each other in the circles. The breeze cooled them when they broke away to rest and flirt. Then they started in again, laughing and clapping hands.

"Maybe we should stay," Caesar repeated. It was decided.

The social ended at midnight. The musicians put out a hat for donations, but most people were deep in scrip by Saturday night so it remained empty. Cora said good night to Caesar and was on her way home when she witnessed an incident.

The woman ran through the green near the schoolhouse. She was in her twenties, of slender build, and her hair stuck up wildly. Her blouse was open to her navel, revealing her breasts. For an instant, Cora was back on Randall and about to be educated in another atrocity.

Two men grabbed the woman and, as gently as they could, stopped her flailing. A crowd gathered. One girl went to fetch the proctors from over by the schoolhouse. Cora shouldered her way in. The woman blubbered incoherently and then said suddenly, "My babies, they're taking away my babies!"

The onlookers sighed at the familiar refrain. They had heard it so many times in plantation life, the lament of the mother over her tormented offspring. Cora remembered Caesar's words about the men at the factory who were haunted by the plantation, carrying it here despite the miles. It lived in them. It still lived in all of them, waiting to abuse and taunt when chance presented itself.

The woman calmed down somewhat and was led back to the dormitory at the very rear of the line. Despite the comfort brought by their decision to stay, it was a long night for Cora as her thoughts returned to the woman's screams, and the ghosts she called her own.

"Will I be able to say goodbye? To the Andersons and the children?" Cora asked.

Miss Lucy was sure that could be arranged. The family was fond of her, she said.

"Did I do a bad job?" Cora thought she had made a fine adjustment to the more delicate rhythms of domestic work. She ran her thumb across the pads of her fingers. They were so soft now.

"You did a splendid job, Bessie," Miss Lucy said. "That's why when this new placement came up, we thought of you. It was my idea and Miss Handler seconded it. The museum needs a special kind of girl," she said, "and not many of the residents have adapted as well as you have. You should take it as a compliment."

Cora was reassured but lingered in the doorway.

"Anything else, Bessie?" Miss Lucy asked, squaring her papers.

Two days after the incident at the social, Cora was still troubled. She asked after the screaming woman.

Miss Lucy nodded in sympathy. "You're referring to Gertrude," she said. "I know it was upsetting. She's fine. They're keeping her in bed for a few days until she's herself again." Miss

Lucy explained that there was a nurse on hand checking on her. "That's why we reserved that dormitory for residents with nervous disorders. It doesn't make sense for them to mix with the larger population. In number 40, they can get the care they require."

"I didn't know 40 was special," Cora said. "It's your Hob."

"I'm sorry?" Miss Lucy asked, but Cora didn't elaborate. "They're only there for a short time," the white woman added. "We're optimistic."

Cora didn't know what *optimistic* meant. She asked the other girls that night if they were familiar with the word. None of them had heard it before. She decided that it meant *trying*.

The walk to the museum was the same route she took to the Andersons', until she turned right at the courthouse. The prospect of leaving the family made her sorrowful. She had little contact with the father, as he left the house early and his office window was one of those in the Griffin that stayed lit the latest. Cotton had made him a slave, too. But Mrs. Anderson had been a patient employer, especially after her doctor's prescriptions, and the children were pleasant. Maisie was ten. By that age on the Randall plantation all the joy was ground out. One day a pickaninny was happy and the next the light was gone from them; in between they had been introduced to a new reality of bondage. Maisie was spoiled, doubtless, but there were worse things than being spoiled if you were colored. The little girl made Cora wonder what her own children might be like one day.

She'd seen the Museum of Natural Wonders many times on her strolls but never knew what the squat limestone building was for. It occupied an entire block. Statues of lions guarded the long flat steps, seeming to gaze thirstily at the large fountain. Once Cora walked into its influence, the sound of the splashing water dampened the street noise, lifting her into the auspices of the museum.

Inside, she was taken through a door that was off-limits to the public and led into a maze of hallways. Through half-opened doors, Cora glimpsed curious activities. A man put a needle and thread to a dead badger. Another held up yellow stones to a bright light. In a room full of long wooden tables and apparatus she saw her first microscopes. They squatted on the tables like black frogs. Then she was introduced to Mr. Field, the curator of Living History.

"You'll do perfectly," he said, scrutinizing her as the men in the rooms had scrutinized the projects on their worktables. His speech at all times was quick and energetic, without a trace of the south. She later discovered that Mr. Fields had been hired from a museum in Boston to update the local practices. "Been eating better since you came, I see," he said. "To be expected, but you'll do fine."

"I start cleaning in here first, Mr. Fields?" Cora had decided on the way over that in her new position she would avoid the cadences of plantation speech the best she could.

"Cleaning? Oh, no. You know what we do here—" He stopped. "Have you been here before?" He explained the business of museums. In this one, the focus was on American history—for a young nation, there was so much to educate the public about. The untamed flora and fauna of the North American continent, the minerals and other splendors of the world beneath their feet. Some people never left the counties where they were born, he said. Like a railroad, the museum permitted them to see the rest of the country beyond their small experience, from Florida to Maine to the western frontier. And to see its people. "People like you," Mr. Fields said.

Cora worked in three rooms. That first day, gray drapes covered the large glass windows that separated them from the public. The next morning the drapes were gone and the crowds arrived.

The first room was Scenes from Darkest Africa. A hut dominated the exhibit, its walls wooden poles lashed together under a peaked thatch roof. Cora retreated into its shadows when she needed a break from the faces. There was a cooking fire, the flames represented by shards of red glass; a small, roughly made bench; and assorted tools, gourds, and shells. Three large black birds hung from the ceiling on a wire. The intended effect was that of a flock circling over the activity of the natives. They reminded Cora of the buzzards that chewed the flesh of the plantation dead when they were put on display.

The soothing blue walls of Life on the Slave Ship evoked the Atlantic sky. Here Cora stalked a section of a frigate's deck, around the mast, various small barrels, and coils of rope. Her African costume was a colorful wrap; her sailor outfit made her look like a street rascal, with a tunic, trousers, and leather boots. The story of the African boy went that after he came aboard, he helped out on deck with various small tasks, a kind of apprentice. Cora tucked her hair under the red cap. A statue of a sailor leaned against the gunwale, spyglass pointed. The eyes, mouth, and skin color were painted on its wax head in disturbing hues.

Typical Day on the Plantation allowed her to sit at a spinning wheel and rest her feet, the seat as sure as her old block of sugar maple. Chickens stuffed with sawdust pecked at the ground; from time to time Cora tossed imaginary seed at them. She had numerous suspicions about the accuracy of the African and ship scenes but was an authority in this room. She shared her critique. Mr. Fields did concede that spinning wheels were not often used outdoors, at the foot of a slave's cabin, but countered that while authenticity was their watchword, the dimensions of the room forced certain concessions. Would that he could fit an entire field of cotton in the display and had the budget for a dozen actors to work it. One day perhaps.

Cora's criticism did not extend to Typical Day's wardrobe, which was made of coarse, authentic negro cloth. She burned with shame twice a day when she stripped and got into her costume.

Mr. Fields had the budget for three actors, or types as he referred to them. Also recruited from Miss Handler's schoolhouse, Isis and Betty were similar in age and build to Cora. They shared costumes. On their breaks, the three discussed the merits and disadvantages of their new positions. Mr. Fields let them be, after a day or two of adjustments. Betty liked that he never showed his temper, as opposed to the family she had just worked for, who were generally nice but there was always the possibility of a misunderstanding or a bad mood that was none of her doing. Isis enjoyed not having to speak. She hailed from a small farm where she was often left to her own devices, save on those nights when the master needed company and she was forced to drink the cup of vice. Cora missed the white stores and their abundant shelves, but she still had her evening walks home, and her game with the changing window displays.

On the other hand, ignoring the museum visitors was a prodigious undertaking. The children banged on the glass and pointed at the types in a disrespectful fashion, startling them as they pretended to fuss with sailor's knots. The patrons sometimes yelled things at their pantomimes, comments that the girls couldn't make out but that gave every indication of rude suggestions. The types rotated through the exhibits every hour to ease the monotony of pretending to swab the deck, carve hunting tools, and fondle the wooden yams. If Mr. Fields had one constant instruction, it was that they not sit so much, but he didn't press it. They teased Skipper John, as they nicknamed the dummy sailor, from their stools as they fiddled with the hemp rope.

THE exhibits opened the same day as the hospital, part of a celebration trumpeting the town's recent accomplishments. The new mayor had been elected on the progress ticket and wanted to ensure that the residents associated him with his predecessor's forward-looking initiatives, which had been implemented while he was still a property lawyer in the Griffin Building. Cora did not attend the festivities, although she saw the glorious fireworks that night from the dormitory window and got to see the hospital up close when her checkup came around. As the colored residents settled into South Carolina life, the doctors monitored their physical well-being with as much dedication as the proctors who took measure of their emotional adjustments. Some day, Miss Lucy told Cora one afternoon while they walked the green, all the numbers and figures and notes would make a great contribution to their understanding of colored life.

From the front, the hospital was a smart, sprawling single-floor complex that seemed as long as the Griffin Building was tall. It was stark and unadorned in its construction in a way Cora had never seen before, as if to announce its efficiency in its very walls. The colored entrance was around the side but apart from that was identical to the white entrance, in the original design and not an afterthought, as was so often the case.

The colored wing was having a busy morning when Cora gave her name to the receptionist. A group of men, some of whom she recognized from socials and afternoons on the green, filled the adjacent room while they waited for their blood treatments. She hadn't heard of blood trouble before arriving in South Carolina, but it afflicted a great number of the men in the dormitories and was the source of tremendous effort on the part of the town doctors. The specialists had their own section it seemed, the patients disappearing down a long hall when their name was called.

She saw a different physician this time, one more pleasant than Dr. Campbell. His name was Stevens. He was a northerner, with black curls that verged on womanish, an effect he tempered with his carefully tended beard. Dr. Stevens seemed young for a doctor. Cora took his precociousness as a tribute to his talents. As she moved through the examination, Cora got the impression she was being conveyed on a belt, like one of Caesar's products, tended down the line with care and diligence.

The physical examination was not as extensive as the first. He consulted the records from her previous visit and added his own notes on blue paper. In between he asked her about dormitory life. "Sounds efficient," Dr. Stevens said. He declared the museum work "an intriguing public service."

After she dressed, Dr. Stevens pulled over a wooden stool. His manner remained light as he said, "You've had intimate relations. Have you considered birth control?"

He smiled. South Carolina was in the midst of a large public health program, Dr. Stevens explained, to educate folks about a new surgical technique wherein the tubes inside a woman were severed to prevent the growth of a baby. The procedure was simple, permanent, and without risk. The new hospital was specially equipped, and Dr. Stevens himself had studied under the man who pioneered the technique, which had been perfected on the colored inmates of a Boston asylum. Teaching the surgery to local doctors and offering its gift to the colored population was part of the reason he was hired.

"What if I don't want to?"

"The choice is yours, of course," the doctor said. "As of this week, it is mandatory for some in the state. Colored women who have already birthed more than two children, in the name of population control. Imbeciles and the otherwise mentally unfit, for obvious reasons. Habitual criminals. But that doesn't apply to you, Bessie. Those are women who already have enough burdens. This is just a chance for you to take control over your own destiny."

She wasn't his first recalcitrant patient. Dr. Stevens put the matter aside without losing his warm demeanor. Her proctor had more information about the program, he told Cora, and was available to talk about any concern.

She walked down the hospital corridor briskly, hungry for air. Cora had become too accustomed to escaping unscathed from encounters with white authority. The directness of his questions and his subsequent elaborations threw her. To compare what had happened the night of the smokehouse with what passed between a man and his wife who were in love. Dr. Stevens's speech made them the same. Her stomach twisted at the idea. Then there was the matter of *mandatory*, which sounded as if the women, these Hob women with different faces, had no say. Like they were property that the doctors could do with as they pleased. Mrs. Anderson suffered black moods. Did that make her unfit? Was her doctor offering her the same proposal? No.

As she turned these thoughts over, she found herself in front of the Andersons' house. Her feet took over when her mind was elsewhere. Perhaps underneath, Cora was thinking about children. Maisie would be at school, but Raymond might be home. She had been too busy the last two weeks to make a proper goodbye.

The girl who opened the door looked at Cora with suspicion, even after she explained who she was.

"I thought her name was Bessie," the girl said. She was skinny and small, but she held on to the door as if more than happy to throw her weight against it to keep out intruders. "You said you was Cora."

Cora cursed the doctor's distraction. She explained that her master named her Bessie, but in the quarter everyone called her Cora because she looked so much like her mother.

"Mrs. Anderson is not at home," the girl said. "And the children are playing with they friends. You best come back when she's home." She shut the door.

For once, Cora took the shortcut home. Talking to Caesar would have helped, but he was at the factory. She lay in her bed until supper. From that day on, she took a route to the museum that avoided the Anderson home.

Two weeks later Mr. Fields decided to give his types a proper tour of the museum. Isis and Betty's time behind the glass had improved their acting skills. The duo affected a plausible interest as Mr. Fields held forth on the cross-sections of pumpkins and the life rings of venerable white oaks, the cracked-open geodes with their purple crystals like glass teeth, the tiny beetles and ants the scientists had preserved with a special compound. The girls chuckled at the stuffed wolverine's frozen smile, the red-tailed hawk caught mid-dive, and the lumbering black bear that charged the window. Predators captured in the moment they went in for the kill.

Cora stared at the wax faces of the white people. Mr. Fields's types were the only living exhibits. The whites were made of plaster, wire, and paint. In one window, two pilgrims in thick wool breeches and doublets pointed at Plymouth rock while their fellow voyagers looked on from ships in the mural. Delivered to safety after the hazardous passage to a new beginning. In another window, the museum arranged a harbor scene, where white colonists dressed like Mohawk Indians hurled crates of tea over the side of the ship with exaggerated glee. People wore different kinds of chains across their lifetimes, but it wasn't hard to interpret rebellion, even when the rebels wore costumes to deny blame.

The types walked before the displays like paying customers. Two determined explorers posed on a ridge and gazed at the mountains of the west, the mysterious country with its perils and discoveries before them. Who knew what lay out there? They were masters of their lives, lighting out fearlessly into their futures.

In the final window, a red Indian received a piece of parchment from three white men who stood in noble postures, their hands open in gestures of negotiation.

"What's that?" Isis asked.

"That's a real tepee," Mr. Fields said. "We like to tell a story in each one, to illuminate the American experience. Everyone knows the truth of the historic encounter, but to see it before you—"

"They sleep in there?" Isis said.

He explained. And with that, the girls returned to their own windows.

"What do you say, Skipper John," Cora asked her fellow sailor. "Is this the truth of our historic encounter?" She had lately taken to making conversation with the dummy to add some theater for the audience. Paint had flaked from his cheek, exposing the gray wax beneath.

The stuffed coyotes on their stands did not lie, Cora supposed. And the anthills and the rocks told the truth of themselves. But the white exhibits contained as many inaccuracies and contradictions as Cora's three habitats. There had been no kidnapped boys swabbing the decks and earning pats on the head from white kidnappers. The enterprising African boy whose fine leather boots she wore would have been chained belowdecks, swabbing his body in his own filth. Slave work was sometimes spinning thread, yes; most times it was not. No slave had ever keeled over dead at a spinning wheel or been butchered for a tangle. But nobody wanted to speak on the true disposition of the world. And no one wanted to hear it. Certainly not the white monsters on the other side of the exhibit at that very moment, pushing their greasy snouts against the window, sneering and hooting. Truth was a changing display in a shop window, manipulated by hands when you weren't looking, alluring and ever out of reach.

The whites came to this land for a fresh start and to escape the tyranny of their masters, just as the freemen had fled theirs. But the ideals they held up for themselves, they denied others. Cora had heard Michael recite the Declaration of Independence back on the Randall plantation many times, his voice drifting through the village like an angry phantom. She didn't understand the words, most of them at any rate, but *created equal* was not lost on her. The white men who wrote it didn't understand it either, if *all men* did not truly mean all men. Not if they snatched away what belonged to other people, whether it was something you could hold in your hand, like dirt, or something you could not, like freedom. The land she tilled and worked had been Indian land. She knew the white men bragged about the efficiency of the massacres, where they killed women and babies, and strangled their futures in the crib.

Stolen bodies working stolen land. It was an engine that did not stop, its hungry boiler fed with blood. With the surgeries that Dr. Stevens described, Cora thought, the whites had begun stealing futures in earnest. Cut you open and rip them out, dripping. Because that's what you do when you take away someone's babies—steal their future. Torture them as much as you can when they are on this earth, then take away the hope that one day their people will have it better.

"Ain't that right, Skipper John?" Cora asked. Sometimes, if

Cora turned her head fast, it looked as if the thing were winking at her.

A few nights later, she noticed the lights in number 40 were out, even though it was early in the evening. She asked the other girls. "They were moved to the hospital," one said. "So they can get better."

———◆———

The night before Ridgeway put an end to South Carolina, Cora lingered on the roof of the Griffin Building, trying to see where she had come from. There was an hour until her meeting with Caesar and Sam and she didn't relish the idea of fretting on her bed, listening to the chirping of the other girls. Last Saturday after school, one of the men who worked in the Griffin, a former tobacco hand named Martin, told her that the door to the roof was unlocked. Access was easy. If Cora worried about one of the white people who worked on the twelfth floor questioning her when she got off the elevator, Martin told her, she could take the stairs for the final flights.

This was her second twilight visit. The height made her giddy. She wanted to jump up and snatch the gray clouds roiling overhead. Miss Handler had taught the class about the Great Pyramids in Egypt and the marvels the slaves made with their hands and sweat. Were the pyramids as tall as this building, did the pharaohs sit on top and take the measure of their kingdoms, to see how diminished the world became when you gained the proper distance? On Main Street below workmen erected three- and four-story buildings, taller than the old line of two-floor establishments. Cora walked by the construction every day. Nothing as big as the Griffin yet, but one day the building would have brothers and sisters, striding over the land. Whenever she let her dreams take her down hopeful avenues, this notion stirred her, that of the town coming into its own.

To the east side of the Griffin were the white people's houses and their new projects—the expanded town square, the hospital, and the museum. Cora crossed to the west, where the colored dormitories lay. From this height, the red boxes crept up on the uncleared woods in impressive rows. Is that where she would live one day? A small cottage on a street they hadn't laid yet? Putting the boy and the girl to sleep upstairs. Cora tried to see the face of the man, conjure the names of the children. Her imagination failed her. She squinted south toward Randall. What did she expect to see? The night took the south into darkness.

And north? Perhaps she would visit one day.

The breeze made her shiver and she headed for the street. It was safe to go to Sam's now.

Caesar didn't know why the station agent wanted to see them. Sam had signaled as he passed the saloon and told him, "Tonight." Cora had not returned to the railroad station since her arrival, but the day of her deliverance was so vivid she had no trouble finding the road. The animal noises in the dark forest, the branches snapping and singing, reminded her of their flight, and then of Lovey disappearing into the night.

She walked faster when the light from Sam's windows fluttered through the branches. Sam embraced her with his usual enthusiasm, his shirt damp and reeking with spirits. She had been too distracted to notice the house's disarray on her previous visit, the grimed plates, sawdust, and piles of clothes. To get to the kitchen she had to step over an upturned toolbox, its contents jumbled on the floor, nails fanned like pick-up-sticks. Before she left, she would recommend he contact the Placement Office for a girl.

Caesar had already arrived and sipped a bottle of ale at the kitchen table. He'd brought one of his bowls for Sam and ran his fingers over its bottom as if testing an imperceptible fissure. Cora had almost forgotten he liked to work with wood. She had not seen much of him lately. He had bought more fancy clothes from the colored emporium, she noted with pleasure, a dark suit that fit him well. Someone had taught him how to tie a tie, or perhaps that was a token of his time in Virginia, when he had believed the old white woman would free him and he had worked on his appearance.

"Is there a train coming in?" Cora asked.

"In a few days," Sam said.

Caesar and Cora shifted in their seats.

"I know you don't want to take it," Sam said. "It's no matter."

"We decided to stay," Caesar said.

"We wanted to make sure before we told you," Cora added.

Sam huffed and leaned back in the creaky chair. "It made me happy to see you skipping the trains and making a go of things here," the station agent said. "But you may reconsider after my story."

Sam offered them some sweetmeats—he was a faithful customer of Ideal Bakery off Main Street—and revealed his purpose. "I want to warn you away from Red's," Sam said.

"You scared of the competition?" Caesar joked. There was no question on that front. Sam's saloon did not serve colored patrons. No, Red's had exclusive claim to the residents of the dormitories with a hankering for drink and dance. It didn't hurt that they took scrip.

"More sinister," Sam said. "I'm not sure what to make of it, to be honest." It was a strange story. Caleb, the owner of the Drift, possessed a notoriously sour disposition; Sam had a reputation as the barkeep who enjoyed conversation. "You get to know the real life of a place, working there," Sam liked to say. One of Sam's regulars was a doctor by the name of Bertram, a recent hospital hire. He didn't mix socially with the other northerners, preferring the atmosphere and salty company at the Drift. He had a thirst for whiskey. "To drown out his sins," Sam said.

On a typical night, Bertram kept his thoughts close until his third drink, when the whiskey unstoppered him and he rambled animatedly about Massachusetts blizzards, medical-school hazing rituals, or the relative intelligence of Virginia opossum. His discourse the previous evening had turned to female companionship, Sam said. The doctor was a frequent visitor at Miss Trumball's establishment, preferring it to the Lanchester House, whose girls had a saturnine disposition in his opinion, as if imported from Maine or other gloom-loving provinces.

"Sam?" Cora said.

"I'm sorry, Cora." He abridged. Dr. Bertram enumerated some of the virtues of Miss Trumball's, and then added, "Whatever you do, man, keep out of Red's Café, if you have a taste for nigger gals." Several of his male patients frequented the saloon, carrying on with the female patrons. His patients believed they were being treated for blood ailments. The tonics the hospital administered, however, were merely sugar water. In fact, the niggers were participants in a study of the latent and tertiary stages of syphilis.

"They think you're helping them?" Sam asked the doctor. He kept his voice neutral, even as his face got hot.

"It's important research," Bertram informed him. "Discover how a disease spreads, the trajectory of infection, and we approach a cure." Red's was the only colored saloon in the town proper; the proprietor got a break on the rent for a watchful eye. The syphilis program was one of many studies and experiments under way at the colored wing of the hospital. Did Sam know that the Igbo tribe of the African continent is predisposed to nervous disorders? Suicide and black moods? The doctor recounted the story of forty slaves, shackled together on a ship, who jumped overboard en masse rather than live in bondage. The kind of mind that could conceive of and execute such a fantastic course! What if we performed adjustments to the niggers' breeding patterns and removed those of melancholic tendency? Managed other attitudes, such as sexual aggression and violent natures? We could protect our women and daughters from their jungle urges, which Dr. Bertram understood to be a particular fear of southern white men.

The doctor leaned in. Had Sam read the newspaper today?

Sam shook his head and topped off the man's drink.

Still, the barkeep must have seen the editorials over the years, the doctor insisted, expressing anxiety over this very topic. America has imported and bred so many Africans that in many states the whites are outnumbered. For that reason alone, emancipation is impossible. With strategic sterilization—first the women but both sexes in time—we could free them from bondage without fear that they'd butcher us in our sleep. The architects of the Jamaica uprisings had been of Beninese and Congolese extraction, willful and cunning. What if we tempered those bloodlines carefully over time? The data collected on the colored pilgrims and their descendants over years and decades, the doctor said, will prove one of the boldest scientific enterprises in history. Controlled sterilization, research into communicable diseases, the perfection of new surgical techniques on the socially unfit—was it any wonder the best medical talents in the country were flocking to South Carolina?

A group of rowdies stumbled in and crowded Bertram to the end of the bar. Sam was occupied. The doctor drank quietly for a time and then slipped out. "You two are not the sort that goes to Red's," Sam said, "but I wanted you to know."

"Red's," Cora said. "This is more than the saloon, Sam. We have to tell them they're being lied to. They're sick."

Caesar was in agreement.

"Will they believe you over their white doctors?" Sam asked. "With what proof? There is no authority to turn to for redress—the town is paying for it all. And then there are all the other towns where colored pilgrims have been installed in the same system. This is not the only place with a new hospital."

They worked it out over the kitchen table. Was it possible that not only the doctors but everyone who ministered to the colored population was involved in this incredible scheme? Steering the colored pilgrims down this or that path, buying them from estates and the block in order to conduct this experiment? All those white hands working in concert, committing their facts and figures down on blue paper. After Cora's discussion with Dr. Stevens, Miss Lucy had stopped her one morning on her way to the museum. Had Cora given any thought to the hospital's birth control program? Perhaps Cora could talk to some of the other girls about it, in words they could understand. It would be very appreciated, the white woman said. There were all sorts of new positions opening up in town, opportunities for people who had proven their worth.

Cora thought back to the night she and Caesar decided to stay, the screaming woman who wandered into the green when the social came to an end. "They're taking away my babies." The woman wasn't lamenting an old plantation injustice but a crime perpetrated here in South Carolina. The doctors were stealing her babies from her, not her former masters.

"They wanted to know what part of Africa my parents hailed

from," Caesar said. "How was I to know? He said I had the nose of a Beninese."

"Nothing like flattery before they geld a fellow," Sam said.

"I have to tell Meg," Caesar said. "Some of her friends spend evenings at Red's. I know they have a few men they see there."

"Who's Meg?" Cora said.

"She's a friend I've been spending time with."

"I saw you walk down Main Street the other day," Sam said. "She's very striking."

"It was a nice afternoon," Caesar said. He took a sip of his beer, focusing on the black bottle and avoiding Cora's eyes.

They made little progress on a course of action, struggling with the problem of whom to turn to and the possible reaction from the other colored residents. Perhaps they would prefer not to know, Caesar said. What were these rumors compared to what they had been freed from? What sort of calculation would their neighbors make, weighing all the promises of their new circumstances against the allegations and the truth of their own pasts? According to the law, most of them were still property, their names on pieces of paper in cabinets kept by the United States Government. For the moment, warning people was all they could do.

Cora and Caesar were almost to town when he said, "Meg works for one of those Washington Street families. One of those big houses you see?"

Cora said, "I'm glad you have friends."

"You sure?"

"Were we wrong to stay?" Cora asked.

"Maybe this is where we were supposed to get off," Caesar said. "Maybe not. What would Lovey say?"

Cora had no answer. They didn't speak again.

SHE slept poorly. In the eighty bunks the women snored and shifted under their sheets. They had gone to bed believing themselves free from white people's control and commands about what they should do and be. That they managed their own affairs. But the women were still being herded and domesticated. Not pure merchandise as formerly but livestock: bred, neutered. Penned in dormitories that were like coops or hutches.

In the morning, Cora went to her assigned work with the rest of the girls. As she and the other types were about to get dressed, Isis asked if she could switch rooms with Cora. She was feeling poorly and wanted to rest at the spinning wheel. "If I could just get off my feet for a bit."

After six weeks at the museum, Cora hit upon a rotation that suited her personality. If she started in Typical Day on the Plantation, she could get her two plantation shifts finished just after the midday meal. Cora hated the ludicrous slave display and preferred to get it over as soon as possible. The progression from Plantation to Slave Ship to Darkest Africa generated a soothing logic. It was like going back in time, an unwinding of America. Ending her day in Scenes from Darkest Africa never failed to cast her into a river of calm, the simple theater becoming more than theater, a genuine refuge. But Cora agreed to Isis's request. She would end the day a slave.

In the fields, she was ever under the merciless eye of the overseer or boss. "Bend your backs!" "Work that row!" At the Andersons', when Maisie was at school or with her playmates and little Raymond was asleep, Cora worked unmolested and unwatched. It was a small treasure in the middle of the day. Her recent installation in the exhibition returned her to the furrows of Georgia, the dumb, open-jawed stares of the patrons stealing her back to a state of display.

One day she decided to retaliate against a red-haired white woman who scowled at the sight of Cora's duties "at sea." Perhaps the woman had wed a seaman of incorrigible appetites and hated the reminder—Cora didn't know the source of her animus, or care. The woman irked her. Cora stared into her eyes, unwavering and fierce, until the woman broke, fairly running from the glass toward the agricultural section.

From then on Cora selected one patron per hour to evil-eye. A young clerk ducking out from his desk in the Griffin, a man of enterprise; a harried matron corralling an unruly clutch of children; one of the sour youths who liked to batter the glass and startle the types. Sometimes this one, sometimes that one. She picked the weak links out from the crowd, the ones who broke under her gaze. The weak link—she liked the ring of it. To seek the imperfection in the chain that keeps you in bondage. Taken individually, the link was not much. But in concert with its fellows, a mighty iron that subjugated millions despite its weakness. The people she chose, young and old, from the rich part of town or the more modest streets, did not individually persecute Cora. As a community, they were shackles. If she kept at it, chipping away at weak links wherever she found them, it might add up to something.

She got good at her evil eye. Looking up from the slave wheel or the hut's glass fire to pin a person in place like one of the beetles or mites in the insect exhibits. They always broke, the people, not expecting this weird attack, staggering back or looking at the floor or forcing their companions to pull them away. It was a fine lesson, Cora thought, to learn that the slave, the African in your midst, is looking at you, too.

The day Isis felt under the weather, during Cora's second rotation on the ship, she looked past the glass and saw pigtailed Maisie, wearing one of the dresses Cora used to wash and hang on the line. It was a school trip. Cora recognized the boys and girls who accompanied her, even if the children did not remember her as the Andersons' old girl. Maisie didn't place her at first. Then Cora fixed her with the evil eye and the girl knew. The teacher elaborated on the meaning of the display, the other children pointed and jeered at Skipper John's garish smile—and Maisie's face twitched in fear. From the outside, no one could tell what passed between them, just like when she and Blake faced each other the day of the doghouse. Cora thought, I'll break you, too, Maisie, and she did, the little girl scampering out of the frame. She didn't know why she did it, and was abashed until she took off her costume and returned to the dormitory.

—

SHE called upon Miss Lucy that evening. Cora had been figuring on Sam's news all day, holding it up to the light like a hideous bauble, tilting it so. The proctor had aided Cora many times. Now her suggestions and advice resembled maneuvers, the way a farmer tricks a donkey into moving in line with his intentions.

The white woman was gathering a stack of her blue papers when Cora poked her head into the office. Was her name written down there, and what were the notes beside it? No, she corrected: Bessie's name, not hers.

"I only have a moment," the proctor said.

"I saw people moving back into number 40," Cora said. "But no one who used to live there. Are they still in the hospital for their treatment?"

Miss Lucy looked at her papers and stiffened. "They were moved to another town," she said. "We need room for all the new arrivals, so women like Gertrude, the ones who need help, are being sent to where they can get more suitable attention."

"They're not coming back?"

"They are not." Miss Lucy appraised her visitor. "It troubles you, I know. You're a smart girl, Bessie. I still hope you'll take on the mantle of leadership with the other girls, even if you don't think the operation is what you need right now. You could be a true credit to your race if you put your mind to it."

"I can decide for myself," Cora said. "Why can't they? On the plantation, master decided everything for us. I thought we were done with that here."

Miss Lucy recoiled from the comparison. "If you can't see the

152

difference between good, upstanding people and the mentally disturbed, with criminals and imbeciles, you're not the person I thought you were."

I'm not the person you thought I was.

One of the proctors interrupted them, an older woman named Roberta who often coordinated with the Placement Office. She had placed Cora with the Andersons, those months ago. "Lucy? They're waiting on you."

Miss Lucy grumbled. "I have them all right here," Miss Lucy told her colleague. "But the records in the Griffin are the same. The Fugitive Slave Law says we have to hand over runaways and not impede their capture—not drop everything we're doing just because some slave catcher thinks he's onto his bounty. We don't harbor murderers." She rose, holding the stack of papers to her chest. "Bessie, we'll take this up tomorrow. Please think about our discussion."

Cora retreated to the bunkhouse stairs. She sat on the third step. They could be looking for anyone. The dormitories were full of runaways who'd taken refuge here, in the wake of a recent escape from their chains or after years of making a life for themselves elsewhere. They could be looking for anyone.

They hunted murderers.

Cora went to Caesar's dormitory first. She knew his schedule but in her fright could not remember his shifts. Outside, she didn't see any white men, the rough sort she imagined slave catchers to look like. She sprinted across the green. The older man at the dormitory leered at her—there was always a licentious implication when a girl visited the men's housing—and informed her that Caesar was still at the factory. "You want to wait with me?" he asked.

It was getting dark. She debated whether or not to risk Main Street. The town records had her name as Bessie. The sketches on the fliers Terrance had printed after their escape were crudely drawn but resembled them enough that any savvy hunter would look at her twice. There was no way she would rest until she conferred with Caesar and Sam. She took Elm Street, parallel to Main, until she reached the Drift's block. Each time she turned a corner, she expected a posse on horses, with torches and muskets and mean smiles. The Drift was full with early-evening carousers, men she recognized and those she did not. She had to pass by the saloon's window twice before the station agent saw her and motioned for her to come around back.

The men in the saloon laughed. She slipped through the light cast in the alley from inside. The outhouse door was ajar: empty. Sam stood in the shadows, his foot on a crate as he laced his boots. "I was trying to figure out how to get word," he said. "The slave catcher's name is Ridgeway. He's talking to the constable now, about you and Caesar. I've been serving two of his men whiskey."

He handed her a flier. It was one of the bulletins Fletcher had described in his cottage, with one change. Now that she knew her letters, the word *murder* hooked her heart.

There was a ruckus from inside the bar and Cora stepped

farther into the shadows. Sam couldn't leave for another hour, he said. He'd gather as much information as he could and try to intercept Caesar at the factory. It was best if Cora went ahead to his house and waited.

She ran as she had not in a long time, sticking to the side of the road and darting into the woods at the sound of a traveler. She entered Sam's cottage through the back door and lit a candle in the kitchen. After pacing, unable to sit, Cora did the only thing that calmed her. She had cleaned all the dishware when Sam returned home.

"It's bad," the station agent said. "One of the bounty hunters came in right after we spoke. Had a ring of ears around his neck like a red Indian, a real tough character. He told the others that they knew where you were. They left to meet their man in front, Ridgeway." He panted from the run over. "I don't know how, but they know who you are."

Cora had grabbed Caesar's bowl. She turned it over in her hands.

"They got a posse together," Sam said. "I couldn't get to Caesar. He knows to come here or the saloon—we had a plan. He may already be on his way." Sam intended to return to the Drift to wait for him.

"Do you think anyone saw us talking?"

"Maybe you should go down to the platform."

They dragged the kitchen table and the thick gray rug. Together they lifted the door in the floor—it was a tight fit—and the musty air flickered the candles. She took some food and a lantern and descended into the darkness. The door closed above her and the table rumbled back into place.

She had avoided the services at the colored churches in town. Randall forbade religion on his plantation to eliminate the distraction of deliverance, and churching never interested her once she came to South Carolina. It made her seem strange to the other colored residents, she knew, but seeming strange had not bothered her for a long time. Was she supposed to pray now? She sat at the table in the thin lamplight. It was too dark on the platform to make out where the tunnel began. How long would it take them to root out Caesar? How fast could he run? She was aware of the bargains people made in desperate situations. To reduce the fever in a sick baby, to halt the brutalities of an overseer, to deliver one from a host of slave hells. From what she saw, the bargains never bore fruit. Sometimes the fever subsided, but the plantation was always still there. Cora did not pray.

She fell asleep waiting. Later, Cora crawled back up the steps, perching just beneath the door, and listened. It might be day or night in the world. She was hungry and thirsty. She ate some of the bread and sausage. Moving up and down the steps, putting her ear to the door and then retreating after a time, she passed the hours. When she finished the food, her despair was complete. She listened by the door. There was not a sound.

The thundering above woke her, terminating the void. It was not one person, or two, but many men. They ransacked the house and shouted, knocking over cabinets and upending furniture. The noise was loud and violent and so near, she shrank down the steps. She could not make out their words. Then they were done.

The seams in the door permitted no light and no draft. She could not smell the smoke, but she heard the glass shatter and the pop and crackle of the wood.

The house was on fire.

Stevens

THE Anatomy House of the Proctor Medical School was three blocks away from the main building, second from last on the dead-end street. The school wasn't as discriminating as the better-known medical colleges in Boston; the press of acceptances necessitated an expansion. Aloysius Stevens worked nights to satisfy the terms of his fellowship. In exchange for tuition relief and a place to work—the late-night shift was quiet and conducive to study—the school got someone to admit the body snatcher.

Carpenter usually delivered just before dawn, before the neighborhood roused, but tonight he called at midnight. Stevens blew out the lamp in the dissection room and ran up the stairs. He almost forgot his muffler, then remembered how cold it had been last time, when autumn crept in to remind them of the bitter season to come. It rained that morning and he hoped it wouldn't be too muddy. He had one pair of brogues and the soles were in a miserable state.

Carpenter and his man Cobb waited in the driver's seat. Stevens settled in the cart with the tools. He slid down until they got a healthy distance away, in case any of the faculty or students were about. It was late, but a bone expert from Chicago had presented that night and they might still be carousing in the local saloons. Stevens was disappointed about missing the man's talk—his fellowship often prevented his attendance at guest lectures—but the money would remove some of the sting. Most of the other students came from well-off Massachusetts families, spared worries over rent or food. When the cart passed McGinty's and he heard the laughter inside, Stevens pulled his hat down.

Cobb leaned around. "Concord tonight," he said, and offered his flask. As a matter of policy Stevens declined when Cobb shared his liquor. Though still in his studies he was certain of various diagnoses he'd made about the state of the man's health. But the wind was brisk and mean and they had hours in the dark and mud before the return to the Anatomy House. Stevens took a long pull and choked on fire. "What is this?"

"One of my cousin's concoctions. Too strong for your taste?" He and Carpenter chortled.

More likely he had collected last night's dregs at the saloon. Stevens took the prank in good cheer. Cobb had warmed to Stevens over the months. He could imagine the man's complaints when Carpenter suggested that he stand in whenever one of their gang was too besotted, or incarcerated, or otherwise unavailable for their nocturnal missions. Who's to say this fancy rich boy could keep his tongue? (Stevens was not rich and was fancy only in his aspirations.) The city had started hanging grave robbers lately—which was ironic or fitting depending on one's perspective, as the bodies of the hanged were given to medical schools for dissection.

"Don't mind the gallows," Cobb had told Stevens. "It's quick enough. The people are the thing—it should be a private viewing, if you ask me. Watching a man shit his guts, it's indecent."

Digging up graves had fastened the bonds of friendship. Now when Cobb called him Doctor, it was with respect and not derision. "You're not like that other sort," Cobb told him one night when they carried a cadaver through the back door. "You're a wee shady."

That he was. It helped to be a wee disreputable when you were a young surgeon, especially when it came to materials for postmortem dissection. There had been a body shortage ever since the study of anatomy came into its own. The law, the jail, and the judge provided only so many dead murderers and prostitutes. Yes, persons afflicted with rare diseases and curious deformities sold their bodies for study after their demise, and some doctors donated their cadavers in the spirit of scientific inquiry, but their numbers scarcely met the demand. The body game was fierce, for buyers and sellers alike. Rich medical schools outbid the less fortunate ones. Body snatchers charged for the body, then added a retainer, then a delivery fee. They raised prices at the start of the teaching period when demand was high, only to offer bargains at the end of the term when there was no longer a need for a specimen.

Morbid paradoxes confronted Stevens daily. His profession worked to extend life while secretly hoping for an increase in the deceased. A malpractice suit called you before the judge for want of a skill, but get caught with an ill-gotten cadaver and the judge punished you for trying to obtain that skill. Proctor made its students pay for their own pathological specimens. Stevens's first anatomy course required two complete dissections—how was he supposed to pay for that? Back home in Maine, he'd been spoiled by his mother's cooking; the women on her side were gifted. Here in the city, tuition, books, lectures, and rent had him subsisting on crusts for days on end.

When Carpenter invited Stevens to work for him, he did not hesitate. His appearance scared Stevens, that first delivery months before. The grave robber was an Irish giant, imposing in frame, uncouth in manner and speech, and carried with him the reek of damp earth. Carpenter and his wife had six children; when two of them passed from yellow fever, he sold them for anatomical study. Or so it was said. Stevens was too scared to ask for refutation. When trafficking in cadavers, it helped to be immune to sentimentality.

He wouldn't be the first body snatcher to open a grave to find the face of a long-lost cousin or a dear friend.

Carpenter recruited his gang at the saloon, rowdies all. They slept the day, drank well into the evening, and then set off for their pastime. "The hours are not great, but suit a certain character." Criminal character, incorrigible by any measure. It was a low enterprise. Raiding cemeteries was the least of it. The competition was a pack of rabid animals. Leave a prospect to too late in the evening and you were liable to discover someone else had pilfered the body first. Carpenter reported his competition's clients to the police, broke into dissection rooms to mutilate their deliveries. Brawls erupted when rival gangs converged on the same pauper's field. They smashed one another's faces among the tombstones. "It was raucous," Carpenter always said when he finished one of his stories, grinning through his mossy teeth.

In his glory days, Carpenter elevated the ploys and chicanery of his trade to a devilish art. He brought rocks in wheelbarrows for undertakers to bury and carried away the deceased. An actor taught his nieces and nephews to cry on demand, the craft of bereavement. Then they made the rounds of the morgue, claiming bodies as long-lost relatives—although Carpenter was not above simply stealing bodies from the coroner when he had to. On more than one occasion, Carpenter sold a cadaver to an anatomical school, reported the body to the police, and then had his wife, dressed in mourning clothes, claim it as her son. Whereupon Carpenter sold the body again to another school. It saved the county the expense of burial; no one looked too closely.

Eventually the body trade grew so reckless that relatives took to holding graveside vigils, lest their loved ones disappear in the night. Suddenly every missing child was perceived to have been a victim of foul play—snatched, dispatched, and then sold for dissection. The newspapers took up the cause in outraged editorials; the law stepped in. In this new climate, most body snatchers extended their territory, riffling the graves of distant cemeteries to space out their raids. Carpenter turned to niggers exclusively.

The niggers did not post sentries over their dead. Niggers did not pound on the door of the sheriff, they did not haunt the offices of the newspapermen. No sheriff paid them any mind, no journalist listened to their stories. The bodies of their loved ones disappeared into sacks and reappeared in the cool cellars of medical schools to relinquish their secrets. Every one of them a miracle, in Stevens's view, providing instruction into the intricacies of God's design.

Carpenter snarled when he said the word, a mangy dog hoarding his bone: *nigger.* Stevens never used the word. He disapproved of racial prejudice. Indeed, an uneducated Irishman like Carpenter, steered by society to a life of rummaging graves, had more in common with a negro than a white doctor. If you considered the matter at length. He wouldn't say that aloud, of course. Sometimes Stevens wondered if his views weren't quaint, given the temper of the modern world. The other students uttered the most horrible things about the colored population of Boston, about their smell, their intellectual deficiencies, their primitive drives. Yet when his classmates put their blades to a colored cadaver, they did more for the cause of colored advancement than the most high-minded abolitionist. In death the negro became a human being. Only then was he the white man's equal.

On the outskirts of Concord, they stopped at the small wooden gate and waited for the custodian's signal. The man waved his lantern back and forth and Carpenter drove the cart inside the cemetery. Cobb paid the man's fee and he directed them to this night's bounty: two large, two medium, and three infants. The rain had softened the earth. They'd be done in three hours. After they refilled the graves, it would be as if they were never there.

"Your surgeon's knife." Carpenter handed Stevens a spade.

He'd be a medical student again in the morning. Tonight he was a resurrection man. Body snatcher was an accurate name. Resurrection man was a bit florid, but it held a truth. He gave these people a second chance to contribute, one denied them in their previous life.

And if you could make a study of the dead, Stevens thought from time to time, you could make a study of the living, and make them testify as no cadaver could.

He rubbed his hands to stir the blood and started to dig.

North Carolina

Runaway or conveyed off, From the subscriber's residence, near Henderson, on the 16th inst. a negro girl named MARTHA, belonging to the Subscriber. Said girl is of a dark brown complexion, slightly made, and very free spoken, about 21 years of age; she wore a black silk bonnet with feathers; and had in her possession two calico bed quiltings. I understand she will try to pass as a free girl.

RIGDON BANKS
GRANVILLE COUNTY, AUGUST 28, 1839

She lost the candles. One of the rats woke Cora with its teeth and when she settled herself, she crawled across the dirt of the platform in her search. She came up with nothing. It was the day after Sam's house collapsed, though she couldn't be sure. Best to measure time now with one of the Randall plantation's cotton scales, her hunger and fear piling on one side while her hopes were removed from the other in increments. The only way to know how long you are lost in the darkness is to be saved from it.

By then Cora only needed the candlelight for company, having collected the particulars of her prison. The platform was twenty-eight paces long, and five and a half from wall to tracks' edge. It was twenty-six steps up to the world above. The trapdoor was warm when she placed her palm against it. She knew which step snagged her dress when she crawled up (the eighth) and which liked to scrape her skin if she scrabbled down too fast (the fifteenth). Cora remembered seeing a broom in a corner of the platform. She used it to tap the ground like the blind lady in town, the way Caesar had probed the black water during their flight. Then she got clumsy or cocky and fell onto the tracks, losing both the broom and any desire beyond huddling on the ground.

She had to get out. In those long hours, she could not keep from devising cruel scenes, arranging her own Museum of Terrible Wonders. Caesar strung up by the grinning mob; Caesar a brutalized mess on the floor of the slave catcher's wagon, halfway back to Randall and the waiting punishments. Kind Sam in jail; Sam tarred and feathered, interrogated about the underground railroad, broken-boned and senseless. A faceless white posse sifted through the smoldering remains of the cabin, pulled up the trapdoor and delivered her into wretchedness.

Those were the scenes she decorated in blood when awake. In nightmares the exhibits were more grotesque. She strolled back and forth before the glass, a customer of pain. She was locked in Life on the Slave Ship after the museum had closed, ever between ports and waiting for the wind while hundreds of kidnapped souls screamed belowdecks. Behind the next window, Miss Lucy cut open Cora's stomach with a letter opener and a thousand black spiders spilled from her guts. Over and over, she was transported back to the night of the smokehouse, held down by nurses from the hospital as Terrance Randall grunted and thrusted above her. Usually the rats or bugs woke her when their curiosity became too much, interrupting her dreams and returning her to the darkness of the platform.

Her stomach quivered under her fingers. She had starved before, when Connelly got it in his mind to punish the quarter for mischief and cut off rations. But they needed food to work and the cotton demanded the punishment be brief. Here, there was no way to know when she would eat next. The train was late. The night Sam told them about the bad blood—when the house still stood—the next train was due in two days. It should have arrived. She didn't know how late it was, but the delay signified nothing good. Maybe this branch was shut down. The entire line exposed and canceled. No one was coming. She was too weak to walk the unknowable miles to the next station, in the dark, let alone face whatever waited at the following stop.

Caesar. If they had been sensible and kept running, she and Caesar would be in the Free States. Why had they believed that two lowly slaves deserved the bounty of South Carolina? That a new life existed so close, just over the state line? It was still the south, and the devil had long nimble fingers. And then, after all the world had taught them, not to recognize chains when they were snapped to their wrists and ankles. The South Carolina chains were of new manufacture—the keys and tumblers marked by regional design—but accomplished the purpose of chains. They had not traveled very far at all.

She could not see her own hand in front of her but saw Caesar's capture many times. Seized at his factory station, snatched en route to meet Sam at the Drift. Walking down Main Street, arm in arm with his girl Meg. Meg cries out when they seize him, and they knock her to the sidewalk. That was one thing that would be different if she had made Caesar her lover: They might have been captured together. They would not be alone in their separate prisons. Cora drew her knees to her chest and wrapped her arms around them. In the end she would have disappointed him. She was a stray after all. A stray not only in its plantation meaning—orphaned, with no one to look after her—but in every other sphere as well. Somewhere, years ago, she had stepped off the path of life and could no longer find her way back to the family of people.

The earth trembled faintly. In days to come, when she remembered the late train's approach, she would not associate the vibration with the locomotive but with the furious arrival of a truth she had always known: She was a stray in every sense. The last of her tribe.

The light of the train shuddered around the bend. Cora reached for her hair before realizing that after her interment there was no improving her appearance. The engineer would not judge her; their secret enterprise was a fraternity of odd souls. She waved her hands animatedly, savoring the orange light as it expanded on the platform like a warm bubble.

The train sped past the station and out of sight.

She almost keeled over into the tracks as she howled after the train, her throat raspy and raw after days of privation. Cora stood and shook, incredulous, until she heard the train stop and back up on the tracks.

The engineer was apologetic. "Will you take my sandwich, as well?" he asked as Cora guzzled from his waterskin. She ate the sandwich, oblivious to his jest, even though she had never been partial to hog tongue.

"You're not supposed to be here," the boy said, adjusting his spectacles. He was no older than fifteen, raw-boned and eager.

"Well, you see me, don't you?" She licked her fingers and tasted dirt.

The boy cried "Gosh!" and "Sweet mother!" at every complication in her story, tucking his thumbs into the pockets of his overalls and rocking on his heels. He spoke like one of the white children Cora had observed in the town square playing kick-the-ball, with a carefree authority that did not jibe with the color of his skin, let alone the nature of his job. How he came to command the locomotive was a story, but now was not the time for the unlikely histories of colored boys.

"Georgia station is closed," he said finally, scratching his scalp beneath his blue cap. "We're supposed to stay away. Patrollers must have smoked it out, I figure." He clambered into his cabin after his pisspot, then went to the edge of the tunnel and emptied it. "The bosses hadn't heard from the station agent, so I was running express. This stop wasn't on my schedule." He wanted to leave immediately.

Cora hesitated, unable to stop herself from looking at the stairs for a last-minute addition. The impossible passenger. Then she started for the cabin.

"You can't go up here!" the boy said. "It's regulations."

"You can't expect me to ride on that," Cora said.

"All passengers ride coach on this train, miss. They're pretty strict about that."

To call the flatcar a coach was an abuse of the word. It was a boxcar like the one she rode to South Carolina, but only in foundation. The plane of wooden planks was riveted to the undercarriage, without walls or ceiling. She stepped aboard and the train jolted with the boy's preparations. He turned his head and waved at his passenger with disproportionate enthusiasm.

Straps and ropes for oversize freight lay on the floor, loose and serpentine. Cora sat in the center of the flatcar, wrapped one around her waist three times, grabbed another two and fashioned reins. She pulled tight.

The train lurched into the tunnel. Northward. The engineer yelled, "All aboard!" The boy was simple, Cora decided, responsibilities of his office notwithstanding. She looked back. Her underground prison waned as the darkness reclaimed it. She wondered if she was its final passenger. May the next traveler not tarry and keep moving up the line, all the way to liberty.

In the journey to South Carolina, Cora had slept in the turbulent car, nestled against Caesar's warm body. She did not sleep on her next train ride. Her so-called coach was sturdier than the boxcar, but the rushing air made the ride into a blustery ordeal. From time to time, Cora had to turn her body to catch her breath. The engineer was more reckless than his predecessor, going faster, goading the machine into velocity. The flatcar jumped whenever they took a turn. The closest she had ever been to the sea was her term in the Museum of Natural Wonders; these planks taught her about ships and squalls. The engineer's crooning drifted back, songs she did not recognize, debris from the north kicked up by the gale. Eventually she gave up and lay on her stomach, fingers dug into the seams.

"How goes it back there?" the engineer asked when they stopped. They were in the middle of the tunnel, no station in sight.

Cora flapped her reins.

"Good," the boy said. He wiped the soot and sweat from his forehead. "We're about halfway there. Needed to stretch my legs." He slapped the side of the boiler. "This old girl, she bucks."

It wasn't until they were moving again that Cora realized she forgot to ask where they were headed.

A careful pattern of colored stones decorated the station beneath Lumbly's farm, and wooden slabs covered the walls of Sam's station. The builders of this stop had hacked and blasted it from the unforgiving earth and made no attempt at adornment, to showcase the difficulty of their feat. Stripes of white, orange, and rust-colored veins swam through the jags, pits, and knobs. Cora stood in the guts of a mountain.

The engineer lit one of the torches on the wall. The laborers hadn't cleaned up when they finished. Crates of gear and mining equipment crowded the platform, making it a workshop. Passengers chose their seating from empty cases of explosive powder. Cora tested the water in one of the barrels. It tasted fresh. Her mouth was an old dustpan after the rain of flying grit in the tunnel. She drank from the dipper for a long time as the engineer watched her, fidgeting. "Where is this place?" she asked.

"North Carolina," the boy replied. "This used to be a popular stop, from what I'm told. Not anymore."

"The station agent?" Cora asked.

"I've never met him, but I'm sure he's a fine fellow."

He required fine character and a tolerance for gloom to

operate in this pit. After her days beneath Sam's cottage, Cora declined the challenge. "I'm going with you," Cora said. "What's the next station?"

"That's what I was trying to say before, miss. I'm in maintenance." Because of his age, he told her, he was entrusted with the engine but not its human freight. After the Georgia station shut down—he didn't know the details, but gossip held it had been discovered—they were testing all the lines in order to reroute traffic. The train she had been waiting for was canceled, and he didn't know when another one would be through. His instructions were to make a report on conditions and then head back to the junction.

"Can't you take me to the next stop?"

He motioned her to the edge of the platform and extended his lantern. The tunnel terminated fifty feet ahead in a ragged point.

"We passed a branch back there, heads south," he said. "I've got just enough coal to check it out and make it back to the depot."

"I can't go south," Cora said.

"The station agent will be along. I'm sure of it."

She missed him when he was gone, in all of his foolishness.

Cora had light, and another thing she did not have in South Carolina—sound. Dark water pooled between the rails, fed in steady drips from the station ceiling. The stone vault above was white with splashes of red, like blood from a whipping that soaked a shirt. The noise cheered her, though. As did the plentiful drinking water, the torches, and the distance she had traveled from the slave catchers. North Carolina was an improvement, beneath the surface.

She explored. The station abutted a rough-hewn tunnel. Support struts shored up the wooden ceiling and stones embedded in the dirt floor made her stumble. She chose to go left first, stepping over spill that had come loose from the walls. Rusting tools littered the path. Chisels, sledges, and picks—weaponry for battling mountains. The air was damp. When she ran her hand along the wall it came back coated in cool white dust. At the end of the corridor, the ladder bolted into the stone led up into a snug passage. She lifted the torch. There was no telling how far the rungs extended. She braved the climb only after discovering that the other end of the corridor narrowed into a glum dead end.

A few feet into the level above, she saw why the equipment had been abandoned by the work gangs. A sloping mound of rocks and dirt, floor to ceiling, cut off the tunnel. Opposite the cave-in, the tunnel terminated after a hundred feet, confirming her fear. She was trapped once more.

Cora collapsed on the rocks and wept until sleep overtook her.

The station agent woke her. "Oh!" the man said. His round red face poked through the space he'd made at the top of the rubble. "Oh, dear," he said. "What are you doing here?"

"I'm a passenger, sir."

"Don't you know this station is closed?"

She coughed and rose, straightening her filthy dress.

"Oh dear, oh dear," he said.

His name was Martin Wells. Together they widened the hole in the wall of stone and she squeezed through to the other side. The man helped her clamber down to level ground as if helping a lady from the finest carriage. After several turns, the mouth of the tunnel extended a dim invitation. A breeze tickled her skin. She gulped the air like water, the night sky the best meal she had ever had, the stars made succulent and ripe after her time below.

The station agent was a barrel-shaped man deep in his middle age, pasty-complected and soft. For an agent of the underground railroad, presumably no stranger to peril and risk, he evinced a nervous personality. "You're not supposed to be here," he said, repeating the engineer's assessment. "This is a very regrettable turn."

Martin huffed through his explanation, washing his sweaty gray hair from his face as he spoke. The night riders were on patrol, he explained, casting agent and passenger into dangerous waters. The old mica mine was remote, to be sure, exhausted long ago by Indians and forgotten by most, but the regulators routinely checked the caves and mines, anyplace a fugitive might seek refuge from their justice.

The cave-in that had so distressed Cora was a ruse to camouflage the operation below. Despite its success, the new laws in North Carolina had rendered the station inoperable—he was visiting the mine merely to leave a message for the underground railroad that he could accept no more passengers. When it came to harboring Cora, or any other runaway, Martin was unprepared in every way. "Especially given the present circumstances," he whispered, as if the patrollers waited at the top of the gully.

Martin told her he needed to fetch a wagon and Cora wasn't convinced he was coming back. He insisted he wouldn't be long—dawn was approaching and after that it would be impossible to move her. She was so grateful to be outside in the living world that she decided to believe him, and almost threw her arms around him when he reappeared, driving a weather-beaten wagon pulled by two bony draft horses. They repositioned the sacks of grain and seed to make a slim pocket. The last time Cora needed to hide in this manner, they required room for two. Martin draped a tarpaulin over his cargo and they rumbled out of the cut, the station agent grumbling profane commentary until they gained the road.

They had not traveled long when Martin stopped the horses. He removed the tarpaulin. "It will be sunrise soon, but I wanted you to see this," the station agent said.

Cora did not immediately know what he meant. The country road was quiet, crowded on both sides by the forest canopy. She saw one shape, then another. Cora got out of the wagon.

The corpses hung from trees as rotting ornaments. Some of them were naked, others partially clothed, the trousers black where their bowels emptied when their necks snapped. Gross wounds and injuries marked the flesh of those closest to her, the two caught by the station agent's lantern. One had been castrated, an ugly mouth gaping where his manhood had been. The other was a woman. Her belly curved. Cora had never been good at knowing if a body was with a child. Their bulging eyes seemed to rebuke her stares, but what were the attentions of one girl, disturbing their rest, compared to how the world had scourged them since the day they were brought into it?

"They call this road the Freedom Trail now," Martin said as he covered the wagon again. "The bodies go all the way to town."

In what sort of hell had the train let her off?

When she next emerged from the wagon, Cora sneaked around the side of Martin's yellow house. The sky was growing light. Martin had brought the wagon as far back into his property as he dared. The homes on either side of his were quite close—anyone awakened by the horses' noise could see her. Toward the front of the house, Cora saw the street, and beyond that, a grass field. Martin urged her on and she crept onto the back porch and then inside. A tall white woman in her night-clothes leaned against the wainscoting in the kitchen. She sipped a glass of lemonade and did not look at Cora as she said, "You're going to get us murdered."

This was Ethel. She and Martin had been married for thirty-five years. The couple did not speak as he washed his trembling hands in the basin. They had quarreled over her while she waited at the mine, Cora knew, and would resume that argument once they dealt with the matter before them.

Ethel led Cora upstairs while Martin returned the wagon to

his store. Cora got a brief look at the parlor, which was modestly furnished; after Martin's warnings, the morning light through the window quickened her step. Ethel's long gray hair extended halfway down her back. The woman's manner of walking unnerved Cora—she seemed to float, aloft on her fury. At the top of the stairs, Ethel stopped and pointed to the washroom. "You smell," she said. "Be quick about it."

When Cora stepped into the hallway again, the woman summoned her up the stairs to the attic. Cora's head almost brushed the ceiling of the small, hot room. Between the sloping walls of the peaked roof, the attic was crammed with years of castoffs. Two broken washboards, piles of moth-eaten quilts, chairs with split seats. A rocking horse, covered in matted hide, sat in the corner under a curl of peeling yellow wallpaper.

"We're going to have to cover that now," Ethel said, referring to the window. She moved a crate from the wall, stood on it, and nudged the hatch in the ceiling. "Come, come," she said. Her face set in a grimace. She still had not looked at the fugitive.

Cora pulled herself up above the false ceiling, into the cramped nook. It came to a point three feet from the floor and ran fifteen feet in length. She moved the stacks of musty gazettes and books to make more room. Cora heard Ethel descend the stairs, and when her host returned she handed Cora food, a jug of water, and a chamber pot.

Ethel looked at Cora for the first time, her drawn face framed by the hatch. "The girl is coming by and by," she said. "If she hears you, she'll turn us in and they will kill us all. Our daughter and her family arrive this afternoon. They cannot know you are here. Do you understand?"

"How long will it be?"

"You stupid thing. Not a sound. Not a single sound. If anyone hears you, we are lost." She pulled the hatch shut.

The only source of light and air was a hole in the wall that faced the street. Cora crawled to it, stooping beneath the rafters. The jagged hole had been carved from the inside, the work of a previous occupant who'd taken issue with the state of the lodgings. She wondered where the person was now.

That first day, Cora acquainted herself with the life of the park, the patch of green she'd seen across the street from the house. She pressed her eye to the spy hole, shifting around to capture the entire view. Two- and three-story wood-frame houses bordered the park on all sides, identical in construction, distinguished by paint color and the type of furniture on their long porches. Neat brick walkways crisscrossed the grass, snaking in and out of the shadows of the tall trees and their luxurious branches. A fountain warbled near the main entrance, surrounded by low stone benches that were occupied soon after sunup and remained popular well into the night.

Elderly men with handkerchiefs full of crusts for the birds, children with their kites and balls, and young couples under the spell of romance took their shifts. A brown mutt owned the place, known to all, yipping and scampering. Across the afternoon, children chased it through the grass and onto the sturdy white bandstand at the edge of the park. The mutt dozed in the shade of the benches and the gigantic oak that dominated the green with majestic ease. It was well-fed, Cora observed, gobbling down the treats and bones offered by the citizens. Her stomach never failed to rumble at the sight. She named him Mayor.

As the sun approached its zenith, and the park bustled with midday traffic, the heat transformed the hidey-hole into a wretched furnace. Crawling to different sections of the attic nook, searching for imaginary oases of cool, became her principal activity after her vigil over the park. She learned that her hosts would not visit her during the day, when their girl Fiona was working. Martin tended to his store, Ethel came and went on her social rounds, but Fiona was always downstairs. She was young, with a prominent Irish accent. Cora heard her going about her duties, sighing to herself and muttering invectives toward her absent employers. Fiona did not enter the attic that first day, but the sound of her steps turned Cora as stiff as her old sailing mate Skipper John. Ethel's warnings the first morning made their intended impression.

On her arrival day there were additional visitors—Martin and Ethel's daughter, Jane, and her family. From the daughter's bright and pleasant manner, Cora decided she took after her father, and filled in her broad face using Martin as a template. The son-in-law and the two granddaughters were an unceasing commotion, thundering through the house. At one point the girls started for the attic but reconsidered after a discussion about the habits and customs of ghosts. There was indeed a ghost in the house, but she was done with chains, rattling or no.

In the evening the park remained busy. The main street must be nearby, Cora thought, funneling the town. Some older women in blue gingham dresses nailed white-and-blue bunting to the bandstand. Garlands of orange leaves added a flourish. Families staked out spots before the stage, unrolling blankets and removing supper from baskets. Those who lived next to the park gathered on their porches with jugs and glasses.

Preoccupied by her uncomfortable refuge and the parade of misfortunes since the slave catchers found them out, Cora did not immediately notice an important feature of the park: Everyone was white. She had never left the plantation before she and Caesar ran away, so South Carolina gave Cora her first glimpse of the mingling of races in towns and cities. On Main Street, in stores, in factories and offices, in every sector, black and white mixed all day as a matter of course. Human commerce withered without it. In liberty or bondage, the African could not be separated from the American.

In North Carolina the negro race did not exist except at the ends of ropes.

Two able young men helped the matrons hang a banner over the bandstand: Friday Festival. A band took its place onstage, the sounds of their warming up gathering the scattered parkgoers. Cora hunkered and pressed her face to the wall. The banjo man displayed some talent, the horn player and fiddler less so. Their melodies were bland in comparison to those of the colored musicians she'd heard, on Randall and off, but the townspeople enjoyed the denatured rhythms. The band closed with spirited renditions of two colored songs Cora recognized, which proved the most popular of the night. On the porch below, Martin and Ethel's grandchildren squealed and clapped.

A man in a rumpled linen suit took the stage to deliver a brief welcome. Martin told Cora later that this was Judge Tennyson, a respected figure in town when abstemious. This night he tottered. She couldn't make out the judge's introduction of the next act, a coon show. She'd heard of them but had never witnessed their travesties; the colored evening at the theater in South Carolina offered different fare. Two white men, their faces blackened by burned cork, capered through a series of skits that brought the park to exuberant laughter. Dressed in mismatched, gaudy clothes and chimney-pot hats, they molded their voices to exaggerate colored speech; this seemed to be the source of the humor. A sketch where the skinnier performer took off his dilapidated boot and counted his toes over and over again, constantly losing his place, generated the loudest reaction.

The final performance, following a notice from the judge regarding the chronic drainage issues at the lake, was a short play. From what Cora put together from the actors' movements and the bits of dialogue that traveled to her suffocating nook, the play concerned a slave—again, a white man in burned cork, pink showing on his neck and wrists—who ran north after a light rebuke from his master. He suffered on his journey, delivering a pouty soliloquy on hunger, cold, and wild beasts. In the north, a saloon keeper took him on. The saloon keeper was a ruthless boss, beating and insulting the wayward slave at every turn, stealing wages and dignity, the hard image of northern white attitudes.

The last scene depicted the slave on his master's doorstep, having once again run away, this time from the false promises of the Free States. He begged after his former position, lamenting his folly and asking for forgiveness. With kind and patient words, the master explained that it was impossible. In the slave's absence, North Carolina had changed. The master whistled and two patrollers ushered the prostrate slave from the premises.

The town appreciated the moral of the performance, their applause resounding through the park. Toddlers clapped from the shoulders of their fathers, and Cora caught Mayor nipping at the air. She had no idea of the size of the town but felt that every citizen was in the park now, waiting. The true purpose of the evening revealed itself. A sturdy-built man in white trousers and a bright red coat took command of the stage. Despite his size, he moved with force and authority—Cora recalled the mounted bear in the museum, posed at the dramatic moment of his charge. He twisted one end of his handlebar mustache with patient amusement as the crowd quieted. His voice was firm and clear and for the first time that evening Cora did not miss a single word.

He introduced himself as Jamison, though every soul in the park was aware of his identity. "Each Friday I awake full of vigor," he said, "knowing that in a few hours we'll gather here again and celebrate our good fortune. Sleep used to come so hard to me, in the days before our regulators secured the darkness."

He gestured to the formidable band, fifty-strong, who had assembled at the side of the bandstand. The town cheered when the men waved and nodded at Jamison's acknowledgment.

Jamison caught the crowd up. God had given one regulator the gift of a newborn son, and two others had observed their birthdays. "We have a new recruit with us tonight," Jamison continued, "a young man from a fine family who joined the ranks of the night riders this week. Come on up, Richard, and let them have a look at you."

The slender red-haired boy advanced tentatively. Like his fellows, he wore his uniform of black trousers and white shirt of thick cloth, his neck swimming in the collar. The boy mumbled. From Jamison's side of the conversation, Cora gathered that the recruit had been making the rounds of the county, learning the protocols of his squad.

"And you had an auspicious start, didn't you, son?"

The lanky boy bobbed his head. His youth and slight frame reminded Cora of the engineer of her last train trip, inducted by circumstance into the work of men. His freckled skin was lighter-hued, but they shared the same fragile eagerness. Born the same day, perhaps, then steered by codes and circumstances to serve disparate agencies.

"It's not every rider who makes a catch his first week out," Jamison said. "Let's see what young Richard has for us."

Two night riders dragged a colored girl onstage. She had a house girl's tender physique and shrank further in her simpering. Her gray tunic was torn and smeared with blood and filth, and her head had been crudely shaved. "Richard was searching the hold of a steamship bound for Tennessee when he found this rascal hiding below," Jamison said. "Louisa is her name. She absconded from her plantation in the confusion of the reorganization and hid in the woods these many months. Believing she had escaped the logic of our system."

Louisa rolled over to survey the crowd, lifted her head briefly, and was still. It would have been difficult to make out her tormentors with all the blood in her eyes.

Jamison raised his fists in the air, as if daring something in the sky. The night was his opponent, Cora decided, the night and the phantoms he filled it with. In the dark, he said, colored miscreants lurked to violate the citizens' wives and daughters. In the deathless dark, their southern heritage lay defenseless and imperiled. The riders kept them safe. "We have each of us made sacrifices for this new North Carolina and its rights," Jamison said. "For this separate nation we have forged, free from northern interference and the contamination of a lesser race. The black horde has been beaten back, correcting the mistake made years ago at this nation's nativity. Some, like our brothers just over the state line, have embraced the absurd notion of nigger uplift. Easier to teach a donkey arithmetic." He bent down to rub Louisa's head. "When we find the odd rascal, our duty is clear."

The crowd separated, tutored by routine. With Jamison leading the procession, the night riders dragged the girl to the great oak in the middle of the park. Cora had seen the wheeled platform in the corner of the park that day; children climbed and jumped on it all afternoon. At some point in the evening it had been pushed beneath the oak tree. Jamison called for volunteers, and people of all ages rushed to their places on either side of the platform. The noose lowered around Louisa's neck and she was led up the stairs. With the precision born of practice, a night rider threw the rope over the thick, sturdy branch with a single toss.

One of those who had gathered to push the ramp away was ejected—he'd already taken his turn at a previous festival. A young brunette in a pink polka-dot dress rushed to take his place.

Cora turned away before the girl swung. She crawled to the opposite side of the nook, in the corner of her latest cage. Over the next several months, on nights when it was not too suffocating, she preferred that corner for sleeping. It was as far from the park, the miserable thumping heart of the town, as she could get.

The town hushed. Jamison gave the word.

To explain why he and his wife kept Cora imprisoned in their attic, Martin had to go back a ways. As with everything in the south, it started with cotton. The ruthless engine of cotton required its fuel of African bodies. Crisscrossing the ocean, ships brought bodies to work the land and to breed more bodies.

The pistons of this engine moved without relent. More slaves led to more cotton, which led to more money to buy more land to farm more cotton. Even with the termination of the slave trade, in less than a generation the numbers were untenable: all those niggers. Whites outnumbered slaves two to one in North Carolina, but in Louisiana and Georgia the populations neared parity. Just over the border in South Carolina, the number of blacks surpassed that of whites by more than a hundred thousand. It was not difficult to imagine the sequence when the slave cast off his chains in pursuit of freedom—and retribution.

In Georgia and Kentucky, South America and the Caribbean Isles, the Africans turned on their masters in short but disturbing encounters. Before the Southampton rebellion was smothered, Turner and his band murdered sixty-five men, women, and children. Civilian militias and patrollers lynched three times that in response—conspirators, sympathizers, and innocents—to set an example. To clarify the terms. But the numbers remained, declaring a truth unclouded by prejudice.

"Around here, the closest thing to a constable was the patroller," Martin said.

"Most places," Cora said. "Patroller will harass you anytime they feel like." It was after midnight, her first Monday. Martin's daughter and her family had returned home, as had Fiona, who lived down the road in Irishtown. Martin perched on a crate in the attic, fanning himself. Cora paced and stretched her sore limbs. She had not stood in days. Ethel declined to appear. Dark blue drapes hid the windows and the small candle licked at the gloom.

Despite the hour, Martin spoke in a whisper. His next-door neighbor's son was a night rider.

As the slave owners' enforcers, the patrollers were the law: white, crooked, and merciless. Drawn from the lowest and most vicious segment, too witless to even become overseers. (Cora nodded in agreement.) The patroller required no reason to stop a person apart from color. Slaves caught off the plantation need passes, unless they wanted a licking and a visit to the county jail. Free blacks carried proof of manumission or risked being conveyed into the clutches of slavery; sometimes they were smuggled to the auction block anyway. Rogue blacks who did not surrender could be shot. They searched slave villages at will and took liberties as they ransacked the homes of freemen, stealing hard-earned linens or making licentious advances.

In war—and to put down a slave rebellion was the most glorious call to arms—the patrollers transcended their origins to become a true army. Cora pictured the insurrections as great, bloody battles, unfurling beneath a night sky lit by vast fires. From Martin's accounts, the actual uprisings were small and chaotic. The slaves walked the roads between towns with their scavenged weapons: hatchets and scythes, knives and bricks. Tipped by colored turncoats, the white enforcers organized elaborate ambushes, decimating the insurgents with gunfire and running them down on horseback, reinforced by the might of the United States Army. At the first alarms, civilian volunteers joined the patrollers to quell the disturbance, invading the quarters and putting freemen's homes to the torch. Suspects and bystanders crammed the jails. They strung up the guilty and, in the interest of prevention, a robust percentage of the innocent. Once the slain had been avenged—and more important, the insult to white order repaid with interest—the civilians returned to their farms and factories and stores, and the patrollers resumed their rounds.

The revolts were quashed, but the immensity of the colored population remained. The verdict of the census lay in glum columns and rows.

"We know it, but don't say it," Cora told Martin.

The crate creaked as Martin shifted.

"And if we say, we don't say it for anyone to hear," Cora said. "How big we are."

On a chilly evening last autumn, the powerful men of North

Carolina convened to solve the colored question. Politicians attuned to the shifting complexities of the slavery debate; wealthy farmers who drove the beast of cotton and felt the reins slipping; and the requisite lawyers to fire the soft clay of their schemes into permanence. Jamison was present, Martin told Cora, in his capacities as a senator and local planter. It was a long night.

They assembled in Oney Garrison's dining room. Oney lived atop Justice Hill, so named because it allowed one to see everything below for miles and miles, placing the world in proportion. After this night their meeting would be known as the Justice Convention. Their host's father had been a member of the cotton vanguard and a savvy proselytizer of the miracle crop. Oney grew up surrounded by the profits of cotton, and its necessary evil, niggers. The more he thought about it—as he sat there in his dining room, taking in the long, pallid faces of the men who drank his liquor and overstayed their welcome—what he really wanted was simply more of the former and less of the latter. Why were they spending so much time worrying about slave uprisings and northern influence in Congress when the real issue was who was going to pick all this goddamned cotton?

In the coming days the newspapers printed the numbers for all to see, Martin said. There were almost three hundred thousand slaves in North Carolina. Every year that same number of Europeans—Irish and Germans mostly, fleeing famine and political unpleasantness—streamed into the harbors of Boston, New York, Philadelphia. On the floor of the state house, in the editorial pages, the question was put forth: Why cede this supply to the Yankees? Why not alter the course of that human tributary so that it fed southward? Advertisements in overseas papers promoted the benefits of term labor, advance agents expounded in taverns and town meetings and poorhouses, and in due course the charter ships teemed with their willing human cargo, bringing dreamers to the shores of a new country. Then they disembarked to work the fields.

"Never seen a white person pick cotton," Cora said.

"Before I came back to North Carolina, I'd never seen a mob rip a man limb from limb," Martin said. "See that, you stop saying what folks will do and what they won't."

True, you couldn't treat an Irishman like an African, white nigger or no. There was the cost of buying slaves and their upkeep on one hand and paying white workers meager but livable wages on the other. The reality of slave violence versus stability in the long term. The Europeans had been farmers before; they would be farmers again. Once the immigrants finished their contracts (having paid back travel, tools, and lodging) and took their place in American society, they would be allies of the southern system that had nurtured them. On Election Day when they took their turn at the ballot box, theirs would be a full vote, not three-fifths. A financial reckoning was inevitable, but come the approaching conflict over the race question, North Carolina would emerge in the most advantageous position of all the slave states.

In effect, they abolished slavery. On the contrary, Oney Garrison said in response. We abolished niggers.

"All the women and children, the men—where did they go?" Cora asked. Someone shouted in the park, and the two in the attic were still for a while.

"You saw," Martin said.

The North Carolina government—half of which crowded into Garrison's dining room that night—purchased existing slaves from farmers at favorable rates, just as Great Britain had done when it abolished slavery decades ago. The other states of the cotton empire absorbed the stock; Florida and Louisiana, in their explosive growth, were particularly famished for colored hands, especially the seasoned variety. A short tour of Bourbon Street forecast the result to any observer: a repulsive mongrel state in which the white race is, through amalgamation with negro blood, made stained, obscured, confused. Let them pollute their European bloodlines with Egyptian darkness, produce a river of half-breeds, quadroons, and miscellaneous dingy yellow bastards—they forge the very blades that will be used to cut their throats.

The new race laws forbid colored men and women from setting foot on North Carolina soil. Freemen who refused to leave their land were run off or massacred. Veterans of the Indian campaigns earned generous mercenary coin for their expertise. Once the soldiers finished their work, the former patrollers took on the mantle of night riders, rounding up strays—slaves who tried to outrun the new order, dispossessed freemen without the means to make it north, luckless colored men and women lost in the land for any number of reasons.

When Cora woke up that first Saturday morning, she put off looking through the spy hole. When she finally steeled herself, they had already cut down Louisa's body. Children skipped underneath the spot where she had dangled. "The road," Cora said, "the Freedom Trail, you called it. How far does it go?"

It extended as far as there were bodies to feed it, Martin said. Putrefying bodies, bodies consumed by carrion eaters were constantly replaced, but the heading always advanced. Every town of any real size held their Friday Festival, closing with the same grim finale. Some places reserved extra captives in the jail for a fallow week when the night riders returned empty-handed.

Whites punished under the new legislation were merely hung, not put on display. Although, Martin qualified, there was the case of a white farmer who had sheltered a gang of colored refugees. When they combed through the ashes of the house it was impossible to pick his body from those he had harbored, as the fire had eliminated the differences in their skin, leveling them. All five bodies were hung on the trail and nobody made much of a fuss over the breach in protocol.

With the topic of white persecution, they had arrived at the reason for her term in the nook. "You understand our predicament," Martin said.

Abolitionists had always been run off here, he said. Virginia or Delaware might tolerate their agitating, but no cotton state. Owning the literature was enough for a spell in jail, and when you were released you did not stay in town long. In the amendments to the state's constitution, the punishment for possessing seditious writings, or for aiding and abetting a colored person, was left to the discretion of local authorities. In practice, the verdict was death. The accused were dragged from their homes by their hair. Slave owners who refused to comply—from sentiment or a quaint notion about property rights—were strung up, as well as kindhearted citizens who hid niggers in their attics and cellars and coal bins.

After a lull in white arrests, some towns increased the rewards for turning in collaborators. Folks informed on business rivals, ancient nemeses, and neighbors, recounting old conversations where the traitors had uttered forbidden sympathies. Children tattled on their parents, taught by schoolmistresses the hallmarks of sedition. Martin related the story of a man in town who had been trying to rid himself of his wife for years, to no avail. The details of her crime did not hold up under scrutiny, but she paid the ultimate price. The gentleman remarried three months later.

"Is he happy?" Cora asked.

"What?"

Cora waved her hand. The severity of Martin's account had sent her down an avenue of odd humor.

Before, slave patrollers searched the premises of colored individuals at will, be they free or enslaved. Their expanded powers permitted them to knock on anyone's door to pursue an accusation and for random inspections as well, in the name of public safety. The regulators called at all hours, visiting the poorest trapper and wealthiest magistrate alike. Wagons and carriages were stopped at checkpoints. The mica mine was only a few miles away—even if Martin had the grit to run with Cora, they would not make it to the next county without an examination.

Cora thought that the whites would be loath to give up their freedoms, even in the name of security. Far from instilling resentment, Martin told her, the patrollers' diligence was a point of pride from county to county. Patriots boasted of how often they'd been searched and given a clean bill. A night rider's call on the home of a comely young woman had led to more than one happy engagement.

They twice searched Martin and Ethel's house before Cora appeared. The riders were perfectly pleasant, complimenting Ethel on her ginger cake. They did not look askance at the attic hatch, but that was no guarantee that next time things would proceed along the same lines. The second visit caused Martin to resign from his duties with the railroad. There were no plans for the next leg of Cora's journey, no word from associates. They would have to wait for a sign.

Once again, Martin apologized for his wife's behavior. "You understand she's scared to death. We're at the mercy of fate."

"You feel like a slave?" Cora asked.

Ethel hadn't chosen this life, Martin said.

"You were born to it? Like a slave?"

That put an end to their conversation that night. Cora climbed up into the nook with fresh rations and a clean chamber pot.

Her routine established itself quickly. It could not have been otherwise, given the constraints. After she knocked her head into the roof a dozen times, her body remembered the limits on her movement. Cora slept, nestled between the rafters as if in the cramped hold of a ship. She watched the park. She worked on her reading, making the best of the education that had been cut short in South Carolina, squinting in the spy hole's dim light. She wondered why there were only two kinds of weather: hardship in the morning, and tribulation at night.

Every Friday the town held its festival and Cora retreated to the opposite side of the nook.

The heat was impossible most days. On the worst she gulped at the hole like a fish in a bucket. Sometimes she neglected to ration her water, imbibing too much in the morning and staring with bitterness at the fountain the rest of the day. That damned dog cavorting in the spray. When the heat made her faint, she awoke with her head smeared into a rafter, her neck feeling like a chicken's after Alice the cook tried to wring it for supper. The meat she put on her bones in South Carolina melted away. Her host replaced her soiled dress with one his daughter had left behind. Jane was scarce-hipped and Cora now fit into her clothes with room.

Near midnight, after all the lights in the houses facing the park were extinguished and Fiona had long gone home, Martin brought food. Cora descended into the attic proper, to stretch and breathe different air. They talked some, then at a certain point Martin would stand with a solemn expression and Cora clambered back into the nook. Every few days Ethel permitted Martin to give her a brief visit to the washroom. Cora always fell asleep following Martin's visit, sometimes after an interval of sobbing and sometimes so quickly she was like a candle being blown out. She returned to her violent dreams.

She tracked the regulars on their daily transits through the park, assembling notes and speculations like the compilers of her almanacs. Martin kept abolitionist newspapers and pamphlets in the nook. They were a danger; Ethel wanted them gone, but they had been his father's and predated their residence in the house so Martin figured they could deny ownership. Once Cora had gleaned what she could from the yellowed pamphlets, she started on the old almanacs, with their projections and ruminations about the tides and stars, and bits of obscure commentary. Martin brought her a Bible. On one of her short interludes down in the attic, she saw a copy of *The Last of the Mohicans* that had been warped and swollen by water. She huddled by the spy hole for reading light, and in the evening curled around a candle.

Cora opened Martin's visits with the same question. "Any word?"

After a few months, she stopped.

The silence from the railroad was complete. The gazettes printed reports of raided depots and station agents brought to raw justice, but those were common slave-state fables. Previously, strangers knocked on Martin's door with messages concerning routes, and once, news of a confirmed passenger. Never the same person twice. No one had come in a long time, Martin said. By his lights, there was nothing for him to do.

"You won't let me leave," Cora said.

His reply was a whimper: "The situation is plain." It was a perfect trap, he said, for everyone. "You won't make it. They'll catch you. Then you'll tell them who we are."

"On Randall, when they want you in irons, they put you in irons."

"You'll bring us to ruin," Martin said. "Yourself, me, and Ethel, and all who helped you up and down the line."

She wasn't being fair but didn't much care, feeling mulish. Martin gave her a copy of that day's newspaper and pulled the hatch into place.

Any noise from Fiona sent her stock-still. She could only imagine what the Irish girl looked like. Occasionally Fiona dragged junk up to the attic. The stairs complained loudly at the slightest pressure, an efficient alarm. Once the maid moved on, Cora returned to her tiny range of activities. The girl's vulgarities reminded Cora of the plantation and the stream of oaths delivered by the hands when master's eye was not on them. The small rebellion of servants everywhere. She assumed Fiona spat in the soup.

The maid's route home did not include a cut across the park. Cora never saw her face even as she became a student of the girl's sighs. Cora pictured her, scrappy and determined, a survivor of famine and the hard relocation. Martin told her she'd come to America on a Carolina charter with her mother and brother. The mother got lung sickness and died a day out from land. The boy was too young to work and had a puny constitution overall; older Irish ladies passed him around most days. Was Irishtown similar to the colored streets in South Carolina? Crossing a single street transformed the way people talked, determined the size and condition of the homes, the dimension and character of the dreams.

In a few months it would be the harvest. Outside the town, in the fields, the cotton would pop into bolls and travel into sacks, picked this time by white hands. Did it bother the Irish and Germans to do nigger work, or did the surety of wages erase dishonor? Penniless whites took over the rows from penniless blacks, except at the end of the week the whites were no longer penniless. Unlike their darker brethren, they could pay off their contracts with their salaries and start a new chapter.

Jockey used to talk on Randall about how the slavers needed to roam deeper and deeper into Africa to find the next bunch of slaves, kidnapping tribe after tribe to feed the cotton, making the plantations into a mix of tongues and clans. Cora figured that a new wave of immigrants would replace the Irish, fleeing a different but no less abject country, the process starting anew. The engine huffed and groaned and kept running. They had merely switched the fuel that moved the pistons.

The sloping walls of her prison were a canvas for her morbid inquiries, particularly between sundown and Martin's late-night visit. When Caesar had approached her, she envisioned two outcomes: a contented, hard-won life in a northern city, or death. Terrance would not be content to merely discipline her for running away; he would make her life an ornate hell until he got bored, then have her dispatched in a gory exhibition.

Her northern fantasy, those first weeks in the attic, was a mere sketch. Glimpses of children in a bright kitchen—always a boy and a girl—and a husband in the next room, unseen but loving. As the days stretched, other rooms sprouted off the kitchen. A parlor with simple but tasteful furniture, things she had seen in the white shops of South Carolina. A bedroom. Then a bed covered in white sheets that shone in the sun, her children rolling on it with her, the husband's body half visible at the edges. In another scene, years hence, Cora walked down a busy street in her city and came across her mother. Begging in the gutter, a broken old woman bent into the sum of her mistakes. Mabel looked up but did not recognize her daughter. Cora kicked her beggar's cup, the few coins flew into the hubbub, and she continued on her afternoon errand to fetch flour for her son's birthday cake.

In this place to come, Caesar occasionally came for supper and they laughed ruefully about Randall and the travails of their escape, their eventual freedom. Caesar told the children how he got the small scar over his eyebrow, dragging a finger across it: He was caught by a slave catcher in South Carolina but got free.

Cora rarely thought of the boy she had killed. She did not need to defend her actions in the woods that night; no one had the right to call her to account. Terrance Randall provided a model for a mind that could conceive of North Carolina's new system, but the scale of the violence was hard to settle in her head. Fear drove these people, even more than cotton money. The shadow of the black hand that will return what has been given. It occurred to her one night that she was one of the vengeful monsters they were scared of: She had killed a white boy. She might kill one of them next. And because of that fear, they erected a new scaffolding of oppression on the cruel foundation laid hundreds of years before. That was Sea Island cotton the slaver had ordered for his rows, but scattered among the seeds were those of violence and death, and that crop grew fast. The whites were right to be afraid. One day the system would collapse in blood.

An insurrection of one. She smiled for a moment, before the facts of her latest cell reasserted themselves. Scrabbling in the walls like a rat. Whether in the fields or underground or in an attic room, America remained her warden.

It was a week before the summer solstice. Martin stuffed one of the old quilts into a chair without a seat and sank into it by degrees over the course of his visit. As was her habit, Cora asked for help with words. This time they came from the Bible, through which she made desultory progress: *gainsay, ravening, hoar*. Martin admitted he didn't know the meanings of gainsay and ravening. Then, as if to prepare for the new season, Martin reviewed the series of bad omens.

The first had occurred the previous week, when Cora knocked over the chamber pot. She'd been in the nook for four months and made noise before, knocking her head against the roof or her knee against a rafter. Fiona had never reacted. This time the girl was puttering around in the kitchen when Cora kicked the pot against the wall. Once Fiona came upstairs she wouldn't be able to overlook the dripping sound of the mess leaking between the boards into the attic, or the smell.

The noon whistle had just sounded. Ethel was out. Fortunately, another girl from Irishtown visited after lunch and the two gossiped in the parlor for so long that afterward Fiona had to speed through her chores. She either didn't notice the odor or pretended not to, shirking the responsibility for cleaning after whatever rodent's nest was up there. When Martin came that night and they cleaned, he told Cora it was best if he didn't mention the close call to Ethel. Her nerves were especially brittle with the rise in the humidity.

Informing Ethel was up to Martin. Cora hadn't seen the woman since the night of her arrival. As far as she could tell, her host didn't speak of her—even when Fiona was off the premises—beyond infrequent mentions of *that creature*. The slam of the bedroom door often preceded Martin's upstairs visit. The only thing that kept Ethel from turning her in, Cora decided, was complicity.

"Ethel is a simple woman," Martin said, sinking in the chair. "She couldn't foresee these troubles when I asked for her hand."

Cora knew that Martin was about to recount his accidental recruitment, which meant extra time outside the nook. She stretched her arms and encouraged him. "How could you, Martin."

"Lord, how could I," Martin said.

He was a most unlikely instrument of abolition. In Martin's recollection, his father, Donald, had never expressed an opinion about the peculiar institution, although their family was rare in their circle in not owning slaves. When Martin was little, the stock boy at the feed store was a wizened, stooped man named Jericho, freed many years previously. To his mother's dismay, Jericho came over every Thanksgiving bearing a tin of turnip mash. Donald grunted in disapproval or shook his head at newspaper items about the latest slave incident, but it wasn't clear if he judged the brutality of the master or the intransigence of the slave.

At eighteen, Martin left North Carolina and after a period of lonesome meandering took a position as a clerk in a Norfolk shipping office. The quiet work and sea air suited him. He developed a fondness for oysters and his constitution improved generally. Ethel's face appeared one day in a crowd, luminous. The Delanys had old ties to the region, pruning the family tree into a lopsided sight: abundant and many-cousined in the north, sparse and faceless in the south. Martin rarely visited his father. When Donald fell while fixing the roof, Martin hadn't been home in five years.

The men had never communicated easily. Before Martin's mother passed, it was her lot to translate the ellipses and muttered asides that constituted conversation between father and son. At Donald's deathbed, there was no interpreter. He made Martin promise to finish his work, and the son assumed the old man meant him to take over the feed store. That was the first misunderstanding. The second was taking the map he discovered in his father's papers for directions to a cache of gold. In his life, Donald wrapped himself in a kind of quiet that, depending on the observer, signaled imbecility or a reservoir of mystery. It would be just like his father, Martin thought, to comport himself like a pauper while hiding a fortune.

The treasure, of course, was the underground railroad. Some might call freedom the dearest currency of all, but it was not what Martin expected. Donald's diary—set on a barrel on the station platform and surrounded by colored stones in a kind of shrine—described how his father had always been disgusted by his country's treatment of the Ethiopian tribe. Chattel slavery was an affront to God, and slavers an aspect of Satan. Donald had provided aid to slaves his whole life, whenever possible and with whatever means at hand, ever since he was a small boy and misdirected some bounty men who badgered him over a runaway.

His many work trips during Martin's childhood were in fact abolitionist missions. Midnight meetings, riverbank chicanery, intrigue at the crossroads. It was ironic that given his communication difficulties, Donald functioned as a human telegraph, relaying messages up and down the coast. The U.G.R.R. (as he referred to it in his notes) operated no spurs or stops in North Carolina until Donald made it his mission. Working this far south was suicide, everyone said. He added the nook to the attic nonetheless, and if the false ceiling was not without seams, it kept his charges aloft. By the time a loose shingle undid him, Donald had conveyed a dozen souls to the Free States.

Martin helped a considerably smaller number. Both he and Cora decided his skittish personality had not helped them during the close call the previous night, when in another bad omen the regulators knocked on the front door.

IT had been just after dark and the park was full of those afraid to go home. Cora wondered what waited for them that they lingered so purposefully, the same people week after week. The fast-walking man who sat on the fountain's rim, dragging his fingers through his wispy hair. The slovenly, wide-hipped lady who always wore a black bonnet and muttered to herself. They weren't here to drink the night air or sneak a kiss. These people slumped on their distracted circuits, looking this way and that, never in front. As if to avoid the eyes of all the ghosts, the dead ones who had built their town. Colored labor had erected every house on the park, laid the stones in the fountain and the paving of the walkways. Hammered the stage where the night riders performed their grotesque pageants and the wheeled platform that delivered the doomed men and women to the air. The only thing colored folks hadn't built was the tree. God had made that, for the town to bend to evil ends.

No wonder the whites wandered the park in the growing darkness, Cora thought, her forehead pressed into the wood. They were ghosts themselves, caught between two worlds: the reality of their crimes, and the hereafter denied them for those crimes.

Cora was informed of the night riders' rounds by the ripple passing through the park. The evening crowd turned to gawk at a house on the opposite side. A young girl in pigtails let a trio of regulators inside her home. Cora remembered the girl's father had trouble with their porch steps. She hadn't seen him for weeks. The girl clutched her robe to her neck and closed the door behind them. Two night riders, tall and densely proportioned, idled on the porch smoking their pipes with complacent sloth.

The door opened half an hour later and the team huddled on the sidewalk in a lantern's circle, consulting a ledger. They crossed the park, eventually stepping beyond the spy hole's domain. Cora had closed her eyes when their loud rapping on the front door shocked her. They stood directly beneath.

The next minutes moved with appalling slowness. Cora huddled in a corner, making herself small behind the final rafter. Sounds furnished details of the action below. Ethel greeted the night riders warmly; anyone who knew her would be certain she was hiding something. Martin made a quick tour of the attic to make sure nothing was amiss, and then joined everyone downstairs.

Martin and Ethel answered their questions quickly as they showed the group around. It was just the two of them. Their daughter lived elsewhere. (The night riders searched the kitchen and parlor.) The maid Fiona had a key but no one else had access to the house. (Up the stairs.) They had been visited by no strangers, heard no strange noises, noted nothing out of the ordinary. (They searched the two bedrooms.) Nothing was missing. There was no cellar—surely they knew by now that the park houses did not have cellars. Martin had been in the attic that very afternoon and noticed nothing amiss.

"Do you mind if we go up?" The voice was gruff and low. Cora assigned it to the shorter night rider, the one with the beard.

Their footfalls were loud on the attic stairs. They navigated around the junk. One of them spoke, startling Cora—his head was inches below her. She kept her breath close. The men were sharks moving their snouts beneath a ship, looking for the food they sensed was close. Only thin planks separated hunter and prey.

"We don't go up here that much since the raccoons made a nest," Martin said.

"You can smell their mess," the other night rider said.

The regulators departed. Martin skipped his midnight rounds in the attic, scared that they were in the teeth of an elaborate trap. Cora in her comfortable darkness patted the sturdy wall: It had kept her safe.

They had survived the chamber pot and the night riders. Martin's final bad omen happened that morning: A mob strung up a husband and wife who hid two colored boys in their barn. Their daughter turned them in, jealous of the attention. Despite their youth, the colored boys joined the grisly gallery on the Freedom Trail. One of Ethel's neighbors told her about it in the market and Ethel fainted dead away, pitching into a row of preserves.

Home searches were on the rise. "They've been so successful rounding up people that now they have to work hard to meet their quotas," Martin said.

Cora offered that perhaps it was good the house had been searched—it would be some time before they returned. More time for the railroad to reach out, or for another opportunity to present itself.

Martin always fidgeted when Cora raised the idea of initiative.

He cradled one of his childhood toys in his hands, a wooden duck. He'd worried the paint from it these last months. "Or it means the roads will be twice as hard to pass," he said. "The boys'll be hungry for a souvenir." His face lit up. "Ravening—I think it means very hungry."

Cora had been feeling poorly all day. She said good night and climbed into her nook. For all the close calls, she was in the same place she had been in for months: becalmed. Between departure and arrival, in transit like the passenger she'd been ever since she ran. Once the wind picked up she would be moving again, but for now there was only the blank and endless sea.

What a world it is, Cora thought, that makes a living prison into your only haven. Was she out of bondage or in its web: how to describe the status of a runaway? Freedom was a thing that shifted as you looked at it, the way a forest is dense with trees up close but from outside, from the empty meadow, you see its true limits. Being free had nothing to do with chains or how much space you had. On the plantation, she was not free, but she moved unrestricted on its acres, tasting the air and tracing the summer stars. The place was big in its smallness. Here, she was free of her master but slunk around a warren so tiny she couldn't stand.

Cora hadn't left the top floors of the house in months but her perspective roved widely. North Carolina had its Justice Hill, and she had hers. Looking down over the universe of the park, she saw the town drift where it wanted, washed by sunlight on a stone bench, cooled in the shadows of the hanging tree. But they were prisoners like she was, shackled to fear. Martin and Ethel were terrified of the watchful eyes behind every darkened window. The town huddled together on Friday nights in the hope their numbers warded off the things in the dark: the rising black tribe; the enemy who concocts accusations; the child who undertakes a magnificent revenge for a scolding and brings the house down around them. Better to hide in attics than to confront what lurked behind the faces of neighbors, friends, and family.

The park sustained them, the green harbor they preserved as the town extended itself outward, block by block and house by house. Cora thought of her garden back on Randall, the plot she cherished. Now she saw it for the joke it was—a tiny square of dirt that had convinced her she owned something. It was hers like the cotton she seeded, weeded, and picked was hers. Her plot was a shadow of something that lived elsewhere, out of sight. The way poor Michael reciting the Declaration of Independence was an echo of something that existed elsewhere. Now that she had run away and seen a bit of the country, Cora wasn't sure the document described anything real at all. America was a ghost in the darkness, like her.

THAT night she took ill. Spasms in her belly woke her. In her dizziness, the nook lurched and rocked. She lost the contents of her stomach in the small space, and control of her bowels. Heat besieged the tiny room, firing the air and inside her skin. Somehow she made it to morning's light and the lifting of the veil. The park was still there; in the night she had dreamed she was at sea and chained belowdecks. Next to her was another captive, and another, hundreds of them crying in terror. The ship bucked on swells, dove and slammed into anvils of water. She heard footsteps on the stairs, the sound of the hatch scraping, and she closed her eyes.

Cora woke in a white room, a soft mattress cupping her body. The window delivered more than a stingy puncture of sunlight. Park noise was her clock: It was late afternoon.

Ethel sat in the corner of her husband's childhood bedroom. Her knitting piled in her lap, she stared at Cora. She felt her patient's forehead. "Better," Ethel said. She poured a glass of water, then brought a bowl of beef broth.

Ethel's attitude had softened during Cora's delirium. The runaway made so much noise moaning in the night and was so ill when they lowered her from the attic nook that they were obliged to let Fiona go for a few days. Martin had the Venezuelan pox, they told the Irish girl, caught from a tainted bag of feed, and the doctor forbid anyone to enter the house until it had run its course. He'd read about one such quarantine in a magazine, the first excuse that came into his head. They paid the girl her wages for the week. Fiona tucked the money into her purse and asked no more questions.

It was Martin's turn to absent himself while Ethel assumed responsibility for their guest, nursing Cora through two days of fever and convulsions. The couple had made few friends during their time in the state, making it easier to abstain from the life of town. While Cora twisted in her delirium, Ethel read from the Bible to speed her recuperation. The woman's voice entered her dreams. So stern the night Cora emerged from the mine, it now contained a quality of tenderness. She dreamed the woman kissed her forehead, motherly. Cora listened to her stories, drifting. The ark delivered the worthy, bringing them to the other side of the catastrophe. The wilderness stretched for forty years before others found their promised land.

The afternoon stretched the shadows like taffy and the park entered its period of diminished popularity as supper approached. Ethel sat in the rocking chair, smiled, and looked through the Scripture, trying to find an appropriate section.

Now that she was awake and could speak for herself, Cora told her host that the verses were unnecessary.

Ethel's mouth formed a line. She closed the book, one thin finger holding her place. "We are all in need of our Savior's grace," Ethel said. "It wouldn't be very Christian of me to let a heathen into my house, and not share His word."

"It has been shared," Cora said.

It had been Ethel's childhood Bible that Martin gave to Cora, smudged and stained by her fingers. Ethel quizzed Cora, dubious as to how much their guest could read and understand. To be sure, Cora was not a natural believer, and her education had been terminated sooner than she wished. In the attic she had struggled with the words, pressed on, doubled back to difficult verses. The contradictions vexed her, even half-understood ones.

"I don't get where it says, He that stealeth a man and sells him, shall be put to death," Cora said. "But then later it says, Slaves should be submissive to their masters in everything—and be well-pleasing." Either it was a sin to keep another as property, or it had God's own blessing. But to be well-pleasing in addition? A slaver must have snuck into the printing office and put that in there.

"It means what it says," Ethel said. "It means that a Hebrew may not enslave a Hebrew. But the sons of Ham are not of that tribe. They were cursed, with black skin and tails. Where the Scripture condemns slavery, it is not speaking of negro slavery at all."

"I have black skin, but I don't have a tail. As far as I know—I never thought to look," Cora said. "Slavery is a curse, though, that much is true." Slavery is a sin when whites were put to the yoke, but not the African. All men are created equal, unless we decide you are not a man.

Under the Georgia sun, Connelly had recited verses while scourging field hands for infractions. "Niggers, obey your earthly masters in everything and do it not only when their eye is on you and to win their favor but with sincerity of heart and reverence for the Lord." The slash of the cat-o'-nine-tails punctuating every syllable, and a wail from the victim. Cora remembered other passages on slavery in the Good Book and shared them with her host. Ethel said she didn't wake up that morning to get into a theological argument.

Cora enjoyed the woman's company and frowned when she left. For her part, Cora blamed the people who wrote it down.

People always got things wrong, on purpose as much as by accident. The next morning Cora asked for the almanacs.

They were obsolete, last year's weather, but Cora adored the old almanacs for containing the entire world. They didn't need people to say what they meant. The tables and facts couldn't be shaped into what they were not. The vignettes and parodies between the lunar tables and weather reports—about cranky old widows and simple darkies—confused her as much as the moral lessons in the holy book. Both described human behavior beyond her ken. What did she know, or need to know, of fancy wedding manners, or moving a herd of lambs through the desert? One day she might use the almanac's instructions, at least. Odes to the Atmosphere, Odes to the Cocoa-Tree of the South Sea Islands. She hadn't heard of odes or atmospheres before, but as she worked through the pages, these creatures took up residence in her mind. Should she ever own boots, she now knew the trick of tallow and wax that extended their use. If one of her chickens got the snuffles one day, rubbing asafetida in butter on their nostrils would set them straight.

Martin's father had needed the almanacs to plan for the full moon—the books held prayers for runaways. The moon grew fat and thin, there were solstices, first frosts, and spring rains. All these things proceeded without the interference of men. She tried to imagine what the tide looked like, coming in and going out, nipping at the sand like a little dog, heedless of people and their machinations. Her strength returned.

On her own, she couldn't understand all the words. Cora asked Ethel, "Can you read some to me?"

Ethel growled. But she opened an almanac where the spine broke and in compromise with herself used the same cadences she used for the Bible. "'Transplanting the Evergreens. It seems not very material whether evergreen trees are transplanted in April, May, or June ...'"

When Friday arrived, Cora was much improved. Fiona was set to come back on Monday. They agreed that in the morning Cora should return to the nook. Martin and Ethel would invite a neighbor or two for cake to dispel any gossip or speculation. Martin practiced a wan demeanor. Perhaps even host someone for the Friday Festival. Their porch had a perfect view.

That evening Ethel let Cora stay in the extra bedroom, provided she kept the room dark and stayed away from the window. Cora had no intention of watching the weekly spectacle but looked forward to one last stretch in the bed. In the end, Martin and Ethel thought better of inviting people over, so the only guests were the uninvited ones that stepped out of the crowd at the start of the coon show.

The regulators wanted to search the house.

The performance stopped, the town buzzing at the commotion at the side of the park. Ethel tried to stall the night riders. They pushed past her and Martin. Cora started for the stairs but they complained reliably, warning her so often these last few months, that she knew she wouldn't be able to make it. She crawled under Martin's old bed and that's where they found her, snatching her ankles like irons and dragging her out. They tossed her down the stairs. She jammed her shoulder into the banister at the bottom. Her ears rang.

She laid eyes on Martin and Ethel's porch for the first time. It was the stage for her capture, a second bandstand for the town's amusement as she lay on the planks at the feet of four regulators in their white and black uniforms. Another four restrained Martin and Ethel. One more man stood on the porch, dressed in a worsted plaid vest and gray trousers. He was one of the tallest men Cora had ever seen, solidly built with an arresting gaze. He surveyed the scene and smiled at a private joke.

The town filled the sidewalk and the street, jostling each other for a view of this new entertainment. A young redheaded girl pushed through. "Venezuelan pox! I told you they had someone up there!"

So here was Fiona, finally. Cora propped herself up for a look at the girl she knew so well but had never seen.

"You'll get your reward," the night rider with the beard said. He'd been to the house on the previous search.

"You say, you lummox," Fiona said. "You said you checked the attic last time, but you didn't, did you?" She turned to the town to establish witnesses for her claim. "You all see—it's my reward. All that food missing?" Fiona kicked Cora lightly with her foot. "She'd make a big roast and then the next day it was gone. Who was eating all that food? Always looking up at the ceiling. What were they looking at?"

She was so young, Cora thought. Her face was a round and

freckled apple, but there was hardness in her eyes. It was difficult to believe the grunts and cusses she'd heard over the months had come out of that little mouth, but the eyes were proof enough.

"We treated you nice," Martin said.

"You have an awful queer way, both of you," Fiona said. "And you deserve whatever you get."

The town had seen justice served too many times to count, but the rendering of the verdict was a new experience. It made them uneasy. Were they a jury now, in addition to the gallery? They looked at each other for cues. An old-timer made his hand into a cone and hollered nonsense through it. A half-eaten apple hit Cora's stomach. On the bandstand, the coon-show players stood with their disheveled hats in their hands, deflated.

Jamison appeared, rubbing his forehead with a red handkerchief. Cora had not seen him since the first night, but she had heard every speech of the Friday-night finales. Every joke and grandiose claim, the appeals to race and statehood, and then the order to kill the sacrifice. The interruption in the proceedings confounding him. Absent its usual bluster, Jamison's voice squeaked. "This is something," he said. "Aren't you Donald's son?"

Martin nodded, his soft body quivering with quiet sobs.

"I know your daddy would be ashamed," Jamison said.

"I had no idea what he was up to," Ethel said. She tugged against the night riders who gripped her tight. "He did it himself! I didn't know anything!"

Martin looked away. From the people on the porch, from the

town. He turned his face north toward Virginia, where he had been free of his hometown for a time.

Jamison gestured and the night riders pulled Martin and Ethel to the park. The planter looked Cora over. "A nice treat," Jamison said. Their scheduled victim was in the wings somewhere. "Should we do both?"

The tall man said, "This one is mine. I've made it clear."

Jamison's expression curdled. He was not accustomed to ignorance of his status. He asked for the stranger's name.

"Ridgeway," the man said. "Slave catcher. I go here, I go there. I've been after this one for a long time. Your judge knows all about me."

"You can't just come in here, muscling about." Jamison was aware that his usual audience, milling outside the property, observed him with undefined expectations. At the new tremor in his words two night riders, young bucks both, stepped forward to crowd Ridgeway.

Ridgeway exhibited no bother over the display. "You all have your local customs going on here—I get that. Having your fun." He pronounced *fun* like a temperance preacher. "But it doesn't belong to you. The Fugitive Slave Law says I have a right to return this property to its owner. That's what I aim to do."

Cora whimpered and felt her head. She was dizzy, like she'd been after Terrance struck her. This man was going to return her to him.

The night rider who threw Cora down the stairs cleared his throat. He explained to Jamison that the slave catcher had led them to the house. The man had visited Judge Tennyson that afternoon and made an official request, although the judge had been enjoying his customary Friday whiskey and might not remember. No one was keen on executing the raid during the festival, but Ridgeway had insisted.

Ridgeway spat tobacco juice on the sidewalk, at the feet of some onlookers. "You can keep the reward," he told Fiona. He bent slightly and lifted Cora by her arm. "You don't have to be afraid, Cora. You're going home."

A little colored boy, about ten years old, drove a wagon up the street through the crowd, shouting at the two horses. On any other occasion the sight of him in his tailored black suit and stovepipe hat would have been a cause of bewilderment. After the dramatic capture of the sympathizers and the runaway, his appearance nudged the night into the realm of the fantastical. More than one person thought what had just transpired was a new wrinkle in the Friday entertainment, a performance arranged to counter the monotony of the weekly skits and lynchings, which, to be honest, had grown predictable.

At the foot of the porch, Fiona held forth to a group of girls from Irishtown. "A girl's got to look after her interests if she's going to get ahead in this country," she explained.

Ridgeway rode with another man in addition to the boy, a tall white man with long brown hair and a necklace of human ears around his neck. His associate shackled Cora's ankles, and then ran the chains through a ring in the floor of the wagon. She arranged herself on the bench, her head pulsing in agony with every heartbeat. As they pulled away, she saw Martin and Ethel. They had been tied to the hanging tree. They sobbed and heaved at their bonds. Mayor ran in mad circles at their feet. A blond girl picked up a rock and threw it at Ethel, hitting her in the face. A segment of the town laughed at Ethel's piteous shrieks. Two more children picked up rocks and threw them at the couple. Mayor yipped and jumped as more people bent to the ground. They raised their arms. The town moved in and then Cora couldn't see them anymore.

Ethel

EVER since she saw a woodcut of a missionary surrounded by jungle natives, Ethel thought it would be spiritually fulfilling to serve the Lord in dark Africa, delivering savages to the light. She dreamed of the ship that would take her, a magnificent schooner with sails like angel wings, cutting across the violent sea. The perilous journey into the interior, up rivers, wending mountain passes, and the dangers escaped: lions, serpents, man-killing plants, duplicitous guides. And then the village, where the natives receive her as an emissary of the Lord, an instrument of civilization. In gratitude the niggers lift her to the sky, praising her name: Ethel, Ethel.

She was eight years old. Her father's newspapers contained tales of explorers, unknown lands, pygmy peoples. The nearest she could get to the image in the newspaper was playing missionary and native with Jasmine. Jasmine was like a sister to her. The game never lasted long before they switched to husband and wife, practicing kisses and arguments in the cellar of Ethel's house. Given the color of their skins, there was never any doubt over their roles in either game, Ethel's habit of rubbing soot onto her face notwithstanding. Her face blackened, she practiced expressions of amazement and wonder in front of the mirror so she'd know what to expect when she met her heathens.

Jasmine lived in the upstairs room with her mother, Felice. The Delany family owned Felice's mother, and when little Edgar Delany turned ten, he received Felice as a present. Now that he was a man, Edgar recognized that Felice was a miracle, tending to the affairs of his house as if she were born to it. He recounted her darky wisdom as a matter of routine, sharing her parables about human nature with guests whenever she disappeared into the kitchen so that when she returned their faces glowed with affection and jealousy. He gave her passes to visit the Parker plantation every New Year's Day feast; Felice's sister was a washwoman there. Jasmine was born nine months after one such visit, and now the Delanys owned two slaves.

Ethel thought that a slave was someone who lived in your house like family but was not family. Her father explained the origin of the negro to disabuse her of this colorful idea. Some maintained that the negro was the remnant of a race of giants who had ruled the earth in an ancient time, but Edgar Delany knew they were descendants of cursed, black Ham, who had survived the Flood by clinging to the peaks of a mountain in Africa. Ethel thought that if they were cursed, they required Christian guidance all the more.

On her eighth birthday, Ethel's father forbid her to play with Jasmine so as not to pervert the natural state of relations between the races. Ethel did not make friends easily, even then. She sobbed and stomped for days; Jasmine was more adaptable.

Jasmine assumed simple duties around the household and took over her mother's position when Felice's heart seized and she fell mute and paralyzed. Felice lingered for months, her mouth open and pink, eyes foggy, until Ethel's father had her removed. Ethel observed no disturbance in her old playmate's face when they loaded her mother into the cart. By then the two did not speak outside of household matters.

The house had been built fifty years before and the stairs creaked. A whisper in one room carried into the next two. Most nights after supper and prayers, Ethel heard her father going up the crooked stairs, guided by the bobbing light of the candle. Sometimes she sneaked to her bedroom door and caught a glimpse of his white bedclothes disappearing around the corner.

"Where are you going, Father?" she asked one night. Felice had been gone two years. Jasmine was fourteen.

"Going upstairs," he said, and both experienced a strange relief now that they had a term for his nocturnal visits. He was going upstairs—where else did the stairs lead? Her father had given one explanation for the separation of the races in fratricidal punishment. His nighttime trips elaborated on the arrangement. Whites lived downstairs and blacks lived upstairs, and to bridge that separation was to heal a biblical wound.

Her mother held a low opinion about her husband going upstairs but was not without resources. When their family sold Jasmine to the coppersmith on the other side of town, Ethel knew it was her mother's doing. There was no more going upstairs when the new slave took residence. Nancy was a grandmother, slow in her steps and half blind. Now it was her wheezing that penetrated the walls, not footsteps and squeals. The house had not been so clean and orderly since Felice; Jasmine had been efficient but distracted. Jasmine's new home was across the way in colored town. Everyone whispered that the child had his father's eyes.

One day over lunch Ethel announced that when she was old enough, she intended to spread the Christian word to African primitives. Her parents scoffed. It was not something that good young women from Virginia did. If you want to help savages, her father said, teach school. The brain of a five-year-old is more savage and unruly than the oldest jungle darky, he said. Her course was set. Ethel filled in for the regular teacher when she was under the weather. Little white children were primitive in their own way, chirping and undeveloped, but it wasn't the same. Her thoughts of the jungle and a ring of dark admirers remained in her private preserve.

Resentment was the hinge of her personality. The young women in her circle comported themselves in a foreign ritual, undecipherable. She had little use for boys and, later, men. When Martin appeared, introduced by one of her cousins who worked at the shipping company, she had tired of the gossip and long relinquished an interest in happiness. A panting badger, Martin wore her down. The game of husband and wife was even less fun than she supposed. Jane, at least, turned out to be an unexpected mercy, a tidy bouquet in her arms, even if conception proved yet another humiliation. Over the years life on Orchard Street passed with a tedium that eventually congealed into comfort. She pretended not to see Jasmine when they passed on the street, especially when her former playmate was in the company of her son. His face was a dark mirror.

Then Martin was summoned to North Carolina. He arranged Donald's funeral on the hottest day of the year; they thought she fainted from sadness when it was just the barbaric humidity. Once they got a taker for the feed shop, they were done, he assured her. The place was backward. If it wasn't the heat, it was the flies; if not the mice, then the people. At least in Virginia, lynch mobs maintained a pretext of spontaneity. They didn't string up people practically on your front lawn, the same time every week, like church. North Carolina was to be a brief interlude, or so she thought until she came across the nigger in her kitchen.

George had dropped out of the attic for some food, the lone slave Martin helped before the girl arrived. It was a week before the race laws went into effect and violence against the colored population was on the rise in rehearsal. A note on their doorstep had directed Martin to the mica mine, he told her. George waited for him, hungry and irritated. The tobacco picker thumped around the attic for a week before a railroad agent took him on the next leg, boxing him up in a crate and shoving the thing through the front door. Ethel was livid, then despairing—George acted as Donald's executor, illuminating Martin's secret inheritance. He'd lost three fingers on his hand cutting cane.

Slavery as a moral issue never interested Ethel. If God had not meant for Africans to be enslaved, they wouldn't be in chains. She did, however, have firm ideas about not getting killed for other people's high-minded ideas. She and Martin argued over the underground railroad as they hadn't argued in a long time, and that was before the murderous fine print of the race laws manifested itself. Through Cora—that termite in the attic— Donald reached from beyond the grave to punish her for her joke those many years before. When their families met for the first time, Ethel made a remark about Donald's simple country suit. She was trying to call attention to the two families' different ideas of proper attire, to get it out of the way so they could all enjoy the meal Ethel had spent so much time planning. But Donald had never forgiven her, she told Martin, she was sure of it, and now they were going to swing from the branches of the tree right outside their front door.

When Martin went upstairs to help the girl it was not in the same way her father had gone upstairs, but both men came down transformed. They reached across the biblical rift for a selfish purpose.

If they could, why not her?

Everything had been denied Ethel her whole life. To mission, to help. To give love in the way she wanted. When the girl got sick, the moment Ethel awaited for so long had finally arrived. In the end she had not gone to Africa, Africa had come to her. Ethel went upstairs, as her father had done, to confront the stranger who lived in her house as family. The girl lay on the sheets, curved like a primeval river. She cleaned the girl, washing her filth from her. She kissed the girl on her forehead and neck in her restless slumber with two kinds of feeling mixed up in those kisses. She gave her the Holy Word.

A savage to call her own, at last.

Tennessee

25 DOLLARS REWARD

RAN AWAY from the subscriber on the 6th of February last, his Negro Girl PEGGY. She is about 16 years of age, and is a bright mulatto, about the ordinary height, with straight hair and tolerable good features—she has a ragged scar on her neck occasioned by a burn. She will no doubt attempt to pass for a free girl, and it is likely she has obtained a free pass. She has a down look when spoken to, and not remarkably intelligent. She speaks quick, with a shrill voice.

JOHN DARK.
CHATHAM COUNTY, MAY 17.

"JESUS, carry me home, home to that land . . ."

Jasper wouldn't stop singing. Ridgeway shouted from the head of their little caravan for him to shut his mouth, and sometimes they halted so Boseman could climb into the wagon and clout the runaway on the head. Jasper sucked the scars on his fingers for a short interval, then resumed his crooning. Quietly at first so that only Cora could hear. But soon he'd be singing again, to his lost family, to his god, to everyone they passed on the trail. He'd have to be disciplined again.

Cora recognized some of the hymns. She suspected he made up many of them; the rhymes were crooked. She wouldn't have minded it so much if Jasper had a better voice, but Jesus had not blessed him in that department. Or with looks—he had a lopsided frog face and oddly thin arms for a field hand—or with luck. Luck least of all.

He and Cora had that in common.

They picked up Jasper three days out of North Carolina. Jasper was a delivery. He absconded from the Florida cane fields and made it to Tennessee before a tinker caught him stealing food from his pantry. After a few weeks the deputy located his owner, but the tinker had no means of transport. Ridgeway and Boseman were drinking in a tavern around the corner from the jail while little Homer waited with Cora and the wagon. The town clerk approached the famous slave catcher, brokered an arrangement, and Ridgeway now had the nigger chained in the wagon. He hadn't reckoned the man for a songbird.

The rain tapped on the canopy. Cora enjoyed the breeze and then felt ashamed for enjoying something. They stopped to eat when the rain let up. Boseman slapped Jasper, chuckled, and unchained the two fugitives from the wagon floor. He offered his customary vulgar promise as he knelt before Cora, sniffing. Jasper's and Cora's wrists and ankles remained manacled. It was the longest she had ever been in chains.

Crows glided over. The world was scorched and harrowed as far as they could see, a sea of ash and char from the flat planes of the fields up to the hills and mountains. Black trees tilted, stunted black arms pointing as if to a distant place untouched by flame. They rode past the blackened bones of houses and barns without number, chimneys sticking up like grave markers, the husked stone walls of ravaged mills and granaries. Scorched fences marked where cattle had grazed; it was not possible the animals survived.

After two days of riding through it, they were covered in black grime. Ridgeway said it made him feel at home, the blacksmith's son.

This is what Cora saw: Nowhere to hide. No refuge between those black stalks, even if she weren't fettered. Even if she had an opportunity.

An old white man in a gray coat trotted by on a dun horse. Like the other travelers they passed on the black road, he slowed in curiosity. Two adult slaves were common enough. But the colored boy in the black suit driving the wagon and his queer smile discomfited strangers. The younger white man with the red derby wore a necklace adorned with pieces of shriveled leather. When they figured out these were human ears, he bared a line of intermittent teeth browned by tobacco. The older white man in command discouraged all conversation with his glowering. The traveler moved on, around the bend where the road limped between the denuded hills.

Homer unfolded a moth-eaten quilt for them to sit on and distributed their portions on tin plates. The slave catcher allowed his prisoners an equal share of the food, a custom dating to his earliest days in the job. It reduced complaints and he billed the client. At the edge of the blackened field they ate the salt pork and the beans Boseman had prepared, the dry flies screeching in waves.

Rain agitated the smell of the fire, making the air bitter. Smoke flavored every bite of food, each sip of water. Jasper sang, "Jump up, the redeemer said! Jump up, jump up if you want to see His face!"

"Hallelujah!" Boseman shouted. "Fat little Jesus baby!" His words echoed and he did a dance, splashing dark water.

"He's not eating," Cora said. Jasper had foregone the last few meals, screwing his mouth shut and crossing his arms.

"Then it doesn't eat," Ridgeway said. He waited for her to say something, having grown used to her chirping at his remarks. They were on to each other. She kept silent to interrupt their pattern.

Homer scampered over and gobbled down Jasper's portion. He sensed Cora staring at him and grinned without looking up.

The driver of the wagon was an odd little imp. Ten years old, Chester's age, but imbued with the melancholy grace of an elderly house slave, the sum of practiced gestures. He was fastidious about his fine black suit and stovepipe hat, extracting lint from the fabric and glaring at it as if it were a poison spider before flicking it. Homer rarely spoke apart from his hectoring of the horses. Of racial affinity or sympathy, he gave no indication. Cora and Jasper might as well have been invisible most of the time, smaller than lint.

Homer's duties encompassed driving the team, sundry maintenance, and what Ridgeway termed "bookkeeping." Homer maintained the business accounts and recorded Ridgeway's stories in a small notebook he kept in his coat pocket. What made this or that utterance from the slave catcher worthy of inclusion, Cora could not discern. The boy preserved worldly truism and matter-of-fact observations about the weather with equal zeal.

Prompted by Cora one night, Ridgeway maintained that he'd never owned a slave in his life, save for the fourteen hours Homer was his property. Why not? she asked. "What for?" he said. Ridgeway was riding through the outskirts of Atlanta— he'd just delivered a husband and wife to their owner, all the way from New York—when he came upon a butcher trying to square a gambling debt. His wife's family had given them the boy's mother as a wedding gift. The butcher had sold her during his previous stretch of bad luck. Now it was the boy's turn. He painted a crude sign to hang around the boy's neck advertising the offer.

The boy's strange sensibility moved Ridgeway. Homer's shining eyes, set in his round pudgy face, were at once feral and serene. A kindred spirit. Ridgeway bought him for five dollars and drew up emancipation papers the next day. Homer remained at his side despite Ridgeway's halfhearted attempts to shoo him away. The butcher had held no strong opinions on the subject of colored education and had permitted the boy to study with the children of some freemen. Out of boredom, Ridgeway helped him with his letters. Homer pretended he was of Italian extraction when it suited him and let his questioners sit with their bewilderment. His unconventional attire evolved over time; his disposition remained unchanged.

"If he's free, why don't he go?"

"Where?" Ridgeway asked. "He's seen enough to know a black boy has no future, free papers or no. Not in this country. Some disreputable character would snatch him and put him on the block lickety-split. With me, he can learn about the world. Find purpose."

Each night, with meticulous care, Homer opened his satchel and removed a set of manacles. He locked himself to the driver's seat, put the key in his pocket, and closed his eyes.

Ridgeway caught Cora looking. "He says it's the only way he can sleep."

Homer snored like a rich old man every night.

BOSEMAN, for his part, had been riding with Ridgeway for three years. He was a rambler out of South Carolina and found his way to slave catching after a hardscrabble sequence: dockhand, collection agent, gravedigger. Boseman was not the most intelligent fellow but had a knack for anticipating Ridgeway's wishes in a manner equal parts indispensable and eerie. Ridgeway's gang numbered five when Boseman joined, but his employees drifted off one by one. The reason was not immediately clear to Cora.

The previous owner of the ear necklace had been an Indian named Strong. Strong had promoted himself as a tracker, but the only creature he sniffed out reliably was whiskey. Boseman won the accessory in a wrestling contest, and when Strong disputed the terms of their match, Boseman clobbered the red man with a shovel. Strong lost his hearing and ditched the gang to work in a tannery in Canada, or so the rumor went. Even though the ears were dried and shriveled, they drew flies when it was hot. Boseman loved his souvenir, however, and the revulsion on a new client's face was too delectable. The flies hadn't harassed the Indian when he owned it, as Ridgeway reminded him from time to time.

Boseman stared at the hills between bites and had an uncharacteristically wistful air. He walked off to urinate and when he came back said, "My daddy passed through here, I think. He said it was forest then. When he came back, it had all been cleared by settlers."

"Now it's doubly cleared," Ridgeway responded. "It's true what you say. This road was a horse path. Next time you need to make a road, Boseman, make sure you have ten thousand starving Cherokee on hand to clear it for you. Saves time."

"Where did they go?" Cora asked. After her nights with Martin, she had a sense of when white men were on the brink of a story. It gave her time to consider her options.

Ridgeway was an ardent reader of gazettes. The fugitive bulletins made them a requirement in his line of work—Homer maintained a thorough collection—and current affairs generally upheld his theories about society and the human animal. The type of individuals in his employ had made him accustomed to explaining the most elementary facts and history. He could hardly expect a slave girl to know the significance of their environs.

They sat on what was once Cherokee land, he said, the land of their red fathers, until the president decided otherwise and ordered them removed. Settlers needed the land, and if the Indians hadn't learned by then that the white man's treaties were entirely worthless, Ridgeway said, they deserved what they got. Some of his friends had been with the army at that time. They rounded up the Indians in camps, the women and children and whatever they could carry on their backs, and marched them west of the Mississippi. The Trail of Tears and Death, as one Cherokee sage put it later, not without cause, not without that Indian flair for rhetoric. Disease and malnutrition, not to mention the biting winter that year, which Ridgeway himself remembered without fondness, claimed thousands. When they got to Oklahoma there were still more white people waiting for them, squatting on the land the Indians had been promised in the latest worthless treaty. Slow learners, the bunch. But here they were on this road today. The trip to Missouri was much more comfortable than it had been previously, tamped by little red feet.

"Progress," Ridgeway said. "My cousin got lucky and won some Indian land in the lottery, in the north part of Tennessee. Grows corn."

Cora cocked her head at the desolation. "Lucky," she said.

On their way in, Ridgeway told them that a lightning strike must have started the fire. The smoke filled the sky for hundreds of miles, tinting the sunset into gorgeous contusions of crimson and purple. This was Tennessee announcing itself: fantastic beasts twisting in a volcano. For the first time, she crossed into another state without using the underground railroad. The tunnels had protected her. The station master Lumbly had said that each state was a state of possibility, with its own customs. The red sky made her dread the rules of this next territory. As they rode toward the smoke, the sunsets inspired Jasper to share a suite of hymns whose central theme was the wrath of God and the mortifications awaiting the wicked. Boseman made frequent trips to the wagon.

The town at the edge of the fire line was overrun with escapees. "Runaways," Cora declared and Homer turned in his seat to wink. The white families swarmed in a camp off the main street, inconsolable and abject, the meager possessions they were able to save piled around their feet. Figures staggered through the street with demented expressions, wild-eyed, their clothes singed, rags tied around burns. Cora was well-accustomed to the screams of colored babies in torment, hungry, in pain, confused by the mania of those charged to protect them. Hearing the screams of so many little white babies was new. Her sympathies lay with the colored babies.

Empty shelves greeted Ridgeway and Boseman in the general store. The shopkeeper told Ridgeway that homesteaders had started the fire while trying to clear some scrub. The fire escaped them and ravaged the land with bottomless hunger until the rains came finally. Three million acres, the shopkeeper said. The government promised relief but no one could say when it would arrive. The biggest disaster in as long as anyone could remember.

The original residents had a more thorough list of wildfires and floods and tornadoes, Cora thought when Ridgeway shared the shopkeeper's words. But they were not here to contribute their knowledge. She didn't know which tribe had called this territory home, but knew it had been Indian land. What land hadn't been theirs? She had never learned history proper, but sometimes one's eyes are teacher enough.

"They must have done something to make God angry," Boseman said.

"Just a spark that got away is all," Ridgeway said.

They lingered by the road after their lunchtime meal, the white men smoking pipes by the horses and reminiscing an escapade. For all his talk of how long he had hunted her, Ridgeway displayed no urgency about delivering Cora to Terrance Randall. Not that she hurried toward that reunion. Cora stutter-stepped into the burned field. She'd learned to walk with irons. It was hard to believe it had taken this long. Cora had always pitied the downcast coffles marching in their pathetic line past the Randall place. Now look at her. The lesson was unclear. In one respect she had been spared an injury for many years. In another, misfortune had merely bided time: There was no escape. Sores puckered on her skin beneath the iron. The white men paid her no mind as she walked to the black trees.

By then she had run a few times. When they stopped for supplies, Boseman was distracted by a funeral procession rounding the corner and she made it a couple of yards before a boy tripped her. They added a neck collar, iron links dropping to her wrists like moss. It gave her the posture of a beggar or praying mantis. She ran when the men stopped to relieve themselves at the side of the trail and made it a little farther that time. She ran once at dusk, by a stream, the water making a promise of movement. The slick stones sent her tumbling into the water, and Ridgeway thrashed her. She stopped running.

THEY seldom spoke the first days after leaving North Carolina. She thought the confrontation with the mob had exhausted them as much as it had exhausted her, but silence was their policy in general—until Jasper came into their midst. Boseman whispered his rude suggestions and Homer turned back from the driver's seat to give her an unsettling grin on his inscrutable schedule, but the slave catcher kept his distance at the head of the line. Occasionally he whistled.

Cora caught on that they were heading west instead of south. She'd never paid attention to the sun's habits before Caesar. He told her it might aid their escape. They stopped in a town one morning, outside a bakery. Cora steeled herself and asked Ridgeway about his plans.

His eyes widened, as if he'd been waiting for her to approach. After this first conversation Ridgeway included her in their plans as if she had a vote. "You were a surprise," he said, "but don't worry, we'll get you home soon enough."

She was correct, he said. They were headed west. A Georgia planter named Hinton had commissioned Ridgeway to return one of his slaves. The negro in question was a wily and resourceful buck who had relatives in one of the colored settlements in Missouri; reliable information confirmed Nelson plied his trade as a trapper, in broad daylight, without concern of retribution. Hinton was a respected farmer with an enviable spread, a cousin of the governor. Regrettably, one of his overseers had gossiped with a slave wench and now Nelson's behavior made his owner an object of ridicule on his own land. Hinton had been grooming the boy to be a boss. He promised Ridgeway a generous bounty, going so far as to present a contract in a pretentious ceremony. An elderly darky served as witness, coughing into his hand the while.

Given Hinton's impatience, the most sensible course was to travel on to Missouri. "Once we have our man," Ridgeway said, "you can be reunited with your master. From what I've seen, he'll prepare a worthy welcome."

Ridgeway didn't hide his disdain for Terrance Randall; the man had what he called an "ornate" imagination when it came to nigger discipline. This much was plain from the moment his gang turned down the road to the big house and saw the three gallows. The young girl was installed in hers, hooked through her ribs by a large metal spike and dangling. The dirt below dark with her blood. The other two gallows stood waiting.

"If I hadn't been detained upstate," Ridgeway said, "I'm sure I'd have scooped up the three of you before the trail got cold. Lovey—was that its name?"

Cora covered her mouth to keep in her scream. She failed. Ridgeway waited ten minutes for her to regain her composure. The townspeople looked at the colored girl laying there collapsed on the ground and stepped over her into the bakery. The smell of the snacks filled the street, sweet and beguiling.

Boseman and Homer waited in the drive while he talked to the master of the house, Ridgeway said. The house had been lively and inviting when the father was alive—yes, he had been there before to search for Cora's mother and come up empty-handed. One minute with Terrance and the cause of the terrible atmosphere was evident. The son was mean, and it was the kind of meanness that infected everything around. The daylight was gray and sluggish from the thunderheads, the house niggers slow and glum.

The newspapers liked to impress the fantasy of the happy plantation and the contented slave who sang and danced and loved Massa. Folks enjoyed that sort of thing and it was politically useful given the combat with the northern states and the antislavery movement. Ridgeway knew that image to be false—he didn't need to dissemble about the business of slavery—but neither was the menace of the Randall plantation the truth. The place was haunted. Who could blame the slaves their sad comportment with that corpse twisting on a hook outside?

Terrance received Ridgeway into the parlor. He was drunk and had not bothered to dress himself, lounging on the sofa in a red robe. It was tragic, Ridgeway said, to see the degeneration that can happen in just one generation, but money does that to a family sometimes. Brings out the impurities. Terrance remembered Ridgeway from his earlier visit, when Mabel disappeared into the swamp, just like this latest trio. He told Ridgeway that his father had been touched that he came in person to apologize for his incompetence.

"I could have slapped the Randall boy twice across the face without losing the contract," Ridgeway said. "But in my mature years I decided to wait until I had you and the other one in hand. Something to look forward to." He assumed from Terrance's eagerness and the size of the bounty that Cora was her master's concubine.

Cora shook her head. She had stopped sobbing and stood now, her trembling under control, hands in fists.

Ridgeway paused. "Something else, then. At any rate, you exert a powerful influence." He resumed the story of his visit to Randall. Terrance briefed the slave catcher on the state of affairs since Lovey's capture. Just that morning his man Connelly had been informed that Caesar frequented the premises of a local shopkeeper—the man sold the nigger boy's woodwork, supposedly. Perhaps the slave catcher might visit this Mr. Fletcher and see what developed. Terrance wanted the girl alive but didn't care how the other one came back. Did Ridgeway know that the boy came from Virginia originally?

Ridgeway did not. This was some sort of jousting about his home state. The windows were closed and yet a disagreeable smell had moved into the room.

"That's where he learned his bad habits," Terrance had said. "They're soft up there. You make sure he learns how we do things in Georgia." He wanted the law kept out of it. The pair was wanted for the murder of a white boy and wouldn't make it back once the mob got wind. The bounty accounted for his discretion.

The slave catcher took his leave. The axle of his empty wagon complained, as it did when there was no weight to quiet it. Ridgeway promised himself it would not be empty when he returned. He wasn't going to apologize to another Randall, certainly not that whelp who ran the place now. He heard a sound and turned back to the house. It came from the girl, Lovey. Her arm fluttered. She was not dead after all. "Lingered another half day, from what I heard."

Fletcher's lies collapsed immediately—one of those weak religious specimens—and he relinquished the name of his associate on the railroad, a man named Lumbly. Of Lumbly there was no sign. He never returned after taking Cora and Caesar out of state. "To South Carolina was it?" Ridgeway asked. "Was he also the one who conveyed your mother north?"

Cora kept her tongue. It was not hard to envision Fletcher's fate, and perhaps his wife's as well. At least Lumbly made it out. And they hadn't discovered the tunnel beneath the barn. One day another desperate soul might use that route. To a better outcome, fortune willing.

Ridgeway nodded. "No matter. We have plenty of time to catch each other up. It's a long ride to Missouri." The law had caught up with a station master in southern Virginia, he said, who gave up the name of Martin's father. Donald was dead, but Ridgeway wanted to get a sense of the man's operation if he could, to understand the workings of the larger conspiracy. He hadn't expected to find Cora but had been utterly delighted.

Boseman chained her to the wagon. She knew the sound of the lock now. It hitched for a moment before falling into place. Jasper joined them the next day. His body shivered like that of a beaten dog. Cora tried to engage him, asking after the place he fled, the business of working cane, how he took flight. Jasper responded with hymns and devotions.

—

THAT was four days ago. Now she stood in a black pasture in bad-luck Tennessee, crunching burned wood beneath her feet.

The wind picked up, and the rain. Their stop was over. Homer cleaned after their meal. Ridgeway and Boseman tapped out their pipes and the younger man whistled for her to return. Tennessee hills and mountains rose around Cora like the sides of a black bowl. How awful the flames must have been, how fierce, to make such ruin. We're crawling in a bowl of ashes. What's left when everything worthwhile has been consumed, dark powder for the wind to take.

Boseman slid her chains through the ring in the floor and secured them. Ten rings were bolted to the wagon floor, two rows of five, enough for the occasional big haul. Enough for these two. Jasper claimed his favorite spot on the bench, crooning with vigor, as if he'd just gobbled down a Christmas feast. "When the Savior calls you up, you're going to lay the burden down, lay that burden down."

"Boseman," Ridgeway said softly.

"He's going to look in your soul and see what you done, sinner, He's going to look in your soul and see what you done."

Boseman said, "Oh."

The slave catcher got into the wagon for the first time since he picked up Cora. He held Boseman's pistol in his hand and shot Jasper in the face. The blood and the bone covered the inside of the canopy, splashing Cora's filthy shift.

Ridgeway wiped his face and explained his reasoning. Jasper's reward was fifty dollars, fifteen of that for the tinker who brought the fugitive to jail. Missouri, back east, Georgia—it would be weeks before they delivered the man to his owner. Divide thirty-five dollars by, say, three weeks, minus Boseman's share, and the lost bounty was a very small price to pay for silence and a restful mind.

Homer opened his notebook and checked his boss's figures. "He's right," he said.

⊷⊷ ⚏✦⚏ ⊶⊶

Tennessee proceeded in a series of blights. The blaze had devoured the next two towns on the cindered road. In the morning the remains of a small settlement emerged around a hill, an arrangement of scorched timber and black stonework. First came the stumps of the houses that had once contained the dreams of pioneers, and then the town proper in a line of ruined structures. The town farther along was larger but its rival in destruction. The heart was a broad intersection where ravaged avenues had converged in enterprise, now gone. A baker's oven in the ruins of the shop like a grim totem, human remains bent behind the steel of a jail cell.

Cora couldn't tell what feature of the landscape had persuaded the homesteaders to plant their futures, fertile earth or water or vistas. Everything had been erased. If the survivors returned it would be to confirm the resolution to try again somewhere else, scurrying back east or ever west. No resurrection here.

Then they escaped the wildfire's reach. The birches and wild grasses vibrated with impossible color after their time in the burned land, Edenic and fortifying. In jest, Boseman imitated Jasper's singing, to mark the change in mood; the black scenery had worked on them more than they knew. The robust corn in the fields, already two feet high, pointed to an exuberant harvest; with equal force the ruined territory had advertised reckonings to come.

Ridgeway called for a stop shortly after noon. The slave catcher stiffened as he read aloud the sign at the crossroads. The town up the road was overcome by yellow fever, he said. All travelers warned away. An alternative trail, smaller and uneven, led southwest.

The sign was new, Ridgeway observed. Most likely the sickness had not run its course.

"My two brothers passed of yellow fever," Boseman said. He grew up on the Mississippi, where the fever liked to visit when the weather turned warm. His younger brothers' skin turned jaundiced and waxen, they bled from their eyes and asses and seizures wracked their tiny bodies. Some men took away their corpses in a squeaky wheelbarrow. "It's a miserable death," he said, his jokes taken from him again.

Ridgeway knew the town. The mayor was a corrupt boor, the food turned your guts runny, but he held a good thought for them. Going around would add considerable time to their trip. "The fever comes on the boats," Ridgeway said. From the West Indies, all the way from the dark continent, following in the wake of trade. "It's a human tax on progress."

"Who's the taxman came to collect it?" Boseman said. "I never saw him." His fear made him skittish and petulant. He didn't want to linger, even this crossroads too close to the fever's embrace. Not waiting for Ridgeway's order—or obeying a signal shared only by the slave catcher and the boy secretary—Homer drove the wagon away from the doomed town.

Two more signs along the southwesterly course maintained the warning. The trails feeding into the quarantined towns displayed no sign of the danger ahead. Traveling through the handiwork of the fire for so long made an unseeable menace more terrifying. It was a long time, after dark, before they stopped again. Time enough for Cora to take stock of her journey from Randall and make a thick braid of her misfortunes.

List upon list crowded the ledger of slavery. The names gathered first on the African coast in tens of thousands of manifests. That human cargo. The names of the dead were as important as the names of the living, as every loss from disease and suicide—and the other mishaps labeled as such for accounting purposes—needed to be justified to employers. At the auction block they tallied the souls purchased at each auction, and on the plantations the overseers preserved the names of workers in rows of tight cursive. Every name an asset, breathing capital, profit made flesh.

The peculiar institution made Cora into a maker of lists as well. In her inventory of loss people were not reduced to sums but multiplied by their kindnesses. People she had loved, people who had helped her. The Hob women, Lovey, Martin and Ethel, Fletcher. The ones who disappeared: Caesar and Sam and Lumbly. Jasper was not her responsibility, but the stains of his blood on the wagon and her clothes might as well have represented her own dead.

Tennessee was cursed. Initially she assigned the devastation of Tennessee—the blaze and the disease—to justice. The whites got what they deserved. For enslaving her people, for massacring another race, for stealing the very land itself. Let them burn by flame or fever, let the destruction started here rove acre by acre until the dead have been avenged. But if people received their just portion of misfortune, what had she done to bring her troubles on herself? In another list, Cora marked the decisions that led her to this wagon and its iron rings. There was the boy Chester, and how she had shielded him. The whip was the standard punishment for disobedience. Running away was a transgression so large that the punishment enveloped every generous soul on her brief tour of freedom.

Bouncing on the wagon springs, she smelled the damp earth and the heaving trees. Why had this field escaped while another burned five miles back? Plantation justice was mean and constant, but the world was indiscriminate. Out in the world, the wicked escaped comeuppance and the decent stood in their stead at the whipping tree. Tennessee's disasters were the fruit of indifferent nature, without connection to the crimes of the homesteaders. To how the Cherokee had lived their lives.

Just a spark that got away.

No chains fastened Cora's misfortunes to her character or actions. Her skin was black and this was how the world treated black people. No more, no less. Every state is different, Lumbly said. If Tennessee had a temperament, it took after the dark personality of the world, with a taste for arbitrary punishment.

No one was spared, regardless of the shape of their dreams or the color of their skin.

A young man with curly brown hair, pebbly eyes dark beneath his straw hat, drove a team of workhorses from the west. His cheeks were sunburned a painful red. He intercepted Ridgeway's gang. A big settlement lay ahead, the man said, with a reputation for a rambunctious spirit. Free of yellow fever as of that morning. Ridgeway told the man what lay ahead of him and gave his thanks.

Immediately the traffic on the road resumed, even the animals and insects contributing activity. The four travelers were returned to the sights and sounds and smells of civilization. On the outskirts of the town, lamps glowed in the farmhouses and shacks, the families settling in for the evening. The town rose into view, the biggest Cora had seen since North Carolina, if not as long established. The long main street, with its two banks and the loud row of taverns, was enough to bring her back to the days of the dormitory. The town gave no indication of quieting for the night, shops open, citizens a-prowl on the wooden sidewalks.

Boseman was adamant about not spending the night. If the fever was so close it might strike here next, perhaps it already churned in the bodies of the townspeople. Ridgeway was irritated but gave in, even though he missed a proper bed. They'd camp up the road after they resupplied.

Cora remained chained to the wagon as the men pursued errands. Strollers caught her face through the openings in the canvas and looked away. They had hard faces. Their clothes were coarse and homespun, less fine than the white people's clothes in the eastern towns. The clothes of settlers, not of the settled.

Homer climbed in the wagon whistling one of Jasper's more monotonous ditties. The dead slave still among them. The boy held a bundle wrapped in brown paper. "This is for you," he said.

The dress was dark blue with white buttons, soft cotton that gave off a medicinal smell. She held up the dress so that it blocked the blood stains on the canvas, which were stark on the fabric from the streetlamps outside.

"Put it on, Cora," Homer said.

Cora raised her hands, the chains making a noise.

He unlocked her ankles and wrists. As she did every time, Cora considered the chances of escape and came up with the dead result. A town like this, rough and wild, made good mobs, she figured. Had news of the boy in Georgia reached here? The accident she never thought about and which she didn't include in her list of transgressions. The boy belonged on his own list—but what were its terms?

Homer watched her as she dressed, like a valet who had waited on her since the cradle.

"I'm caught," Cora said. "You choose to be with him."

Homer looked puzzled. He took out his notebook, turned to the last page, and scribbled. When he was finished, the boy fixed her manacles again. He gave her ill-fitting wooden shoes. He was about to chain Cora to the wagon when Ridgeway said to bring her outside.

Boseman was still out after a barber and a bath. The slave catcher handed Homer the gazettes and the fugitive bulletins he'd collected from the deputy in the jail. "I'm taking Cora for some supper," Ridgeway said, and led her into the racket. Homer dropped her filthy shift into the gutter, the brown of the dried blood seeping into the mud.

The wooden shoes pinched. Ridgeway didn't alter his stride to accommodate Cora's hindered pace, walking ahead of her and unconcerned that she might run. Her chains were a cowbell. The white people of Tennessee took no notice of her. A young negro leaned against the wall of a stable, the only person to register her presence. A freeman from his appearance, dressed in striped gray trousers and a vest of cowhide. He watched her move as she had watched the coffles trudge past Randall. To see chains on another person and be glad they are not your own—such was the good fortune permitted colored people, defined by how much worse it could be any moment. If your eyes met, both parties looked away. But this man did not. He nodded before passersby took him from view.

Cora had peeked inside Sam's saloon in South Carolina but never crossed the threshold. If she was an odd vision in their midst, one look from Ridgeway made the patrons return to their own business. The fat man tending the bar rolled tobacco and stared at the back of Ridgeway's head.

Ridgeway led her to a wobbly table against the rear wall. The smell of stewed meat rose above that of the old beer soaked into the floorboards and the walls and the ceiling. The pigtailed maid was a broad-shouldered girl with the thick arms of a cotton loader. Ridgeway ordered their food.

"The shoes were not my first choice," he told Cora, "but the dress suits you."

"It's clean," Cora said.

"Now, well. Can't have our Cora looking like the floor of a butcher's shop."

He meant to elicit a reaction. Cora declined. From the saloon next door, a piano started up. It sounded as if a raccoon ran back and forth, mashing on the keys.

"All this time you haven't asked about your accomplice," Ridgeway said. "Caesar. Did it make the newspapers up in North Carolina?"

This was going to be a performance then, like one of the Friday-night pageants on the park. He had her dress up for night at the theater. She waited.

"It's so strange going to South Carolina," Ridgeway said, "now that they have their new system. Had many a caper there in the old days. But the old days aren't that far off. For all their talk of negro uplift and civilizing the savage, it's the same hungry place it always was."

The maid delivered bread heels and bowls full of beef and potato stew. Ridgeway whispered to her while looking at Cora, something she couldn't hear. The girl laughed. Cora realized he was drunk.

Ridgeway slurped. "We caught up with it at the factory at the end of its shift," he said. "These big colored bucks around it, finding their old fear again after thinking they'd put it behind them. At first, wasn't no big fuss. Another runaway caught. Then word spread that Caesar was wanted for the murder of a little boy—"

"Not little," Cora said.

Ridgeway shrugged. "They broke into the jail. The sheriff opened the door, to be honest, but that's not as dramatic. They broke into the jail and ripped its body to pieces. The decent people of South Carolina with their schoolhouses and Friday credit."

News of Lovey had broken her down in front of him. Not this time. She was prepared—his eyes brightened when he was on the verge of a cruelty. And she had known Caesar was dead for a long time now. No need to ask after his fate. It appeared before her one night in the attic like a spark, a small and simple truth: Caesar did not make it out. He was not up north wearing a new suit, new shoes, new smile. Sitting in the dark, nestled into the rafters, Cora understood that she was alone again. They had got him. She had finished mourning him by the time Ridgeway came knocking on Martin's door.

Ridgeway plucked gristle from his mouth. "I made a little silver for the capture at any rate, and returned another boy to its master along the way. Profit in the end."

"You scrape like an old darky for that Randall money," Cora said.

Ridgeway laid his big hands on the uneven table, tilting it to his side. Stew ran over the rim of the bowls. "They should fix this," he said.

The stew was lumpy with the thickening flour. Cora mashed the lumps with her tongue the way she did when one of Alice's helpers had prepared the meal and not the old cook herself. Through the wall the piano player bit into an upbeat ditty. A drunken couple dashed next door to dance.

"Jasper wasn't killed by no mob," Cora said.

"There are always unexpected expenses," Ridgeway said. "I'm not going to get reimbursed for all the food I fed it."

"You go on about reasons," Cora said. "Call things by other names as if it changes what they are. But that don't make them true. You killed Jasper in cold blood."

"That was more of a personal matter," Ridgeway conceded, "and not what I'm talking about here. You and your friend killed a boy. You have your justifications."

"I was going to escape."

"That's all I'm talking about, survival. Do you feel awful about it?"

The boy's death was a complication of her escape, like the absence of a full moon or losing the head start because Lovey had been discovered out of her cabin. But shutters swung out inside her and she saw the boy trembling on his sickbed, his mother weeping over his grave. Cora had been grieving for him, too, without knowing it. Another person caught in this enterprise that bound slave and master alike. She moved the boy from the lonely list in her head and logged him below Martin and Ethel, even though she did not know his name. X, as she signed herself before she learned her letters.

Nonetheless. She told Ridgeway, "No."

"Of course not—it's nothing. Better weep for one of those burned cornfields, or this steer swimming in our soup. You do what's required to survive." He wiped his lips. "It's true, though, your complaint. We come up with all sorts of fancy talk to hide things. Like in the newspapers nowadays, all the smart men talking about Manifest Destiny. Like it's a new idea. You don't know what I'm talking about, do you?" Ridgeway asked.

Cora sat back. "More words to pretty things up."

"It means taking what is yours, your property, whatever you deem it to be. And everyone else taking their assigned places to allow you to take it. Whether it's red men or Africans, giving up themselves, giving of themselves, so that we can have what's rightfully ours. The French setting aside their territorial claims. The British and the Spanish slinking away.

"My father liked his Indian talk about the Great Spirit," Ridgeway said. "All these years later, I prefer the American spirit, the one that called us from the Old World to the New, to conquer and build and civilize. And destroy that what needs to be destroyed. To lift up the lesser races. If not lift up, subjugate. And if not subjugate, exterminate. Our destiny by divine prescription—the American imperative."

"I need to visit the outhouse," Cora said.

The corners of his mouth sank. He gestured for her to walk in front. The steps to the back alley were slippery with vomit and he grabbed her elbow to steady her. Closing the outhouse door, shutting him out, was the purest pleasure she'd had in a long while.

Ridgeway continued his address undeterred. "Take your mother," the slave catcher said. "Mabel. Stolen from her master by misguided whites and colored individuals in a criminal conspiracy. I kept an eye out all this time, turned Boston and New York upside down, all the colored settlements. Syracuse. Northampton. She's up in Canada, laughing at the Randalls and me. I take it as a personal injury. That's why I bought you that dress. To help me picture her wrapped like a present for her master."

He hated her mother as much as she did. That, and the fact they both had eyes in their head, meant they had two things in common.

Ridgeway paused—a drunk wanted to use the privy. He shooed him away. "You absconded for ten months," he said. "Insult enough. You and your mother are a line that needs to be extinguished. A week together, chained up, and you sass me without end, on your way to a bloody homecoming. The abolitionist lobby loves to trot out your kind, to give speeches to white people who have no idea how the world works."

The slave catcher was wrong. If she'd made it north she would have disappeared into a life outside their terms. Like her mother. One thing the woman had passed on to her.

"We do our part," Ridgeway said, "slave and slave catcher. Master and colored boss. The new arrivals streaming into the harbors and the politicians and sheriffs and newspapermen and the mothers raising strong sons. People like you and your mother are the best of your race. The weak of your tribe have been weeded out, they die in the slave ships, die of our European pox, in the fields working our cotton and indigo. You need to be strong to survive the labor and to make us greater. We fatten hogs, not because it pleases us but because we need hogs to survive. But we can't have you too clever. We can't have you so fit you outrun us."

She finished her business and picked out a fugitive bulletin from the stack of paper to wipe herself. Then she waited. A pitiful respite, but it was hers.

"You heard my name when you were a pickaninny," he said. "The name of punishment, dogging every fugitive step and every thought of running away. For every slave I bring home, twenty others abandon their full-moon schemes. I'm a notion of order. The slave that disappears—it's a notion, too. Of hope. Undoing what I do so that a slave the next plantation over gets an idea that it can run, too. If we allow that, we accept the flaw in the imperative. And I refuse."

The music from next door was slow now. Couples coming together to hold each other, to sway and twist. That was real conversation, dancing slow with another person, not all these words. She knew that, even though she had never danced like that with another person and had refused Caesar when he asked. The only person to ever extend a hand to her and say, Come closer. Maybe everything the slave catcher said was true, Cora thought, every justification, and the sons of Ham were cursed and the slave master performed the Lord's will. And maybe he was just a man talking to an outhouse door, waiting for someone to wipe her ass.

CORA and Ridgeway returned to the wagon to find Homer rubbing his small thumbs on the reins and Boseman sipping whiskey from a bottle. "This town is sick with it," Boseman said, slurring. "I can smell it." The younger man led the way out of town. He shared his disappointments. The shave and bath had gone well; with a fresh face the man looked almost innocent. But he had not been able to perform like a man at the brothel. "The madam was sweating like a pig and I knew they had the fever, her and her whores." Ridgeway let him decide how far was far enough to camp.

She had been asleep for a short time when Boseman crept in and put his hand over her mouth. She was ready.

Boseman put his fingers to his lips. Cora nodded as much as his grip permitted: She would not cry out. She could make a fuss now and wake Ridgeway; Boseman would give him some excuse and that would be the end of it. But she had thought about this moment for days, of when Boseman let his carnal desires get the best of him. It was the most drunk he'd been since North Carolina. He complimented her dress when they stopped for the night. She steeled herself. If she could persuade him to unshackle her, a dark night like this was made for running.

Homer snored loudly. Boseman slipped her chains from the wagon ring, careful not to let the links sound against each other. He undid her ankles and cinched her wrist chains to silence them. He descended first and helped Cora out. She could just make out the road a few yards away. Dark enough.

Ridgeway knocked him to the ground with a growl and started kicking him. Boseman started his defense and Ridgeway kicked him in the mouth. She almost ran. She almost did. But the quickness of the violence, the blade of it, arrested her. Ridgeway scared her. When Homer came to the back of the wagon with a lantern and revealed Ridgeway's face, the slave catcher was staring at her with untempered fury. She'd had her chance and missed it and at the look on his face was relieved.

"What are you going to do now, Ridgeway?" Boseman wept. He was leaning against the wagon wheel for support. He looked at the blood on his hands. His necklace had snapped and the ears made it look like the dirt was listening. "Crazy Ridgeway, does as he pleases. I'm the last one left. Only Homer left to beat on when I'm gone," he said. "I think he'll like it."

Homer chuckled. He got Cora's ankle chains from the wagon. Ridgeway rubbed his knuckles, breathing heavily.

"It is a nice dress," Boseman said. He pulled out a tooth.

"There'll be more teeth if any of you fellows move," the man said. The three of them stepped into the light.

The speaker was the young negro from town, the one who nodded at her. He didn't look at her now, monitoring Ridgeway. His wire spectacles reflected the lantern's glow, as if the flame burned inside him. His pistol wavered between the two white men like a dowser's stick.

A second man held a rifle. He was tall and well-muscled,

dressed in thick work clothes that struck her as a costume. He had a wide face and his long red-brown hair was combed up into a fan like a lion's mane. The man's posture said that he did not enjoy taking orders, and the insolence in his eyes was not slave insolence, an impotent pose, but a hard fact. The third man waved a bowie knife. His body shook with nerves, his quick breathing the night sound between his companion's talk. Cora recognized his bearing. It was that of a runaway, one unsure of the latest turn in the escape. She'd seen it in Caesar, in the bodies of the new arrivals to the dormitories, and knew she'd exhibited it many times. He extended the trembling knife in Homer's direction.

She had never seen colored men hold guns. The image shocked her, a new idea too big to fit into her mind.

"You boys are lost," Ridgeway said. He didn't have a weapon.

"Lost in that we don't like Tennessee much and would rather be home, yes," the leader said. "You seem lost yourself."

Boseman coughed and traded a glance with Ridgeway. He sat up and tensed. The two rifles turned to him.

Their leader said, "We're going to be on our way but we thought we'd ask the lady if she wanted to come with us. We're a better sort of traveling companion."

"Where you boys from?" Ridgeway said. He talked in a way that told Cora he was scheming.

"All over," the man said. The north lived in his voice, his accent from up there, like Caesar. "But we found each other and now we work together. You settle down, Mr. Ridgeway."

He moved his head slightly. "I heard him call you Cora. Is that your name?"

She nodded.

"She's Cora," Ridgeway said. "You know me. That's Boseman, and that's Homer."

At his name, Homer threw the lantern at the man holding the knife. The glass didn't break until it hit the ground after bouncing off the man's chest. The fire splashed. The leader fired at Ridgeway and missed. The slave catcher tackled him and they both tumbled into the dirt. The red-headed rifleman was a better shot. Boseman flew back, a black flower blooming suddenly on his belly.

Homer ran to get a gun, followed by the rifleman. The boy's hat rolled into the fire. Ridgeway and his opponent scuffled in the dirt, grunting and hollering. They rolled over to the edge of the burning oil. Cora's fear from moments ago returned—Ridgeway had trained her well. The slave catcher got the upper hand, pinning the man to the ground.

She could run. She only had chains on her wrists now.

Cora jumped on Ridgeway's back and strangled him with her chains, twisting them tight against his flesh. Her scream came from deep inside her, a train whistle echoing in a tunnel. She yanked and squeezed. The slave catcher threw his body to smear her into the ground. By the time he shook her off, the man from town had his pistol again.

The runaway helped Cora to her feet. "Who's that boy?" he said.

Homer and the rifleman hadn't returned. The leader instructed the man with the knife to have a look, keeping the gun on Ridgeway.

The slave catcher rubbed his thick fingers into his ravaged neck. He did not look at Cora, which made her fearful again.

Boseman whimpered. He burbled, "He's going to look in your soul and see what you done, sinner ... " The light from the burning oil was inconstant, but they had no trouble making out the widening puddle of blood.

"He's going to bleed to death," Ridgeway said.

"It's a free country," the man from town said.

"This is not your property," Ridgeway said.

"That's what the law says. White law. There are other ones." He addressed Cora in a gentler tone. "If you want, miss, I can shoot him for you." His face was calm.

She wanted every bad thing for Ridgeway and Boseman. And Homer? She didn't know what her heart wanted for the strange black boy, who seemed an emissary from a different country.

Before she could speak, the man said, "Though we'd prefer to put irons on them." Cora retrieved his spectacles from the dirt and cleaned them with her sleeve and the three of them waited. His companions returned empty-handed.

Ridgeway smiled as the men shackled his wrists through the wagon wheel.

"The boy is a devious sort," the leader said. "I can tell that. We have to go." He looked at Cora. "Will you come with us?"

Cora kicked Ridgeway in the face three times with her new

wooden shoes. She thought, If the world will not stir itself to punish the wicked. No one stopped her. Later she said it was three kicks for three murders, and told of Lovey, Caesar, and Jasper to let them live briefly again in her words. But that was not the truth of it. It was all for her.

Caesar

THE excitement over Jockey's birthday allowed Caesar to visit his only refuge on Randall. The dilapidated schoolhouse by the stables was generally empty. At night lovers sneaked in, but he never went there at night—he required light, and he was not going to risk lighting a candle. He went to the schoolhouse to read the book Fletcher gave him after much protest; he went when feeling low, to weep over his burdens; he went to watch the other slaves move about the plantation. From the window it was as if he were not one of their unlucky tribe but only observing their commerce, as one might watch strangers stroll past one's front door. In the schoolhouse it was as if he were not there at all.

Enslaved. In fear. Sentenced to death.

If his scheme came to fruition, this would be the last time he celebrated Jockey's birthday. God willing. Knowing him, the old man was apt to announce another one next month. The quarter was so jubilant over the tiny pleasures they scavenged together on Randall. A made-up birthday, a dance after toiling under the harvest moon. In Virginia the celebrations were spectacular. Caesar and his family rode in the widow's buggy to the farms of freemen, they visited relatives on estates for the Lord's holidays and New Year's Day. The pigs and venison steaks, ginger pies and corn-bread cakes. The games went all day long, until Caesar and his companions fell in panting collapse. The masters in Virginia kept their distance those festival days. How could these Randall slaves truly enjoy themselves with that dumb menace waiting at the sidelines, poised to swoop? They didn't know their birthdays so had to invent them. Half these folks didn't know their mothers and fathers.

I was born on August 14th. My mother's name is Lily Jane. My father is Jerome. I don't know where they are.

Through the schoolhouse window, framed by two of the older cabins—their whitewash smeared to gray, worn down like those who slept inside them—Cora huddled with her favorite at the starting line. Chester, the boy who prowled the quarter with such enviable cheer. Obviously he'd never been beaten.

The boy turned his head shyly from something Cora said. She smiled—quickly. She smiled at Chester, and Lovey and the women from her cabin, with brevity and efficiency. Like when you see the shadow of a bird on the ground but look up and nothing's there. She subsisted on rations, in everything. Caesar had never spoken to her but had this figured out about her. It was sensible: She knew the preciousness of what little she called her own. Her joys, her plot, that block of sugar maple she perched on like a vulture.

He was drinking corn whiskey with Martin in the barn loft one night—the boy wouldn't say where he got the jug—when they started talking about the women of Randall. Who was most likely to mush your face into their titties, who'd scream so loud the whole quarter would know, and who would never tell. Caesar asked about Cora.

"Nigger don't fool with no Hob woman," Martin said. "They cut your thing off and make soup with it." He told him the old story of Cora and her garden and Blake's doghouse, and Caesar thought, That sounds about right. Then Martin said she liked to sneak out to fornicate with swamp animals, and Caesar realized the cotton picker was dumber than he thought.

None of the Randall men was that bright. The place had undone them. They joked and they picked fast when the bosses' eyes were on them and they acted big, but at night in the cabin after midnight they wept, they screamed from nightmares and wretched memories. In Caesar's cabin, in the next cabins over, and in every slave village near and far. When the work was done, and the day's punishments, the night waited as an arena for their true loneliness and despair.

Cheers and shouts—another race done. Cora set her hands on her hips, head tilted as if hunting after a tune hidden in the noise. How to capture that profile in wood, preserve her grace and strength—he didn't trust himself not to botch it. Picking had ruined his hands for delicate woodwork. The slope of a woman's cheek, lips in the midst of a whisper. His arms trembled at the end of the day, muscles throbbing.

How the old white bitch had lied! He should have been living with his mother and father in their cottage, rounding off barrels for the cooper or apprenticed to another of the town's craftsmen.

His prospects were limited by his race, to be sure, but Caesar had grown up believing he was free to choose his own fate. "You can be whatever you want to be," his father said.

"Even go to Richmond?" From all reports, Richmond sounded far away and splendid.

"Even Richmond, if you like."

But the old woman had lied and now his crossroad was reduced to one destination, a slow death in Georgia. For him, for his entire family. His mother was slight and delicate and not made for field labor, she was too kind to endure the plantation's battery of cruelties. His father would hold out longer, donkey that he was, but not much. The old woman had destroyed his family so thoroughly it couldn't have been accidental. It wasn't her niece's greed—the old woman had played a trick on them the whole time. Tightening the knots every time she held Caesar in her lap and taught him a word.

Caesar pictured his father cutting cane in a Florida hell, burning his flesh as he stooped over the big kettles of molten sugar. The cat-o'-nine-tails biting into his mother's back when she failed to keep the pace with her sack. Stubborn breaks when it don't bend, and his family had spent too much time with the kindly white folks in the north. Kindly in that they didn't see fit to kill you fast. One thing about the south, it was not patient when it came to killing negroes.

In the old crippled men and women of the plantation he saw what lay in store for his mother and father. In time, what would become of him. At night, he was certain they were dead; in the daylight, merely maimed and half dead. Either way he was alone in the world.

Caesar approached her after the races. Of course she waved him away. She didn't know him. It could've been a prank, or a trap laid by the Randalls in a fit of boredom. Running was too big an idea—you had to let it set a while, turn it around in your head. It took Caesar months to permit it into his thoughts, and he needed Fletcher's encouragement to let it truly live. You need someone else to help you along. Even if she didn't know she'd say yes, he did. He'd told her he wanted her for good luck—her mother was the only one to ever make it out. Probably a mistake, if not an insult, to someone like her. She wasn't a rabbit's foot to carry with you on the voyage but the locomotive itself. He couldn't do it without her.

The terrible incident at the dance proved it. One of the house slaves told him the brothers were drinking at the big house. Caesar took it as a bad omen. When the boy carried the lantern down to the quarter, his masters following, violence was assured. Chester had never been beaten. Now he had been, and tomorrow he'd get his first hiding. No more children's games for him, races and hide-and-seek, but the grim trials of slave men. No one else in the village made a move to help the boy—how could they? They'd seen it a hundred times before, as victim or witness, and would see it a hundred times more until they died. But Cora did. She shielded the boy with her own body and took his blows for him. She was a stray through and through, so far off the path it was like she'd already run from the place long ago.

After the beating Caesar visited the schoolhouse at night for the first time. Just to hold the book in his hands. To make sure it was still there, a souvenir from a time when he had all the books he wanted, and all the time to read them.

What became of my companions in the boat, as well as those who escaped on the rock, or were left in the vessel, I cannot tell; but conclude they were all lost. The book will get him killed, Fletcher warned. Caesar hid *Travels into Several Remote Nations* in the dirt under the schoolhouse, wrapped in two swatches of burlap. Wait a little longer until we can make the preparations for your escape, the shopkeeper said. Then you can have any book you want. But if he didn't read, he was a slave. Before the book the only thing to read was what came written on a bag of rice. The name of the firm that manufactured their chains, imprinted in the metal like a promise of pain.

Now a page here and there, in the golden afternoon light, sustained him. Guile and pluck, guile and pluck. The white man in the book, Gulliver, roved from peril to peril, each new island a new predicament to solve before he could return home. That was the man's real trouble, not the savage and uncanny civilizations he encountered—he kept forgetting what he had. That was white people all over: Build a schoolhouse and let it rot, make a home then keep straying. If Caesar figured the route home, he'd never travel again. Otherwise he was liable to go from one troublesome island to the next, never recognizing where he was, until the world ran out. Unless she came with him. With Cora, he'd find the way home.

Indiana

50 **REWARD.**

LEFT my house on Friday evening the 26th about 10 o'clock P.M. (without provocation whatever) my negro girl SUKEY. She is about 28 years of age, of rather a light complexion, has high cheek bones, is slender in her person, and very neat in her appearance. Had on when she went away, a striped jean frock. Sukey was lately owned by L. B. Pearce, Esq. and formerly belonged to William M. Heritage, deceased. She is at present (from appearance) a strict member of the Methodist Church in this place, and is no doubt known to a majority of the members.

JAMES AYKROYD
OCTOBER 4

THEN she became the one lagging in her lessons, surrounded by impatient children. Cora was proud of the progress she made with her reading in South Carolina and the attic. The shaky footing of every new word, an unknown territory to struggle through letter by letter. She claimed each circuit through Donald's almanacs as a victory, then returned to the first page for another round.

Georgina's classroom revealed the smallness of her accomplishments. She didn't recognize the Declaration of Independence the day she joined them in the meeting house. The children's pronunciation was crisp and mature, so distant from Michael's stiff recitations back on Randall. Music lived in the words now, the melody asserting itself as each child took their turn, bold and confident. The boys and girls stood from the pews, turned over the paper where they'd copied the words, and sang the promises of the Founding Fathers.

With Cora, the class numbered twenty-five. The youngest— the six- and seven-year-olds—were exempt from the recital. They whispered and fussed in the pews until Georgina hushed them. Nor did Cora participate, being new to the class, the farm, their way of doing things. She felt conspicuous, older than all of them and so far behind. Cora understood why old Howard had wept, back in Miss Handler's schoolhouse. An interloper, like a rodent that had chewed through the wall.

One of the cooks rang the bell, drawing the lesson to a close. After the meal, the younger students would return to their lessons while the older ones took to their chores. On their way out of the meeting house, Cora stopped Georgina and said, "You taught these pickaninnies how to give a proper talk, that's for sure."

The teacher checked to make sure her students hadn't heard Cora. She said, "Here we call them children."

Cora's cheeks got hot. She'd never been able to make out what it meant, she added quickly. Did they know what was in all those big words?

Georgina hailed from Delaware and had that vexing way of Delaware ladies, delighting in puzzles. Cora had met a few of them on Valentine and didn't care for that regional peculiarity, even if they knew how to bake a good pie. Georgina said the children make of it what they can. What they don't understand today, they might tomorrow. "The Declaration is like a map. You trust that it's right, but you only know by going out and testing it yourself."

"You believe that?" Cora asked. From the teacher's face, she didn't know what to make of her.

Four months had passed since that first class. The harvest was done. Fresh arrivals to the Valentine farm made it so Cora was no longer the greenhorn, bumbling about. Two men Cora's age joined the lessons in the meeting house, eager runaways more ignorant than she was. They ran their fingers over the books as if the things were goofered, hopping with magic. Cora knew her way around. When to prepare her own meal because today's cook would muddle the soup, when to bring a shawl because Indiana nights were a shiver, colder than she'd ever known. The quiet places of shade to be alone.

Cora sat in the front of the class nowadays, and when Georgina corrected her—on her penmanship or arithmetic or speech—she no longer smarted. They were friends. Georgina was such a dedicated gossip that the lessons provided a reprieve from her constant reports on the farm's goings-on. *That strapping man from Virginia has a mischievous look, don't you think? Patricia ate all the pig's feet when we turned our backs.* Delaware women liked to flap their gums, that was another thing.

This particular afternoon, Cora walked out with Molly once the bell sounded. She shared a cabin with the girl and her mother. Molly was ten years old, almond-eyed and reserved, careful with her affections. She had many friends but preferred to stand just outside the circle. The girl kept a green jar in her room for her treasures—marbles, arrowheads, a locket without a face—and got more pleasure from spreading them on the cabin floor, feeling the cool of blue quartz on her cheek, than playing outside.

Which was why their routine of late delighted Cora. Cora had started braiding the girl's hair on the mornings when her mother left for work early, and the last few days Molly had reached for her hand when school ended. A new thing between them. Molly tugged her along, squeezing hard, and Cora enjoyed being led. She hadn't been chosen by one of the little ones since Chester.

There was no noon meal on account of that night's big Saturday supper, the smell of which impelled the students to the barbecue pits. The barbecue men had been cooking the hogs since midnight, casting a spell property-wide. More than one of the residents had dreamed of gorging on a magnificent banquet, only to wake up devastated. Hours to go. Cora and Molly joined the hungry spectators.

Over the smoky greenwood coals, long sticks splayed out the two hogs. Jimmy was the pit master. His father had grown up in Jamaica and had passed down the fire secrets of the Maroons. Jimmy poked the roasting meat with his fingers and nudged the coals, prowling around the fire as if sizing up a grappling partner. He was one of the more wizened residents on the farm, late from North Carolina and the massacres, and preferred his meat melting soft. He only had two teeth.

One of his apprentices shook a jug of vinegar and pepper. He motioned to a little girl at the edge of the fire and guided her hands to mop the insides of the hog with the mixture. The drippings popped on the coals in the trenches. White plumes of smoke sent the crowd back and the girl squealed. It would be a fine meal.

CORA and Molly had an appointment at home. It was a short walk. Like most of the farm's work buildings, the older log cabins bunched on the eastern edge, put up in a hurry before they knew how big the community would become. Folks came from all over, plantations that had favored this or that arrangement of quarters, so the cabins came in various shapes. The newer ones—the latest additions the men put up now that the corn was picked—followed an identical style, with more spacious rooms, and were distributed on the property with more care.

Since Harriet had married and moved out, Cora, Molly, and Sybil were the only inhabitants of their cabin, sleeping in the two rooms off the main living area. In general, three families lived in each house. Newcomers and visitors shared Cora's room from time to time, but for the most part the other two beds were empty.

Her own room. Another unlikely gift from the Valentine farm after all her prisons.

Sybil and her daughter were proud of their house. They'd whitewashed the exterior with quicklime, tinted it pink. Yellow paint with white trim made the front room hum in the sunlight. Decorated with wildflowers in the warm season, the room remained pleasant in the autumn with wreaths of red and gold leaves. Purple curtains bunched in the windows. Two carpenters who lived on the farm lugged in furniture now and again—they were sweet on Sybil and kept their hands busy to distract from her indifference. Sybil had dyed some burlap sacks to make a carpet, which Cora laid on when she got one of her headaches. The front room had a nice breeze that took the bite out of the attacks.

Molly called after her mother when they reached the porch. Sarsaparilla boiled for one of Sybil's tonics, overpowering the aroma of the roasting meat. Cora headed straight to the rocking chair, which she'd claimed as hers on her first day. Molly and Sybil didn't mind. It creaked extravagantly, the handiwork of Sybil's less talented suitor. Sybil was of the mind that he'd made it loud on purpose, to remind her of his devotion.

Sybil emerged from the back, wringing her hands on her apron. "Jimmy working hard out there," she said, shaking her head in hunger.

"I can't wait," Molly said. The girl opened the pine chest by the hearth and removed their quilting. She was steadfast on finishing her latest project by supper.

They got to it. Cora hadn't picked up a needle apart from simple mending since Mabel left. Some of the Hob women tried to teach her to no avail. As she did in the classroom, Cora kept looking over at her companions for guidance. She cut out a bird, a cardinal; it came out looking like something dogs had fought over. Sybil and Molly encouraged her—they had badgered her into their pastime—but the quilt was botched. Fleas had found the batting, she insisted. The seams puckered, her corners unjoined. The quilt betrayed a crookedness in her thinking: run it up a pole as the flag of her wild country. She wanted to set it aside but Sybil forbid her. "You start something else when this one finished," Sybil said. "But this ain't finished yet."

Cora needed no advice on the virtues of perseverance. But

she picked up the creature in her lap and picked at where she'd left off.

Sybil was twelve years her senior. Her dresses made her look slightly built, but Cora knew that it was merely her time away from the plantation working on the woman in the best way: Her new life required a different sort of strength. She was meticulous in her posture, a walking spear, in the manner of those who'd been made to bend and will bend no more. Her master had been a terror, Sybil told Cora, a tobacco man who competed with the neighboring planters every year over the biggest crop. His poor showing stirred him to malice. "He work us hard," she'd say, her thoughts lighting out to old miseries. Molly would come over from wherever she was and sit on her lap, nuzzling.

The three of them worked wordlessly for a while. A cheer went up over by the barbecue pit, as it did each time they turned the hogs. Cora was too distracted to reverse her mistakes in the quilt. The silent theater of Sybil and Molly's love moved her always. The way the child asked for assistance without speaking and the mother pointed, nodded, and pantomimed her child out of a fix. Cora wasn't accustomed to a quiet cabin—on Randall there was always a shriek or cry or sigh to break a moment—and certainly not accustomed to this type of maternal performance.

Sybil had absconded with Molly when her daughter was only two, toting her child all the way. Rumors from the big house held that their master meant to dispose of some property to cover debts from the disappointing crop. Sybil faced a public sale. She left that night—the full moon gave its blessing and guidance through the forest. "Molly didn't make no sound," Sybil said. "She knew what we were up to." Three miles over the Pennsylvania border they risked a visit to the cottage of a colored farmer. The man fed them, whittled toys for the little girl, and, through a line of intermediaries, contacted the railroad. After a spell in Worcester working for a milliner, Sybil and Molly made their way to Indiana. Word had spread of the farm.

So many fugitives had passed through Valentine—there was no telling who might have spent time there. Did Sybil happen to make the acquaintance of a woman from Georgia? Cora asked her one evening. Cora had been with them for a few weeks. Slept the night through once or twice, put back some of the weight she'd lost in the attic. The dry flies cut out their noise, leaving an opening in the night for a question. A woman from Georgia, maybe went by the name of Mabel, maybe not?

Sybil shook her head.

Of course she hadn't. A woman who leaves her daughter behind becomes someone else to hide the shame of it. But Cora asked everyone on the farm sooner or later, the farm being its own kind of depot, attracting people who were between places. She asked those who'd been on Valentine for years, she asked all the new people, pestered the visitors who came to the farm to see if what they'd heard was true. The free men and women of color, the fugitives who stayed and the ones who moved on. She asked them in the cornfield between a work song, rumbling in the back of a buggy on the way to town: gray eyes, scar across the back of her right hand from a burn, maybe went by the name of Mabel, maybe not?

"Maybe she in Canada," Lindsey answered when Cora decided it was her turn. Lindsey being a slim, hummingbird woman fresh out of Tennessee, who maintained a demented cheer that Cora couldn't understand. From what she saw, Tennessee was fire, disease, and violence. Even if it was there that Royal and them had rescued her. "Lot of folks, they fond of Canada now," Lindsey said. "Though it's awful cold."

Cold nights for the coldhearted.

Cora folded her quilt and retired to her room. She curled up, too distracted thinking on mothers and daughters. Fretting over Royal, three days overdue. Her headache approached like a thunderhead. She turned her face to the wall and did not move.

SUPPER was held outside the meeting house, the biggest building on the property. Legend had it that they put it up in a single day, before one of the first big gatherings, when they realized the assembled no longer fit inside Valentine's farmhouse. Most days it served as a schoolhouse. Sundays, a church. On Saturday evenings the farm got together for a common meal and diversions. Masons who worked on the courthouse downstate came back hungry, seamstresses returned from daywork for local white ladies and put on their nice dresses. Temperance was the rule except for Saturday night, when those with a taste for spirits partook and had something to think about at the next morning's sermon.

The hogs were the first order of business, chopped on the long pine table and covered in dipney sauce. Smoky collards, turnips, sweet potato pie, and the rest of the kitchen's concoctions sat in the Valentines' nice dishes. The residents were a reserved bunch, save for when Jimmy's barbecue came out—prim ladies used their elbows. The pit master lowered his head at every compliment, already thinking of improvements for the next roast. In a deft maneuver Cora tugged off a crispy ear, Molly's favorite, and presented it to the girl.

Valentine no longer kept count of how many families lived on his land. One hundred souls was a sturdy number to stop at—a fantastic figure by any measure—and that didn't account for the colored farmers who'd purchased adjacent land and got their own operations going. Of the fifty or so children, most were under the age of five. "Liberty make a body fertile," Georgina said. That, and the knowledge they will not be sold, Cora added. The women in the colored dormitories of South Carolina believed they knew liberty, but the surgeons' knives cut them to prove otherwise.

Once the hogs disappeared, Georgina and some of the younger women took the children to the barn for games and sing-alongs. The children didn't sit still for all the talk at the meetings. Their absence placed the stakes of the discussions into relief; ultimately, it was for the young ones that they schemed. Even if the adults were free of the shackles that had held them fast, bondage had stolen too much time. Only the children could take full advantage of their dreaming. If white men let them.

The meeting house filled. Cora joined Sybil in a pew. Tonight was to be a subdued affair. Next month after the shucking bee, the farm would host the most important gathering yet, to address the recent debates about picking up stakes. In advance, the Valentines had reduced the Saturday-night entertainments. The pleasant weather—and the warnings of the coming Indiana winter, which scared those who'd never seen snow—kept them occupied. Trips to town turned into dallying expeditions. Social calls stretched into the evening now that so many colored settlers had put down roots, the advance guard of a great migration.

Many of the farm's leaders were out of town. Valentine himself was in Chicago meeting with the banks, his two sons in tow now that they were old enough to help with the farm's accounts. Lander traveled with one of the new abolitionist societies in New York, on a speaking tour of New England; they kept him busy. What he learned during this latest excursion into the country would doubtless shape his contribution to the big meeting.

Cora studied her neighbors. She'd held out hope that Jimmy's hogs would lure Royal back in time, but he and his partners were still engaged in their mission for the underground railroad. There was no word from their party. Gruesome reports reached the farm concerning a posse that had strung up some colored troublemakers the previous night. It had happened thirty miles downstate, and the victims supposedly worked for the railroad, but nothing specific on top of that. A freckled woman unfamiliar to Cora—so many strangers these days—carried on about the lynchings in a loud voice. Sybil turned and shushed her, then gave Cora a quick hug as Gloria Valentine stepped to the lectern.

Gloria had been working in the laundry of an indigo plantation when John Valentine met her. "The most delicious vision these eyes ever beheld," Valentine liked to tell the new arrivals, drawing out *delicious* as if ladling hot caramel. Valentine didn't make a habit of visiting slavers in those days, but he'd gone in on a shipment of feed with Gloria's owner. By the end of the week he had purchased her freedom. A week after that they wed.

She was still delicious, and as graceful and composed as if she'd gone to a finishing school for white ladies. She protested that she didn't enjoy filling in for her husband, but her ease in front of a crowd argued otherwise. Gloria worked hard on eliminating her plantation inflections—Cora heard her slip when conversation took a folksy turn—but she was naturally impressive, whether she spoke colored or white. When Valentine's addresses took a stern tone, his practical disposition overcoming his generosity, Gloria stepped in to smooth matters.

"Did you all have a pleasant day?" Gloria said when the room quieted. "I was down in the root cellar all day and then I come up to see what a gift God gave us today. That sky. And them hogs . . ."

She apologized for her husband's absence. John Valentine wanted to take advantage of the big harvest to renegotiate their loan. "Lord knows, there's so much in the offing, it's nice to have a little peace of mind." She bowed at Mingo, who sat in front, next to the empty space usually reserved for Valentine. Mingo was a stoutly made man of middle stature, with a West Indian complexion that was livened by his red checkered suit tonight. He gave an amen and turned to nod at his allies in the meeting house.

Sybil nudged Cora at this acknowledgment of the farm's political arguments, an acknowledgment that legitimized Mingo's position. There was frequent talk now of lighting out west, where colored towns sprouted up on the other side of the Arkansas River. To places that didn't share a border with slave states, had never countenanced the abomination of slavery. Mingo advocated staying in Indiana, but with a severe reduction in those they sheltered: the runaways, the lost. People like Cora. The parade of famous visitors spreading the farm's renown made the place into a symbol of colored uplift—and a target. After all, the specter of colored rebellion, all those angry dark faces surrounding them, had stirred white settlers to leave the south. They come to Indiana, and right next door is a black nation rising. It always ended in violence.

Sybil scorned Mingo, his greasy personality and constant jockeying; an imperious nature lurked beneath his gregariousness. Yes, the man wore an honorable legend: After he hired himself out from his master for weekend labor, he had purchased the freedom of his wife, then his children, and finally himself. Sybil dismissed this prodigious feat—the man got lucky with regards to his master is all. Mingo would never be more than an opportunist, harassing the farm with his own notions about colored advancement. With Lander, he would take the lectern at next month's gathering to decide their future.

Cora declined to join her friend in her derision. Mingo had been distant to her on account of the attention that runaways brought to the farm, and when he heard she was wanted for murder, shunned Cora altogether. Still, the man had saved his family and could've died before completing his task—it was a mighty thing. Her first day in the schoolhouse his two girls, Amanda and Marie, had delivered the Declaration with poise. They were admirable girls. But no, Cora didn't like his smart talk. Something in his smile reminded her of Blake, that preening buck from the old days. Mingo didn't need a place to put his dog-house, but surely he was on the lookout to expand his domain.

They'd get to the music in short order, Gloria reassured them. There weren't what Valentine called "dignitaries" among them tonight—in fancy clothes, with Yankee accents—although some guests from the county had come down the road. Gloria asked them to stand up and identify themselves for a welcome. Then it was time for the diversions. "While you digest that fine meal, we have a sweet treat," she said. "You may recognize his face from his earlier visit to Valentine, a most distinguished young man of the arts."

The previous Saturday, it had been a pregnant opera singer from Montreal. The Saturday before that, a violinist from Connecticut who made half the women weep, so overcome were they with feeling. Tonight belonged to the poet. Rumsey Brooks was solemn and slim, dressed in a black suit with a black bow tie. He looked like a traveling preacher.

—

HE'D been there three months prior with a delegation out of Ohio. Did the Valentine farm deserve its reputation? An old white lady devoted to the cause of negro uplift had organized the expedition. The widow of a big Boston lawyer, she collected funds for various ventures, the publication and dissemination of colored literature a particular concern. After hearing one of Lander's orations, she arranged for the distribution of his autobiography; the printer had previously put out a line of Shakespeare's tragedies. The volume's first run sold out in days, a handsome edition with Elijah Lander's name in gold leaf. Rumsey's own manuscript was forthcoming next month, Gloria said.

The poet kissed his host's hand and asked permission to share some of his poetry. He was not without charisma, Cora had to admit. According to Georgina, Rumsey courted one of the milkhouse girls, but was so liberal with flattery that he was obviously a young man open to the sweet mysteries of fate. "Who knows what destiny has in store for us," he asked Cora on his first visit, "and what kind of people we will have the pleasure to know?" Royal suddenly appeared at her side and pulled her away from the poet's honey words.

She should have recognized Royal's intentions. If she'd known how out of sorts his disappearances made her, she would have rebuffed him.

With Gloria's blessing, the poet cleared his throat. "'Ere I saw a dappled wonder," he recited, his voice rising and dipping as if battling a headwind. "Settling 'cross the fields, hovering on angel wings and brandishing a blazing shield ..."

The meeting house amened and sighed. Rumsey tried not to smile at their reaction, the effect of his performance. Cora couldn't make much out of his poems: a visitation of a magnificent presence, a seeker awaiting a message. A conversation between an acorn, a sapling, and a powerful oak. Also a tribute to Benjamin Franklin and his ingenuity. Versifying left her cold. Poems were too close to prayer, rousing regrettable passions. Waiting for God to rescue you when it was up to you. Poetry and prayer put ideas in people's heads that got them killed, distracting them from the ruthless mechanism of the world.

After the poetry the musicians were set to perform, some players who had just joined the farm. The poet prepared the dancing circles well, intoxicating them with visions of flight and release. If it made them happy, who was Cora to belittle them? They put bits of themselves into his characters, grafting their faces onto the figures in his rhymes. Did they see themselves in Benjamin Franklin or his inventions? Slaves were tools, so maybe the latter, but no one here was a slave. Counted as property by someone far away, perhaps, but not here.

The entire farm was something beyond her imagination. The Valentines had performed a miracle. She sat among the proof of it; more than that, she was part of that miracle. She had given herself too easily to the false promises of South Carolina. Now a bitter part of her refused the treasures of the Valentine farm, even as every day some blessing part came into bloom. In a young girl taking her hand. In her fears for a man she'd come to feel for.

Rumsey closed with an appeal for nurturing the artistic

temperament in young and old alike, "to stoke that Apollonian ember in all mortal beings." One of the newcomers shoved the lectern across the stage. A cue for the musicians, and a cue for Cora. Sybil knew her friend's ways by now and kissed her farewell. The hall stifled; outside it was cold and dark. Cora left to the sound of the large pews scraping to make room to dance. She passed someone on the path who declared, "You going the wrong way, girl!"

When she got home, Royal was leaning against a post of her porch. His silhouette, even in the dark. "I thought you'd be along once that banjo got on," he said.

Cora lit the lamp and saw his black eye, the yellow-purple lump. "Oh," she said, hugging him, putting her face into his neck.

"A scuffle is all," he said. "We got away." Cora shuddered and he whispered, "I know you were worried. I didn't feel like mixing with folks tonight, reckoned I'd wait here."

On the porch, they sat on the lovelorn carpenters' chairs and took in the night. He moved over so their shoulders touched.

She told him what he'd missed, the poet and the meal.

"There'll be more," he said. "I got you something." He rummaged in his leather satchel. "It's this year's edition, but I thought you'd appreciate it even though it's October. When I get to a place where they got next year's, I'll pick it up."

She grabbed his hand. The almanac had a strange, soapy smell and made a cracking noise like fire as she turned the pages. She'd never been the first person to open a book.

Royal took her to the ghost tunnel after a month on the farm.

Cora started working her second day, thoughts in a knot over Valentine's motto: "Stay, and contribute." A request, and a cure. She contributed first in the washhouse. The head of the laundry was a woman named Amelia who'd known the Valentines in Virginia and followed two years later. Gently she warned Cora against "abusing the garments." Cora was quick with her labor on Randall. Working with her hands stirred her old, fearful industry. She and Amelia decided that she might prefer another chore. She helped in the milk house for a week and did a stint with Aunty, watching the babies while their parents worked. After that, she spread manure in the fields when the leaves of the Indian corn turned yellow. As Cora bent in the rows she looked out for an overseer, haunted.

"You look weary," Royal told her one August evening after Lander delivered one of his speeches. Lander's talk verged on a sermon, concerning the dilemma of finding your purpose once you've slipped the yoke of slavery. The manifold frustrations of liberty. Like the rest of the farm, Cora regarded the man with awe. He was an exotic prince, traveling from a far land to teach them how people conducted themselves in decent places. Places so far away they eluded all maps.

Elijah Lander's father was a rich white lawyer in Boston who lived openly with his colored wife. They suffered the rebukes of their circle and in midnight whispers characterized their offspring as the union of an African goddess and a pale mortal. A demigod. To hear the white dignitaries tell it in their long-winded introductions to his speeches, Lander demonstrated his brilliance from an early age. A sickly child, he made the family library his playground, poring over volumes he struggled to lift from the shelves. At the age of six, he played the piano like a European master. He performed concerts to the empty parlor, bowing to silent applause.

Family friends interceded to make him the first colored student at one of the prestigious white colleges. "They gave me a slave pass," as he described it, "and I used it for mischief." Lander lived in a broom closet; no one would room with him. After four years his fellows elected him valedictorian. He skittered between obstacles like a primeval creature who had outwitted the modern world. Lander could have been anything he wanted. A surgeon, a judge. Brahmins urged him to go to the nation's capital to make his mark in politics. He'd broken through into a small corner of American success where his race did not curse him. Some might have lived in that space happily, rising alone. Lander wanted to make room for others. People were wonderful company sometimes.

In the end, he chose to give speeches. In his parents' parlor to an audience of distinguished Bostonians, then in the homes of those distinguished Bostonians, in colored meeting houses and Methodist churches and lecture halls throughout New England. Sometimes he was the first colored person to set foot in the buildings apart from the men who built them, the women who cleaned them.

Red-faced sheriffs arrested him for sedition. He was jailed for inciting riots that weren't riots but peaceful gatherings. The Honorable Judge Edmund Harrison of Maryland issued a warrant for his arrest, accusing him of "promulgating an infernal orthodoxy that imperils the fabric of good society." A white mob beat him before he was rescued by those who had come to hear him read from his "Declarations of the Rights of the American Negro." From Florida to Maine his pamphlets, and later his autobiography, were burned in bonfires along with his effigy. "Better in effigy than in person," he said.

What private aches nagged him beneath that placid demeanor, none could say. He remained imperturbable and strange. "I'm what the botanists call a hybrid," he said the first time Cora heard him speak. "A mixture of two different families. In flowers, such a concoction pleases the eye. When that amalgamation takes its shape in flesh and blood, some take great offense. In this room we recognize it for what it is—a new beauty come into the world, and it is in bloom all around us."

WHEN Lander finished his address that August night, Cora and Royal sat on the meeting-house steps. The other residents streamed past them. Lander's words had set Cora in a melancholy place. "I don't want them to put me out," she said.

Royal turned over her palm and slid a thumb across her fresh calluses. No need to fret about that, he said. He proposed a trip to see more of Indiana, as a break from her labors.

The next day they set out in a buggy pulled by two piebald horses. With her wages she had bought a new dress and bonnet. The bonnet covered the scar on her temple, for the most part. The scar made her nervous lately. She'd never thought overlong about brands before, the Xs and Ts and clovers slave masters burned into their chattel. A horseshoe puckered on Sybil's neck, ugly and purple—her first owner had raised draft horses. Cora thanked the Lord that her skin had never been burned in such a way. But we have all been branded even if you can't see it, inside if not without—and the wound from Randall's cane was the very same thing, marking her as his.

Cora had been to town plenty, even climbed the steps of the white bakery to buy a cake. Royal took them in the opposite direction. The sky was a sheet of slate but it was still warm, an August afternoon that let you know its kind was running out. They stopped for a picnic at the side of a meadow, under a crab apple tree. He'd packed some bread, jam, and sausage. She let him put his head in her lap. She considered running her hands through the soft black curls by his ears but refrained when a memory of old violence reared up.

On the way back Royal turned the buggy down an overgrown path. Cora wouldn't have seen it otherwise. Cottonwood swallowed the entrance. He said he wanted to show her something. She thought it might be a pond or a quiet place no one knew about. Instead they rounded a turn and stopped at a forlorn, ramshackle cottage, gray like chewed-up meat. Shutters slanted off, wild grasses bowing from the roof. Weather-beaten was the word—the house was a whipped mutt. She hesitated at the threshold. The grime and moss gave her a lonesome feeling, even with Royal there.

Weeds pushed out of the floor of the main room as well. She covered her nose from the stench. "It makes that manure smell sweet," she said. Royal laughed and said he'd always thought manure smelled sweet. He uncovered the trapdoor to the cellar and lit a candle. The stairs creaked. Animals scurried in the cellar, outraged over the intrusion. Royal counted off six paces and started digging. He stopped when he had exposed the second trapdoor, and they descended to the station. He warned her about the steps, which were slick with a gray slime.

It was the sorriest, saddest station yet. There was no drop to the tracks—the rails started at the end of the steps and jetted into the dark tunnel. A small handcar rested on the tracks, its iron pump waiting for a human touch to animate it. As in the mica mine in North Carolina, long wooden planks and struts buttressed the walls and ceiling.

"It's not made for a locomotive," Royal said. "The tunnel is too small, see. It doesn't connect to the rest of the line."

No one had been there in a long time. Cora asked where it went.

Royal grinned. "It's from before my time. The conductor I replaced showed me when I took over this section. I took that handcar a few miles in, but it was too unsettling. The walls hugging and coming close." Cora knew better than to ask who built it. All the railroad men, from Lumbly to Royal, countered with a variation of "Who do you think made it? Who makes everything?" She'd get him to tell her one day, she decided.

The ghost tunnel had never been used, Royal said, as far as anyone knew. No one knew when it was dug, or who had lived above. Some engineers told him the house had been built by one of the old surveyors, like Lewis and Clark, who had explored and mapped the American wilderness. "If you saw the entire country," Royal said, "from the Atlantic to the Pacific, the great Niagara Falls and the Rio Grande, would you make a home here, in the woods of Indiana?" An old station master offered that it had been the home of a major general in the Revolutionary War, a man who had witnessed much bloodshed and had withdrawn from the young nation after helping to bring it into existence.

A recluse story contained more sense, but Royal thought the army part was claptrap. Did Cora notice that there was no sign that someone had lived there, not even an old toothpick or a nail in the wall?

A notion crept over her like a shadow: that this station was not the start of the line but its terminus. Construction hadn't started beneath the house but at the other end of the black hole. As if in the world there were no places to escape to, only places to flee.

In the cellar above, the scavengers roused to activity, scraping.

Such a dank little hole. Any trip with this point of origin could only be ill-fated. The last time she'd been in one of the railroad's departure stations it had been brightly lit, generous in its comforts, and had delivered her to the bounty of Valentine. That was in Tennessee, when they waited to be carried away from the dangerous escapade with Ridgeway. The events of that night still made her heart quicken.

ONCE they left the slave catcher and his wagon, her rescuers gave their names. Royal was the man who'd spied her in town; his partner was Red, owing to the rusty color of his curly hair. The timid one was Justin, a fugitive like her and unaccustomed to waving bowie knives at white men.

After Cora agreed to go with them—never had an inevitability been so politely proposed—the three men made haste to hide the signs of the altercation. Homer's looming presence, somewhere in the dark, magnified the urgency. Red kept watch with his rifle as Royal and Justin chained first Boseman and then Ridgeway to the wagon. The slave catcher did not speak, sneering at Cora with his bloody mouth the while.

"That one," she said, pointing, and Red chained him to the ring her captors had used for Jasper.

They drove the slave catcher's wagon to the far edge of the pasture, hiding it from the road. Red shackled Ridgeway five times over, using every chain in the wagon's boot. He tossed the keys into the grass. They chased away the horses. Of Homer, there was no sound; perhaps the boy skulked just outside the lantern light. Whatever head start these measures gave would have to suffice. Boseman let out a mortifying gasp as they departed, which Cora took as his death rattle.

Her rescuers' cart was a short walk down the road from Ridgeway's camp. She and Justin hid under a thick blanket in the back and they charged off, at dangerous velocity given the darkness and the uniformly poor quality of Tennessee roads. So agitated by the fight were Royal and Red that they forgot to blindfold their cargo for several miles. Royal was bashful about it. "It's for the safety of the depot, miss."

That third trip on the underground railroad began beneath a stable. By now a station meant a descent down impossibly deep steps and the revelation of the next station's character. The owner of the premises was away on business, Royal told them as he untied the rags from their eyes, a ruse to hide his part in their enterprise. Cora never got his name, nor that of the town of departure. Just that he was another person of subterranean inclinations—and a taste for imported white tile. The walls of the station were covered with it.

"Every time we come down here, there's something new," Royal said. The four of them waited for the train at a table covered with a white tablecloth, sitting in heavy chairs upholstered in crimson. Fresh flowers jutted from a vase and paintings of farmland hung on the walls. There was a cut-crystal pitcher full of water, a basket of fruit, and a big loaf of pumpernickel for them to eat.

"This is a rich folk's house," Justin said.

"He likes to maintain a mood," Royal answered.

Red said he liked the white tiles, which were an improvement over the pine boards that had been there formerly. "I don't know how he put them up himself," he added.

Royal said he hoped the help had a still tongue.

"You killed that man," Justin said. He was numb. They had discovered a jug of wine inside a cupboard and the fugitive drank with abandon.

"Ask the girl if he had it coming," Red said.

Royal grabbed Red's forearm to stop the man's trembling. His friend had never taken a man's life before. The premise of their misadventure was enough to get them hanged, but the murder ensured grim abuse before they swung. Royal was taken aback when Cora told him later that she was wanted for murder in Georgia. He recovered and said, "Then our course was already set from the moment I laid eyes on you, on that dirty street."

Royal was the first freeborn man Cora had ever met. There were many freemen in South Carolina who'd relocated for the so-called opportunities, but they'd served their time as chattel. Royal took in liberty with his first breath.

He was raised in Connecticut; his father was a barber and his mother a midwife. They were freeborn as well, hailing from New York City. On their orders, Royal apprenticed with a printer as soon as he was old enough to labor. His parents believed in the dignity of the honest trades, envisioning the generations of their family branching into the future, each more accomplished than the last. If the north had eliminated slavery, one day the abominable institution would fall everywhere. The negro's story may have started in this country with degradation, but triumph and prosperity would be his one day.

Had his parents realized the power of their reminiscences on the boy, they might have been more reserved in their stories of their native city. Royal lit out for Manhattan at eighteen, and his first sight of the majestic city from the rail of the ferry confirmed his fate. He took a room with three other men in a colored boardinghouse in Five Points and hung a shingle as a barber until he met the famous Eugene Wheeler. The white man started a conversation with Royal at an antislavery meeting; impressed, Wheeler told him to come to his office the next day. Royal had read of the man's exploits in the newspaper—lawyer, abolitionist crusader, bane of slavers and those who did their dirty work. Royal scouted the city jail for runaways the lawyer might defend, ran messages between enigmatic persons, and distributed funds from antislavery societies to relocated fugitives. By his official induction into the underground railroad, he had been its instrument for some time.

"I oil the pistons," he liked to say. Royal placed the coded messages in the classifieds that informed runaways and conductors of departures. He bribed ship captains and constables, rowed shivering pregnant women across rivers in leaky skiffs, and delivered judges' release orders to frowning deputies. In general he was paired with a white ally, but Royal's quick wits and proud bearing made it clear the color of his skin was no impediment. "A free black walks different than a slave," he said. "White people recognize it immediately, even if they don't know it. Walks different, talks different, carries himself different. It's in the bones." Constables never detained him and kidnappers kept their distance.

His association with Red began with the Indiana posting. Red was from North Carolina, absconding after the regulators strung up his wife and child. He walked the Freedom Trail for miles, searching for their bodies to say goodbye. He failed—the trail of corpses went on forever it seemed, in every direction. When Red made it north, he took up with the railroad and dedicated himself to the cause with a sinister resourcefulness. On hearing of Cora's accidental killing of the boy in Georgia, he smiled and said, "Good."

The Justin mission was unusual from the start. Tennessee lay outside Royal's posting, but the railroad's local represent-ative had been out of contact since the wildfire. To cancel the train would be disastrous. With no one else available, Royal's superiors reluctantly sent the two colored agents deep into the Tennessee badlands.

The guns were Red's idea. Royal had never held one before.

"It fits in your hand," Royal said, "but it's as heavy as a cannon."

"You looked fearsome," Cora said.

"I was shaking, but inside," he told her.

Justin's master often hired him out for masonry work and a sympathetic employer made arrangements with the railroad on his behalf. There was one condition—that Justin hold off on making tracks until he finished the stone wall around the man's property. They agreed that a gap of three stones was acceptable, if Justin left thorough instructions for completion.

On the appointed day, Justin set off for work one last time. His absence wouldn't be noticed until nightfall; his employer insisted that Justin never showed up that morning. He was in the back of Royal and Red's cart by ten o'clock. The plan changed when they came upon Cora in town.

The train pulled into the Tennessee station. It was the most splendid locomotive yet, its shiny red paint returning the light even through the shroud of soot. The engineer was a jolly character with a booming voice, opening the door to the passenger car with no little ceremony. Cora suspected a kind of tunnel madness afflicted railroad engineers, to a man.

After the rickety boxcar and then the cargo platform that had conveyed her to North Carolina, to step into a proper passenger car—well-appointed and comfortable like the ones she'd read about in her almanacs—was a spectacular pleasure. There were seats enough for thirty, lavish and soft, and brass fixtures gleamed where the candlelight fell. The smell of fresh varnish made her feel like the inaugural passenger of a magical, maiden voyage. Cora slept across three seats, free from chains and attic gloom for the first time in months.

The iron horse still rumbled through the tunnel when she woke. Lumbly's words returned to her: *If you want to see what this nation is all about, you have to ride the rails. Look outside as you speed through, and you'll find the true face of America.* It was a joke, then, from the start. There was only darkness outside the windows on her journeys, and only ever would be darkness.

Justin talked in the seat in front of her. He said that his brother and three nieces he'd never met lived up in Canada. He'd spend a few days at the farm and then head north.

Royal assured the fugitive that the railroad was at his disposal. Cora sat up and he repeated what he'd just told her fellow fugitive. She could continue on to a connection in Indiana, or stay on the Valentine farm.

White people took John Valentine as one of theirs, Royal said. His skin was very light. Any person of color recognized his Ethiopian heritage immediately. That nose, those lips, good hair or no. His mother was a seamstress, his father a white peddler who passed through every few months. When the man died, he left his estate to his son, the first time he acknowledged the boy outside of the walls of their house.

Valentine tried his hand at potato farming. He employed six freemen to work his land. He never claimed to be that which he was not, but did not disabuse people of their assumptions. When Valentine purchased Gloria, no one thought twice. One way of keeping a woman was to keep her in bondage, especially if, like John Valentine, you were new to romantic liaisons. Only John, Gloria, and a judge on the other side of the state knew she was free. He was fond of books and taught his wife her letters. They raised two sons. The neighbors thought it broad-minded, if wasteful, that he set them free.

When his eldest boy was five, one of Valentine's teamsters was strung up and burned for reckless eyeballing. Joe's friends maintained that he hadn't been to town that day; a bank clerk friendly with Valentine shared the rumor that the woman was trying to make a paramour jealous. As the years pass, Valentine observed, racial violence only becomes more vicious in its expression. It will not abate or disappear, not anytime soon, and not in the south. He and his wife decided that Virginia was an unfit place to raise a family. They sold the farm and picked up stakes. Land was cheap in Indiana. There were white people there, too, but not so close.

Valentine learned the temperament of Indian corn. Three lucky seasons in a row. When he visited relations back in Virginia, he promoted the advantages of his new home. He hired old cronies. They could even live on his property until they found their footing; he'd expanded his acreage.

Those were the guests he invited. The farm as Cora discovered it originated one winter night after a blur of slow, heavy snow. The woman at the door was an awful sight, frozen half to death. Margaret was a runaway from Delaware. Her journey to the Valentine farm had been fraught—a troupe of hard characters took her on a zigzag route away from her master. A trapper, the pitchman of a medicine show. She roamed from town to town with a traveling dentist until he turned violent. The storm caught her between places. Margaret prayed to God for deliverance, promised an end to the wickedness and moral shortcomings she had expressed in her flight. The lights of Valentine emerged in the gloom.

Gloria tended to her visitor the best she could; the doctor came around on his pony. Margaret's chills never subsided. She expired a few days later.

The next time Valentine went east on business, a broadsheet promoting an antislavery meeting stopped him in his tracks. The woman in the snow was the emissary of a dispossessed tribe. He bent himself to their service.

By that autumn, his farm was the latest office of the underground railroad, busy with fugitives and conductors. Some runaways lingered; if they contributed, they could stay as long as they liked. They planted the corn. In an overgrown patch, a former plantation bricklayer built a forge for a former plantation blacksmith. The forge spat out nails at a remarkable rate. The men crosscut trees and erected cabins. A prominent abolitionist stopped for a day en route to Chicago and stayed for a week. Luminaries, orators, and artists started attending the Saturday-night discussions on the negro question. One freewoman had a sister in Delaware who'd gotten into difficulties; the sister came out west for a new start. Valentine and the farm's parents paid her to teach their children, and there were always more children.

With his white face, Royal said, Valentine went down to the county seat and bought parcels for his friends with black faces, the former field hands who had come west, the fugitives who had found a haven on his farm. Found a purpose. When the Valentines arrived, that neck of Indiana was unpopulated. As the towns erupted into being, quickened by the relentless American thirst, the black farm was there as a natural feature of the landscape, a mountain or a creek. Half the white stores depended on its patronage; Valentine residents filled the squares and Sunday markets to sell their crafts. "It's a place of healing," Royal told Cora on the train north. "Where you can take stock and make preparations for the next leg of the journey."

The previous night in Tennessee, Ridgeway had called Cora and her mother a flaw in the American scheme. If two women were a flaw, what was a community?

ROYAL didn't mention the philosophical disputes that dominated the weekly meetings. Mingo, with his schemes for the next stage in the progress of the colored tribe, and Lander, whose elegant but opaque appeals offered no easy remedy. The conductor also avoided the very real matter of the white settlers' mounting resentment of the negro outpost. The divisions would make themselves known by and by.

As they hurtled through the underground passage, a tiny ship on this impossible sea, Royal's endorsement achieved its purpose. Cora slapped her hands on the cushions of the parlor car and said the farm suited her just fine.

Justin stayed two days, filled his belly, and joined his relations in the north. He later sent a letter describing his welcome, his new position at a building company. His nieces had signed their names in different-colored ink, frisky and naïve. Once Valentine lay before her in its seductive plenty, there was no question of Cora leaving. She contributed to the life of the farm. This was labor she recognized, she understood the elemental rhythms of planting and harvest, the lessons and imperatives of the shifting seasons. Her visions of city life clouded—what did she know about places like New York City and Boston? She'd grown up with her hands in the dirt.

One month after her arrival, at the mouth of the ghost tunnel, Cora remained certain of her decision. She and Royal were about to return to the farm when a gust swept out of the tunnel's murky depths. As if something moved toward them, old and dark. She reached for Royal's arm.

"Why did you bring me here?" Cora said.

"We're not supposed to talk about what we do down here," Royal said. "And our passengers aren't supposed to talk about how the railroad operates—it'd put a lot of good people in danger. They could talk if they wanted to, but they don't."

It was true. When she told of her escape, she omitted the tunnels and kept to the main contours. It was private, a secret about yourself it never occurred to you to share. Not a bad secret, but an intimacy so much a part of who you were that it could not be made separate. It would die in the sharing.

"I showed you because you've seen more of the railroad than most," Royal continued. "I wanted you to see this—how it fits together. Or doesn't."

"I'm just a passenger."

"That's why," he said. He rubbed his spectacles with his shirt-tail. "The underground railroad is bigger than its operators—it's all of you, too. The small spurs, the big trunk lines. We have the newest locomotives and the obsolete engines, and we have

318

handcars like that one. It goes everywhere, to places we know and those we don't. We got this tunnel right here, running beneath us, and no one knows where it leads. If we keep the rail-road running, and none of us can figure it out, maybe you can."

She told him she didn't know why it was there, or what it meant. All she knew is that she didn't want to run anymore.

November sapped them with Indiana cold, but two events made Cora forget about the weather. The first was Sam's appearance on the farm. When he knocked on her cabin, she hugged him tight until he pleaded for her to stop. They wept. Sybil brewed cups of root tea while they composed themselves.

His coarse beard was entwined with gray and his belly had grown large, but he was the same garrulous fellow who'd taken in her and Caesar those long months past. The night the slave catcher came to town had cleaved him from his old life. Ridgeway snatched Caesar at the factory before Sam could warn him. Sam's voice faltered as he told her how their friend was beaten in the jail. He kept mum about his comrades, but one man said he'd seen the nigger talking to Sam on more than one occasion. That Sam abandoned the saloon in the middle of his shift—and the fact some in town had known Sam since they were children and disliked his self-satisfied nature—sufficed to get his house burned to the ground.

"My grandfather's house. My house. Everything that was mine." By the time the mob tore Caesar from the jail and mortally assaulted him, Sam was well on his way north. He paid a peddler for a ride and was on a ship bound for Delaware the next day.

A month later under cover of night, operatives filled in the entrance to the tunnel beneath his house, per railroad policy. Lumbly's station had been dealt with in similar fashion. "They don't like to take chances," he said. The men brought him back a souvenir, a copper mug warped from the fire. He didn't recognize it but kept it anyway.

"I was a station agent. They found me different things to do." Sam drove runaways to Boston and New York, hunkered over the latest surveys to devise escape routes, and took care of the final arrangements that would save a fugitive's life. He even posed as a slave catcher named "James Olney," prying slaves from jail on the pretext of delivering them to their masters. The stupid constables and deputies. Racial prejudice rotted one's faculties, he said. He demonstrated his slave-catcher voice and swagger, to Cora's and Sybil's amusement.

He had just brought his latest cargo to the Valentine farm, a family of three who'd been hiding out in New Jersey. They had insinuated themselves into the colored community there, Sam said, but a slave catcher nosed around and it was time to flee. It was his final mission for the underground railroad. He was western bound. "Every pioneer I meet, they like their whiskey. They'll be needing barkeeps in California."

It heartened her to see her friend happy and fat. So many of those who had helped Cora had come to awful fates. She had not got him killed.

Then he gave her the news from her plantation, the second item that took the sting out of the Indiana cold.

Terrance Randall was dead.

From all accounts, the slave master's preoccupation with Cora and her escape only deepened over time. He neglected the plantation's affairs. His day to day on the estate consisted of conducting sordid parties in the big house and putting his slaves to bleak amusements, forcing them to serve as his victims in Cora's stead. Terrance continued to advertise for her capture, filling the classifieds in far-off states with her description and details of her crime. He upped the considerable reward more than once—Sam had seen the bulletins himself, astounded—and hosted any slave catcher who passed through, to provide a fuller portrait of Cora's villainy and also to shame the incompetent Ridgeway, who had failed first his father and then him.

Terrance died in New Orleans, in a chamber of a Creole brothel. His heart relented, weakened by months of dissipation.

"Or even his heart was tired of his wickedness," Cora said. As Sam's information settled, she asked about Ridgeway.

Sam waved his hand dismissively. "He's the butt of humor now. He'd been at the end of his career even before"—here he paused—"the incident in Tennessee."

Cora nodded. Red's act of murder was not spoken of. The railroad discharged him once they got the full story. Red wasn't bothered. He had new ideas about how to break the stranglehold of slavery and refused to give up his guns. "Once he lays his hand to the plow," Royal said, "he is not one to turn back." Royal was sad to see his friend ride off, but there was no bringing their methods into convergence, not after Tennessee. Cora's own act of murder he excused as a matter of self-protection, but Red's naked bloodthirstiness was another matter.

Ridgeway's penchant for violence and odd fixations had made it hard to find men willing to ride with him. His soiled reputation, coupled with Boseman's death and the humiliation of being bested by nigger outlaws, turned him into a pariah among his cohort. The Tennessee sheriffs still searched for the murderers, of course, but Ridgeway was out of the hunt. He had not been heard of since the summer.

"What about the boy, Homer?"

Sam had heard about the strange little creature. It was he who eventually brought help to the slave catcher, out in the forest. Homer's bizarre manner did nothing for Ridgeway's standing—their arrangement fed unseemly speculations. At any rate, the two disappeared together, their bond unbroken by the assault. "To a dank cave," Sam said, "as befits those worthless shits."

Sam stayed on the farm for three days, pursuing the affections of Georgina to no avail. Long enough to mix it up with the shucking bee.

THE competition unfolded on the first night of the full moon. The children spent all day arranging the corn into two mammoth piles, inside a border of red leaves. Mingo captained one team—the second year in a row, Sybil observed with distaste. He picked a team full of allies, heedless of representing the breadth of farm society. Valentine's eldest son, Oliver, gathered a diverse group of newcomers and old hands. "And our distinguished guest, of course," Oliver said finally, beckoning Sam.

A little boy blew the whistle and the shucking began in a frenzy. This year's prize was a large silver mirror Valentine had picked up in Chicago. The mirror stood between the piles, tied with a blue ribbon, reflecting the orange flicker of the jack-o'-lanterns. The captains shouted orders to their men while the audience hooted and clapped. The fiddler played a fast and comical accompaniment. The smaller children raced around the piles, snatching the husks, sometimes before they even touched the ground.

"Get that corn!"

"You best hurry up over there!"

Cora watched from the side, Royal's hand resting on her hip. She had permitted him to kiss her the night before, which he took, not without reason, as an indication Cora was finally allowing him to step up his pursuit. She'd made him wait. He'd wait more. But Sam's report on Terrance's demise had softened her, even as it bred spiteful visions. She envisioned her former master tangled in linens, purple tongue poking from his lips. Calling for help that never arrived. Melting to a gory pulp in his casket, and then torments in a hell out of Revelation. Cora believed in that part of the holy book, at least. It described the slave plantation in code.

"This wasn't harvest on Randall," Cora said. "It was full moon when we picked, but there was always blood."

"You're not on Randall anymore," Royal said. "You're free."

She kept ahold of her temper and whispered, "How so? Land is property. Tools is property. Somebody's going to auction the Randall plantation, the slaves, too. Relations always coming out when someone dies. I'm still property, even in Indiana."

"He's dead. No cousin is going to bother over getting you back, not like he did." He said, "You're free."

Royal joined the singing to change the subject and to remind her that there were things a body could feel good about. A community that had come together, from seeding to harvest to the bee. But the song was a work song Cora knew from the cotton rows, drawing her back to the Randall cruelties and making her heart thud. Connelly used to start the song as a signal to go back to picking after a whipping.

How could such a bitter thing become a means of pleasure? Everything on Valentine was the opposite. Work needn't be suffering, it could unite folks. A bright child like Chester might thrive and prosper, as Molly and her friends did. A mother raise her daughter with love and kindness. A beautiful soul like Caesar could be anything he wanted here, all of them could be: own a spread, be a schoolteacher, fight for colored rights. Even be a poet. In her Georgia misery she had pictured freedom, and it had not looked like this. Freedom was a community laboring for something lovely and rare.

Mingo won. His men chaired him around the piles of naked cobs, hoarse with cheers. Jimmy said he'd never seen a white man work so hard and Sam beamed with pleasure. Georgina remained unswayed, however.

On the day of Sam's departure, Cora embraced him and kissed his whiskered cheek. He said he'd send a note when he settled, wherever that was.

They were in the time of short days and long nights. Cora visited the library frequently as the weather turned. She brought Molly when she could coax the girl. They sat next to each other, Cora with a history or a romance, and Molly turning the pages of a fairy tale. A teamster stopped them one day as they were about to enter. "Master said the only thing more dangerous than a nigger with a gun," he told them, "was a nigger with a book. That must be a big pile of black powder, then!"

When some of the grateful residents proposed building an addition to Valentine's house for his books, Gloria suggested a separate structure. "That way, anyone with a mind to pick up a book can do so at their leisure." It also gave the family more privacy. They were generous, but there was a limit.

They put up the library next to the smokehouse. The room smelled pleasantly of smoke when Cora sat down in one of the big chairs with Valentine's books. Royal said it was the biggest collection of negro literature this side of Chicago. Cora didn't know if that was true, but she certainly didn't lack for reading material. Apart from the treatises on farming and the cultivation of various crops, there were rows and rows of histories. The ambitions of the Romans and the victories of the Moors, the royal feuds of Europe. Oversize volumes contained maps of lands Cora had never heard of, the outlines of the unconquered world.

And the disparate literature of the colored tribes. Accounts of African empires and the miracles of the Egyptian slaves who had erected pyramids. The farm's carpenters were true artisans—they had to be to keep all those books from jumping off the shelves, so many wonders did they contain. Pamphlets of verse by negro poets, autobiographies of colored orators. Phillis Wheatley and Jupiter Hammon. There was a man named Benjamin Banneker who composed almanacs—almanacs! she devoured them all—and served as a confidant to Thomas Jefferson, who composed the Declaration. Cora read the accounts of slaves who had been born in chains and learned their letters. Of Africans who had been stolen, torn from their homes and families, and described the miseries of their bondage and then their hair-raising escapes. She recognized their stories as her own. They were the stories of all the colored people she had ever known, the stories of black people yet to be born, the foundations of their triumphs.

People had put all that down on paper in tiny rooms. Some of them even had dark skin like her. It put her head in a fog each time she opened the door. She'd have to get started if she was going to read them all.

Valentine joined her one afternoon. Cora was friendly with Gloria, who called Cora "the Adventuress," owing to the many complications of her journey, but she hadn't spoken to Gloria's husband beyond greetings. The enormity of her debt was inexpressible, so she avoided him altogether.

He regarded the cover of her book, a romance about a Moorish boy who becomes the scourge of the Seven Seas. The language was simple and she was making quick work of it. "I never did read that," Valentine said. "I heard you like to spend time here. You're the one from Georgia?"

She nodded.

"Never been there—the stories are so dismal, I'm liable to lose my temper and make my wife a widow."

Cora returned his smile. He'd been a presence in the summer months, looking after the Indian corn. The field hands knew indigo, tobacco—cotton, of course—but corn was its own beast. He was pleasant and patient in his instructions. With the changing of the season he was scarce. Feeling poorly, people said. He spent most of his time in the farmhouse, squaring the farm's accounts.

He wandered to the shelves of maps. Now that they were in the same room, Cora was compelled to rectify her months of silence. She asked after the preparations for the gathering.

"Yes, that," Valentine said. "Do you think it will happen?"

"It has to," Cora said.

The meeting had been postponed twice on account of Lander's speaking engagements. Valentine's kitchen table started the culture of debate on the farm, when Valentine and his friends—and later, visiting scholars and noted abolitionists—stayed up past midnight arguing over the colored question. The need for trade schools, colored medical schools. For a voice in Congress, if not a representative then a strong alliance with liberal-minded whites. How to undo slavery's injury to the mental faculties—so many freed men continued to be enslaved by the horrors they'd endured.

The supper conversations became ritual, outgrowing the house and migrating to the meeting house, whereupon Gloria stopped serving food and drink and let them fend for themselves. Those favoring a more gradual view of colored progress traded barbs with those on a more pressing schedule. When Lander arrived—the most dignified and eloquent colored man any of them had seen—the discussions adopted a more local character. The direction of the nation was one matter; the future of the farm, another.

"Mingo promises it will be a memorable occasion," Valentine said. "A spectacle of rhetoric. These days, I hope they get the spectacle done early so I can retire at a decent hour." Worn down by Mingo's lobbying, Valentine had ceded organization of the debate.

Mingo had lived on the farm for a long time, and when it came to addressing Lander's appeals, it was good to have a native voice. He was not as accomplished a speaker, but as a former slave spoke for a large segment of the farm.

Mingo had taken advantage of the delay to press for improved relations with the white towns. He swayed a few from Lander's camp—not that it was clear exactly what Lander had in mind. Lander was plainspoken but opaque.

"What if they decide that we should leave?" Cora was surprised at her difficulty in mustering the words.

"They? You're one of us." Valentine took the chair that Molly favored on her visits. Up close, it was plain the burden of so many souls had exacted its toll. The man was weariness

329

itself. "It may be out of our hands," he said. "What we built here . . . there are too many white people who don't want us to have it. Even if they didn't suspect our alliance with the railroad. Look around. If they kill a slave for learning his letters, how do you think they feel about a library? We're in a room brimming with ideas. Too many ideas for a colored man. Or woman."

Cora had come to cherish the impossible treasures of the Valentine farm so completely that she'd forgotten how impossible they were. The farm and the adjacent ones operated by colored interests were too big, too prosperous. A pocket of blackness in the young state. Valentine's negro heritage became known years before. Some felt tricked that they'd treated a nigger as an equal—and then to have that uppity nigger shame them with his success.

She told Valentine of an incident the previous week, when she'd been walking up the road and was almost trampled by a wagon. The driver yelled disgusting epithets as he passed. Cora was not the only victim of abuse. The new arrivals to the nearby towns, the rowdies and low whites, started fights when residents came for supplies. Harassed the young women. Last week a feed store hung a shingle saying WHITES ONLY—a nightmare reaching up from the south to claim them.

Valentine said, "We have a legal right as American citizens to be here." But the Fugitive Slave Law was a legal fact as well. Their collaborations with the underground railroad complicated things. Slave catchers didn't show their faces often, but it wasn't unheard of. Last spring, two catchers appeared with a warrant to search every house on the farm. Their quarry was long gone, but the reminder of the slave patrols exposed the precarious nature of the residents' lives. One of the cooks urinated in their canteens as they ransacked the cabins.

"Indiana was a slave state," Valentine continued. "That evil soaks into the soil. Some say it steeps and gets stronger. Maybe this isn't the place. Maybe Gloria and I should have kept going after Virginia."

"I feel it when I go to town now," Cora said. "See that look in their eyes I know." It wasn't just Terrance and Connelly and Ridgeway she recognized, the savage ones. She'd watched the faces in the park in North Carolina during the daytime, and at night when they gathered for atrocities. Round white faces like an endless field of cotton bolls, all the same material.

Taking in Cora's downcast expression, Valentine told her, "I'm proud of what we've built here, but we started over once. We can do it again. I have two strong sons to help now, and we'll get a nice sum for the land. Gloria has always wanted to see Oklahoma, although for the life of me I don't know why. I try to make her happy."

"If we stay," Cora said, "Mingo wouldn't allow people like me. The runaways. Those with nowhere to go."

"Talk is good," Valentine said. "Talk clears the air and makes it so you can see what's what. We'll see what the mood of the farm is. It's mine, but it's everybody's, too. Yours. I'll abide by the decision of the people."

Cora saw the discussion had depleted him. "Why do all this," she asked. "For all of us?"

"I thought you were one of the smart ones," Valentine said. "Don't you know? White man ain't going to do it. We have to do it ourselves."

If the farmer had come in for a specific book, he left empty-handed. The wind whistled through the open door and Cora pulled her shawl tight. If she kept reading, she might start another book by suppertime.

The final gathering on Valentine farm took place on a brisk December night. In the years to come, the survivors shared their versions of what happened that evening, and why. Until the day she died, Sybil insisted Mingo was the informer. She was an old lady then, living on a Michigan lake with a gang of grandchildren who had to listen to her familiar stories. According to Sybil, Mingo told the constables that the farm harbored fugitives and provided the particulars for a successful ambush. A dramatic raid would put an end to relations with the railroad, the endless stream of needy negroes, and ensure the longevity of the farm. When asked if he anticipated the violence, she pressed her lips into a line and said no more.

Another survivor—Tom the blacksmith—observed that the law had hunted Lander for months. He was the intended target. Lander's rhetoric inflamed passions; he fomented rebellion; he was too uppity to allow to run free. Tom never learned to read but liked to show off his volume of Lander's *Appeal*, which the great orator had signed to him.

Joan Watson was born on the farm. She was six years old that night. In the aftermath of the attack she wandered the forest for three days, chewing acorns, until a wagon train discovered her. When she got older, she described herself as a student of American history, attuned to the inevitable. She said that white towns had simply banded together to rid themselves of the black stronghold in their midst. That is how the European tribes operate, she said. If they can't control it, they destroy it.

If anyone on the farm knew what was to come, they gave no sign. Saturday proceeded in lazy calm. Cora spent most of the day in her bedroom with the latest almanac Royal had given her. He'd picked it up in Chicago. He knocked on her door 'round midnight to give it to her; he knew she was awake. It was late and she didn't want to disturb Sybil and Molly. Cora took him into her room for the first time.

She broke down at the sight of next year's almanac. Thick as a book of prayer. Cora had told Royal about the attic days in North Carolina, but seeing the year on the cover—an object conjured from the future—spurred Cora to her own magic. She told him about her childhood on Randall where she had picked cotton, tugging a sack. About her grandmother Ajarry who'd been kidnapped from her family in Africa and tilled a small corner of land, the only thing to call her own. Cora spoke of her mother, Mabel, who absconded one day and left her to the inconstant mercy of the world. About Blake and the doghouse and how she had faced him down with a hatchet. When she told Royal about the night they took her behind the smokehouse and she apologized to him for letting it happen, he told her to hush.

She was the one due an apology for all her hurts, he said. He told her that every one of her enemies, all the masters and overseers of her suffering, would be punished, if not in this world then the next, for justice may be slow and invisible, but it always renders its true verdict in the end. He folded his body into hers to quiet her shaking and sobs and they fell asleep like that, in the back room of a cabin on the Valentine farm.

She didn't believe what he said about justice, but it was nice to hear him say it.

Then she woke up the next morning and felt better, and had to admit that she did believe it, maybe just a little.

Thinking Cora was laid up with one of her headaches, Sybil brought her some food around noon. She teased Cora about Royal staying the night. She was mending the dress she'd wear to the gathering when he "come sneaking out of here holding his boots in his hand and looking like a dog that'd stolen some scraps." Cora just smiled.

"Your man ain't the only one come around last night," Sybil said. Lander had returned.

That accounted for Sybil's playfulness. Lander impressed her mightily, every one of his visits fortifying her for days after. Those honeyed words of his. Now he had finally come back to Valentine. The gathering would happen, to an unknowable outcome. Sybil didn't want to move west and leave her home, which everyone assumed to be Lander's solution. She'd been adamant about staying ever since the talk of resettling started. But she wouldn't abide Mingo's conditions, that they stop providing shelter to those in need. "There ain't no place like here, not anywhere. He wants to kill it."

"Valentine won't let him spoil it," Cora said, though after talking with the man in the library it seemed he'd already packed up in his mind.

"We'll see," Sybil said. "I may have to give a speech my own self, and tell these people what they need to hear."

That night Royal and Cora sat in the front row next to Mingo and his family, the wife and children he had rescued from slavery. His wife, Angela, was silent, as always; to hear her speak, you had to hide under the window of their cabin as she counseled her man in private. Mingo's daughters wore bright blue dresses, their long pigtails entwined with white ribbons. Lander played guessing games with the youngest one as the residents filled the meeting hall. Her name was Amanda. She held a bouquet of cloth flowers; he made a joke about them and they laughed. When Cora caught Lander at a moment such as this, in a brief lapse between performances, he reminded her of Molly. For all his friendly talk, she thought he'd prefer to be home by himself, playing concerts in empty rooms.

He had long, dainty fingers. How curious that one who'd never picked a boll or dug a trench or experienced the cat-o'-nine-tails had come to speak for those who had been defined by those things. He was lean in build, with glowing skin that announced his mixed parentage. She had never seen him rush or hurry. The man moved with exquisite calm, like a leaf drifting on the surface of a pond, making its own way on gentle currents.

Then he opened his mouth, and you saw that the forces steering him to your presence were not gentle at all.

There were no white visitors this night. Everyone who lived and worked on the farm was in attendance, as well as the families from the neighboring colored farms. Seeing them all in one room, Cora got an idea of how large they were for the first time. There were people she'd never seen before, like the mischievous little boy who winked at her when their eyes met. Strangers but family, cousins but never introduced. She was surrounded by men and women who'd been born in Africa, or born in chains, who had freed themselves or escaped. Branded, beaten, raped. Now they were here. They were free and black and stewards of their own fates. It made her shiver.

Valentine gripped the lectern for support. "I didn't grow up the way you did," he said. "My mother never feared for my safety. No trader was going to snatch me in the night and sell me south. The whites saw the color of my skin, and that sufficed to let me be. I told myself I was doing nothing wrong, but I conducted myself in ignorance all my days. Until you came here and made a life with us."

He left Virginia, he said, to spare his children the ravages of prejudice and its bully partner, violence. But saving two children is not enough when God has gifted you with so much. "A woman came to us out of the bitter winter—sick and desperate. We could not save her." Valentine's voice rasped. "I neglected my duty. As long as one of our family endured the torments of bondage, I was a freeman in name only. I want to express my gratitude to everyone here for helping me to put things right. Whether you have been among us for years or just a few hours, you have saved my life."

He faltered. Gloria joined him and gathered his body in hers. "Now some of our family have things they want to share with you," Valentine said, clearing his throat. "I hope you'll listen to them like you listen to me. There's room enough for different notions when it comes to charting our path through the wilderness. When the night is dark and full of treacherous footing."

The farm's patriarch withdrew from the lectern and Mingo replaced him. Mingo's children trailed him, kissing his hands for good luck before returning to the pews.

Mingo opened with the story of his journey, the nights he spent begging the Lord for guidance, the long years it took to purchase his family's freedom. "With my honest labor, one by one, just as you saved yourselves." He rubbed a knuckle in his eye.

Then he changed course. "We accomplished the impossible," Mingo said, "but not everyone has the character we do. We're not all going to make it. Some of us are too far gone. Slavery has twisted their minds, an imp filling their minds with foul ideas. They have given themselves over to whiskey and its false comforts. To hopelessness and its constant devils. You've seen these lost ones on the plantations, on the streets of the towns and cities—those who will not, cannot respect themselves. You've seen them here, receiving the gift of this place but unable to fit in. They always disappear in the night because deep in their hearts they know they are unworthy. It is too late for them."

Some of his cronies in the back of the room amened. There are realities we have to face, Mingo explained. White people aren't going to change overnight. The farm's dreams are worthy and true, but require a gradual approach. "We can't save everyone, and acting as if we can will doom us all. You think the white folks—just a few miles from here—are going to endure our impudence forever? We flaunt their weakness. Harboring runaways. Underground railroad agents with guns coming and going. People who are wanted for murder. Criminals." Cora made fists as Mingo's gaze fell on her.

The Valentine farm had taken glorious steps into the future, he said. White benefactors supplied schoolbooks for their children—why not ask them to pass the hat for entire schools? And not just one or two, but dozens more? By proving the negro's thrift and intelligence, Mingo argued, he will enter into American society as a productive member with full rights. Why jeopardize that? We need to slow things down. Reach an accommodation with our neighbors and, most of all, stop activities that will force their wrath upon us. "We've built something astounding here," he concluded. "But it is a precious thing, and it needs to be protected, nourished, or else it will wither, like a rose in a sudden frost."

During the applause, Lander whispered to Mingo's daughter and they giggled again. She removed one of the cloth flowers from her bouquet and twisted it into the top buttonhole of his green suit. Lander pretended to sniff its fragrance and mock-swooned.

"It's time," Royal said as Lander shook Mingo's hand and assumed his place at the lectern. Royal had spent the day with him, walking the grounds and talking. Royal didn't share what Lander would speak on that night, but he had an optimistic air. Formerly, when the subject of relocating came up, Royal told Cora he favored Canada over the west. "They know how to treat free negroes there," he said. And his work with the railroad? Have to settle down sometime, Royal said. Can't raise a family while running around on railroad errands. Cora changed the subject when he engaged in such talk.

Now she'd see for herself—they'd all see—what the man from Boston had in mind.

"Brother Mingo made some good points," Lander said. "We can't save everyone. But that doesn't mean we can't try. Sometimes a useful delusion is better than a useless truth. Nothing's going to grow in this mean cold, but we can still have flowers.

"Here's one delusion: that we can escape slavery. We can't. Its scars will never fade. When you saw your mother sold off, your father beaten, your sister abused by some boss or master, did you ever think you would sit here today, without chains, without the yoke, among a new family? Everything you ever knew told you that freedom was a trick—yet here you are. Still we run, tracking by the good full moon to sanctuary.

"Valentine farm is a delusion. Who told you the negro deserved a place of refuge? Who told you that you had that right? Every minute of your life's suffering has argued otherwise. By

340

every fact of history, it can't exist. This place must be a delusion, too. Yet here we are.

"And America, too, is a delusion, the grandest one of all. The white race believes—believes with all its heart—that it is their right to take the land. To kill Indians. Make war. Enslave their brothers. This nation shouldn't exist, if there is any justice in the world, for its foundations are murder, theft, and cruelty. Yet here we are.

"I'm supposed to answer Mingo's call for gradual progress, for closing our doors to those in need. I'm supposed to answer those who think this place is too close to the grievous influence of slavery, and that we should move west. I don't have an answer for you. I don't know what we should do. The word *we*. In some ways, the only thing we have in common is the color of our skin. Our ancestors came from all over the African continent. It's quite large. Brother Valentine has the maps of the world in his splendid library, you can look for yourself. They had different ways of subsistence, different customs, spoke a hundred different languages. And that great mixture was brought to America in the holds of slave ships. To the north, the south. Their sons and daughters picked tobacco, cultivated cotton, worked on the largest estates and smallest farms. We are craftsmen and midwives and preachers and peddlers. Black hands built the White House, the seat of our nation's government. The word *we*. We are not one people but many different people. How can one person speak for this great, beautiful race—which is not one race but many, with a million desires and hopes and wishes for ourselves and our children?

341

"For we are Africans in America. Something new in the history of the world, without models for what we will become.

"Color must suffice. It has brought us to this night, this discussion, and it will take us into the future. All I truly know is that we rise and fall as one, one colored family living next door to one white family. We may not know the way through the forest, but we can pick each other up when we fall, and we will arrive together."

WHEN the former residents of the Valentine farm recalled that moment, when they told strangers and grandchildren of how they used to live and how it came to an end, their voices still trembled years later. In Philadelphia, in San Francisco, in the cow towns and ranches where they eventually made a home, they mourned those who died that day. The air in the room turned prickly, they told their families, quickened by an unseen power. Whether they had been born free or in chains, they inhabited that moment as one: the moment when you aim yourself at the north star and decide to run. Perhaps they were on the verge of some new order, on the verge of clasping reason to disorder, of putting all the lessons of their history to bear on the future. Or perhaps time, as it will, lent the occasion a gravity that it did not possess, and everything was as Lander insisted: They were deluded.

But that didn't mean it wasn't true.

The shot hit Lander in the chest. He fell back, dragging down the lectern. Royal was the first one to his feet. As he ran to the fallen man, three bullets bit into his back. He jerked like one of Saint Vitus's dancers and dropped. Then came a chorus of rifle fire, screams, and broken glass, and a mad scramble overtook the meeting hall.

The white men outside whooped and howled over the carnage. Pell-mell the residents hastened to the exits, squeezing between pews, climbing over them, climbing over one another. Once the main entrance bottlenecked, people crawled over the windowsills. More rifles crackled. Valentine's sons helped their father to the door. To the left of the stage, Gloria crouched over Lander. She saw there was nothing to be done and followed her family out.

Cora held Royal's head in her lap, just as she had the afternoon of the picnic. She ran her fingers through his curls and rocked him and wept. Royal smiled through the blood that bubbled on his lips. He told her not to be afraid, the tunnel would save her again. "Go to the house in the woods. You can tell me where it goes." His body went slack.

Two men grabbed her and removed her from Royal's body. It's not safe here, they said. One of them was Oliver Valentine, come back to help others escape the meeting house. He cried and shouted. Cora broke from her rescuers once they got her outside and down the steps. The farm was a commotion. The white posse dragged men and women into the dark, their hideous faces awash with delight. A musket cut down one of Sybil's carpenters—he held a baby in his arms and they both crashed to the ground. No one knew where best to run, and no reasonable voice could be heard above the clamor. Each person on their own, as they ever had been.

Mingo's daughter Amanda shook on her knees, her family absent. Desolate in the dirt. Her bouquet had shed its petals. She gripped the naked stems, the iron wires the blacksmith had drawn out on the anvil last week, just for her. The wires cut her palms, she gripped them so tight. More blood in the dirt. As an old woman she would read about the Great War in Europe and recall this night. She lived on Long Island then, after roaming all over the country, in a small house with a Shinnecock sailor who doted on her to excess. She'd spent time in Louisiana and Virginia, where her father opened colored institutions of learning, and California. A spell in Oklahoma, where the Valentines resettled. The conflict in Europe was terrible and violent, she told her sailor, but she took exception to the name. The Great War had always been between the white and the black. It always would be.

Cora called for Molly. She didn't see anyone she recognized; their faces had been transformed by fear. The heat from the fires washed over her. Valentine's house was ablaze. A jar of oil exploded against the second floor and John and Gloria's bedroom caught. The windows of the library shattered and Cora saw the books burning on the shelves inside. She made two steps toward it before Ridgeway grabbed her. They struggled and his big arms encircled her, her feet kicking against the air like those of one hanging from a tree.

Homer was at his side—he was the boy she'd seen in the pews, winking at her. He wore suspenders and a white blouse, looking like the innocent child he would have been in a different world. At the sight of him, Cora added her voice to the chorus of lamentation that echoed across the farm.

"There's a tunnel, sir," Homer said. "I heard him say it."

Mabel

‖‖‖‖‖‖‖‖‖‖‖‖‖‖‖‖‖‖‖‖‖‖‖‖‖‖‖‖‖‖‖‖

‖‖‖‖‖‖‖‖‖‖‖‖‖‖‖‖‖‖‖‖‖‖‖‖‖‖‖‖‖‖‖‖

‖‖‖‖‖‖‖‖‖‖‖‖‖‖‖‖‖‖‖‖‖‖‖‖‖‖‖‖‖‖‖‖

THE first and last things she gave to her daughter were apologies. Cora slept in her stomach, the size of a fist, when Mabel apologized for what she was bringing her into. Cora slept next to her in the loft, ten years later, when Mabel apologized for making her a stray. Cora didn't hear either one.

At the first clearing Mabel found the north star and reoriented. She gathered herself and resumed her escape through the black water. Kept her eyes forward because when she looked back she saw the faces of those she left behind.

She saw Moses's face. She remembered Moses when he was little. A twitching bundle so frail no one expected him to survive until he was old enough for pickaninny work, the trash gang, or offering a ladle of water in the cotton. Not when most children on Randall died before their first steps. His mother used the witch-woman cures, the poultices and root potions, and sang to him every night, crooning in their cabin. Lullabies and work tunes and her own maternal wishes in singsong: Keep the food in your stomach, break the fever, breathe until morning. He outlived most of the boys born that year. Everybody knew it was his mother, Kate, who saved him from affliction and the early winnowing that is every plantation slave's first trial.

Mabel remembered when Old Randall sold off Kate once her arm went numb and wasn't fit for labor. Moses's first whipping for stealing a potato, and his second whipping for idleness, when Connelly had the boy's wounds washed out with hot pepper until he howled. None of that made Moses mean. It made him silent and strong and fast, faster than any other picker in his gang. He wasn't mean until Connelly made him a boss, the master's eyes and ears over his own kind. That's when he became Moses the monster, Moses who made the other slaves quake, black terror of the rows.

When he told her to come to the schoolhouse she scratched his face and spat at him and he just smiled and said if you're not game I'll find someone else—how old is your Cora now? Cora was eight. Mabel didn't fight him after that. He was quick and he wasn't rough after that first time. Women and animals, you only have to break them in once, he said. They stay broke.

All those faces, living and dead. Ajarry twitching in the cotton, bloody foam on her lips. She saw Polly swinging on a rope, sweet Polly, who she'd come up with in the quarter, born the same month. Connelly transferred them from the yard to the cotton fields the same day. Always in tandem until Cora lived but Polly's baby didn't—the young women delivered within two weeks of each other, with one baby girl crying when the midwife pulled her out and the other making no sound at all. Stillborn and stone. When Polly hung herself in the barn with a loop of hemp, Old Jockey said, You did everything together. Like Mabel was supposed to hang herself now, too.

She started to see Cora's face and she looked away. She ran.

Men start off good and then the world makes them mean. The world is mean from the start and gets meaner every day. It uses you up until you only dream of death. Mabel wasn't going to die on Randall, even if she'd never been a mile away from the grounds in her life. One midnight she decided, up in the sweltering loft, *I am going to survive*—and the next midnight she was in the swamp, tracking after the moon in stolen shoes. She turned her escape over in her head all day, let no other thought intrude or dissuade. There were islands in the swamp—follow them to the continent of freedom. She took the vegetables she raised, flint and tinder, a machete. Everything else she left behind, including her girl.

Cora, sleeping back in the cabin she was born in, that Mabel was born in. Still a girl, before the worst of it, before she learns the size and heft of a woman's burdens. If Cora's father had lived, would Mabel be here now, tramping through the marsh? Mabel was fourteen when Grayson arrived on the southern half, sold down south by a drunken indigo farmer in North Carolina. Tall and black, sweet-tempered with a laughing eye. Swaggering even after the hardest toil. They couldn't touch him.

She picked him out that first day and decided: him. When he grinned it was the moon shining down on her, a presence in the sky blessing her. He scooped her up and twirled her when they danced. I'm going to buy our freedom, he said, hay in his hair from where they lay down. Old Randall didn't go in for that, but he'd convince him. Work hard, be the best hand on the plantation—he'd earn his way out of bondage and take her, too. She said, You promise? Half believing he could do it. Grayson the Sweet, dead of fever before she knew she carried their child. His name never again crossed her lips.

Mabel tripped over a cypress root and went sprawling into the water. She staggered through the reeds to the island ahead and flattened on the ground. Didn't know how long she had been running. Panting and tuckered out.

She took a turnip from her sack. It was young and tender-soft, and she took a bite. The sweetest crop she'd ever raised in Ajarry's plot, even with the taste of marsh water. Her mother had left that in her inheritance, at least, a tidy plot to watch over. You're supposed to pass on something useful to your children. The better parts of Ajarry never took root in Mabel. Her indomitability, her perseverance. But there was a plot three yards square and the hearty stuff that sprouted from it. Her mother had protected it with all her heart. The most valuable land in all of Georgia.

She lay on her back and ate another turnip. Without the sound of her splashing and huffing, the noises of the swamp resumed. The spadefoot toads and turtles and slithering creatures, the chattering of black insects. Above—through the leaves and branches of the black-water trees—the sky scrolled before her, new constellations wheeling in the darkness as she relaxed. No patrollers, no bosses, no cries of anguish to induct her into another's despair. No cabin walls shuttling her through the night seas like the hold of a slave ship. Sandhill cranes and warblers, otters splashing. On the bed of damp earth, her breathing slowed and that which separated herself from the swamp disappeared. She was free.

This moment.

She had to go back. The girl was waiting on her. This would have to do for now. Her hopelessness had gotten the best of her, speaking under her thoughts like a demon. She would keep this moment close, her own treasure. When she found the words to share it with Cora, the girl would understand there was something beyond the plantation, past all that she knew. That one day if she stayed strong, the girl could have it for herself.

The world may be mean, but people don't have to be, not if they refuse.

Mabel picked up her sack and got her bearings. If she kept a good pace, she'd be back well before first light and the earliest risers on the plantation. Her escape had been a preposterous idea, but even a sliver of it amounted to the best adventure of her life.

Mabel pulled out another turnip and took a bite. It really was sweet.

The snake found her not long into her return. She was wending through a cluster of stiff reeds when she disturbed its rest. The cottonmouth bit her twice, in the calf and deep in the meat of her thigh. No sound but pain. Mabel refused to believe it. It was a water snake, it had to be. Ornery but harmless. When her mouth went minty and her leg tingled, she knew. She made it another mile. She had dropped her sack along the way, lost her course in the black water. She could have made it farther—working Randall land had made her strong, strong in body if nothing else—but she stumbled onto a bed of soft moss and it felt right. She said, Here, and the swamp swallowed her up.

The North

RAN AWAY

from her legal but not rightful master fifteen months past, a slave girl called CORA; of ordinary height and dark brown complexion; has a star-shape mark on her temple from an injury; possessed of a spirited nature and devious method. Possibly answering to the name BESSIE.

Last seen in Indiana among the outlaws of John Valentine Farm.

She has stopped running.

Reward remains unclaimed.

SHE WAS NEVER PROPERTY.

December 23

HER point of departure that final voyage on the underground railroad was a tiny station beneath an abandoned house. The ghost station.

Cora led them there after her capture. The posse of blood-thirsty whites still rampaged across the Valentine farm when they left. The gunfire and screams came from farther away, deeper in the property. The newer cabins, the mill. Perhaps as far as the Livingston spread, the mayhem encompassing the neighboring farms. The whites meant to rout the entirety of colored settlers.

Cora fought and kicked as Ridgeway carried her to the wagon. The burning library and farmhouse illuminated the grounds. After a barrage to his face, Homer finally gathered her feet together and they got her inside, chaining her wrists to her old ring in the wagon floor. One of the young white men watching the horses cheered and asked for a turn when they were done. Ridgeway clopped him in the face.

She relinquished the location to the house in the woods when the slave catcher put his pistol to her eye. Cora lay down on the bench, seized by one of her headaches. How to snuff her thoughts like a candle? Royal and Lander dead. The others who were cut down.

"One of the deputies said it reminded him of the old days of proper Indian raids," Ridgeway said. "Bitter Creek and Blue Falls. I think he was too young to remember that. Maybe his daddy." He sat in the back with her on the bench opposite, his outfit reduced to the wagon and the two skinny horses that pulled it. The fire danced outside, showing the holes and long tears in the canvas.

Ridgeway coughed. He had been diminished since Tennessee. The slave catcher was completely gray, unkempt, skin gone sallow. His speech was different, less commanding. Dentures replaced the teeth Cora ruined in their last encounter. "They buried Boseman in one of the plague cemeteries," he said. "He would have been appalled, but he didn't have much of a say. The one bleeding on the floor—that was the uppity bastard who ambushed us, yes? I recognized his spectacles."

Why had she put Royal off for so long? She thought they had time enough. Another thing that might have been, snipped at the roots as if by one of Dr. Stevens's surgical blades. She let the farm convince her the world is other than what it will always be. He must have known she loved him even if she hadn't told him. He had to.

Night birds screeched. After a time Ridgeway told her to keep a lookout for the path. Homer slowed the horses. She missed it twice, the fork in the road signaling they'd gone too far. Ridgeway slapped her across the face and told her to mind him. "It took me awhile to find my footing after Tennessee," he said. "You and your friends did me a bad turn. But that's done. You're going home, Cora. At last. Once I get a look-see at the famous underground railroad." He slapped her again. On the next circuit she found the cottonwoods that marked the turn.

Homer lit a lantern and they entered the mournful old house. He had changed out of his costume and back into his black suit and stovepipe hat. "Below the cellar," Cora said. Ridgeway was wary. He pulled up the door and jumped back, as if a host of black outlaws waited in a trap. The slave catcher handed her a candle and told her to go down first.

"Most people think it's a figure of speech," he said. "The underground. I always knew better. The secret beneath us, the entire time. We'll uncover them all after tonight. Every line, every one."

Whatever animals lived in the cellar were quiet this night. Homer checked the corners of the cellar. The boy came up with the spade and gave it to Cora.

She held out her chains. Ridgeway nodded. "Otherwise we'll be here all night." Homer undid the shackles. The white man was giddy, his former authority easing into his voice. In North Carolina, Martin had thought he was onto his father's buried treasure in the mine and discovered a tunnel instead. For the slave catcher the tunnel was all the gold in the world.

"Your master is dead," Ridgeway said as Cora dug. "I wasn't surprised to hear the news—he had a degenerate nature. I don't know if the current master of Randall will pay your reward. I don't rightly care." He was surprised at his words. "It wasn't going to be easy, I should have seen that. You're your mother's daughter through and through."

The spade struck the trapdoor. She cleared out a square. Cora had stopped listening to him, to Homer's unwholesome snickering. She and Royal and Red may have diminished the slave catcher when they last met, but it was Mabel who first laid him low. It flowed from her mother, his mania over their family. If not for her, the slave catcher wouldn't have obsessed so over Cora's capture. The one who escaped. After all it cost her, Cora didn't know if it made her proud or more spiteful toward the woman.

This time Homer lifted the trapdoor. The moldy smell gusted up.

"This is it?" Ridgeway asked.

"Yes, sir," Homer said.

Ridgeway waved Cora on with his pistol.

He would not be the first white man to see the underground railroad, but the first enemy. After all that had befallen her, the shame of betraying those who made possible her escape. She hesitated on the top step. On Randall, on Valentine, Cora never joined the dancing circles. She shrank from the spinning bodies, afraid of another person so close, so uncontrolled. Men had put a fear in her, those years ago. Tonight, she told herself. Tonight I will hold him close, as if in a slow dance. As if it were just the two of them in the lonesome world, bound to each other until the end of the song. She waited until the slave catcher was on the third step. She spun and locked her arms around him like a chain of iron. The candle dropped. He attempted to keep his footing with her weight on him, reaching out for leverage against the wall, but she held him close like a lover and the pair tumbled down the stone steps into the darkness.

They fought and grappled in the violence of their fall. In the jumble of collisions, Cora's head knocked across the stone. Her leg was ripped one way, and her arm twisted under her at the bottom of the steps. Ridgeway took the brunt. Homer yelped at the sounds his employer made as he fell. The boy descended slowly, the lantern light shakily drawing the station from shadow. Cora untwined herself from Ridgeway and crawled toward the handcar, left leg in agony. The slave catcher didn't make a sound. She looked for a weapon and came up empty.

Homer crouched next to his boss. His hand covered in blood from the back of Ridgeway's head. The big bone in the man's thigh stuck out of his trousers and his other leg bent in a gruesome arrangement. Homer leaned his face in and Ridgeway groaned.

"Are you there, my boy?"

"Yes, sir."

"That's good." Ridgeway sat up and howled in anguish. He looked over the station's gloom, recognizing nothing. His gaze passed over Cora without interest. "Where are we?"

"On the hunt," Homer said.

"Always more niggers to hunt. Do you have your journal?"

"Yes, sir."

"I have a thought."

Homer removed his notes from the satchel and opened to a fresh page.

"The imperative is ... no, no. That's not it. The American imperative is a splendid thing ... a beacon ... a shining beacon." He coughed and a spasm overtook his body. "Born of necessity and virtue, between the hammer ... and the anvil ... Are you there, Homer?"

"Yes, sir."

"Let me start again ... "

Cora leaned into the pump of the handcar. It didn't move, no matter how much weight she heaved on it. At her feet on the wooden platform was a small metal buckle. She snapped it and the pump squeaked. She tried the lever again and the handcar crawled forward. Cora looked back at Ridgeway and Homer. The slave catcher whispered his address and the black boy recorded his words. She pumped and pumped and rolled out of the light. Into the tunnel that no one had made, that led nowhere.

She discovered a rhythm, pumping her arms, throwing all of herself into movement. Into northness. Was she traveling through the tunnel or digging it? Each time she brought her arms down on the lever, she drove a pickax into the rock, swung a sledge onto a railroad spike. She never got Royal to tell her about the men and women who made the underground railroad. The ones who excavated a million tons of rock and dirt, toiled in the belly of the earth for the deliverance of slaves like her.

Who stood with all those other souls who took runaways into their homes, fed them, carried them north on their backs, died for them. The station masters and conductors and sympathizers. Who are you after you finish something this magnificent—in constructing it you have also journeyed through it, to the other side. On one end there was who you were before you went underground, and on the other end a new person steps out into the light. The up-top world must be so ordinary compared to the miracle beneath, the miracle you made with your sweat and blood. The secret triumph you keep in your heart.

She put miles behind her, put behind her the counterfeit sanctuaries and endless chains, the murder of Valentine farm. There was only the darkness of the tunnel, and somewhere ahead, an exit. Or a dead end, if that's what fate decreed—nothing but a blank, pitiless wall. The last bitter joke. Finally spent, she curled on the handcar and dozed, aloft in the darkness as if nestled in the deepest recess of the night sky.

When she woke, she decided to go the rest of the way on foot—her arms were empty. Limping, tripping over crossties. Cora ran her hand along the wall of the tunnel, the ridges and pockets. Her fingers danced over valleys, rivers, the peaks of mountains, the contours of a new nation hidden beneath the old. *Look outside as you speed through, and you'll find the true face of America.* She could not see it but she felt it, moved through its heart. She feared she'd gotten turned around in her sleep. Was she going deeper in or back from where she came? She trusted the slave's choice to guide her—anywhere, anywhere but where you are escaping from. It had gotten her this far. She'd find the terminus or die on the tracks.

She slept twice more, dreaming of her and Royal in her cabin. She told him of her old life and he held her, then turned her around so they faced each other. He pulled her dress over her head and took off his trousers and shirt. Cora kissed him and ran her hands over the territory of his body. When he spread her legs she was wet and he slid inside her, saying her name as no one had ever said it and as no one ever would, sugary and tender. She awoke each time to the void of the tunnel and when she was done weeping over him she stood and walked.

The mouth of the tunnel started as a tiny hole in the dark. Her strides made it a circle, and then the mouth of a cave, hidden by brush and vines. She pushed aside the brambles and entered the air.

It was warm. Still that stingy winter light but warmer than Indiana, the sun almost overhead. The crevice burst open into a forest of scrub pine and fir. She didn't know what Michigan or Illinois or Canada looked like. Perhaps she wasn't in America anymore but had pushed beyond it. She kneeled to drink from the creek when she stumbled on it. Cool clear water. She washed the soot and grime from her arms and face. "From the mountains," she said, after an article in one of the dusty almanacs. "Snowmelt." Hunger made her head light. The sun told her which way was north.

It was getting dark when she came upon the trail, worthless and pocked rut that it was. She heard the wagons after she'd been sitting on the rock awhile. There were three of them, packed for a long journey, laden with gear, inventories lashed to the sides. They were headed west.

The first driver was a tall white man with a straw hat, gray-whiskered and as impassive as a wall of rock. His wife sat beside him on the driver's box, pink face and neck poking out of a plaid blanket. They regarded her neutrally and passed on. Cora made no acknowledgment of their presence. A young man drove the second wagon, a redheaded fellow with Irish features. His blue eyes took her in. He stopped.

"You're a sight," he said. High in pitch, like a bird's chirping. "You need something?"

Cora shook her head.

"I said, do you need anything?"

Cora shook her head again and rubbed her arms from the chill.

The third wagon was commanded by an older negro man. He was thickset and grizzled, dressed in a heavy rancher's coat that had seen its share of labor. His eyes were kind, she decided. Familiar though she couldn't place it. The smoke from his pipe smelled like potatoes and Cora's stomach made a noise.

"You hungry?" the man asked. He was from the south, from his voice.

"I'm very hungry," Cora said.

"Come up and take something for yourself," he said.

Cora clambered to the driver's box. He opened the basket. She tore off some bread and gobbled it down.

"There's plenty," he said. He had a horseshoe brand on his neck and pulled up his collar to hide it when Cora's eyes lingered. "Shall we catch up?"

"That's good," she said.

He barked at the horses and they proceeded on the rut.

"Where you going?" Cora said.

"St. Louis. From there the trail to California. Us, and some people we going to meet in Missouri." When she didn't respond he said, "You come from down south?"

"I was in Georgia. I ran away." She said her name was Cora. She unfolded the blanket at her feet and wrapped herself in it.

"I go by Ollie," he said. The other two wagons came into view around the bend.

The blanket was stiff and raspy under her chin but she didn't mind. She wondered where he escaped from, how bad it was, and how far he traveled before he put it behind him.

ACKNOWLEDGMENTS

Thanks to Nicole Aragi, Bill Thomas, Rose Courteau, Michael Goldsmith, Duvall Osteen, and Alison Rich (still) for getting this book into your hands. At Hanser over the years: Anna Leube, Christina Knecht, and Piero Salabe. Also: Franklin D. Roosevelt for funding the Federal Writers' Project, which collected the life stories of former slaves in the 1930s. Frederick Douglass and Harriet Jacobs, obviously. The work of Nathan Huggins, Stephen Jay Gould, Edward E. Baptist, Eric Foner, Fergus Bordewich, and James H. Jones was very helpful. Josiah Nott's theories of "amalgamation." *The Diary of a Resurrectionist.* Runaway slave advertisements come from the digital collections of the University of North Carolina at Greensboro. The first one hundred pages were fueled by early Misfits ("Where Eagles Dare [fast version]," "Horror Business," "Hybrid Moments") and Blanck Mass ("Dead Format"). David Bowie is in every book, and I always put on *Purple Rain* and *Daydream Nation* when I write the final pages; so thanks to him and Prince and Sonic Youth. And finally, Julie, Maddie, and Beckett for all the love and support.

◇◇

Read on for an exclusive extract from *The Intuitionist*, Colson Whitehead's debut novel and a 1999 *New York Times* Notable Book, which is now available as a Fleet paperback and ebook.

FLEET

◇◇

It's a new elevator, freshly pressed to the rails, and it's not built to fall this fast.

*   *   *

She doesn't know what to do with her eyes. The front door of the building is too scarred and gouged to look at, and the street behind her is improbably empty, as if the city had been evacuated and she's the only one who didn't hear about it. There is always the game at moments like this to distract her. She opens her leather field binder and props it on her chest. The game gets harder the farther back she goes. Most of the inspectors from the last decade or so are still with the Guild and are easy to identify: LMT, MG, BP, JW. So far she doesn't particularly like the men who have preceded her at 125 Walker. Martin Gruber chews with his mouth open and likes to juggle his glass eye. Big Billy Porter is one of the Old Dogs, and proud of it. On many occasions Lila Mae has returned to the Pit from an errand only to hear Big Billy

Porter regaling the boys about the glory days of the Guild, before. While his comments are never specific, it is clear to everyone just what and who Big Billy is referring to in his croaking, muddy voice. Rebellious among the bureaucratic rows of the Pit, Big Billy's oak desk juts out into the aisle so he can seat his bulk directly beneath one of the ceiling fans. He says he overheats easily and on the hottest days of the summer his remaining hair slides away from how he's combed it, the strands easing into nautilus whorls. It's a slow process and watching it is like waiting for a new hour. But it happens eventually.

All the inspectors who have visited 125 Walker in the past have been Empiricists. As far as she can tell. When she gets fifteen years back in the record there are no more faces to put to the initials. She recognizes the initials from the inspection records of other elevators in other buildings but has never met the people they belong to. JM, for example, is also listed in the inspection record of the elevator Lila Mae departed just half an hour ago, and EH, she's learned over time, has a thing for worn guide shoes, something no one ever looks at except the real stickler types. Checking guide shoes is a losing proposition. Some of the initial men must be in the pictures along the walls of the Pit. The men in those pictures sport the regulation haircuts the Guild required back then, respectable haircuts fit for men of duty and responsibility. The haircuts are utilitarian mishaps that project honor, fidelity, brotherhood unto death. The barber shop two doors down from the Guild, the one that always has big band music coming from inside, used to specialize. Or so they say. Some of the younger inspectors have started wearing the haircut again. It's called a Safety. Lila Mae's hair parts in the middle and cups her round face like a thousand hungry fingers.

The light at this hour, on this street, is the secondhand gray of ghetto twilight, a dull mercury color. She rings the superintendent again and hears a tinny bleating sound. Down twenty years in the record she finds one of the treasures that make the game real:

James Fulton and Frank Chancre inspected 125 Walker within six months of each other. From Lila Mae's vantage, it is easy to read into this coincidence the passing of the crown. Not clear why Fulton left his office to hit the field again, though. Twenty years ago he would have been Dean of the Institute and long past making the rounds of the buildings, ringing superintendents, waiting on worn and ugly stoops. Then she remembers Fulton liked to go into the field every now and again so he wouldn't forget. Fulton with his mahogany cane, rapping impatiently on one of the three windows set in the front door of 125 Walker. Perhaps they weren't cracked then. Perhaps he cracked them. Across from his initials the inspection record notes a problem with the limit switch, a 387. She recognizes the handwriting from Fulton's room at the Institute, from the tall wooden display cases where his most famous papers are kept behind glass, in controlled atmospheres.

As for Chancre, he would have been a young and rising inspector back then. A little thinner, fewer exploded capillaries in his nose. He wouldn't have been able to afford his double-breasted navy suits on a rookie's salary, but his position has changed since those days. Lila Mae sees Chancre swallowing the super's hands with his oversized mitts in faltering camaraderie. It takes a long time to become a politician, but he was born with the smile. You can't fake smiles like that. Nice building you got here, chum. Nice to see a man who takes pride in his craft. Sometimes you walk into these places, you never know what you're going to see, bless my heart. You want to say to yourself, how can people live like this, but then we are all dealt differently and you have to play what you're dealt. Back home, we . . . He gave 125 Walker a clean bill. Lots on his mind, lots on his mind.

The wind is trapped in one of Walker Street's secret nooks, pushing through, whistling. The elevator is an Arbo Smooth-Glide, popular with residential building contractors when 125 went up. Lila Mae remembers from an Institute class on elevator marketing that Arbo spent millions promoting the Smooth-Glide in the trades and at conventions. They were the first to understand the dark powers of the bikini. On a revolving platform festooned with red, white and blue streamers, slender fingers fan the air, summoning the contractors hither. The models have perfect American navels and the air is stuffy in the old convention hall. A placard overlooked for red-blooded distraction details in silver script Arbo's patented QuarterPoint CounterWeight System. Has this ever happened to you? You've just put the finishing touches on your latest assignment and are proud as a peacock to show off for your client. As you ride to the top floor, the Brand X elevator stops and refuses to budge. You won't be working with *them* anymore! Say goodbye to sticky, stubborn counterweights with the new Smooth-Glide Residential Elevator from Arbo. Over two million Arbo elevators are in use worldwide. Going up?

A bald head girdled by loose curls of red hair appears at the door's window. The man squints at Lila Mae and opens the door, hiding his body behind the gray metal. He leaves it to her to speak.

"Lila Mae Watson," she says. "I've come to inspect your elevator."

The man's lips arch up toward his nose and Lila Mae understands that he's never seen an elevator inspector like her before. Lila Mae has pinpointed a spot as the locus of metropolitan disaffection. A zero-point. It is situated in the heart of the city, on a streetcorner that clots with busy, milling citizens during the day and empties completely at night except for prostitutes and lost encyclopedia salesmen. It's a two-minute walk from the office. With that zero-point as reference, she can predict just how much suspicion, curiosity and anger she will rouse in her cases. 125 Walker is at the outer edges of the city, near the bank of the polluted river that keeps the skyscrapers at bay from the suburbs, and quite a distance from the streetcorner: He doesn't like her. "Let me see your badge," the man says, but Lila Mae's hand is already fishing in her jacket pocket. She flips open her identification and holds it up to the man's face. He doesn't bother to look at it. He just asked for effect.

The hallway smells of burning animal fat and obscure gravies boiling to slag. Half the ceiling lights are cracked open or missing. "Back here," he says. The superintendent seems to be melting as he leads Lila Mae across the grime-caulked black and white hexagonal tile. His bulbous head dissolves into shoulders, then spreads into a broad pool of torso and legs. "How come Jimmy didn't come this time?" the super asks. "Jimmy's good people." Lila Mae doesn't answer him. Dark oil streaks his forearms and clouds his green T-shirt. A door bangs open upstairs and a loud female voice yells something in the chafing tones reserved for disciplining children and pets.

The lumpy, pitted texture of the cab's door tells her that management has painted it over a few times, but Lila Mae still recognizes the unusually wide dimensions of an Arbo Smooth-Glide door. Taking their cue from the early days of passenger-response criticism, Arbo equipped their newest model with an oversized door to foster the illusion of space, to distract the passenger from what every passenger feels acutely about elevators. That they ride in a box on a rope in a pit. That they are in the void. If the super doesn't strip the old paint the next time he renovates, it will eventually impede the movement of the door. (Of course a lot of graffiti in this neighborhood.) Already the elevator door halts in its furrows when it opens. A violation waiting to be born, the nascent outlines of a 787. Lila Mae decides against saying anything to the super. It's not her job. "You'll want to start in the machine room, I guess," the super says. He's fixated on the ideal triangularity of Lila Mae's tie knot, its grid of purple and blue squares. The tie disappears near her bosom, gliding beneath the buttons of her dark blue suit.

Lila Mae does not answer him. She leans against the dorsal wall of the elevator and listens. 125 Walker is only twelve floors high, and the vibration of the idling drive doesn't diminish that much as it swims through the gritty loop of the diverting pulley, descends down the cables, navigates the suspension gear, and grasps the car. Lila Mae can feel the idling in her back. She hears the door operator click above her in the dark well and then the door shuts, halting a small degree as the strata of paint chafes. Three Gemco helical springs are standard-issue buffers on Arbo elevators. They wait fifteen feet below her like stalagmites. "Press twelve," Lila Mae orders the super. Even with her eyes closed she could have done it herself, but she's trying to concentrate on the vibrations massaging her back. She can almost see them now. This elevator's vibrations are resolving themselves in her mind as an aqua-blue cone. Her pen rests in her palm and her grip loosens. It might fall. She shuts out the sound of the super's breathing, which is a low rumble lilting into a wheeze at the ultimate convexity of his exhalation. That's noise. The elevator moves. The elevator moves upward in the well, toward the grunting in the machine room, and Lila Mae turns that into a picture, too. The ascension is a red spike circling around the blue cone, which doubles in size and wobbles as the elevator starts climbing. You don't pick the shapes and their behavior. Everyone has their own set of genies. Depends on how your brain works. Lila Mae has always had a thing for geometric forms. As the elevator reaches the fifth floor landing, an orange octagon cartwheels into her mind's frame. It hops up and down, incongruous with the annular aggression of the red spike. Cubes and parallelograms emerge around the eighth floor, but they're satisfied with half-hearted little jigs and don't disrupt the proceedings like the mischievous orange octagon. The octagon ricochets into the foreground, famished for attention. She knows what it is. The triad of helical buffers recedes farther from her, ten stories down at the dusty and dark floor of the well. No need to continue. Just before she opens her eyes she tries to think of what the super's expression must be. She doesn't come close, save for that peculiar arching of his lips, but that doesn't count because she already saw that from when he opened the front door.

The super's eyes are two black lines that withdraw indistinguishably into the skein of his hieroglyphic squint. His lips push up so far that his nostrils seem to suck them in. "I'm going to have to cite you for a faulty overspeed governor," Lila Mae says. The door opens slowly in its track and the drive's idling vibration is full and strong, up here so close to the machine room.

"But you haven't even looked at it," the super says. "You haven't even seen it." He is confused, and tiny pricks of blood speckle his pink cheeks.

"I'm going to have to cite you for a faulty overspeed governor," Lila Mae repeats. She's removing the tiny screws from the glass inspection plate on the left anterior wall of the elevator. The side of her screwdriver reads, PROPERTY OF THE DEPARTMENT OF ELEVATOR INSPECTORS. "It catches every six meters or so," Lila Mae adds as she withdraws the inspection slip from beneath the glass. "If you want, I can get my handbook from the car and you can see the regulations for yourself."

"I don't want to look at the damn book," the super says. He runs his thumbs animatedly across his fingers as she signs the slip and replaces the plate. "I know what the book says. I want you to look at the damn thing yourself. It's running fine. You haven't even been upstairs."

"Nevertheless," Lila Mae says. She opens her field binder and writes her initials at the bottom of the ID column. Even from the twelfth floor, she can still hear the woman downstairs yelling at her children, or what Lila Mae supposes to be children. You never know these days.

"You aren't one of those voodoo inspectors, are you? Don't need to see anything, you just feel it, right? I heard Jimmy make jokes about you witch doctors."

She says, "Intuitionist." Lila Mae rubs the ballpoint of the pen to get the ink flowing. The W of her initials belongs to a ghost alphabet.

The super grins. "If that's the game you want to play," he says,

"I guess you got me on the ropes." There are three twenty-dollar bills in his oily palm. He leans over to Lila Mae and places the money in her breast pocket. Pats it down. "I haven't ever seen a woman elevator inspector before, let alone a colored one, but I guess they teach you all the same tricks."

The door of apartment 12-A cracks behind Lila Mae. "What's all this noise in the hall?" a high, reedy voice asks. "Who's that hanging out there? What you want?"

The super pulls 12-A's door firmly shut and says, "You just mind your own business, Missus LaFleur. It's just me." He turns back to Lila Mae and smiles again. He sticks his tongue into the hole where his two front teeth used to be. Arbo didn't lie about their QuarterPoint CounterWeight System. It rarely fails. A regrettable incident in Atlanta kicked up a lot of fuss in the trades a few years back, but an inquiry later absolved Arbo of any wrongdoing. As they say. The model's overspeed governors are another matter, though, notoriously unreliable, and probability says their famous manufacturing defect should have emerged long ago. Sixty bucks is sixty bucks.

"You'll get a copy of the official citation in a few days in the mail, and it'll inform you how much the fine is," Lila Mae says. She writes *333* in 125 Walker's inspection record.

The super slaps the door of 12-A with his big hand. "But I just gave you sixty dollars! Nobody has ever squeezed me for more than sixty." He's having trouble keeping his trembling arms still at his chest. No, he wouldn't mind taking a swipe at her.

"You placed sixty dollars in my pocket. I don't think I implied by my behavior that I wanted you to bribe me, nor have I made any statement or gesture, such as an outstretched palm, for example, saying that I would change my report because you gave me money. If you want to give away your hard-earned money"—Lila Mae waves her hand toward a concentration of graffiti—"I see it as a curious, although in this case fortuitous, habit of yours that has nothing whatsoever to do with me. Or why I'm here." Lila Mae starts down the stairs. After riding elevators all day, she looks forward to walking down stairs. "If you want to try and take your sixty dollars off me, you're welcome to try, and if you want to challenge my findings and have another person double-check the overspeed governor, that's your right as a representative of this building. But I'm correct." Lila Mae abandons the super on the twelfth floor with the Arbo Smooth-Glide. The super cusses. She is right about the overspeed governor. She is never wrong.

She doesn't know yet.

*   *   *

All of the Department's cars are algae green and shine like algae, thanks to the diligent ministrations of the motor pool. On the night of his inauguration Chancre gripped the lectern with his sausage fingers and announced his Ten Point Plan. The gold badge of his office hung over his shoulders by a long, patriotic ribbon. "Department vehicles," he thundered, "must be kept in a condition befitting the Department." To much applause in the dim banquet room of the Albatross Hotel. Those seated at the long oval tables, gathered around Mrs. Chancre's unholy floral arrangements, easily translated Point Number Seven to the more succinct "Those colored boys better put a shine on those cars." One of the mechanics, Jimmy, has a secret crush on Lila Mae. Not completely secret: Lila Mae's sedan is the only one that gets vacuumed daily, and each morning when she leaves the garage for the field the rearview mirror has been adjusted from the night shift's contortions, to just the way she likes it. Jimmy is a slender character among the burly crew of the motor pool, and the youngest. The calluses on his hands are still tiny pebbles in his flesh.

The traffic at quitting time is a bother. Radio station WCAM equips men with binoculars and positions them at strategic overpasses to describe the gnarls and tangles. Lila Mae is never able to differentiate these men from the meandering isolates who linger at the margins of freeways. All of them make obscure, furtive gestures, all share a certain stooped posture that says they lack substantive reasons for being where they are, at the side of the road. Impossible to distinguish a walkie-talkie from a bottle of cheap wine at such distances.

They don't have alibis, Lila Mae appraises the men at the side of the road.

Her sedan limps through black glue. The WCAM sentry warns of an accident up ahead: A schoolbus has overturned, and as the passing commuters rubberneck and bless themselves, the traffic clots.

Over here, honks a woman in a red compact. The light trilling of her car horn reveals its foreign birth, cribside cooing in alien tongues. Lila Mae thinks car horns work backward: they don't prod and urge the laggard ahead but summon those behind, come up, follow me. Lila Mae listens to the sporadic summons, listens to the news reports of WCAM, the red brake lights smoldering on the road ahead. Each of the announcer's words have the routine elegance, the blank purity Lila Mae associates with geometry. The announcer says that a low-pressure system is rolling east. The announcer says that there's been an accident at the Fanny Briggs Memorial Building. An elevator has fallen.

Now we're cooking.

Lila Mae turns on her Department radio and hears the dispatcher call her inspector's code. "Come in, Z34. Report Zulu-three-four."

"This is Z34 reporting to base," Lila Mae says.

"Why haven't you reported back, Z34?" Contrary to prevailing notions, the elevator inspector dispatch room is not filled with long consoles staffed by an able company who furiously plug and unplug wires from myriad inputs, busily routing. The dispatch room is a small box on the top floor of the office and there's only one person on duty at a time. It is very neat and has no windows. Craig's on dispatch now, and in Lila Mae's imagination he is a skinny man with brown hair who withers in his revolving chair, dressed in suspendered slacks and a sleeveless undershirt. She's never seen a dispatcher, and she's only seen their room once, on her first day of work. He must have been in the bathroom, or making coffee.

"I was on a call," Lila Mae responds. "125 Walker. I just stepped in the car." No one is going to catch her in that lie. Lila Mae always turns off the radio when she's finished for the day. Occasionally one of the night shift calls in sick and Craig wants her to fill in for a few hours. Until the city and the Department work out their overtime policies there's no way Lila Mae is going to fill in for the night shift. If you haven't killed your hangover by six o'clock, you should take your lumps, is what she thinks.

"You're to report back to HQ immediately," Craig says. Then he adds, "Zulu-thirty-four."

"What's this crap about the Briggs building?" Lila Mae asks.

"You're to report back here immediately, Z34. Chancre wants to talk to you. And I don't think I have to quote you Department regs on profanity over city frequencies. Dispatch out."

Lila Mae returns to WCAM, hoping for more details. For some reason Craig's being a hardass, and that's not good. She considers steering over to the shoulder to bypass the traffic, brandishing her inspector credentials should a policeman stop her. But the police and the elevator inspectors have a difficult past, and it's doubtful a cop would let her off the hook, even for city business. Of course the city has never answered Chancre's repeated requests for sirens. No one outside the Guild seems to think they're necessary for some reason. Over the radio, one of the WCAM sentries ahead comments on how long it's taking the emergency techs to remove the children from the schoolbus.

Lila Mae once delivered an oral report on Fanny Briggs in the third grade. Fanny Briggs was in the newer encyclopedias. Some even had her picture. Fanny Briggs looked tired in the marginalia; her eyelids drooped and her jowls oozed down from her cheekbones. Lila Mae stood in front of Ms. Parker's third-grade class and trembled as she started her report. She preferred to fade into the back rows, next to the rabbit cages, beneath the awkward pastels of the spring art project. There she was at Ms. Parker's desk, and her index cards shook in her tiny hands.

"Fanny Briggs was a slave who taught herself how to read."

One time a radio program featured Dorothy Beechum, the most famous colored actress in country, reading parts of Fanny Brigg's account of her escape North. Lila Mae's mother called her into the drawing room. Lila Mae's legs dangled over her mother's lap as she leaned toward the brown mesh of the radio speaker. The actress's voice was iron and strong and did not fail to summon applause from the more liberal quarters of her audience, who murmured about noble struggle. Tiny particles of darkness pressed beyond the cracked, wheaty mesh of the speaker, the kind of unsettling darkness Lila Mae would later associate with the elevator well. Of course she'd do her oral report on Fanny Briggs. Who else was there?

Not much progress in this traffic.

The times are changing. In a city with an increasingly vocal colored population—who are not above staging tiresome demonstrations for the lowlier tabloids, or throwing tomatoes and rotten cabbages during otherwise perfectly orchestrated speeches and rallies—it only makes sense to name the new municipal building after one of their heroes. The Mayor is not stupid; you don't become the ruler of a city this large and insane by being stupid. The Mayor is shrewd and understands that this city is not a Southern city, it is not an old money city or a new money city but the most famous city in the world, and the rules are different here. The new municipal building has been named the Fanny Briggs Memorial Building, and there have been few complaints, and fewer tomatoes.

When Lila Mae was assigned the Fanny Briggs Memorial

Building, she thought nothing of it. It made sense that it would be either her or Pompey, the only two colored inspectors in the Department. Chancre's no fool. There are, after all, election years in the Elevator Guild too, and this is one of them, and all sorts of unexpected things have been happening. The Department-wide $1.25 raise, for example, which according to Chancre really adds up to a pretty penny after a while. Not that the elevator inspectors, civil-servant to the core despite their maverick reputations and occasionally flashy antics, needed to be convinced of the importance of a $1.25 raise. A government job is a government job, whether it's inspecting elevators or railroad cars full of hanging meat, and anything that brings their salaries into closer proportion to their contributions to the American good are accepted cheerfully, election-year ploy or no. Same thing with the screwdrivers. When a memo circulating soon after the raises announced that the new screwdrivers were on their way, few cared that the Guild Chair was so naked in his attempt to score points with the electorate. For the new screwdrivers were quite beautiful. Ever since the city granted license to the Department, bulky and ungainly screwdrivers had poked and bulged in the jacket pockets of the elevator inspectors, completely ruining any attempts at dapperness and savoir faire. It's difficult to look official and imposing while listing to one side. The new screwdrivers have mother-of-pearl handles and heads the exact width of an inspection-plate screw. They fold out like jackknives and lend themselves to baroque fantasies about spies and secret missions. And who can argue with that?

So when the word spread that Lila Mae had been assigned the 18-deep elevator stack in the Fanny Briggs Memorial Building (18-deep!), a career-making case for any inspector, few were surprised and whatever ground Chancre lost among the Old Dogs of the Guild was more than compensated for by the goodwill generated by the raise and the new mother-of-pearl jackknife screwdrivers. Lila Mae knew when she got the assignment that it was meant to draw attention from Chancre's opponent in the race for the Guild Chair, the liberal Orville Lever, who apparently thinks that only Intuitionists are capable of building coalitions, shaking hands with fundamentally different people, etc. Lila Mae (who, by the way, is still not making much headway in the evening traffic) may be an Intuitionist, but she is a colored woman, which is more to the point. Chancre's assistant left a note on her desk: *Your good service won't be forgotten after the election.* As if she needed to be bribed with a vague promise of promotion (and probably a lie anyway). It's her job. She's taken an oath and such things are to be taken seriously. Lila Mae held the note in her small hands, and even though she did not look up from her desk she knew that all of them, the Old Dogs and the New Guys in their retrograde Safety haircuts, were looking at her. The way the gossip flows in the Pit (Lila Mae is situated quite far downstream), they probably knew she got the case before she did. Probably skinny Ned, that vapor, that meandering cumulus masquerading as a man, sentenced to desk duty after the infamous Johnson Towers debacle, talked to a guy who talked to a guy in Chancre's inner circle and the word came down: the colored gal gets the job. Not any of them, not Pompey. There are no surprises in election years, just a bit more static.

And here's Chancre now, arms struts at the tails of his signature double-breasted suit, twenty feet tall on a billboard for the United Elevator Co. Lila Mae's car creeps through the bottleneck at the entrance to the tunnel so there's no missing him. No more honking for this glum procession—they can see the tunnel now, and there is always the mandatory period of pensive anticipation on entering the tunnel. ALL SAFE declares the copy across his feet, a play on Otis's famous declaration at the 1853 Crystal Palace Exposition. The reference doesn't mean much to the people in the cars around Lila Mae—elevator ads probably only register in civilian heads as a dim affirmation of modernity, happy progress to be taken for granted and subconsciously cherished—but Otis's phrase is the hoist pulling her and her fellow inspectors out of bed each morning. The sacred motto.

Even long observers of the mysterious ways of corporate vanity are hard-pressed to understand the sudden ubiquity of elevator ads. In addition to billboards like the one towering over Lila Mae right now, the elevator industry's advertisements line park benches, adorn the buses and subways of the city's transit system, brace the outfield walls of baseball stadiums, bright non sequiturs. Other places, too. One time before the start of a double feature at her favorite movie house—the Marquee on Twenty-third Street, notorious among those in the know for its free popcorn refills—Lila Mae sat astonished as a thirty-second movie reel introduced American Elevator's new frictionless drive. From time to time Lila Mae still catches herself humming the spot's elastic doo-wop chorus, never mind that the frictionless drive in question is just American's old 240–60 drive in a smart new housing. It's a relatively recent phenomenon, the vocality of the international short-range vertical transport industry, and there's no one to explain it. How much Chancre makes in endorsements each year is anyone's guess, but it goes without saying that he has a lot riding on his reelection to Guild Chair. Just look at him up there. So far Lila Mae thinks her role in the campaign is limited to window dressing—evidence for the new, progressive face of the Elevator Guild, and by extension, city government.

She doesn't know yet.

She's almost inside the tunnel when WCAM finally decides to update the situation at the Fanny Briggs Memorial Building. The yellow tiles inside the tunnel glisten and Lila Mae sees a long throat strangled by mucus. In his geometric voice, so full of planes, WCAM's radio announcer says that Chancre and the Mayor will be holding a press conference to discuss what transpired at the new municipal building early this afternoon. But before he can say something more, something tangible that Lila Mae can use to prepare herself, the tunnel eats the transmission. Like that. Then there's just the agitated scratch of static inside her sedan and the earnest humming of multiple tires on the tunnel floor outside. Near silence, to better contemplate the engineering marvel they travel through, the age of miracles they live in. The air is poisonous.

Something happened. It was her case. Lila Mae drums her fingers on the steering wheel and relives her call to the Briggs building the day before. Those looking for a correlative to Fanny Briggs's powerful, lumpy body in the shape of the building dedicated to her will have to bear in mind the will to squat that roosts in the soul of every city architect. Government buildings are generally squat rather than tall, presumably to better accommodate deep file drawers of triplicate ephemera. So it has been for generations. But who can resist the seductions of elevators these days, those stepping stones to Heaven, which make relentless verticality so alluring? While the architects understand that the future is up, the future is in how high you can go, it is difficult to shake old habits. Habits clamp down on the ankle and resist all entreaties, no matter how logical. As it is in politics, the only victor in the end was ugly compromise. The Fanny Briggs Memorial Building hunkers down on the northern edge of Federal Plaza in the renovated section of downtown, burly and squat for five floors before launching into space with another forty stories of pure, unsullied steel. The net effect is chrysalid, a photograph of a glass insect emerging from a stone cocoon. When Lila Mae first walked up the broad stone steps of the building, she looked up at the monolith above and felt a trembling instant of vertigo: It was a big responsibility. The mandatory Latinate motto was engraved above the entrance.

Lila Mae is outside the tunnel now and can't think of what she did wrong. She needs a plan.

Keep cool, Lila Mae.